THE ROUTLEDGE INTERNATIONAL HANDBOOK OF SHARED PARENTING AND BEST INTEREST OF THE CHILD

This multidisciplinary volume offers an essential, comprehensive study of perspectives on the scope and application of the best interests of the child and focuses mainly on its application in relation to child custody.

With expert contributions from psychological, sociological and legal perspectives, it offers scientific analysis and debate on whether it should be the primary consideration in deciding child custody cases in cases of divorce or separation or whether it should be one of several primary considerations. It explores complex dilemmas inherent in shared parenting and whether the advantages it offers children are sufficient when compared to attributing custody to one parent and limiting visitation rights of the other. Offering a comprehensive analysis of this complex topic, chapters provide detailed insight into the current state of research in this area, as well as expert guidelines aimed at resolving the controversies when parents agree or disagree over their children's living arrangements. Cutting-edge topics explored include: transnational shared parenting; alternative dispute resolution; breastfeeding parents; religious disputes between parents and the psychological, social and economic factors that affect shared parenting.

The Routledge International Handbook of Shared Parenting and Best Interest of the Child will be essential reading for scholars and graduate students in law, psychology, sociology and economics interested in shared parenting and family law.

José Manuel de Torres Perea is Associate Professor of Civil Law at the University of Málaga, Spain, specialising in Family Law. He is the author of significant contributions on shared parenting and the best interests of the child in Spanish legal literature.

Edward Kruk is Associate Professor of Social Work at the University of British Columbia, specialising in child and family policy. He has published extensively on shared parental responsibility, child custody determination, parental alienation, family mediation and the role of fathers in child development. He is the inaugural president of the International Council on Shared Parenting (ICSP).

Margarita Ortiz-Tallo is a Clinical Psychologist and Professor of Psychology at the University of Málaga, Spain, and has lectured in several countries. She has written numerous articles published in scientific journals, several specialist books on psychopathology and books for the general public on different psychological subjects.

THE ROUTLEDGE INTERNATIONAL HANDBOOK OF SHARED PARENTING AND BEST INTEREST OF THE CHILD

Edited by José Manuel de Torres Perea, Edward Kruk and Margarita Ortiz-Tallo

Routledge
Taylor & Francis Group
LONDON AND NEW YORK

First published 2021
by Routledge
2 Park Square, Milton Park, Abingdon, Oxon OX14 4RN

and by Routledge
605 Third Avenue, New York, NY 10158

Routledge is an imprint of the Taylor & Francis Group, an informa business

© 2021 selection and editorial matter, José Manuel de Torres Perea, Edward Kruk and Margarita Ortiz-Tallo; individual chapters, the contributors

The right of José Manuel de Torres Perea, Edward Kruk and Margarita Ortiz-Tallo to be identified as the authors of the editorial material, and of the authors for their individual chapters, has been asserted in accordance with sections 77 and 78 of the Copyright, Designs and Patents Act 1988.

All rights reserved. No part of this book may be reprinted or reproduced or utilised in any form or by any electronic, mechanical, or other means, now known or hereafter invented, including photocopying and recording, or in any information storage or retrieval system, without permission in writing from the publishers.

Trademark notice: Product or corporate names may be trademarks or registered trademarks, and are used only for identification and explanation without intent to infringe.

British Library Cataloguing-in-Publication Data
A catalogue record for this book is available from the British Library

Library of Congress Cataloging-in-Publication Data
Names: Torres Perea, José Manuel de, editor. | Kruk, Edward, editor. |
Ortiz-Tallo Alarcón, Margarita, editor.
Title: The Routledge international handbook of shared parenting and
best interest of the child / edited by José Manuel de Torres Perea,
Edward Kruk and Margarita Ortiz-Tallo.
Description: Abingdon, Oxon; New York, NY: Routledge, 2021. |
Includes bibliographical references and index.
Identifiers: LCCN 2020053607 (print) | LCCN 2020053608 (ebook) |
ISBN 9780367691448 (hbk) | ISBN 9780367691455 (pbk) |
ISBN 9781003140566 (ebk)
Subjects: LCSH: Custody of children. | Conflict of laws–Custody of children.
Classification: LCC K707.R68 2021 (print) | LCC K707 (ebook) |
DDC 346.01/73–dc23
LC record available at https://lccn.loc.gov/2020053607
LC ebook record available at https://lccn.loc.gov/2020053608

ISBN: 978-0-367-69144-8 (hbk)
ISBN: 978-0-367-69145-5 (pbk)
ISBN: 978-1-003-14056-6 (ebk)

Typeset in Bembo
by Newgen Publishing UK

CONTENTS

List of contributors   x
Preface by   xix
José Manuel de Torres Perea, Edward Kruk and Margarita Ortiz-Tallo

   Introduction   1
   José Manuel de Torres Perea and Martin Widrig

PART I
Best interest of the child and shared parenting   13

1   Children's experiences of shared care   15
   Patrick Parkinson and Judith Cashmore

2   Shared parenting: Twelve experts exchange views in
   panel discussions   27
   Michael E. Lamb and Sanford L. Braver

3   Joint versus sole physical custody: Which is best for children?   40
   Linda Nielsen

4   Best interest of the child: "A" or "the" primary consideration?   51
   José Manuel de Torres Perea

5   Does joint physical custody "cause" children's better outcomes?   63
   Sanford L. Braver and Ashley M. Votruba

6 When children's rights are undermined in the name of the 'best interests of the child': Switzerland's long road to child-centred custody legislation 78
   Martin Widrig

7 Rights and guarantees of unaccompanied minors: Researching the best interest of the child principle in the Spanish welfare state 95
   Elena Avilés Hernández

8 The right of parents to ensure the religious and moral education of their children: Parental conflicts—an analysis of Spanish case law 106
   Rosa García Vilardell

9 The best interests of the child in shared parenting judgments according to Spanish law 117
   Elena Goñi Huarte

10 Informational physiology of individual development 129
   Peter Beyerlein

11 Shared parenting as a protective factor in children's and adults' health 142
   Vittorio Carlo Vezzetti

PART II
Socioeconomic profile of shared parenting 155

12 Legislation and family: Divorce and granting of custody 157
   Diego Becerril Ruíz and José Manuel Jiménez-Cabello

13 Family structure, parental practices, and child wellbeing in post-divorce situations: The case of shared parenting 170
   Ana María López Narbona, Almudena Moreno Mínguez and Marta Ortega Gaspar

14 Factors that affect judicial decisions in relocation cases: Bridging the gap between the empirical evidence and socio-legal practice 183
   Yoav Mazeh

15	Shared parenting versus relocation disputes María Dolores Cano Hurtado	198
16	Shared parenting and financial interests Jesús Martín Fuster	210
17	Having additional children: Should the state regulate family relations? Yoav Mazeh	222

PART III
Shared parenting and parental alienation 231

18	Shared parenting as preventive of parental alienation Edward Kruk	233
19	Shared parenting and politics: Background of equal opportunities in the German context Jorge Guerra González	248
20	Child sexual abuse, parental alienation syndrome and custody Margarita Ortiz-Tallo and Marta Ferragut	262
21	Parental alienation syndrome and the 'friendly parent' concept as examples of perversion of the system Carmen R. Iglesias Martín	271
22	Compensation for "parental alienation": Analysis of ECtHR Judgement 23641/17 Hildegund Sünderhauf-Kravets and Martin Widrig	283
23	The Cooperative Parenting Triangle: A tool to help divorced parents Päivi Hietanen	297

PART IV
Alternative dispute resolution on shared parenting and joint parenting plan 305

24	Mandatory mediation and legal presumption for shared parenting Hildegund Sünderhauf-Kravets	307

25 Parenting coordination as an alternative dispute resolution
    system in Spanish family law   317
    Yolanda De Lucchi López-Tapia

26 PIFE – an intervention aimed at restoring the parent–child bond
    ruptured by acute separation conflict or parental alienation   327
    Celia Lillo

27 Co-responsibility plan and shared parenting   341
    Belén Casado Casado

PART V
Recent evolution of shared parenting in a comparative scenario 353

28 Recent developments in shared parenting in Western countries   355
    José Manuel de Torres Perea

29 What happens when there is presumptive 50/50 parenting
    time? An evaluation of Arizona's new child custody statute   370
    *William V. Fabricius, Michael Aaron, Faren R. Akins,
    John J. Assini and Tracy McElroy*

30 The best interests of the child and parental authority in
    Philippine family law   384
    Ryan Jeremiah Donato Quan and Blesscille V. Guerra-Termulo

31 Meeting their parents: A right always ignored for
    divorce-affected minors   397
    Fahad Ahmad Siddiqi

32 The best interest of the child in the case law of the
    Spanish Supreme Court   403
    José Manuel Martín Fuster

33 Divorce and loss of paternal contact: A perspective
    from Norway   414
    Eivind Meland

34 Trying to put shared parenting into Scottish law   419
    Ian Maxwell

35 Features of joint custody and shared parenting in Slovakia 431
Dagmar Kopčanová

36 The merits of the "Zaunegger approach" of the European
Court of Human Rights 440
Martin Widrig

Conclusion 452
José Manuel de Torres Perea, Edward Kruk and Martin Widrig

Index 470

CONTRIBUTORS

Michael Aaron is enjoying his fifth decade of practising law. Michael was appointed by Chief Justice Scott Bales to the Attorney Ethics Advisory Committee in December 2018 and reappointed December in 2019 by Chief Justice Brutinel. He is a frequent presenter and organizer at AFCC and family law seminars. He was instrumental in setting up a new Friday FUNdamentals series of seminars through the Pima County Bar Association and serves as the Chair of the Family Law Section. Michael was named 2018 Professional of the Year by Strathmore's *Who's Who* worldwide publication. Michael was honored to be named by Best Lawyers and is AV rated by Martindale-Hubbell and as one of the Top Lawyers of Arizona by his peers. Michael is now serving as a Trustee on the Pima County Bar Foundation Board.

Faren R. Akins is a Psychologist and Attorney licensed in Arizona and California. His professional history includes teaching, research, publishing, clinical and forensic psychology practice, and private practice as an attorney.

John J. Assini (Jack) began practising law in 1994 and was in private practice, handling family law matters, including premarital agreements, dissolutions of marriage, child support, paternity actions, spousal maintenance and parenting time issues until he was appointed to the Arizona Superior Court Pima County bench in March of 2015. He is currently doing a three-year family law trial rotation. He received his BA from the University of Arizona in Elementary Education, taught first grade for four years, could not find a rich wife, so returned to the University of Arizona for his JD degree. Jack is the Past Chair of the Executive Council of the Family Law Section of the State Bar of Arizona, a past board member of the Arizona – Association of Family and Conciliation Courts and continues to be a member at large with the Executive Council of the Family Law Section of the State Bar of Arizona.

Contributors

Elena Avilés Hernández holds two degrees, one in Political Science and one in Administration and Law, and two Master's (International Cooperation and Development Policies and Criminal Law and Criminal Policy). Since working for the United Nations Development Programme (UNDP) in Bolivia, she has focused her research work on the field of criminal law, through the University of Málaga. In addition to participating in various projects, she has published articles in journals (*Estudios de Deusto, Revista General de Derecho Penal*) and book chapters for prestigious publishing houses (Tirant lo Blanch, Ediciones Universidad de Salamanca. In the teaching field, she was involved in an international seminar at the University of Incheon, South Korea

Diego Becerril Ruíz is a Professor in the School of Political Science and Sociology at the University of Granada, Spain. He is also Director of the SEJ131 research group, "Analysis of Social Life". His main lines of research are family, youth and social structure. He is a researcher on multiple projects and visiting professor at international universities.

Peter Beyerlein is a professor and Head of the Institute of Biomedical Informatics at the Technical University of Applied Sciences, Wildau, Germany. He teaches mathematics, signal processing, systems theory and computational biology. His is a known expert in machine intelligence and computational biology and, together with Andreas Beutler of the Mayo Clinic, authored a paper on the development of chronic pain as a result of cell reprogramming. He is co-founder of the Institute of Family Law and Social Pediatrics (Institut für familienrechtliche Sozialpädiatrie, IFS).

Sanford L. Braver was a faculty member in the Department of Psychology at Arizona State University for over 40 years, retiring in 2011 as Emeritus Professor. To support his work on the dynamics of divorcing families, he was the recipient of 17 competitively reviewed, primarily federal, research grants, totalling almost $20 million. His work has been published in well over 125 peer-reviewed professional journals and book chapters, as well as in the acclaimed 1998 book. *Divorced Dads: Shattering the Myths* (Penguin Putnam).

María Dolores Cano Hurtado is a Doctor in Law at the University of Alicante, Spain. She is a research academic with a focus on civil law and family law. She is Lecturer in a Civil Law at the University CEU Cardenal Herrrera (Valencia-Elche), Spain. She is a member of the *Cuestión de Orden Público: problemática jurídica actual* research group.

Belén Casado Casado is an academic researcher and expert in civil law, obligations and contracts and family law. She works in the Department of Civil Law at the University of Málaga, Spain. Over the years she has published articles on the rights of minors, parental functions and shared parenting.

Contributors

Judith Cashmore is Professor of Social Legal Research and Policy at Sydney Law School, and Professorial Research Fellow in the Research Centre for Children and Families at the University of Sydney. The focus of her research has been on children's experience of and involvement in family law, child protection and criminal proceedings and other processes in which decisions are made about their lives and the implications for law, social policy and practice.

William V. Fabricius is an Associate Professor of Psychology at Arizona State University. He received his PhD in Developmental Psychology from the University of Michigan. His research in children's socio-cognitive development, parenting and adolescent health has been supported by grants from the National Institutes of Health.

Marta Ferragut, PhD, is an expert on the postgraduate course in child and youth psychology at the University of Málaga, Spain, the main researcher of the I+D+I project "Evaluation and prevention of the APC in Spain". She has made notable contributions focusing on children and adolescents, especially on aspects of violence, sexism and positive psychology. She is the secretary of the Con.ciencia Association, whose objective is the study and prevention of child sexual abuse.

Elena Goñi Huarte is a research scholar focusing on civil and family law. She works in the Department of Legal and Political Sciences at the European University of Madrid, Spain. She is also a member of the "Studies in Private and Comparative Law" research group at the University of Almeria, Spain.

Rosa García Vilardell is a Lecturer at the Universidad CEU Cardenal Herrera. She is Director of the Department of Legal Sciences at the Universidad CEU UCH in Elche (Valencia), Spain. Her research focuses on public freedoms and the family, and she has made various contributions in this field.

Jorge Guerra González is a Researcher at Leuphana University in Lüneburg, Germany. He is a family mediator, guardian ad litem and contact facilitator. He has a PhD in Law as well and a Master's in Social Economy. At present he is completing a Bachelor's in Psychology. His main areas of interest are child protection at family courts, BIC-friendly transformation of the family support system and equal access to opportunities for all family members to spend time with each other and to societal goods irrespective of their personal conditions. He has published, given speeches and provided training on these issues at regional, national and international levels.

Blesscille V. Guerra-Termulo holds a Bachelor of Arts in Psychology (2008) from the University of the Philippines, a Juris Doctor degree (2012) from the Ateneo de Manila University School of Law, and a Master of Arts in Pastoral Counseling (2020) from the Asian Theological Seminary. She was admitted to the Philippine Bar in 2013. She was previously a litigation associate in a law firm and is currently engaged in development work.

Contributors

Päivi Hietanen holds a Master's degree in social sciences, works as a family mediator and holds divorce seminars. Hietanen acts as a specialist with divorcing families with children at the Federation of Mother and Child Homes and Shelters, where she focuses on promoting cooperative parenting and keeping the focus on the rights and status of the child during divorce. In her work, she develops divorce services in cooperation with professionals and volunteers, and provides training on topics such as parental divorce, cooperative parenting and the rights of the child.

Carmen R. Iglesias Martín is an academic researcher focused on family law, tort law, electronic contracting and new technologies. She has made numerous doctrinal contributions. She is Professor of Civil Law at the University of Salamanca, Spain, and a founding member of RIIDE, an international research network on educational law.

José Manuel Jiménez-Cabello is a Professor and Researcher in the Department of Sociology at the University of Granada, Spain. His main line of research focuses on the sociology of the family, specifically on divorce and the assignment of child custody. He received a national award on his university studies (Spanish Ministry of Education).

Dagmar Kopčanová is an educational psychologist, researcher, consultant and lecturer with long-term practical experiences in the area of psychological counselling and school psychology. She currently works in the Research Institute for Child Psychology and Pathopsychology. Dr Kopčanová has been published widely in Slovak, English, Russian and German language national and international professional journals. As a co-author she contributed to the monography, *Counselling Psychology*, with the chapter "Beginning and development of psychological counselling and guidance services in former Czechoslovakia until today". In the last few years, she has been mostly involved in research and counselling families who are experiencing family breakdown. For this reason, she became more involved with the International Committee for Shared Parenting.

Edward Kruk is Associate Professor of Social Work at the University of British Columbia and President of the International Council on Shared Parenting. He has published extensively in the areas of co-parenting after separation, family mediation, the impact of divorce on children and families, parental alienation, and women and addiction. The most recent of his five books is *The Equal Parent Presumption*, published by McGill-Queen's University Press.

Michael E. Lamb is Emeritus Professor of Psychology at the University of Cambridge. He has long studied parent–child relationships and child development in various family and cultural circumstances and the role of children in the legal system. That research has led to several international awards and honorary degrees. Michael is currently editor of the American Psychological Association's journal, *Psychology, Public Policy, and Law*.

Celia Lillo is a clinical psychologist, family mediator and parenting coordinator practising in Montreal, Canada. Her work focuses on intervention with high conflict families, primarily in situations where a loss or risk of loss of the parent–child bond, including parental alienation, is present. In 2014 she participated in the creation and development of the PIFE, a supervised family intervention protocol aimed at restoring contact and re-establishing the parent–child bond degraded by parental conflict.

Ana María López Narbona is a Professor and Research Academic with a focus on family, social inclusion and exclusion, migrations, racism and xenophobia, and sociology of the law. She works in the Department of Sociology at the University of Málaga, Spain. She is a member of national and international sociological associations.

Yolanda De Lucchi López-Tapia is an Associate Professor of Procedural Law at the University of Málaga, Spain. Her main research work focuses on justice and vulnerability, dealing with issues related to children and families, people with disabilities and consumers. She is a member of the Ibero-American Network of Researchers "100 Rules of Brasilia" on access to justice for people in vulnerable situations.

Jesús Martín Fuster is a Professor and Researcher in the Civil Law Department at the University of Málaga, Spain. He has an international doctorate from the University of Málaga, and a Master's in Legal Practice, with an extraordinary award for the best academic record, having made important contributions to the field of private law.

José Manuel Martín Fuster is a Professor and Academic Researcher. His main focus is the area of civil law, especially consumer and family law. He works in the Department of Private Law at the University of Málaga and has made important contributions to the field of civil law.

Ian Maxwell is the national manager of Shared Parenting Scotland, formerly Families Need Fathers Scotland. He has worked with charities supporting separated parents since 1993. He was a lay member of the Scottish Civil Justice Council from 2014–2019, the statutory body that produces court rules in Scotland. Versions of this chapter have been delivered at international conferences in Boston, Strasbourg and Málaga between 2016 and 2019.

Yoav Mazeh (LL.B. Heb. U., M.St. Oxford, D.Phil. Oxford) is a law professor at Ono Academic College in Israel, and a leading divorce attorney (mazeh.co.il). His academic work focuses on family law, particularly on aspects relating to children within divorce. His publications are often cited by the courts and have led various changes in Israeli family law, including a shift towards joint parenting, gender neutral child support and changes relating to parental alienation.

Tracy McElroy is currently the Director of Pinal County Family Services of the Conciliation Court in Arizona. She has been working for Conciliation Services since

2007 in various capacities and has been the Director since 2015. She has a Master's degree in Psychology and currently serves on several state-wide committees focused on improving court processes for families.

Eivind Meland has worked as a family physician since 1978 and is still engaged in clinical work. He is now Professor Emeritus at the University of Bergen, where he has worked since 1990. His main research interests are motivational psychology, lifestyle changes and adolescent and family health.

Almudena Moreno Mínguez is Professor of Sociology at the University of Valladolid, Spain. She is a specialist in family, public policy and gender issues. Her research work has been recognised by the International Award for Young Sociologists from the International Sociological Association. She is a member of the European Sociological Association's Advisory Board on Family Research. She is the author of more than 100 scientific publications, including articles and books.

Linda Nielsen is a Professor of Education at Wake Forest University in Winston Salem, NC. She is an internationally recognised expert on shared physical custody for children with separated parents and on father–daughter relationships. In addition to her many academic journal articles, she has written three books on father–daughter relationships and three editions of the college textbook, *Adolescence: A Contemporary View* (Cengage Learning). Her work has been featured in many forums, including a PBS documentary, National Public Radio, *New York Times*, *Wall Street Journal* and *Time* magazine.

Marta Ortega Gaspar is a Senior Lecturer of Sociology at the University of Málaga, Spain. Her research focuses on sociology of the family, work–life balance, ageing, child well-being and gender. She has been a visiting researcher at the University of Oxford (Oxford Institute of Population Ageing) and at City, University of London. She is currently co-leader of a national research project: "Child well-being and material privation in the new family scenario of precariousness in Spain" (www.researchgate.net/profile/Marta_Ortega_Gaspa).

Margarita Ortiz-Tallo has written extensively on domestic violence and child abuse, including sexual abuse. She is Professor of Psychology at the University of Málaga, Spain, and a clinical psychologist. She has given lectures in several countries and has had a special impact on many Spanish-speaking countries. She has published numerous articles in scientific journals, specialist books on psychopathology and, for the general public, on diverse topics in the field of psychology. One of her best-known works is *Psicopatología Clínica* [*Clinical Psychopathology*].

Patrick Parkinson is a Professor of Law at the University of Queensland. He was the President of the International Society of Family Law, 2011–2014. He has held numerous positions in Australia involving reform of family law and the child protection system.

Contributors

Ryan Jeremiah Donato Quan is a full-time law professor at the Ateneo de Manila University School of Law in the Philippines. His areas of teaching, research, and published writing include international human rights law, women's rights and gender issues, child rights, labor and employment law, business and human rights, and human rights dimensions of environmental issues. He is also currently a legal specialist (advisor) at the Commission on Human Rights of the Philippines. He holds Bachelor's degrees in Development Studies and Legal Management (2004) from De La Salle University – Manila, a Juris Doctor degree (2008) from Ateneo, and a Master of Law degree in International Human Rights Law, summa cum laude, (2015) from the University of Notre Dame, USA.

Fahad Ahmad Siddiqi is a lawyer from Pakistan, practising exclusively in child custody. He is the author of *Non-Custodial Fathers and the Guardian and Wards Act 1890* and *Shared Parenting: A Socio Legal Perspective* and numerous articles on the subject of child custody litigation published on a local legal webportal, courtingthelaw.com.

Hildegund Sünderhauf-Kravets has been a professor of family law for more than 20 years in the education of social workers at the Lutheran University of Applied Sciences in Nuremberg, Germany. For ten years her research has focused on shared parenthood. She is the author of the standard scientific book on the legal, psychological and practical aspects of shared parenthood after parental separation in German-speaking countries and a guide for parents. She influenced the ICSP as a co-founder and permanent board member. She lives with her family in Bavaria and also practises family mediation.

José Manuel de Torres Perea is Associate Professor of Civil Law at the University of Málaga, Spain. He specialises in Family Law. He is the author of important contributions on shared parenting and the best interests of the child in Spanish legal literature. He has been a visiting professor, among others, at Goethe University, Frankfurt, Germany; Northwestern University, Chicago; and Pennsylvania University, Philadelphia, USA. His latest publication is the English-language book *Spanish Modern Family Law through an Analysis of Eighty Landmark Decisions*, published by Thomson Reuters.

Vittorio Carlo Vezzetti is a paediatrician working for the Insubria Health Agency. He has presented and taught at more than 100 conferences in Italy and abroad regarding the crisis of the family and child custody. He has contributed to Italian parliamentary debates on changing the national law on joint custody and has addressed several official questions to the Italian and European parliaments. He has also written many articles on child custody and an Italian bestseller on this topic: *Nel nome dei Figli* [*In the Name of the Sons*]. His comparative research "The European children and the divorce of their parents" was presented at the European Parliament in Strasbourg and to the High Commissioner for Human Rights. He is co-founder of Colibri Europe and focuses on the biological health consequences of childhood adversity.

Contributors

Ashley M. Votruba is an Assistant Professor in the Law-Psychology Program at the University of Nebraska–Lincoln. She received her PhD in social psychology from Arizona State University and her Juris Doctor from the Sandra Day O'Connor College of Law in 2017. Her primary research area is how social perception influences legal decision-making and conflict management.

Martin Widrig is a research academic with a focus on human rights and constitutional and family law. He works in the Department of Public Law at the University of Fribourg, Switzerland, is a founding member of the International Council on Shared Parenting and has made important contributions to Switzerland's latest physical custody legislation.

PREFACE

Over the past two decades, there have been significant advances in our collective understanding of the essential needs and best interests of children whose parents are undergoing separation and divorce, and the extent to which shared parental responsibility for the care and upbringing of children is commensurate with those needs and interests. A paradigm shift has occurred in scientific thinking about children and families undergoing the separation transition, with an emerging consensus that we have reached a watershed in understanding the best interests of children in situations of family separation and divorce. These changes in society have revolutionised child custody determination in contested cases of separation and divorce. Over sixty research studies over this time has demonstrated the degree to which shared parenting offers benefits and advantages to children and families, and overcomes the many drawbacks of traditional adversarial approaches such as "winner-take-all" legal determinations that award primary care and control of children to one parent only.

This volume addresses the vital question of how shared parenting meets the needs and best interests of children in cases of parental conflict regarding custody, through contributions from experts in the fields of sociology, psychology, social work and law. Experts from different areas met to share and discuss the results of their research during the International Scientific Conference on Best Interest of the Child and Shared Parenting, 2–3 December 2019, University of Malaga, Spain. This conference was preceded by four others, held in Strasbourg in 2018, Boston in 2017 and Bonn in 2014 and 2015, all organised by the International Council on Shared Parenting (ICSP). This book brings together a selection of contributions presented at these conferences.

This book is essentially a current interdisciplinary guide to shared parenting and the best interests of the child with an international focus. Written by researchers into divorce and legal and mental health practitioners in the fields of shared parenting and the best interests of the child, we find varied opinions on crucial, sometimes conflicting, issues. Thus, some authors make the case for a legal rebuttable presumption in favour of shared parenting, while others consider that such a possibility is incompatible with the principle of the best interests of the child and defend the status quo. Some chapters oppose the idea of considering parental alienation as a decision-making tool, while others make the case that, as a form of family violence and child abuse, it is an essential consideration in child custody determination. These controversies are only a reflection of some of the key issues in academic and professional practice debate examined here. Our aim is to provide readers with the state of current scientific knowledge in this arena and to also give them a glimpse of the guidelines proposed by the experts to resolve the different controversies raised. However, we point out from the outset that some of these questions must remain open and pending further studies to provide data from which to draw definitive conclusions.

The book focuses on the legal, social and psychological elements of shared parenting and the best interests of children, and the convergences, divergences and interactions among these perspectives. It traces the evolution of child custody from a maternal deference standard to a discretionary best interest of the child standard to the present-day focus on an evidence-based "best interests of the child from the perspective of the child" criterion.

The International Council on Shared Parenting was established to develop evidence-based approaches to the needs and rights of children whose parents are living apart. The purpose of the association is, first, the dissemination and advancement of scientific knowledge on the needs and rights ("best interests") of children whose parents are living apart and, second, to formulate evidence-based recommendations concerning the legal, judicial and practical implementation of shared parenting. Its aim is to find solutions for reducing the problems of children known to arise from family breakdown, such as diminished self-esteem, depression and possible parental alienation, as well as educational failure, substance abuse and trouble with the law.

Thus, the stage was set for the University of Malaga International Scientific Conference on Best Interest of the Child and Shared Parenting. We invite readers to consider the range of viewpoints offered on these and other pertinent questions and debates and to come to their own conclusions respecting the needs and best interests of children and families undergoing the separation transition.

José Manuel de Torres Perea
Edward Kruk
Margarita Ortiz-Tallo

INTRODUCTION

José Manuel de Torres Perea and Martin Widrig

In this *The Routledge International Handbook on Shared Parenting and Best Interest of the Child*, some of the world's leading scholars in the field provide answers to and essential information on a selection of the most important questions raised in the current family law arena. What does research say on shared parenting? Is it still justified to give preference to sole physical custody? Is a presumption in favour of shared parenting a viable solution? If so, under what conditions? How should we address conflict? How can we improve research to gain better guidance for policy and practice? What is the most efficient way to use the undefined legal term "best interests of the child"?

The reader of this book receives first-hand answers to these and many other important questions, primarily from the perspectives of psychology, sociology and law. In addition, going beyond these established fields, our contributors offer insights from the standpoints of biochemistry, psychobiology and developmental biology.

In this introduction, we will first explain the reasons for the strong focus on Spain and what makes this country particularly interesting in the study of shared parenting and then present the structure of the book and the main questions asked in each contribution.

Introductory considerations

The family is a reality that experienced a dramatic change during the twentieth century. The patriarchal model has now been replaced by a new system based on respect for human rights, that is, the protection of family life, equality between spouses or cohabitees and the protection of children, who are considered the most vulnerable subjects in families and our society. From a legal perspective, this situation has evolved into the principle of the best interests of the child as the new Gordian knot of family relations. In fact, the trend has increased during the first two decades of the current century. This is a crucial time, in which many indicators show that significant social change is about to take place.

What is certain is that traditional family models are outdated and have completed their life cycle. The romantic idealisation of loving relationships fuelled by the Hollywood film industry fostered a conventional model of a married couple, whereby each spouse has long-term possession of the other. Newly-weds are led to believe that their happiness lies in finding a prince charming or a princess to live with forever. The frustration created by these unrealistic expectations is enormous, resulting in an exponential increase in divorce rates. Divorce is a worldwide reality that affects millions of couples and children. In addition, women have entered the labour market and childcare is now a task for both parents. This joint care of children that is an undisputed norm during marriage is, however, not always accepted after a marriage break-up. Thus, custody of children post-separation is a crucial issue that society must resolve. Moreover, psychological studies suggest that children love and identify with both parents and that to reject one of them is to reject a part of the child. They also remind us that it is important to consider the long-term benefits resulting from addressing children's needs for coming generations. When we take care of our children's well-being, we are also taking care of future generations.

It appears that, even after four decades of research, the main questions about shared parenting still await an answer. Bruce Smyth distinguishes between two types of question: those posed during the first generation of shared parenting studies, which were mainly developed in the United States, and those asked during the second generation of studies resulting from worldwide concern regarding this issue. The basic questions of the first group were: Does joint custody work? When is it most likely to work? When is it likely to fail? Should the courts impose shared parenting?[1] The second set of more comprehensive questions was: What particular dimensions of shared parenting benefit different types of families and under which conditions[2] and "for which children, at what age and under what parenting conditions do shared parenting arrangements pose a developmental strain?"[3]

Answering these questions is a difficult task that, on the one hand, must be the result of thoughtful reflection and, on the other, based on reliable data. We propose taking the study carried out by Smyth in 2017 and published in a special issue of *Family Court Review* as a starting point. The study takes a comparative approach to shared-time parenting around the world by asking leading international researchers to present their latest work.

We can summarise Smyth's findings as follows. On the one hand, although presumptions of equal parenting time are not welcomed by legislators, several countries promote timeshare arrangements as a starting point, always conditioned by the best interests of the child and the safety of family members. On the other hand, during the first two decades of the twenty-first century it seems that timeshare agreements have gradually increased. This popularity is due to wider social, cultural and legislative change[4] and likely also results from the idea that shared parenting coincides with some of the most fundamental values of our societies.

However, the study mentions two problems. First, the diversity of terminology, which makes it very difficult to interpret the different laws. In fact, shared parenting is a term that can be expressed and interpreted as parenthood with shared time, shared physical custody, shared custody, shared care, shared residence, alternative residence and co-parenthood, depending on the legislation of the particular state. However, the concepts may also differ. If we compare the terminology used in the United States with that used in Spain, for example, the term "custody" is used in the latter as the equivalent of "physical custody" and the term "parental responsibility" as "legal custody". As Smyth states,[5] shared parenting is a term that can refer to a wide range of the time a child spends with each of his or her parents, from 25 to 50%. For this reason, definitions also differ from one legislation to another.

Second, the pool of reliable data[6] is scarce. Population data is crucial for assessing trends and understanding the effects that implementation of a specific legal measure may have on a given society. In any case, trying to adapt the conclusions of data from one country to another may be risky, if social and cultural patterns diverge. Likewise, as Girard points out, it may be counter-productive to imitate the wishes and ways of lives of others.[7]

Strong focus on Spain

This book is largely the fruit of a family law conference held in Málaga, Spain, in December 2019, which explains the high number of contributions from Spanish authors. Spanish family law is a melting pot in which different cultural and legal traditions come together. On the one hand, it is a bridge between the Western European legal world and Latin-American law. There is even a strong connection between Spanish and Philippine family law resulting from historical legal bonds. On the other hand, it is a meeting point between the Northern European Lutheran vision of family and society and the Mediterranean vision, resulting from efforts over the last forty years to modernise Spanish law and society. Finally, it is law that is halfway between Continental Law and Common Law. This is due to the important reform resulting from the adoption of the new Procedural Law that has given a new role to the case law of the Spanish Supreme Court. This special juncture is what makes Spanish family law so special. In fact, due to its dynamism and innovative spirit, it could be considered as a true research laboratory, in which the transition to twenty-first century reality is taking place.

It is worthwhile mentioning that Spain is a particularly interesting case for the study of shared parenting and the effect of different legislations. Spain has a special legal system, in which, for historical reasons, certain autonomous communities (*comunidades autonomas*, which are equivalent to American states) are able to legislate custody matters on their own. Most of the autonomous communities entitled to do so have adopted more favourable legislation relating to shared physical custody than that provided by the Spanish Civil Code, which makes shared physical custody the exception and is binding for the other communities.[8] An interesting observation can be made here: with the exception of the Balearic Islands, in autonomous communities with laws favouring shared custody, the percentage of children living in such an arrangement is above the national average. In the others, it is below.[9] Some of our contributors have analysed the influence of legislation on the promotion of shared parenting.[10]

Figure 0.1 shows the evolution of the percentage of shared custody in Spanish autonomous communities in recent years. There is a notable difference between the

SP DECISIONS 2017

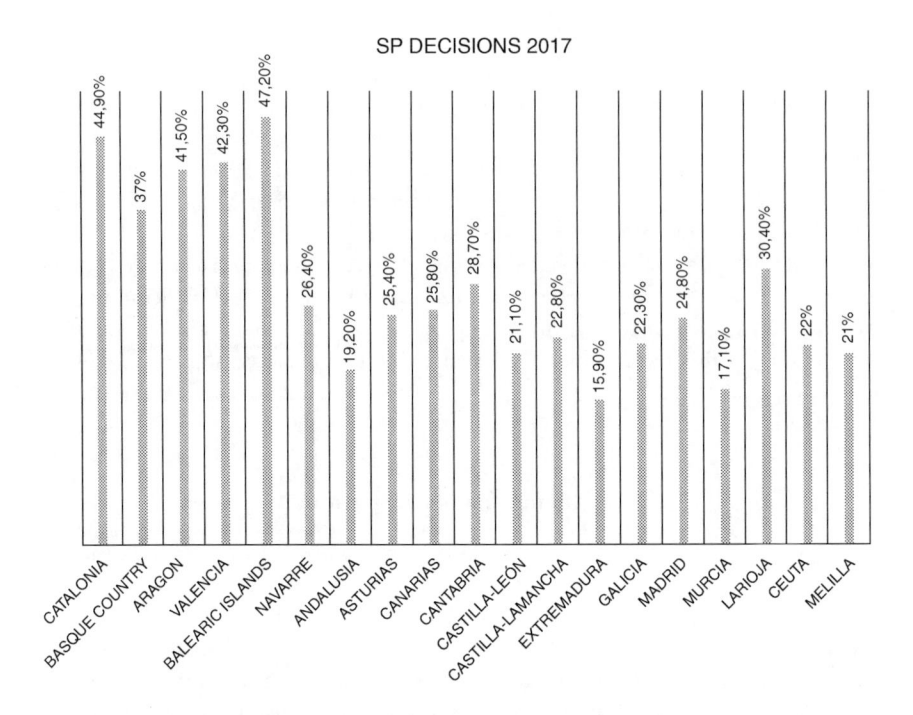

Region	Percentage
CATALONIA	44.90%
BASQUE COUNTRY	37%
ARAGON	41.50%
VALENCIA	42.30%
BALEARIC ISLANDS	47.20%
NAVARRE	26.40%
ANDALUSIA	19.20%
ASTURIAS	25.40%
CANARIAS	25.80%
CANTABRIA	28.70%
CASTILLA-LEÓN	21.10%
CASTILLA-LAMANCHA	22.80%
EXTREMADURA	15.90%
GALICIA	22.30%
MADRID	24.80%
MURCIA	17.10%
LARIOJA	30.40%
CEUTA	22%
MELILLA	21%

Figure 0.1 Percentage of shared custody rulings in autonomous communities in Spain

autonomous communities with laws more in favour of shared parenting than those of the Civil Code, in which shared custody is considered an exception in the absence of an agreement. Perhaps the most obvious exception is the case of the Balearic Islands which, despite not having passed legislation in favour of shared custody, nonetheless have a higher percentage of children looked after in this way. The explanation could possibly be the fact that the Balearic Islands are within the circle of influence of Catalan and Valencian law. Legislation in favour of shared custody in these two areas may have influenced the courts in the Balearic Islands.

In addition, another interesting phenomenon has occurred in Spain in this respect. Since 2009 and especially due to the intervention of Judge Encarna Roca, the Spanish Supreme Court has developed case law in favour of shared parenting. In accordance with this line of case law, the Supreme Court issued a ruling in 2013 that created a precedent by stating that, despite the provisions of Article 92.8 of the Spanish Civil Code, in the absence of an agreement, shared parenting should not be considered as the exception but as the best possible measure to be considered.[11] Since then, the total percentage of children living in shared custody in Spain has multiplied exponentially, as shown in Figure 0.2. These two figures suggest a connection between the percentage of shared parenting arrangements and legislative measures or case law positions, which is an interesting issue to consider, especially if we want to promote shared parenting. This approach is developed in depth by Becerril Ruiz and Jiménez Cabello in Chapter 12.

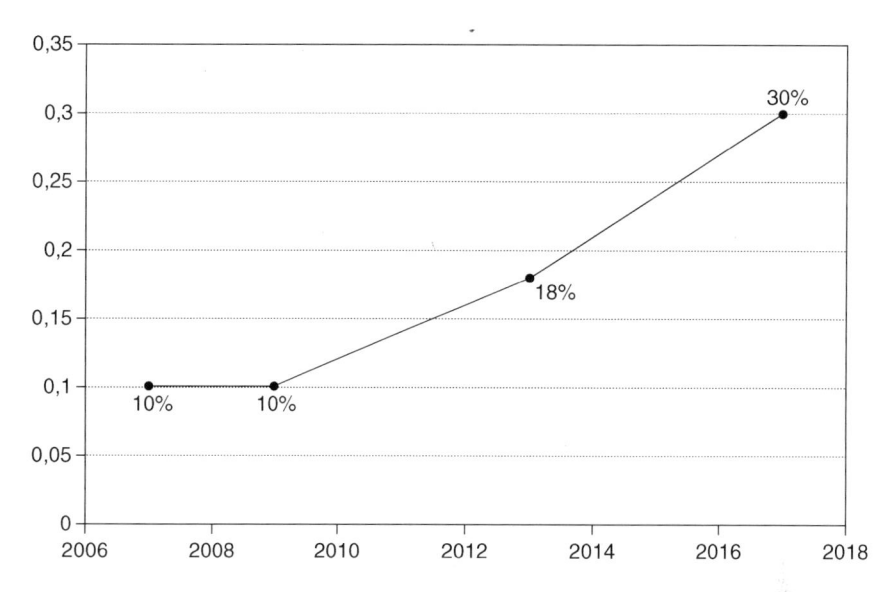

Figure 0.2 Evolution of the percentage of shared custody in Spain since the Supreme Court changed its jurisprudence. The percentage reflects the number of shared custody with respect to the total number of separations and divorces with children that have taken place in Spain from year 2006 to year 2018
Source: Instituto Nacional de Estadística, Spain

Main issues discussed in this volume

We now focus on the issues discussed in the contributions to this book. As mentioned in the Preface, we find varied opinions on crucial, sometimes conflicting, issues. Some authors make the case for a legal rebuttable presumption in favour of shared parenting, while others consider that such a possibility is incompatible with the principle of the best interests of the child and defend the status quo. Some chapters oppose the idea of considering parental alienation as a decision-making tool, while others claim that, as a form of family violence and child abuse, parental alienation is an essential consideration in child protection or custody decisions. These disputes are just a reflection of some of the key issues in the academic and professional practice debate examined in this volume. Our aim is to provide readers with the state of current scientific knowledge in this area and also a glimpse of the guidelines proposed by experts to resolve the different controversies that have arisen. However, we point out from the outset that some of these issues remain open and require further studies that provide data from which we can draw final conclusions.

In search of the right approach

The first thing to consider is what approach should be taken when deciding on the type of parenting that is appropriate for a child. Should it be a parent- or child-centred approach? In the case of a child-centred approach, the next question to be answered is how to make it effective. If we reflect on this question, we realise that the most appropriate way to make it effective might be to put ourselves into the child's shoes. This may require a change in approach, which is undoubtedly a difficult task that is not always understood by professionals, especially in the legal field. Parkinson and Cashmore (Chapter 1), however, succeed when presenting their findings on children's experiences with shared parenting in Australia.

This approach requires a certain commitment to how parents relate to their child. It will be necessary to determine how parents should behave in order to build a relationship that is focused on their child. Furthermore, it should be questioned whether a child-centred approach is crucial only when a decision on the parenting arrangement is taken or whether it is equally vital to maintain this approach for the duration of the arrangement. Finally, it will be necessary to determine what it means to have a "meaningful relationship" with a parent and what this involves.

Factors to consider at the outset when deciding on parenting arrangements

Another important issue to be addressed relates to the logistical factors necessary for shared custody to be viable. It will be important to identify the benefits and risks that a shared custody system can create. This assessment may be useful to reveal which risk factors may make shared custody inadvisable.

Traditional positions claim that shared parenting is conditioned by three factors: the absence of parental conflict, the family income, which should be medium or high and, finally, the quality of parenting skills and the parent–child relationships. With respect to the latter, it has been argued that the better outcomes for joint physical custody of children are *caused* by better relationships and parenting skills at the outset and that more time does not increase the child's well-being. Therefore, there is no benefit in sharing parenting. It is important to note that, in support of these assumptions, the quantity of time was often considered as equivalent to frequency of contact.

The impact of these factors traditionally used to limit the possibility of shared parenting must be analysed to determine whether they actually justify excluding limitations. It must also be investigated whether it is appropriate to reduce parenting decisions to a single factor, such as the existence of parental conflict.

Questions to be answered include whether, in the case of shared parenting: the parents have little in common with parents who opt for sole custody with regard to family income, level of conflict and "quality"; children in sole physical custody have better outcomes than children in joint physical custody; income, conflict and quality levels are the same; shared physical custody leads to worse results for children than sole physical custody; and "quality", income and conflict levels are not optimal.

Perhaps the most controversial issue is whether parental conflict is compatible with shared parenting. Questions relating to this topic may include: is it true that shared parenting is the worst arrangement for children if it leaves them "in the middle of a war zone" in a high-conflict divorce? Or, in contrast, is it possible for children to benefit from shared parenting even when the parents have high levels of conflict? In other words: can positive effects associated with shared parenting reduce the negative impact of conflict on a child's well-being? Are there different types of conflict? Is all conflict (equally) toxic for children? Is it possible to limit children's exposure to parental conflict? Can conflict be unilaterally instigated? What consequences would this have? Is conflict generally static or dynamic? Does conflict tend to decrease when litigation concludes?

The answers to these questions require data provided by scientific studies and its correct interpretation. Several of the chapters in this book refer to studies carried out in recent years. Nielsen (Chapter 3), to our knowledge, provides the most complete existing summary of the results of quantitative studies comparing the well-being of children in joint and sole physical custody. She also refers to what the results of the studies imply for the aforementioned questions on conflict, income and quality.

Is there persuasive evidence that shared parenting provides real benefits to children?

Perhaps the central focus of shared parenting research is limited to one simple question: Is there evidence that shared parenting, understood as a living arrangement in which the child lives at least 35% of the time with each parent, benefits the child after separation or divorce? The answer to this question cannot be found in the legal sphere, but rather in the experience of psychology professionals. However, an objective answer requires a previous series of studies that provide data. These studies should not only be approached from the point of view of psychology but also sociology. Lamb and Braver (Chapter 2) focus on this question and dedicate their chapter to presenting the conclusions of twelve experts at a conference held in Boston in 2017. Other authors have addressed these important issues concerning the reliability of existing shared parenting research and what its results may imply for policy and practice. In addition, they suggest how future research can be improved to provide better answers (Braver and Votruba, Chapter 5; López Narbona, Moreno Mínguez and Ortega Gaspar, Chapter 13).

This prompts the question: assuming that children fare better if parenting is shared, are these better outcomes actually *caused* by shared parenting and not by other factors, such as those mentioned above. Other questions are: Is there evidence that, on average, children prefer to spend substantial and even equal time with both parents? Could it be said that children are at a disadvantage if they do not have a secure attachment to both the adult caregivers? Is there evidence that, during their first three years of life, children should be cared for by their mother only? In the chapters mentioned above, many of the answers to these questions can be found.

Should there be a shared parenting rebuttable presumption?

As Lamb and Braver state in Chapter 2, a *presumption* in law is an assumption made by a court as the basis for decisions. Generally, presumptions in family law are considered rebuttable and are accepted by the court until and unless proven otherwise. For this reason, the relevant question is whether there should be a legal rebuttable presumption in favour of shared parenting in the event that the parents do not reach an agreement. It seems necessary to mention this explicitly, as those suggesting a presumption have been accused of "forcing all parents" into shared parenting (including those who voluntarily choose sole physical custody), thus discrediting their proposal.

This presumption is perhaps the issue behind the most heated debates, not only among academics, but also or even mainly between different social bodies. This debate has reached the parliaments in several nations. In fact, we are now at a decisive moment in which proposals for and against this presumption are being put forward.

A number of questions arise when reflecting on this issue. Is there currently sufficient evidence to allow social scientists to recommend that politicians cautiously adopt the presumption in favour of shared custody? Would it be necessary for researchers to continue their work before making any recommendations? Have sufficient studies of a sufficient scope been conducted to show new evidence in support of shared parenting? Braver and Votruba attempt to answer these questions in Chapter 5. Can it be said that the legal admission of this presumption would be detrimental to mothers who suffer from violence? Could shared parenting prevent parental alienation?

If a presumption were to be accepted, we should consider in which exceptional cases and based upon which factors could it be rebutted. Could these exceptions include the risk of negligence on the part of one of the parents? The risk of family abduction? The fact that the child requires special care? The existence of gender or domestic violence? Could the existence of a high level of parental conflict or the opposition of one of the parents to shared parenting be considered as factors to rebut the presumption? Kruk, Guerra González, Ortiz-Tallo, Ferragut, Iglesias Martín, Sünderhauf-Kravets and Widrig deal with these issues, offering different perspectives, in Chapters 18–22 of this book.

The book, however, does not stop at a mere debate of this topic. A presumption in favour of shared parenting has been introduced into the legislation of Arizona, USA, and the impact of these legislative changes on those concerned has been analysed by Fabricius, Aaron, Akins, Assini and McElroy. You can find the results of their study in Chapter 29.

Are the best interests of the child "a" or "the" primary consideration?

Directly connected to the above issue is the debate on the scope of the principle of the best interests of the child. This is because one of the main objections to a presumption in favour of shared parenting is the view that it is incompatible with the principle of the best interests of the child. Thus, it is suggested that this principle requires a case-by-case examination and an ad hoc solution for each issue affecting the child.

This objection must be considered in relation to two very different approaches used with respect to the best interests of the child (BIC). In the first, the BIC are applied as "a" primary consideration and, in the second, as "the" primary consideration. Different legal systems have adopted either the first or the second of these approaches. This has led to different perspectives and outcomes. De Torres Perea

(Chapter 4) writes extensively on this topic. He finds that one of the most interesting issues related to this divergence is the compatibility of a shared parenting presumption with the BIC principle. However, we must also ask ourselves whether the flexibility and generality inherent in the undefined legal term BIC leads to more problems than the intended child-friendly outcomes.

In Chapter 6, Widrig also addresses concerns expressed in the doctrine about the BIC standard, pointing out that legislation, which violated most fundamental rights of the child, was justified by the claim that it serves the BIC and suggests interpreting the BIC in the light of the United Nations Convention on the Rights of the Child.

Tools and approaches to facilitate practice

A factor that could produce better results in practice is an open-minded attitude on the part of parents to alternative means of resolving disputes rather than adversarial proceedings before courts. Sünderhauf-Kravets (Chapter 24) explores mandatory mediation, its advantages and requirements, and how to make it work using the successful Australian family relationship centres as a reference. De Lucchi López-Tapia (Chapter 25) does the same with respect to parenting coordination.

Lillo (Chapter 26) explains the PIFE intervention method to restore parent–child bonds that have been ruptured by conflict or alienation dynamics. Hietanen (Chapter 23) presents the Cooperative Parenting Triangle, developed by the Federation of Mother and Child Homes and Shelters in Finland, to support parents of divorce. Widrig (Chapter 36) highlights the "Zaunegger approach", developed by the European Court of Human Rights, as a tool to ensure respect for most fundamental rights of the child. Mazeh (Chapter 14) provides an interesting list of criteria to take into account when deciding on the custody of children.

Insights from all over the world

In the final part of the book, you will find a series of essays on diverse experiences in relation to shared parenting in different geographical areas. De Torres Perea (Chapter 28) provides a comparative scenario on the evolution of shared parenting regulations in Western countries in. Maxwell (Chapter 34) gives insights into Scotland, Kopčanová (Chapter 35) into Slovakia, Martín Fuster (Chapter 32) and Casado Casado (Chapter 27) into Spain, Siddiqi (Chapter 31) into Pakistan, Quan and Guerra-Termulo (Chapter 30) into the Philippines and Meland (Chapter 33) into Norway.

Many other topics

Our scholars address many other important topics. Although we can only mention them briefly, they provide valuable insights for interested readers. Cano Hurtado (Chapter 15) and Mazeh (Chapter 14) explore questions on relocation; Martín Fuster (Chapter 16) refers to the impact of shared parenting on the parties' economic interests; Avilés Hernándes (Chapter 7) addresses the delicate situation of unaccompanied minors migrating to Spain; García Vilardell (Chapter 8) provides solutions for parental conflict over children's religious and moral education; Goñi Huarte (Chapter 9) explores the compatibility of custody decisions with child welfare legislation in Spain ; and Mazeh (Chapter 17) addresses the discrimination of children from second families in relation to children from first families.

New approaches

To conclude this Introduction, we would like to refer to a whole new way of understanding family law matters, determined by scientific fields that, until now, have not been taken into consideration when studying the best interests of the child or shared parenting. We refer to the fields of biochemistry, psychobiology, epigenetics and development biology. As Beyerlein (Chapter 10) describes, after two decades of genome sequencing research we are able to reconstruct and understand the physiologic mechanisms leading to cell differentiation, organ differentiation and development of a person's character, that is, developing into the physiological individuum. The amount of biologic information generated throughout individual development is calling for a new way of thinking about the requirements for the environment in which children grow up. A new understanding of our developmental biology offers a wide range of explanations regarding when, why and how missing biological parents and/or a substitution of biological parents by foster parents will have a significant impact on the biology of the developing child and its long-term future. Vezzetti (Chapter 11) investigates, from a biological perspective, the impact of parental loss and other childhood adversities in relation to parental separation on the well-being of children. He analyses the impact of this on public health and suggests means by which policy and practice could be improved.

Conclusion

This chapter presents the roadmap for this book. The main issues, questions and doubts raised by both academics and practitioners regarding shared parenting and the best interests of the child have been formulated systematically. We now invite the reader to become immersed in the different chapters selected for this book. We hope that reading this material enables the reader to find answers to many questions and formulate new ones – as this is how science advances.

Notes

1 Smyth, B. M. 2017. Special issue on shared-time parenting after separation. *Family Court Review* 55/4: 494–495.
2 Pruett, M., and Barker, C. 2009. Joint custody: A judicious choice for families – but how, when and why? In R. Galatzer-Levy, L. Kraus, and L. Galatzer-Levy (eds), *The scientific basis of child custody decisions*, 2nd ed. Hoboken, NJ: Wiley, p. 417 f.
3 McIntosh, J. 2009. Legislating for shared parenting: Exploring some underlying assumptions. *Family Court Review* 47: p. 397.
4 Smyth. n. 23.

5 Ibid.
6 Ibid.
7 Girard, R. 2012. *Resurrection from the underground: Feodor Dostoevsky*. East Lansing: Michigan State University Press, p. 88 f. In this respect, we would like to mention the controversy created in Bhutan after it started broadcasting television channels. In fact, criticism has been raised as to whether TV really brings happiness or rather contributes to breaking up family life by reproducing previously unknown behaviours in that geographical area.
8 Extensively hereto: Solsona Pairó, M., Ajenjo Cosp, M., Brullet Tenas, C., and Gómez-Casillas, A. 2020. *La custodia compartida en los tribunales*. Barcelona: Icaria Editorial, p. 53 ff.
9 Ibid., p. 25 ff. In 2017, there was one exception from this observation: Navarra, with its own legislation, fell below the national average, and behind Cantabria and La Rioja (both bound by the Spanish Civil Code). Also, La Rioja made it just above the national average.
10 See D. Becerril Ruiz and J Jimenez-Cabello, this handbook, Chapter 12.
11 Judgement of the Spanish Supreme Court, of 29 April 2013 (RJ\2013\3269). Reporting Judge: José Antonio Seijas Quintana.

PART I

Best interest of the child and shared parenting

1
CHILDREN'S EXPERIENCES OF SHARED CARE

Patrick Parkinson and Judith Cashmore

Introduction

In many parts of the world, there has been huge controversy about whether the law should be reformed to encourage more shared parenting, or shared care, if parents live apart.[1] The term 'shared care' is used in this chapter to refer to a parenting arrangement that involves children spending at least five nights every two weeks, on average, in each parent's home. That is, even if the arrangement gives primary care to one parent, the children spend nights with the other, not only at weekends but also during the school week.

Calm and reasoned debate on the issue of shared care, informed by the available evidence, has not been assisted by the polarised way in which some advocates have framed the issue as being about fathers' rights rather than children's interests.[2] Some opposition to shared parenting reforms has been apocalyptic in its tone.[3] Notwithstanding the opposition to change, the trend of law reform in Europe, North America and Australasia has been towards encouraging the greater involvement of both parents in children's lives after separation, and some jurisdictions require courts to consider the option of an equal time or other shared care arrangement.[4]

While much has been written *about* children in shared parenting arrangements, there is still only a limited body of research that has involved actually listening to the children themselves to hear about their experiences, needs and interests.

This chapter draws upon Australian research in which we have been involved, interviewing children and young people in several studies. Comparisons are made with other studies. As can be expected, children's experiences of shared parenting arrangements are quite varied, but this qualitative research does provide insights about when shared parenting arrangements work for children and young people, and why.

Research on children's views and experiences

For the most part, the studies that have actually interviewed children are small-scale qualitative studies. One such study was conducted in Britain by Carol Smart and colleagues.[5] In interviews with 30 children and young people in shared parenting arrangements in Britain, they found that some children were much more positive about shared care than others. For some, where the arrangement was inflexible and the idea of 'equal time' was invested with heavy ideological or emotional significance by a parent, it could be very oppressive. For others, the arrangement worked very well and provided benefits not only in having the regular involvement of both parents, but also in giving chances for a brief 'sabbatical' in the relationship with each of them, as the child moved from one household to the other.

In a follow-up of these children, three–four years later, Smart identified three factors that made the difference between successful and unsuccessful shared care arrangements.[6] These were whether: (1) the arrangement was based on the needs and wishes of the parents or those of the children; (2) the arrangements were flexible enough to accommodate changing needs and circumstances; and (3) the children felt equally 'at home' in both of their parents' homes.

Carlberg et al.'s study in Sweden involved responses from 22 young people in shared care arrangements. Like Smart et al., they also found a range of reactions to shared care. Interviewees valued the opportunity to spend a great deal of time with both parents; but some, at least, found the constant transition between homes a problem. Some would have preferred to have one primary abode.[7] The authors reported:[8]

> The young people who are most satisfied with alternating residency are those who have parents who are flexible, can cooperate, and live near each other. Many youths think that the parents have succeeded well with coming to agreements and finding solutions that work for the children. Those with parents who live near each other are very satisfied with this and highlight it as something that their parents have really done well.

Haugen's study in Norway involved interviews with 5 girls and 10 boys, aged 9–18, who were in shared care.[9] All except one child had homes that were within walking distance of one another. Several reported a flexible arrangement, whereby they were allowed to visit the other parent's home when they wanted to, outside of the normal shared care schedule. This worked well for them. Others valued the equal time arrangement but expressed some reservations about how well it was working for them. Only one child was in a rigid time-sharing arrangement – enforced strictly at her father's insistence.

A Utah study involving 17 children aged 5–11 in 10 families found that joint physical custody arrangements, as they were known in that jurisdiction, do not imperil children's neighbourhood friendships.[10] This was so even though sometimes their friends had to be turned away when they came around inviting the child to play and he or she was at the other parent's house. Parents knew their children's friends and would facilitate play dates.

Various Australian studies add to the picture. Lodge and Alexander conducted telephone interviews with 623 adolescents, aged 12–18 years.[11] About 17 per cent, over 100 adolescents, reported that they were in shared care arrangements. This was more common for 12–14 year olds than for older adolescents. Overall, 61 per cent of adolescents in equal time arrangements were very happy with this arrangement and 32 per cent were somewhat happy. While 7 per cent were unhappy with the arrangement, this percentage was not dissimilar to the percentage of those unhappy with other care arrangements. However, those who were in equal time arrangements were more likely to desire changes, for example, to have more consistency of place.[12]

Sadowski and MacIntosh interviewed 16 children, aged 8–12 years, from 11 different families.[13] The study employed a descriptive phenomenological methodology, focused upon children's experiences of security and contentment in shared care, or the absence thereof. They found that time was not a central issue for the children. No child mentioned the allotment of time with each parent as having any bearing on their sense of security.[14] Far more important was the way in which the parents behaved towards one another and created a sense of continuing family. The authors identified a number of factors that were core to creating security and contentment, including the parents' willingness and ability to[15]:

- Be together from time to time in the same physical space, conflict-free in front of the child;
- Share simple enjoyment and pride in their child, on occasions of meaning to the child, such as school functions, sporting events, family gatherings
- Create benign intimacy when together in the child's presence (such as genuine intent when saying hello, sharing a laugh);
- Enable the child to connect with the 'absent' parent, especially to reach out to this parent in times of need, without guilt or worry about hurting the other parent's feelings;
- Cultivate the sense of living in a separated but still integrated family (through actions such as joining together for events of significance to the child, and communicating openly to keep apprised of the child's day-to-day life); and
- Prioritise the needs of the child.

In another Australian study, Campo et al. interviewed 12 boys and 10 girls, aged 10–18, from 15 different families.[16] Nine of these children were in equal time arrangements and another three had at least 30–45 per cent of nights with each parent. There were changes in the patterns of parenting arrangements over time. Six children in equal time arrangements said their arrangements had not changed at all. These children were more likely to be satisfied with their living arrangements if their parents lived close to one another and parented in a cooperative manner, without on-going conflict. Logistical problems, such as the time taken to get from one home to school by bus, impeded satisfaction with the arrangements. Indeed, four children who were no longer in equal time arrangements cited travel between homes as a reason for seeking changes to the arrangements. Children in shared time arrangements spoke about shared time as being 'fair' and consistent with loving their parents equally.

University of Sydney studies

We conducted a number of studies at the University of Sydney involving interviews with children who have experienced parental separation.[17] In most cases, the children have been caught up in legal disputes about the parenting arrangements.

In the *Children's Voices* project, we interviewed 90 parents and 47 children and young people who had had a family law dispute of some kind.[18] In the *Relocation* study, we interviewed 80 parents in 70 families up to three times over a five-year period. These were almost all cases in which the mother wanted to relocate a considerable distance with the children.[19] In one case, it was the mother who was opposing the relocation. We also interviewed 33 children.[20] In the *Adolescent Views* study,[21] we conducted an analysis of telephone interviews with 60 adolescents aged 12–19 (average age of 14.7 years) in Australia concerning their views on parenting arrangements.[22] In the *Shared Care* study, we reported findings from an online survey of 136 children and adolescents (aged 8–17 years) as part of a larger study of shared care arrangements commissioned by the Australian Government.[23] Overall, 20 were in shared care arrangements. Details of the methodology of each study are contained in the relevant publications.

A number of themes emerged from these studies that add to the body of other research on children's views and experiences.

Heterogeneity of children's views and experiences

In working out what is best for children, so much depends on the circumstances, and the relationships between them and their parents. There were children in our studies who were completely estranged from one parent, and others who were very close to both. It was common in our studies for children to express greater closeness to their mothers than their fathers, and in some cases they experienced difficulties in the relationship with their father. Some wanted their fathers to be more involved in their lives than the fathers were, it seems, willing to be.

The quality of relationship that children have with each parent will vary from one child to another; so generalisations about what will be best for them need to be made cautiously. Siblings may also differ in their views, illustrated by two sisters in our Relocation study, both of whom were in a week-about equal time arrangement. The mother wanted to move with the children about two hours away to facilitate a relationship with a new partner. Melinda, the older daughter, was interviewed at age 10, before any decision had been made about the relocation. She said she did not want to go, but had experienced some difficulty in making that clear to her mother:

> Has Mum asked you about how you feel about moving?
> Yeah.
> And what have you told her?
> 'Yeah', and then she asked me again and I said 'no' and then asked me again and I said 'yes', and then again and I said 'no'.

Melinda felt very close to both parents, was happy in an equal time arrangement and was stressed about being caught up in the conflict between her parents. However, her eight-year-old sister, Zoe, had a very different view. She going 'backwards and forwards' between her parents difficult and wanted to live most of the time with her mother. When we interviewed Zoe again, two years later, she expressed the wish that her parents would reconcile: 'I want to live with both. I just wish they'd join up together.' While children's views, from our studies, do not suggest that there is one parenting arrangement that is best for children and young people in the abstract, there were numerous positives that emerged from our studies that support the serious consideration of shared care arrangements as being a very workable and suitable arrangement.

An equal time arrangement is a preferred option for many children

Many children and young people express a preference, even a strong preference, for a shared care arrangement, particularly children in their middle years of schooling. In our Relocation study, a recurring theme in the interviews of children was a preference for an equal time arrangement among those who had good relationships with both parents. Many younger children would have preferred that their parents had not separated.[24]

A preference for shared care was evident, also, in the Adolescent Views study. Half the young people said that they did not have enough time with their non-resident parent. Having a continuing and meaningful relationship with both parents, and with siblings, was very important to them. In answer to a question about optimal parenting arrangements if parents divorce, the most common preference (22/66, 33.3 per cent) was that the time should be evenly divided.

The preference for an equal time arrangement did not necessarily mean that this was feasible for the young people interviewed. There were various factors that impacted upon whether a shared care arrangement was possible, not least the parents' respective locations. Our finding that shared care was nonetheless a preferred option for many children in the abstract is consistent with the findings of Fabricius and Hall, who reported that 70 per cent of adult students from divorced families believed that the best living arrangement for children was equal time with each parent.[25] However, only about 20 per cent of the students in that study said they had wanted equal time themselves, 'given their particular family circumstances'.[26]

Many children who are not in shared care want more time with the other parent

In our Shared Care study, we found that nearly 40 per cent of the children who were living primarily with one parent wanted to see the other parent more often. Indeed, there were children who clearly equated their parents' time and the amount of effort they made to see them as a marker of their parents' love for them.

Twelve children ranging in age from 11 to 17, all in the primary care of one parent, wanted equal time arrangements. Their reasons included wanting to protect one or both parents and to improve their relationships with them.

Children want to be fair to both parents

One factor leading so many children and young people to favour an equal time arrangement may be their 'ethic of fairness'.[27] In their interviews with 30 children and young people in shared parenting arrangements in Britain, Carol Smart and her colleagues found that children took on a sense of responsibility about being fair to each parent. Their own sense about what arrangements were fair was thus influenced by how they saw those arrangements through the eyes of their parents.

This was a theme also in our studies. Some children indicated that they felt some responsibility for keeping their parents happy. Shared care was seen as a way of doing this. For example, in the Adolescent Views study, young people who expressed a preference for shared care explained their rationale in terms of what was fair for the parents:

> They should have half and half so they both get a chance to be involved with the kids.
>
> *(13-year-old child living with her mother)*

> Half and half; spend one week with one parent and one week with the other provided they live near each other and the kid is happy doing it.
>
> *(14-year-old child living with her mother)*

A similar theme emerged in the Shared Care study. For example, children in shared care arrangements said:

> I see both my mum and dad equally which makes them happy as well.
>
> *(12-year-old boy)*

> It keeps both my parents happy, or happy enough.
>
> *(16-year-old girl)*

Children's sense of fairness is correlated with participation

Norwegian researchers who surveyed 527 parents with equal time arrangements found that 25 per cent of the children participated to a significant degree in the decision; 21 per cent reported that the child had some influence in the decision; and 55 per cent said that the child had no influence at all. Age was, of course, a significant factor in whether children's views were taken into account.[28]

Likewise, in the Adolescent Voices study, we found that half of the young people reported that they had no say at all in where they would live after separation. There was a strong relationship between young people's perceptions of the fairness of the parenting arrangements and the extent to which they were allowed to participate in making those arrangements.

In our Shared Care study, children who felt they had some say in the arrangements were significantly happier with the arrangements than those who had not. When asked what advice, if any, they would give to other children after their parents separate, the most common response was to 'have a say if you want to'. A consistent theme was to have a say and not be forced into arrangements by parents.

Participation was also an important theme in our Children's Voices project. The interviews with 47 children concerned their understanding of, and participation in, decision making about parenting arrangements following the separation of their parents. Thirty-five children were re-interviewed 18–30 months after the first interview, to explore any changes in their arrangements and their views about being involved in making or changing those arrangements.

Sixty per cent of the children said they had had some say (either 'a bit' or 'a fair bit') at some stage in the arrangements about where they would live and when they would see their parents after the separation. For some children, especially those who had been very young, this was not in the immediate aftermath of their parents' separation but some years later when circumstances changed or the children wanted them to change. Most children (91 per cent) said that they should be involved, though not necessarily in *making* the decisions. Most of the children who expressed strong and unqualified views were involved in contested matters, whereas those who said that they wanted to be involved but did not want to make the decision themselves were more likely to be involved in non-contested matters without high levels of conflict or violence.

There were several themes in children's comments concerning the reasons they wanted to be involved, themes that have emerged in other studies.[29] These included the need to be acknowledged, the belief that this would ensure more informed decisions and better outcomes, and the view that they had the right to have some say in the arrangements that would affect them most. Emma, 13, explained her rationale as follows:

> I think that it's important for them to have a say because it's their lives and they're going to have to deal with it and it's a choice that I think personally is up to them. It's not whether the parents want them to be with them because I'm hoping both of the parents want to be with their kids.

Having their voice heard and their views taken into account is very important to children and young people, even though they do not want to determine the outcome. Being listened to and having their concerns recognised is also an indicator to children of the quality of their relationship with parents.

Closeness

In the Shared Care study, we found that children in shared care were closer to their mothers than their fathers, but no less close than the children who were living with their mothers most of the time. Similarly, there was no significant difference between children in shared care and those living most of the time with their fathers regarding how close they felt to their fathers. Several of the children in shared care arrangements thought they were closer to their father than they would have been if they spent most of the time living with their mother and only saw their father on weekends.

This view is consistent with a finding from the Adolescent Views study that children who stayed overnight with their (non-resident) fathers were not less close to their mothers than those who did not stay overnight, and the frequency of overnight stays with the non-resident parent made no difference.[30]

Logistics

An important aspect of living in more than one home for both adults and children is managing the practical issues: keeping in contact with friends, getting from one place to another and to school or work, and managing one's belongings so that things that are needed are not left behind.

In the Shared Care study, children were asked to rate how much of a problem it was if they left something behind at the other parent's home – from 'not a problem at all' to 'a really big problem'. Children in shared care did not report that it was significantly more of a problem if they left things behind than children living mostly with one parent, although there was a trend in that direction ($p = 0.06$). The more of a problem children said it was, however, the less happy they were with their living arrangements.

While leaving things behind was a problem for some children in shared care, it was also a problem for many who were not in shared care as well. The issue here was often more the degree of angst associated with the conflict between the parents, which created or exacerbated any practical difficulty.

Stability

One of the main objections to shared care in the literature is that children, and especially young children, need a stable place to live and to call home. Moving between homes too frequently is seen as disrupting that sense of stability for children. In our Shared Care study, some children who were currently in, or had experienced, shared care expressed similar concerns about 'moving back and forth all the time' and not having one place to call home. Older adolescents indicated that they preferred to be in one place as they needed to concentrate more on studying in their senior years of high school.

Conflict

Another consistent concern about shared care arrangements is that it is contraindicated or much more difficult if the parents are in continuing conflict and cannot work cooperatively or in parallel without tension. These complaints about parents fighting were more common among children who lived most of their time with one parent, but the children who were unhappy in shared care, with one exception, were those who complained about their parents fighting.

Conclusion

The question about whether shared parenting is better or worse than other patterns of parenting after separation is often discussed in the abstract, comparing outcomes for children in the primary care of one parent, usually the mother, with those in shared parenting arrangements.[31] However, this is not a choice that is available in many cases when parents separate, and, even when it is, may not be sustainable in the years afterwards as parents' and children's circumstances change.

For there to be a functional shared care arrangement, the parents need to be able to afford two viable homes that are sufficiently well furnished to allow children to stay comfortably in each. They need to live reasonably close to one another so that the children can get to school from either home without undue difficulty or time expended in travel. Parents also need to have sufficient flexibility in their working arrangements (or sufficient support in terms of child care) to make the arrangement practicable.

These logistical issues need to be considered carefully in determining whether shared care is even feasible. There are many other factors, beyond the structure of the care arrangement, which affect children's wellbeing, in particular the closeness of the child's relationship to each parent, parental capacity, interparental conflict, safety issues, and adjustments to new partners or stepfamilies.

In determining what parenting arrangement is best for children, it is important to try to see the issues through the eyes of the child. Children are the ones required to do the switching from one home to another, not parents, and their views need to be taken into account. Summarising a number of studies concerning children's experiences of shared care, Birnbaum and Saini found some common themes:[32]

> Participants across the studies seem to favour shared care when they were provided input into the decision-making process, when parents respect and integrate their feelings and concerns, when the parenting plan emphasised and maximised their time with both parents, and when the plan supported a continuous and meaningful relationship with both parents and their siblings post separation and divorce.

It is clear from the various studies of children's views and experiences that there were benefits resulting from shared care for many children. The main benefit was maintaining a relationship with both parents. Having equal time was also seen to be fair. Feeling comfortable and at home in both places could also be both an outcome and a prerequisite for shared parenting to work. Having some respite from one parent in the move to the other was also a perceived benefit for some children.

The costs or disadvantages were the moves back and forth, the lack of one place to call home, especially with the demands of the senior years of high school, and the risk of leaving things behind. However, we found in our studies that these problems were not necessarily unique to shared care. One stable home is very important for some children who feel more comfortable in one home than the other and for whom the costs of moving back and forth exceed the rewards of the extra time with the non-resident parent.

An arrangement that works well at some stages of children's lives may not continue to be suitable as they get older and the demands of education and their social commitments increase. Time with peers becomes progressively more important as children mature. Teenagers spend less time at home than when younger and tend to rely increasingly on their friends. They also tend to argue more frequently with their parents, with typical arguments including issues surrounding the teenagers' desire for greater freedom.

It follows from all of this that not only is it important to listen to children when parenting arrangements are initially made, but to keep on listening as children get older and circumstances change. There are no bright line rules; however, the consistent findings of so many studies into children's views point to common themes. A child-focused shared care arrangement can be excellent for children who have close relationships with both parents. Making it work can take effort, but that is not a challenge that arises only in shared care arrangements. All parenting after separation has its challenges and requires an effort to cooperate with the other parent. Shared care may at times require more cooperation, but to model this well is, in itself, a benefit to the children who can see that their family life continues, albeit in a different way than before the separation.

Notes

1 For discussion of the arguments, see Jenn McIntosh, 'Legislating for Shared Parenting: Exploring Some Underlying Assumptions' (2009) 47 *Family Court Review* 389; Patrick Parkinson, 'The Payoffs and Pitfalls of Laws that Encourage Shared Parenting: Lessons from the Australian Experience' (2014) 37 *Dalhousie Law Journal* 301. See also, William Fabricius, 'Equal Parenting Time: The Case for a Legal Presumption' in Jim Dwyer (ed), *Oxford Handbook of Children and the Law*, Oxford: Oxford University Press, 2020.

2 See, for example, Susan Armstrong, '"We told you so…" Women's Legal Groups and the Family Law Reform Act 1995' (2001) 15 *Australian Journal of Family Law* 129; Michael Flood, '"Fathers' Rights" and the Defense of Paternal Authority in Australia' (2010) 16 *Violence Against Women* 328; Regina Graycar, 'Family Law Reform In Australia, or Frozen Chooks Revisited Again?' (2012) 13 *Theoretical Inquiries in Law* 24; Helen Rhoades, 'The Rise and Rise of Shared Parenting Laws' (2002) 19 *Canadian Journal of Family Law* 75.

3 This has been so particularly in Canada. See, for example, Marie Laing, 'For the Sake of the Children: Preventing Reckless New Laws' (1999) 16 *Canadian Journal of Family Law* 229; Jonathan Cohen and Nikki Gershbain, 'For the Sake of the Fathers? Child Custody Reform and the Perils of Maximum Contact' (2001) 19 *Canadian Family Law Quarterly* 121. See also, Nicholas Bala, 'A Report from Canada's "Gender War Zone": Reforming the Child Related Provisions of the Divorce Act' (1999) 16 *Canadian Journal of Family Law* 163; Nicholas Bala et al., 'Shared Parenting in Canada: Increasing Use but Continued Controversy' (2017) 55 *Family Court Review* 513.

4 Patrick Parkinson, *Family Law and the Indissolubility of Parenthood* (New York: Cambridge University Press, 2011). The research for this book was funded by the Australian Research Council.

5 Carol Smart, Bren Neale & Amanda Wade, *The Changing Experience of Childhood: Families and Divorce* (Cambridge: Polity Press, 2001); Carol Smart, 'From Children's Shoes to Children's Voices' (2002) 40 *Family Court Review* 307.
6 Carol Smart, C. 'Equal Shares: Rights for Fathers or Recognition for Children?' (2004) 24 *Critical Social Policy* 484.
7 M. Carlberg, A. Hardy, E. Elver-Lindstrom & S. Julin, *Växelvis boende: Att bo hos både pappa och mamma fast de inte bor tillsammans* [Alternating *Residency: Living with Both Mother and Father Even Though They Do Not Live Together*] (Stockholm: Socialstyrelsen, 2004).
8 Ibid., 30 (translated from Swedish).
9 Gry Mette D. Haugen, 'Children's Perspectives on Everyday Experiences of Shared Residence: Time, Emotions and Agency Dilemmas' (2010) 24 *Children and Society* 112.
10 Ariana Prazen, Nick Wolfinger, Caitlin Cahill & Lori Kowalesji-Jones, 'Joint Physical Custody and Neighborhood Friendships in Middle Childhood' (2011) 81 *Sociological Inquiry* 247.
11 Jodie Lodge & Michael Alexander, *Views of Adolescents in Separated Families*, Attorney-General's Department, Canberra, December 2010.
12 Ibid., 20–21.
13 Christine Sadowski & Jennifer McIntosh, 'On Laughter and Loss: Children's Views of Shared Time, Parenting and Security Post-separation' (2016) 23 *Childhood* 69.
14 Ibid., 82.
15 Ibid., 82–83.
16 Monica Campo, Belinda Fehlberg, Christine Millward & Rachel Carson, 'Shared Parenting Time in Australia: Exploring Children's Views' (2012) 34 *Journal of Social Welfare and Family Law* 295.
17 We were assisted in various projects by Dr Judi Single (data collection) and Dr Alan Taylor (data analysis).
18 Patrick Parkinson & Judith Cashmore, *The Voice of a Child in Family Law Disputes* (Oxford: Oxford University Press, 2008). See also, Judith Cashmore & Patrick Parkinson, 'Children's and Parents' Perceptions of Children's Participation in Decision-making after Parental Separation and Divorce' (2008) 40 *Family Court Review* 90. The research was funded by the Australian Research Council.
19 For the findings generally, see Patrick Parkinson & Judith Cashmore, 'Reforming Relocation Law: An Evidence-based Approach' (2015) 53 *Family Court Review* 23. The research was funded by the Australian Research Council.
20 Judith Cashmore & Patrick Parkinson, 'Children's "Wishes and Feelings" in Relocation Disputes' (2016) 28 *Child and Family Law Quarterly* 151.
21 This was part of a study associated with the Australian Divorce Transitions Project (ADTP) conducted by the Australian Institute of Family Studies. The principal investigators on the adult project were Kathleen Funder, Grania Sheehan, Bruce Smyth and Belinda Fehlberg. The principal investigators on the children's study were Kate Funder and Grania Sheehan. The Australian Institute of Family Studies invited us to analyse this data.
22 Patrick Parkinson, Judith Cashmore & Judi Single, 'Adolescents' Views on the Fairness of Parenting and Financial Arrangements after Separation' (2005) 43 *Family Court Review* 429; Judith Cashmore, Patrick Parkinson & Alan Taylor, 'Overnight Stays and Children's Relationship with Resident and Nonresident Parents after Divorce' (2008) 29 *Journal of Family Issues* 707.
23 J. Cashmore, P. Parkinson, R. Weston, R. Patulny, G. Redmond, L. Qu, J. Baxter, M. Rajkovic, T. Sitek & I. Katz, *Shared Care Parenting Arrangements since the 2006 Family Law Reforms*, Report to the Australian Government, Attorney-General's Department (2010).
24 Patrick Parkinson, & Judith Cashmore, 'Relocation and the Indissolubility of Parenthood' (2018) 15 *Journal of Child Custody* 76–87.
25 William Fabricius & Jeff Hall, 'Young Adults' Perspectives on Divorce: Living Arrangements' (2000) 38 *Family & Conciliation Courts Review* 446.

26 Ibid., 457.
27 Carol Smart, Amanda Wade & Bren Neale, 'Objects of Concern? Children and Divorce' (1999) 11 *Child and Family Law Quarterly* 365.
28 Kristin Skjørten & Rolf Barlindhaug, 'The Involvement of Children in Decisions about Shared Residence' (2007) 21 *International Journal of Law, Policy and the Family* 373.
29 See, for example, Megan Gollop, Anne Smith & Nicola Taylor, 'Children's Involvement in Custody and Access Arrangements after Parental Separation' (2000) 12 *Child and Family Law Quarterly* 383; Carol Smart & Bren Neale, '"It's My Life Too": Children's Perspectives on Post-divorce Parenting' (2000) 30 *Family Law* 163.
30 Cashmore, Parkinson & Taylor, Note 22.
31 Linda Neilsen, 'Joint versus Sole Physical Custody: Children's Outcomes Independent of Parent–Child Relationships, Income, and Conflict in 60 Studies' (2018) 59 *Journal of Divorce and Remarriage* 1.
32 Rachel Birnbaum & Michael Saini, 'A Qualitative Synthesis of Children's Experiences of Shared Care Post Divorce' (2015) 23 *International Journal of Children's Rights* 109, 126.

2
SHARED PARENTING
Twelve experts exchange views in panel discussions[1]

Michael E. Lamb and Sanford L. Braver

A rather extraordinary event happened in Boston in late May 2017. Expert researchers and scholars of child custody and divorce family law around the world gathered together for two days at a conference jointly sponsored by the National Parents Organization (NPO) and the International Council of Shared Parenting (ICSP) to discuss and explore possible consensus regarding the benefits of shared parenting (SP; also called joint custody, shared care, shared custody, etc.). The program included the usual lectures and presentations (46 in all), but, rather uniquely, the organizers also staged two two-hour panel discussions. These videotaped sessions were moderated by a skilled facilitator, Prof. Donald Hubin, who encouraged all participants to express their views on a series of topics and to answer questions from the audience.

Below, we summarize the panel discussions of the seven interrelated topics that were highlighted after first introducing the 12 panelists.

Dr. Kari Adamsons is Associate Professor of Human Development and Family Studies at the University of Connecticut, who has published many peer-reviewed articles and chapters on fathering, co-parenting, and divorce. She is particularly known for her work on nonresident father involvement and father identity, and is considered one of the leaders of the next generation of fathering scholars.

Dr. William Austin is a nationally recognized expert on child custody evaluations, who has published numerous professional articles and book chapters on this topic and co-chaired the task force that developed the Model Standards of Practice for Child Custody Evaluation for the Association of Family and Conciliation Courts (AFCC).

Dr. Malin Bergström, of the Karolinska Institute in Sweden, has written several books about child development, attachment theory, and parenting. Dr. Bergström's research focuses on children's health and welfare in shared parenting arrangements and she has led rigorous research evaluating the Swedish experience with shared parenting.

Dr. Sanford Braver is Professor Emeritus at Arizona State University, where he served in the Psychology Department for 41 years and was the recipient of 18 competitively reviewed, primarily federal, research grants, totaling over $28 million. His work has been published in nearly 130 peer-reviewed professional articles and chapters, and he is author of three books, including *Divorced Dads: Shattering the Myths* (Braver & O'Connell, 1998).

Prof. Jennifer Harman is Associate Professor of Psychology at Colorado State University. She specializes in the study of intimate relationships and has published many peer-reviewed articles and textbooks on this topic. Her 2016 TEDx talk on parental alienation showcased several ideas from her most recent co-authored and well-received book, *Parents Acting Badly* (Harman & Biringen, 2016).

Dr. Michael Lamb is Professor of Psychology at the University of Cambridge. He has focused his scholarship on the role of father– and mother–child relationships in development over the last 40 years, publishing over 500 professional articles and 50 books, including five editions of *The Role of the Father in Child Development*. He is currently president of APA's Division 7 (Developmental Psychology).

Dr. Pamela Ludolph is a clinical and forensic psychologist in the Department of Psychology at the University of Michigan and in the Child Advocacy Law Clinic at the University's Law School. She is a published author who conducts complex child custody evaluations and frequently lectures to officials, judges, attorneys, and mental health professionals in the US and abroad.

Dr. Linda Nielsen is Professor of Adolescent and Educational Psychology at Wake Forest University. She is an internationally recognized expert on shared physical custody research and father–daughter relationships, and adolescence. She has written three books on father–daughter relationships and three editions of the college textbook, *Adolescence: A Contemporary View*.

Prof. Patrick Parkinson is Professor of Law at the University of Sydney, Australia, and was president of the International Society of Family Law, 2011–2014. He played a major role in the development of legislation and practice in family law and child protection in Australia and helped persuade the Australian government to invest in a national network of Family Relationship Centers, offering mediation and other services to parents going through separation. He has written six books and authored approximately 100 journal articles and book chapters.

Dr. Irwin Sandler is Regents Professor Emeritus in the Department of Psychology at Arizona State University. For over 25 years he directed a national center for research on the development and evaluation of programs to prevent adverse outcomes for children following parental divorce, including by focusing on post-divorce parenting. He is the author of over 200 scientific papers, and has served on several scientific advisory boards and committees.

Prof. Hildegund Sünderhauf has been Professor of Family Law and Youth Welfare Law at the Lutheran University of Applied Sciences in Nuremberg (Germany) for 17 years. She initiated Resolution 2079 of the Parliamentary Assembly of the Council of Europe that calls on the member states to provide for shared residence following a separation, wrote the only monograph about shared parenting in Germany, and co-founded the International Council on Shared Parenting.

Dr. Richard Warshak is Clinical Professor of Psychiatry at the University of Texas Southwestern Medical Center and is one of the world's most respected authorities on divorce, child custody, and the psychology of alienation. He has written 14 books and more than 75 articles in 18 languages that have had a broad impact on family law. His book, *Divorce Poison: How to Protect Your Family from Bad-mouthing and Brainwashing* (2010), has been particularly influential.

Theme 1: Is there indeed persuasive evidence that SP provides real benefit to children of divorce?

This question was the implicit focus of every presentation and discussion during the conference, and there was a remarkable degree of consensus. The empirical evidence currently available strongly suggests that children of divorce, on average, benefit substantially from SP. Findings from well over 50 individual studies (see reviews by Bauserman, 2002; Nielsen, 2015, 2017) indicate that children whose parents have SP fare better than those with sole custody. The beneficial effects are evident on a plethora of outcome measures, including (1) lower levels of depression, anxiety, and dissatisfaction; (2) lower aggression, and reduced alcohol and substance abuse; (3) better school performance and cognitive development; (4) better physical health; (5) lower smoking rates; and (6) better father–child relationships. Of course, some studies have failed to show such benefits, but almost none show that SP *harms* children (at worst, they show no significant difference between children with different custody arrangements). Panelists and participants broadly agreed that a tipping point had been reached, and that the benefits of SP for most children could no longer be doubted.

One of the papers (Braver & Votruba, 2018) presented at the conference addressed the *causal* status of this evidence. Because most of the published studies were cross-sectional or static group comparisons between two or more *pre-existing* groups (Campbell & Stanley, 1963), it was not clear that SP actually caused the better outcomes achieved by children in shared care. Instead, the outcomes could plausibly be attributed to self-selection because SP is generally not granted if either or both parents are unalterably opposed to such arrangements. As a result, whatever factors led both parents to accept the SP arrangements could have explained the children's superior outcomes. After a thorough review of the literature, however, Braver and Votruba ruled out this self-selection explanation and concluded that a causal role for SP was the only viable interpretation. Moreover, findings in jurisdictions such as Sweden, where 50–50 SP is now normative (Bergstrom et al., 2015), imply that the benefits of SP will be obtained even when those arrangements are imposed on parents against their will. As perhaps another sign that public attitudes have changed, perhaps faster than courts and legal scholars recognize, researchers have shown that jury-eligible Americans and Britons recognize the superiority of SP arrangements (Braver et al., 2011).

Theme 2: What is the "active ingredient" of SP and what specific elements make it beneficial?

Most panelists argued that it was beneficial for children to have two involved parents rather than only one. Researchers have shown that if *either* mother or father evinces good parenting, the parenting skills of the other matter far less (Elam et al., 2016; Sandler, Wheeler, & Braver, 2013). Put another way, a good father can "cover" for a less-skilled mother, and vice versa. In an SP arrangement, the child has two chances of receiving good parenting, whereas if a sole parent has deficient parenting skills, the child will suffer because the second parent cannot "come to the rescue". In the language of attachment theory (Bowlby, 1969; Lamb, 2002), children are disadvantaged if they lack secure attachments to adult caregivers/ protectors. Contrary to Bowlby's earlier assumption, children can – and usually do – have more than one such attachment (Lamb & Lewis, 2005), ensuring that the temporary deficiencies or unavailability of one parent are readily compensated for by the other (Braver & Lamb, 2012).

Enhanced access to "social capital" may also explain the superiority of SP (Austin, 2011; Coleman, 1990; Hetherington, 1999). According to this view, social capital describes the array of social resources and mechanisms that promote individuals' well-being and chances of success. The greater the number and effectiveness of these resources, the better off individuals will be. For children of divorce, sole custody deprives them of one of the key sources of social capital, the second parent, whereas SP restores that deficiency, to the children's advantage.

Panelists also pointed out that parenting characteristics are not static. Adults' abilities to parent effectively are affected by what else is going on in their lives. At various times, any parent's attention can be diverted by other events, while parenting skills may be undermined by stress, other demands, and, perhaps, impatience with the child. These are the very times when a second engaged parent can pick up the slack, helping to explain why children in two-parent households are better adjusted, on average (Clarke-Stewart & Brentano, 2006; McLanahan & Teitler, 1999; Simons et al., 1999). Similarly, in SP – but not in sole parenting conditions – the second parent is available to step in. Many decrees capture this sense through *right of first refusal* provisions, which stipulate that one parent must first offer the other parent the opportunity to look after the child before a babysitter or other family member is asked to do so (Meyer, 2016). Accordingly, Fransson et al. (2017) found that the living conditions of children in SP were "on par with children who live with two custodial parents in the same household", especially with regard to economic and material conditions, relations with parents, and health-related outcomes. Children in sole parenting experienced poorer living conditions.

According to the panelists, such compensatory dynamics developed when children had opportunities to build and maintain relationships with both parents, which requires spending adequate amounts of time with both in a variety of circumstances or contexts. Writing on behalf of 18 experts on the effects of divorce, Lamb, Sternberg, and Thompson (1997, p. 400) observed two decades ago that:

> To maintain high-quality relationships with their children, parents need to have sufficiently extensive and regular interactions with them, but the amount of time involved is usually less important than the quality of the interaction that it fosters. Time distribution arrangements that ensure the

involvement of both parents in important aspects of their children's everyday lives and routines … are likely to keep nonresidential parents playing psychologically important and central roles in the lives of their children.

Many recent studies show that attachment relationships, too, are not static and fixed in the first year or so of the child's life, as was earlier thought (see review by Thompson, 2006). Instead, attachments grow and change in quality over time, throughout childhood and adolescence and into adulthood (Lamb & Lewis, 2005). Thus, parenting time allocations must be flexible, and subject to change as the children mature. Laws like those in Michigan, which allow SP to phase in over time, are a step in the right direction (Michigan Friend of the Court, 2016). As one expert pithily put it, "would you want to build and enrich and nurture a relationship with a new spouse based on being together only alternating weekends?"

Children with SP also have better outcomes, it was opined, because such arrangements are preferred by the children themselves. There is convincing evidence (Fabricius & Hall, 2000; Parkinson, Cashmore & Single, 2005; Warshak, 2003) that, on average, children would prefer to spend substantial – even equal – amounts of time with both parents. Fabricius and Hall, for example, found that 48 per cent of now-college-age young people whose parents had divorced would have preferred to spend almost equal or equal time with both parents, although most had been in sole maternal custody. In some states, in fact, decision-makers are required to consider children's preferences when they are over a certain age.

Because many factors can explain the advantages and benefits of SP, it may be helpful for researchers to "unpack" or "unravel" these various elements to determine which are critical to improved outcomes. Such research might have both theoretical and practical importance, perhaps allowing courts, when necessary, to consider the relevant aspects while ignoring others.

The panelists identified research supporting the importance of virtually every one of these factors. For example, the benefits of more time (not necessarily equal time) with both parents were documented by research reviewed by Nielsen (2017) and Adamsons and Johnson (2013). The fact that better quality child–parent interaction typically enhances children's well-being was the conclusion reached by Amato and Gilbreth (1999), whose report also suggested that high-quality parenting is not promoted when the amount of time is too minimal. The consensus is that a minimum of approximately 35 per cent is required to promote the development and maintenance of meaningful parent–child relationships (Lamb, 2004; Braver & O'Connell, 1998; Fabricius et al., 2010). Overnight time, including mid-week overnight time (when school is in session), is beneficial (Kelly, 2005; Finley & Schwartz, 2007; Braver & Lamb, 2012) because it makes possible the parents' involvement in a variety of activities (help with bedtime routines, help with morning getting-ready-for-school routines, and homework discipline, for example).

Joint physical custody is almost always accompanied by joint legal custody, but the reverse is not the case (Maccoby & Mnookin, 1992). Joint legal custody, in which parents share legal authority to make medical, educational, and religious decisions for the child, has independent positive effects on children's welfare, even when it is not accompanied by shared physical parenting (Seltzer, 1998; Gunnoe & Braver, 2001). To some, this latter finding is surprising, because the relevant major decisions are rare and it is hard to enforce joint decision-making. Indeed, Albiston et al, (1990) found that fathers with joint legal custody were no more involved in everyday decisions than those who did not have legal custody. However, shared decision-making carries very substantial *symbolic* benefits, if not actual, pragmatic, ones. The legal authority to make or share in important life decisions communicates to the child, the other parent, the school, and medical authorities – to the world – that both parents have responsibility for shaping the child into a functioning adult.

Theme 3: The symbolic value of SP, norms, public opinion, and public education

Similarly, SP arrangements have *symbolic* weight. Panelists agreed that SP arrangements signaled that both parents mattered, that both retained their parental roles and responsibilities, that both were necessary to the child's well-being, and that neither could be discarded or reduced to secondary or purely financial roles. This more or less public announcement may affect both parents and their children. Knowing that he or she mattered to *each* parent powerfully affects the emotional functioning of adolescents (Schenck et al., 2009). Velez et al. (2020) also found that mattering to the father after divorce had a greater impact on adjustment than mattering to the mother.

Recognizing the symbolic advantage of SP arrangements, over and above any practical advantages, the panel discussed how the status could be signaled most effectively. It was noted that the prevalence of joint legal custody arrangements is highly variable, not only from jurisdiction to jurisdiction, but also over time within jurisdictions, even without changes in applicable legal statutes or binding precedents (Fabricius et al., 2010). This underlined the importance of cultural norms and understanding, especially among the professionals from whom separating parents might get advice. When a lawyer tells a divorcing parent that SP is good for children, and is therefore likely to be awarded, this changes not only the parent's calculus but also the way she or he thinks about the other parent. Similarly, because many separating parents attend (often mandatory court-ordered) "divorce education" classes (Blaisure & Geasler, 2000; Pollet & Lambreglia, 2008) they are widely exposed to the message that both parents matter, and that the courts will honor and vindicate the value of both parents (DeLuse & Braver, 2015).

The fact that fathers play nurturing roles is gaining currency and the content of commercials featuring fathers and children has shifted noticeably (Flores, 2017; Tropp & Kelly, 2015). Nielsen has, for example, been hired as a consultant by advertisers trying to bring their commercials more into line with contemporary understandings of how men interact with their young daughters, not simply as bunglers (Huffman, 2017). This obvious recognition of the idea that fathers are typically necessary and important, not useless or destructive, can make, and has made, for change in both practical and legal domains.

Sünderhauf described a different but analogous social and normative change in Austria, where corporal punishment by parents was legally banned 20 years ago. Two years after the ban, research showed that parents still spanked but felt *guilty* about doing so. Five years later, however, rates of corporal punishment actually declined, underlining the lesson that changes in normative *beliefs* about appropriate parenting practices need to precede changes in behavior. As noted earlier, the fact that almost 70 per cent of the general public think equal parenting time is preferable in typical divorce cases (Braver et al., 2011) suggests that there is public support for SP.

In the UK, current law discourages judges from adjudicating custody. Instead, through "private ordering", parents are encouraged to make decisions by themselves. In such a system, the parents' cultural and familial understandings become crucial. This automatically turns attention from "parental rights" and ownership to public education. In fact, it makes public ideology the dominant factor determining post-separation parenting plans. More generally, this underlines the fact that we will not see policy changes without changes in public perception.

The slow but unmistakable shift toward insisting on substantial parenting roles for fathers after divorce has become evident, with many American, European, and Australasian societies having turned the corner. Tracing patterns of change over the last 20–30 years, one panelist suggested that "the effort to allow divorced fathers a greatly enhanced role in their children's lives is on the right side of history. The completion of the effort seems inevitable. It appears just a matter of time until it predominates."

Theme 4: Should SP be a legal presumption and, if so, what factors should make for exceptions?

A *presumption* in law is an assumption made by a court as the basis on which decisions can be made. Generally, presumptions in family law are considered rebuttable and are accepted by the court until and unless disproved. Thus, to make SP the presumption would make it the default arrangement; naturally, such a default could be overridden when evidence convinced the decision-maker that application of the presumption would be inappropriate. Only one US state (Arizona) and some European nations (Belgium, Sweden) currently make SP the presumptive arrangement. In Australia, a 2006 law requires courts to "consider" equal time, or at least "substantial and significant" time, when establishing post-divorce parenting plans. Many participants in the conference believed that more jurisdictions would embrace this presumption in the future. Would this be warranted, based on the available social scientific literature?

Most, but not all, panelists believed that the evidence favored such a posture. As one noted,

> the evidence is now sufficiently deep and consistent to permit social scientists to *cautiously* recommend presumptive SP to policy-makers. As always, the presumption should be rebuttable; that is, although on average JPC can now be confidently predicted to bestow benefits on children, there are certainly situations where JPC would be unwise. Researchers can assist the enterprise of identifying these exceptions by engaging in systematic efforts to identify subgroups for whom the usual conclusion does not fit. One way

to do this is to investigate interaction effects (e.g.,custody arrengements by conflict interactions) on the child outcomes. We might aptly characterize the current state of the evidence as "the preponderance of the evidence", meaning that there is substantially more evidence for the presumption than against it. A great many studies, with various inferential strengths, suggest that SP will bestow benefits on children on average, and few if any studies show that it might instead harm them.

(Braver & Votruba, 2018 11–12)

By contrast, one panelist, a custody evaluator, preferred that recommendations for or against SP be based exclusively on the facts of each case, without any presumptions. Even this panelist, however, favored a presumption of "at least 35% time" for each parent, rather than a 50–50 presumption.

All panelists were appropriately wary of a one-size-fits-all standard, cautioning that exceptions need to be recognized as appropriate bases for rebuttal. Among the factors that should lead decision-makers to make exceptions were: credible risk to the child of abuse or neglect; large geographic separations; threat of abduction; and unreasonable or excessive gate-keeping. Furthermore, some children with special needs may require the care of a single parent.

There was extended discussion of whether the mere existence of intimate partner violence (IPV) should constitute a rebuttal factor as well, especially in light of the increasingly sophisticated understanding of IPV, based largely on the typology introduced by Michael Johnson (2010). Johnson distinguished among four distinct patterns of IPV, of which only one should preclude SP: coercive controlling violence – the stereotypical male battering pattern (Kelly & Johnson, 2008). Researchers, evaluators, and courts must explore not simply whether there is evidence of IPV, but also its nature when considering implications for parenting plans.

Theme 5: Should high parental conflict or parents' failure to agree to SP be grounds for an exception?

Previous commentators have argued that SP should be precluded in the presence of high degrees of interparental conflict. For example, Buchanan (2001) wrote that "when parents remain in high conflict, joint custody is … ill-advised" (p. 234). Similarly, in his guide for professional custody evaluators, Stahl (1999) opined that "high conflict parents cannot share parenting" (p. 99). In the same vein, Emery (2009) argued that "joint physical custody is the worst arrangement for children when [it] leaves [them] in the middle of a war zone … In high conflict divorces, children do worse in joint physical custody than in other arrangements."

Most members of the panel eschewed this view, in view of the plethora of recent evidence to the contrary. In particular, Nielsen (2017) had reviewed 27 distinct studies showing that children benefitted significantly from SP even when the parents had high levels of conflict. Several other cautions were raised as well. One was that not all conflict was toxic to children, in either intact or separated families. Indeed, exposure to some degrees of disagreement between adults has been shown to promote children's adjustment (Cummings & Davies, 1994; Grych, Seid, & Fincham, 1992). Further, various mechanisms (such as drop off and pick up at school) can be used to limit children's *exposure* to conflict. This may lead to more parallel than cooperative parenting, which can be problematic in some cases.

Panelists also noted the need for a more sophisticated view of parent conflict. Although conflict is often viewed simplistically as a couple-level construct ("it takes two to tango"), more detailed analyses show that (in perhaps a third of cases, according to Kelly, 2003) only one of the parents may be fomenting hostility, while the other has "moved on" and is (fruitlessly) pursuing relative harmony. Professionals thus need to determine whether the conflict is unilaterally instigated, and make decisions accordingly (Braver et al., 2011).

Finally, it is important to recognize that conflict is malleable, dynamic, and subject to change as a result of numerous factors, including simply the passage of time. Intervention can mitigate the degree of conflict between parents, even when only one parent participates (Cookston et al., 2007). Indeed, the court environment itself often foments conflict, which diminishes after litigation ends (Kelly, 2007; Pruett & Jackson, 1999). Moreover, the belief that proclaiming high levels of conflict may preclude SP provides an incentive both for exaggeration about and proliferation of conflict.

In the past, decision-makers have often avoided SP when one or both parents were opposed to it (Maccoby & Mnookin, 1992). This idea was strongly opposed by most of the panelists. First, it unwisely gave veto power to less-cooperative parents. Second, agreement to SP arrangement is not fixed but highly dependent on context, especially court-related factors (Fabricius et al., 2010). When parents are educated by courts, lawyers, and related professionals that SP is beneficial and *normative*, opposition often dissipates.

Theme 6: Should parental alienating dynamics preclude shared parenting?

Although the concepts of conflict and violence are often related and commonly confused – by researchers, courts, and separating parents – links between both constructs to the concept of parental alienation are often overlooked. Panelists, especially those who conducted custody evaluations, noted that parents may foment discord in children's relationships with their other parent in order to reduce the amount of contact between them, ultimately excluding them from the children's lives (Warshak, 2010). These actions sometimes have the desired effect of disrupting children's relationships with otherwise worthy and blameless parents. However, SP arrangements can successfully undermine those attempts at alienation because they ensure that children can directly evaluate the behavior of both parents, recognizing for themselves discrepancies between the parents' actual characteristics and those described by the alienating parents. Among the factors influencing outcomes in these cases are the initial quality of the child–parent relationship, whether or not there have been breaks in contact, the mental health of the parents, and the temperament and mental health of the children.

Theme 7: What should happen when one parent wants to relocate?

Increases in the numbers of children whose involved parents live apart have resulted in a growing number of cases in which courts must decide whether one of those parents can be allowed to relocate with the children, thereby attenuating children's relationships with the non-moving parent. In eras dominated by single-parent custody arrangements, custodial parents (typically mothers) faced very few restrictions on their ability to move as and where they chose, but that situation has now changed.

Jurisdictions approach these disputes differently, with some placing the burden of proof on the party who wishes to relocate and others on the non-moving party to show why the move should not be allowed. The panelists noted that these decisions should be individualized, without presumptions either favoring or eschewing relocation, but with attention paid to the underlying rationale, the "moving" parent's need to move and the possibility that both parents might move, and the projected impact on the parent–child-relationships and the children's adjustment. Although many relocations threaten to have negative effects on the latter, panelists also noted that decisions needed to take into account the history of involvement by the non-moving parent when adjudicating these cases (Kelly & Lamb, 2003; Parkinson & Cashmore, 2015). Where children have meaningful relationships with both parents but the relocation of one parent is deemed appropriate, it is important that courts and parents establish new parent plans that take the changed circumstances into account when ensuring that children are able to maintain significant relationships with both parents.

Note

1 This chapter was previously published in the *Journal of Divorce & Remarriage* (2018), *59*(5), 372–387. DOI:10.1080/10502556.2018.1454195

References

Adamsons, K., & Johnson, S. K. (2013). An updated and expanded meta-analysis of nonresident fathering and child well-being. *Journal of Family Psychology, 27*(4), 589–599.

Albiston, C. R., Maccoby, E. E., & Mnookin, R. R. (1990). Does joint legal custody matter? *Stanford Law & Policy Review, 2*, 167–179.

Amato, P. R., & Gilbreth, J. G. (1999). Nonresident fathers and children's well-being: A meta-analysis. *Journal of Marriage and the Family, 61*, 557–573.

Austin, W. G. (2011). Parental gatekeeping in custody disputes: Mutual parental support in divorce. *American Journal of Family Law, 25*(4), 148–153.

Bauserman, R. (2002). Child adjustment in joint-custody versus sole-custody arrangements: A meta-analytic review. *Journal of Family Psychology, 16*(1), 91–102.

Bergström, M., Fransson, E., Modin, B., Berlin, M., Gustafsson, P. A., & Hjern, A. (2015). Fifty moves a year: Is there an association between joint physical custody and psychosomatic problems in children? *Journal of Epidemiology and Community Health, 69*(8), 769–774.

Blaisure, K. R., & Geasler, M. J. (2000). The divorce education intervention model. *Family Court Review, 38*(4), 501–513.

Bowlby, J. (1969). *Attachment and Loss: Volume 1. Attachment.* New York: Basic Books.

Braver, S. L. & Lamb, M. E. (2012). Marital dissolution. In G. W. Peterson & K. R. Bush (eds), *Handbook of Marriage and the Family* (3rd ed.). New York: Springer, 487–516.

Braver, S. L. & O'Connell, D. (1998). *Divorced Dads: Shattering the Myths.* New York: Putnam.

Braver, S. L. & Votruba, A. M. (2018). Does shared parenting "cause" better outcomes for children? Empirical and research design considerations. University of Nebraska, Lincoln, Faculty Publications, Department of Psychology.

Braver, S. L., Ellman, I. M. Votruba, A., & Fabricius, W. V. (2011). Lay judgments about child custody after divorce. *Psychology, Public Policy and the Law, 17*(2), 212–240.

Buchanan, C. M. (2001). Divorce. In J. V. Lerner, R. M. Lerner, & J. Finkelstein (eds), *Adolescence in America: An Encyclopedia.* Santa Barbara, CA: ABC-CLIO, 232–235.

Campbell, D. T., & Stanley, J. C. (1963). *Experimental and Quasi-experimental Designs for Research on Teaching.* Boston, MA: Houghton Mifflin.

Clarke-Stewart, A., & Brentano, C. (2006). *Divorce: Causes and Consequences.* New Haven, CT: Yale University Press.

Coleman, J. S. (1990). *Foundations of Social Capital.* Cambridge: Belknap Press.

Cookston, J. T, Braver, S. L., Griffin, W. A., DeLusé, S. R., & Miles, J. C. (2007). Effects of the Dads For Life intervention on coparenting in the two years after divorce. *Family Process, 46*(1), 123–137.

Cummings, E. M., & Davies, P. (1994). *Children and marital conflict: The impact of family dispute and resolution.* New York: Guilford Press.

DeLuse, S., & Braver, S. L. (2015). A rigorous quasi-experimental evaluation of a mandatory divorce education program. *Family Court Review, 53*(1), 66–78.

Elam, K. K., Sandler, I., Wolchik, S., & Tein, J. Y. (2016). Non-residential father–child involvement, interparental conflict and mental health of children following divorce: A person-focused approach. *Journal of Youth and Adolescence, 45*(3), 581–593.

Emery, R. (2009, May 18). Joint physical custody: Is joint physical custody best – or worst – for children? Retrieved from www.psychologytoday.com/blog/divorced-children/200905/joint-physical-custody

Fabricius, W. V., & Hall, J. A. (2000). Young adults' perspectives on divorce: Living arrangements. *Family and Conciliation Courts Review, 38,* 446–461.

Fabricius, W. V., Braver, S. L., Diaz, P., & Velez, C. E. (2010). Custody and parenting time: Links to family relationships and well-being after divorce. In M. E. Lamb (ed.), *Role of the Father in Child Development* (5th ed.). Chichester: Wiley, 245–289.

Finley, G. E., & Schwartz, S. J. (2007). Father involvement and long-term young adult outcomes: The differential contributions of divorce and gender. *Family Court Review, 45*(4), 573–587.

Flores, A. M. (2017). Parent interaction in primetime family themed television portrayals: A replication and extension of Dail and Way's (1985) content analysis. Doctoral dissertation, Wayne State University.

Fransson, E., Låftman, S. B., Östberg, V., Hjern, A., & Bergström, M. (2017). The living conditions of children with shared residence: The Swedish example. *Child Indicators Research, 11*(3), 861–883.

Grych, J. H., Seid, M., & Fincham, F. D. (1992). Assessing marital conflict from the child's perspective: The Children's Perception of Interparental Conflict Scale. *Child Development, 63*(3), 558–572.

Gunnoe, M. L., & Braver, S. L. (2001). The effects of joint legal custody on mothers, fathers, and children, controlling for factors that predispose a sole maternal vs. joint legal award. *Law and Human Behavior, 25,* 25–43.

Harman, J. J. & Biringen, Z. (2016). *Parents Acting Badly: How Institutions and Societies Promote the Alienation of Children from Their Loving Families.* Fort Collins, CO: Colorado Parental Alienation Project.

Hetherington, E. M. (1999). Social capital and the development of youth from nondivorced, divorced, and remarried families. In W. A. Collins & B. Laursen (eds), *Relationships as*

Developmental Contexts: The Minnesota Symposia on Child Psychology (Vol. 30). Mahwah, NJ: Lawrence Erlbaum, 177–209.

Huffman, S. (2017). How this professor's research motivated a new Barbie ad campaign. Retrieved from www.bizjournals.com/bizwomen/news/latest-news/2017/01/how-thisprofessors-research-motivated-a-new-barbie.html?page=all

Johnson, M. P. (2010). *A Typology of Domestic Violence: Intimate Terrorism, Violent Resistance, and Situational Couple Violence*. Lebanon, NH: Northeastern University Press.

Kelly, J. B. (2003). Parents with enduring child disputes: Multiple pathways to enduring disputes. *Journal of Family Studies*, 9(1), 37–50.

Kelly, J. B. (2005). Developing beneficial parenting plan models for children following separation and divorce. *Journal of the American Academy of Matrimonial Law*, 19, 237–401.

Kelly, J. B. (2007). Children's living arrangements following separation and divorce: Insights from empirical and clinical research. *Family Process*, 46(1), 35–52.

Kelly, J. B., & Johnson, M. P. (2008). Differentiation among types of intimate partner violence: Research update and implications for interventions. *Family Court Review*, 46(3), 476–499.

Kelly, J. B., & Lamb, M. E. (2003). Developmental issues in relocation cases involving young children: When, whether, and how? *Journal of Family Psychology*, 17, 193–205.

Lamb, M. E. (2002). Infant–father attachments and their impact on child development. In C. S. Tamis-LeMonda & N. Cabrera (eds), *Handbook of Father Involvement: Multidisciplinary Perspectives*. Mahwah, NJ: Lawrence Erlbaum, 93–117.

Lamb, M. E. (2004) Divorce and parenting. In C. B. Fisher & R. M. Lerner (eds), *Encyclopedia of Applied Developmental Science*. New York: Sage, 794–796.

Lamb, M. E., & Lewis, C. (2005). The role of parent–child relationships in child development. In M. H. Bornstein & M. E. Lamb (eds), *Developmental Science: An Advanced Textbook* (5th ed.). Mahwah, NJ: Lawrence Erlbaum, 429–468.

Lamb, M. E., Sternberg, K. J., & Thompson, R. A. (1997). The effects of divorce and custody arrangements on children's behavior, development, and adjustment. *Family and Conciliation Courts Review*, 35, 393–404.

Maccoby, E. E., & Mnookin, R. H. (1992). *Dividing the Child: Social and Legal Dilemmas of Custody*. Cambridge, MA: Harvard University Press.

McLanahan, S. S., & Teitler, J. (1999). The consequences of father absence. In M. E. Lamb (ed.), *Parenting and Child Development in "Nontraditional" Families*. Mahwah, NJ: Lawrence Erlbaum, 83–102.

Meyer, C. (2016). What is right of first refusal during child custody? Retrieved from www.liveabout.com/what-is-right-of-first-refusal-during-child-custody-1103331

Michigan Friend of the Court (2016). Michigan Parenting Time Guideline. Retrieved from http://courts.mi.gov/administration/scao/resources/documents/publications/manuals/focb/pt_gdlns.pdf

Nielsen, L. (2015). Shared physical custody: Does it benefit children? *Journal of the American Academy of Matrimonial Lawyers*, 28, 79–139.

Nielsen, L. (2017). Re-examining the research on parental conflict, coparenting, and custody arrangements. *Psychology, Public Policy, and Law*, 23(2), 211–231.

Parkinson, P., & Cashmore, J. (2015). Reforming relocation law: An evidence-based approach. *Family Court Review*, 53, 23–39.

Parkinson, P., Cashmore, J., & Single, J. (2005). Adolescents' views on the fairness of parenting and financial arrangements after separation. *Family Court Review*, 43(3), 429–444.

Pollet, S. L. & Lombreglia, M. (2008). A nationwide survey of mandatory parent education. *Family Court Review*, 46(2), 375–394.

Pruett, M. K., & Jackson, T. D. (1999). The lawyer's role during the divorce process: Perceptions of parents, their young children, and their attorneys. *Family Law Quarterly*, 33, 283–310.

Sandler, I. N., Wheeler, L. A., & Braver, S. L. (2013). Relations of parenting quality, interparental conflict, and overnights with mental health problems of children in divorcing families with high legal conflict. *Journal of Family Psychology*, 27(6), 915–924.

Schenck, C. E., Braver, S. L., Wolchik, S. A., Saenz, D., Cookston, J. T., & Fabricius, W. V. (2009). Relations between mattering to step- and non-residential fathers and adolescent mental health. *Fathering*, 7(1), 70–90.

Seltzer, J. A. (1998). Father by law: Effects of joint legal custody on nonresident fathers' involvement with children. *Demography*, 35(2), 135–146.

Simons, R. L., Lin, K. H., Gordon, L. C., Conger, R. D., & Lorenz, F. O. (1999). Explaining the higher incidence of adjustment problems among children of divorce compared with those in two-parent families. *Journal of Marriage and the Family*, 61, 1020–1033.

Stahl, P. M. (1999). *Complex Issues in Child Custody Evaluations*. New York: Sage.

Thompson, R. A. (2006). Early sociopersonality development. In W. Damon, R. A. Lerner, & N. Eisenberg (eds), *Handbook of Child Development* (Vol. 3. *Social, Emotional, and Personality Development* (6ed.). Hoboken, NJ: Wiley.

Tropp, L., & Kelly, J. (2015). *Deconstructing Dads: Changing Images of Fathers in Popular Culture*. Lanham, MD: Lexington Books.

Velez, C. S., Braver, S. L., Cookston, J. T. Fabricius, W. V., & Parke, R. D. (2020). Does mattering to parents "matter" to adolescent mental health? *Family Relations*, 69(1), 180–194.

Warshak, R. A. (2003). Payoffs and pitfalls of listening to children. *Family Relations*, 52(4), 373–384.

Warshak, R. (2010). *Divorce Poison: How To Protect Your Family from Bad-mouthing and Brainwashing*. New York: William Morrow.

3

JOINT VERSUS SOLE PHYSICAL CUSTODY

Which is best for children?

Linda Nielsen

Which type of custody arrangement is best for most children—joint physical custody (JPC), whereby they continue to live with each parent at least 35 per cent of the time, or sole physical custody (SPC), whereby they live primarily or exclusively with one parent? If JPC children have better outcomes, is this largely because their parents have far more money, less conflict, better parenting skills, or higher quality relationships with their children to begin with? Put differently, are JPC parents exceptional people who share very little in common with SPC parents?

Arguments against joint physical custody

These questions are at the root of the fears and assumptions raised in relation to JPC—fears and assumptions that have persisted throughout the past decade.[1] Two of the most frequently voiced concerns relate to conflict and the age of the child. The critics claim that JPC only benefits children when their parents get along well. When there is ongoing conflict between the parents, children will supposedly fare better living with one parent. The assumption is that whatever advantages JPC children accrue by continuing to live with each parent will be undone by the negative impact of the parents' conflict—and that the negative impact of conflict will be worse if the children are living in a JPC family.

The second popular claim is that children under the age of three will not benefit from JPC. Indeed, frequent overnighting away from their mother or living in two homes is supposedly harmful to infants, toddlers, and preschoolers. The assumption is that being away from the mother overnight in the father's care undermines a young child's bond with her and leads to stress-related problems such as irritability, inattentiveness, and wheezing. And if overnighting is harmful, then living in a JPC family is surely going to be damaging for the very young.

Given these concerns, opponents of JPC contend that custody laws should not be revised to grant more equal parenting time to both parents. Some also believe that if laws encourage shared physical custody, then parental conflict and domestic violence will increase. Fortunately, two studies have addressed these fears. In 2014 Arizona enacted a shared parenting statute, which has been functioning as a rebuttable presumption of equal parenting time. Four years later, lawyers, judges, and mental health professionals were asked to evaluate the impact of the law. They viewed the law favorably in terms of children's best interests and perceived it as having no impact on the level of legal or personal conflict between parents.[2] Likewise, in Kentucky equal shared time became the rebuttable presumption in custody laws in 2018.[3] The year before the shared parenting law was enacted, 22,512 cases were filed in family court. This number dropped to 19,991 one year after the law took effect and the number of domestic violence claims declined by 445.

Opponents of JPC also tend to dismiss the research showing better outcomes for JPC children by insisting that these benefits are not due to the custody arrangement. They contend that, compared to SPC parents, JPC parents have far more money, far less conflict and far better relationships with their children from the outset. Moreover, the quality of the child's relationship with the father is what matters, not the amount of time the father and children spend together in the years after the family breakup. There are a number of problems, however, with these assumptions about fathering time, income, and conflict.

Quality or quantity?

The "quality versus quantity" argument has been around for a long time, despite having been repeatedly debunked by reviews of the research. The worn-out old argument goes like this. So long as the children have a quality relationship with their dad, the quantity of time they spend with him after the family breakup has little to no impact. In the years after the parents separate, it's not the amount of fathering time that matters; it's the "quality" of their relationship. Following this line of reasoning, if a married couple has a good relationship while they are living together, then living apart and spending very little time together over the next 10 to 15 years will have virtually no impact on the quality of their marriage. This ignores the reality that married parents build relationships with their children by spending enough time with them doing the day to day, ordinary things together that strengthen their bond. To toss that reality out of the window because the parents are no longer living together is hardly in a child's best interests.

More importantly, the two most thorough reviews of the research on this issue conclude that spending time in person with a loving, involved father *is* beneficial to children after their parents separate.[4,5] These studies were measuring only the father's in-person or phone "contact" with the children, and did not include fathers and children who were living together in JPC families. Even so, frequent face-to-face fathering time was linked to better outcomes for children. As we would expect, brief, occasional, or sporadic "contact" with the father had no significant impact on children's outcomes. Based on this large body of research documenting the benefits of frequent, face-to-face, involved fathering time, it is not surprising that increasing fathering time through JPC arrangements would lead to better outcomes for children.

Then, too, unless parents are abusive or terribly negligent when they are with their children, maximizing their time together may give them opportunities to build a better relationship. For example, in a study with seventh graders, children who spent the most time with their dads after the parents separated (including living with him up to 50 percent of the time) had better relationships with him three years later—even those whose relationships were not very good in the seventh grade.[6] This finding merits repeating. The fathering time was beneficial over the three-year period in the best *and in the worst* relationships. In short, quality relationships cannot be created or maintained without quantity of time.

There are also several problems with the assumption that JPC children have better outcomes because their parents have higher incomes than SPC parents. According to a large body of research over the past three decades, unless children are living in poverty, family income is not closely linked to their behavioral, emotional or mental health problems, drug and alcohol use, or the quality of their relationships with their parents.[7,8,9,10] In married or divorced families, children from higher income families are not more advantaged in these ways. Not surprisingly, then, in the 25 custody studies where family income was factored in before comparing the children's outcomes, JPC children still came out ahead.[16]

Co-parenting conflict: The myth of exceptional couples

Contrary to popular belief, JPC parents do *not* generally have significantly less conflict or more cooperative relationships than SPC parents, according to the 20 studies that have investigated this question.[11] In fact, it is not uncommon in JPC families for one of the parents to initially want sole physical custody and having to be persuaded to share. This finding is extremely important because many people try to dismiss the benefits of JPC by claiming that these parents get along so well that their children would have the best outcomes even in SPC arrangements. Moreover, when conflict is high and co-parenting is poor, children do *not* have worse outcomes in JPC than in SPC families. Not surprisingly, the quality of the parent–child relationship is a better predictor than parents' conflicts of children's outcomes. The exception, of course, is when children need to be protected from witnessing intense or ongoing physical conflict or violence between their parents. The bottom line is that we should be focusing less on the issue of parental conflict and more on how to strengthen children's relationships with both of their parents.

Conclusions from previous reviews of the research

My summaries of the 60 studies reached the same conclusions as those of the only two meta-analyses that have compared children's outcomes in JPC and SPC families: children who live with each parent at least 35 percent of the time generally have better outcomes than children who live primarily or exclusively with only one parent. It is worth noting that a meta-analysis differs from a review or summary of the studies. A meta-analysis determines the size of the differences between JPC and SPC children's outcomes.

The first analysis, by Bauserman, included 11 studies from peer-reviewed academic journals and 22 doctoral dissertations.[12] The dissertations and published articles reached the same conclusions. JPC children had better outcomes even after accounting for parental conflict.

The second analysis, by Baude et al., included only 18 of the 55 studies that existed at the time and did not consider conflict.[13] Like Bauserman, these researchers concluded that JPC children had better outcomes, though the links were weak, especially in the older studies. However, these researchers addressed another important question: Do JPC children who live 50 percent of the time with each parent have better outcomes than JPC children who live only 35 percent of the time with each parent? The answer was yes. This finding is important because it suggests that, if researchers only considered those studies where the children lived "equally" with both parents, the outcomes for the JPC children would have been even better than what is generally reported.

Two other summaries of some of the 60 available studies reached similar conclusions to those of these two meta-analyses and to my review of all 60 studies. In Steinbach's summary of 29 studies, JPC children generally had better outcomes than SPC children.[14] In most of the studies Steinbach chose, however, JPC parents tended to have higher incomes than SPC parents. The second summary included only 10 studies. All of them were qualitative, meaning that the researchers were merely asking older children to share their personal experiences about JPC or SPC in earlier years.[15] Based on their personal stories, no conclusion could be drawn about the actual impact of either type of custody arrangement.

The 60 research studies

So, let's address the three questions. First, do JPC parents have very little in common with SPC parents in terms of higher income, lower conflict, and better relationships with their children? Second, do JPC children have better outcomes than SPC children? Third, when the parents do not get along well in coparenting, do children have worse outcomes in JPC than in SPC families?

To answer these questions, I reviewed all 60 studies published before 2019 that compared JPC and SPC children's outcomes. I paid special attention to those studies where parental conflict, income, or the quality of the parent–child relationship were factored in to the analysis before comparing the children's outcomes. All 60 studies were quantitative whereby the researchers used various kinds of standardized tests to compare the outcomes for JPC and SPC children across a wide range of measures of well-being.[16,17] Fifty-three studies were published in peer-reviewed academic journals. The other seven were published in Australian government reports by teams of researchers assessing various aspects of JPC and SPC families' lives. The entire list of studies, with detailed descriptions, findings, and limitations, are available from me upon request.

Data from the 60 studies can be grouped into five broad categories of child well-being: (1) academic or cognitive outcomes; (2) emotional or psychological outcomes; (3) behavioral problems, which include teenage drug, nicotine or alcohol use;

(4) physical health or stress-related physical problems; and (5) quality of parent–child relationships.

Overall conclusion

The overall conclusion is that JPC children have better outcomes than SPC children. Compared to SPC children, JPC children had better outcomes on all measures in 34 studies; equal outcomes on some measures and better outcomes on other measures in 14 studies; and equal outcomes on all measures in six studies. In six studies JPC children had worse outcomes on one of the measures but equal or better outcomes on all other measures.

Family income

Did JPC children still have better outcomes when the researchers considered family income? Yes. In the 25 studies that considered family income before comparing the children, JPC children had better outcomes on all measures in 18 studies, equal outcomes on some measures and better outcomes on other measures in four studies, and equal outcomes on all measures in one study. In only two income studies did the JPC children have worse outcomes than SPC children on one of the measures—with equal or better outcomes on all other measures.

Parent conflict

What about parent conflict? When parent conflict was high, did children fare worse in JPC than SPC families? In the 19 studies that considered conflict, JPC children still had better outcomes on all measures in nine studies, equal outcomes on some measures and better outcomes on other measures in five studies, and equal outcomes on all measures in two studies. In only three of the 19 studies did JPC children have worse outcomes than SPC children on one of the measures of well-being when conflict was high and ongoing. Still, even in those three studies, JPC had equal or better outcomes than SPC children in high conflict families. This is not to say that being continually exposed to and dragged into the middle of high conflict has no impact on children. What these studies are saying is that high conflict is not more important than the custody arrangement, that it has no worse impact on children living in two homes than those living in one home, and that the quality of the parent–child relationship matters more than the conflict, as we will now see.

Quality of parent–child relationships

Do JPC parents have much better relationships with their children than SPC parents to begin with? Does the custody arrangement have an impact on the quality of those relationships? Does the parent–child relationship have more impact than income, parent conflict, or the custody arrangement?

Unfortunately, we do not know if JPC parents have better relationships with their children than SPC parents before the breakup. None of the 60 studies measured the quality of parent–child relationships while the parents were still together. Without measuring the quality of the relationship with *both* parents at the outset, we have no way of knowing whether JPC children had better relationships or how much impact the custody arrangement has on those relationships over time.

What we do know is that JPC children have much better relationships with both parents than SPC children in the years after the separation. In fact, of all the measures of well-being, the greatest advantage for JPC children was better relationships with both parents. In 22 of 23 studies that assessed family bonds, JPC children had closer, more communicative relationships with both parents. It would be a serious mistake, however, to interpret this as meaning that JPC parents had better relationships with their children all along.

Only three studies that I am aware of have considered whether the quality of parent–child relationships affects children differently in JPC and SPC families. In a study conducted in Arizona, teenagers who had bad relationships with their father had more behavioral problems when they lived with him in a JPC family than when they lived with their mother.[18] But children who had good relationships with their father only had better outcomes when they were living with him in a JPC family. In short, a good relationship did not compensate for having too little time with their father. Likewise, in a study in Belgium, teenagers who got along poorly with their father felt more depressed and more dissatisfied when they lived with him in a JPC family.[19] And in another study from Belgium, the quality of the teenagers' relationships with each parent was more closely linked to their well-being than was conflict between the parents or the custody arrangement.[20]

It stands to reason that, during the teenage years, those children who get along badly with their father will probably not do as well when they are having to live with him as when they can minimize their time together by living with their mother. The same would probably be true for teenagers who have bad relationships with their mother and have to live with her in a JPC family, though no study to my knowledge has investigated this question.

Shared parenting for babies, infants, and preschoolers

Only six of the 60 studies focused exclusively on children ages zero to five. These six studies have been critiqued by many scholars, including a group of 110 international experts, who all reached the same conclusions.[21–23,24]

These scholars concurred that two of the six studies were too methodologically flawed to be applied to the general population of parents. Because these two seriously flawed studies have been widely cited in the media and by policy makers as evidence that overnighting and JPC are harmful to young children, it is extremely important to recognize these two studies whenever we encounter them in discussions about JPC. One is an Australian study led by Jennifer McIntosh, commissioned and published by the Australian government.[25] Among its numerous shortcomings were the use of non-standardized tests, questionable interpretations of their test results, extremely small sample sizes largely from families where the parents had never been married or lived together, and downplaying those findings where there were no differences or more positive outcomes for the overnighting or JPC children.

The other seriously flawed, yet highly publicized study, is American and conducted by Robert Emery and his graduate student, Samantha Tornello.[26] Among its most serious flaws were reliance on inner city, impoverished, never married minority parents with high rates of violence, substance abuse problems and mental health issues, and use of non-standardized tests. Like the Australian researchers, these researchers also emphasized the few negative outcomes and ignored or downplayed the majority of findings showing no differences or better outcomes for the overnighting/JPC children compared to the non-overnighting or SPC children.

Based on the four methodologically sound studies,[24,27-29] these groups of scholars concluded that babies, toddlers, and preschoolers who frequently overnight away from their mother or who spend up to half of their time living with their father generally have better outcomes than those who spend almost all of their overnight time in their mother's care.

Other noteworthy findings

Several other noteworthy findings emerged from the 60 studies. First and foremost, in no study did JPC children have worse outcomes on all, or even on most, measures than SPC children. JPC and SPC children were the most alike in regard to academic achievement or cognitive skills. It appears that the custody arrangement has less impact on grades and cognitive development than on all other areas of children's lives.

The greatest advantage for JPC children was better family relationships. In 22 of 23 studies that assessed family bonds, JPC children had closer, more communicative relationships with both parents. The second greatest advantage for JPC children was better physical and mental health. In 13 of 15 studies that addressed physical health, JPC children had fewer psychosomatic, stress-related physical problems. Forty-two studies assessed children's emotional health: depression, life-satisfaction, anxiety, and self-esteem. In 24 studies, JPC children had better outcomes and in 12 studies there were no significant differences between the two groups. In six studies, the results were "mixed" depending on gender and which measure of emotional well-being was being assessed.

As teenagers, JPC children also had better outcomes. Twenty-four studies assessed one or more of these behaviors: drinking, smoking, using drugs, being aggressive, bullying, committing delinquent acts, getting along poorly with peers. In 21 studies, JPC teenagers had better outcomes on all measures. In three studies, the results were "mixed" because the differences between JPC and SPC teenagers depended on gender or on which measure was being assessed.

What about children's relationships with their grandparents—and why should we care? In all four studies that addressed this question, JPC children had closer relationships with their grandparents than SPC children. This matters because children who have close relationships with their grandparents after their parents separate tend to be better adjusted emotionally and behaviorally. Especially when the family is experiencing the stress of the parents' separation, strong relationships with grandparents can be a protective factor for children.

Worse outcomes for JPC children

Despite the benefits of JPC for most children, in six of the 60 studies JPC children had worse outcomes than SPC children on one of the measures of well-being. Two of the six studies were the two "baby" studies previously discussed—studies whose findings have been refuted by numerous scholars. To be clear, no study has ever found that JPC children were worse off on *all* measures of well-being. So, let's look at the four studies in which JPC teenagers had worse outcomes than SPC teenagers on any measure of well-being.

In a study with Australian teenagers, eight of the 50 JPC boys said they "sometimes did not get along well with peers" compared to 32 of the 200 SPC boys.[30] But the reverse was true for girls. JPC girls were four times *less* likely than SPC girls to say they "sometimes" did not get along with friends. In another study, involving 74 SPC and 68 JPC adolescents in high conflict families in Arizona, those who had bad relationships with their father had more behavioral problems in JPC than in SPC families.[31] Similarly, in a study conducted in Belgium, those teenagers who had bad relationships with their fathers were more depressed and more dissatisfied in JPC than in SPC. And when parental conflict remained high *eight years after the divorce*, girls were more depressed in JPC than in SPC—but boys were less depressed in JPC.[19] In another Belgian study, teenagers who were extremely "conscientious" (very task oriented, very rule oriented) felt more depressed in JPC than in SPC.[20]

Why is JPC beneficial even when parental conflict is high?

The fact that JPC children still have better outcomes even after factoring in parent conflict undermines the claim that children do not benefit from JPC unless their parents have a low conflict, cooperative relationship. This might be partly explained by the fact that, in a separate analysis of 19 studies, JPC couples did not have significantly less conflict or more cooperative, communicative relationships than SPC couples at the time they separated or in the years after their separation.[11] Even in those studies where the JPC parents had not initially agreed to the plan, the JPC children had better outcomes than SPC children. Both parents did not have to mutually agree to the custody plan in order for JPC to benefit the children.

Moreover, in an analysis of 11 studies, children whose parents were in high conflict in the first few years after their separation did not have worse outcomes than children with low conflict parents.[32] And even when conflict remained high many years after the divorce, the negative impact on the children was offset by having a high quality relationship with one or both parents.

Accepting limitations versus dismissing the research

Some opponents of JPC dismiss or downplay the positive findings from the 60 studies because the effect sizes are relatively small and the studies are correlational. An effect size is a measure of how strongly the variables are correlated with one another. And it is true that the effect sizes in the JPC studies, especially the older studies, are generally small. But dismissing social science studies with small effect sizes is a mistake.[33] First, small effect sizes are very common in social science studies showing a correlation between children's well-being and factors such as parental conflict, poverty, and domestic violence. Yet we still take the findings from those studies seriously, as we should. Moreover, even small effect sizes in social science and medical studies have important implications for large numbers of children.

Similarly, most social science studies, especially those involving families, are correlational. It would be impossible and unethical to design studies that proved causality. The reality is that we rely on correlational studies on such issues as family violence, poverty, and poor parenting to try to figure out what might be causing children's problems. And on the basis of those correlational studies, we create policies designed to protect and benefit children. Moreover, many of the 60 JPC studies factored in conflict and income before comparing the children's outcomes. This makes a stronger case for JPC being the cause of the better outcomes by eliminating other competing explanations.

The bottom-line messages

To be clear, the 60 studies are not saying that being dragged into the middle of parents' ongoing conflicts has no negative impact on children. And the studies are not claiming that JPC is the *only* reason why these children have better outcomes or that JPC has a greater impact than the quality of the child's relationship with both parents. What the studies are saying is that, even when conflict is high—with the exception of physically abusive conflict—and even after considering family income, most children still benefit more from JPC than from SPC. It is not fair to children or to the researchers who have conducted these studies to frame the situation as if one single factor—conflict, income, JPC, or quality of parent–child relationships—has to be the sole winner of some imaginary contest. Our goal should be to provide children with as many situations as possible that have been linked to their well-being after their parents separate. It is abundantly clear that one of those beneficial factors is continuing to live with each parent for at least 35 percent of the time after they separate.

The conclusion reached by at least three separate groups of researchers is clear: shared physical custody is in the best interests of children of all ages, with the exception of children whose parents are abusive or negligent. The largest group included 110 internationally recognized scholars and mental health practitioners.[23] Members of the second group, comprising 12 researchers, were chosen to be the keynote speakers at the 2018 International Conference on Shared Parenting.[34] The third group consisted of 31 social scientists and family law scholars, who were invited to a 2016 think tank on shared parenting sponsored by the Association of Family and Conciliation Courts.[35] To dismiss, downplay, or denigrate the conclusions of so many scholars and a large body of research is a disservice to children and to the parents who love them.

Notes

1. Kruk E. Arguments against a presumption of shared parenting in family law. *Journal of Divorce & Remarriage* 2018; 59: 388–400.
2. Fabricius W, Aaron M, Akins F, Assini J, McElroy T. What happens if there is presumptive 50/50 parenting time? An evaluation of Arizona's new child custody statute. *Journal of Divorce & Remarriage* 2018; 59: 414–428.
3. Hale M. Kentucky's popular joint custody law shows why it's the most effective at helping families. *Courier Journal*, August 30, 2019.
4. Adamsons K. Quantity versus quality of nonresident father involvement: Deconstructing the argument that quantity doesn't matter. *Journal of Child Custody* 2018; 15: 26–34.
5. Amato P, Gilbreth J. Nonresident fathers and children's well being: A meta-analysis. *Journal of Marriage and Family* 1999; 61: 557–573.
6. Fabricius W, Sokol K, Diaz P, Braver S. The missing link between parenting time and children's mental and physical health. In: Drozd R, Saini M, editors. *Parenting plan evaluations: Applied research for the family court*. New York: Oxford University Press, 2016, 74–85.
7. Gershoff E, Aber L, Raver C, Lennon M. Income is not enough: Incorporating material hardship into models of income associations with parenting and child development. *Child Development* 2007; 78: 70–95.
8. Luthar S, Barkin S, Crossman E. I can, therefore I must: Fragility in the upper middle classes. *Development and Psychopathology* 2013; 25: 1529–1549.
9. Mayer S. *What money can't buy: Family income and children's life chances*. Cambridge, MA: Harvard University Press, 1997.
10. Lareau A. *Unequal childhoods: Class, race, and family life*. Berkeley, CA: University of California Press, 2003.
11. Nielsen L. Re-examining the research on parental conflict, coparenting and custody arrangements. *Psychology, Public Policy and Law* 2017; 23: 211–231.
12. Bauserman R. A meta-analysis of parental adjustment and conflict in joint physical custody and sole custody following divorce. *Journal of Divorce & Remarriage* 2012; 53: 464–488.
13. Baude A, Pearson J, Drapeau S. Children's adjustment in joint physical custody versus sole custody: A meta-analytic review. *Journal of Divorce and Remarriage* 2016; 57: 338–360.
14. Steinbach A. Children's and parents' well-being in joint physical custody: A literature review. *Family Process* 2018; 58: 353–369.
15. Birnbaum R, Saini M. A qualitative synthesis of children's experiences of shared care post divorce. *International Journal of Children's Rights* 2015; 23: 109–132.
16. Nielsen L. Joint versus sole physical custody: Children's outcomes independent of parent–child relationships, income, and conflict in 60 studies. *Journal of Divorce & Remarriage* 2018; 59: 247–281.
17. Nielsen L. Joint versus sole physical custody: Outcomes for children in 60 studies independent of income and conflict. *Journal of Child Custody* 2018; 15: 35–54.
18. Elam K, Sandler I, Wolchik S, Tein J. Non-residential father–child involvement, interparental conflict and mental health of children following divorce. *Journal of Youth and Adolescence* 2016; 45: 581–593.
19. Vanassche S, Sodermans A, Matthijs K, Swicegood G. Commuting between two parental households: The association between joint physical custody and adolescent wellbeing following divorce. *Journal of Family Studies* 2013; 19: 139–158.

20 Sodermans K, Matthijs K. Joint physical custody and adolescents' subjective well-being: A personality x environment interaction. *Journal of Family Psychology* 2014; 28: 346–356.
21 Lamb M. Does shared parenting by separated parents affect the adjustment of young children? *Journal of Child Custody* 2018; 25: 1–12.
22 Nielsen L. Woozles: Their role in custody law reform, parenting plans and family court. *Psychology, Public Policy and Law* 2014; 20: 164–180.
23 Warshak R. Social science and parenting plans for young children: With the endorsement of the researchers and practitioners listed in the Appendix. *Psychology, Public Policy and Law* 2014; 20: 46–67.
24 Fabricius W, Suh G. Should infants and toddlers have frequent overnight parenting time with fathers? The policy debate and new data. *Psychology, Public Policy and Law* 2017; 23: 68–84.
25 McIntosh J, Smyth B, Kelaher M, Wells YLC. Post separation parenting arrangements: Outcomes for infants and children. Sydney, Australia: Attorney General's Office, 2010.
26 Tornello S, Emery R, Rowen J, Potter D, Ocker B, Xu Y. Overnight custody arrangements, attachment and adjustment among very young children. *Journal of Marriage and Family* 2013; 75: 871–885.
27 Solomon J. Infants after divorce: Overnight visitation and family relationships. Washington, DC: National Center for Education in Maternal and Child Health, 1998.
28 Bergstrom M, Fransson E, Fabian H, Hjern, Sarkadi A, Salari R. Preschool children living in joint physical custody arrangements show less psychological symptoms than those living mostly or only with one parent. *Acta Paediatrica* 2017; July: 1–7.
29 Pruett M, Ebling R, Insabella G. Critical aspects of parenting plans for young children. *Family Court Review* 2004; 42: 39–59.
30 Lodge J, Alexander M. Views of adolescents in separated families. Sydney, Australia: Australian Institute of Family Studies, 2010.
31 Sandler I, Wheeler L, Braver S. Relations of parenting quality, interparental conflict, and overnights with mental health problems of children in divorcing families with high legal conflict. *Journal of Family Psychology* 2013; 27: 915–924.
32 Mahrer N, O'Hara K, Sandler I, Wolchik S. Does shared parenting help or hurt children in high conflict divorced families? *Journal of Divorce & Remarriage* 2018; 59: 324–347.
33 McCartney K, Rosenthal R. Effect size, practical importance and social policy for children. *Child Development* 2000; 71: 173–180.
34 Braver S, Lamb M. Shared parenting after parental separation: The views of 12 experts. *Journal of Divorce & Remarriage* 2018; 59: 372–387.
35 Pruett M, DiFonzo H. Closing the gap: Research, policy, practice and shared parenting. *Family Court Review* 2014; 44: 152–174.

4
BEST INTEREST OF THE CHILD
"A" or "the" primary consideration?

José Manuel de Torres Perea

Introduction

In this chapter, we study the principle of the best interest of the child (BIC) and its application as "a" primary consideration or "the" primary consideration. Each of these options has been adopted by different legal systems, resulting in two different perspectives and approaches to the BIC, thus producing different outcomes. One of the most interesting issues related to this divergence refers to the acceptability of a rebuttable presumption in favour of shared parenting.

As an initial approach, I should briefly explain the conceptual map that provides the framework in which we are currently moving when we refer to the best interests of the child. The point of departure is Article 3 of the United Nations Convention on the Rights of the Child (UNCRC), which states that, "In all actions concerning children ... the best interest of the child shall be a primary consideration." This rule is adopted by national regulations in different areas. We can distinguish between two important ones: first, national law commonly repeats the literal wording of the UN Convention; second, national law sometimes changes its wording significantly and gives a new meaning to the concept. The latter is the option taken by certain important legal systems, such as those in England and Wales, Scotland and Spain. In English law, Section 1 of the Children Act 1989 (ChA) states that, "the child's welfare shall be the court's paramount consideration". In addition, Article 16(1) of the Children (Scotland) Act (ChSA) 1995 states that, "where under or by virtue of this Part of this Act, F1 ... a court determines, any matter with respect to a child the welfare of that child throughout his childhood shall be F2 its paramount consideration." Finally, in Spain, Article 2 of the Children Act (LOPJM[1]) states that, "the best interest of the child will prevail over any other legitimate interest".[2]

On the other hand, most countries follow a strict interpretation of Article 3 of the UNCRC. This is also the case for the European Court of Human Rights (ECtHR), which applies the BIC according to context and circumstances and does not consider that it is the sole consideration to take into account, allowing for presumptions.

With respect to English law, some authors[3] claim that a distinction must be made between decisions about the child and decisions on other matters that indirectly affect the child. Only when a decision directly affects a child is it possible to consider it the sole determining consideration, but not in other cases. However, when there are indirect measures, the best interest principle should be "a primary" consideration that may coincide with other primary considerations. This difference would also be based on General Comment No. 14 (2012) of Article 3 of the UNCRC, which interprets the expression "concerning" as referring, first, to "to measures and decisions directly concerning a child, children as a group or children in general, and secondly, to other measures that have an effect on an individual child, children as a group or children in general, even if they are not the direct targets of the measure".[3]

At this point, the question is what other primary considerations can be taken into account by lawmakers or courts that could be as important as the BIC principle? To answer this question, we analyse certain court cases in which this issue has been raised. Let us start by looking at two interesting Spanish cases. In spite of the fact that Spanish law establishes that the BIC is the only primary consideration, on occasions the Spanish courts have strayed from this rule. The first case is related to the dignity of human beings and their right to lead a decent life. The second is connected to the need to avoid human commodification.

First, we refer to a decision by the Cordoba Court of Appeal, in Spain.[4] In this case, the parents got divorced and the father refused to agree to his children having overnight stays at his home. However, the Court of Appeal considered that the mother was overwhelmed by the sole custody of the children and it was therefore a critical family situation. As a result, it was decided that the best option was to establish parity between the parents in the care of their two children and shared parenting was imposed upon the father.

The court based this decision on the best interest of the child. However, when referred to psychologists, they always agree that the imposition of cohabitation against the will of one parent cannot be beneficial for a child. Therefore, a credible alternative is that, in this case, the imposition of shared parenting was not really based on the BIC but, rather, on another consideration. This other consideration could be the protection of the right of a spouse to live in dignity, giving priority to the interests of a mother to be able to reconcile family and working life, or even the consideration that parity between the parents in the care of their two children is a priority.

Second, we refer to a decision by the Spanish Supreme Court on gestational surrogacy[5] and the BIC. In this case, a Spanish married gay couple entered into a contract in California, USA, with a woman who agreed to be the surrogate mother of their children. The Spanish authorities denied the registration of the Californian certification of filiation in favour of the Spanish couple because Article 10 of the Spanish law on the Application of Human Assisted Reproduction Techniques (LTRHA) prohibits contracts with a surrogate mother.

The gay spouses filed a claim with the General Directorate of the Registries and Notaries (DGRN). They requested the revocation of the consular decision that had refused the registration of the Californian certification in order to be recognized as legal parents of the two children. Finally, the DGRN agreed. However, as far as we are concerned, this significant judgement is interesting in relation to what it establishes in relation to the BIC. The Supreme Court stated that:

> this general clause must be applied on a case by case basis. It is a controversial principle whose application does not authorize the court to adopt any type of result. In fact, this general clause is a useful tool to interpret the law or to fill legal gaps, but does not give free rein to approve what is expressly prohibited by a mandatory law.[6]

In addition, the Supreme Court stated that:

> art. 3 of the United Nations Convention of the Rights of the Child states that the best interest of the child must be a primordial consideration. Consequently, this consideration is not the only one to take into account. Other considerations may be taken into account and all of them must be balanced by the court. These other considerations may be: respect for the dignity and integrity of a pregnant woman, the fight against the exploitation of women in a state of necessity and the commodification of women. These principles are enshrined by constitutional texts and international conventions.[7]

Another primary consideration is applied by the ECtHR. It implies that national authorities are obliged to make the necessary progress to facilitate contact between children and parents as reasonably can be demanded, depending on the specific case. We refer to this case in the sections below.

Is the BIC principle compatible with legal presumptions?

The results of a literal or modified interpretation of Article 3 of the UNCRC can differ. If the BIC is regarded as the court's paramount consideration, close judicial control of the situation of the child in every case should be necessary. As mentioned above, this would prevent the use of general presumptions. In the UK, where this approach is applied, a significant question arises: How is it possible for the ECtHR to act as if it would apply general presumptions when referring to the welfare of children, when these presumptions can diverge from the BIC in a specific case?

The ECtHR has stated in different cases that Article 8 of the Convention on Human Rights establishes that national authorities are obliged to make the necessary progress to facilitate contact between children and parents as reasonably can be demanded, while taking into consideration the facts of the specific case. This approach by the European Court has been interpreted as the existence of a rebuttable presumption in favour of contact between children and parents.

However, there is another possible explanation: what the European Court follows is that this benefit to children of remaining with their families is considered as a matter of fact.[8] Therefore, it is stated that there is not a presumption, but a fact that is a common feature of the world and of human nature.

This explanation is provided by English scholars, who are influenced by English law. In fact, Sir James Munby, President of the Family Division of the High Court of England and Wales until 2018, stated that presumptions cannot be made in a case governed by Section 1 of the Children Act 1989.[9] Moreover, Andrew Bainham, a leading commentator on family law, considered that the welfare principle required "a court to consider all circumstances bearing on welfare, rather than the basic facts of a presumption simply prevailing in the absence of evidence to the contrary".[10] It is true that a presumption was introduced into the Children Act according to which "with respect to each parent within subsection (6a) to presume, unless the contrary is shown, that involvement of that parent in the life of the child concerned will further the child's welfare". However, this presumption has been interpreted in the sense that the Court still has discretion despite operation of the presumption. In other words, no contact could be ordered even if the presumption is not rebutted. Apparently, this presumption is only "one of the factors that the court has to take into account when applying the principle that the child's welfare is paramount".[11]

These conclusions are a consequence of the fact that UK regulations apply the BIC as the only possible primary consideration. In fact, in order to answer the previous question, it is necessary to take into account an issue normally ignored by English scholars. According to Herring, Probert and Gilmore,[12] the ECtHR does not apply and interpret the BIC as the sole consideration; on the contrary, the ECtHR applies the BIC as a significant tool to protect the child and in specific cases, and due to its nature, it can override the interests of the child's parents.[13] However, Herring et al. refer to the fact that the English courts have asserted that any difference between the requirements of Article 8 of the ECHR and Section 1 of the Children's Act 1989 is merely semantic. In reality, the English courts consider that the best interest is automatically decisive and the ECtHR that it is not; this is an oft-ignored distinction by English courts and scholars. Spanish authors also fall into this trap.

Therefore, from the perspective of the ECtHR, there are other possible primary considerations besides the BIC, for example the right of a spouse to lead a decent life, the need to avoid human commodification, the benefit of contact between children and parents, parity between parents in the care of their children and others. Moreover, a presumption linked to one of these primary considerations could be possible in spite of the fact that it could contradict another primary consideration. In this way, we can understand the convenience of a presumption in favour of facilitating contact between children and parents, as the ECtHR does, or a presumption in favour of shared parenting. In fact, these two presumptions could result from the obligation of national authorities to make the necessary progress to facilitate contact between children and parents as reasonably can be demanded, depending on the specific case.

Of course, a presumption can be linked to the BIC if the psychological studies support its application. Obviously, a court may decide not to apply a presumption in favour of shared parenting, if it considers that the BIC in a specific case is sole custody. Nevertheless, if we admit that the BIC is not automatically applied, there is no problem accepting a presumption as a departure point, whenever it is rebuttable.

In any case, it is the job of psychologists to determine if a presumption in favour of shared parenting is in the best interest of the child. In order to do so, their research should be supported by empirical data.[14] Legal professionals should therefore take a more sceptical approach marked by a wait-and-see attitude.

Equally, a presumption cannot be based on any specific primary consideration, but on the measures that courts normally adopt when deciding on the custody of children. In this case, statistics could help to find a starting point. From this perspective, there is no really significant objection to accepting a rebuttable presumption in favour of shared parenting, in spite of the fact that it may contradict the BIC. It is the function of the court to balance the pros and cons of applying a rebuttable presumption to a specific case. In fact, it has been said that these types of rebuttable presumption can offer protection against the indeterminacy of the best interest principle.

If we accept that the best interest of the child may be served by several possible primary considerations and that it is not necessarily automatic, there would not be a problem in applying a rebuttable presumption that could contradict the BIC, as mentioned above. The Gordian knot is to decide which one is the most acceptable legal option: the BIC as "a" or "the" primary consideration.

The ECtHR approach

To understand how a presumption could be applied in cases that affect the best interest of the child, we believe that it is of great interest to explore the approach followed by the European Court of Human Rights (ECtHR) approach. As mentioned above, the ECtHR does not consider that the best interest should be automatically applied and, on the contrary, that it should be applied as a significant tool, which, in specific cases, depending on context, circumstances and significance, may override the interests of the parents, as decided in *Johansen* v. *Norway*,[15] *TP and KM* v. *United Kingdom*[16] and *Pisica* v. *Moldova*.[17] Therefore, according to this case law, the child's welfare or best interest of the child is not the sole consideration.

In any case, the European Court of Human Rights (ECtHR) case law is of paramount importance[18] when applying Article 8 of the ECHR.[19] This article is interpreted as taking into consideration "the best interest of the child and his or her right"[20] in this way.[21]

Some specific statements of the European Court are very significant. In *Kosmopoulou* v. *Greece*,[22] it was stated that Article 8 implies a right of parents to measures being adopted to be reunited with their children and an obligation for the national authorities to take such measures. *Glaser* v. *United Kingdom*[23] and, mutatis mutandis, *Kuppinger* v. *Germany*, no. 62198/11, § 101, 15 January 2015, state that what is decisive is whether the national authorities have taken all necessary steps to facilitate contact that can reasonably be demanded in the special circumstances of each case. In addition, in *A. V.* v. *Slovenia*,[24] the European Court stated, in relation to parental contact rights, that the State initially has an obligation to take measures with a view to reuniting parents with their children and an obligation to facilitate such reuniting, in so far as the interests of the child dictate that everything must be done to preserve personal relations.

In fact, in *C v. Finland*,[25] there is a strict screening of actions by the state authorities because the consequence of denying contact is to curtail the parent–child relationship.[26] In fact, the ECtHR takes into account Article 9(3) of the UNCRC when it states that the members of the Convention should: "respect the right of the child who is separated from one or both parents to maintain personal relations and direct contact with both parents on a regular basis, except if it is contrary to the child's best interests."[27]

According to the majority of legal experts, Article 8 of the ECHR establishes a right of contact that implies a contact presumption that can only be rebutted for a good reason, normally the welfare of the child.[28] However, other scholars have a different point of view, stating that what the Convention protects is the right to respect for family life, with contact being only a particular form of this relationship; another aspect of this family life is the right to remain safe from the risk of domestic violence.[29] Therefore, this would advocate a two-fold approach, as in *Gnahoré v. France*.[30] However, the existence of a rebuttable presumption in favour of contact between children and their parents or, better yet, a general assumption that contact is beneficial, is the common starting point of the ECtHR decisions on these matters.[31]

Pros and cons of the child's welfare as the court's paramount consideration

We have referred to the two different existing approaches in order to apply the best interest of the child principle and how they can influence the acceptance of presumptions when decisions must be made on issues that concern children.

We now focus on analysis of the pros and cons of the child's welfare as the court's paramount consideration. The emergence of the child's welfare as a court's paramount consideration may result in advantages and disadvantages. The most important advantages are that it introduces an important social and moral value when protecting children from harm.[32] In addition, it creates a flexible way to adapt the law to a specific case and the social reality. Finally, this approach is well-accepted and understood by the mass media and therefore a good tool for achieving a negotiated solution.[33]

The disadvantages are also significant, the most relevant one being the indeterminate nature of the welfare principle and the subsequent uncertainty that it creates.[34] This indeterminate nature is related to something that does not have verifiable, defined and specified limits. In other words, a court needs to have a lot of information in order to be able to determine what is best for a child in a specific case of separation. This could mean a long delay in reaching a judicial decision.[35] Another difficult point could be how to define the criteria to be followed in order to decide what is best for the welfare of a child, for example should it be a short- or long-term assessment? In addition, some believe that such a presumption would introduce a rule that would then mean applying a rigid solution to different cases.[36] Herring et al.[37] refer to the lack of transparency that the welfare principle may introduce: "other values, or reasons for the decision, can be smuggled in under the guise of the child's welfare".[38]

Finally, there is another danger that may result from considering the BIC as a "general clause": when the BIC is applied as "the" only possible paramount consideration, the temptation to shoe-horn it into a general clause may exist, as adopted by German doctrine.[39] In fact, Michael Coster in *Das Kindeswohl als Rechtsbegriff*[40] translated the English expression "best interest of the child" into the German term: "Generalklauseln des Kindeswohl". According to German doctrine, the concept "general clause" can be defined as a legal provision that makes reference to values and can exercise an auxiliary legislative role. A general clause contains a general, abstract and undetermined concept that can only be specified by its application to a particular case. Its function is to develop the law and adapt it to the ever-changing social reality.[41] On occasions, a judge faces difficulties caused by a lack of legislative action and, in spite of a legal gap, must make a decision. In these cases, general clauses can be very useful. It is claimed that the main function of a general clause is to correct a law when its application is contrary to the values contained in the general clause and causes unjust effects.[42] As general clauses are included in legal provisions, it is not possible to claim that they are contrary to law. On the other hand, what their application may cause is a conflict between laws. In fact, they are considered essential tools to complete and make the legal system more flexible.[43]

To understand the functioning of a general clause according to German doctrine, we can refer to Article 242 of the German Civil Code (BGB) that contains the principle of good faith, which is considered aa general clause that is at the same level as the law. In 1923, the German Supreme Court (*Reichsgericht*) applied Article 242 BGB to avoid the application of a compulsory law, as it considered that its application would lead to a result contrary to good faith. The German Parliament then decided to repeal the provision. The Supreme Court subsequently declared that it would not obey Parliament and added that:

> The idea of good faith is above the law, above any legal disposition. No legal system, that merits its name, can survive without this principle. Moreover, the lawmaker cannot use the power of his words to thwart an outcome imperatively demanded by good faith.[44]

Therefore, the general clause of good faith is considered a tool to create and correct law.[45]

However, the use of general clauses has been criticized on the basis of the uncertainty and arbitrariness it may cause.[46] If we connect this doctrine to the approach that describes the BIC as the sole paramount consideration, the risk arises of shoehorning the BIC into a general clause that applies as a good faith principle. This is what has happened in Spain, where case law interpreted the BIC in this way, considering it to be above the law.[47]

The dissident vote of four members of the Spanish Supreme Court in the abovementioned decision on gestational surrogacy is of great interest. The dissenting members stated that Article 10 of Act 14/2006 (LTRHA) prohibiting contracts with a surrogate mother could not be applied, as it was against the BIC, the regulation of which is of a constitutional nature and must be applied by courts. They stated that the

BIC is a priority and added that a child is a living being of flesh and blood that should never be ignored when applying the law. Consequently, they argued that the appealed judgment that applied Article 10 of the LTRHA should be revoked.[48]

Another interesting example is a decision by the Spanish Supreme Court of 2013[49] that has created judicial doctrine. In this case, the Court had to apply Article 92.8 CC, which states that, if there is no agreement between the parents, shared parenting is an exceptional measure. However, the judgment stated that, in the absence of an agreement, shared parenting should not be considered an exceptional measure but, rather, a standard and preferable one, because this measure allows the child to maintain their relationship with both parents. In fact, the reporting judge, José Antonio Seijas Quintana, is fond of saying that the best interest of the child moves mountains.

Finally, we refer to the decision by the Spanish Supreme Court in a case of assisted reproduction techniques whereby the filiation of two babies was declared in favour of the lesbian live-in partner of the mother. The plaintiff did not comply with the requirements of Article 7.3 of the Act 14/2006 (LTRHA) and, therefore, the Court applied Article 131 of the Civil Code that allows the declaration of filiation to be based on a biological fact. This decision, based on the BIC, can be considered contrary to a law intended to provide legal certainty to a biological link.[50] A deeper study of this line of case law was discussed in two recent articles.[51] In any case, the risk and danger posed by this case law approach to legal certainty is obvious.

The Kantian ethic objection

We have analyzed two approaches that interpret and apply the best interest of the child in different and even opposed ways. We have also referred to the pros and cons of both options. Now we want to focus on a philosophical aspect of this controversy.

In fact, there is a philosophical argument against the conceptualization of the BIC as the only primary consideration: this view may conflict with the Kantian ethic that orders us not to use a human being as a tool but to respect him/her as an end.[52] Therefore, the protection of a child cannot imply ignorance of the interest of that child's parents, at the expense of those parents' own welfare. Achievement of the child's protection at too high a price, such as acting against a sense of justice and ignoring the parents' interests, cannot be justified. It is true that this Kantian concept of dignity has been discussed recently. There are new proposals to define the concept, for example the "capacity approach" of Nobel Prize winner, Amartya Sen.[53] This theory, applied to animals by his disciple Martha Nussbaum, has given room to a new concept of dignity.[54] However, we believe that the Kantian formula remains on the table and is the basis of the International Declaration of Human Rights and our democratic systems. Therefore, this keynote objection is essential and any legal doctrine that could harm it should be avoided.

This issue probably causes the different mismatches that occur when the BIC is adopted as the only primary consideration. English scholars state that, on occasion, the BIC may not be the guideline if its application can be detrimental to one of the parents.[55] A similar conclusion was reached by the Provincial Court of Cordoba, Spain, in the case mentioned above, in which it gave priority to the interests of the working mother. It is not good to oversimplify all of the circumstances, feelings, needs, interests, rights, wishes and priorities that may be involved when a decision that concerns a child has to be adopted. In fact, the reduction of all these factors to only one consideration may imply a violation of the dignity of the other involved persons. This violation can be manifested in different ways, for example in decisions that contribute to the exploitation of women in a state of need or the commodification of women, as mentioned in relation to gestational surrogacy.

If we combine this philosophical perspective with the balance of pros and cons of the two different approaches analyzed, we can conclude that the most reasonable option should be the one that makes the BIC compatible with other significant considerations.

Conclusion

The final question is: how to balance the different interests concerned when an adult's decision can affect a child? We believe that, in special circumstances, the BIC should be preferred. However, the BIC should not be applied automatically applied – or exclusive.[56] The right approach should be the one adopted by the ECHR case law when applying Article 8 of the Convention, in accordance with Article 3 of the United Nations Convention on the Rights of the Child. Therefore, after studying this matter, we agree with this case law and consider the BIC one of the principles to be taken into consideration, which may override the interests of the parents.[57] This approach makes room for presumptions, especially for a rebuttable presumption in favour of shared parenting as a starting point. If the BIC is not automatically applied, there is no problem in accepting a presumption, provided it is rebuttable.

Notes

1 Ley Orgánica de protección jurídica del menor (Ley 1/1996 adopted on 15 January 1996) that is the equivalent of the Children Act 1989.
2 Article 2 Ley Orgánica de Protección Jurídica del Menor (LOPJM):

> Best interest of the child must be valued and considered as primary in all the actions and decisions concerning children, both in the public and private sphere. This valuation and consideration shall be a right of the child. In the event of another legitimate interest coinciding with the best interest of the child, the application of the latter must respect the former. However, if this is not possible, the best interest of the child must prevail over any other legitimate interest.

3 United Nations Convention on the Rights of the Child, General comment No. 14 (2013) on the right of the child to have his or her best interests taken as a primary consideration (art. 3, para. 1) (www2.ohchr.org/English/bodies/crc/docs/GC/CRC_C_GC_14_ENG.pdf).
4 Judgement of the Court of Appeals of Cordoba of 23 January 2018 (JUR\2018\46596), reporting judge: Miguel Ángel Navarro Robles.
5 Judgement of the Supreme Court of Spain, 6 February 2014, reporting judge: Rafael Saraza Jimena.
6 Judgement of the Supreme Court of Spain, 6 February 2014, reporting judge: Rafael Saraza Jimena.

7 Ibid.
8 Eekelaar (2015), 25, refers to *YC* v. *United Kingdom*, Application No. 4547/16 (2012) FLR 332: "In identifying the child's best interest in a particular case, two considerations must be borne in mind: first it is in the child's best interest that his ties with his family be maintained except in cases where the family has proved particularly unfit …"
9 Munby, L.J., in Re F, Relocation, 2012, EWCA Civ 1364, 2013, 1 FLR 645, 2013 1 FLR 645, at para. 37.
10 www.legislation.gov.uk/ukpga/2014/6/section/11.
11 Kaganas, Felicity (2018). Parental involvement: A discretionary presumption. *Legal Studies*, *38*(4), 549–570 (quotation taken from 557).
12 Herring, Jonathan, Probert, Rebecca and Gilmore, Stephen (2015). *Great debates in family law* (2nd ed.), Ch. 4. London: Red Globe Press, 11.
13 *Johansen* v. *Norway*, 1996, 23 EHRR 33, 72 at para. 78; and *TP and KM* v. *United Kingdom*, 2002, 34 EHRR 2, para.172.
14 In fact, other chapters of this volume delve into this issue, and they refer to interesting studies based on empirical data that can provide support to a presumption in favour of shared parenting. See Kruk, Edward (2018). Arguments against a presumption of shared physical custody in family law. *Journal of Divorce & Remarriage*, *59*(1), 1–13.
15 *Johansen* v. *Norway*, 1996, 23 EHRR 33, 72 at para. 78
16 *TP and KM* v. *United Kingdom*, 2002, 34 EHRR 2, para.172.
17 See *Pisica* v. *Moldova* (Application no. 23641/17), 23641/17, [2019] ECHR 779; see also *K.B. and Others* v. *Croatia*, no. 36216/13, § 143, 14 March 2017; *V.D. and Others* v. *Russia*, no. 72931/10, § 114, 9 April 2019. In *Pisica* v. *Moldova* the ECtHR states that, while the Court's case law requires children's views to be taken into account, those views are not necessarily immutable, and children's objections, which must be given due weight, are not necessarily sufficient to override the parents' interests, especially their interest in having regular contact with their child.
18 In any case, there is currently a broad consensus in support of the idea that, in all decisions concerning children, their best interests must be paramount. See *Neulinger and Shuruk* v. *Switzerland* [GC], no. 41615/07, § 135, 6 July 2010; *X.* v. *Latvia* [GC], no. 27853/09, § 96, ECHR 2013; *Strand Lobben and Others* v. *Norway* [GC], no. 37283/13, § 179, 10 September 2019).
19 In this paragraph we follow the approach of Herring et al. (2015).
20 *Glaser* v. *United Kingdom*, no. 32346/96, 2001, 33 EHRR 1, 2001, FLR 153, at para. 65.
21 It is also interesting to note that *A.V.* v. *Slovenia*, no. 878/13, § 73, 9 April 2019, states that children having the right to express their own views should not be interpreted as effectively giving them an unconditional power of veto without any other factors being considered and an examination being carried out to determine their best interests.
22 *Kosmopoulou* v. *Greece* (application no. 60457/00), 2004, 1 FLR 800, para. 4.
23 *Glaser* v. *United Kingdom*, no. 32346/96, 2001, 33 EHRR 1, 2001, FLR 153, at para. 66.
24 *A.V.* v. *Slovenia*, no. 878/13, § 73, 9 April 2019.
25 *C* v. *Finland* (application no. 18249/02), 2008, 46 EHRR 485, 2006, 2 FLR 597, at para. 60.
26 In addition, the State authorities play a significant role in striking a fair balance between the interests and rights of a child and the contact with his/her parents, when such "contact with the parent might appear to threaten this interest or interfere with those rights", *Glaser* v. *United Kingdom*, no. 32346/96, 2001, 33 EHRR 1, 2001, FLR 153, at para. 65.
27 1577 UNTS 3, opened to signature 20 November 1989 (UNCRC).
28 Beinham, Andrew (2003). Contact as a right and obligation. In Andrew Bainham, Bridget Lindley, Martin Richards and Liz Trinder (eds), *Children and their families: Contact, rights and welfare*. London: Bloomsbury, 62–75.
29 Gilmore, Stephen (2006). Disputing contact: Challenging some assumptions. *Child and Family Law Quarterly*, *20*(3), 285–311, para 59.
30 *Gnahoré* v. *France Case Digest*. 11(9–10), 479–484, 2000.

31 Bainham and Gilmore (2015), 635.
32 King, Michael (1987). Playing the symbols: Custody and the Law Commission. *Family Law*, 186 (17).
33 Herring, Jonathan (1999). The welfare principle and the rights of parents In Andrew Bainham, Shelley Day Sclater and Martin Richards (eds), *What is a parent? A socio-legal analysis*. Oxford: Hart Publishing, 100, 163.
34 Mnookin, Robert (1975). Child-custody adjudication: Judicial functions in the face of indeterminacy. *Law and Contemporary Problems*, *39*(3), 226.
35 Herring (1999), 100, 160.
36 Schneider, Carl (1992). Discretion and rules: A lawyer's view. In K. Hawkins (ed.), *The uses of discretion*. Oxford: Clarendon Press.
37 Herring et al. (2015), 10. In fact, I follow these authors when analysing this point in this paragraph and the preceding one.
38 Helen Reece gives us an example dated from the 1980s, when same-sex parents were the object of social censure, which could negatively influence the decision of courts under the veil of the welfare principle.
39 See Lüderssen, Klaus (1978). *Generalklauseln asl Gegenstand der Sozialwissenschaften*. Baden-Baden: Nomos-Verlagsgesellschaft; Teubner, Gunther (1971). *Standards und Direktiven in Generalklauseln*. Frankfurt am Mein: Verlagsort, 56 & ff.
40 Coester, Michael (1983). *Das Kindeswohl als Rechtsbegriff*. Frankfurt am Main: Verlagsort, 89.
41 Beater, A. (1994). Generalklauseln und Fallgruppen. *AcP*, *194*, 82–89.
42 Miquel González, José María (1997). Clausulas generales y desarrollo judicial del Derecho. *AFDUAM*, *1*, 297–326, 316.
43 See Teubner, Gunther (1993). *Law as an autopoietic system*. Fiesole, Italy: European University Institute Press, 115 & ff.
44 Weber, R. (1992). Entwicklung und Ausdehnung des § 242 BGB zum "königlichen Paragraphen". *JuS*, 633 & ff.
45 Rüthers, Bernd (1968). *Die unbegrenzte Auslegung. Zum Wandel der Privatrechtsordnung in Nationalsozialismus*. Tübingen, Germany: Mohr Siebeck, 55.
46 Justus Wilhelm Hedemann, in *Die Fucht in die Generalklauseln*, Tubinga, 1933, was able to forecast the consequences of the application of general clauses by a social-nationalist totalitarian regime, due to the arbitrariness that they can cause.
47 This jurisprudential approach has been accompanied by a doctrinal sector. In 1994 Professor Encarna Roca was the first Spanish author to affirm that the best interest of the child was a general clause. See Roca, Encarna (1993). Contestación: El interés del menor como factor de progreso y unificación del Derecho internacional privado. *Revista Jurídica de Cataluña*, *4*, 975 & ff.
48 Judgement of the Supreme Court of Spain, 6 February 2014, reporting judge: Rafael Saraza Jimena. Dissenting vote of Justices José Antonio Seijas Quintana, José Ramón Ferrándiz Gabriel, Francisco Javier Arroyo Fiesta and Sebastian Sastre Papiol.
49 Judgement of the Spanish Supreme Court, 29 April 2013 (RJ\2013\3269), reporting judge: José Antonio Seijas Quintana.
50 Judgement of the Supreme Court (STS), 5 December 2013 (RJ\2013\7640), reporting judge: José Antonio Seijas Quintana.
51 Torres Perea, José Manuel de (2016). Estudio de la función atribuida al interés del menor como cláusula general por una relevante línea jurisprudencial. *Diario La Ley* n.8737, 8 April 2016, Ref. D-147, p.1143 and ff; and (2017). Das Kindeswohl im spanischen Familienrecht: Eine vergleichende Analyse mit dem US-Recht. *European Review of Private Law*, *1*, 3 & ff.
52 Elster, J. (1987). Solomonic judgments: Against the best interest of the child', *University of Chicago Law Review*, *54*(1).
53 Claassen (2014).

54 Nussbaum, Martha (2008). Human dignity and political entitlements. In *Human dignity and bioethics*. Washington, DC: The President's Council on Bioethics. Retrieved from https://bioethicsarchive.georgetown.edu/pcbe/reports/human_dignity/chapter14.html; (2002). Animal rights: The need for a theorical basis. *Havard Law Review*, *114*(5), 1506–2549.
55 Eekelaar, John (2002). Beyond the welfare principle. *Child and Family Law Quarterly*, *14*(3), 243.
56 Chourdhy, S. and Fenwick, H. (2005). Taking the rights of parents and children seriously: Confronting the welfare principle under the Human Rights Act. *Oxford Journal of Legal Studies*, *25*(3), 453.
57 Ibid.

References

Bainham, Andrew and Gilmore, Stephen (2015). The English Children and Families Act 2014. *VUWLR*, *46*, 627–648.

Chourdhy, Shazia and H. Fenwick, Helen (2005). Taking the rights of parents and children seriously: Confronting the welfare principle under the Human Rights Act", *Oxford Journal of Legal* Studies, *25*(3), 453.

Claassen, Rutger (2014). Human dignity in the capacity approach. In Marcus Düwell, Jens Braarvig, Roger Brownsword & Dietmar Mieth (eds), *The Cambridge Handbook of Human Dignity*. Cambridge: Cambridge University Press, 240–249.

Eekelaar, John (2015). The role of the best interest principle in decisions affecting children and decisions about children. *International Journal of Children's Rights*, *23*, 3–26.

Kruk, Edward (2018). Arguments against a presumption of shared physical custody in family law. *Journal of Divorce & Remarriage*, *59*(1), 1–13.

Torres Perea, José Manuel de (2016). Estudio de la función atribuida al interés del menor como cláusula general por una relevante línea jurisprudencial. *Diario La Ley*, n. 8737, 8 Abril, ref. D-147, 1143 & ff.

5
DOES JOINT PHYSICAL CUSTODY "CAUSE" CHILDREN'S BETTER OUTCOMES?[1]

Sanford L. Braver and Ashley M. Votruba

Research generally suggests that children of divorce are at increased risk for social, psychological, and educational difficulties (Braver & Lamb, 2012; Chase-Lansdale, Cherlin, & Kiernan, 1995; Cherlin et al., 1991). Thus, when it comes to family law and custody determination, policymakers and researchers are concerned with knowing what types of postseparation parenting arrangements are generally the most beneficial for children. More specifically, interest has focused on whether joint physical custody (JPC) produces better outcomes for children than sole maternal physical custody (SPC). Another related question is how well JPC works when there is parental conflict or when one or both parents did not want JPC.

A handful of review articles have examined the large number of studies that have addressed these questions and generally found that children with JPC arrangements were significantly better off than those in SPC (generally maternal custody) arrangements (Baude, Pearson, & Drapeau, 2016; Bauserman, 2002; Nielsen, 2015, 2017). Bauserman (2002) performed a meta-analysis on 33 studies with a combined sample size of more than 2,650 children, of whom about one-third had JPC arrangements. Children with JPC plans scored significantly higher on adjustment measures compared to children in sole custody. This was true for nearly all categories of adjustment (except academic adjustment), including general measures of adjustment, family relations, self-esteem, emotional adjustment, behavioral adjustment, and divorce-specific adjustment. This suggests that JPC can benefit children in a wide range of domains. Baude et al. (2016) replicated this finding in a meta-analysis of 17 studies that included some 36,000 families.

Nielsen also updated the Bauserman (2002) review in 2015, citing 40 studies, then again in 2017, summarizing 54 studies, and most recently summarizing 61 studies (Nielsen, 2018). In all three reviews she found that children with JPC arrangements were generally better off than children with sole custody arrangements. Across these studies, children with JPC arrangements showed: (a) better grades and cognitive development; (b) lower levels of depression, anxiety, and dissatisfaction; (c) lower aggression, drug use, and alcohol use; (d) better physical health and lower smoking rates; and (e) better father–child relationships. Nielsen (2015) also concluded that the benefits of JPC arrangements occur even when there is parental conflict. She explicitly noted that, in 11 of the 40 studies, the researchers stated that their sample included high-conflict and litigating parents. Further, in 16 of the studies, either the parents with a JPC arrangement had as much conflict as those with sole custody arrangements, or the outcomes remained better for JPC children even controlling for parental conflict.

Despite being armed with this robust and consistent recent literature attesting to the substantial benefits of JPC, advocates have run into consistent opposition in converting the findings into a legal presumption: an assumption made and accepted by a court as a basis for their decision in the case to be decided. Generally, presumptions in family law are considered rebuttable and are accepted by the court until disproved. The assumption "will stand as a fact unless someone comes forward to contest it and prove otherwise" (Rebuttable Presumption Law and Legal Definition, 2017). In family law, for example, the child support amount arising from each state's child support guidelines constitutes a rebuttable presumption of the proper child support award (Elrod, 1990). Proponents of JPC have engaged in many unsuccessful attempts to pass laws making JPC a presumption that is rebuttable on showing that, for some specifiable legal reason, such an arrangement should not be considered in the child's best interest in the particular case.

One of the key sources of opposition to making JPC a legal presumption arises because of scientific considerations.[2] The objection focuses on a certain limitation of the research design historically used by the vast majority of the studies comparing the impact of JPC and SPC arrangements. This research design has been termed the static group comparison (Campbell & Stanley, 1963) and is often also referred to as a cross-sectional study. A static group design compares two or more preexisting groups. In this case the research compared families with JPC arrangements to those with SPC arrangements—generally maternal custody. The term *cross-sectional* (implying a single point in time, with preexisting groups) is generally contrasted with the longitudinal study (implying multiple points in time). The limitation of this design generally ensues from the fact that there is "no formal means of certifying that the groups would have been equivalent had it not been for" the custody arrangement (Campbell & Stanley, 1963, p. 12). Whatever the basis on which the individuals become sorted into groups it represents *selection*, which constitutes a substantial threat to the internal validity of the causal conclusion.

For the issue at hand, it is mostly *self*-selection that comprises the most plausible alternative explanation for the differences found between JPC and SPC children. Specifically, during the historical period when many of the JPC studies were conducted, families were granted JPC only if both parents (more or less) freely declared that this was the arrangement they preferred. If either parent declared that he or she was unalterably opposed to such an arrangement, the courts would typically not grant it. Thus, JPC was virtually never imposed on consistently unwilling families—in some instances because the statutes specifically precluded it. Thus, couples in which both parents wished for JPC—which was a distinct minority (Braver & O'Connell, 1998; Maccoby & Mnookin, 1992)—were compared to couples in which one or both parents opposed it. Hence, the sorting into the two comparison groups was based nearly entirely on the parents' own decisions, resulting in self-selection. It is also well known that many discernable factors, as identified later in this chapter, might discriminate between couples making these two choices and that these factors often are also associated with better child outcomes regardless of the custody arrangement. This is an important methodological limitation because it could be these self-selection factors, rather than the custody arrangement per se, that accounts entirely for the advantages found for JPC children.

The reality of this methodological limitation found in much of the research on JPC has implications both for scientific inquiry and for policy development. Scientifically speaking, when exploring a cause–effect relationship, if any plausible alternative explanation happens to be entirely responsible for the effect, the causal conjecture is thereby invalidated. Specifically, if selection accounts for the entirety of an effect, then enacting the "cause" variable will not have the anticipated impact on the "effect" variable. In terms of custody policy, if the JPC arrangement is not the cause of the benefits, if instead self-selection happens to account for all the positive findings, imposing JPC (rather than letting parents choose it) will not have the mostly beneficial effects indicated by the research, as noted by Bauserman (2002) and Fehlberg and colleagues (2011). Thus, a presumptive law, which would impose JPC over the opposition of one of the parents, might fail to create the intended benefits. As Emery, Otto, and O'Donohue (2005) concluded from research using this methodology, "we cannot extrapolate from voluntary joint physical custody to circumstances when joint physical custody is imposed upon parents by laws favoring joint physical custody … or by judges who order it" (pp. 16–17).

Although the static group research design with self-selection into comparison groups has clear limitations for assessing causality, other methodological approaches offer greater promise. The gold standard methodological approach that can fully overcome the barriers to drawing causal conclusions is the randomized experiment (Cook & Campbell, 1979). For example, if couples were assigned at random to either JPC or SPC, any subsequent differences in children's well-being could be unambiguously attributed to the custody arrangement. It is true that family courts have on relatively rare but increasingly common occasions been convinced to deploy random assignment for various purposes (Ballard, Holtzworth-Munroe, Applegate, D'Onofrio, & Bates, 2013; Beck et al., 2009; Braver, Sandler, Hita, & Wheeler, 2016; Mauricio et al., 2017; Rossi et al., 2015; Sandler et al., 2016; Winslow et al., 2017). Nonetheless, there has never been and never will be an instance of judges assigning custody of children at random. Thus, although conducting a randomized experiment would clearly be the best methodological option for assessing the causal mechanism, it is out of the question.

Research designs that probe causality

There are, however, a number of additional methodological approaches that would allow researchers to probe causality, albeit not prove it. The inability—for practical, ethical, or physical reasons—to assign treatments at random is an extremely common one in social science and even physical science. This problem has prompted a great deal of recent scholarly work devoted to going beyond static group comparisons to render causal inferences more credible. These approaches include: (a) employing statistical controls; (b) propensity score analysis; (c) natural experiments; and (d) regression discontinuity or interrupted time-series quasi-experiments. In regard to JPC and SPC children's outcomes, two more approaches present themselves: (e) differentiating the findings on the basis of parents' initial custody preferences; and (f) examining outcomes in jurisdictions where JPC is already a presumption or a norm.

Statistical controls

The most common approach to strengthening the possibility of establishing causality is to employ statistical controls. The intent of this technique is to statistically hold constant, adjust for differences in, covary out, partial out, control for, correct for, or equate for (all preceding terms are essentially synonyms) these self-selection factors. According to the *Berkeley Glossary of Statistical Terms*, "to control for a variable is to try to separate its effect from the treatment effect, so it will not confound with the treatment" (in this case, the custody arrangement; Stark, 2017). It is important to recognize that such research takes place under one of two distinct statistical approaches. The first is the group-oriented approach that treats JPC and SPC families as two distinct classes of people. Group-oriented approaches, in general, use independent group *t*-tests and analysis of variance (ANOVA) as their main statistical tools. When they attempt to control for any variables, they move to an analysis of covariance (ANCOVA), to "covary out" the possible confound. The second approach treats most of the variables as continuous ones, not as classes or groups. This approach uses multiple regression as its main statistical tool. Typically, multiple regressions will treat JPC versus SPC as a dummy or binary variable and enter it into the analysis after the control variables have been entered. In this (or in another equivalent) way, the self-selection variables are controlled for or partialed out, allowing a firmer inference that it is the custody arrangement per se that is responsible for the outcomes. The regression approach and the ANCOVA approach yield virtually identical results and are merely two different but equivalent approaches (Huitema, 2011).

In JPC and SPC studies, most researchers consider parent conflict and family income to be the two most important self-selection factors in that they are thought to powerfully affect both the self-selection of JPC arrangements and child well-being. Accordingly, quite a large number of recent studies have attempted to control for these two factors in evaluating the impact of JPC. Nielsen (2018) cataloged these 60 studies. Of the 36 studies that considered parental conflict, JPC children had better outcomes on all measures in 18 studies, equal to better in 11 studies, equal in 3 studies, and worse outcomes on 1 of the measures in 4 studies. In the 42 studies that considered family income, JPC children had better outcomes on all measures in 25 studies, equal to better outcomes in 9 studies, equal outcomes in 4 studies, and worse outcomes on 1 measure but equal or better outcomes on other measures in 4 studies. As Nielsen (2018) also pointed out, the links between income and children's well-being in the vast literature on this topic actually find only weak and indirect effects, with the exception of children growing up in poverty.

Although the two self-selection factors of income and parental conflict are often seen as the most consequential, they certainly do not exhaust the list of potential factors influencing children's outcomes. This fact is critical because the effectiveness of the statistical control approach is greatly compromised if other selection factors are strongly at work. Among these additional factors might be mother's and father's level of education, the child's age, the parents' ages, which parent wanted the divorce, each parent's mental health, how guilty each parent felt about the breakup, and so on.

One study was quite comprehensive in identifying which factors might set JPC and SPC parents apart (Gunnoe & Braver, 2001). This study was somewhat unique in that it was both longitudinal and captured data before the divorce was final—that is, before any custody arrangement became official. In fact, the initial interview with the parents took place within a short 2.5 months after the initial petition for divorce, which starts the legal process of divorcing. The study assessed fully 71 predivorce variables, including all those mentioned earlier, that might plausibly differentiate between families that ultimately obtained joint legal versus sole legal custody (with maternal physical custody). Twenty of the 71 factors indeed discriminated at a statistically significant level parents who ultimately obtained sole or joint legal custody. All 20 factors were then simultaneously controlled in a subsequent ANCOVA comparison of the 52 sole and 26 joint legal custody families 2 years postdivorce. The children in the families with joint legal custody continued to have fewer adjustment problems than children in sole custody families, over and above the predivorce selection factors. It should be noted that it was legal custody, rather than physical custody that was at issue here, because the study was conducted at a time before there were sufficient numbers of JPC cases to yield adequate statistical power. Note, however, that Bauserman's (2002) meta-analysis found that joint legal custody and JPC bestowed largely equal benefits. It is also important that the more positive outcomes for JPC children were not moderated by the level of predivorce conflict between the parents.

In conclusion, statistical controls, the most ubiquitous approach to dealing with the self-selection confound, have shown rather overwhelmingly that JPC confers substantial benefits to children over and above, or independent of, self-selection factors.

Propensity score analysis

Propensity score analysis is a relatively new technique that deals with the issue of static or preexisting groups by providing another means for equating the groups on a large number of variables (covariates) measured at a baseline point (West, Cham, Thoemmes et al., 2014). Once they are "equated" at baseline (via matching, stratification, weighting or ANCOVA) on all the covariates (e.g., parental conflict) that predict group selection, the comparison of the groups' differential outcomes rules out the effect of these potential confounding factors (Shadish, Cook, & Campbell, 2002; West, Cham, & Liu, 2014). This strongly enhances the internal validity of the study and thereby the inference of causal impact.

Propensity score analysis is an upgrade from traditional approaches that equate groups on only a few variables, instead allowing equating on a large number of baseline covariates simultaneously by creating a single propensity score that summarizes all of the covariates. The score is typically constructed using a logistic regression equation in which the full set of covariates is used to predict group membership. Unlike traditional approaches, however, it leaves out simultaneous consideration at this stage of the outcome variable of interest. Essentially, the "propensity score is the predicted probability that the person will be assigned to the treatment group based on his or her scores on each of the full set of covariates" (West, Cham, Thoemmes et al., 2014, p. 908). If the groups are successfully equated, then it is possible to arrive at an unbiased estimate of the causal effect of the treatment. In our case, it would thus be possible to examine what causal effect JPC or SPC had on child well-being. However, propensity score analysis has advantages over regression-oriented statistical controls because it assesses overlap of the two groups being compared; it makes no assumptions about the functional form of the relationship between the covariate and selection, such as linearity; it allows nonparametric as well as parametric conditioning; and it allows checks of the putative selection model.

One of the challenges of performing propensity score analysis is that, to get an accurate propensity score, it is necessary to measure all or nearly all covariates that might be confounded with self-selection into JPC or SPC arrangements and child well-being (West, Cham, Thoemmes et al., 2014). This could mean measuring a very large number of potential covariates at baseline. In addition to new data collection efforts, researchers can consider secondary analysis of data sets that included many potential such covariates that have already been collected, as did Gunnoe and Braver (2001).

To our knowledge, no researcher has yet attempted to use this powerful and sophisticated methodology to examine the causal effect of custody arrangements on child well-being. Because propensity score analysis achieves results close to those of a randomized experiment (Cook, Shadish, & Wong, 2008; Shadish, Clark, & Steiner, 2008), we believe this is a strong candidate for future research.

Natural experiments

Natural experiments also often allow causal conclusions to be fairly made. In natural experiments, the assignment to a treatment condition is not made at random by the researcher but is made instead by some independent event, for example nature, the weather, sickness, or policy changes. The key to whether the causal inference is valid in any natural experiment is whether "the event ... allows for the random or *seemingly random* assignment of study subjects to different groups" (Messer, 2017, italics added).

Because custody laws are a matter of much legal and cultural ferment and change, new laws and new court holdings are constantly coming into being. Comparing couples assigned by some means to JPC to couples assigned to SPC could plausibly constitute a natural experiment that would allow causal inferences about the custody arrangement's impact on child outcomes. The validity of such an inference rests completely on the exact nature of the design, however. Consider, for example, a hypothetical study comparing couples who divorced before a JPC presumption took effect to another group of couples who divorced after the presumption took effect. Only to the degree that we might fairly regard as "random or seemingly random" whether the exact date of each specific case's divorce decree fell either before or after the law change would the causal inference about the impact of the JPC presumption on the child's well-being be valid. When other potential causes of any differences in child outcomes found might also be plausible, they constitute clear threats to the internal validity of the inference. For example, if "other change-producing events" (p. 7) that might affect the children's outcomes have occurred between the two observation points (e.g., economic downturns, housing collapses), the inference risks invalidity. Such an "other" event "becomes a more plausible rival explanation of change the longer" (p. 7) the interval between the two observations. Thus, studies that let only small intervals (i.e., a few months) intervene between the divorce dates of the couples in the two regimes are on more solid footing with causal claims.

We are aware of no solid empirical investigations of JPC's impact on child outcomes that employed such a natural experiment but are mindful, however, that these could be profitably deployed by alert investigators whenever the passage of a presumptive law seems imminent. With more than 20 states and numerous countries currently debating new JPC presumption laws (Leading Women for Shared Parenting, 2017), researchers should note the important opportunity that exists to study a random sample of families before and another random sample after such a law takes effect.

It might appear that another natural experiment opportunity exists by comparing two nearby jurisdictions with different custody laws, but this rarely is valid. For example, Douglas (2003) compared a sample of parents from New Hampshire, which had recently passed a presumptive joint legal custody law, to a sample from Maine, which did not have such a presumption. The samples were chosen from six counties matched on several demographic factors. However, although matched on some variables, many other differences between the jurisdictions exist, such as radically different child support regimes. Many, or all, of these differences could plausibly account for any impact of the new presumption. Thus, Douglas (2003, p. 9) admitted that "more well-controlled designs are greatly needed" for sound inference. In summary, comparing different jurisdictions at the same time generally constitutes an invalid variant of natural experiment with which to evaluate the causal impact of JPC on child outcomes.

Quasi-experimental designs: Regression discontinuity or interrupted time-series

One of the most important contributions of Campbell and Stanley's (1963) work was to identify an extremely important class of research designs, new at the time, which they termed *quasi-experiments*. These designs are admittedly less conclusive than randomized experiments, but, when well conducted, only marginally so. The two quasi-experimental designs we highlight here are the ones best suited to the evaluation of JPC arrangements or presumptions on child well-being: regression discontinuity or interrupted time-series. For our purposes, these terms are largely interchangeable, and we refer to them as RD–ITS, accordingly.

Whereas a simple pre- and post-test design is very susceptible to the argument that other causes might have intervened between the two measurement occasions, the RD–ITS approach minimizes that threat to internal validity by considering many pre-test points and many post-test points. Figure 5.1 illustrates this approach: It gathers a sample of many pre-law-change cases and many post-law-change cases and plots them all on the horizontal axis by the date of the final decree. The child well-being measure(s) for each case is plotted on the vertical axis. If the law had an impact on child well-being (or any other relevant outcome measure) it should be evidenced by an abrupt discontinuity or jump in the trend line tracing the average outcomes over time. Any alternative explanation of the child outcome results other than the causal impact of the JPC presumptive law taking effect would have to pass the considerable hurdle of explaining why the impact occurred at that one exact point in time.

Although we are aware of no existing study that used such a design to study the impact of JPC presumptions on child outcomes, work preliminary to an analysis of the introduction of Arizona law has been conducted by Fabricius and Millar. Moreover, the design can be used to evaluate other interventions in the family law environment. For example, DeLusé and Braver (2015) used such a design to evaluate a divorce education program and deemed such an evaluation rigorous.

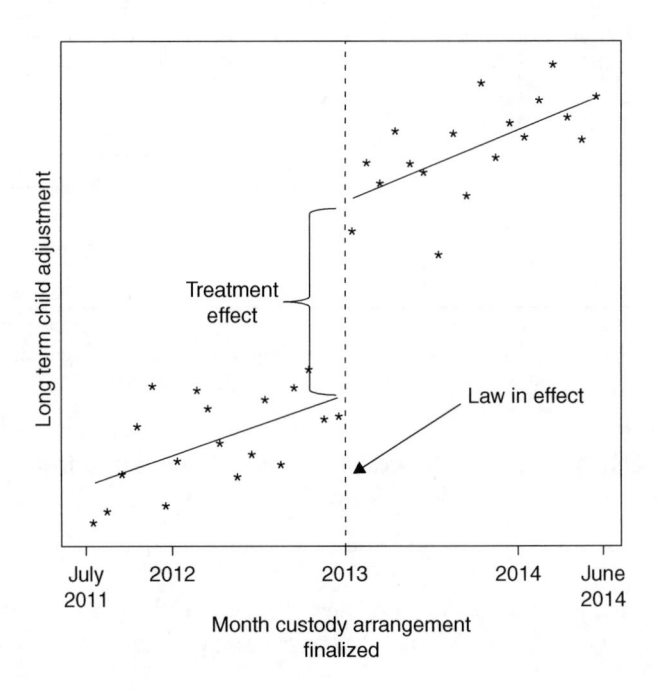

Figure 5.1 Regression discontinuity design

Differentiating on the basis of parents' initial preferences

In evaluating the causal impact of JPC arrangements on child well-being, another methodological strategy rather uniquely presents itself. This occurs because there are two parents, and they might in fact agree initially on a JPC arrangement or they might initially disagree. With one parent initially against it, JPC sometimes nevertheless prevailed, infrequently because a court decision overruled that parent and, more commonly, because the opposing parent later withdrew his or her opposition, perhaps because of professional advice or under pressure of some kind. Braver and O'Connell (1998) and Maccoby and Mnookin (1992) found that initial mutual agreement on joint custody is relatively rare, between 18 and 23 percent. Fabricius, Braver, Diaz, and Velez (2010), among others, discussed the many avenues in which the bargaining process between the ex-spouses can be influenced by the "guidance about their chances they receive from judges, attorneys, custody evaluators, parent educators, and mediators" (p. 257). Mnookin and Kornhauser (1979) famously called this "bargaining in the shadow of the law." Braver, Cookston, and Cohen (2002) presented evidence that it is the parents' lawyers, in particular, who often influence the process, leading parents to not pursue their initial preferences by advising them about their "likelihood of prevailing" in seeking the arrangements they prefer. If analysts have access to information about the two parents' initial preferences prior to the decree, they could compare the child outcomes of the "both initially agree on shared" to the "one initially wanted sole but 'caved'" groups to probe the impact of the self-selection alternative explanation. If self-selection is responsible for the benefits of JPC that have been documented, we should expect that children for whom both parents voluntarily selected JPC will have better outcomes than those for whom one parent initially opposed it. Nielsen (2014) identified six studies that catalog parents' initial agreements or lack thereof concerning the eventual parenting plan (Braver & O'Connell, 1998; Brotsky, Steinman, & Zemmelman, 1988; Fabricius & Suh, 2017; Luepnitz, 1986; Maccoby & Mnookin, 1992; Pearson & Thoennes, 1990). Most of these are longitudinal, having assessed parents' initial preferences before the decree was final. The study by Luepnitz (1986), however, is not longitudinal and simply stated, without explanation of how it was determined, that "in only 54% of the joint cases had parents agreed from the outset on some form of shared custody. In the remaining cases there was conflict over the question of custody initially" (p. 3). Finally, Fabricius and Suh (2017) assessed initial agreement about custody arrangements by retrospective report. The six studies in general do not find lower benefits of JPC for the group of parents who initially disagreed; rather, the benefits of JPC held even when one parent disagreed on the arrangement, undermining the notion that self-selection accounts for the totality of JPC benefits.

We encourage researchers with longitudinal data sets with parents' initial custody preferences recorded to harness this power with additional secondary analyses. Notably, Maccoby and Mnookin (1992) have a large data set that is publicly available at www.socio.com/fam2527.php. This could be leveraged to address this and other important causal questions, but to our knowledge it has not been done.

We should also note the inferential power of longitudinal studies more generally. Analyses such as cross-lagged panel studies and structural equation models at different periods of time are generally regarded as greatly enhancing the ability to make causal inferences even without random assignment. It has long been noted that family law research needs more longitudinal studies (e.g., Braver & Lamb, 2012; Braver et al., 1993).

Examining outcomes in jurisdictions where it is already a presumption or a norm

Finally, yet another inferential approach is, or is rapidly becoming, available in the present instance to evaluate this chapter's central question. However, this final approach skirts the causal question per se and instead addresses the related question of whether the benefits of JPC arrangements found in the literature will continue to hold when such arrangements are a rebuttable presumption or when imposed on parents against their will. It turns out we have such evidence by examining jurisdictions where JPC is already a presumption or where there are already strong norms upholding it. Because JPC practices are rapidly becoming more widespread throughout the United States and world, several jurisdictions now have large portions of the recent divorce cases adopting JPC, some of which were presumably initially disinclined. Among these jurisdictions are several European countries, including Sweden and Belgium, Australia, and several US states, including Arizona and Wisconsin. By examining child well-being or other relevant outcomes in samples of recent divorces in these locales it is possible to glean answers regarding how well it works when it is imposed, perhaps over the initial objections of one of the parents.

Most of these law reforms are too fresh to permit sensitive analyses of longer-term impacts of the presumption or practice. Consequently, it is too soon to have many published evaluations. The Arizona presumptive law, however, had a recent cursory evaluation that is summarized in Fabricius, Aaron, Akins, Assini, and McElroy (2018). It found that the law appears to be having a positive effect and is in the child's best interests.

The country with the most mature law and practice as well as rigorous recent evaluations is Sweden. Articles by Nielsen (2018) and Fransson, Hjern and Bergström (2018) summarizing the Swedish research indicate both that the arrangement has become a "new norm" and that children who spent equal time living with both parents after a separation reported better well-being than children in predominantly single-parent care.

As noted, the move toward making JPC the substantially normative option is very recent. Thus, it is premature to expect a plethora of these types of well-designed studies assessing what happens when large swaths of couples, which include the many couples where at least one of the parents is unenthusiastic about the arrangement, have JPC imposed on them because of legal reform. Scholars, advocates, and decision makers should be very alert to evaluations of these situations emerging and becoming part of the literature. It is noteworthy, though, that virtually all of the studies to date support the proposition that JPC is in children's best interests even when one parent opposes it.

Conclusion

The central aim of this chapter was to ask whether JPC causes better outcomes for children and to describe those research designs that can better help us answer this question. It is difficult to draw causal conclusions from older research in this area because the studies use primarily static group comparison research designs with self-selection into comparison groups, which confounds the causal question. Because a random assignment experiment is unlikely to ever occur, it is a certainty that such causality will never be answered conclusively. However, several other approaches that can probe causality are beginning to be employed with more frequency. Some recent studies exploiting such analyses have already been reported, and others should be expected in the near future.

The weight of the recent evidence indicates that self-selection effects do not largely account for the benefits of JPC in the empirical literature. Over a wide variety of methodological approaches, and for the vast majority of findings to date, it appears that the benefits of JPC for children are not primarily due to the fact that a unique set of families choose it. Thus, evidence from recent research is discrediting the major rival explanation—that the better child outcomes observed in JPC are merely the result of self-selection. Infirming the primary alternative explanation has the compensatory effect of supporting the original causal proposition (Cook & Campbell, 1979). Thus, we conclude that JPC probably does cause benefits to children, on average. It should go without saying that the final two words in the preceding sentence are absolutely necessary. Although the general tendency across all individuals merits this conclusion, it certainly might not apply to all individual child custody cases. However, whether we currently have the requisite expertise to permit inferences about the likely impact in any particular case is debatable (Emery, Otto, & O'Donahue, 2005; Kelly & Ramsey, 2009; Stevenson, Braver, Ellman, & Votruba, 2012). According to Braver (2014, p. 177):

> Bottom line: much as it may be desirable, we may really *not know how* to properly individualize, tailor, or custom-fit parenting plans to achieve the best possible outcomes in each case. If this is true, the effort and expense and time and trouble taken in the futile pursuit of case-specific fittings come with little in the way of corresponding benefits. And, in such a case, it is better to have a rule or starting place that covers the majority of cases and families, with, of course, the ability to deviate when the fit is obviously bad.

Similarly, with the recent increased use of methodologically advanced research designs, we regard the evidence to now be sufficiently deep and consistent as to permit social scientists to provisionally recommend presumptive JPC to policymakers. As always, the presumption should be rebuttable; that is, although on average JPC can now be confidently predicted to bestow benefits on children, there are certainly situations in which JPC would be unwise. Researchers can assist the enterprise of identifying these exceptions by engaging in systematic efforts to identify subgroups for whom the usual conclusion does not fit. One way to do this is to investigate interaction effects (e.g., custody arrangement by conflict interactions) on the child outcomes.

The term *provisionally* is used here because we hope and expect researchers will keep studying the matter, especially with rigorous analyses of the type identified in this chapter. Consumers of this research also need to be alert to new findings that continue to affirm the conclusions here—or perhaps that oppose it. We might aptly characterize the current state of the evidence as "the preponderance of the evidence," meaning that there is substantially more evidence for the presumption than against it. A great many studies, with various inferential strengths, suggest that JPC will bestow benefits on children on average, and few if any studies show that it instead harms them. We note a kind of personal natural before and after experiment in this regard. About 20 years ago, the first author wrote, "There is simply not enough evidence available at present to substantiate routinely imposing joint residential custody ... there are too few cases adopting [it] to perform statistical analyses" (Braver & O'Connell, 1998, p. 223). That was before. A large number of those studies have since been performed, and the state of the newer evidence is almost completely supportive. On this basis, we contend that the burden of persuasion has shifted to those who oppose a presumption of JPC.

Notes

1 This chapter was previously published in the *Journal of Divorce & Remarriage*, 2018, 1–17. DOI: 10.1080/10502556.2018.1454203.
2 There is also, of course, a very substantial literature that opposes shared parenting presumptions when domestic violence is evident or alleged (e.g., Greenberg, 2004; Morrill, Dai, Dunn, Sung, & Smith, 2005). Although these voices are persuasive, in general, the articles provide arguments, not quantitative empirical research findings. Because this chapter is devoted to research design issues within the quantitative empirical research literature, papers presenting arguments only are outside its scope. In any event, proposed statutes often explicitly note that the existence of chronic, one-sided domestic violence should be a rebuttal factor. There are also voices that oppose shared parenting when there is high interparental conflict. For example, Stahl (1999), in his guide for professional custody evaluators, opined, "high conflict parents cannot share parenting" (p. 99). Similarly, Buchanan (2001) wrote, "when parents remain in high conflict, joint custody is ... ill-advised" (p. 234). Emery (2009) wrote, "joint physical custody is the worst arrangement for children when [it] leaves [them] in the middle of a war zone ... In high conflict divorces, children do worse in joint physical custody than in other arrangements." Such claims are supposedly based on the quantitative empirical literature and therefore are included in our review here.

References

Ballard, R., Holtzworth-Munroe, A., Applegate, A., D'Onofrio, B., & Bates, J. (2013). A randomized controlled trial of child-informed mediation. *Psychology, Public Policy, and Law, 19*, 271–281.

Baude, A., Pearson, J., & Drapeau, S. (2016). Child adjustment in joint physical custody versus sole custody: A meta-analytic review. *Journal of Divorce & Remarriage, 57*, 338–360.

Bauserman, R. (2002). Child adjustment in joint-custody versus sole-custody arrangements: A metaanalytic review. *Journal of Family Psychology, 16*, 91–102.

Beck, C., Holtzworth-Munroe, A., D'Onofrio, B., Fee, H., William, C., Hill, H., & Frances, G. (2009). Collaboration between judges and social science researchers in family law. *Family Court Review, 47*, 451–467.

Braver, S. L. (2014). Costs and pitfalls of individualizing decisions and incentivizing conflict: A comment on AFCC's think tank report on shared parenting. *Family Court Review, 52*, 175–180.

Braver, S. L., & Lamb, M. E. (2012). Marital dissolution. In G. W. Peterson & K. R. Bush (eds), *Handbook of marriage and the family* (3rd ed., pp. 487–516). New York: Springer.

Braver, S. L., & O'Connell, D. (1998). *Divorced dads: Shattering the myths.* New York: Tarcher/Putman.

Braver, S. L., Cookston, J., & Cohen, B. (2002). Experiences of family law attorneys with current issues in divorce practice. *Family Relations, 51*, 325–334.

Braver, S. L., Sandler, I. N., Hita, L. C., & Wheeler, L. A. (2016). A randomized comparison trial of two court-connected programs for high conflict families. *Family Court Review, 54*, 349–363.

Braver, S. L., Wolchik, S. A., Sandler, I. N., Sheets, V., Fogas, B., & Bay, R. C. (1993). A longitudinal study of noncustodial parents: Parents without children. *Journal of Family Psychology, 7*, 9–23.

Brotsky, M., Steinman, S., & Zemmelman, S. (1988). Joint custody through mediation. *Conciliation Courts Review, 26*, 53–58.

Buchanan, C. M. (2001). Divorce. In J. V. Lerner, R. M. Lerner, & J. Finkelstein (eds), *Adolescence in America: An encyclopedia* (pp. 232–235). Santa Barbara, CA: ABC-CLIO.

Campbell, D. T., & Stanley, J. C. (1963). *Experimental and quasi-experimental designs for research on teaching.* Boston, MA: Houghton Mifflin.

Chase-Lansdale, P. L., Cherlin, A. J., & Kiernan, K. E. (1995). The long-term effects of parental divorce on the mental health of young adults: A developmental perspective. *Child Development, 66*, 1614–1634.

Cherlin, A. J., Furstenberg, F. F., Jr., Chase-Lansdale, L., Kiernan, K. E., Robins, P. K., Morrison, D. R., & Teitler, J. O. (1991). Longitudinal studies of effects of divorce on children in Great Britain and the United States. *Science, 252*, 1386–1389.

Cook, T. D., & Campbell, D. T. (1979). *Quasi-experimentation: Design and analysis for field settings.* New York: Rand-McNally.

Cook, T. D., Shadish, W. R., & Wong, V. C. (2008). Three conditions under which experiments and observational studies produce comparable causal estimates: New findings from within-study comparisons. *Journal of Policy Analysis and Management, 27*, 724–750.

DeLusé, S., & Braver, S. L. (2015). A rigorous quasi-experimental evaluation of a mandatory divorce education program. *Family Court Review, 53*, 66–78.

Douglas, E. M. (2003). The impact of a presumption for joint legal custody on father involvement. *Journal of Divorce & Remarriage, 39*(1–2), 1–10.

Elrod, L. H. (1990). The federalization of child support guidelines. *Journal of the American Academy of Matrimonial Law, 6*, 103–130.

Emery, R. (2009, May 18). *Joint physical custody: Is joint physical custody best—or worst—for children?* [web log post]. Retrieved from www.psychologytoday.com/blog/divorced-children/200905/joint-physical-custody

Emery, R., Otto, R., & O'Donohue, W. (2005). A critical assessment of child custody evaluations: Limited science and a flawed system. *Psychological Science, 6*(1), 1–29.

Fabricius, W. V., & Suh, G. W. (2017). Should infants and toddlers have frequent overnight parenting time with fathers? The policy debate and new data. *Psychology, Public Policy, and Law, 23*, 68–84.

Fabricius, W. V., Aaron, M., Akins, F. R., Assini, J. J., and McElroy, T. (2018). What happens when there is presumptive 50/50 parenting time? An evaluation of Arizona's New Child Custody Statute. *Journal of Divorce & Remarriage*, 59(5), 414–428.

Fabricius, W. V., Braver, S. L., Diaz, P., & Velez, C. E. (2010). Custody and parenting time: Links to family relationships and well-being after divorce. In M. E. Lamb (ed.), *Role of the father in child development* (5th ed., pp. 245–289). Hoboken, NJ: Wiley.

Fehlberg, B., Smyth, B., Maclean, M., & Roberts, C. (2011). Legislating for shared time parenting after separation: A research review. *International Journal of Law, Policy and the Family*, 25, 318–337.

Fransson, E., Hjern, A. & Bergström, M. (2018) What can we say regarding shared parenting arrangements for Swedish children? *Journal of Divorce & Remarriage*, 59(5), 349–358.

Greenberg, J. G. (2004). Domestic violence and the danger of joint custody presumptions. *Northern Illinois University Law Review*, 25, 403–515.

Gunnoe, M. L., & Braver, S. L. (2001). The effects of joint legal custody on mothers, fathers, and children, controlling for factors that predispose a sole maternal vs. joint legal award. *Law and Human Behavior*, 25, 25–43.

Huitema, B. (2011). *The analysis of covariance and alternatives: Statistical methods for experiments, quasiexperiments, and single-case studies* (2nd ed.). Hoboken, NJ: Wiley.

Kelly, R. F., & Ramsey, S. H. (2009). Child custody evaluations: The need for systems-level outcome assessments. *Family Court Review*, 47, 286–303.

Leading Women for Shared Parenting. (2017). *Twenty five states consider shared parenting bills in 2017*. Retrieved from http://lw4sp.org/blog/2017/2/24/twenty-five-states-considershared-parenting-billsin-2017

Luepnitz, D. (1986). A comparison of maternal, paternal and joint custody. *Journal of Divorce*, 9, 1–12.

Maccoby, E. E., & Mnookin, R. H. (1992). *Dividing the child: Social and legal dilemmas of custody*. Cambridge, MA: Harvard University Press.

Mauricio, A. M., Mazza, G. L., Berkel, C., Tein, J. Y., Sandler, I. N., Wolchik, S. A., & Winslow, E. (2017). Attendance trajectory classes among divorced and separated mothers and fathers in the new beginnings program. *Prevention Science*, 19(5), 620–629.

Messer, L. C. (2017). *Natural experiment*. Retrieved from www.britannica.com/topic/natural-experiment

Mnookin, R. H., & Kornhauser, L. (1979). Bargaining in the shadow of the law: The case of divorce. *The Yale Law Journal*, 88, 950–997.

Morrill, A. C., Dai, J., Dunn, S., Sung, I., & Smith, K. (2005). Child custody and visitation decisions when the father has perpetrated violence against the mother. *Violence Against Women*, 11, 1076–1107.

Nielsen, L. (2014). Shared physical custody: Summary of 40 studies on outcomes for children. *Journal of Divorce & Remarriage*, 55(8), 613–635.

Nielsen, L. (2015). Shared physical custody: Does it benefit children? *Journal of the American Academy of Matrimonial Lawyers*, 28, 79–139.

Nielsen, L. (2017). Re-examining the research on parental conflict, coparenting, and custody arrangements. *Psychology, Public Policy, and Law*, 23, 211–231.

Nielsen, L. (2018). Joint versus sole physical custody: Outcomes for children independent of family income or parental conflict. *Journal of Child Custody*.

Pearson, J., & Thoennes, N. (1990). Custody after divorce: Demographic and attitudinal patterns. *American Journal of Orthopsychiatry*, 60, 233–249.

Rebuttable Presumption Law and Legal Definition. (2017). *USLegal*. Retrieved from https://definitions.uslegal.com/r/rebuttable-presumption/

Rossi, F. S., Holtzworth-Munroe, A., Applegate, A. G., Beck, C. J., Adams, J. M., & Hale, D. F. (2015). Detection of intimate partner violence and recommendation for joint family mediation: A randomized controlled trial of two screening measures. *Psychology, Public Policy, and Law*, 21, 239.

Sandler, I. N., Wolchik, S. A., Berkel, C., Jones, S., Mauricio, A. M., Tein, J.-Y., & Winslow, E. (2016). Effectiveness trial of the New Beginnings Program (NBP) for divorcing and separating parents: Translation from and experimental prototype to an evidence-based community service. In M. Israelashvili & J. L. Romano (eds), *Cambridge handbook of international prevention science* (pp. 81–106). Cambridge: Cambridge University Press.

Shadish, W. R., Clark, M. H., & Steiner, P. M. (2008). Can nonrandomized experiments yield accurate answers? A randomized experiment comparing random and nonrandom assignments. *Journal of the American Statistical Association, 103*, 1334–1344.

Shadish, W. R., Cook, T. D., & Campbell, D. T. (2002). *Experimental and quasi-experimental designs for generalized causal inference.* Boston, MA: Houghton Mifflin.

Stahl, P. M. (1999). *Complex issues in child custody evaluations.* New York: Sage.

Stark, P. B. (2017). Control for a variable. In *Berkeley glossary of statistical terms*. Retrieved from www.stat.berkeley.edu/~stark/SticiGui/Text/gloss.htm

Stevenson, M. M., Braver, S. L., Ellman, I. M., & Votruba, A. M. (2012). Fathers, divorce and custody. In N. C. Cabrera & C. S. Tamis-LeMonda (eds), *Handbook of father involvement: Multidisciplinary perspectives* (2nd ed., pp. 379–396). New York: Psychology Press.

West, S. G., Cham, H., & Liu, Y. (2014). Causal inference and generalization in field settings: Experimental and quasi-experimental designs. In H. T. Reis & C. M. Judd (eds), *Handbook of research methods in social and personality psychology* (2nd ed., pp. 49–80). New York: Cambridge University Press.

West, S. G., Cham, H., Thoemmes, F., Renneberg, B., Schulze, J., & Weiler, M. (2014). Propensity score as a basis for equating groups: Basic principles and application in clinical treatment outcome research. *Journal of Consulting & Clinical Psychology, 82*, 906–919.

Winslow, E. B., Braver, S., Cialdini, R., Sandler, I., Betkowski, J., Tein, J.Y., ... Lopez, M. (2017). Video-based approach to engaging parents into a preventive parenting intervention for divorcing families: Results of a randomized controlled trial. *Prevention Science*, 19(5), 674–684.

6

WHEN CHILDREN'S RIGHTS ARE UNDERMINED IN THE NAME OF THE 'BEST INTERESTS OF THE CHILD'

Switzerland's long road to child-centred custody legislation

Martin Widrig

Introduction

One of the biggest achievements of the UN Convention on the Rights of the Child (CRC) is that children became *subjects of law*. Two norms emphasize this new status: Article 3 CRC, in particular, which requests that the child's best interests are *a primary consideration in all decisions* concerning children; and Article 12 CRC, which awards all children the right to have their *voices heard and considered in all decisions* concerning them.[1] According to the UN Committee on the Rights of the Child, these articles are two of four considered to be the 'general principles of the Convention'.[2] The doctrine emphasizes these articles' particular importance as well.[3]

Frequently, decision-makers bring these norms into the context of the so-called 'best interests of the child (BIC) standard'.[4] Using this standard, decision-makers intend to find the best possible solution for children in each particular case, while the interests of parents or others must yield.[5] This standard is particularly common when questions about legal or physical custody arise.[6]

Although the goal of the BIC standard is very noble, well-known scholars of psychology and law openly criticize its use and recommend replacing it by clearer standards, such as the primary caretaker rule,[7] the approximation rule,[8] the equal parenting presumption[9] or even 'flipping the coin.'[10,11]

After a brief introduction into these scholar's concerns below, we then explain how Swiss authorities and other important actors used the BIC as an argument to defend legislation that violated most fundamental rights of the child. Finally, we look at the solution provided by the Convention on the Rights of the Child.

Critique concerning the BIC standard

The two major problems scholars identified concerning the BIC standard are the *indeterminacy* of the best possible solution for the child and the *broad and unreviewable discretion* given to decision-makers by the *vagueness* of the standard itself. We discuss these in the sub-sections below and then discuss the question of why this standard persists.

Indeterminacy of the BIC

The first problem is simple. Whatever we try to do, it is nearly impossible to determine the best solution for a child's future in each case. To do so, we always ought to consider all possible options, all possible outcomes of each option, the probabilities of each outcome and the value attached to each outcome.[12] Given that 'present day knowledge ... provides no basis for the kind of individualized predictions required by the best-interests standard' and that no social consensus about the values to attach to each outcome exists, the ambition to find the best solution for each child in each case proves to be largely impossible.[13] In addition, individualized decision-making costs valuable time,[14] consumes a lot of money that will no longer be available for the child[15] and likely leads to worse outcomes than decisions based upon a simple set of rules.[16]

Broad and unreviewable discretion of the BIC

With respect to the second problem concerning unreviewable discretion, as Elster[17] pointed out, throughout history decision-makers have used the BIC standard to justify the paternal preference rule, the fault-based presumption, the maternal preference rule and the primary caretaker assumption alike. All these presumptions are common in the history of family law.[18] Some of them assume the exact opposite.

Many other examples suggest that people use the BIC as an argument to justify almost anything. For instance, in the early 1970s, when Swiss men decided, by a binding plebiscite, on women's right to vote, opponents promoted the view that women's access to politics would jeopardize the well-being of our children. They published advertisements featuring babies lying crying on the ground in a messy living room and a black cat in the crib and crying boys and girls looking for their mothers.[19] Similarly, in the 1970s, the German legislator used the BIC to justify the obligation of one parent to finance the other parent's ability to stay at home and take care of the child. Ironically, although single fathers existed, until 1997 only single mothers were eligible for this support.[20] Finally, in Great Britain, the authorities used the BIC to send many children to the colonies, thus separating them from their families.[21]

Understandably, scholars expressed concern that the BIC standard leads to intuitive decision-making rather than logical thinking and that personal values may influence decisions.[22] Similarly, Justice Brennan, judge of the High Court of Australia, pointed out that, 'in the absence of legal rules or a hierarchy of values, the best interests approach depends upon the value system of the decision-maker ... [and] simply creates an unexaminable discretion in the repository of the power.'[23] As a result, the standard leads to unpredictable outcomes, increases litigation and impedes parental cooperation.[24]

The 'puzzling persistence' of the BIC

As Emery and Scott put it: 'There is unanimous critique concerning the BIC standard. Nevertheless, it persists.'[25] They give as a possible reason for its use that decision-makers want to maintain the wide discretion offered by adherence to the BIC. Furthermore, the standard is likely the result of a 'political compromise' between the interests of fathers who want to remain involved in their children's lives and to be treated equally to mothers and the interests of those who defend mothers who want to care for their children on their own and, in practice, fare quite well under adherence to the BIC standard.[26]

Swiss custody legislation and children's rights

Below, we discuss Swiss custody legislation and its most recent revisions, show how those rules violated most important rights of the child and look for possible reasons for the failure to comply with these rights.

Swiss custody legislation and its revisions

Over the last 25 years, three revisions of the Swiss Civil Code (ZGB) greatly affected Swiss custody legislation. Before 1 January 2000, joint custody existed only during marriage. After divorce, the law excluded joint legal custody and joint physical custody (JPC) – even if both parents agreed.[27] In 1988, the Swiss Federal Court overruled the maternal preference rule.[28] However, for children out of wedlock, the law excluded paternal custody, even when the parents lived together and the father stayed at home to take care of the children.[29]

After 1 January 2000, it became possible to maintain legal and physical custody beyond marriage, but only if both parents agreed and the solution was considered to be in the BIC.[30] The same rule applied for children out of wedlock if the mother agreed to share custody, authorities found that the solution was compatible with the BIC and the fathers signed a contract.[31] In practice, that contract meant that fathers were obliged to cede taking care of their children and to pay maintenance to the mother as soon as she wanted that to be the case – even if the father had been the primary caretaker of the child.

Since 1 July 2014, the ZGB has included the rebuttable presumption that joint legal custody is in the BIC (Article 296 ZGB). With respect to physical custody, the government wanted, in each case, the best possible solution for the child.[32] Nevertheless, there remained opposition from some scholars[33] and some courts continued to exclude JPC automatically unless both parents agreed.[34] To clarify the issue, and to promote JPC, on 17 March 2015, the parliament decided to amend Articles 298 and 298b ZGB. The modified articles request explicitly that decision-makers have to consider JPC as a possible care solution if one parent or the child request.[35] Thus, the legislator imposed an approach developed by the European Court of Human Rights in the judgement *Zaunegger v. Germany*.[36,37]

Two months later, in May 2015, the Swiss Federal Court decided to adopt the same approach.[38] According to its case law, the BIC is the decisive factor in care decisions. Thus, the Federal Court adopted the BIC standard. However, importantly and as clarified recently, if the necessary requirements for JPC are met, the Swiss Federal Court presumes JPC with equal distribution of time to be in the BIC.[39]

Incompatibilities with the rights of the child

Articles 3 and 12 CRC request that children's interests and their will be considered in all decisions concerning them. Decisions about custody or care are particularly important for children, which makes it even more important that these rules are applied.

While the Swiss Civil Code after 2014 complies with these standards, the earlier custody legislation did not. A rule that excludes joint legal or physical custody automatically because of divorce, lack of marriage, or any other reason, excludes the consideration of the BIC as well as the child's wishes by default. Hence, such rules are contrary to Articles 3 and 12 CRC.

The same is valid for the requirement that both parents agree to joint legal or physical custody. If a rule automatically excludes joint legal or physical custody because there is no consent by both parents, the consideration of the BIC and the child's wishes become dependent upon the decision of one parent. As a result, if one parent refuses to agree, such rules preclude the consideration of the BIC and the child's will. This is incompatible with both articles in question. Such regulations have been criticised by the Committee on the Rights of the Child and the European Court of Human Rights alike.[40]

Failure to comply

Articles 3 and CRC are quite easy to understand and apply. Anyone who thinks about the problem will realize that the former Swiss custody legislation precluded respect for these fundamental rights of the child. Nevertheless, not before, during or even after the revision was this topic an issue.[41] In contrast, many fought changes and defended the old jurisdiction as it related to the BIC.[42]

Some actors seem to have been convinced that the old jurisdiction (always) served the BIC. For instance, when asked at a conference whether Article 3 CRC requests that JPC be allowed if it is in the BIC but opposed by one parent, even a European Court of Human Rights' judge answered no, 'because we have to think about the children'.[43] The same was true for the Swiss legislator, which, in 1995, considered joint legal custody generally contrary to the BIC if one parent opposed it.[44] Moreover, some taught that rule and claimed simultaneously that the BIC is the only relevant criteria upon which to base custody decisions.[45]

Interestingly, at the same time, Members of Parliament, the government and the Swiss Federal Court all claimed that a similar automatic application of a new Swiss constitutional norm violates Article 3 CRC.[46] According to that norm, noncitizens lose their residence permit automatically if they commit a serious crime.[47] This may affect and exclude consideration of the rights of their children.

Possible reasons

An explanation for such convictions is given by Joan B. Kelly, probably the most respected divorce specialist of our time. She argued that, when divorce became common, only very limited research, focusing primarily on the importance of mothers, was available. This and traditional role models strongly influenced legal answers that had to be found back then. Ever since, decision-makers have considered those solutions to be in the BIC, while they largely ignore the vast body of newer and better research.[48] Similarly, Felix Schöbi, judge of family law at the Swiss Federal Court, the highest court in Switzerland, concludes: 'To change the law, ten years may be enough. However, the change of mentalities requires decades – judges are no exception.'[49]

This seems to be true for Switzerland. When, in 1974, the Swiss government proposed new custody standards, it officially shared the view that 'according to educational science and child psychology contact rights are frequently the source of severe difficulties … [and] predominantly considered as an evil.'[50] In 2005, influential scholars still described the strongly criticized views of Goldstein, Freud, and Solnit from the 1970s as 'ground-breaking'.[51] Others do not seem to question the 'dominance of the mother–child relationship'.[52] Moreover, contact rights remain low if parents disagree. In some regions, children under school age see their non-resident parent for only a few hours every fortnight or one to half a day per month.[53] Older children see their non-resident parent every other weekend from Saturday morning to Sunday evening and two to three of their thirteen weeks of holidays per year.[54] In comparison, in Swiss families in which both parents live together, fathers do approximately 40 per cent of active childcare.[55]

Another factor, which might be less evident for professionals from a background other than law, backs Kelly's view: An important function of law is to create 'legal certainty'. Legal certainty provides stability and reliability for actors subject to law. It preserves the status quo and creates a rather rigid system that is reluctant to change. This is an advantage in many situations. However, it also slows down the adaptation of a legal system to an evolving society.

Further obstacles to change were strong opposition on the part of special interest groups, and sometimes legal or other family law professionals who expressed concerns about the practicability of new legislation. Moreover, limited funding of the family law system and the high workloads of the professionals involved might also have prevented their readiness for innovation.

Interim conclusion

Many scholars openly criticize the BIC standard. The Swiss experience provides an illustrative example of problems that arise with the BIC if we consider it an indefinite legal term. Wide discretion in determination of the BIC even led to the situation whereby our jurisdiction violated the most fundamental rights of children. This largely happened unnoticed. For this reason, doubts about the BIC standard leading to child friendly outcomes appear to be legitimate.

Clearly, a state governed by the rule of law could and should avoid such mistakes and the needless suffering, sorrow and grief caused by them. For a jurisdiction that claims to act in the BIC, such mistakes are unacceptable and suggest a need to critically evaluate and rethink the family law system.

Switzerland was not the only country with such problems. Even Germany, for instance, has allowed care by both parents in the absence of a parental agreement only since 2017.[56] It seems that we are dealing with a much more global problem.

As pointed out earlier, well-known scholars suggest that a possible way to improve the family law system may be to limit the discretion of decision-makers and stick to a clear set of rules or guidelines during the decision-making process. Such guidance could protect decision-makers from the undue influence of their beliefs while taking decisions and assure respect for important legal norms, such as Articles 3 and 12 CRC. Furthermore, guidelines seem to be common in other fields of law and may lead to faster and better outcomes than wide discretion.[57]

In custody and care decisions, scholars recommend using an alternative to the BIC standard. However, there might be an easier option, which does not require changing the law: we can start by taking the guiding principles and values of our international human rights instruments more seriously. The UN Convention on the Rights of the Child, in particular, the most important human rights instrument for children in existence, provides clear guidance on the meaning and determination of the BIC.

The BIC and the CRC

The Convention on the Rights of the Child (CRC)[58] outlines clear and unmistakable principles. After a look at the principal purpose of Articles 3 and 12 CRC, we interpret the BIC in the light of this Convention. In a further step, we consider the consequences for legal practice.

Essence of Articles 3 and Art. 12 CRC

The UN created several human rights treaties, which, together, form the UN human rights protection system. The older and more general human rights conventions, the International Covenant on Civil and Political Rights and the International Covenant on Economic, Social and Cultural Rights, both of 1966, protect essentially the same rights of children as the Convention on the Rights of the Child (CRC).

From this perspective, the reformulation of children's rights in a more specific convention for children primarily raises awareness of the importance of protecting in particular the rights of some of the most vulnerable individuals in society: our children.

Historically, children were treated like objects belonging to their parents or others – rather than as subjects of law, with their own rights that must be taken into consideration in legal decisions. Decisions were simply imposed on them, treating them as though they did not exist as separate entities. This is incompatible with human dignity.

That today children are usually considered subjects of law is one of the biggest achievements of the CRC. This new status was achieved because decision-makers were obliged to consider the BIC and children's wishes in all decisions concerning children, as proscribed by Articles 3 and 12 CRC. These norms assure children the status of subjects of law, one of the most important objectives of the Convention.[59]

Interpretation of the BIC

The creators of the Convention wanted it to be in the BIC. For this reason, it seems evident that the rights given to the child by the Convention are an expression of what the creators of the Convention thought to be in the BIC. Bearing this in mind, it makes sense that, according to the UN Committee on the Rights of the Child, we must interpret the BIC in the light of the rights of the Convention.[60] This alone reduces a decision-maker's discretion significantly.

If we interpret Article 3 CRC with respect to custody and care, the relevant norms are those in Articles 7, 9 and 18 CRC. According to Article 7 CRC, 'the child shall have ... the *right to ... be cared for by his or her parents*' (emphasis added). Like all human rights, this right can be restricted, but only if this is necessary and justified. According to Article 9 (1) CRC, 'a child shall *not be separated from his or her parents ..., except when ... such separation is necessary* for the best interests of the child' (emphasis added). The same norm specifies that such determination '*may be necessary* in a particular case such as one involving abuse or neglect ... or one *where the parents are living separately*' (emphasis added). Article 18 CRC emphasizes that parental responsibilities are *common* responsibilities.

Hence, the child has a right to care by both parents.[61] Moreover, the CRC presumes that care by both parents is in the BIC.[62]

Consequences for legal practice and research

Although the norms leave some room for interpretation, the legal principles provided are unmistakably clear: decision-makers have to assess the BIC in each particular case (Article 3 CRC). In custody and care decisions, the CRC presumes care or responsibility provided by both parents to be in the BIC (Articles 7 and 18 CRC). This is the *starting point* for the assessment. Interventions remain possible at any time and are sometimes even required (Articles 9 and 19 CRC) if there are reasons to believe that care or responsibility provided by both parents is contrary to the BIC. According to ordinary human rights standards, the intervening authority must justify why it is intervening.[63]

The most relevant questions deriving from these principles are: (1) when is care or responsibility provided by both parents contrary to the BIC and (2) are there better alternatives for children than care by both parents and, if yes, under what circumstances?

It is important to mention that these principles derive from a 'purely' legal perspective, based on the values expressed by the fundamental rights of the child. No psychological or other knowledge has been considered. Such knowledge is relevant for family law policy and practice as well.

Furthermore, the application of these principles does not necessarily imply that most children will live with both parents. The Convention requests an assessment of the BIC in each particular case. How many children live in a specific living arrangement will largely depend on the results of these assessments.

Finally, these principles primarily concern children whose parents disagree on the living arrangements for their children. The CRC leaves it to the parents to decide how they want to care for their children, if they agree and the children are safe (Articles 5, 9 (1) and 18 CRC). For parents who do agree, the principles have symbolic value. They indicate an ideal from a children's rights perspective. Hence, the CRC does what any good policy and law should do: it provides a clear ideal that serves as an orientation for the general population and decision-makers. At the same time, it offers room for exceptions and guidance for appropriate solutions in problematic cases.

Compatibility with psychological research

From a purely legal perspective, the guiding principles are clear. But what does psychological research say? In particular, is there evidence that proves the legal principles underlying the CRC to be wrong in general or in specific circumstances?

In an attempt to get closer to an answer to these questions with limited space, we will, in a first step, look at the *results* of those studies that compared the well-being of children in *joint* physical custody (JPC) with that of children in *sole* physical custody (SPC). In a second step, we will consider the *interpretation* of these results by *larger groups* of scholars. We focus on disagreement and conflict because these situations are particularly important for family law practice. Then we look at what young adults said about their experience as children of divorce and reach our conclusion with respect to the aforementioned legal principles of the CRC. The chapter closes with a cautionary note concerning the interpretation of social science research and reasons for the conclusion drawn.

Results of studies

According to the most extensive summary of studies of which the author is aware, in 2018 there existed 60 quantitative studies comparing the well-being of children in JPC and SPC, 10 qualitative studies and 2 meta-analyses, which only considered a limited number of studies. The ten qualitative studies had mixed outcomes. In both meta-analyses, JPC children fared better. One of the studies checked for conflict and identified that, even with conflict between parents, the results were better for children in JPC. In the other meta-analysis, JPC children showed better results when they received equal care, in terms of time, from both parents.[64] Malin Bergström, Emma Fransson and their team found the latter result in several studies conducted within their Elvis Project on Swedish children.[65]

The 60 quantitative studies described as JPC living arrangements whereby children lived at least 35 per cent of the time with either parent. Although the studies used different methods, had different sample sizes and were conducted in different Western countries, the results were quite similar. Under normal conditions, JPC children had better outcomes on all measures in 34 studies; better or equal outcomes in 14 studies; equal outcomes on all measures in 6 studies; and worse outcomes on 1 of the measures but equal or better outcomes on all other measures in 6 studies.[66]

In 19 of these quantitative studies, parental conflict levels were similar (no significant difference) in either form of physical custody (15 studies), or the authors of the study controlled for conflict in the statistical analysis so that conflict did not affect the outcome (4 studies). In 9 studies, JPC children fared better than SPC children on all measures; in 5 studies they fared better or equal; in 2 studies they fared equal; and in 3 studies they fared worse on 1 measure but equal or better on all other measures.[67]

Six additional studies, in which conflict levels between JPC and SPC were different, provided an unexpected result: In two of these studies, parental conflict was *higher* when children lived in JPC. Nevertheless, the JPC children fared *better* in both studies. In the other four studies, conflict was *lower* in the JPC families. Nevertheless, *only in one* of these four studies did JPC children fare better on all measures. In the other three studies, they fared equally on all measures.[68] According to the author of the summary, children fared worse in JPC with high conflict when their relationship with their father was bad.[69]

Two studies are interesting because they compared the outcomes for children in JPC and SPC in 36 different countries. The results were positive and similar for all countries.[70]

Groups of experts

In a 2014 consensus report, all 111 experts in psychology shared the view that, in the light of existing evidence, JPC, defined as living arrangements with at least 35 per cent of care provided by each parent, should be the norm for children of all ages.[71] Rather than excluding JPC if there is parental conflict, they provided suggestions on how to approach the problem, such as choosing neutral sites for the transfer of children, promoting parenting plans through a non-adversarial process or identifying the dynamics of conflict to inform a more appropriate intervention.[72]

Another consensus report dates from 1997. At that time, reaching definite conclusions concerning physical custody was not possible. However, the participants suggested that qualitative parental involvement is beneficial for children and that quality relationships require sufficient time.[73]

In 2014, a group of 32 experts in psychology and law agreed that the promotion of shared physical custody, considered as living arrangements with at least 35 per cent of care provided by each parent, is a public health issue.[74] The majority shared the view that research strongly suggests that JPC is in the BIC if both parents agree. They also referred to some evidence suggesting that JPC can be beneficial for children if there are lower forms of conflict. Nevertheless, the majority rejected an equal parenting presumption and favoured a case by case approach. Finally, they decided against a general exclusion of JPC in the case of high conflict and domestic violence.[75]

In 2018, in a group of 12 experts in psychology and law, most concluded that research evidence now supports a rebuttable presumption in favour of JPC under normal conditions. They recommended reversing the presumption if there is a credible risk of abuse or neglect, too great a distance between parents' homes, a threat of abduction, excessive gate-keeping, special needs of the child and coercive controlling violence (one of the four types of domestic violence). They also stated that neither conflict nor parental alienation dynamics should preclude JPC.[76]

Young adults' perspectives

Looking back at their time as children of divorce, many young adults explained that one of their biggest sorrows with respect to divorce was the reduced or lost contact with one parent. Usually, they would have wanted to spend more time with both parents.[77]

One study questioned which care solution these young adults considered best. Approximately 70 per cent considered JPC to be the best solution. Of those who lived in JPC when they were young, more than 90 per cent thought it was the best possible solution for them. According to the interviewed students, their fathers wanted to spend more time with them as well, but their mothers did not want that.[78]

Interim conclusion

Joan B. Kelly states that psychological research convincingly demonstrates that limited time with one parent is not in the child's best interests. More expansive time patterns should be the norm not the exception. Moreover, for decades, most children of divorce wished they had more time with both parents. It is time to take their wish seriously.[79]

These points bring together the results of our review quite well. That is, that care provided by both parents is usually in the BIC when both parents agree and even, in many cases, where they disagree. Furthermore, the promotion of care provided by both parents seems to be a public health issue.

It seems that the principles outlined by the CRC, based on fundamental human rights values, are compatible with the current state of psychological research and adequate for practice, as long as there is sufficient room for exceptions. Research may not 'prove' causally that, in most cases, care provided by both parents is better for children than care by one parent. However, it 'proves' even less that care by both parents is, mostly, and under normal conditions, bad for children or worse than care provided by one parent, which are the more relevant questions from a children's (human) rights perspective.

Cautionary note

Many scholars caution against inappropriate presentation of facts in social science and provide useful suggestions on how to interpret data.[80] There are many examples of delicate but influential statements with respect to psychological research on shared parenting. For instance, in 2014 in Switzerland, influential scholars claimed: '*Psychological research makes it clear* that JPC, imposed by a court or an authority, without basic willingness of both parents to contribute that it works, has little chances of success' (emphasis added).[81] They did not provide references. For this reason, it is impossible to verify how and why they reached their conclusion.

Another Swiss example concerns a government-commissioned report on JPC, published in 2017. It included a six-page review of psychological research on JPC. The authors cited *psychologically relevant information*[82] from only 3 of approximately 50 quantitative studies available at that time: five times from the same Australian study on high conflict,[83] once from an Australian study on overnight care patterns for young children by the same authors[84] and once from a third Australian study.[85] According to Nielsen, who wrote the most extensive review on conflict studies of which the author is aware, the study on high conflict was the only one out of 17 studies that statistically controlled for conflict and found a negative outcome for children in JPC.[86] In addition, many scholars expressed concerns about the validity of those findings.[87] It is important to mention and consider that conflict study as well. However, the picture provided by a review is likely more accurate, if all studies are mentioned or, at least, reasons are given for their selection. After all, the authors of the Swiss report ought to have known that other studies existed since they cited a 2014 summary[88] that discussed this topic extensively, twice.[89]

Inaccurate statements and subjectivity in the choice and interpretation of sources do not necessarily imply 'bad faith' – providing well-balanced and accurate information, especially in soft sciences, is challenging. However, the lack of transparency, 'cherry-picking' and so on may lead to a distorted view of facts. It is important that readers are aware of such problems when reading this review also.

The attempts made here to reduce subjectivity are transparency about the information provided and reasons given for the selection of information. Furthermore, the author tried to present all information (rather than a selection), provided precise sources (allowing for verification and critique), focused on results of studies (rather than individual interpretations), considered, due to limited space, interpretations of larger groups of scholars only, was careful with conclusions and raised reader awareness regarding possible weaknesses of and problems inherent in reviews.

Conclusion

Many well-known scholars criticize the BIC standard and the way in which it is being used. They ask for clearer rules and presumptions. The Swiss example provides evidence that even legal scholars, practitioners and judges use the BIC as an argument to justify and defend a system that violates most fundamental rights of the child. This passes unnoticed while, at the same time, the same actors consider a similar problem incompatible with the same fundamental rights of the child.

Such mistakes suggest a need to rethink the family law system and support considering replacing the vague BIC standard with a more child-friendly presumption or better guidance on how to interpret the indefinite legal term BIC.

A presumption, which seems to be in line with children's wishes and needs, already exists. It indicates how to proceed to determine the BIC and is easy to apply and review. As any good legislation and policy should, it provides not only guiding principles for the concerned and decision-makers at large but also the tools needed to solve problematic individual cases. In addition, it is founded upon the most fundamental values of our societies: those expressed by the Convention on the Rights of the Child.

The Convention presumes care provided by both parents to be in the BIC. This is the starting point in care decisions. Nevertheless, the Convention requests that the child's interests be considered in each particular case and an intervention be made, if necessary.

Notes

1 Zermatten (2010).
2 Committee on the Rights of the Child, General Comment No. 14 (2013) on the right of the child to have his or her best interests taken as a primary consideration (art. 3, para. 1), May 29, 2013, CRC/C/GC/14, n. 1; Committee on the Rights of the Child, General Comment No. 12 (2009): The right of the child to be heard, July 20, 2009, CRC/C/GC/12, n. 2; Committee on the Rights of the Child, General comment no. 5 (2003): General measures of implementation of the Convention on the Rights of the Child, November 27, 2003, CRC/GC/2003/5, n. 12.
3 Eekelaar and Tobin (2019), p. 74; UNICEF (2007), p. 35; Zermatten (n. 1), p. 492.
4 BGE 132 III 359 (Swiss Federal Court, Judgement 4C.178/2005 of December 20, 2005), Cons. 4.4.2; Reusser R., and Lüscher, K. 2014. Commentary on art. 11 Swiss-Cst. In B. Ehrenzeller, B., Schindler, R. J. Schweizer and K. Vallender (eds), *Die schweizerische Bundesverfassung, St. Galler Kommentar* (3rd ed.). Zurich: DIKE, p. 27.
5 BGE 143 I 2 (Swiss Federal Court, Judgement 2C_27/2016 of November 17, 2016), Cons. 5.5.3.
6 BGE 142 III 612 (Swiss Federal Court, Judgement 5A_991/2015 of September 29, 2016), Cons. 4.2 ff.
7 Chambers (1984), p. 569.
8 Scott (2014), p. 201.
9 Kruk (2013).
10 Elster (1987), p. 40 ff.
11 Emery and Scott (2014), p. 76; Eekelaar (2002), p. 237.
12 Elster (n. 10), p. 12 ff.; Mnookin (1975), p. 256 ff.
13 Mnookin (2014), p. 251 ff.; Braver (2014), p. 176 ff.; Emery and Scott. (n. 11), p. 92.
14 Braver (n. 13), p. 177; Lamb (2014), p. 195.
15 Braver (n. 13), p. 177.
16 Lamb (n. 14), p. 195 f.; Braver (n. 13), p. 177; Emery and Scott (n. 11), p. 76.
17 Elster (n. 10), p. 7 ff.
18 See, for Switzerland, Bernard and Meyer Löhrer (2014), n. 10 ff.
19 Imhof (2011).

20 German Constitutional Court, Judgement of the Order of the First Senate, 1 BvL 9/04, of February 28, 2007, § 6–8.
21 Eekelaar (n. 11), p. 237.
22 Mnookin (n. 13), p. 252.
23 Judge Brennan in Judgement of the High Court of Australia, *Secretary, Department of Health and Community Services* v. *JWB and SMB (Re Marion)* (1992) FLC 92–293 of 6.5.1992, n. 79,191.
24 Mnookin (n. 13), p. 251 ff.; Braver (n. 13), p. 176 f.; Emery and Scott (n. 11), p. 69.
25 Emery and Scott (n. 11), p. 76.
26 Emery and Scott (n. 11), p. 76, 81 and 108.
27 Former art. 297 ZGB (as found in AS 1977 237); BGE 117 II 523 (Swiss Federal Court, Judgement K. v. K of December 12, 1991), Cons. 1h); BGE 123 III 445 (Swiss Federal Court, Judgement Ps. v. Ms of November 20, 1997), Cons. 2.
28 BGE 114 II 200 (Swiss Federal Court, Judgement B. v. M. of April 28, 1988), Cons. 5b.
29 Former art. 298 ZGB (as found in AS 1977 237).
30 Former art. 133 ZGB (as found in AS 1999 1118).
31 Former art. 298a ZGB (as found in AS 1999 1118).
32 Government report concerning the revision of Swiss custody legislation of November 16, 2011, BBl 2011 9077, p. 9094.
33 Kilde (2015), n. 299; Gloor (2015), p. 342.
34 See, e.g., Protocol of the parliamentary debates AB 2015 N 81 [Nidegger], AB 2015 S 188 [Stadler], and AB 2015 S 189 [Janiak].
35 See, e.g., Protocol of the parliamentary debates AB 2015 N 423 f. [Sommaruga], AB 2015 S 188 [Stadler], AB 2015 S 187 [Engler], AB 2015 N 82 [Visher], AB 2015 N 80 [v. Graffenried], and AB 2014 S 1121 f. [Janiak].
36 *Zaunegger* v. *Germany*, App. No. 22028/04 (ECtHR, judgment of December 3, 2009).
37 See Widrig, this handbook.
38 Swiss Federal Court, Judgement 5A_46/2015 of May 26, 2015, Cons. 4.4.5.
39 Swiss Federal Court, Judgement 5A_46/2015 of May 26, 2015, Cons. 4.4.5; Swiss Federal Court, Judgement 5A_367/2020 of October 19, 2020, Cons. 3.4–3.7; Swiss Federal Court, Judgement 5A_629/2019 of November 13, 2020, Cons. 8.
40 Committee on the Rights of the Child 2009. 41st session, Consideration of Reports submitted by states parties under article 44 of the Convention, Concluding observations: Liechtenstien. March 16, 2006, CRC/C/LIE/CO/2, n. 18 f.; *Zaunegger* v. *Germany*, App. No. 22028/04 (ECtHR, Judgement of December 3, 2009), para. 59; *Sporer* v. *Austria*, App. No. 35637/03 (ECtHR, Judgement of February 3, 2011), para. 70 and 90; *Doring* v. *Germany*, App. No. 50216/09 (ECtHR, Decision of February 21, 2009); *Sude* v. *Germany*, App. No. 38102/04 (ECtHR, Decision of October 7, 2010).
41 MP *Alec* v. *Graffenried* pointed out the problem out (Protocol of the parliamentary debates AB 2014 N 79 and AB 2015 N 422). However, unfortunately, it seems to have been overlooked.
42 See, e.g., BGE 117 II 523 (Swiss Federal Court, Judgement K. v. K of December 12, 1991), Cons. 1d); Schwenzer (2005), p. 15; protocol of parliamentary debates AB 2005 N 1496 [Fehr].
43 The author attests to having witnessed that situation.
44 Government report concerning a revision of divorce law of November 15, 1996, BBl 1996 I 1, p. 129 f.
45 See, e.g., Hausheer et al. (2007), p. 151 n. 10.126.
46 See, e.g., BGE 139 I 16 (Swiss Federal Court, Judgement 2C_828/2011 of October 12, 2012), Cons. 4.3.3; Government report concerning the plebiscite "für die Ausschaffung krimineller Ausländer (Ausschaffungsinitiative)" and a modification of the "Bundesgesetz über die Ausländerinnen und Ausländer" of June 24 2009, BBl 2009 5097, p. 5106 ff.; Government report concerning the plebiscite "Zur Durchsetzung der Ausschaffung krimineller Ausländer (Durchsetzungsinitiative)" of November 20, 2013, BBl 2013 9459,

p. 9501 ff.; see also Protocol of the parliamentary debates AB 2014 N 525 [Gross]; AB 2015 N 530 [Sommaruga]; AB 2014 S 1258 [Niederberger]; AB 2014 S 1262 [Diener Lenz]; Diggelmann, O. 2015. Commentary on art. 13 BV. In *Basler Kommentar, Bundesverfassung*, ed. Waldmann, B., Belser, E. M., Epiney, A., Basel, n. 23; Achermann A. 2015, Commentary on art. 121 BV. In *Basler Kommentar, Bundesverfassung*, ed. Waldmann, B., Belser, E. M., Epiney, A., Basel, n. 36; Weber F. 2012. *Die gesetzlichen Umsetzungsvarianten der SVP-Ausschaffungsinitiative im Lichte des FZA und der Rechtsprechung des EGMR zu Art. 8 EMRK*. Aktuelle Juristische Praxis, p. 1436 ff., p. 1445 ff.; Gächter, T., and Kradolfer, M. 2008. *Von schwarzen Schafen—Gedanken zur Ausschaffungsinitiative aus juristischer Sicht*. Asyl, p. 12 ff., p. 17; *El Ghatet v. Switzerland*, App. No. 56971/10 (ECtHR, Judgement of November 8, 2016) para. 47; *M.P.E.V. a.o. v. Switzerland*, App. no. 3910/13 (ECtHR, Judgement of July 8, 2014) para. 57; Swiss Federal Court, Judgement 2C_327/2010 of May 19, 2011, E. 5.1.3. Interestingly, the party that was responsible for this norm, was the only *big* Swiss party whose MPs voted (almost) completely for art. 298 and 298b ZGB to assure the respect of art. 3 CRC. MP Yvette Estermann seems to have played an important role in that outcome. However, many MPs of other big parties who criticized the plebiscite (a.o. because of art. 3 CRC), voted against art. 298 and 298b ZGB.

47 Art. 121 (3 ff.) Cst. This new norm was imposed by a plebiscite, which is possible in Switzerland (see art. 139 Cst).
48 Kelly (2007), p. 35 f.
49 Schöbi (2016), p. 86.
50 Government report concerning a revision of family law of June 5, 1974, BBl 1974 II 1, p. 54.
51 Schwenzer (n. 42), p. 15. For critique on Goldstein et al. (1973), see, e.g., Lamb (n. 14), p. 193 ff. or Pruett and DiFonzo (2014a), p. 209 f.
52 Cottier et al. (2017), n. 156.
53 Büchler (2019); Bernard and Meyer Löhrer (n. 18), n. 3 ff.
54 Ibid.
55 Swiss Federal Statistical Office (2017). As confirmed by the Swiss Federal Statistical Office via email, March 8, 2017. From that data we can deduce that fathers do 39 per cent (13.9 hours) of *active childcare* when children are under the age of seven and 42 per cent (8.9 hours) when children are between the ages of 7 and 17. The data allows for a rough estimate only and provides no information on how much time parents are present.
56 German Federal Court, Decision of the XII. civil-senate, XII ZB 601/15 of February 1, 2017.
57 Lamb (n. 14), p. 195 f.; see also the 'Critique concerning the BIC standard' section in this chapter.
58 Convention on the Rights of the Child of November 20, 1989.
59 Zermatten (n. 1), p. 483 f.
60 Committee on the Rights of the Child 2013 (n. 2), n. 32.
61 UNICEF (n. 3), art. 7 p. 108, art. 9 p. 127 and art. 18 p. 235.
62 Ibid. (n. 3), art. 7 p. 109, art. 9 p. 130 and art. 18 p. 237.
63 See, e.g., *Pisică v. the Republic of Moldova*, App. No. 23641/17 (ECtHR, Judgement of October 29, 2019), para. 78; Kilkelly (2003), p. 23 ff.
64 Nielsen (2018), p. 248 ff.
65 See, e.g., Bergström et al. (2015). For all 15 studies of the Elvis Project concerning JPC and Swedish children see: www.su.se/publichealth/english/research/research-projects/the-elvis-project.
66 Nielsen (n. 54), p. 258.
67 Ibid., p. 271.
68 Ibid.
69 Ibid., p. 272.
70 Bjarnason et al. (2012); Bjarnason and Arnarsson (2011).
71 Warshak (2014), p. 59.

72 Ibid., p. 56 f.
73 Lamb et al. (1997), p. 400.
74 Pruett and DiFonzo (2014b). Similar also is Vezzetti (2016).
75 Pruett and DiFonzo (2014b), p. 154.
76 Braver and Lamb (2018), p. 380 ff.
77 Finley and Schwartz (2007), p. 582; Laumann-Billings and Emery (2000), p. 683; Kelly and Emery (2003), p. 359.
78 Fabricius (2003), p. 387.
79 Kelly (2014), p. 17 f.
80 See, e.g., Cashmore and Parkinson (2014); Emery et al. (2016); Sandler et al. (2016); Nielsen (2015).
81 Schwenzer and Cottier (2014).
82 The report also mentioned psychologically non-relevant information from a few other studies, e.g. one of Bergstrom et al.'s to state that, in Sweden in 2009, 30 per cent of all children with separated parents lived in JPC and one of Cashmore et al.'s to state that, in Australia in 2008, 8 per cent of these children lived in JPC.
83 McIntosh et al. (2010), p. 23 ff.
84 Ibid., p. 85 ff.
85 Cottier et al. (n. 52), p. 28 ff.
86 Nielsen (2017), p. 221.
87 See, e.g., Cashmore and Parkinson; Kelly (2014) (n. 79), p. 17 f.; Lamb (2012); Ludolph (2012); Warshak (n. 71). See also McIntosh et al. (2015); Warshak (2017).
88 Nielsen (2014).
89 They cited the 2014 summary to affirm that the number of children living in JPC is increasing and that this development mirrors the evolution of society (Cottier et al. (n. 52), p. 64, footnote 368 f.).

References

Achermann, A. 2015. Commentary on art. 121 BV. In B. Waldmann, E. M. Belser, A. Epiney (eds), *Basler Kommentar, Bundesverfassung*. Basel: Helbing Lichtenhahn Verlag.
Bergström, M., Fransson, E., Modin, B. et al. 2015. Fifty moves a year: Is there an association between joint physical custody and psychosomatic problems in children? *Journal of Epidemiol and Community Health* 69: 769–774.
Bernard, S. and Meyer Löhrer, B. 2014. Kontakte des Kindes zu getrennt lebenden Eltern – Skizze eines familienrechtlichen Paradigmenwechsels. Jusletter of May 12.
Bjarnason, T. and Arnarsson, A. M. 2011. Joint physical custody and communication with parents: A cross-national study of children in 36 Western countries. *Journal of Comparative Family Studies* 42: 871–890.
Bjarnason, T., Bendtsen, P., Arnarsson, A. M. and Borup, I. 2012. Life satisfaction among children in different family structures: A comparative study of 36 Western societies. *Children & Society* 26: 51–62.
Braver, S. 2014. The costs and pitfalls of individualizing decisions and incentivizing conflict: A comment on AFCC's think tank report on shared parenting. *Family Court Review* 52/2: 175–180.
Braver, S. L. and Lamb, M. E. 2018. Shared parenting after parental separation: The views of 12 experts. *Journal of Divorce & Remarriage* 59/5: 372–387.
Büchler, A. 2019. *'Das gerichtsübliche' Besuchsrecht Betrachtungen zum angemessenen Besuchsrecht im Lichte der Rechtsprechung und der jüngsten Gesetzesentwicklungen*. Presentation at the 5th Zürcher Tagung zum Scheidungsrecht.
Cashmore, J. and Parkinson, P. 2014. The use and abuse of social science research evidence in children's cases. *Psychology, Public Policy and Law* 20/3: 239–250.

Chambers, D. L. 1984. Rethinking the substantive rules for custody disputes in divorce. *Michigan Law Review* 83/3: 477–569.
Cottier, M., Widmer, E. D., Tornare, S. and Girardin, M. 2017, *Interdisziplinäre Studie zur alternierenden Obhut*. Geneva: University of Geneva.
Diggelmann, O. 2015. Commentary on art. 13 BV. In B. Waldmann, E. M. Belser, A. Epiney (eds), *Basler Kommentar, Bundesverfassung*. Basel: Helbing Lichtenhahn Verlag.
Eekelaar, J. 2002. Beyond the welfare principle. *Child and Family Law Quarterly* 14/3: 237–249.
Eekelaar, J. and Tobin, J. 2019. Commentary on art. 3 CRC. In J. Tobin (ed.), *The UN Convention on the Rights of the Child, A commentary*. Oxford: Oxford University Press, 73–107,
Elster, J. 1987. Solomonic judgements: Against the best interests of the child. *University of Chicago Law Review* 54/1: 1–45.
Emery, R. E. and Scott, E. S. 2014. Gender politics and child custody: The puzzling persistence of the best-interests standard. *Law and Contemporary Problems* 77: 69–108.
Emery, R., Holtzworth-Munroe, A., Johnston, J. R. et al. 2016. 'Bending' evidence for a cause: Scholar-advocacy bias in family law. *Family Court Review* 54/2: 134–149.
Fabricius, W. V. 2003. Listening to children of divorce: New findings that diverge from Wallerstein, Lewis, and Blakeslee. *Family Relations* 52/4: 385–396.
Finley, G. E. and Schwartz, S. J. 2007. Father involvement and long-term young adult outcomes: The differential contributions of divorce and gender. *Family Court Review* 45/4: 573–587.
Gächter, T. and Kradolfer, M. 2008. Von schwarzen Schafen—Gedanken zur Ausschaffungsinitiative aus juristischer Sicht. *Asyl* 23/1: 12–20.
Gloor, N. 2015. Der Begriff der Obhut. *Praxis des Familienrechts* 2: 331–353.
Goldstein, J., Freud, A. and Solnit, A. J. 1973. *Beyond the best interests of the child*. New York: Free Press.
Imhof, I. 2011. Der lange Weg zum Frauenstimmrecht. Neue Zürcher Zeitung, February 4, 2011. Retrieved from: www.nzz.ch/frauenstimmrecht-1.9350588?reduced=true
Hausheer, H., Geiser, T. and Aebi-Müller, R. E. 2007. *Das Familienrecht des Schweizerischen Zivilgesetzbuches* (3rd ed). Bern: Stämpfli Verlag AG.
Kelly, J. B. 2007. Children's living arrangements following separation and divorce: Insights from empirical and clinical research. *Family Process* 46/1: 35–52.
Kelly, J. B. 2014. Paternal involvement and child and adolescent adjustment after separation and divorce: Current research and implications for policy and practice. *International Family Law, Policy and Practice* 2/1: 5–23.
Kelly, J. B. and Emery, R. E. 2003. Children's adjustment following divorce: Risk and resilience perspectives. *Family Relations* 52/4: 352–362.
Kilde, G. 2015. *Der persönliche Verkehr: Eltern-Kind-Dritte, Zivilrechtliche und interdisziplinäre Lösungsansätze*. PhD diss., University of Freiburg, Zurich, n. 299.
Kilkelly U. 2003. *The right to respect for private and family life: A guide to the implementation of Art. 8 of the European Convention on Human Rights*. Strasbourg: Cedex.
Kruk, E. 2013. *The equal parent presumption: Social justice in the legal determination of parenting after divorce*. Kingston, Ontario: McGill-Queen's University Press.
Lamb, M. E. 2012. A wasted opportunity to engage with the literature on the implications of attachment research for family court professionals. *Family Court Review* 50: 481–485.
Lamb, M. E. 2014. Dangers associated with the avoidance of evidence-based practice. *Family Court Review* 52/2: 193–197.
Lamb, M. E., Sternberg, K. J. and Thompson, R. A. 1997. The effects of divorce and custody arrangements on children's behaviour, development, and adjustment. *Family and Conciliation Courts Review* 35/4: 393–404.
Laumann-Billings, L. and Emery, R. E. 2000. Distress among young adults from divorced families. *Journal of Family Psychology* 14/4: 671–687.
Ludolph, P. 2012. Special issue on attachment: Overreaching theory and data. *Family Court Review* 50: 486–495.

McIntosh, J. E., Smyth, B. M. and Kelaher, M. A. 2015. Responding to concerns about a study of infant overnight care postseparation, with comments on consensus: Reply to Warshak (2014). *Psychology, Public Policy, and Law* 21: 111–119.

McIntosh, J., Smyth, B., Kelaher, M., Wells, Y. and Long, C. 2010. *Post-separation parenting arrangements: Outcomes for infants and children*. Melbourne: Australian Institute of Family Studies.

Mnookin, R. H. 1975. Child-custody adjudication: Judicial functions in the face of indeterminacy. *Law and Contemporary Problems* 39/3: 226–293.

Mnookin, R. H. 2014. Child custody revisited. *Law and Contemporary Problems* 77/1: 249–269.

Nielsen, L. 2014. Shared physical custody: Summary of 40 studies on outcomes for children. *Journal of Divorce & Remarriage* 55/8: 613–635.

Nielsen, L. 2015. Pop goes the woozle: Being misled by research on child custody and parenting plans. *Journal of Divorce & Remarriage* 56/8: 595–633.

Nielsen, L. 2017. Re-examining the research on parental conflict, coparenting, and custody arrangements. *Psychology, Public Policy, and Law* 23/2: 211–231.

Nielsen, L. 2018. Joint versus sole physical custody: Children's outcomes independent of parent–child relationships, income, and conflict in 60 studies. *Journal of Divorce & Remarriage* 59/4: 247–281.

Pruett M. K. and DiFonzo, J. H. 2014a. Advancing the shared parenting debate, one step at a time: Responses to the commentators. *Family Court Review* 52/2: 207–212.

Pruett, M. K. and DiFonzo, J. H. 2014b. Closing the gap: Research, policy, practice, and shared parenting. *Family Court Review* 52/2: 152–174.

Sandler I., Saini, M., Pruett, M. K. et al. 2016. Convenient and inconvenient truths in family law: Preventing scholar-advocacy bias in the use of social science research for public policy. *Family Court Review* 54/2: 150–166.

Schöbi, F. 2016. La garde alternée, ça marche? In *Les nouvelles formes de parentalité: Le temps du partage ... et l'enfant?* Geneva: University of Geneva.

Schwenzer, I. 2005. Die elterliche Sorge–die Sicht des Rechts von aussen auf das Innen. *Praxis des Familienrechts* 6/1: 12–24.

Schwenzer I. and Cottier M. 2014. Commentary on art. 298 ZGB. In H. Honsell, N. P. Vogt and T. Geiser (eds), *Basler Kommentar, Zivilgesetzbuch I, Art. 1–456 ZGB* (5th ed.) Basel. Art. 298 ZGB n. 7.

Scott, E. S. 2014. Planning for Children and resolving custodial disputes: A comment on the think tank report. *Family Court Review* 52/2: 200–206.

Swiss Federal Statistical Office 2017. *Haus- und Familienarbeit: Durchschnittlicher Zeitaufwand in Stunden pro Woche (table je-d-03.06.02.01)*. Retrieved from www.bfs.admin.ch/bfs/en/home/news/whats-new.assetdetail.2922666.html

UNICEF 2007. *Implementation handbook for the Convention on the Rights of the Child*. Geneva: UNICEF.

Vezzetti, C. V. 2016. New approaches to divorce with children: A problem of public health. Health Psychology Open 3/2: 1–13.

Warshak, R. A. 2014. Social science and parenting plans for young children: A consensus report. *Psychology, Public Policy, and Law* 20/1: 46–67. Warshak, R. A. 2017. Stemming the tide of misinformation: International Consensus on Shared Parenting and Overnighting. *Journal of the American Academy of Matrimonial Lawyers* 30: 177–217.

Weber, F. 2012. Die gesetzlichen Umsetzungsvarianten der SVP-Ausschaffungsinitiative im Lichte des FZA und der Rechtsprechung des EGMR zu Art. 8 EMRK. *Aktuelle Juristische Praxis* 21/10: 1436–1451.

Zermatten, J. 2010. The best interests of the child principle: Literal analysis and function. *International Journal of Children's Rights* 18: 483–499.

7

RIGHTS AND GUARANTEES OF UNACCOMPANIED MINORS

Researching the best interest of the child principle in the Spanish welfare state[1]

Elena Avilés Hernández

Introduction

To say that Europe has great cultural diversity and a linguistic pluralism is not something new. A clear example is the mixture of ethnic groups, cultures and religions that have lived together in the continent throughout its history, with Islam being one of the most relevant ones.[2] In this sense, Spain has not been an exception. Although multiculturalism has become a prominent topic due to the migratory movements that have taken place in recent decades,[3] it is not an unknown phenomenon either at the social level or in the political sphere. The situation has also posed a challenge from the legal perspective: how to address, in the most appropriate way, those needs raised at the social level and how to achieve a response that guarantees the exercise of the rights and freedoms of a welfare state? Based on this premise, I will focus on one of the most vulnerable social groups: unaccompanied foreign minors. In particular, in this investigation, I will analyse the situation of Moroccan children who arrive in Andalusia, as this is the group with the highest incidence in the country, the same area with the highest numbers,[4] as I will explain below. Therefore, I will first assess how Spanish legislation has tried to regulate this situation. The theoretical basis will serve to verify its implementation and, above all, its effective execution in practice. It will allow us to assess whether policies applied to the integration of minors have, as their ultimate objective, the best interests of the child and to identify the most effective means of achieving that goal.

Europe in numbers: A brief review

Migration of unaccompanied children to countries in the European Union began to occur in the 1990s (with the exception of Germany, which had received young asylum seekers since the end of the 1970s). Although Germany reached its peak during the 1980s, the arrival of asylum-seeking and migrant children in the rest of the countries had significantly increased by 2000 and during the first years of the present decade.[5] Almost 20 years later, the situation is even worse. In the European Union, in 2015, there were 1,321,600 asylum applicants; 29% of them were children and 23% of those child applicants were unaccompanied by an adult. In total, 88,245 unaccompanied children applied for asylum in that year. Of those unaccompanied child applicants, 91% were male.[6] In Spain, the data reflects a similar trend. According to the General Commissioner for Aliens and Borders, in 2018, 7,026 unaccompanied minors arrived by sea. The number represents a spectacular increase of 199.61% compared to 2017 (2,345 children). The increment is even higher if we compare this figure to the number of minors who arrived in 2014 (223 children). The figure implies massive growth compared to past years. The vast majority are boys (96.9%); the rest are girls. Most of them come from Morocco (61.89%), Republic of Guinea (14.10%), Mali (8.15%), Algeria (5.6%), Côte d'Ivoire (4.5%) and Gambia (1.69%). On 31 December 2018, a total of 13,796 minors were registered under the guardianship or care of the protection services.[7] Of this number, 12,825 were boys and 971 were girls. Consequently, there has been an increase of 115% from the 6,414 registered in 2017. Andalusia received most of these children (6,294 minors), followed by Catalonia (1,842) and Melilla (1,322).[8] Focusing on Andalusia, if we look at the figures provided by the children's ombudsman in 2018, the Andalusian system recorded 7,783 new admissions of unaccompanied migrant minors. These numbers represent a 135% increase from 2017 (3,306 new entries)[9]; 94.9% were boys and 5.1% were girls. By age group, most of them were between 16 and 17 years old (60.3%). Of migrant children in the Andalusian child protection system throughout 2018, 62.5% came from Morocco, 13.2% from Guinea, 8.0% from Mali, 4.9% from Côte d'Ivoire and 2.1% from Algeria.[10]

The best interest principle in the regulatory framework

According to the 1989 Convention on the Rights of the Child, decisions taken at the political and legal levels must serve the best interest of the child.[11] Since then, many international and European texts have adopted this precept as a guiding principle for their actions. It can be understood from a threefold perspective: (1) as a substantive right, it creates an intrinsic obligation for States, is directly applicable and can be invoked in a court; (2) as an interpretative legal principle, if a lawful provision is open to more than one interpretation, it is mandatory to choose the one that most effectively serves the child's best interest; and (3) as a rule of procedure, assessing and determining the best interest of the child requires procedural guarantees. States must justify how their decision has weighed the child's interests.[12] To know what most benefits a child, it is necessary to understand different aspects of the child's identity and needs; therefore, allowing the child access to the territory is a prerequisite to this initial assessment process.[13] Thus having a procedure that can be personalised to elucidate what is in the best interest of the child in each case is the key to guaranteeing such access.

Foreign minor in Spain: Minor or foreigner?

At the Spanish national level, *Ley Orgánica 1/1996, de 15 de enero, de Protección Jurídica del Menor, de modificación parcial del Código Civil y de la Ley de Enjuiciamiento Civil* continues the trend set by the rest of Europe. To assess the best interest of the child requires considering the protection of their right to life, survival and development, satisfaction of their core needs, consideration of their wishes and opinions and preservation of their identity, culture or religion. To this end, some weighting elements should be taken into account: the age and maturity of the child; the need to ensure equality and non-discrimination on the grounds of particular vulnerability; the effect of the passage of time; the stability of solutions or the transition to adulthood; and consideration of the principles of necessity and proportionality. In addition, any measure focusing on the best interest of the child must be taken following due process of law.[14]

However, the problem is that they are not only minors but also foreigners. So, the situation not only encounters the legal system for the protection of children but also the Aliens Law.[15] Unfortunately, when it comes to immigrant minors, special protection takes second place.

When unaccompanied minors arrive on national territory, in the majority of cases it is the police or themselves who report the situation of abandonment.[16] Once these children are considered minors, based on their documentation or the results of medical tests, and they are included in the registry of unaccompanied foreign minors, the regional communities are in charge of taking care of them. They have the duty of guardianship when a minor is in the situation of abandonment.[17]

The aspect I consider most worrying is paragraph 5 of the Spanish Framework Protocol on actions regarding unaccompanied minors.[18] It prioritises, as a general rule, the return to their country of origin, assuming that this decision is in the best interests of the child. This statement contrasts with the European Commission's Action Plan on Unaccompanied Minors (2010–2014), which states, as the most relevant aspects, (1) a durable solution (2) based on the best interests of the child. This solution shall consist of one of these three options, according to the particularities of the case:

- Return and reintegration in the country of origin;
- Granting of international protection status or other legal status allowing minors to successfully integrate into the Member State of residence;
- Resettlement.[19]

Although, at first sight, it may seem that these two approaches are the same, the nuance introduced by Spanish legislation changes everything. It means that the entire legal structure focuses on doing everything possible to return the minor to the place from which he or she came, without having sufficient economic and human resources to examine all cases individually. Furthermore, even when the child is already legally resident in Spain, he or she can still be returned to his or her place of origin when it is considered that it is in his or her best interest.[20] In this case, the child is not being deported from the country but 'returned' to his or her family. For this reason, the child is in a constant state of uncertainty, which makes it difficult for him or her to fulfil their life plan and integrate into society.

Procedure: Disadvantages and limitations of an incomplete system

A residence authorisation as a minor is granted only once the child's return to his or her country of origin has proven to be impossible, their best interest has been taken into account and nine months have elapsed since he or she was placed under the care of the relevant social services.[21] However, that is not the only problem the child has to face, as seen below:

> One of the issues implies the closing of the file when the minor is over eighteen years old. The situation is worrying if the child reaches the legal age while the documentation is being processed. The main consequence is that the young person leaves the protection system without permission to reside and no support network. In this case, the young person cannot access the specific public programmes for young people over 18 because the decree of abandonment is a requirement. The young person cannot obtain their regularisation because he or she cannot prove their means of subsistence. Neither can her or she go to the employment services or social-labour insertion programmes because they cannot demonstrate that they have been a minor under guardianship.[22]

Another problem is the risk children face when they decide to leave juvenile facilities. During 2018, 6,853 minors were discharged from the Andalusian System of Protection; 64.8% of them were from Morocco. Discharges based on minors reaching legal age represented 13.4% of the total. Contrary to what might be expected, family reunification represented less than 4% of the total: 3.5% were reunified in Spain and 0.3% in the country of origin. However, 73.5% of the withdrawals from the Child Protection System in 2018 were associated with voluntary departures (74.7% were boys; 49.7% were girls).[23] Before the 2015 Spanish reform, some centres decreed 'voluntary leave' for the child if he or she was absent from the juvenile facility. The problem is that, via the Spanish legal system which informs procedures for the protection of children and adolescents, *Ley 26/2015, de 28 de julio, de modificación del sistema de protección a la infancia y a la adolescencia*, this practice now has the status of law: Article 172 of the Spanish Civil Code establishes as one of the cases of cessation of the situation of abandonment as being when six months have passed since the minor voluntarily left the protection centre and his or her whereabouts are unknown. In most cases, it is assumed that the child who leaves the centre does so voluntarily. For that reason, the police are not alerted and no one starts the searching procedure.[24]

The situation of children who have formalised their condition before coming of legal age is also not as beneficial as might be expected. *Ley Orgánica 1/1996, de 15 de enero, de Protección Jurídica del Menor, de modificación parcial del Código Civil y de la Ley de Enjuiciamiento Civil* includes Article 22a, which refers to the programmes of preparation for independent living.[25] These programmes are designed for young people who are under a protection measure, specifically in residential care or in a vulnerable situation. For that reason, these programmes are particularly important in the case of unaccompanied foreign minors. They seek to provide tools to help them overcome the problem of having no family in the country; the bureaucratic difficulties they face in regularising their situation; or the limitations on obtaining minimum means of subsistence through work due to lack of authorisation. However, care for young people who come of legal age, having previously been under government supervision, is one of the most significant deficits of the current protection system. The latest report from the Chamber of Accounts that audits the Andalusian Regional Government's childcare programme demonstrates this problem. The report, published in June 2020, reflects a series of structural problems and non-compliance during 2017. Both in terms of control of resources and in the care provided to minors, Article 11.4 of Law 26/2015 states that public entities must have programmes and resources in place to support and guide those who, being under their guardianship, reach legal age and leave the protection system. Nevertheless, of the total obligations recognised for the 31E programme of the Andalusian Regional Government in 2017, only 2% of the expenditure was allocated to the Legal Age Programme. These data reflect that 62% of minors who reached the age of 18, and were therefore no longer under guardianship, were left without any form of care.[26]

A final issue highlighted in the report, which I consider particularly severe, is the illegalities that occurred in the procedural area[27]: if a foreign child arrives at a police station during the weekend, he or she must remain there until Monday. This situation arises because no one responsible for their custody attends to collect the child. This procedure is illegal: *Ley Orgánica 1/1996, de 15 de enero, de Protección Jurídica del Menor, de modificación parcial del Código Civil y de la Ley de Enjuiciamiento Civil* establishes 24 hours as a maximum period of detention. If no one collects the child, it is the police officers themselves who must transfer him or her, even though it is not their responsibility to do so.[28]

The situations described above are clear examples of failure to apply the principle of the best interest of the child, for lack of financial resources or material or human means. When the law on aliens comes into play, the fact that the child is vulnerable takes second place. All these cases are also clear examples of the circumstances of exclusion and particular vulnerability that characterise this social group.

Some answers to a multi-level problem

It is not easy to assert the best interest of the child when this principle clashes with immigration policies. That is why it is so difficult to find a balance. In many cases, the argument of returning based on the general interest is nothing more than an easy justification for problems such as the lack of places in care centres or the disruptive behaviour of a child. More often than not, staff try to do their best at each stage of the process; the problem is caused by the lack of human or financial means to carry out the procedures individually. Each child has a personal, individual history and situation but, on many occasions, it is difficult to assess them. To ensure the best interest of the child it is necessary to analyse case by case.

Lack of coordination between different regions also makes the task more difficult. Each regional government has full competence in this area and, for that reason, a minor can move around various communities without the knowledge of previous ones. In some cases, this displacement occurs because a certain community was not the final intended destination of the minor; in others, he or she believes that larger cities will provide better opportunities. Once more, the consequence is the vulnerability of the minor; when the child 'voluntarily' leaves a centre to move between regions, it is difficult to track his or her entire migration process.

My research confirms that, although in theory policies tend to guarantee the best interest of the child, in practice implementation is inadequate and fails to deliver the desired results.

Double objective of policies to protect unaccompanied foreign minors

Based on General Comment No. 14 (2013) on the right of the child to have his or her best interests taken as a primary consideration (art. 3, para. 1)[29] and the subsequent Spanish reform in 2015, development of tools to assess and determine the best interest of the child has been prioritised. Save the Children published one such tool: the Instrument for the Evaluation and Determination of the Best Interest of the Child in the Declaration of a Situation of Abandonment – an 11-pages document that helps professionals to determine, on a case-by-case basis, the interest of every single child.[30] Although this is a first and fundamental step towards achieving the objective of identifying the best interest of the child, it does not overcome one of the disadvantages initially raised: the lack of human and technical resources that allow a case-by-case study. The advantage of this form is that it makes the standardisation of some criteria possible. This element is crucial when it comes to providing coordinated action at the state level, even though the regions are actually responsible for unaccompanied minors. However, I believe that addressing this situation from the perspective of one area only is not enough; rather, it is necessary to provide a multi-level response to a multi-level problem. Only in this way can all existing gaps be addressed.

Therefore, policies focused on this field should have a dual objective:

- First, to follow a procedure that enables guaranteeing the real best interests of the child. So far, the regulations state that the best interest of the child is, as a general rule, repatriation with his or her family to the place of origin. However, the figures indicate something completely different: family reunification accounted for less than 4% of all repatriations. There are two possible reasons for this fact: the first is that there are not enough resources to carry out all planned repatriations and the second is that repatriation is not in the real best interest of the minor. Hence the

importance of determining this approach based on an assessment process that takes into account all the elements raised above.
- Second, policies should aim to create as durable a solution as possible. In the case of children who do not return to their country of origin, the best outcome is their integration into the society where they live. To this end, it is essential to work on the inclusion of these young people before they come of legal age and are no longer supported by institutions.

Role of NGOs in integration policies: 'Asociación Marroquí para la Integración de los Inmigrantes' as a successful case

The role of NGOs is crucial in achieving lasting solutions. Not only do they carry out projects that favour the integration of the child into the environment in which he or she lives, they also constitute a support network as a whole – a place where children and families can ask for help if they need to. One of the most important at the regional level is the *Asociación Marroquí para la Integración de los Inmigrantes* in Málaga; it also has offices in Granada, Sevilla, Almería and Algeciras. It provides migrants living in Spain with services or resources that favour their inclusion in society and tries to alleviate the situations of vulnerability or social exclusion that migrants face by giving them individualised and specific care and attention.[31] Although it works with a large number of projects (and a diverse age range of migrants), I will highlight only the two[32] most pertinent to this research.

The first one is called 'Sheltering Dreams'. During 2019, it worked with 40 young adults and helped them to meet their food and accommodation needs. It also delivered an overall intervention focused on the promotion of emancipation and social and labour inclusion. This project seeks to mitigate the difficulties that young people face once they leave the state protection system because they are over 18 years of age.

I consider it crucial to carry out this intervention in a gradual, progressive way as soon as unaccompanied minors are within the care system, that is when they are younger than 18. If this process is successful, when they come of legal age they will be able to continue developing by themselves. For this reason, the most relevant intervention for me is that carried out through the 'Join Me' project, which focused on aiding the inclusion of 124 unaccompanied minors and young people between the ages of 16 and 18. It encourages the creation of links between local or international volunteers and young people and works to provide them with institutional and informal support during their emancipation process. Here, then, is addressing the real best interest of the child, which is, after all, nothing more than the successful integration into the environment in which he or she lives.

In conclusion, it is not easy to migrate to a different country, especially for minors. They are the most vulnerable victims in a whole chain of actors and events; continuously exposed to dangers such as human trafficking[33] or even death. For this reason, the system must guarantee the fulfilment of their rights and try to change what is not working effectively. However, I believe that this task does not belong only to the institutional sphere. A lasting solution involves working together to make integration as successful as possible. It can only be achieved with the support of the host society.

This is why this stage must begin years before the child is left without the tools of protection provided by the system. Only in this way can the best interest of the child be defended and guaranteed throughout the entire process.

Notes

1 This chapter is part of the 'Derechos y garantías de las personas vulnerables en el Estado de bienestar' research project (UMA18-FEDERJA-175), supported by the aids to R&D+I projects in the framework of the Regional Operational Programme of the European Regional Development Fund (ERDF ROP) 2014–2020. The main researchers are Octavio García Pérez and Carmen Sánchez Hernández. It is also part of the 'Inmigración y Derecho: retos actuales desde un enfoque interdisciplinar' project (PPIT.UMA.B1.2018/04), conducted by the University of Malaga. The main researcher is Carmen Rocío Fernández Díaz (elenaavileshernandez@uma.es).
2 Justo Lacunza Balda, 'La diversidad geográfica del islam', in *El Islam y los musulmanes hoy. Dimensión internacional y relaciones con España*, ed. Olivia Orozco de la Torre and Gabriel Alonso García, Cuadernos de la escuela diplomática 48 (Madrid: Ministerio de Asuntos Exteriores y Cooperación, 2013), 64. Retrieved from www.exteriores.gob.es/Portal/es/Ministerio/EscuelaDiplomatica/Documents/el_islam_y_los_musulmanes_hoy%2048.pdf
3 Ana I Planet Contreras and Jordi Moreras, 'Islam e inmigración: Elementos para un análisis y propuestas de gestión', in *Islam e inmigración*, Ministerio de la Presidencia, Foro Inmigración y Ciudadanía (Madrid: Centro de Estudios Politicos y Constitucionales, 2015), 9–10.
4 Elisa García España, 'Menores inmigrantes en el sistema tutelar andaluz', *Boletín criminológico*, no. 74 (2004), 1.
5 Daniel Senovilla Hernández, 'Situación y tratamiento de los menores extranjeros no acompañados en Europa un estudio comparado de 6 países: Alemania, Bélgica, España, Francia, Italia y Reino Unido' (Belgium: Observatorio Internacional de Justicia Juvenil, 2007), 20. Retrieved from www.oijj.org/sites/default/files/documental_5573_es.pdf
6 House of Lords, European Union Committee, 'Children in Crisis: Unaccompanied Migrant Children in the EU' (Authority of the House of Lords, 2016), 5. Retrieved from www.parliament.uk/business/committees/committees-a-z/lords-select/eu-home-affairs-subcommittee/news-parliament-2015/unaccompanied-minors-report-published/
7 The main challenge for Spain concerning unaccompanied foreign minors is correct coordination between all institutions and administrations involved. The situation makes it difficult or impossible for children to be re-entered on the Register.
8 State's Attorney, 'Memoria de la Fiscalía General del Estado' (Madrid: Ministerio de Justicia, 2019), 837–38. Retrieved from www.fiscal.es/documents/20142/133838/MEMORIA+-+2019.pdf/a63c133c-dff3-6cf9-1a74-55d658be912a?version=1.0&t=1568023202838
9 It is important to highlight a small variation in the figures provided by the central government compared to the regional government. Different issues are addressed, among them: failure to update Registry data, errors or duplicates in the entries, etc. María Martín and Jesús A. Cañas, 'España no sabe cuántos menores extranjeros no acompañados acoge', *EL PAÍS*, 13 May 2020, sec. España. Retrieved from https://elpais.com/espana/2020-05-13/espana-no-sabe-cuantos-menores-extranjeros-no-acompanados-acoge.html. Andalusia is not an exception; the rest of the regions suffer from the same problem. In any case, these differences show the difficulty of accurately counting the number of unaccompanied foreign minors in each regional community.
10 Andalusian Ombudsman for Children, 'Informe Anual del Menor de Andalucía 2018' (Sevilla, 2019), 38–41. Retrieved from www.defensordelmenordeandalucia.es/sites/default/files/informe-anual-de-menores-2018/desgloses/pdf/dma2018D-6-2-5-2.pdf

Rights & guarantees of unaccompanied minors

11 Office of the High Commissioner for Human Rights (OHCHR), 'Convention on the Rights of the Child', GA Res. 44/25, Annex § (1989). Retrieved from www.ohchr.org/en/professionalinterest/pages/crc.aspx. Art. 3, para. 1.
12 UN Committee on the Rights of the Child (CRC), 'General Comment No. 14 (2013) on the Right of the Child to Have His or Her Best Interests Taken as a Primary Consideration (Art. 3, para. 1)', Pub. L. No. CRC/C/GC/14, 1 (2013), 4. Retrieved from www.refworld.org/docid/51a84b5e4.html. Para. 6.
13 UN Committee on the Rights of the Child (CRC), 'General Comment No. 6 (2005): Treatment of Unaccompanied and Separated Children Outside Their Country of Origin', Pub. L. No. CRC/GC/2005/6, 1 (2005), 9. Retrieved from www.refworld.org/docid/42dd174b4.html. Para. 20.
14 Head of State, 'Ley Orgánica 1/1996, de 15 de Enero, de Protección Jurídica Del Menor, de Modificación Parcial Del Código Civil y de La Ley de Enjuiciamiento Civil', Pub. L. No. BOE-A-1996–1069, 1 (1996). Retrieved from www.boe.es/eli/es/lo/1996/01/15/1/con. Art. 2.
15 See *Ley Orgánica 4/2000, de 11 de enero, sobre derechos y libertades de los extranjeros en España y su integración social* (Art. 35) and its Implementing Regulation: *Real Decreto 557/2011, de 20 de abril, por el que se aprueba el Reglamento de la Ley Orgánica 4/2000, sobre derechos y libertades de los extranjeros en España y su integración social, tras su reforma por Ley Orgánica 2/2009*.
16 García España, 'Menores inmigrantes en el sistema tutelar andaluz', 3.
17 See Article 172 of the Spanish Civil Code and Article 148.1 of the Spanish Constitution.
18 See *Protocolo Marco sobre determinadas actuaciones en relación con los menores Extranjeros no Acompañados*: 'The policy on foreign unaccompanied minors must be aimed at the return of the minor to his or her country of origin, either with his or her family or in a care centre in his or her country, as a lasting solution and provided that this is in the best interests of the minor', para. 5.
19 European Commission, 'Action Plan on Unaccompanied Minors (2010–2014). Communication from the Commission to the European Parliament and the Council', 2010, 12, doi:10.1163/2210-7975_HRD-4679-0058. The Action Plan also clarify the duty of taking this decision 'by the competent authorities within the shortest possible period … taking into account the obligation to try to trace the family, explore other possibilities for reintegration in their home society and assess which solution is in the best interests of the child', p. 12.
20 See *Ley Orgánica 4/2000, de 11 de enero, sobre derechos y libertades de los extranjeros en España y su integración social* Art. 35, para. 8.
21 European Migration Network (EMN), 'Policies, Practices and Data on Unaccompanied Minors. Spain 2014' (Madrid: European Commission, 2014), 16. Retrieved from http://extranjeros.mitramiss.gob.es/es/redeuropeamigracion/Estudios_monograficos/ficheros/Estudio_REM_menores_no_acompanados_2014_EN.pdf
22 María Martín, 'España mantiene sin papeles a casi 10.000 menores inmigrantes tutelados', *El País*, 19 November 2019 (translated by author). Retrieved from https://elpais.com/politica/2019/11/18/actualidad/1574096323_979962.html See also Margarita De la Rasilla, 'La protección jurídica y social de los Menores Extranjeros No Acompañados en Andalucía' (Políticas públicas y Menores Extranjeros No Acompañados, Sevilla: Save the Children, 2007), 112–13. Retrieved from www.savethechildren.es/sites/default/files/imce/docs/proteccion_juridica_menores_extranjeros_no_acompanados_andalucia.pdf
23 Andalusian Ombudsman for Children, 'Informe Anual del Menor de Andalucía 2018', 42–43.
24 García España, 'Extranjeros sospechosos, condenados y excondenados: Un mosaico de exclusión', 11.
25 See *Ley Orgánica 1/1996, de 15 de enero, de Protección Jurídica del Menor, de modificación parcial del Código Civil y de la Ley de Enjuiciamiento Civil*: 'Public entities shall offer programmes of preparation for independent living to young people who are under a protective measure,

particularly in residential care or in a situation of special vulnerability, from two years before their coming of legal age, once they have reached the age, whenever they need it, with a commitment to their active participation and use. The programmes must provide socio-educational follow-up, accommodation, social and occupational integration, psychological support and economic aid'. Art. 22 bis.

26 Audit Chamber of Andalusia, 'Fiscalización del programa presupuestario 31e 'Atención a la infancia'. Ejercicio 2017' (Sevilla: Junta de Andalucía, 27 April 2020), 20. Retrieved from www.ccuentas.es/junta-de-andalucia
27 This is not the only regulatory irregularity detected. The Chamber of Accounts has found infringement of the right to a child's hearing in cases of change of centre. Article 32.2.c of Decree 355/2003, of 16 December, on Residential Care for Minors, guarantees this procedural safeguard as a right of the child.
28 Audit Chamber of Andalusia, 'Fiscalización del programa presupuestario 31e 'Atención a la infancia'. Ejercicio 2017', 41–42.
29 See General Comment No. 14 (2013): 'Assessment and determination of the child's best interests are two steps to be followed when required to make a decision', para. 47.
30 Julieta Moreno-Torres Sánchez, 'Instrumento para la evaluación y determinación del Interés Superior del Menor en la declaración de situación de desamparo' (Madrid: Save the Children, 2017). Retrieved from www.savethechildren.es/sites/default/files/imce/docs/ism_pdf_6_octubre_docx_0.pdf
31 Asociación Marroquí para la Integración de los Inmigrantes, 'Memoria 2019' (Málaga, España, 2020), 8. Retrieved from https://issuu.com/asociacionmarroquiparalaintegracion/docs/memoria_2019_-_asociacion_marroqui?fbclid=IwAR2Th3vFd02SAwI_68vc1uUvs-X5oOrtHFywsPC-8Wh2Quj_MgY29RVksvs
32 Ibid., 50–51.
33 For academic commentary on this topic, see, Raquel Vela Díaz, 'Trata de personas y su incidencia sobre menores extranjeros', in *Tratamiento normativo y social de los menores inmigrantes*, ed. Consejería de justicia e Interior. Junta de Andalucía, Formación en Interculturalidad y Migraciones (Sevilla: Junta de Andalucía, n.d.), 29–38.

References

Andalusian Ombudsman for Children. 'Informe Anual del Menor de Andalucía 2018'. Sevilla, 2019. Retrieved from www.defensordelmenordeandalucia.es/sites/default/files/informe-anual-de-menores-2018/desgloses/pdf/dma2018D-6–2–5–2.pdf
Asociación Marroquí para la Integración de los Inmigrantes. 'Memoria 2019'. Málaga, España, 2020. Retrieved from https://issuu.com/asociacionmarroquiparalaintegracion/docs/memoria_2019_-_asociacion_marroqui?fbclid=IwAR2Th3vFd02SAwI_68vc1uUvs-X5oOrtHFywsPC-8Wh2Quj_MgY29RVksvs
Audit Chamber of Andalusia. 'Fiscalización del programa presupuestario 31e 'Atención a la infancia'. Ejercicio 2017'. Sevilla: Junta de Andalucía, 27 April 2020. Retrieved from www.ccuentas.es/junta-de-andalucia
De la Rasilla, Margarita. 'La protección jurídica y social de los Menores Extranjeros No Acompañados en Andalucía', 109–18. Sevilla: Save the Children, 2007. Retrieved from www.savethechildren.es/sites/default/files/imce/docs/proteccion_juridica_menores_extranjeros_no_acompanados_andalucia.pdf
European Commission. 'Action Plan on Unaccompanied Minors (2010–2014): Communication from the Commission to the European Parliament and the Council', 2010. doi:10.1163/2210-7975_HRD-4679-0058.
European Migration Network (EMN). 'Policies, Practices and Data on Unaccompanied Minors. Spain 2014'. Madrid: European Commission, 2014. Retrieved from http://extranjeros.mitramiss.gob.es/es/redeuropeamigracion/Estudios_monograficos/ficheros/Estudio_REM_menores_no_acompanados_2014_EN.pdf

García España, Elisa. 'Extranjeros sospechosos, condenados y excondenados: Un mosaico de exclusión'. *Revista Electrónica de Ciencia Penal y Criminología*, no. 19–15 (2017): 1–28.

———. 'Menores inmigrantes en el sistema tutelar andaluz'. *Boletín criminológico*, no. 74 (2004): 1–4.

Head of State. Ley 26/2015, de 28 de julio, de modificación del sistema de protección a la infancia y a la adolescencia., Pub. L. No. BOE-A-2015–8470, 1 (2015). Retrieved from www.boe.es/eli/es/l/2015/07/28/26/con

———. Ley Orgánica 1/1996, de 15 de enero, de Protección Jurídica del Menor, de modificación parcial del Código Civil y de la Ley de Enjuiciamiento Civil, Pub. L. No. BOE-A-1996–1069, 1 (1996). Retrieved from www.boe.es/eli/es/lo/1996/01/15/1/con

———. Ley Orgánica 4/2000, de 11 de enero, sobre derechos y libertades de los extranjeros en España y su integración social, Pub. L. No. BOE-A-2000–544, 1 (2000). Retrieved from www.boe.es/eli/es/lo/2000/01/11/4/con

House of Lords. European Union Committee. 'Children in Crisis: Unaccompanied Migrant Children in the EU'. Authority of the House of Lords, 2016. Retrieved from www.parliament.uk/business/committees/committees-a-z/lords-select/eu-home-affairs-subcommittee/news-parliament-2015/unaccompanied-minors-report-published/

Lacunza Balda, Justo. 'La diversidad geográfica del islam'. In *El Islam y los musulmanes hoy. Dimensión internacional y relaciones con España*, edited by Olivia Orozco de la Torre and Gabriel Alonso García, 47–74. Cuadernos de la escuela diplomática 48. Madrid: Ministerio de Asuntos Exteriores y Cooperación, 2013. Retrieved from www.exteriores.gob.es/Portal/es/Ministerio/EscuelaDiplomatica/Documents/el_islam_y_los_musulmanes_hoy%2048.pdf

Martín, María. 'España mantiene sin papeles a casi 10.000 menores inmigrantes tutelados'. *El País*. 19 November 2019. Retrieved from https://elpais.com/politica/2019/11/18/actualidad/1574096323_979962.html

Martín, María, and Jesús A. Cañas. 'España no sabe cuántos menores extranjeros no acompañados acoge'. *EL PAÍS*. 13 May 2020, sec. España. Retrieved from https://elpais.com/espana/2020-05-13/espana-no-sabe-cuantos-menores-extranjeros-no-acompanados-acoge.html

Moreno-Torres Sánchez, Julieta. 'Instrumento para la evaluación y determinación del Interés Superior del Menor en la declaración de situación de desamparo'. Madrid: Save the Children, 2017. Retrieved from www.savethechildren.es/sites/default/files/imce/docs/ism_pdf_6_octubre_docx_0.pdf

Planet Contreras, Ana I, and Jordi Moreras. 'Islam e inmigración: Elementos para un análisis y propuestas de gestión'. In *Islam e inmigración*, Ministerio de la Presidencia., 1–79. Foro Inmigración y Ciudadanía. Madrid: Centro de Estudios Politicos y Constitucionales, 2015.

Senovilla Hernández, Daniel. 'Situación y tratamiento de los menores extranjeros no acompañados en Europa un estudio comparado de 6 países: Alemania, Bélgica, España, Francia, Italia y Reino Unido'. Belgium: Observatorio Internacional de Justicia Juvenil, 2007. Retrieved from www.oijj.org/sites/default/files/documental_5573_es.pdf

State's Attorney. 'Memoria de la Fiscalía General del Estado'. Madrid: Ministerio de Justicia, 2019. Retrieved from www.fiscal.es/documents/20142/133838/MEMORIA+-+2019.pdf/a63c133c-dff3–6cf9–1a74–55d658be912a?version=1.0&t=1568023202838

UN Committee on the Rights of the Child (CRC). General Comment No. 6 (2005): Treatment of Unaccompanied and Separated Children Outside their Country of Origin, Pub. L. No. CRC/GC/2005/6, 1 (2005). Retrieved from www.refworld.org/docid/42dd174b4.html

———. General Comment No. 14 (2013) on the right of the child to have his or her best interests taken as a primary consideration (art. 3, para. 1), Pub. L. No. CRC/C/GC/14, 1 (2013). Retrieved from www.refworld.org/docid/51a84b5e4.html

Vela Díaz, Raquel. 'Trata de personas y su incidencia sobre menores extranjeros'. In *Tratamiento normativo y social de los menores inmigrantes*, edited by Consejería de justicia e Interior. Junta de Andalucía, 27–39. Formación en Interculturalidad y Migraciones. Sevilla: Junta de Andalucía, n.d.

8
THE RIGHT OF PARENTS TO ENSURE THE RELIGIOUS AND MORAL EDUCATION OF THEIR CHILDREN

Parental conflicts—an analysis of Spanish case law

Rosa García Vilardell

Introductory aspects: The joint exercise of parental responsibility in the case of separation and divorce

The child is considered by the Spanish legal system as a person who should be protected in a unique way due to their lack of maturity.[1] In this respect, during this state of being a minor, parents are granted care and representation of the children while their ability to act is limited.

The protection of family and childhood is one of the principles governing social and economic policy, being expressly guaranteed in a mandate of care addressed to parents. Paragraph 3 of Article 39 of the Spanish Constitution states: "Parents shall provide all forms of assistance to children born in or out of wedlock, during their minority and in other cases where the law so provides."

Articles 154 and following from the Civil Code (CC), which regulate relations between parents and children, attempt to respond to this constitutional mandate:

> Unemancipated children are under the protection of their father and mother. Parental authority shall always be exercised in the interest of the children, in accordance with their personality, and includes the following duties and powers:
>
> 1 Take care of them, be with them, to feed them, to educate them and provide them with integral formation.
> 2 Represent them and manage their assets.

This is the general context in which the institution of parental authority should be understood today. Since reform of family law by enactment of the Law of 13 May 1981,[2] the concept of civil and patriarchal law, in which the parent had exclusive authority, has been replaced by a new concept that places special emphasis on the functionality of said institution, as it is not exercised in the interest of the parent but always in the interest of the child.[3]

Parental custody, which can only be exercised by parents, is currently configured as an institution whose central focus is the best interest of the child. Therefore, it is conceived as a function, which implies that it is the children who have the right to be cared for while the parents are seen as "organs to play a role: the care and education of the child".[4] We are faced with a set of rights that legislation grants to its holders not to satisfy their own interests, but to fulfil the function of care of children. As stated, they are of a compulsory, non-waivable and imprescriptible nature, so that their exercise is no longer merely optional for the holder—an inherent feature of subjective rights in general. As a consequence of the obligatory nature of its exercise, it is non-unrenounceable and imprescriptible, as we stated, which means that the legitimate holder cannot abandon the purposes for which it is asked to comply, and likewise, not exercising it, whether voluntarily or by force, lacks all potential for extinction of the same.[5]

That said, and as is established by Article 156 of the Spanish Civil Code, parental authority is exercised jointly by both parents or by one with express or tacit consent by the other. This is the general rule that, logically, remains intact in instances of crisis or termination of the couple. Therefore, in the event of separation or divorce, the attribution of custody to one of the parents will not affect parental authority, nor entitlement to it, nor its exercise, which is held jointly. In no case can it be understood that the custodial parent is granted a greater right of decision than the parent with visiting rights.

In this regard, for the conciliation between single-parent custody and the joint exercise of parental authority, a distinction is usually drawn between acts of ordinary and extraordinary scope.[6] Given the lack of legal specification, we can define the former using the words of Navarro Michel (2015)[7] as: "those [acts] which relate to the normal development of the child's daily life, and those which are repeated relatively frequently in practice". Extraordinary acts can be defined as: "those which affect more fundamental decisions with a greater impact on the child's life". In other words, the custody holding parent, or the parent who holds visiting rights at the time, usually makes decisions in the context of ordinary acts involving those that affect the child's daily routine, education and development. These include issues related to extracurricular activities, school outings and trips, tutoring, doctor's appointments or health issues that are not of a serious nature, as well as application for passports or identity cards. On the other hand, acts of extraordinary scope, referring to more relevant decisions, must be adopted by both parents since they are, for example, questions that may influence more fundamental matters for the child's development, such as: the choice of formal education (state or private school, secular or religious, bilingual or not), determining the place of residence, non-urgent but substantial health matters, psychological treatment or similar, or religious celebrations.

As is easily conceivable, being a function exercised by two people, it is highly probable that conflict will arise between the parents when making certain decisions related to the children of both spouses.[8] Which type of religious or moral education is chosen for the children has huge implications and significance for their development. Therefore, it falls outside the scope of custody and is among the acts of extraordinary scope of parental authority and subject therefore to the joint decision of both parents. This aspect has become one of the points of conflict that the Courts deal with today, precisely because of confrontations between parents on religious matters, such as those related to worship and religious observance, adherence to certain religious beliefs or whether or not children should receive religious education.

The child's religious freedom and the right of parents to ensure the religious and moral education of their children: Conflicting rights or is it possible to reconcile them?

Before delving into the aforementioned conflict, given the nature of the rights involved in the subject matter, it is essential that we first focus our attention on these rights. Specifically, we refer to the parents' right to educate their child in accordance with their own beliefs, and the child's right to religious freedom, both of which are expressly guaranteed by the Spanish Constitution as fundamental rights of the individual.

Article 27.3 of the Spanish Constitutional text expressly guarantees "the right that helps parents to have their children receive a religious and moral education in accordance with their own beliefs".

Given the crucial significance of the institution of parental authority, for the correct development and evolution of the child, the legal system has granted extensive powers to the parents for the performance of their duties related to education, some of which are constituted, as is the case, precisely, of the law under consideration.

The parental right to choose religious and moral education has a double dimension, both positive and negative.[9] On the positive side, it implies the parents' right to transmit their own beliefs and, therefore, to choose both within and outside the school environment, the religious and moral education of their children, in accordance with the same. On the negative side, it implies the recognition of a sphere of autonomy that protects them from any interference by public authorities, upon which a specific demand of respect for the beliefs of the student is placed.

However, the wording used in Article 27.3 of the Constitution, to which we have just referred, cannot be interpreted as a subjective right of parents before their children, since we are within the area of conscience or, in other words, before rights closely connected to human dignity, so the entitlement to and exercise of the same correspond to the child by virtue of the fact that he or she is a person.

Article 16 of the Constitution enforces and guarantees "the freedom of ideology, religion and worship of individuals and communities with no limitation, other than those necessary to maintain public order guaranteed by law". In the same way, the most important international texts on human rights—which, by virtue of the mandate provided in Article 10.2 of the Magna Carta, should be complementary to the rules concerning fundamental rights and freedoms that are recognised by the Spanish legal system—propagate the right to freedom of ideology, religion and worship for "every individual", without making distinctions, as can be seen, regarding entitlement to the same. It can therefore be said that the minor is a bearer of the aforementioned right, as expressly recognised in the most characteristic instrument of the denominated child law. Examples of such include: the Convention on the Rights of the Child, adopted by the General Assembly of the United Nations on 20 November 1989; The European Charter of Children's Rights, issued by the European Parliament in 1992; and, within the scope of Spanish law, the Organic Law on the Legal Protection of Children and Young People that must be highlighted and lays out textually: "Minors will enjoy the rights available to them in the Constitution and the International Treaties in which Spain participates."

It is clear that the child has the right to freedom of beliefs and the exercising of the same. Although the actual possibility of the latter, i.e. the autonomy of the child, will be determined progressively according to the degree of maturity, the holders of parental authority will guide the exercise of this freedom, so long as this level does not exist. Mature judgement constitutes, therefore, the only limit to the minor's exercise of the freedom of beliefs and, in turn, constitutes a limit to the guiding authority held by parents: maturity and parental guidance are presented, in sum, as two poles whose relationship is inversely proportional: the greater the maturity, the less parental guidance.[10]

This question leads us to ask ourselves about the balance between both rights: the parental right to choose religious education of their children and the religious freedom of the child, which we will address immediately.

The law contained in Article 27.3 of the Spanish Magna Carta is, in this sense, a right that effectively belongs to the parents in relation to the State; it implies the constitutionalisation of a guarantee of protection against teachings with indoctrinating purposes by public authorities.[11]

However, as far as minors are concerned, it is clear from the above that recognition in its own right of the entitlement to educate children's consciences is not possible and nor is it possible to require children to respect the beliefs of society.[12] But it is, in short, a right granted to parents because it is their obligation to care for their children until they reach the necessary capacity to choose. This also implies a faculty expressly granted by the constitutional system to the parents, with the objective of facilitating the fulfilment of the educational obligations involved in parental authority. It also guarantees, as we have stated, the free development of the formation of conscience, in this case of the minor, when they are not capable of making decisions for themselves because they are too young.

The parents' right to choose their children's religious and moral education in accordance with their own beliefs should be understood as a right of a functional nature, as it derives from the duty of care incumbent upon them. Therefore, in any case, the parental right granted by Article 27.3 of the Constitution could constitute a right to impose an ideological model on the child. This is the only plausible interpretation, from our point of view, in relation to reconciling both fundamental rights, taking into account the true role of the institution of parental authority.[13]

Parental conflict concerning the choice of moral and religious education of common children

In the context of family relations, it is clear that the task of education that falls to parents cannot ignore the fact that minors are entitled to their fundamental rights and freedoms. Parents' right to choose religious and moral education for the child, provided that these beliefs are in keeping with public order and, of course, their own beliefs, is thus in the best interests and to the advantage of the child. Likewise, although—as pointed out by Bercovitz Rodriguez-Cano (2000)—difficulties may arise when the minor has sufficient critical judgement and maturity to exercise said freedom with a certain autonomy, the truly conflictive issue in this subject normally arises when there is a lack of agreement between the parents on the education and religious instruction of their common children.[14]

As mentioned above, in cases in which there is a discrepancy of criteria between the holders of parental authority and the will of the minor, the conflict is resolved in accordance with the minor's decision, if they have reached a sufficient level of maturity.

But what happens when there is a lack of unified criteria among parents? It should be noted that, in these cases, probably due to the social confusion that exists on the exclusive powers of parental authority and those of custody, in practice it is not so relevant whether the child is under joint parental authority and custody or joint parental authority and sole custody of one of the parents. Most disputes arise from the intention to modify the award of custody or to modify the original visitation agreement, as follows.

Indeed, on many occasions, the parent who has custody assumes the right to make unilateral decisions about the religious education of the children, despite the fact that this is a decision of critical importance to the child's development, and therefore subject to the prior agreement of both parents. These situations have led to the judicialisation of both family life and relations with children, whereby the judge becomes a "third parent", having to grant the legal capacity to one of the two parents, adopting in this way the definitive solution over education in a particular faith, the reception of a sacrament or the choice of a religious or secular school.

The Provincial Court of Zaragoza (St. No. 154/2006, 23 October), ruled on an appeal lodged by the non-custodial father of a seven-year-old girl, in favour of his daughter receiving a religious education, opting for the Catholic Religious Education class, against the will of the mother, who had been granted care and custody of the child, and who had decided on the Ethics class. The Court ruled in favour of the father's claim, upholding his appeal on the basis of the criteria of continuity, since the child had been attending the Religious Education class during previous years—as decided jointly by the parents at that time—and there was no justified reason for the change demanded by the custody-holding parent.

For its part, the Provincial Court of Castellón issued a ruling on a case in which the mother was opposed to her son being educated in the Catholic faith (Order No. 601/2008, 4 November); the power to do so had been granted to the father in the first instance ruling:

According to the appealing party, the decision adopted by the Court of First Instance … constitutes "an inadmissible civil interference in the field of the integral education of the child, which would be contrary to the spirit and purpose of our Spanish Constitution, on religious freedom".

The appellant argued that educating children in a particular religious faith is only possible when both parents agree, thus, in the present case, Articles 14, 16 and 27.3 of the Constitution were infringed. As a logical consequence, the appellant proposed that the child be given a secular education until they reached the age of majority. The Court of Appeal upheld the contested judgement, applying, as in the previous case, the criteria of continuity, on the understanding that the father's choice was in line with the family's beliefs and in which the child had been initiated up until that time, as the marriage had been celebrated in canonical form and the child had been baptised. Furthermore, the Court of Appeal indicated, that the appellant, at the hearing for the adoption of precautionary measures, expressly declared that she did not oppose the intention of her husband in this matter and that in no way had it been established, by her, that the father's intention to educate his child in the Catholic faith would be harmful or dangerous to their comprehensive development.

On the same basis, in 2011, the Court of First Instance of Barbastro, ruled in favour of a mother who, faced with opposition from the father, called for the right to decide on the option for her children to follow a Catholic religious education (Order 246/2011, 5 December; y, Order 10/12, 30 April 2013). Specifically, it was requested that one of the children take the subject of religious education and that the other attend catechism classes to prepare for First Communion. The order based the decision to grant legal capacity to the mother on the basis that she was merely continuing with the educational model decided on by both parents from the beginning of their cohabitation; that is, understanding that the change had more to do with the parents' separation than with the interests of the children. However, after two years, at which time one of the children was going to receive their First Communion, and due to the father's opposition, the mother brought the petition before the court. In this case, the judge granted the legal capacity to the father, considering that, at that time, it was in the child's interest to leave the decision on whether or not to submit to the rite of communion to a future time when he would be able to form a more informed judgement on the matter. The reason the judge made this decision, without following the common criteria that had been accepted years before, was the observation that the child perceived, in this particular case, that taking or not taking communion would result in conflict, based on the fact that he expressed at the hearing that he did not care either way. Thus, in order to avoid further harm by involving him in conflict, the judge believed that it would be best to postpone said decision.[15]

In the field of regulated education, the Court of First Instance No. 1 of Moncada decided, by order, in 2017 on an action brought by one of the parents, in this case the father, requesting authorisation to enrol his youngest daughter in a state school, against the mother's wishes, who made the case for enrolment in a subsidised religious school. The order argued that the resolution of these cases would require recourse to social or family norms or, when applicable, to the agreement reached by the parties or to the conclusions reached by each of the parents in this regard (Order, 21 June 2017).

The decision under review records that, in the case in question, there was no agreement on the education of the child, as at that time the child was finishing nursery and had not yet started school. It was also suggested that the child had been baptised, but, surprisingly—taking into account the reasoning we have been commenting on—the judge, apparently expressing his own preferences, did not interpret this as an act that identifies the parental decision to educate their offspring in the Catholic faith, nor therefore as a bid for a future religious-type education, as he considered that, in the current context, baptism had become a social tradition. Therefore, given such circumstances, the court's judgement was based on the parents' motives, regarding the father's choice, and awarded him the authority to make decisions. The Court of First Instance considered that, although the mother's reasons may have been legitimate, that is, she stated that she wanted her daughter to enrol in a state-subsidised religious school on the basis of the school's hours and its proximity rather than religious reasons, the father's wish was based on the right to freedom of religion and conscience and the right to educate a child in accordance with his convictions. Both rights are fundamental, and therefore have a preferential protection that can exempt other situations which do not reach the same level of judicial protection.

In the same year, the Provincial Court of Burgos ruled on an appeal made by the mother of a child requesting the revocation of an order issued in the Court of First Instance that had rejected the authorisation she had requested (Order No. 38/2017, 9 February). The mother had submitted the request for judicial authorisation so that her nine-year-old child, against the father's wishes, could receive the Sacraments of Baptism, Penance and Eucharist. By Order dated 31 May, the Court of First Instance agreed not to grant her request, and the mother lodged an appeal, arguing that:

> the appealed Order be revoked, declaring it not to be consistent with the law for not granting her request … to be granted judicial authorisation for her daughter … to receive the Holy Sacraments of Baptism, Penance and Eucharist and a new Resolution be ruled granting the order of this party.

The Court, taking into account the specific circumstances of the case, dismissed the appeal, basing its decision on the initial agreement between the parents that left the decision of exercising her religious freedom to their daughter, without choosing a religious affiliation for her. The judge considered that there was no justification for revoking the parents' agreement on the basis of the child being discriminated against by her classmates if she failed to take Communion, as her mother alleged, given that she attended a public school that did not adhere to an official religion.

Indeed, according to the facts submitted in the analysed resolution, the parents had a canonical marriage, but it is also true that, when the child was born, they had decided by mutual agreement not to baptise her and that she herself should decide on the manner in which to exercise her right to freedom of religion once she reached the age of 13 or 14 years. The issue we want to focus on here, unlike the judicial decision raised above, is that in this case the court clearly emphasised the importance of the fact of being baptised in resolving the conflict,

> insofar as it is not the same that the child already be baptised, which would mean belonging to the Catholic Church due to previous agreement between the parents, or on the contrary, that the child was not baptised because at the time of her birth her parents decided by mutual agreement not to baptise her in order for the child to be able to make this decision once she was mature enough to do so.

We also find in the development of the argument another aspect that, in our view, is crucial to the conflicts we are discussing, that is, court hearings for children. In the case of court orders, the fifth appeal action alleges, the omission of said procedure would constitute the annulment of the same; despite this, in the judicial document, it is neither requested that the proceedings be processed nor annulled, consequently the judge does not have the power to decree. However, he takes the opportunity to elaborate on the meaning and content of said procedure in accordance with the legislation in force, which makes mandatory character court hearings for children from the age of 12 if they are sufficiently mature. At its discretion, taking into account the child's age and the subject of the decision—which is not a question of authorising the taking of the communion of a child who was baptised by her parents, rather that a child whose parents decided in the past not to baptise her, be baptised and also take the Sacraments of Penance and Eucharist—the judge does not consider it opportune, due to her age (surprisingly, in view of the legislation in force[16]), to hear the child as it would entail involving her in responsibility for a decision that is not expected at her age.

The ECHR, in the case of *Rupprecht* v. *Spain* (February 2013), has also expressed an opinion on the reception of the Sacraments by children when the parents maintain opposing positions. The European Court ruled inadmissible the non-custodial father's claim to be given the right to decide on his daughter's religious education. This was a child who had been baptised according to the Catholic rite and enrolled in Catechism classes without the permission of the complainant's father, who maintained that it should be the child herself, having sufficient judgement, who should make the decision on whether or not to adhere to a religious denomination. The Court of First Instance denied the father's request, considering that she had been schooled, without opposition from him, in a school that taught religious education classes, and the girl had expressed, on her own initiative, her wish to take the Communion. The hearing confirmed the reasoning of the decision in this instance, appealed by the non-custodial parent. The claimant lodged an appeal in cassation with the Supreme Court, which declared the appeal inadmissible, and filed subsequently for amparo with the Constitutional Court, which also dismissed it as having no constitutional relevance

As can be observed in this case, the Courts do not consider the fact that the child does not belong to the Catholic Church, by the joint decision of both parents, to be transcendent, and base their decision on two criteria: the education in a religious school and the own desire. This last criterion has absolute preference, provided it be accredited, at the time of deciding on the child's religious education.

By way of conclusion

It is possible to make a few remarks in relation to the issue under consideration, depending on the conflict in question and not forgetting that in such sensitive situations close attention should be paid to the specific circumstances of each case. In the case of conflict between the minor's wishes and the religious beliefs chosen by the parents to educate them, the minor's decision prevails, if they are sufficiently mature. Legislation granting parents authority to carry out their function of guidance and care can under no circumstances be interpreted as a right to impose an ideological model on the child, since in these cases we find ourselves facing an authentic breach of the right to freedom of religious belief. If the minor lacks sufficient capacity to decide, the parents' actions should always, and in all cases, aim to achieve the minor's best interests, taking into account the evolution of their faculties. This implies the prohibition of any coercion, repression or imposition of certain beliefs against their will, even if the minor lacks sufficient maturity.[17]

A separate issue is that of the different criteria existing between parents regarding the religious education of the children, and we find ourselves before young children, whom we cannot imagine exercising their right to religious freedom autonomously.

Case law unanimously asserts that the religious beliefs of the parents cannot be taken into account, on their own, as a determining factor for the modulation of the rights specific to parent–child relations. Conflict caused by the opposing wishes of parents regarding a minor's education in a particular religion are difficult to settlement in Spanish courts, especially when, as on many occasions, a dispute between the parents is the actual underlying issue rather than substantial religious grounds. In any case, and in spite of the absence of clear criteria on behalf of Spanish courts, the commonly followed rule is that of continuity in the education received, although this prevailing criterion will not be followed if the minor does not show themselves in favour of religious education.

The court ruling must be based on the specific circumstances and details of the case in hand, and should be adopted after having weighed up the possible risks and benefits the different options offered by the parents will imply for the minor, taking into account that it is an evolving reality and that, therefore, any estimation of that which constitutes their best interest at the time should be made from the perspective of the correct development of their personality, which is being shaped. In this task the judge should set aside their personal beliefs on the issues being addressed in the trial—which we have seen can be achieved—and decide according to the minor's best interest.[18] The recent reform of the Organic Law on the Protection of Children and Young People has introduced two elements that, for the matter at hand, are in our view of crucial importance for the correct interpretation of the minor's interest:[19] first, the minor's opinion, which should be taken into account in all decisions that affect them, regardless of their age;[20] and, second, the child's identity, which should be preserved with the objective of guaranteeing their harmonious development.[21]

As Rivero Hernández (2000) rightly points out, there is a need to distinguish the child's right to religious freedom—which they are entitled to exercise, as we have seen—from their interest in this matter. The matter revolves around avoiding any negative impact on the minor; "this interest lies outstandingly in the pacific enjoyment of their religious options", avoiding any type of crisis, which can be easily provoked by arguments, pressures or tensions on religious matters. This criterion seems to be met by some of our court decisions, by ruling against the criterion of continuity with the objective of avoiding further damage resulting from involving the child in the conflict between their parents.[22]

Notes

1 The Convention on the Rights of the Child, expressly states: "the child, by reason of his physical and mental immaturity, needs special safeguards and care, including appropriate legal protection, before as well as after birth"; in the same manner, the European Charter on Children's Rights considers a child as "one of the most sensitive categories of the population, with specific needs that must be satisfied and protected"; and in Spanish law, the Organic Law on the Legal Protection of Children and Young People sees children as in need of protection because of their age.
2 Law 11/1981, 13 May, amendment of the Civil Code with regards to parent–child relation, parental authority and the financial regime of marriage. (*BOE* no. 119, of 19 May 1981).
3 On the new consideration of parental authority in the Spanish legal system, see, e.g., Martín Sánchez, I. Patria potestad y libertad religiosa del menor en la jurisprudencia sobre el Convenio europeo de Derechos Humanos. In Castro Jover, A., *Derecho de Familia y libertad de conciencia en los países de la Unión Europea y el Derecho Comparado. Actas del IX Congreso Internacional de Derecho Eclesiástico del Estado* (San Sebastián, 1–3 de junio de 2000): 585–602. Universidad del País Vasco, 2001; Cubillas Recio, M. La enseñanza de la religión en el sistema español y su fundamentación en el derecho de los padres sobre la formación religiosa de sus hijos. Laicidad y libertades. *Escritos jurídicos* 2002; 2: 205–208; Ureña Carazo, B. Hacia una corresponsabilidad parental: la superación de la distinción entre patria potestad y guardia y custodia. *Revista de Derecho de Familia* 2015; 69: 49–69.
4 De Diego-Lora, C. El menor centro de atribución de los derechos en las relaciones paterno-filiales. In Viladrich, P. J. (Dir.) El derecho de visita de los menores en las crisis matrimoniales. *Teoría y praxis*: 443–454. Pamplona; 1982.
5 Judgement of the Supreme Court, 11 October 1994, F. J. 2. See: Ureña Carazo, B. Hacia una corresponsabilidad parental: la superación de la distinción entre patria potestad y guardia y custodia. *Revista de Derecho de Familia* 2015; 69: 49–69.
6 Romero Coloma, A. M. Conflictos derivados del ejercicio de la patria potestad. *Revista Aranzadi Doctrinal* 2015; 4: 179–194.
7 Navarro Michel, M. Comentario a la Sentencia de 11 de diciembre de 2014 (RJ 2014, 6539). *Revista Cuadernos Civitas de Jurisprudencia Civil* 2015; 98: 419–434. See also, Romero Coloma, A. M. Conflictos derivados del ejercicio de la patria potestad. *Revista Aranzadi Doctrinal* 2015; 4: 179–194; Díaz Martínez, A. La determinación del lugar de residencia del menor como conflicto en el ejercicio conjunto de la patria potestad por progenitores no convivientes. *Revista Doctrinal Aranzadi Civil-Mercantil* 2013; 9: 1–11.
8 Article 156 of the Spanish Civil Code empowers either parent to apply to a judge as a means of resolving any disagreements between parents.
9 See: Souto Galván, B. La libertad de creencias y el interés superior del menor. *Revista Europea de Derechos Fundamentales* 2016; 28: 191–220.
10 Puente Alcubilla, V. *Minoría de edad, religión y derecho*. Madrid, 2001.
11 Ruano Espina, L. *El derecho a elegir, en el ámbito escolar, la educación religiosa y moral que esté de acuerdo con las propias convicciones, en el marco de la LOLR. Revista General de Derecho*

Canónico y Derecho Eclesiástico del Estado (RGDCDEE) 2009; 19. Iustel.com. The same, Objeción de conciencia a la Educación para la Ciudadanía. *RGDCDEE* 2008; 17. Iustel. com; Constitucional Court judgement, 13 February 1981, F. J. 9.

12 Aláez Corral, B. *Minoría de edad y derechos fundamentales.* Madrid, 2003.
13 García Vilardell, M. R. La libertad de creencias del menor y las potestades educativas paternas: la cuestión del derecho de los padres a la formación religiosa y moral de sus hijos. *Revista Española de Derecho Canónico* 2009; 66: 325–351.
14 Bercovitz Rodriguez-Cano, R. Derecho de los progenitores a la formación religiosa y moral de sus hijos. *Revista Doctrinal Aranzadi Civil-Mercantil* 2000; 8: 11–12.
15 Roca, M.J. Conflicto entre normas civiles y canónicas en relación con la patria potestad. *Anuario de Derecho Civil* 2015; 68: 63–92; Ramírez Navalón, R.M. Patria potestad y educación religiosa de los hijos menores. *Revista Boliviana de derecho* 2015; 19: 142–163.
16 Article 9.1 of the Organic Law on the Legal Protection of Children and Young People guaranteed the child's right to be heard without age limit.
17 Moreno Antón, M. Minoría de edad y libertad religiosa: estudio jurisprudencial. *Revista General de Derecho Canónico y Derecho Eclesiástico del Estado* 2009; 19: 1–37.
18 Rivero Hernández, F. Límites de la libertad religiosa y las relaciones personales de un padre con sus hijos. (Comentario de la STC 141/2000, de 29 de mayo). *Derecho Privado y Constitución* 2000; 14: 245–299.
19 Souto Galván, B. La libertad de creencias y el interés superior del menor. Revista *Europea de Derechos Fundamentales* 2016; 28: 191–220.
20 Article 9.1 of the Organic Law on the Legal Protection of Children and Young People.
21 Article 2 (d) of the Organic Law on the Legal Protection of Children and Young People.
22 See Note 18.

9

THE BEST INTERESTS OF THE CHILD IN SHARED PARENTING JUDGMENTS ACCORDING TO SPANISH LAW

Elena Goñi Huarte

Reasoning of judgments

The reasoning of judgments is regulated in Article 45 of the Convention for the Protection of Human Rights and Fundamental Freedoms (Rome, November 4, 1950, ratified by Spain on September 26, 1979[1]), which states that: "All judgments and the rulings declaring a claim admissible or inadmissible must be reasoned". Under Spanish law, there is a constitutional obligation to provide the reasoning behind a judgment.[2] Article 120.3 of the Spanish Constitution (hereinafter, CE) states that "judgments shall always be reasoned and announced at a public hearing. Article 117.1. CE also states that the judges and magistrates who belong to the judiciary are independent, irremovable, responsible and subject only to the rule of law. This is why Constitutional Court Decision (STC) 329/2006, of 20 November, considers that the requirement for judgments to be reasoned is directly related to the principles of the rule of law (Article 1.1 CE) and binding for judges and magistrates in exercising their jurisdictional powers (Article 117, paragraphs 1 and 3 CE) (Constitutional Court Judgments 24/1990, of February 15, 1990; 35/2002, of February 11, 2002; and 119/2003, of June 16, 2003).[3]

According to Spanish Civil Law, Article 1.7 of the Civil Code (hereinafter CC) regulates the inexcusable duty of judges and courts to resolve all cases held before them in accordance with the established system of sources of law. In civil procedural law (hereinafter, LEC), Article 218.2 also states that:

> judgments shall be reasoned by expressing the factual and legal reasons that lead to the assessment and evaluation of evidence, as well as the application and interpretation of the law. The reasoning must be based on the

different factual and legal elements of the case, considered both individually and jointly, always observing the rules of logic and reason.

Furthermore, the lack of grounds and reasoning behind a judgment may constitute a breach of the fundamental right recognized in Article 24.1 CE. As the Constitutional Court has repeatedly stated in its case law regarding the right to effective due process (Article 24.1 CE), this fundamental right, which does not guarantee the correct interpretation and application of the law, does however require that the judicial response to the claims filed by the parties and, if applicable, the decisions not to admit them, are based on consistent reasoning according to law. For a court decision to be considered as reasoned, it must not be arbitrary, unreasonable or manifestly mistaken.[4]

The Constitutional Court recognizes that the existence of adequate and sufficient reasoning is an essential guarantee for the defendant, since the expression of the most essential features of the reasoning behind a judicial body's decision allows its rationality to be determined, in addition to facilitating control by higher courts (Constitutional Court Judgment 329/2006, of November 20, 2006).[5] It even considers that Article 24 CE not only imposes an obligation upon judicial bodies to provide a reasoned response to all claims, but also that such a response has a legal content and is not arbitrary (Constitutional Court Judgment 118/2006, of April 24, 2006).[6]

Reasoning of judgments involving minors

Article 3.1 of the UN Convention on the Rights of the Child states that "in all actions concerning children, whether undertaken by public or private social welfare institutions, courts of law, administrative authorities or legislative bodies, the best interests of the child shall be a primary consideration". The current wording of Article 2 LOPJM (following its amendment by Organic Law 8/2015 of July 22, 2015[7]) states that "all minors have the right to have their best interests taken as a primary consideration in all actions or decisions that concern them (in both the public and private spheres". The article then defines the content of a child's best interests by regulating a series of general criteria for its interpretation and application (section 2: basic needs, the child's opinion, the family environment, the child's identity, non-discrimination and the development of personality) and providing a list of general elements or guidelines on the weighting of these criteria (section 3: age and maturity, equality, passage of time, stability, preparation for adult life, etc.).

In addition, Article 2.5 (d) LOPJM emphasizes that,

> all measures in the best interests of the child shall be adopted with due regard for procedural safeguards and, in particular: a decision which includes the criteria used in its reasoning, the elements applied in weighing up the criteria and all other present and future interests and procedural safeguards.

Furthermore, Article 9.3 LOPJM reiterates the obligation to provide the reasoning behind decisions in the best interests of the child, when the appearance or hearing of minors is denied in administrative or judicial proceedings.

This obligation to provide reasoning based on the criteria and elements regulated was also stated in the Preamble to Organic Law 8/2015, of 22 July, 2015, amending the system of protection of children and adolescents (which introduced the current wording of the LOPJM provisions)[8]:

> [I]t is clear that the determining of the best interests of the child in each case must be based on a number of accepted criteria and universal values that are recognized by legislators, taken into account and weighted according to the different facts and circumstances of the case and which must be explained in the reasoning behind the decision, in order to determine whether or not the principle has been correctly applied.

In this regard, when the decisions of judicial bodies involve the best interests of a minor, the Constitutional Court has stated that the constitutional level of reasonableness becomes more demanding, as values and principles of unquestionable constitutional importance are involved, given that the plaintiff invokes the principle of the best interests of the child, which is constitutionally protected by Article 39 CE, which it defines as the guiding principle that must inspire all the acts of both administrative and judicial bodies (STC 138/2014, of September 8, 2014[9]). Constitutional Court Judgment 69/2006, of 13 March, 2006, also considered that the fundamental right to effective due process (Article 24.1 CE) implies, first,

> that the decision must be sufficiently reasoned, in other words, contain the elements and reasons for judgment that led to the legal criteria used to reach the decision and, second, that the reasoning must be based on the law, which entails the guarantee that the decision is not the result of an arbitrary application of the law, nor is it manifestly unreasonable, subject to latent error or an evident contradiction between the fundamental points of law or between such points and the ruling, given that in such case, the application of the law would merely be apparent.[10]

In its ruling 482/2018, of July 23, 2018, the Supreme Court (hereinafter, TS) also required courts to provide special reasoning when adopting measures that affect minors.[11] Furthermore, it insisted on the fact that these cases should not convert the cassation appeal into a third instance, unless the review is necessary because the *a quo* court only provided protection of the minor in an apparent, purely formalistic and stereotyped manner (Supreme Court Judgment 194/2018, of April 6, 2018[12]).

In practice, however, "courts sometimes use the child's best interests and base their decisions on it, without specifying what they mean nor providing proper reasoning, which can lead to a lack of legal protection".[13]

Therefore, it has been claimed (based on a reference to General Comment 14 of the United Nations Committee on the Rights of the Child to "the right of the child to have his or her best interests taken as a primary consideration"),[14] that the

> assessment and defining of the best interests of the child will require procedural guarantees: the reasoning behind the judgment must be explicit in the reasoning of the decision and must specifically explain how the right has been taken into account, in other words, provide an explanation of what was considered as the child's best interests and what was examined to reach this conclusion.[15]

Reasoning in judgments on shared parenting

The granting of judicial guardianship and custody of a minor is one of the decisions that most directly affect minors and must therefore be taken in their best interests (Article 2.1 LOPJM).

The Civil Code regulates the granting of shared parenting in Article 92, after it was expressly established by Law 15/2005 of July 8, 2005. Since then, courts have been in favour of granting shared parenting. According to data published by the National Institute of Statistics, in 2018, shared parenting was granted in 33.8% of cases, as opposed to 17.9% in 2013.[16]

Article 92 CC only refers to the best interests of a minor in paragraph 8, by stating that:

> exceptionally, even when the requirements set forth in paragraph 5 of this article are not met, at the request of the Public Prosecutor, the court may rule shared parenting on the grounds that it is the only way to adequately protect the minor.

Interpreting this article, STS 257/2013, of 29 April, 2013, established case law in matters of shared parenting, by stating that it is not an exceptional measure, but rather a desirable one.[17] Accordingly,

> in a collision between two mandatory provisions, the first requiring shared parenting to be considered as an exceptional case and the second requiring that the minor's best interests take priority, the Supreme Court would have opted for the latter, denying the "exceptional" nature of shared parenting.[18]

However, Article 92 of the CC does not define the content of the minor's best interests nor the criteria for application when adopting measures on custody. It has been case law, in its interpretative role, that has pointed out how the best interests of a minor should be protected.

The first judgment by the Supreme Court that sets out the criteria to be used in order to protect the best interests of the minor when granting shared parenting was that of October 8, 2009, such criteria being the previous acts of the parents in their relations with the minor and their personal aptitudes; the wishes of the minor with capacity to decide; the number of children; fulfilment by the parents of their duties in relation to their children and mutual respect in their personal relations and other persons living in the family home; the agreements reached by the parents; the location of their respective homes, schedules and activities; the results of the mandatory reports and, in short, any other criteria that allow the minor to live an adequate life in a situation that is necessarily more complex than when the parents live together.[19]

The criteria established by case law were subsequently included in Organic Law 8/2015, of July 22, 2015, on the amendment of the system of protection of children and adolescents introduced by the current regulation of Article 2 LOPJM. The Preamble states that,

> in order to provide content to the concept mentioned, Article 2 is amended to include both recent Supreme Court case law and the criteria set forth in General Comment 14, of May 29, 2013 by the United Nations Committee on the Rights of the Child, with respect to the right of the child to have his or her best interests taken as a primary consideration.

The second paragraph of Article 2 LOPJM therefore lists the current general criteria for the interpretation and application of the best interests of the child (his or her basic needs, the child's opinion, the family environment, the child's identity, non-discrimination and the development of personality) and a list of general elements or guidelines for the weighting of the above criteria (paragraph 3: age and maturity, equality, period of time, stability, preparation for adult life, etc.).

This list of criteria and elements is not restricted, given that Article 2.2 LOPJM states that others may be considered appropriate in light of the specific circumstances of the case. Legislators leave "the door open to the possibility of applying the principle to specific cases that do not coincide with the general criteria proposed below, always giving priority to the legitimate interests of the minor over others that may be applicable".[20]

Since 2015, Article 2 LOPJM has included criteria for the application and interpretation of the best interests of minors and a series of elements for the weighting of such criteria. However, it is not a voluntary but a mandatory rule: "the following general criteria shall be taken into account ... These criteria shall be weighted according to the following general elements." The question is, then: are these criteria and elements used to reason the granting of shared parenting? To answer this question, we performed an analysis of Supreme Court case law. We specifically analysed the judgments that resolved extraordinary appeals against procedural infringement in cases of shared parenting from 2009 to 2019 (a total of 22 judgments).[21]

We focused on the resolution of extraordinary appeals for procedural infringement because they are those that allow for appeals against judgments that breach procedural rules (Article 469.1.2° LEC), among them, the need for reasoning, Article 218.2 LEC:

judgments shall be reasoned by expressing the factual and legal reasoning that leads to the assessment and evaluation of the evidence, as well as the application and interpretation of the law. The reasoning must be based on the different factual and legal elements of the case, considered both individually and jointly, always observing the rules of logic and reason.

First, we analysed the existence or not of reasoning, given that, as established in STS 229/2012, of April 19, 2012, the existence of reasoning should not be mistaken for reasoning that best protects the interests of the litigant. The Provincial Court based its argument against shared parenting on the benefit/interests of the minor and the lack of a request from the parents, a requirement established in Article 92 of the Civil Code, as seen in section 5 of this ruling. Therefore, it must be concluded that there is sufficient reasoning for the purposes of Article 218 LEC.[22] Second, we examined how the best interests of the minor were present in the reasoning, given that, as indicated in STC 176/2008, of December 22, 2008, the best interests of the child operate precisely as a counterweight to the rights of each parent and obliges the judicial authority to weigh up both the need and the proportionality of the measure regulating the custody of the child.[23]

Twenty-two Supreme Court judgments resolving extraordinary appeals against procedural infringement in cases of shared parenting were analysed and divided into three groups:

(a) In seven judgments, the Supreme Court acknowledges a lack of sufficient reasoning.

STS 500/2019, of September 27, 2019, states that the challenged judgment in no way reaches the minimum level of sufficient reasoning required and therefore breaches the right to effective due process.[24] STS 215/2019, of April 5, 2019, considers that the contested judgment bases its position on inconsistent, inaccurate and incomplete data and merely mentions the benefits of maintaining the form of custody without contrasting it.[25] STS 630/2018, of November 13, 2018, states that the challenged judgment not only contains a lack, but rather a total absence of reasoning and that the arguments that led the court of appeal to change shared parenting and grant it to the mother are unknown.[26] STS 323/2012, of May 25, 2012, states that the reasons appearing in the contested judgment only rhetorically take into account the interests of the child and that no criteria integrating the interests of the child are applied in granting custody.[27]

STS 759/2011, of November 2, 2011, considered the reasoning to be insufficient, as the judgment subject to appeal was based on the sole grounds of a "lack of communication" between the spouses.[28] STS 496/2011, of July 7, 2011, stated that the reasoning was not sufficient, because it did not clearly express the circumstances that led to the revoking of the measure for the couple's two young children.[29] STS 623/2009, of October 8, 2009, considered that the reasoning was not sufficient to justify the refusal to revoke joint guardianship and custody, because the change in circumstances was not justified and did not state what the circumstances were nor how they could affect the interests of the children.[30]

(b) In eleven judgments, sufficient reasoning was recognized, but not based on the criteria and elements of Article 2 LOPJM.

STS 124/2019, of February 26, 2019, stated that the passing of time and the adaptation of the child to single-parent custody could not be used as grounds to refuse a change to shared parenting.[31] STS 157/2017, of March 7, 2017, stated that there was no lack of reasoning, given that, even if briefly, the ruling expressed the reasons that led to the judgment. In other words, they justified the reasons for establishing a shared parenting regime. However the opinion of the minor was still unknown, as she was not given the opportunity to be heard; an opinion that is especially relevant in view of the circumstance of exclusively living with her father since she was seven years old and her current age.[32]

STS 194/2016, of March 29, 2016, stated that it was sufficient to comply with the reasoning requirement if the grounds for the decision and the reasoning on which the judgment is based are expressed. However, it considered that the judgment not only ignores case law on shared parenting, but also goes beyond the provisions of national and international regulations on the interests of the child and resolves the case without a specific reference to the child, who is seven years old, while maintaining the exclusive custody of the mother.[33] STS 55/2016, of February 11, 2016, stated that the contested judgment is sufficiently reasoned as to ultimately find in the case at hand that routine is established as grounds for the denial of shared parenting.[34]

STS 390/2015, of June 26, 2015, states that the judgment allows both the party now appealing and the Court to know the reasons why the claim for shared parenting was rejected, but adds that it only assesses the previous custody agreement, without specifying the interests of the child, which petrifies the child's situation since the time of the agreement, without taking into account the changes that have occurred since then.[35] STS 658/2015, of November 17, 2015, rejected the appeal, as the judgment takes into account all elements of the debate and considers that the current system of custody is very similar to that of shared parenting, made more flexible by mutual agreement, with both parents maintaining a common educational project and having equal educational skills.[36]

STS 619/2014, of October 30, 2014, states that the reasoning is clearly expressed in the contested judgment, as the provisionally adopted custody system worked to the benefit of the child, regardless of whether or not the reasoning was acceptable.[37] STS 200/2014, of April 25, 2014, acknowledges that the judgment should have been more fully reasoned, but that it met the requirement of reasoning because it expressed the reasons that led to a different solution regarding shared parenting and whether or not this criterion is appropriate is a matter of the dispute itself and not related to the requirement for the judgment to be reasoned.[38]

STS 757/2013, of November 29, 2013, stated that it was true that the judgment does not provide sufficient reasoning in relation to the expert report submitted by the

Court's technical team in relation to the custody of the daughters, nor did it specify the documented evidence supporting its decision.[39] STS 745/2012, of December 10, 2012, stated that a simple reading of the contested judgment showed that it was reasoned, as it states that the children had adapted to the current situation of spending the majority of time with their mother, with very broad visiting rights for the father and that, although the father had the capacity to have custody, there was no reason to change it.[40]

STS 659/2011, of October 3, 2011, considered that the contested judgment contained reasoning that went beyond mere explanation and that the case was analysed according to the applicable regulation of which, although not directly stated, the appellant was aware, while expressly establishing the grounds against granting the appellant's petition with respect to shared parenting.[41]

(c) In four judgments, sufficient reasoning is acknowledged and considered to be based on the criteria and elements of Article 2 LOPJM.

STS 389/2017, of June 20, 2017, recognizes that the examination of the minor was not irrelevant and, following the subsidiary proposal of the Public Prosecutor, agreed to shared parenting on the understanding that it was in the child's best interests. It also refers to the existence of another sister, whose custody is not subject to dispute. All this data shows that the challenged decision was sufficiently reasoned, as it enables the parties to understand the grounds for the decision and control of the judgment by the Supreme Court (Article 218 LEC and Article 24 CE).[42] STS 518/2017, of September 22, 2017, considered that the judgment sufficiently reasons the contested decision, insofar as it takes into account the age of the child, the care that the mother had been providing before the divorce, the availability of time for each parent and the external support they received, the elements of judgment that justify the revoking of the court's judgment having therefore been expressed (Article 218.2 LEC).[43]

STS 23/2017, of January 17, 2017, rejects the claim by the appellant of a lack of reasoning in the first instance court's judgment, for being insufficient and inconsistent (Article 218 LEC) and because the conviction of the husband for threatening his partner and his family and the prohibition of communication prevented the adoption of shared parenting, given that it required a rational relationship that enabled the exchange of information and reasonable consensus on the interests of the children, which was visibly lacking.[44]

STS 276/2016, of April 25, 2016, considered that the Court's ruling, upheld by the National Court, comprehensively and consistently analysed the issue of shared parenting, on which most of the debate was focused, evaluating the evidence in such a way that certain evidence was considered more relevant by the Court (Articles 217 and 218 LEC) with reasoning that guaranteed due process (Article 24 CE). The analysis carried out is not illogical and is based on the witness statements and examination of the minor, evidence that was considered more relevant than the expert reports.[45]

Finally, it should be pointed out that the failure to provide the reasoning of a judgment on shared parenting is also subject to appeal before the Constitutional Court, on the grounds of a breach of the fundamental right to effective due process (Article 24 CE). STC 148/1994, of May 12, 1994, stated that:

> Article 24.1 CE, as this Court has repeatedly declared, does not guarantee the correctness of court decisions, meaning that the choice and interpretation of the applicable legal provision corresponds exclusively to the judicial body, with no other exception than cases in which the judicial decision is manifestly unfounded, arbitrary or may not be considered as an expression of justice, but merely an appearance thereof. For the purposes of Article 24(1) CE, the issue is therefore not one of greater or lesser correctness in the interpretation of the law, but rather one of respect for the very scope of the constitutional appeal for remedy against arbitrariness and manifest unreasonableness and to ensure sufficient reasoning.[46]

With regard to the best interests of the child, in proceedings 28/2001 of February 1, 2001, the Constitutional Court itself declared that it can only verify

> whether the reasoning of a court judgment takes into account such interests, that no fundamental rights have been breached and that the determining of the best interests of the child in each specific case is a matter outside this jurisdiction, as it corresponds to the courts.[47]

To date, the breach of a minor's best interests has been associated with the fundamental right to effective due process in several issues relating to minors. In the area of fostering, the Constitutional Court pointed out that the principle of the best interests of the child should inspire judicial action in all matrimonial and family law proceedings and that, in this context, the reinforced standard of effective due process is applicable (STC 65/2016, of April 11, 2016).[48]

In the area of international child abduction, the Constitutional Court stated that, due to the involvement of a minor, Constitutional Court control extended to ensure that the reasoning specifically included an express weighting that identified the best interests of the minor and the assets and rights at stake that were claimed by each party (STC 16/2016, of February 1, 2016).[49] The Constitutional Court has also stated that the constitutional sufficiency of the reasoning and legal grounds of judgments is also considered in terms of the rationality of the results in terms of the minor's best interests (STC 127/2013, of June 3, 2013).[50]

Finally, with respect to the visiting rights granted to grandparents, STC 138/2014, of September 8, 2014, claimed that there was an absolute lack of weighting of the principle of the child's best interests in this area of decision making, which meant that the decision was unfounded according to the constitutional standard required to exercise the right to effective due process (Article 24.1 CE in relation to Article 39 CE).[51]

Conclusions

To comply with the requirement of reasoning in judgments, it is not sufficient for such reasoning to exist and certain grounds claimed for granting or refusing shared parenting. The reasoning must be based on law. The right of minors to have their best interests taken as a primary consideration (Article 2.1 LOPJM) must prevail in this reasoning. The criteria and elements that allow the application and interpretation of such interests in each specific case (Articles 2.2. and 2.3 LOPJM) must be identified in the reasoning behind judgments on shared parenting.

A lack of reasoning based on the best interests of the child in judgments granting shared parenting may be challenged before the Supreme Court by means of an extraordinary appeal for procedural infringement.

According to this study, we can conclude that, in the majority of the analysed Supreme Court judgments resolving an extraordinary appeal for procedural infringement due to a lack of reasoning, the reasoning is deficient. Of the 22 judgments analysed, it should be highlighted that, in seven cases, there was a lack of sufficient reasoning; in 11 judgments, reasoning was provided but not based on the criteria and elements of Article 2 LOPJM; and in only four judgments was correct reasoning acknowledged, according to the criteria and elements of Article 2 LOPJM.

Finally, it should be pointed out that the failure to provide the reasoning behind a judgment is also subject to appeal before the Constitutional Court for breach of the fundamental right to effective due process (Article 24 CE).

Notes

1 *Official State Gazette* no. 243, October 10, 1979. Retrieved from www.boe.es/buscar/doc.php?id=BOE-A-1979-24010.
2 The abbreviations of the laws and judgments included in this chapter correspond to Spanish legislation and courts.
3 RTC 2006\329.
4 STC of December 15, 2003(RTC 2003\224):

> It is true that, logically, an absence of grounds and reasoning is not the same as grounds and reasoning that should be deemed as inexistent, due to their level of arbitrariness or unreasonableness, but it is also true that this Court would incur an excessive formality if it accepted as grounds and reason-based decisions those which, at first glance and without the need for further intellectual and deductive effort, are proved to be based on non-existent or evidently erroneous premises, or follow a line of reasoning with errors in logic of such a magnitude that the conclusions reached may not be considered as based on any of the alleged reasons.

5 RTC 2006\329.
6 RTC 2006\118.
7 Preamble of LO 8/2015, 22 July, on the amendment of the protection system of children and adolescents:

> to provide content for the aforementioned concept, Article 2 is amended to include both recent Supreme Court case law and the criteria set forth in General Comment 14, of May 29, 2013 by the United Nations Committee on the Rights of the Child, with respect to the right of the child to have his or her best interests taken as a primary consideration ...

8 Following on from the Preamble, above, on the changes introduced by LO 8/2015, 22 July, on the amendment of the protection system of children and adolescents:

> The content of this concept is threefold. Firstly, it is a substantive law, in the sense that the child has the right, when a measure concerning him/her is adopted, for his/her best interests to be taken into consideration and, in the event other interests are present, that they have been analysed when reaching a solution. Secondly, it is a general interpretation principle, which means that if a legal provision can be interpreted in more than one way, the interpretation which best responds to the child's best interests must be chosen. However, ultimately, this principle is a procedural regulation.

9 STC of September 8, 2014 (RCT\2014\138):

> there is an absolute lack of analysis of the principle of the child's best interests in this decision-making area that renders the resolution as unfounded, pursuant to the constitutional standards required by law for effective legal guardianship.
> *(art. 24.1 CE in relation to art. 39 CE)*

10 RTC 2006\69; Constitutional Court Judgments 147/1999, of August 4, 1999; 25/2000, of January 31, 2000; 87/2000, of March 27, 2000; 82/2001, of March 26, 2001; 221/2001, of October 31, 2001; 55/2003, of March 24, 2003; 223/2005, of September 12, 2005; and 276/2006, of September 25, 2006, including many others.
11 (RJ\2018\2966). STS of March 23, 2018, also highlights the need for a psycho-social report that assists the court in its decision and establishes that this procedure cannot be omitted without comprehensive reasoning (RJ\2018\1275).
12 JR\2018\1430.
13 For academic comments on this topic, see Verdera (2019).
14 General Observation 14:

> To demonstrate that the rights of the child have been respected with regard to his/her best interests being taken as a primary consideration, all decisions regarding a child or children must be based on grounds, justified and explained. The reasoning should explicitly state all the factual circumstances relating to the child, the elements that have been deemed pertinent for assessment of his or her best interests, the content of the elements in this specific case and the way in which they have been considered in order to determine such interests.
> *(https://tbinternet.ohchr.org/_layouts/15/treatybodyexternal/Download. aspx?symbolno=CRC%2fC%2fGC%2f14&Lang=en)*

15 Cardona (2013).
16 INE. Statistics on Annulments, Separations and Divorces (SNSD) Year 2013. www.ine.es/prensa/np867.pdf.
17 RJ 2013\3269.
18 De Torres (2016), 8.
19 STS of October 8, 2009 (RJ 2009\2606).
20 De la Iglesia (2015), 2.
21 Although the criteria and elements that define the concept of the child's best interests in the current LOPJM cannot be applied to previous facts, STS of November 19, 2015 states that they are comparable as a hermeneutic model (RJ 2015\5495).
22 RJ 2012\5909.
23 STC of December 22, 2008 (RTC 2008\176).
24 RJ 2019\4034.
25 RJ 2019\1791.
26 RJ 2018\4930.
27 RJ 2012\6542.
28 RJ 2012\1239.
29 RJ 2011\5008.

30 RJ 2009\4606.
31 RJ 2019\631.
32 RJ 2018\703.
33 RJ 2016\995.
34 RJ 2016\249.
35 RJ 2015\2658.
36 RJ 2015\5392.
37 RJ 2014\5268.
38 RJ 2014\2651.
39 RJ 2013\7449.
40 RJ 2013/204.
41 RJ 2011\7381.
42 RJ 2017\3052.
43 RJ 2017\4868.
44 RJ 2017\352.
45 RJ 2016\1703.
46 RTC 1994\148.
47 RTC 2001\28.
48 RTC 2016\65.
49 RTC 2016\16.
50 LA LEY 87218/2013.
51 RTC 2014\138.

References

Cardona J. La evaluación y determinación del interés superior del niño. *Revista española de derecho internacional* 2013; 65.

De Torres J. Estudio de la función atribuida al interés del menor como cláusula general por una relevante línea jurisprudencial, *Diario La Ley* 2016; 8737.

De la Iglesia M. Ley Orgánica de modificación del sistema de protección a la infancia y a la adolescencia: las garantías de una protección uniforme a los menores más vulnerables en base a su supremo interés. *Diario La Ley* 2015; 8590.

Verdera B. *La actual configuración jurídica del interés del menor. De la discrecionalidad a la concreción.* Cizur Menor, Navarra: Aranzadi Thomson Reuters, 2019.

10
INFORMATIONAL PHYSIOLOGY OF INDIVIDUAL DEVELOPMENT

Peter Beyerlein

In 2021 we are able to extract DNA and RNA sequences from each and every organism and we have now learned a lot about the molecular reality of reproduction, inheritance and individual development. Finally, we are able to reconstruct and understand the physiologic mechanisms leading to cell differentiation, organ differentiation, development of a person's character, that is, developing into the physiological individuum.

The *genome* (or genetic code) of a child is 6 billion A,T,G,C letters long, 3 billion from the father, 3 billion from the mother; it is established by only one parental interaction, the procreation of a zygote. The male and female donors of the two involved genomes are called throughout this text 'the biological parents'. The result of procreation fits into 1.5 GByte of binary memory, a small USB stick.

After years, a child has grown into billions of cells, each carrying the same copy of the original (procreated) genome. But all cells are different and follow a different program, although they all have the same genetic code. Identical twins with exactly the same genetic code – although showing quite impressive similarities – are still developing into completely independent and different personalities. All with the same genetic code. The differentiation of the zygote and its daughter cells into different tissues and organs, as a fundamental part of embryonic development, is a known and an undisputed fact. Analysis of genetically identical twins shows precisely that the genetic code at procreation is not sufficient to control the final outcome of development. There is another factor – the 'environment' the twins grow up in (We define here the environment as 'anything other than the genetic code'). Even small environmental differences, e.g. different first names or different locations in their mother's uterus, make them develop (slightly) differently. The longer they live, the more different they are.

But where does all this differentiation come from, where is the code for it, what is the mechanism behind it and ... what has all this to do with shared parentship?

For decades we observed the systematics of embryonic development, followed by child development after birth into a mature person – and realized, following thousands of research studies, that mother nature follows here a well-organized plan. From decades of observation, we also learned that somehow we are influencing this development by shaping the environment around the developing embryo or child. The influence might be healthy or adverse and may, in bad cases, lead to physiological, mental, emotional dysfunction, even though the genetic code of the person did not alter.

The molecular-level mechanism could not be explained due to the absence of observable or measurable facts. Today, however, we can explain it because we can measure it, and here I will provide, hopefully understandable as a result of some simplifications, insights to the reader, whether that person be a judge, lawyer, psychologist, teacher or, even more challenging, politician.

What makes us individual?

In the constitution of my country, Germany, as in the constitutions of many other countries, the first articles define the primary rights of the 'individual' human being to exist, develop optimally and act freely (within certain parameters, e.g. not harming others).

But what makes us individual, what is the physiological (and thus measurable) carrier of 'individuality'? An answer to this question could help answer many other difficult questions.

A first level of individuality is given by the 1.5 GByte of genetic information. So, the DNA molecule[1] is a physiologic carrier of genetic individuality that is inherited from the biological parents. However, it would feel not right if our entire individual personality could fit on a memory stick. From the many conflicts with my wife, I am very certain that we are both much more complex than a mere 1.5 GByte. And I am sure – at least on this question – that she would agree.

The genetic code is obviously important. It is the starting point when it comes to individual development, which makes sense as it is procreated together with – that is, at the same time as – as the zygote, the origin of the embryo. It provides all building plans for the later organism.

But from that procreation point in time onwards, the genetic code is fixed and just copied again and again into all the daughter cells throughout the life of the organism, which finally comprises 30 trillion cells, all of which develop out of this 1.5 GByte information, from this one zygote.

So, the big and important question remains: what physiological mechanism makes us develop out of one fixed 1.5 GByte code set into a complex human being?

The answer is very simple and very small[2-4]: it is a molecular switch, located on each of the DNA letters. Its molecular structure had already been discovered in the 1970s but, due to the absence of whole genome data – and, to be honest, also our underdeveloped understanding of the concepts of 'information' and 'evolution' – we did not discover its fundamental function. It is a switch, i.e. one 'bit' of information. We have *6 billion such bits* per cell, as we have 6 billion DNA letters, each carrying one of these bits, which might hold important information for the cell. In this chapter I call this switch/bit a 'toggle', and the specific on and off status of a set of toggles, a 'toggle pattern', which codes certain low- and higher-level human functions. The whole genome analysis arriving in 2000, combined with tremendous progress in protein research, allowed us to uncover three fundamental myths about how special the human is. Proteins were first in upright gait, proteins were first in information processing and storing Terrabytes of data, and proteins were first in socializing, democratic voting, dictatorship and city-like organizations – and all this already billions of years ago.

The epigenetic toggle and its effect on cell differentiation

We estimate the number of protein species (different kinds of proteins) to be 500.000–1.000.000. The structure of each of the proteins depends on the construction plan, found in the gene sequence in the 1.5 Gbyte individual genetic code of the embryo, child or person. I am referring you here to a nice and regularly updated textbook by the nobel laureate James Watson et al.: *Molecular Biology of the Gene*, 7th edition [1]. In addition to this very informative book thousands of publications exist in which scientists investigate many toggle patterns and their resulting phenotype[5-11]. To go into detail here would not help the reader. Instead, I will try to explain the fundamental concept of this toggling mechanism and its consequences for the developing organism:

1. The toggles are not changing the genetic information, an A stays an A, a T stays a T, a G stays a G and a C stays a C, no matter if the toggle is switched on or off.
2. The toggles change the availability of proteins in the cell by masking out some or many proteins – thus reducing a big 'omnipotent' but also chaotic set of proteins to a specialized set of proteins – thus creating a specially-skilled cell: a stem cell has all toggles switched on – all proteins are produced by the cell. The cell is omnipotent. Differentiation away from the stem cell into a specific cell (e.g. kidney cell) works by toggling off a set of genes; thus toggling of construction plans and regulatory plans of proteins leaves only a subset of specialized proteins (e.g. those required in a kidney cell) remaining toggled on.
3. The goal of this toggling mechanism (as of other similar epigenetic information processing mechanisms) is adaptation and specialization, managing the required protein subset in the cell – and saving the resulting blueprint of this management for the future – to the daughter cells – in the form of the DNA-imprinted toggle pattern.

We herewith uncover myth number 4: We humans did not invent the 'writing'!

The DNA-imprinting of cellular regulation information is highly sophisticated and much more informative than human cave painting or some twenty-first-century literature. And it is performed to protect and transmit knowledge to the next generation of the own 'family' of cells.

4. The mechanism is not acting by chance, it is acting 'smart'. It learns, while interacting with the environment of the cell, to produce optimal reactions. That is, by the way, the only reason why it makes sense to write the resulting information down on the DNA, by chemically 'pressing' the toggles.
5. But there is one big difficulty: once the toggles are pressed they are unable to go back into a neutral position! A wrong toggle pressed – imprinted and inherited by the daughter cells – and all future life of this cell-family or species will have to live with it. (And here you might for the first time realize why a bioinformatician is contributing a chapter to a book about parenting.)

Thus, in short, we have found the answer to why we have only one genetic code in each and every of the 30 trillion cells in our body, but we have many different cell types: each cell type is characterized by its toggle pattern, its 'epigenetic code'.

Summary

The toggle pattern induced by cell-specific epigenetic learning defines the specific cell type. It is noted down as though in a textbook as a chemically implemented imprint on the DNA molecule. Differentiation of cells during embryonic development is facilitated by copying one and the same genetic code plus the cells toggle pattern. Thereafter during the lifetime of the cell it is further changing its pattern into another sub-pattern, by which it becomes a new sub-cell type, with a new sub-function. If the cell works efficiently, it will subdivide further and define a new tissue type.

This is the mechanism, which explains the development at embryonic stage into tissues, organs, body parts. And at the same time a logbook of all the developmental steps is written down by them too: the imprinted toggle patterns on the DNA molecules of all cells are assembling a huge and distributed logbook of each and every part of the development process, another book of life, that is stored for future cellular generations on the DNA molecule. How many pages has this logbook?

Quantitative analysis of the differentiation capacity of the human body

How many cell types can evolve from one genetic code?

Six billion toggles give $2^{6.000.000.000}$ potential toggle patterns, which is about $10^{600.000.000}$. Thus, one parental genetic code can still generate all sorts of cell-types. Those types include everything that can be 'developed' out of the original zygote, e.g. all known

Informational physiology

healthy tissue cells, but also cells carrying all kinds of dysfunction (traumata, drug addiction, diabetes, cancer, etc.). This means that, within the limits of the parental genetic library, individual development is an open-ended process.

How long is the logbook of human development and what is the total number of toggles in a mature person?

A grown human is composed of about 30 trillion cells, e.g. $3·10^{13}$ cells. Each cell contains its DNA with the 6 billion letters genetic code plus the 6 billion toggles, e.g. $6·10^9$ bit. The human body carries, therefore, a total of $3·10^{13}$ cells times $6·10^9$ bit/cell, which sums up to a logbook length of $18·10^{22}$ bit specialization information capacity.

To imagine this capacity, we compare it to the memory capacity of a library and that of the human brain:

Library: If we fill books at 3000 letters per page, 1000 pages makes a thickness of 5cm. We would thus require a bookshelf 375 billion kilometers in length, or about 50–70 times the distance to the outer planet Pluto. Now you can imagine how complicated we are.

Brain: A human brain stores about $2.5·10^{15}$ Byte (2.5 Petabyte) of information. Let's calculate how many brain capacities fit into the specialization capacity: $18·10^{22}$ bit/ $20·10^{15}$ bit. The result is $0.9·10^7 = 9.000.000$, or 9 million brains.

Conclusion: The total logbook (toggle pattern imprint) of our individual development out of the original zygote is 9 million times larger than the total memory capacity of the human brain. That's larger than any computer system in the world, so we can debunk myth no. 5: The human is not the first species to invent and create huge computational machines.

Can such a capacity ever be filled and what are the data rates, then?

Eighteen years (our official formal time for personal development) equates to approximately 9 million minutes. The logbook is 9 million brain capacities large, and these have to be filled within 9 million minutes (this maths exercise should be easy): we arrive at one brain capacity per minute.

On average, within one minute of a child's lifetime, their cellular-level body learns and stores epigenetic information in a volume that is (if totally exploited) equal to the capacity of one complete mature human brain. (This is, of course, simplified and an average to make matters easier for the reader.)

The processing speed of our brain is 30 quadrillion = $3·10^{16}$ bit operations per second or higher. The required time our brain needs for processing all the logbook entries memorized in our body depends on the level of detail and task the brain is trying to solve; that is, ranging from seconds (organ-level compression factor 1 billion) to weeks (uncompressed full epigenome).

The individiuum and the physiological 'me'

Following on from this maths exercise, we now come up with a simple formula for the epigenetic system capacity:

Inherited $6·10^9$ bit genetic code (memory stick size library from our parents)
+ $18·10^{22}$ bit individual toggle pattern (life experience capacity of cells)
= physiological memory of the individual development
= physiological memory of the 'current individual' (the physiological 'me')

Although single cell sequencing is an available technology, we would not be able to read-out the complete information on the individual's development cell by cell because the required storage (remember the 50 bookshelves to Pluto?) is technically not available. It's a funny fact that 7.5 billion such storage systems are walking around on earth but we are not able to read-out one of them in detail. The phrase 'reading another person' also takes on an interesting meaning.
If we cannot read-out, how do we know that we are storing anything?

The practical proof of the existence of a memory carrying all specialization information is again simple and understandable: within about seven years almost all cells of the human body are substituted by their descendent cells. Which means that, after seven years, we are no longer the same physiological person. We are 'new'. In some tissues (digestive system, lung), all cells are renewed within two–nine days. The liver is renewed after between six months to two years. Bones have a long renewal time of 10 years. Some organs also have a long renewal time. Hence, our body will not be the same after days, weeks or months. Many new cells are taking over. Still, the results of our child development persist. We look the same, feeling the same, behave in the same way. What, then, happens to the $18·10^{22}$ bit physiological differentiation information, developed over decades during childhood; does it vanish with the cells carrying it?

The answer is: our development and differentiation never stops; not at 18, 30 or 87 years of age. It continues in the same way but slows down over time. And, of course, in this process cells continue to write the logbook and inherit its content to pass on to the next generation. So, when one cell generation is ending its life, the younger generation is already in possession of the written books and continues to add to them and the process continues. Cells thus also have parentship issues.

Epigenetic health

Epigenetic toggles[9–12] are set by the developing organism over its whole period of individual development. Setting a toggle as a result of interaction of the cell with its environment is called in this chapter 'epigenetic learning'. The learning rate capacity at cellular level is, on average about one brain per minute, so each and every minute in a developing child's life seems to be as important as one brain. This biological learning process, in which the cells, tissues, organs, the whole individuum, is learning in and from its environment has one clear goal: survival of the fittest, that is, to become the most effective, strongest and smartest.

This overall programming approach has two phases:

Phase 1: uploading of the genetic code, i.e. programming the library received from parents
Phase 2: learning to set the toggle mask correctly, i.e. programming the library and writing the results into the logbook

It is a powerful trick performed by nature because it allows for efficient adaptation to the environment in which the organism is growing up: *adaptation by self-programming in the target environment.* That's how the embryo and later the child develops at the biomolecular level.

Unfortunately, there is bad news about the possiblitiy of reversing a 'wrong' epigenetic toggle, i.e. to switch it on again after it has been switched off. According to our current knowledge – and simplified somewhat to aid understanding – toggles can only be switched from the 'on-state' into the 'off-state' during the lifetime of the organism; there is no simple natural option to switch them 'on' again.

Hence, epigenetic learning is in a sense unidirectional as a result of subsequent switching-off of more and more toggles. Switching of the right toggles leads to improved performance, switching of the wrong toggles leads to dysfunction, disorder and disease, to traumatization, drug addiction, depression and, over time, also to diabetes or cancer.

Therefore, our children need the right environment and, as part of that environment the right teacher, to handle their genetic libraries (the National Council of the Developing Child, with a center at Harvard University, calls this library the 'genetic potential' and the epigenetic toggle setting, the 'programming').

Infanticide in mammals

Infanticide is a known concept in lions, apes and other higher-level mammalian groups: a lion who kills the previous pack leader, takes over and kills the children of his predecessor. In chimpanzees, the winning group in a territorial war kills children of the loser group. These well-developed mammal species avoid foster parentship situations, and a brutal and simplistic explanation would be the evolutionary concept of survival (and reproduction) of the fittest. But there is a more reasonable explanation, which is not necessarily putting the lion or the chimpanzee into the role of a survival monster.

Their behaviours might have an epigenetic explanation: once the biological father of the animal children is no longer available, they are not able to copy his behaviour and skills during their childhood development. The new animal foster father would try to train them his own way, which is based on his own genetic setup. So, if the new father had better hunting abilities as a result of running faster to catch his prey, he would solve the task of hunting by ... running at the prey. The biological father (who is unfortunately dead) may instead have had other genetic (and, from his father adopted epigenetic) abilities, like being smarter at sneaking closer to the prey than the new pack leader (and now foster father). So, with this mismatch, the foster father's ability to train children to become successful hunters, which have a different hunting skill to that of his own, will be limited. On top of this issue, the children of the old pack leader might be traumatized as a result of losing their father. This may lead to future social dysfunction in the lion's pack. The (brutal natural) solution that is most efficient is infanticide because it resolves all problems for the new father. The infanticide means the group is then able to procreate and feed a new set of children, which may be better trained than the children of the previous pack leader. Thus, the group finally has a stronger chance of survival. So, this infanticide is not necessarily the lonely decision of a murdering lion but, rather, a decision taken to improve the chances of the pack.

A deep understanding of such natural preconditions and the consequences of these genetic and epigenetic mechanisms is very important in terms of furthering our knowledge of the biological impact of parentship, the true biological difference between biological and foster parentship, the impact of divorce and after-divorce scenarios and childhood trauma following parental separation or the settings in which they find themselves thereafter.

Principiis obsta: Sero medicina parata, cum mala per longas convaluere moras (Publius Ovidius Naso)

Our cells learn and inherit learned information from the previous generations of cells. Childhood traumata is stored epigenetically. Our body does not classify environmental experience according to the ICD10 catalogue. It just stores the information. It wants to be prepared and to act efficiently if the situation is recurring. Throughout the lifespan, our body is optimized to keep this information until it dies. So, our body will fight or bypass therapy because it has lots of tools for keeping the original epigenetic information from its own history. The power of such self-defense is very well-known from the field of drug and alcohol addiction. Drug addiction and epigenetic imprinting are strongly linked. The epigenetic memory will store the trauma as environmental information in the logbook, and it will keep the addiction in the logbook as part of its environmental specialization. The longer we wait to respond to changing conditions, the longer the developing body has to multiply the adverse information, by cell division, copying and further specialization of the distorted, dysfunctional or traumatized cells. It's all one machinery, just with a diversity of impact on our health, depending upon the environment in which this machinery is placed.

Thus, the earlier trauma occurs, the deeper the impact on the developing individuum. We may hope that an individuum could 'develop away' from a trauma, but this will not happen (as the trauma is copied again and again into descendent cells). Once traumatized, the child will develop its future personality with the trauma in its backpack.

Epigenetic disorders, that is, those adopted by the organism during childhood development, are well described in the literature. Many publications analyse a given disorder and its medical symptoms, diagnose it and proscribe potential therapies to alleviate the symptoms.

Can adverse toggle patterns be deleted as a form of therapy?

If we were to take a medication that deletes toggle patterns, our cells would turn into stem cells. Lung tissue, skin tissue, kidney tissue, neural tissue – all would become the same and we would lose our structure and identity. We would turn into a heap of identical looking cells. Identifying the subset of 30 billion cells that has to be treated 'locally' is combinatorially complex and would take longer than the organism would exist. So, there is no real option to delete toggle patterns from the inside.

This and other issues make therapy after trauma very difficult. The best trauma therapy is avoiding the trauma right from the beginning.

Epigenetic impact – examples

The epigenetic health of a child is a moving target, as the environment and society changes. A thousand years ago, violent behaviour was necessary to survive. Today, it is banned by society and its use will not help in a professional career or a family setting. Each society has its own special set of problems, issues I will address here:

1. Foster parents and the conserved genetic regions
2. One-parent families, missing parents and the joint imprint from both genders
3. Constructive and destructive conflict, aggression and violence
4. One home or two homes

Foster parents and the conserved genetic regions

Throughout human history a system of foster parentship has been established. During times of war, disease or hunger, many children lose their biological parents and grow up lonely or find other parents who take over, give them human warmth and kindness, adopt them and treat them like their own biological children.

Our genetic code contains so-called conserved regions. A conserved region is one that did not change during evolution of the human race (or even longer, the evolution of mammals). Some genes (genetic regions) carry low-level metabolic functions, which are the same in all species. One example of a conserved genetic region and the resulting protein function is the respiratory chain. A significant modification by a mutation here would kill the organism, right at the beginning of its lifespan, because it could not metabolize oxygen. Counter-examples are the neural network density of our brain or the structure and efficiency of hormones. A mutation in a non-conserved genetic region will change the performance of the corresponding proteins and thus change the ability of the individuum to perform certain functions; however, it will not kill the individuum. Throughout evolution only those humans who have one and the same code in the conserved regions survive, but a variety of genetic codes has evolved in the non-conserved regions.

Foster parents and biological parents and the child have an identical genetic code in the conserved regions. But they do not have an identical code in non-conserved regions. So foster parents can train their foster children optimally in all the primary functions needed for primary survival and here there is absolutely no difference between foster parents and biological parents. The concept of defining children's wellness by the trinity of:

a. Getting access to food and water
b. Having a safe roof over one's head
c. Receiving the warmth and kindness of adults taking a parental role

is without debate necessary but, in a developed society, is far from sufficient. We should not reduce the child's genetic potential to its conserved genetic code only because this is the minimum condition among animal life forms, following billions of years of evolution. Of course, if a society cannot guarantee even this quality of life, there is no need to talk about the difference between foster parents and biological parents.

Currently, based on comparative genetic calculations, we observe that 5 per cent of the genetic code is highly conserved. The other 95 per cent is variable and, here, the best parents are those who have exactly the same genetic code as the child. They are as good as anybody else in terms of teaching the conserved 5 per cent but, together, they are the best teachers on how to use the other 95 per cent of specific bio-parental genetic library material.

For example, let's look at two biological parents from a village who carry a genetic setup with a high risk of developing diabetes at a young age. The parents inherited the risk from their parents and were (unknowingly) trained by the culture and lifestyle of their ancestors to avoid the onset of the, to them unknown, disease. Without knowing it, they would transfer the same protective culture and lifestyle to their child via said child living and cooperating with them and copying their behaviour. This leads to a protective imprinting, and the child stays healthy. Foster parents may and probably will have a completely different diabetes risk (diabetes risk is a non-conserved property) and will – without knowing it – imprint the foster child in a different way and the child may then develop diabetes.

One-parent families, missing parents and the joint imprint from both genders

Biological parents know, in a very natural sense, how to breathe, drink, eat, think, feel and live with their own genetic library and developed and specialized epigenetic toggle pattern. They have 18–50 years' experience of living with their physiological 'me'. So, they (together) are obviously the best teachers for phase 2 – the development and specialization phase – in which the developing child is creating its physiological 'me'. A missing biological parent means that the one and only teacher for half of the 95 per cent of unconserved genetic code is gone. On top of this, the infanticide issue comes into play: loss of parents is a real life-threatening situation and this fear is deeply implanted in our inherited genetics.

The principle of continuity serves the epigenetic needs of our children perfectly. The most important factor in the healthy development of a child is, taking as a given that it has continuous access to air, water, food, housing and love, *continuous access to both biological parents at all time*. Continuity in terms of epigenetic health at population level thus means forming a legal and social system the highest priority of which is to establish a non-disruptable relationship between each child and both its biological parents. Consequently, no parent should have the right to divorce her/himself from the child, or divorce the other parent from the joint child. By law, unnecessary parent–child separation of any kind should be banned and penalized at the level of assault and battery with reference to children.

If biological parents are dead, or if biological parents are failing in their role as parents, the next best choice for foster parents are the corresponding biological grandparents or, if those are not available, then other biological family members (mature sister, brother, aunts, uncles, etc.).

Constructive and destructive conflict, aggression and violence

My youngest boy is trying out everything, without 'thinking' about consequences. He learned to walk by falling, standing up and falling again. But during this process he experienced moments of frustration and aggression. His twin sister learnt a lot just by watching her brother. So, with fewer trials than him, but much observational effort, she also learnt to walk. Interestingly, she also reacted aggressively when falling down. A very good source of material on aggression of children (and thus in adults) is that written by Jesper Juul [13].

The point about my son's frustration is that he has a brain that is organized as a huge neural network, with electrical impulses travelling fast along the network. His brain sets the task to perform: stand up and walk. But to do so he needs his developing and growing body, which is much larger but also much slower than the brain, as it works chemically and not with electricity. This contradiction between the fast system, which postulates the task, and the slow system, which is not so fast in performing the task, creates frustration. This frustration is good; it is the driving force behind repeating the process again and again. The cells can learn to set their toggles for walking and for growing muscles for walking.

Aggression that aims at a constructive outcome, e.g. learning or cooperation with parents, is termed by Jesper Juul 'constructive aggression'. Constructive aggression is a permanent result of the mismatch between the processing times of our two huge information processing systems: the fast human brain and the slow epigenetic system. If we understand that aggression is a very natural part of development, we should also understand that we are evolutionarily and epigenetically well-trained to handle aggression. It is not a new and unknown disruptive danger; we know it, and everybody feels it. Some of us direct aggression outside (which is healthy); others direct it inward (which leads to unhealthy results). If children cannot express aggression, they will direct it inside and their epigenetic system will learn the corresponding unhealthy patterns.

Children are, as a result of their genetic potential, trained to handle aggression; they are not trained to lose parents. Even worse, they have a phylogenetically inherited fear of losing them. Loss of parents means to children that they are in a life-threatening situation because the new pack leader might come and kill them.

In other words, so long as aggression is not turning into destructive violence, an aggressive but stable parent–child relationship may still be much healthier for the child than observing the loss of one or both biological parents.

One home or two homes

Children need authentic parents. They need constructive aggression in their family in order to learn how to handle the real social environment as personalities who are able to defend their interests while maintaining healthy social relationships. And, of course, the best setting is one home with two biological parents, as this is typically the original setting in which the child was conceived (the principle of continuity!).

If this is not possible and the parents are living in separate places, then one thing is important: keeping both biological parents permanently available for the child; this is more important than financial or relationship issues between the parents. Children are able to constructively adapt to any conditions which mean they avoid the deeply coded fear of the life-threatening parent-loss situation (see the earlier section on infanticide). If the parents cannot live in one home, they will have to live in two or more homes and the child will adapt easily to the two or multi-home situation.

Of course, this is a novel learning process for the child because they must adapt to the two-home situation. Aggression is a very natural consequence in each and every learning phase, and this aggression can be directed against both parents or only one of them. When evaluating such situations, it is important to take into account that the primary goal of the child is to maintain its protection by both parents, and avoid a new pack leader (here, they really cooperate). Hence, the child may direct their aggression toward the 'stronger' parent with whom they have a more resilient relationship, thus reducing the probability of loss by making this (very smart) choice.

Notes

1 Watson, J. D., Baker, T. A., Bell, S. B. et al. (2013). *Molecular biology of the gene* (7th ed.). London: Pearson.
2 Menaney, M. (2010). Epigenetics and the biological definition of gene x environment interactions. *Child Development*, 81(1), 41–79.
3 Bernstein, B. E., Meissner, A., & Lander, E. S. (2007). The mammalian epigenome. *Cell*, 128(4), 669–681.
4 Sweatt, J. D. (2007). An atomic switch for memory. *Cell*, 129(1), 23–24.
5 Dolinoy, D. C., Weidman, J. R., & Jirtle, R. L. (2007). Epigenetic gene regulation: Linking early developmental environment to adult disease. *Reproductive Toxicology*, 23(3): 297–307.
6 Kaminsky, Z. A., Tang, T., Wang, S., Ptak, C., Oh, G. H. T., Wong, A. H., & Petronis, A. (2009). DNA methylation profiles in monozygotic and dizygotic twins. *Nature Genetics*, 42, 240–245.
7 McGowan, P. O., Sasaki, A., D'Alessio, A. C. et al. (2009). Epigenetic regulation of the glucocorticoid receptor in human brain associates with childhood abuse. *Nature Neuroscience*, 12(3), 342–348.
8 Roth, T. L., Lubin, F. D., Funk A., & Sweatt, J. (2009). Lasting epigenetic influence of early-life adversity on the BDNF gene. *Biological Psychiatry*, 65(9), 760–769.

9 Crews, D. (2008). Epigenetics and its implications for behavioral neuroendocrinology. *Frontiers in Neuroendocrinology*, 29(3), 344–357.
10 Champagne, F. A. (2010). Epigenetic influences of social experiences across the lifespan. *Developmental Psychobiology*, 52(4) 1–13.
11 Sweatt, J. D. (2009). Experience-dependent epigenetic modifications in the central nervous system. *Biological Psychiatry*, 65(3), 191–197.
12 Isles, A. R., & Wilkinson, L. S. (2008). Epigenetics: What is it and why is it important to mental disease? *British Medical Bulletin*, 85(1), 35–45.
13 Juul, J. (2013). Aggression, a new and dangerous taboo? Retrieved from http://exunusplures.blogspot.com/2013/07/aggression-dangerous-new-taboo.html.

11
SHARED PARENTING AS A PROTECTIVE FACTOR IN CHILDREN'S AND ADULTS' HEALTH

Vittorio Carlo Vezzetti

Introduction

Science has proven that childhood adversity has direct effects on the health of infants and young adults. This damage can be classified into two different categories: the effects caused by traumatic experiences and the effects caused by chronic stressors. Such effects can result from divorce-correlated situations.

The definition of childhood adversity includes the following:

1. *Traumatic experiences* Physical abuse, verbal abuse, mental abuse, witnessing violence within the home, and severe childhood illness.
2. *Chronic stressors.* Parental loss (and parental lack), parental separation with long-term family conflict, neglect, parental education, parental mental health, poverty, and drug use in the family.

Although it is not always possible to demonstrate a sure causal effect (as it is for animal models), it is important to highlight some psychobiological damage associated with parental loss and other childhood adversities as they touch on so far unsuspected fields and because the consequence can become apparent after 20 or 30 years.

The problem is significant as parental separation is, in fact, the first cause of parental loss in Western countries (it occurs in more than 40% of divorces in some countries) and is often linked to other childhood adversities such as, for example, parental conflict or witnessing violence. In fact, it is noteworthy that, until a few years ago, the research in this area focused on effects of divorce "tout court" without considering whether after divorce the child could still have frequent, satisfying, and regular contact with both parents because shared parenting was rare.

The need for very large data sets to make solid inferences about very small subgroups of the population severely restricted the possibility of statistically validating research on children living in a shared-parenting situation. The systematic error was (and often still is) to attribute the effects of trauma and stress to the consequences of divorce, such as parental loss or family conflict (Vezzetti, 2016a).

Only in recent years has the establishment of shared parenting, especially in Nordic countries, allowed wide comparative research to be conducted and demonstrate that this type of parenting could have a huge influence on the consequences of divorce for child well-being.

Knowledge on biological effects on animal models of health linked to parental separation

We should not be surprised about the effects of trauma and stress experienced in childhood because there is ample evidence of such in several animal species, especially parental loss and parental separation. Usually, this research concerns animals with co-parental care of the offspring: examples include birds, mammals (and also primates). Among a multitude of research, we will cite just two examples: those of Bambico et al. (2015), who showed that father absence in the monogamous California mouse impairs social behavior and modifies dopamine and glutamate synapses in the medial prefrontal cortex; and Ovtscharoff et al. (2006), who analyzed the impact of paternal care, that is, the father's emotional contribution to his offspring, on the synaptic development of the anterior cingulate cortex.

We recall that exposure to enriched or impoverished environmental conditions, experience, and learning are factors that influence brain development, and it has been shown that neonatal emotional experience significantly interferes with the synaptic development of higher associative forebrain areas. Indeed, significantly reduced densities (-33%) of symmetric shaft synapses were found in layer II of the fatherless animals compared to controls. This finding indicates an imbalance between excitatory and inhibitory synapses in the anterior cingulate cortex of father-deprived animals (Ovtscharoff et al., 2006).

Results query the general assumption that a father has less impact on the synaptic maturation of his offspring brain than the mother.

Psychobiological effects on infant health linked to parental separation and other childhood adversities

Although the most well-known effects of the divorce process are commonly described in the behavioral and emotional fields, physical morbidity of the children has also been described in situations of parental loss and often correlated with childhood adversities. For example, a study from Taiwan (Juang et al., 2004) found a clear link between parental divorce and children's daily headaches.

Various studies have, moreover, described increased prevalence of attention deficit and hyperactivity disorder (ADHD) in children in situations of divorce and abuse (and not always following a selection effect) (Cohen et al., 2002).

Much research (but all conducted – selection effect! – in monoparental countries, where shared parenting is uncommon and divorce is often linked to the increasing adverse effect of parental loss, high rates of family conflict, etc.) found a correlation between parental divorce and eating disorders and excessive weight (Igoin-Apfelbaum, 1985; Johnson et al., 2002; Yannakoulia et al., 2008).

A study of almost 1 million children in Sweden observed that children growing up with single parents were more than twice as likely to experience a serious psychiatric disorder, commit or attempt suicide or develop an alcohol addiction (Ringsback-Weitoft et al., 2003).

Although both experiences (parental loss as a consequence of divorce and as a consequence of parental death) can impact economic resources, social resources may be more affected by parental divorce because it can result in changes in the child's relationship with both parents, whereas parental death is less likely to disrupt the child's relationship with the remaining parent (Otowa et al., 2014; Tyrka et al., 2008).

Finally, a key body of research in Israel (Agid et al., 1999) has drawn several conclusions:

1. Increased overall rates of early parental loss are observed in major depression, bipolar disorder, and schizophrenia, but the finding is most striking in major depression followed by schizophrenia. The finding in regard to major depression is consistent with the majority of published studies in which loss is not broken down into categories, while the literature on bipolar disorder and schizophrenia is insufficient for comparison.
2. Patients with major depression manifest a significantly increased rate of early parental loss due to permanent separation but not due to death.
3. Loss of mother may be more significant than loss of father, although, in this analysis, this observation was at a trend level only.
4. Loss at an early age (according to this research, younger than nine) is of greater significance than later loss, as observed by several researchers (Bloch et al., 2007; Breier et al., 1988; Kailaheimo-Lönnqvist and Erola, 2020).

Biological consequences of parental loss and other childhood adversities: Latest knowledge

Nicolson (2004) showed that cortisol levels in adult men are increased if, in their childhood, they were subject to parental loss or other adversities. Similarly, Luecken (1998) found that both childhood loss of a parent and poor quality of care are associated with long-term increases in blood pressure.

In terms of psychological stress, conversely, growth hormone (GH) responses are rarely seen. Rather, there is a GH secretory defect associated with prolonged psychosocial stress, which causes a rare condition called psychosocial dwarfism (PD) (Delitala et al., 1987; Magner et al., 1984; Skuse et al., 1996).

Mitchell et al.'s (2017) interesting research observed that, at nine years of age, children ($N = 2420$) who have experienced father loss have significantly shorter telomeres (a 14% reduction). Paternal death has the largest association (16%), followed by incarceration (10%), and separation and/or divorce (6%). No differences were found by age at father loss or a child's race/ethnicity. Changes in income partially mediate these associations (95% mediation for separation and/or divorce, 30% for incarceration, and 25% for death). Effects are 40% greater for boys and 90% greater for children with the most reactive alleles of the serotonin transporter genes when compared with those with the least reactive alleles. Similarly in nine-year-old African-American children, the researchers found significant associations between low income, low maternal education, unstable family structure, and harsh parenting and telomere length (TL) (−19%) (Mitchell et al., 2014).

A new technique (neuroimaging) has clearly shown that early childhood adversity causes initial stress-induced hypertrophy and hyperactivity of amygdala neurons but eventually leads to neuronal atrophy or cell death by adulthood (Herringa, 2016). This morphological issue is very important as we know that reciprocal connections between the amygdala and medial prefrontal cortex (mPFC) support fundamental aspects of emotional behavior in adulthood.

Opacka-Juffry and Mohiyeddini (2012) provided evidence that adverse experience in early life (such as, but not exclusively, parental loss) is negatively associated with oxytocin system activity in adulthood (correlated with depression and anxiety disorders).

A new topic is the possible correlation between height and familial disruption: Sheppard et al. (2015) argue that familial disruption during early childhood has far-reaching repercussions for the health of both men and women. Their study assesses adult height as one such health-relevant outcome. For men, parental death and divorce during early childhood were associated with later puberty. Later puberty was associated with shorter adult height.

Among women, it was found that the father's death during early childhood was associated with earlier puberty, which was in turn associated with shorter adult stature. The relationship between paternal death and height is entirely mediated by age at puberty; there is no evidence of a direct relationship between childhood family disruption and adult height.

Is shared parenting a preventive or positive influence in relation to childhood adversity and parental loss?

Most studies indicate that divorce has a negative impact on children, but there are many different interpretations of the consequences for children, whether the negative impact arises from the divorce itself or more likely from the process, long-term conflict, inadequate parenting, parental loss (very frequent in most countries) and whether this process can actually sometimes be good for the children involved in some situations.

But, as we saw earlier, today a great deal of evidence shows that the effects of parental separation (now so common in Western countries) on minor children is mainly an issue of public health, and should be treated first using a scientific approach; that is, based on approaches that have demonstrated reduction in the risks associated with parental loss and other childhood adversities.

Parental loss

The preventive effect of shared parenting on parental loss is indisputable. There is a tight inverse correlation between shared parenting and parental loss: in countries where shared parenting has become common, parental loss has decreased significantly, while in countries where shared parenting is rare, it is higher: in Denmark, parental loss after parental separation has actually decreased, to 12%; in Sweden, it has quickly decreased to 13%; in Italy and Greece, it is steady at about 30% (Bergstrom, 2015; Lohse, 2015; Paparigopoulos, 2016; Schiratzki, 2009; Sünderhauf, 2015; Vezzetti, 2009, 2016a).

Some French research (Regnier-Loilier, 2013) observes that there is a 1% probability of a child losing contact with the father when the judge orders joint physical custody, at least in the first six months of the judicial trial, but it increases to 21% if the judge orders the traditional arrangement of single-parent custody.

Yet, in the same study, the researcher observes that the distance between the two parental homes (a parameter on which the judicial system can have a huge influence by allowing the emigration of one parent with the child) has a significant influence. The study shows that the probability of losing contact with the father is 12% if the father and child live close to each other (15 minutes apart), but it increases to 33% if they live more than four hours apart and up to 81% if they are so far apart that the father is not able to quantify the necessary travel time. Finally, a recent study (KiMiss-Studie 2016/17) shows that, when parenting time is less than 17%, the risk of parental estrangement rises to 50% or more.

Moreover, this research identifies that, when parenting time is 30% (which is the minimal standard access arrangement of one weekend every two weeks plus half of holiday time, in countries using the single residency model with the mother), the risk and level of parental estrangement is also circa 30%, but rising steeply if the parenting time is any less than 30% as a result of cases in which the residential parent frustrates the attempts of the other parent to spend time with the children. Finally, this research shows that, when parenting time is 50/50 (shared parenting), the risk and level of parental alienation is still 10%.

Conflict

Extensive research has confirmed the positive effects of shared parenting on several issues correlated with childhood adversity (such as minimizing parental conflict). The Australian experience seems to show that parental conflict has been reduced following the new law on shared parenting enacted in 2006. In 2003/2004, 45,004 claims were brought before the Family Court; in 2006/2007, there were just 27,313; and in 2008/2009, there were 18,633. While claims in family courts (and only these), decreased, all other civil claims increased. So, it is possible argue that JPC law had a direct effect on family conflict; 70,261 claims were brought before the Federal Magistrates Court in 2003/2004, 76,807 in 2006/2007 and 79,441 in 2008/2009 (Sünderhauf, 2015; Vezzetti, 2009).

In Spain, the presumption of joint physical custody (JPC) was introduced only in some regions and at different times. In Catalonia, the law was approved in 2010, when there were 6155 claims of gender violence; by 2013, there were 5403 (−12.22%). In Comunidad Valenciana, the law on JPC was approved in 2011, when there were 4712 claims og gender violence; by 2013, there were 4056 (−13.92%). In Aragon, the law on JPC was introduced in 2010 when there were 603 claims of gender violence; by 2013, the situation remained almost steady at 617 claims (+2.3%). Therefore, it is not possible to discuss the negative effects of shared parenting on family conflict because, conversely, the global number of allegations of domestic violence has decreased. In addition, we recall that, in Sweden and Denmark, similar results were found (Bergstrom, 2015; Lohse, 2015).

In Kentucky, USA, a partial version of the shared parenting law was enacted in July 2017. The following July a full shared parenting law took effect. The year before Kentucky had any shared parenting laws, beginning July 14, 2016, and lasting 365 days, 22,512 family court cases were filed. They declined to 21,847 the year the partial shared parenting law began. When the complete shared parenting law took effect, new cases plummeted to 19,991 (a decline of 11% in two years, despite population growth and an increase in divorces) (Hale, 2019).

Nevertheless, in many jurisdictions, there is a legal presumption against shared parenting in high-conflict cases. Conversely, however, shared parenting provides an incentive for parental cooperation, negotiation, and the development of parenting plans. In fact, a wide body of literature (Buchanan et al., 1996; Cashmore and Parkinson, 2010; Fabricius et al., 2012; Kline et al., 1989; Melli and Brown, 2008; Sodermans et al., 2013; Warshak, 2014) showed that there is no significant difference between conflict experienced in families with joint physical custody arrangements and families with sole custody.

Moreover, Fabricius and Luecken (2007) observed, in a sample of 266 university students whose parents divorced before they were 16 years of age, that there is no interaction between time with father and exposure to parent conflict; thus, more time with the father was beneficial in both high- and low-conflict families, and more exposure to parental conflict was detrimental at both high and low levels of time spent with father.

The Stanford Child Custody Study (1984–1990; Fabricius et al., 2012) found that children in joint physical custody (living at least one-third of the time with their fathers) compared with children in sole physical custody were most satisfied with the custody plan and showed the best long-term adjustments, even after controlling for factors that might predispose parents to select joint physical custody (such as education, income, and initial levels of parental hostility). In fact, in 80% of the joint physical custody families, one or both parents initially did not want and did not agree to the arrangement (Maccoby et al., 1993).

General well-being

Concerning other childhood adversities and the best arrangements for children with parents who have separated, the outcomes of the scientific literature are represented by 74 comparative studies published in peer-reviewed papers or government reports between 1977 and 2014. They were subject to two meta-analyses that compared sole and shared custody between those dates. The most noteworthy meta-analysis is Nielsen (2014).

Nielsen's article summarizes 40 studies that have compared children in joint physical custody (at least 35% of time spent with each parent) and children in sole custody during the past 25 years.

The findings of the studies were grouped into five broad categories of child well-being: academic or cognitive outcomes, which include school grades and scores on tests of cognitive development such as language skills (Vezzetti, 2016a); emotional or psychological outcomes, which include feeling depressed, anxious, or dissatisfied with their lives (Bambico et al., 2015); behavioral problems, which include aggression or delinquency, difficult or unmanageable behavior at home or school, hyperactivity, and drug or alcohol use (Ovtscharoff et al., 2006); physical health and smoking, which also includes stress-related illnesses such as stomach aches and sleep disturbances (Juang et al., 2004); and quality of father–child relationships, which includes how well they communicate and how close they feel to one another (Cohen et al., 2002). The following four conclusions were drawn:

- Shared parenting was linked to better outcomes for children of all ages across a wide range of emotional, behavioral, and physical health measures.
- There was no convincing evidence that overnighting or shared parenting was linked to negative outcomes for infants or toddlers.
- The outcomes are not positive when there is a history of violence or when the children do not like or get along with their father.
- Even though shared-parenting couples tend to have somewhat higher incomes and experience less verbal conflict than other parents, these two factors alone do not explain the better outcomes for the children.

A second meta-analysis, conducted by Sünderhauf (2013, analyzes 50 comparative pieces of research carried out between 1977 and 2013. In this review, the cut-off between sole custody and joint physical custody is at 25% of time spent with each parent (thus, with a lower limit than in the study by Nielsen, 2014). In 37 studies (74%), the outcomes were favorable for joint physical custody; in 11 studies (22%), the outcomes included positive effects balanced by some other negative effects; and only in two studies (4%), were the outcomes negative (but further investigation revealed some significant bias in this research).

A corollary to the meta-analysis cited above is the meta-analysis performed by Warshak (2004), which focused only on revision of international literature related to shared care for babies aged under four years of age. This meta-analysis focuses on 13 papers published between 1987 and 2010 and concludes that "[t]here is no evidence to support postponing the introduction of regular and frequent involvement, including overnights, of both parents with their babies and toddlers" and "[i]n general the results of the studies reviewed in this document are favorable to parenting plans that more evenly balance young children's time between two homes".

Actually, there is a dearth of research on this topic (shared parenting for toddlers), but new broad and thorough research on shared parenting and preschool children (focused on children aged three and four) is in progress in Sweden within the context of the ELVIS Project (coordinated by the Centre for Health Equity Studies). The first preliminary outcomes seem to confirm that preschool children in shared parenting arrangements show fewer psychological symptoms than those in monoparental care (Bergstrom et al., 2015).

In the literature published between 1977 and 2014, we find only three research findings that do not support shared parenting, those of (Johnston et al., 1989), (McIntosh et al., 2008), and (Tornello et al., 2013). These studies are burdened by huge bias and important methodological mistakes (Millar and Kruk, 2014; Nielsen, 2014; Poussin, 2016; Warshak, 2014, 2017).

Wide research on the topic of life satisfaction conducted in Sweden, Greenland, Finland, Iceland, the United States, and Denmark was analyzed by Bjarnason et al. (2012) to identify differences in life satisfaction among children in different family structures in 36 Western, industrialized countries ($N = 184,496$).

Children in joint physical custody reported significantly higher levels of life satisfaction than their counterparts in other types of non-intact families. Controlling for perceived family affluence, the difference between joint physical custody families and single mother or mother–stepfather families became non-significant. Difficulties in communicating with parents were strongly associated with lower life satisfaction but did not mediate the relation between family structure and life satisfaction. Children in the Nordic countries characterized by strong welfare systems reported significantly higher levels of life satisfaction in all living arrangements except in single-father households. Differences in economic inequality between countries moderated the association between certain family structures, perceived family affluence, and life satisfaction. In the same sample, impaired communication with both mother and father was significantly less likely in joint physical custody than in other non-intact families. Indeed, impaired communication with the mother was equally prevalent in intact families and joint physical custody families, while impaired communication with the father was in fact less prevalent in joint physical custody than intact families (Bjarnason and Arnarsson, 2011).

Further research examined children's health-related quality of life after parental separation by comparing children living with both parents in nuclear families to those living in joint physical custody and other forms of domestic arrangement (Bergstrom et al., 2013). Investigating a sample from a national Swedish classroom study of 164,580 children aged between 12 and 15 years of age, the researchers found that living in a nuclear family was positively associated with almost all aspects of well-being in comparison to the children with separated parents.

Children in joint physical custody experienced more positive outcomes, in terms of subjective well-being, family life, and peer relations, than children living mostly or only with one parent.

The 15-year-old adolescents in joint physical custody were more likely than the 12-year-old children to report similar well-being levels on most outcomes to the children in nuclear families. Other Swedish research shows that children with non-cohabitant parents experience more psychosomatic problems than those in nuclear families. Those in joint physical custody do, however, report better psychosomatic health than children living mostly or only with one parent (Bergstrom, 2015).

Finally, I recall Turunen's (2015) analysis of data from the Survey of Living Conditions (ULF), 2001–2003. The cross-sectional survey consisted of a nationally representative sample of the Swedish population aged 18–84 years and child supplements with data collected from children aged 10–18 years living in the household of the main respondent. Like other recent studies of emotional outcomes of shared physical custody, this study observed that sharing residence equally after a parental union disruption may not be harmful for children. On the contrary, children in 50/50 shared residence have a markedly lower likelihood of experiencing high levels of stress, thus confirming positive findings on other aspects of emotional well-being.

These findings were then confirmed by the conclusion of another important study in which data on 15-year-old adolescents from the 2005/2006 to 2009/2010 Swedish HBSC survey were analyzed using logistic regression. Here, the authors found that shared physical custody after marriage breakup seems to constitute a protective factor for adolescents' health and problem behavior (Asa et al., 2012).

In conclusion, the causal effect of shared parenting on general well-being is more controversial than that of conflict and parental loss because it may be more difficult to distinguish between the selection effects and causal effects of different parenting (shared, sole, etc.) on individual well-being. However, even if it is not completely clear how much the outcomes depend on selection effect (where parents opting for shared parenting would be more collaborative, non conflictual, and better care providers than sole-parenting parents) or on causal effect (shared parenting really would lead to better outcomes for children), the sudden and huge increase in shared parenting in Sweden (where joint physical custody increased from 4% in 1998 to 28% in 2006 and to 40% in 2014; Bergstrom, 2015, n. 23), some Spanish regions like Catalonia, and in Kentucky, and according to the observations reported earlier (Buchanan et al., 1996; Cashmore and Parkinson, 2010; Fabricius et al., 2012; Melli and Brown, 2008; Nielsen, 2014; Sodermans et al., 2013; Warshak, 2014) that there is no difference in levels of conflict between families in joint physical custody and sole custody, leads us to think that the positive outcomes of shared parenting cannot depend just on selection effect.

The revolutionary dilemma: Is divorce with minor children a juridical, political or public health problem?

There is much evidence on the significant biomedical and organic consequences of divorce on child health. The effects can appear 10, 20, or even 30 years later and, from a biological and biochemical point of view, also in apparently healthy adults. Shared parenting politics can be a good prevention approach.

This issue indicates that this problem should be primarily faced not from a juridical but from a public health point of view. Unfortunately, in most countries, divorce involving minor children is still considered a simple family law problem, and in most European Union Member States, it is the Ministry of Justice (and not Ministry for Childhood or for Health!) that usually manages this issue. As an example of this approach, we recall the words of Viviane Reding, at that time EU Justice

Commissioner, on behalf of the European Commission, to European Parliament Vice President Angelilli:

> The definition of joint custody belongs to substantive family law. As such, it does not fall within the EU's competence but remains under the sole responsibility of the Member States. This explains why there may be differences in the national systems as regards the definition of joint custody and how it works in practice.
>
> *(European Parliament, 2013)*

This wrong and sectionalist approach leads to significant and unjustifiable differences between the Member States, and so the "paramount interest of the child" (Vezzetti, 2015) changes as a result of simply crossing a border (Ares, 2016; European Parliament, 2014; Vezzetti, 2010, 2015, 2016b).

Conclusion

This review confirms that family courts judgments can have a huge influence on human health. They can affect the probabily of children suffering parental loss (which varies according to jurisprudences) and other adversities such as inadequate parenting and long-term conflict. The opinion of this author is that it is necessary to make practices more harmonized, such as in the medical world where shared and common guidelines usually exist (inside which the operator can work according to a case-by-case method). Maybe countering the negative consequences for children's psychological and physical health will only be possible if the dominant "sectionalist" legal language is replaced with a more universal scientific language that allows all children to have an equal or adequate right to health (as requested by most national constitutions and by the EU's Charter of Fundamental Rights) and the Cartesian wall between Science and Right is crossed (Vezzetti, 2010).

Finally, loss of contact between children and one of their parents will result in a heavy burden for future worldwide generations.

References

Agid O, Shapira B, Zislin J, et al. (1999) Environment and vulnerability to major psychiatric illness: A case control study of early parental loss in major depression, bipolar disorder and schizophrenia. *Molecular Psychiatry* 4: 163–172.

Asa C, Eriksson U, Lofstedt P, et al. (2012) Risk behaviour in Swedish adolescents: Is shared physical custody after divorce a risk or a protective factor? *European Journal of Public Health* 23(1): 3–8.

Bambico FR, Lacoste B, Hattan PR, et al. (2013) Father absence in the monogamous California mouse impairs social behavior and modifies dopamine and glutamate synapses in the medial prefrontal cortex. *Cerebral Cortex* 25(5): 1163–1175.

Bergstrom M (2015) Shared parenting in Sweden and elsewhere: Are children different? Presentation at the International Conference on Shared Parenting, Bonn, 9–11 December.

Bergstrom M, Modin B, Fransson E, et al. (2013) Living in two homes: A Swedish national survey of wellbeing in 12 and 15 year olds with joint physical custody. *BMC Public Health* 13: 868.

Bergstrom M, Modin B, Fransson E, et al. (2015) Fifty moves a year: Is there an association between joint physical custody and psychosomatic problems in children? *Journal of Epidemiology & Community Health* 69:769–774.

Bjarnason T and Arnarsson AM (2011) Joint physical custody and communication with parents: Comparative study of 36 Western societies. *Journal of Comparative Family Studies* 4(6): 871–890.

Bjarnason T, Bendtsen P, Arnarsson AM, et al. (2012) Life satisfaction among children in different family structures: A comparative study of 36 Western societies. *Children & Society* 26: 51–62.

Bloch M, Peleg I, Koren D, Aner H and Klein E (2007) Long-term effects of early parental loss due to divorce on the HPA axis *Hormones and Behavior* 51: 516–523.

Breier A et al. (1998) Early parental loss and development of adult psychopathology. *Archives of General Psychiatry* 45(11): 987–993.

Buchanan CM, Maccoby EE and Dornbusch, SM (1996) *Adolescents after divorce*. Cambridge, MA: Harvard University Press, n. 34.

Cashmore J and Parkinson P (2010) *Shared care parenting arrangements since the 2006 family law reforms*. Sydney, Australia: University of New South Wales Social Research Centre.

Cohen AJ, Adler N, Kaplan SJ, et al. (2002) Interactional effects of marital status and physical abuse on adolescent psychopathology. *Child Abuse & Neglect* 26(3): 277–288.

Consejo general del poder judicial (2014). Observatorio Estatal de Violencia sobre la Mujer. Retrieved from https://violenciagenero.igualdad.gob.es/instituciones/observatorioEstatal/home.htm.

Delitala G, Tomasi P and Virdis R (1987) Prolactin, growth hormone and thyrotropin-thyroid hormone secretion during stress states in man. *Baillieres Clinical Endocrinology and Metabolism* 1(2): 391–414.

European Parliament (2013) Parliamentary questions E 000713/2013. Retrieved from www.europarl.europa.eu/doceo/document/E-7-2013-000713-ASW_EN.html?redirect

European Parliament (2014) Parliamentary questions E-005595–14. Retrieved from www.europarl.europa.eu/doceo/document/E-7-2014-005595_EN.html?redirect

Fabricius WV and Luecken LJ (2007) Postdivorce living arrangements, parent conflict, and long-term physical health correlates for children of divorce. *Journal of Family Psychology* 21(2): 195–205.

Fabricius WV, Sokol KR, Diaz P, et al. (2012) Parenting time, parent conflict, parent–child relationships, and children's physical health. In Kuehnle K and Drozd L (eds), *Parenting plan evaluation: Applied research for the family court: Applied research for the family court*. Oxford: Oxford University Press.

Hale, M. (2019) Kentucky's popular joint-custody law shows why it's the most effective at helping families, *Courier Journal*, 14 December.

Herringa RJ et al. (2016) Enhanced prefrontal-amygdala connectivity following childhood adversity as a protective mechanism against internalizing in adolescence. *Biological Psychiatry: Cognitive Neuroscience and Neuroimaging* 1(4): 326–334.

Igoin-Apfelbaum L (1985) Characteristics of family background in bulimia. *Psychotherapy and Psychosomatics* 43(3): 161–167.

Johnson JG, Cohen P, Kasen S, et al. (2002) Childhood adversities associated with risk for eating disorders or weight problems during adolescence or early adulthood. *American Journal of Psychiatry* 159: 394–400.

Johnston JR, Kline M and Tschann JM (1989) Ongoing postdivorce conflict: Effects on children of joint custody and frequent access. *American Journal of Orthopsychiatry* 59(4): 576–592.

Juang KD, Wang SJ, Fuh JL, et al. (2004) Association between adolescent chronic daily headache and childhood adversity: A community-based study. *Cephalalgia* 24(1): 54–59.

Kailaheimo-Lönnqvist S and Erola J (2020) Child's age at parental death and university education. *European Societies* 22(4): 433–455.

KiMiss-Studie 2016/17 Datenbericht unter besonderer Behandlung der Themen Gemeinsame Sorge, Eltern-Kind-Entfremdung und emotionaler Missbrauch. Germany, Universität Tübingen, KiMiss-Projekt, p. 8.

Lohse J (2015) Ongoing shared parenting reforms in Denmark. Presentation at the International Conference on Shared Parenting, Bonn, 9–11 December.

Luecken LJ (1998) Childhood attachment and loss experiences affect adult cardiovascular and cortisol function. *Psychosomatic Medicine* 60(6): 765–772.

Maccoby EE, Buchanan CM, Mnookin RH, et al. (1993) Postdivorce roles of mothers and fathers in the lives of their children. *Journal of Family Psychology* 24: 34–35.

Magner JA, Rogol AD and Gorden P (1984) Reversible growth hormone deficiency and delayed puberty triggered by a stressful experience in a young adult. *American Journal of Medicine* 76(4): 737–742.

McIntosh JE, Wells YD, Smyth BM, et al. (2008) Child-focused and child-inclusive divorce mediation: Comparative outcomes from a prospective study of post separation adjustment. *Family Court Review* 46(1): 105–124.

Melli MS and Brown PR (2008) Exploring a new family form: The shared time family. *International Journal of Law, Policy and the Family* 22(2): 231–269.

Millar P and Kruk E (2014) Maternal attachment, paternal overnight contact, and very young children's adjustment: Comment on Tornello et al. 2013. *Journal of Marriage and Family* 76: 232–236

Mitchell C. et al. (2014) Social disadvantage, genetic sensitivity, and children's telomere length, *Proceedings of the Naional Academy of Science, USA* 111(16) 5944–5949.

Mitchell C. et al. (2017) Father loss and child telomere length. *Pediatrics* 140(2). e20163245.

Nicolson NA (2004) Childhood parental loss and cortisol levels in adult men. *Psychoneuroendocrinology* 29(8): 1012–1018.

Nielsen L (2014) Shared physical custody: Summary of 40 studies on outcomes for children. *Journal of Divorce & Remarriage* 55: 614–636

Opacka-Juffry J and Mohiyeddini C (2012) Experience of stress in childhood negatively correlates with plasma oxytocin concentration in adult men. *Stress* 15(1): 1–10.

Otowa T, York TP, Gardner CO, et al. (2014) The impact of childhood parental loss on risk for mood, anxiety and substance use disorders in a population-based sample of male twins. *Psychiatry Research* 220(1–2): 404–409.

Ovtscharoff W, Helmeke C, Jr and Braun K (2006) Lack of paternal care affects synaptic development in the anterior cingulate cortex. *Brain Research* 1116(1): 58–63.

Paparigopoulos Y (2016) Shared parenting: The need for institutional reforms. Presented at an international conference at Athens University, Greece, 21 May.

Poussin G (2016) Les nouvelles formes de parentalite: Le temps du partage... et l'enfant? Retrieved from www.childrights.org/documents/publications/livres/2016-05_nouvelles-formes-parentalite.pdf

Regnier-Loilier A (2013) When fathers lose touch with their children after a separation. *Population and Society*, 500: 1–4.

Ringsback-Weitoft G, Hjem A, Haglund B, et al. (2003) Mortality, severe morbidity and injury in children living with single parents in Sweden: A population-based study. *The Lancet* 361: 289–295.

Schiratzki J (2009) Custody of children in Sweden: Recent developments. *Scandinavian Studies in Law* 1: 1–2.

Sheppard P, Garcia JR, Sear R, et al. (2015) *Family disruption and adult height: Is there a mediating role of puberty?* Oxford: Oxford University Press (on behalf of the Foundation for Evolution, Medicine, and Public Health).

Skuse D, Albanese A, Stanhope R, et al. (1996) A new stress-related syndrome of growth failure and hyperphagia in children, associated with reversibility of growth-hormone insufficiency. *The Lancet* 348(9024): 353–358.

Sodermans A, Matthijs K and Swicegood G (2013) Characteristics of joint physical custody families in Flanders. *Demographic Research* 28: 821–848.

Sünderhauf H (2013) *Wechselmodell: Psychologie—Recht— Praxis* (Part 1, Chapter 3.1.5). Wiesbaden: Springer.

Sünderhauf H (2015) The legal development of parental responsibility in Europe. Presentation at the International Conference on Shared Parenting, Bonn, 9–11 December.

Tornello SL, Emery R, Rowen J, et al. (2013) Overnight custody arrangements, attachment, and adjustment among very young children. *Family Relations* 75: 871–885.

Turunen J (2015) Shared physical custody and children's experience of stress. *Families and Societies* 24: 1–26.

Tyrka AE, Wier L, Price LH, et al. (2008) Childhood parental loss and adult psychopathology: Effects of loss characteristics and contextual factors. *International Journal of Psychiatry in Medicine* 38(3): 329–344.

Vezzetti V (2009) Il figlio di genitori separate rivista. *SIPPS, Italian Society for Social and Preventive Pediatrics* 3– 8.

Vezzetti V (2010) *Nel nome dei figli* [*In the name of the children*]. Book sprint edition.

Vezzetti V (2014) European children and the divorce of their parents: A question of right to health? Contribution to Day general discussion: Digital Media and Children's rights. Office of High Commissioner for Human Rights, 12 September.

Vezzetti V (2015) *A comparative research on European children and divorce*. Saarbrucken: Scholar Press.

Vezzetti V (2016a) New approaches to divorce with children: A problem of public health. *Health Psychology Open* 1–13.

Vezzetti V (2016b) Letter received from Věra Jourová, Commissioner, Directorate of the European Commission for Civil Justice, in response to letter regarding 'concern about difficulties encountered by children in international families in cases of family break-up' (available from author on request).

Warshak RA (2014) Social science and parenting plans for young children: A consensus report. *Psychology Public Policy and Law* 20(1): 46.

Warshak, R. A. (2017). Stemming the tide of misinformation: International consensus on shared parenting and overnighting. *Journal of the American Academy of Matrimonial Lawyers*, 30(1): 177–217.

Yannakoulia M. et al. (2008) Association between family divorce and children's BMI and meal patterns: The GENDAI Study. *Obesity* 16: 1382–1387.

PART II

Socioeconomic profile of shared parenting

12
LEGISLATION AND FAMILY
Divorce and granting of custody

Diego Becerril Ruíz and José Manuel Jiménez-Cabello

Introduction

In line with global trends, Spanish society has been rapidly transforming. In recent decades, Spain has experienced a great deal of highly diverse social change. The family context has been one of the areas affected the most, with very recent changes in marital breakdown and the granting of child custody. Merely 15 years ago, it was mandatory to separate before divorce and, in the absence of an agreement, a cause was required. Furthermore, joint custody was hardly ever considered.

In this context, the study analyzes this decisive period, with emphasis on the legal reforms introduced in 2005 that, in overall terms, restrict the process of marriage breakdown, in particular with respect to the custody of minors and/or dependents. In Spain, there is a lack of studies aimed at verifying the existence of a probable relationship to or impact of the legal issues relating to the breakdown of marriage or the granting of child custody. As a result, this study addresses this important issue, which is closely related to the social construction of reality[1].

The context in which this work is set suggests that there are two decisive areas: the importance of the law in divorce and the granting of child custody. First, divorce is addressed by reviewing legislation and studies focused on the clarification of its impact. Second, the work provided information on the legal issues of the granting of child custody and a review of the literature that addresses the matter. The methodology used, results obtained and the main conclusions are presented below.

Analysis of the legal impact in a family context
Impact of legislation on marriage breakdown

In a family context, one of the aspects that has undergone the most profound change is marital breakdown, which has been increasingly accepted in Spanish society. Marital breakdown has evolved in various stages, ranging from a stigmatized vision of the process to its understanding as a solution to an unsatisfactory project of cohabitation[2]. In very few years, broad and unrestricted acceptance has been consolidated, which is legally represented by the amendment of the Spanish Divorce Law[3]. Today, life is characterized by change, by trajectories that are constantly evolving, and breakdown plays a fundamental role in a number of aspects of social life.

The study of divorce in Spain must necessarily and inevitably focus on two key moments. First, Spanish Law 30/1981 of July 7, 1981, which amended the regulation of marriage in the Civil Code and determined the procedure to be followed for annulment, separation and divorce. Second, Spanish Law 15/2005 of July 8, 2005, which updated the legislation.

It should first be pointed out that Law 30/1981 responded to a pre-existing reality[4,5]. Marriage breakdown was defined as a multi-stage process of separation and divorce. Accordingly, separation could be requested after at least one year of marriage. Two situations could therefore occur. If separation was by mutual agreement, it would be admitted. Otherwise, the plaintiff had to accept that his or her spouse would be subject to legal grounds for separation (such as unjustified abandonment of the family home or infidelity, amongst others). Divorce could be requested, so long as there had been separation for at least one year, thus resulting in the total dissolution of the marriage. However, the effective cease of conjugal cohabitation for at least two uninterrupted years or, in any case, cessation for more than five years, was considered as grounds for divorce. Likewise, a final conviction for an attempt to take a spouse's life or that of his/her ascendants or descendants was considered as grounds for divorce.

Law 15/2005 of July 8, 2005, is an example of the speed at which a number of social changes took place in Spain. The implementation of new legislation was necessary due to increasing phenomena, such as the development of de facto relationships and the increased scope of freedom of the spouses to file for the dissolution of marriage, amongst others. One of the main innovations introduced by this legislative change is the possibility of filing for divorce without being separated or having to prove grounds, which led to a transition from a multi-stage to a simpler model. It must be pointed out that separation has not disappeared; however, it is no longer established as a mandatory step prior to divorce and merely constitutes an additional option. The decrease in the minimum term required is another relevant innovation, having changed from one year to three months. Furthermore, this period of time may be shorter if certain situations occur (risk to personal integrity, freedom or sexual indemnity of the plaintiff, children or other family members).

Indeed, this legal amendment serves as the basis for analyzing the possible effects on marital breakdown processes. It is difficult to find research that specifically analyzes the impact of legal amendments on the divorce rate in Spain. The study by Spjker[6], which partly addresses the impact of the 2005 Spanish Law on the granting of child custody, can be quoted, along with the work of Solsona, Spijker and Ajenjo[7], who studied the regional legislative reforms. The results of this research show that these reforms increase the number of mutual consent proceedings, which leads to a decrease in litigation and the consequent reduction in the average duration of legal proceedings. In general, the existing studies on the subject have been focused on the evolution and causes of marital breakdown (Becerril[8]; Solsona and Simó[9]) and the associated legal aspects (Ruiz and Alcázar[10]). The lack of studies makes it necessary to consider the consequences of legislative change on the evolution of divorce.

In overall terms, research on the legal impact of breakdowns has been more continuous and extensive, leading to conflicting conclusions. In the United States, where interest in the impact of legal reforms arose immediately[11], Stetson and Wright[12] concluded that higher legal permissiveness goes hand in hand with a higher divorce rate. These authors questioned the impact of legal norms on the divorce rate by analyzing the degrees of legal permissiveness of said norms and their actual implementation in court. Three years later, Wright and Stetson[13] carried out further work specifically focused on the impact of the legal transformation of divorce. The main conclusion by the researchers was that these changes have had little effect on the divorce rate.

In addition, Becker[14] claimed that there is a relevant part of divorce that is influenced very little by the law: the perception of and negotiation by spouses of their future situation as divorced. Peters[15] argued that the presence of symmetrical information possessed by the spouses would result in legal reforms that only amend the compensation structure between the spouses and not the divorce rate. He concluded that the probability of divorce is not dependent upon legal reforms relating to unilateral divorce in the United States. A few years later, this study was analyzed and reinterpreted by Allen[16], who, after recalculating the data presented by Peters[15], stated that legal reform had led to an increase in the divorce rate. Peters[17] replied and insisted that legal reform only redefines what party has the right to end the marriage but does not affect divorce rates[18].

Another discussion worthy of mention is that between Glenn and Nakonezny, Shull and Rodgers. It began with work by Nakonezny, Shull and Rodgers[19] in which they claim that the introduction of laws that eliminate the need for grounds results in an increase in the divorce rate. Glenn[20] re-analyzed the data presented by these authors, highlighting the weakness of their model as it shows a very limited direct effect. Consequently, Rogers, Nakonezny and Shull[21] reaffirmed their initial 1995 idea, arguing that the same analyses carried out by Glenn validate their claims; in other words, that there is a moderate but existing effect of legal reform. Glenn[22] subsequently focused on the duration of the effect, which is unknown to last more than three years after the legal reform and, again, disagrees with the methodology used and the lack of control of other factors. Finally, Rogers, Nakonezny and Shull[23] replied that it can indeed be inferred that an effect could exist or not, but the majority of States would confirm that there is determination.

Research has also failed to define a predominant position. On the one hand, we have those who defend the relevance of legal change, as it affects the divorce rate (Friedberg[24]; Glendon[25]; González and Viitanen[26]; González and Marcén[27]) because there is an unequal distribution of income or well-being between spouses. On the other hand, some authors argue that there is no effect (Gray[28]; Phillips[29]) or note that it is minimal and temporary (Wolfers[30]). In essence, decades of discussion have failed to shed light on the influence of legal change; rather, the two opposing positions continue to be valid. Nevertheless, the latest research tends to verify the effects of legal reform, although its causes and timing are still under discussion. For this reason, the first objective of this study is to determine whether there is an association between the law and marital breakdown in Spain.

Legal impact and the granting of joint custody

In Spain, Law 15/2005 regulated a situation that was recognized in Europe (Germany in 1997, Holland in 1998, Austria in 2001 and France in 2002): the introduction of the figure of joint custody. Just a few years after the introduction of the law, different Autonomous Communities[1] (hereinafter, ACs) such as Aragon, Catalonia and Navarre, commenced legislative procedures aimed at regulating situations and relations with minors after divorce[7].

This law marked a turning point in the debate on joint custody, due to a set of decisive changes, especially those related to the exercising of custody and custody itself. Thanks to this legislation, evident progress has been made, as parental co-responsibility is what should define family relationships between parents and children, understood in terms of an equitable distribution of the rights and duties of parents based on the right of the child to continue to have direct and regular contact with both parents[31].

For the first time, legislation contemplated the possibility of the spouses deciding whether child custody and guardianship should be carried out on an exclusive or shared basis[32]. The shared option was the novelty that for a long time overshadowed the 2005 reform and became the key novelty of the reform itself, despite the many other changes made[33]. Although its formal inclusion was questioned from the beginning[34], a fundamental reform was achieved with a decisive impact on the granting of custody in Spain[35,6]. However, the law was introduced timidly, which led to the beginning of a process of approval in 2010 and the presence of specific regulations on the relations between parents and children in different ACs since 2010. Briefly, these regulations are:

1. In September 2010, the Community of Aragon was the first AC to regulate joint custody in divorce proceedings, encouraging and promoting it through Law 2/2010 on the equality of family relations in the event of a breakdown of parental cohabitation. The main purpose of the law was to promote the exercising of custody in a shared way by both parents, to guarantee the interests and protection of minors, as well as to promote equality between men and women. The explicit objective was to overcome the legal preference for individual custody and replace it with joint custody, unless proven necessary[36].
2. In the case of Catalonia, legislative change came through Law 25/2010, which was sanctioned in the approval of the second book of the Civil Code on the person and the family. The aim of the Catalan reform is much broader than custody regimes, although it includes a specific article on the issue that encourages the promotion of co-parenting. The Parenting Plan is conceived as a basic instrument that includes the way in which parents exercise their parental responsibilities[37].

3. In the Valencian Community, Law 5/2011 on the family relations of children whose parents no longer cohabitat came into force in 2011. The law stands out from the rest as the most controversial reform. Soon after it came into force, it was provisionally suspended due to an appeal to the Constitutional Court filed by the Spanish government. In December 2011, the Constitutional Court decided to lift the suspension. Finally, in 2016, the law was annulled by a Constitutional Court judgment. From a formal perspective, the Valencian law is specifically developed to regulate family relations, like the Aragonese law, highlighting the critical importance of the regulation of custody[37].
4. The Foral Community of Navarre is the fourth region to pass a law (3/2011) on child custody in cases of disruption of the cohabitation of the parents (2011) and refers to child custody in the context of divorced parents. As the law is the shortest of all, it recommends amending foral family rights, where all these issues are regulated. In any case, support for joint custody as the preferred option is evident[38].
5. Finally, Law 7/2015 on family relations in cases of separation or breakdown of marriage was published in the Basque Country in 2015. Shared custody, which is understood as the most appropriate regime, is specifically regulated and combines the principles of parental co-responsibility with the right of minors to shared custody and equality between men and women.

In general, in all cases the application of parental co-responsibility regimes that lead to more balanced or shared custody is preferred in a more or less mandatory manner. This boost in legal reform also affected other CAs. Some of them, such as Galicia and the Balearic Islands, expressed their intention to regulate the matter. At a national level, during the term of Alberto Ruíz Gallardón as Minister of Justice, the possibility of regulating custody was raised, including some form of shared custody in a more ongoing way. However, this did not materialize. Likewise, another former Minister of Justice, Rafael Catalá, promised to present a bill on parental co-responsibility that would regulate joint custody, which did not materialize before the end of the legislature.

With regard to the importance of the law on the granting of child custody, the issue has been discussed more extensively in other countries. Internationally, we observe a great deal of research on the relationship between the law and the granting of child custody. In the case of Oregon, Allen and Brinig[39] verify that the presence of legislation that favors shared custody is a key variable. Their data shows that legislative reform causes a decrease in the percentage of custody granted to the mother, as well as an increase in exclusive custody by the father; however, surprisingly, little change in shared custody is observed. The narrow timeframe analyzed may condition these results, since the Oregon reform came into force in 1997 and the analyzed data is only up to 2002.

As shown in the example of Austria, other research has confirmed the immediacy of the effect, with a decrease in single-parent custody by the mother[40,41]. Atteneder and Halla[40] point out that, before the reform, mothers were more likely to keep exclusive custody of their daughters but not of their sons. Once the law on custody preference was reformed, the gender of the minor did not have any significance. Böheim, Francesconi and Halla[41] find another added effect of legal reform that encourages shared custody: the decrease in the divorce rate and increase in marriages. They argue that this may be caused by a stronger involvement of men in de facto relationships, something already detected following reforms in the United States[42].

In the case of the Netherlands, the 1998 reform legally regulated joint custody. A decade after these changes, shared custody had tripled, from 5% in 1998 to 16% in 2008 (Spruijt and Duindam[43]). Closer to the Spanish reality, Blasio and Vuri[44] investigated the impact of the 2006 legal reform on the granting of custody in Italy. This study covers the time period of 2000 to 2010. After this legal change, a higher percentage of shared custody was observed, with sole custody granted to the mother continuously decreasing. Thus, in the Western environment, it seems evident that joint custody has been favored after legal reform, as its presence has progressively increased.

In Spain, the research by Briones and Villanueva[45] could be considered a partial precedent. Their analysis of the processes involved in measures modification in a Valencian Community court is quite interesting. Despite the limited size of their sample, it is possible to conclude that, unexpectedly, measures modification did not increase. Indeed, they suffered a decrease in the year after the Valencian law came into force. Another interesting finding is that there is no evident inclination towards joint custody. These results are likely to be influenced by several factors, such as the small sample size and the limited time period analyzed (one year), although they are the most closely related to the purpose of this study. In addition, the Valencian law was immediately challenged by the central government and petitions were slowed down by the uncertainty of the appeal filed. Consequently, the second objective focuses on determining whether there is a relationship between the impact of legal reform on the granting of joint custody.

Methodology

The methodology used is eminently quantitative. Specifically, data from the General Council of the Judiciary and the Statistics on Annulments, Separations and Divorces (ENSD) provided by the National Institute of Statistics (INE) was used. The latter source of information is the only one in which information could be obtained on the evolution of the granting of different types of child custody, both at a State and AC level. It is an annual statistic provided by the INE by virtue of an agreement with the General Council of the Judiciary and based on the information of judgments by different judicial bodies with jurisdiction in the matter. This statistic collects data on annulments, separations and divorces that occur annually in Spain. Among other aspects, it includes variables such as the age and nationality of the spouses, number of minors and adult dependent children, existence of pensions, type of custody granted and the existence of previous separation.

Unlike the data on divorce, the specific facts on the granting of child custody have only been recorded since 2007, which constituted a limitation. Accordingly, a large sample that could, for example, be used to analyze the situation from the 1980s onwards could not be constructed. Nevertheless, as the most significant transformations took place in the last decade and a half, we were able to obtain a relatively long time period for the analysis. The last available year is 2017 and this is the timeframe in which the different statistical techniques were performed. Since the INE offers general results, the acquisition of microdata was the option that allowed us to perform more detailed operations to achieve our objectives.

A descriptive analysis was the technique chosen, which allowed us to offer a fairly complete overview of the evolution of divorce, so that we could observe the impact of law. Likewise, a comprehensive study that focused on each AC provided detailed information on the granting of child custody in Spain and its different forms.

In addition, two multivariate analysis techniques were used to make the results more robust. On the one hand, we applied factor analysis, a data reduction technique aimed at limiting a high number of variables, which reduces the explanation to reality in a simpler way (Ferrán[46]). This technique will sacrifice ease to interpret reality at the lowest possible cost in terms of loss of information. In addition, the correspondence analysis was used to increase knowledge of the impact of the law on the granting of custody. This is a specific application of the ACP and is very useful for graphically observing the form of relations between the categories of the variables chosen.

Results and discussion

The results obtained after applying the techniques described above were then analyzed. The number of breakdowns in Spain decreased progressively until it stabilized at around 100,000 breakdowns per year. Specifically, significant differences were observed in the growth of separations and divorces (see Figure 12.1).

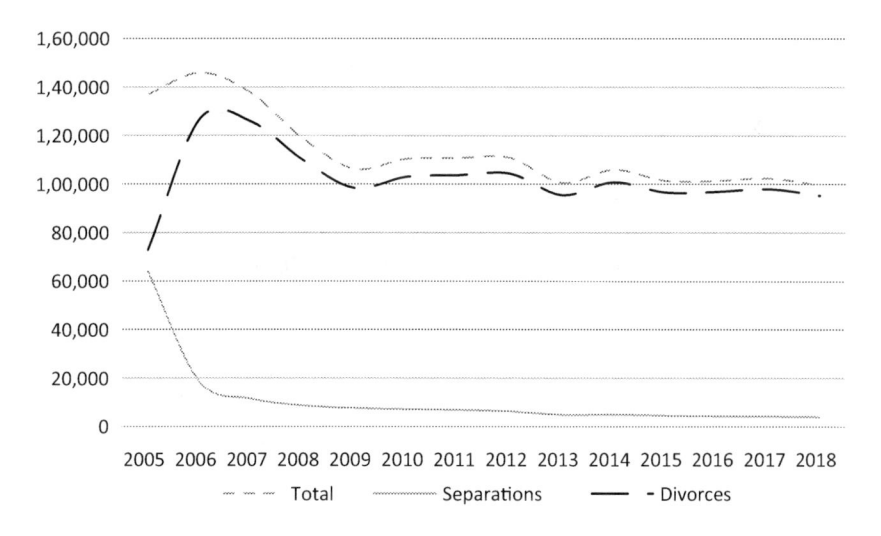

Figure 12.1 Evolution of divorces and separations in Spain

Source: Created by the authors with data from the statistics on annulments, separations and divorces (INE)

Table 12.1 Factor analysis

Variables	2005
Religious beliefs	−0.019
Spouse age	0.074
Spouse educational level	0.006
Nationality of spouse	−0.460
Unemployment rate	−547
Activity rate	0.262
Existence of law	0.829
Cumulative variance: 54.838	**KMO 0.506**
	p-value 0.000

Source: Prepared by the authors based on statistics on annulments, separations and divorces (INE), 2017

Until 2005, there were more separations than divorces. From then on, the legal changes introduced implied a reverse relationship between these forms: separations started to decrease while divorces increased. It should be noted that there was a slight resurge of marital breakdowns at the same time as the legal change was introduced, increasing from 137,044 in 2005 to 145,745 in 2006. Subsequently, the total number of marriage breakdowns decreased from 2007 (137,360) and stabilized as from 2009 (106,039). The relationship between the 2005 law and divorce can be more clearly observed in Table 12.1.

In 2005, the variable "existence of law" appears as the most prominent factor (0.829). It is positive and very high in relation to the rest, where only the female activity rate had a certain weighting (0.262); however, the female activity rate represents approximately less than half of the other value. These results concur with certain research that observed an immediate, short-term effect of the impact of law (Friedberg[24]; Glendon[25]; González and Viitanen[26]; González and Marcén[27]). In this regard, two important aspects can be highlighted: the short-term impact of the law and the potential of the legal reform at the time to trigger a change in the form of breakdown (divorce begins to be predominate).

With regard to the form of custody granted, if we focus on national figures, we observe that there was a remarkable increase in the shared form of custody, from 9.6% in 2007 to 32.8% in 2018. However, this increase is not consistent, which can be explained in certain CAs by the establishment and implementation of their own legislation. Therefore, more detailed information is presented in Figure 12.2, where two sets of CAs are shown (those that have and those that do not have their own legal system).

Although there is a major difference between CAs that apply their own legislation and those that do not, a general trend towards joint custody is increasing. When some CAs began to apply their own regulations in 2011, there were higher percentages of shared custody in comparison to the rest of the communities, as can be observed

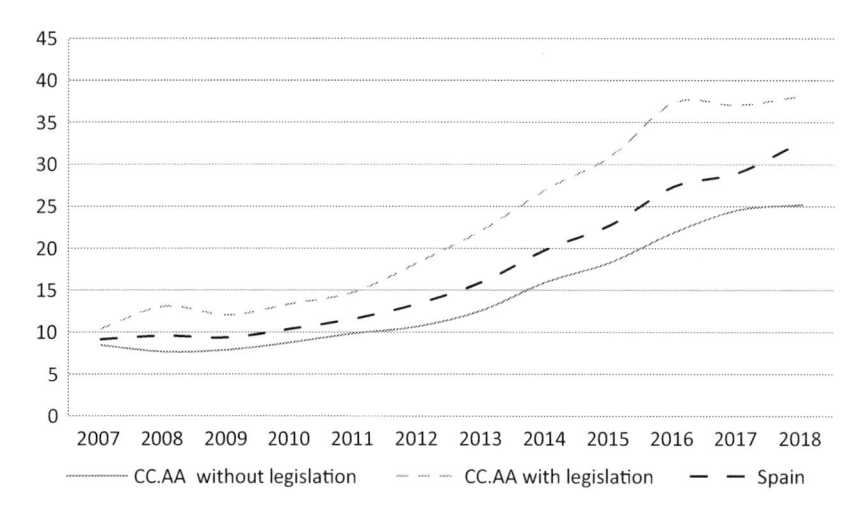

Figure 12.2 Evolution of joint custody in Spain and by groups according to the existence of own law (%)
Source: Created by the authors with data from the statistics on annulments, separations and divorces (INE)

(Figure 12.2). These differences between communities are also due to the fact that the growth of this form in regions of Spain with their own law is much greater than in those without their own legal system. The growth in communities without a specific regulation is delayed and occurs gradually, with an increase of around 16% from 2007 to 2017. The current percentage of shared custody in these communities is 24.5%. In contrast, the CAs with their own legislation had an overall rate of 10.4% of shared custody in 2007 and, 10 years later, had doubled their figures, reaching 37%. This apparent association is more evident after the application of the correspondence analysis.

Catalonia, Aragon, the Balearic Islands and the Valencian Community are the closest CAs with regard to shared custody (Figure 12.3). The remaining communities are quite far away with respect to the shared custody option and closer to the exclusive form for either parent. Furthermore, it is necessary to highlight the evident and significant differences between communities that have and those that do not have their own legal systems.

Therefore, the application of legislation that favors parental co-responsibility and, specifically, the granting of the shared form of custody, has a positive impact, as it increases the percentage of shared custody. However, this increase negatively affects the custody assigned exclusively to the mother. Nevertheless, it should be noted that CAs with their own legal system and higher levels of shared custody have had higher percentages since 2011.

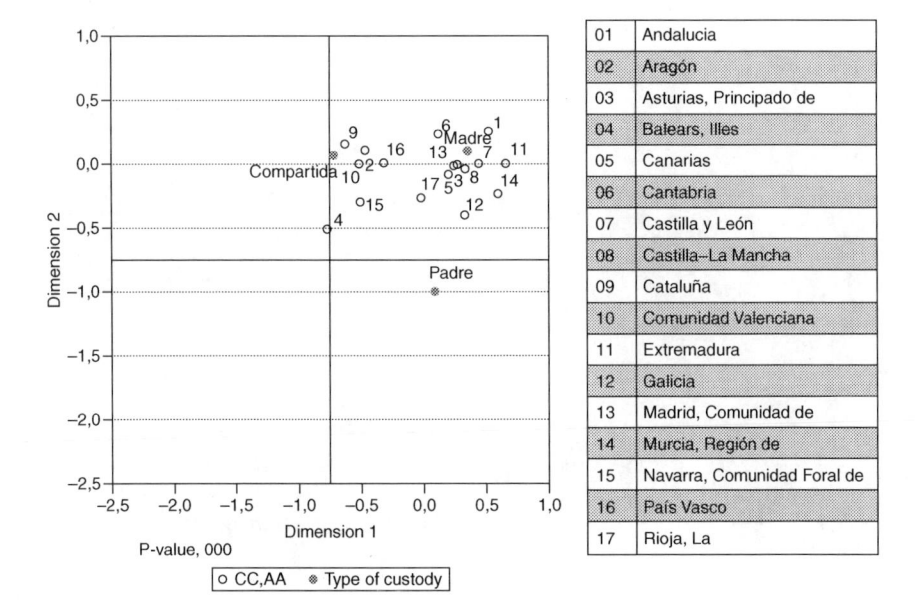

Figure 12.3 Correspondence analysis: Custody modality assigned by Autonomous Community
Source: Created by the authors with data from the statistics on annulments, separations and divorces (INE), 2017

Conclusions

In this chapter, we have addressed the impact of the legal reforms introduced in 2005 that condition both the process of marriage breakdown and the granting of the custody of minors and/or adult dependents. Although divorce and the granting of child custody after a marital breakup, as well as the many issues related to these processes, has been an ongoing field of study in diverse disciplines both nationally and internationally, in Spain there is a dramatic lack of studies. Quantitative methodology was based on the use of the Statistics on Annulments, Separations and Divorces (2005–2018) and the General Council of the Judiciary.

The process of marital breakdown in Spain has undergone several major changes in just a few decades. At present, there are two laws that have or presently regulate the issue: Law 30/1981 of July 7, 1981, and Law 15/2005 of July 8, 2005. The latter introduces substantial changes that enable us to measure the impact of law on the process of divorce.

In terms of marital breakdown, 2005 was a year of radical change. From that time on, divorce became the preferred option to dissolve a marriage rather than separation. Although regulatory change produced an increase in marital breakdowns a year later, in 2006, there was a subsequent reduction followed by a period of stability in 2009. In addition, the form of marital breakdown radically changed: divorce increased and separations decreased. The impact on the divorce rate resulting from legal reform is therefore patent. Nevertheless, this impact is higher in the short term.

A lack of agreement on the impact of law and its relationship with the divorce rate has been evidenced. In fact, a variety of works point to its existence (Friedberg[24]; Glendon[25]; González and Viitanen[26]; González and Marcén[27]) and other research that claims a minimal or non-existent relationship (Gray[28]; Phillips[29]). It should be observed that the key point of the discussion in this chapter is methodological or conceptual issues.

Regarding the granting of child custody, the creation and implementation by several CAs of their own legislation has been progressive. After such legislation was passed, the granting of shared custody increased, at the expense of exclusive custody granted to the mother. Although this has generally occurred at a national level, the increase has been higher in CAs with their own legislation, rising from 15% in 2011 to 35% in 2017. In communities without their own regulations, the increase was from 9% in 2011 to 25% in 2017. We can therefore conclude that the existence of a legal system that somehow favors the granting of joint custody increases its presence. Furthermore, this conclusion concurs with several international research studies (Allen and Brinig[39]; Atteneder and Halla[40]; Böheim, Francesconi and Halla[41]).

In short, this chapter presents the impact of law on both marital breakdown and the granting of child custody, despite the debate that exists on how it actually occurs and is maintained, or not, over time. For this reason, the fact that the issues of divorce and granting of child custody in Spain are important, as they involve a significant element of the population, means that this field of study deserves the necessary attention.

Notes

1 Berger P, Luckmann T. *La construcción social de la realidad*. Buenos Aires: Amorrortu; 2003.
2 Becerril D, Venegas M. *La custodia compartida en España*. Madrid: Dykinson; 2017.
3 Becerril D. La percepción social del divorcio en España. *Revista Española de Investigaciones Sociológicas* 2008; 95: 219–223.
4 Camarero V. *Derecho y conflictividad matrimonial. Datos básicos para una sociología jurídica en la provincia de Castellón (1981–1991)*. Castellón: Diputación provincial de Castellón; 1997.
5 Camarero V. *Estudio jurídico-sociológico de los procesos matrimoniales. Proyección comparativa en la provincia de Castellón (1992–2002)*. Castellón: Diputacion provincial de Castellón; 2008.
6 Spijker J. Trends in custody arrangements in Spain since the divorce reform of 2005. *Papers de Demografia* 2012; 404.
7 Solsona M, Spijker J, Ajenjo A. Calidoscopio de la custodia compartida en España. In *la custodia compartida en España*, edited by Becerril D, Venegas M, 45–72. Madrid: Dykinson; 2017.
8 Becerril D. La ruptura matrimonial en España. In *España 2015. Situación social*, edited by Torres C, 344–350. Madrid: Centros de Investigaciones Sociológicas; 2015.
9 Solsona M, Simó C. Evolución histórica del divorcio en España desde la aprobación de la Ley de 1981 hasta la reforma de 2004. In *La constitución familiar*, edited by Cabré A, 245–296. Bilbao: Fundación BBVA; 2007.
10 Ruiz R, Alcázar R. Propiedades sociométricas del cuestionario de arraigo familiar en supuestos de custodia compartida disputada. *Zerbitzuan* 2018; 66: 21–32.

11 Jacob H. *The silent revolution: The transformation of divorce law in the United States.* University of Chicago Press: Chicago; 1988.
12 Stetson D, Wrighth G. The effects of laws on divorce in American States. *Journal of Marriage and Family* 1975; 37: 537–547.
13 Wright G, Stetson D. The impact of no-fault divorce law reform on divorce in American States. *Journal of Marriage and Family* 1978; 40: 575–580.
14 Becker G. *Tratado sobre la familia.* Madrid: Alianza; 1987.
15 Peters E. Marriage and divorce: Informational constraints and private contracting. *American Economic Review* 1986; 76: 437–454.
16 Allen D. Marriage and divorce: Comment. *American Economic Review* 1992; 82: 679–685.
17 Peters E. Marriage and divorce: Reply. *American Economic Review* 1992; 82: 686–693
18 Härkönen J, Dronkers J. Stability and change in the educational gradient of divorce: A comparison of seventeen countries. *European Sociological Review* 2006; 22; 5: 501–517
19 Nakonezny P, Shull R, Rodgers J. The effect of no-fault divorce law on the divorce rate across the 50 states and its relation to income, education and religiosity. *Journal of Marriage and Family* 1995; 57: 477–488.
20 Glenn N. A reconsideration of the effect of no-fault divorce on divorce rates. *Journal of Marriage and Family* 1997; 59: 1023–1025.
21 Rodgers J, Nakonezny P, Shull, R. The effect of no-fault divorce legislation on divorce rates: A response to a reconsideration. *Journal of Marriage and the Family* 1997; 59: 1026–1030.
22 Glenn N. Discussion of the effects of no-fault divorce on divorce rates. *Journal of Marriage and Family* 1999; 61: 800–802.
23 Rodgers J, Nakonezny P, Shull R. Did no-fault legislation matter? Definitely yes and sometimes no. *Journal of Marriage and Family* 1999; 61: 803–809.
24 Friedberg L. Did unilateral divorce raise divorce rates? Evidence from panel data. *American Economic Review* 1998; 88: 608–627.
25 Glendon M. *The transformation of family law: State, law, and family in the United States and Western Europe.* Chicago: University of Chicago Press; 1989.
26 González L, Viitanen T. The effect of divorce laws on divorce rates in Europe. *IZA Discussion Paper* 2006; 2023.
27 González R, Marcén M. Unilateral divorce versus child custody support in the U.S. *Journal of Economic Behavior & Organization* 2012; 88: 613–643.
28 Gray J. Divorce-law changes, household bargaining, and married women's labor supply. *American Economic Review* 1998; 88(3): 628–642.
29 Phillips, R. *A history of divorce in Western society.* Cambridge: Cambridge University Press; 1988.
30 Wolfers J. Did unilateral divorce laws raise divorce rates? A reconciliation and new results. *American Economic Review* 2006; 96: 1802–1820.
31 Tamayo S. El interés del menor como criterio de atribución de la custodia. *Revista de derecho de familia* 2008; 41: 35–79.
32 Flaquer, L. El avance hacia la custodia compartida o el retorno del padre tras una larga ausencia. In España 2015. *Situación social*, edited by Torres, C. 351–359. Madrid: Centros de Investigaciones Sociológicas; 2015.
33 Becerril, D. La custodia en los procesos de ruptura en España. In *Actas del XI Congreso de Español de sociología. Crisis y cambio: propuestas desde la sociología*, edited by Cairo, H. y Finkel, L. Madrid: Federación Española de Sociología; 2014.
34 Alascio, L. La excepcionalidad de la custodia compartida impuesta (art. 92.8 CC) *Indret. Revista para el análisis del derecho* 2011; 2.
35 Solsona M. Divorcio, generaciones y género. In España 2015. *Situación social*, edited by Torres, C. 117–126. Madrid: Centros de Investigaciones Sociológicas; 2015.
36 Serrano J. La custodia compartida aragonesa en la primera jurisprudencia. 2013. Retrieved from www.eljusticiadearagon.com/gestor/ficheros/_n006014_Custodia%20compartida

37 Gómez, C. El artículo 92 del código civil y la custodia compartida. Cuestiones generales sobre esta institución. 2016. Retrieved from http://digibuo.uniovi.es/dspace/bitstream/10651/34579/6/TFM_GomezHernandez%2CC.pdf
38 Suso A, González I, Pérez A, Velasco M. *Análisis de los modelos de custodia derivados de las situaciones de separación y divorcio en España*. Madrid: Ministerio de sanidad, servicios sociales e igualdad; 2012.
39 Allen D, Brinig, M. Do joint parenting laws make any difference? *Journal of Empirical Legal Studies* 2011; 8: 304–324.
40 Atteneder C, Halla M. Bargaining at divorce: The allocation of custody. *IZA Discussion Paper* 2007; 2544.
41 Böheim R, Francesconi M, Halla M. Does custody law affect family behavior in and out of marriage? *IZA Discussion Paper* 2002; 7064.
42 Halla M. The effect of jont custody on marriage and divorce. *IZA Discussion Paper* 2009; 4314.
43 Spruijt E, Duindam V. Joint physical custody in the Netherlands and the well-being of children. *Journal of Divorce and Remarriage* 2009; 51: 65–82.
44 Blasio G, Vuri, D. Joint custody in the Italian courts. *IZA Discussion Paper* 2013; 7472.
45 Briones P, Villanueva B. Impacto de la ley de custodia compartida de la Comunidad Valenciana en las modificaciones de medida. *Anuario de Psicología Jurídica* 2014; 24: 43–48.
46 Ferrán M. *SPSS para Windows 95. Programación y análisis estadístico*. Madrid: McGraw-Hill; 1996.

13
FAMILY STRUCTURE, PARENTAL PRACTICES, AND CHILD WELLBEING IN POST-DIVORCE SITUATIONS

The case of shared parenting

Ana María López Narbona, Almudena Moreno Mínguez and Marta Ortega Gaspar

Introduction

This chapter provides a critical literature review of empirical sociological studies on shared care (shared parenting [SP], joint custody [JC], joint physical custody [JPC]) and its effects on children's wellbeing (best interest of the child [BIC], subjective wellbeing, satisfaction) in Spain during the years 2015–2019.

The current context of social and family changes is embedded in the second demographic transition (SDT), in which the emergence of phenomena such as a new division of gender roles, decline of the male breadwinner family model, and new parenting styles has gained momentum.[1] In this context, separations and divorces tend to increase, raising growing concern about children's wellbeing.

Despite growing interest in the consequences of shared care on children's wellbeing, our investigation identifies significant deficiencies in the literature on shared care of children when marriages dissolve. First, the field shows serious lack of empirical evidence. Second, concepts are neither defined clearly nor used properly. Third, the field lacks databases. Fourth, studies should consider how parents' wellbeing impacts BIC. Finally, the literature has developed no indicators or indexes based on solid theoretical foundations. Our main conclusion is that these gaps must be addressed to ensure sound grounding of social policies concerning care of children in models that are efficient and in the BIC.

First and second demographic transitions

The first demographic transition explains declines in fertility and mortality (greater longevity, healthier populations) in Western countries from the eighteenth and nineteenth centuries onward. Increases in marriage age also contributed to declines in fertility.

The SDT is characterized by sustained sub-replacement fertility, wide variety of living arrangements other than marriage, disconnect between marriage and procreation, and nonstationary population. In this context, immigration has contributed to increasing fertility, but not at replacement rate.

In the 1950s, divorce rates rose sharply. The SDT brought a change in values, with greater tolerance for diversity and respect for individual choices. Maslow suggests that greater economic development produced a shift from concerns about material needs (subsistence, shelter, physical and economic security) to a focus on nonmaterial needs (free expression, participation and emancipation, self-realization and autonomy, recognition).[2] Inglehart's theory of post-materialism follows similar lines.[3]

Spain has not remained on the sideline of these changes. Since the 1980s, the Spanish population has undergone numerous transformations. Two significant sociodemographic processes in Spanish society, aging and low fertility rates, have produced new family models. Spain has also seen increases in the age of marriage and maternity, unmarried partners with children born out of wedlock, single-parent families, and early divorce.[4]

The economic crisis affected Spain's labor market profoundly. Labor instability since and during the crisis has had a tremendous impact on fertility, which has also modified patterns of family formation.[5] The transformation of family models in Spain is closely linked to reproductive behavior and demographic evolution.

Following studies by Goldscheider, Bernhardt, and Lappegård, and Lesthaege,[6] we conclude that the main vectors of change in the SDT are individualism, labor instability, deinstitutionalization, female revolution and gender equality, and styles of family and social life linked to legal changes. The consequences of the SDT are demographic changes such as fertility reduction, increased divorce and domestic partners, changes in family structure and new forms of family, pluralization, and decline of the breadwinner family model,[7] development of "new paternities" or new styles of fatherhood,[8] economic instability of families,[9] and ultimately an increase in JC.

In the context of the SDT and new fathering styles, both parents share parental responsibility. Furthermore, JC (or SP) is becoming a common form of child custody. The specialized literature supports the conclusion that JC is better for children's wellbeing than sole custody.[10] Children in families with JC have slightly lower satisfaction than those in intact families but slightly higher satisfaction than children in sole custody.

This chapter analyzes concepts closely related to JC, such as children's wellbeing and poverty—key concepts in family policy design. JC poses many other challenges in the policy sphere, such as the debate over equal-time parenting after separation/divorce, a concept currently focused on equalizing mathematical time instead of quality of parent–child relationships in the general SP model.

Children's wellbeing should be understood as a wide-reaching, holistic concept. From this perspective, children's satisfaction in JC depends on many elements: each parent's education level and economic status, conflicts between parents, involvement of parents, and communication between parents and children, among others.[11] For Smyth,[12] the concept of children's wellbeing encompasses "balancing time and responsibility in a way that best suits children's temperament, level of resilience, developmental stage, and age; and that best suits each parent's work responsibilities, personal capacities, and strengths".

A complete critical literature review is crucial to identifying shortcomings, strengths, and weaknesses. One major shortcoming in Spain is the very limited number of studies on JC and children's wellbeing. Another is inadequacy or non-existence of databases and sources. For example, the Health Behaviour in School-aged Children (HBSC) database is one of the few that collects large-scale data on children's wellbeing in Spain.

To overcome these shortcomings, our study provides a critical literature review of empirical sociological studies (qualitative and quantitative) on shared care (SP, JC, JPC, etc.) and its effects on children's wellbeing (BIC, subjective wellbeing, satisfaction, etc.) in Spain from 2015 to 2019. Our review updates that of Marín, Dujo, and Horcajo, which covers publications on JC from 2005 (the year the new Civil Law was enacted) to 2015.[13]

From a sociological perspective, this chapter adopts a very broad focus, as it aims to identify children's wellbeing in the family and in relations between parents and children in the SDT context. We thus review critically the effects on society (focusing mainly on gender relations and roles, and changes in these), the family as institution (e.g., changes in family structure, new parenting styles), children's wellbeing, and parents' wellbeing.

Preliminary conclusions are that no precise definition exists for the concepts involved. Different authors use different terms—JC, JPC, SP, shared residence (SR), shared custody (SC) —with slightly different meanings. SP may indicate equal sharing in which children spend 50% of their time with each parent. Other cases use JPC when either the mother or the father is the primary carer (time spent with child is 25–49%).[14] The literature also lacks consensus on amount of time children spend with parents, cycle of care, and children's age.

Fariña et al.'s report for the American Psychological Association analyzes the consequences of JC practice, observing positive effects on children.[15] Since publication of this report, the United States has defined JC as the best option, as in the BIC (for children's wellbeing and adaptation), essentially making BIC synonymous with JC.[16]

If SP and JC are becoming pervasive in post-divorce situations, full knowledge of the literature on these legal arrangements in Spain is key to sound policy decisions and children's wellbeing.

Methodology

The importance of a good literature review is self-evident: it can build science and shape research, practice, and policy initiatives.[17] This review seeks to provide a full description of the state of the art on shared care and its effects on children's wellbeing as evidenced by empirical studies (qualitative and quantitative) in Spain between 2015 and 2019. The main objective is to contribute to both theory development and direct applicability and policy.

Since a critical literature review can encompass infinite variables, issues, or populations, clarity of purpose is essential. A well-specified purpose facilitates the review's ability to operationalize variables accurately and thus extract appropriate data from primary sources.

Because clear identification of problem and purpose are essential to providing focus and boundaries for the overall review process, we first identified the main problems the review needed to address, that is, its purpose: the consequences of shared care on children's wellbeing. The primary focus is the effects of JC on all population groups involved—children, parents, and families.

We performed an extensive, systematic, critical literature search and review of publications in Spain between 2015 and 2019 using the following key words: *custodia*, custody, *custodia compartida*, shared custody, shared parenting, joint custody, *bienestar infantil*, children's wellbeing, satisfaction, best interest of the child, *estudios empíricos*, empirical studies, *co-parentalidad*, *residencia compartida*, shared residence, *co-responsabilidad parental*, and parental co-responsibility.

The search was conducted on the following platforms: Social Science Citation Index, Sociological Abstracts, Google Scholar, Scopus, International Bibliography of the Social Sciences, JSTOR, Dialnet, and Latindex, among others.

The main problem this study faced was the great difficulty of comparing empirical findings in existing studies because of different concepts used, different samples and sample sizes, and different methods, societal contexts, and outcomes.

Results of the critical review of effects of divorce on children's wellbeing

As stated above, analyzing children's wellbeing requires opening the scope of analysis to include the different population groups whose wellbeing impacts children's wellbeing. We identified four crucial groups: the children themselves, their parents, the family as an institution, and society as a whole.

We then classified the results of the critical review of empirical studies according to importance of effects on the family as institution, on parents, on children, or on all three.

Effects on children

The (above-mentioned) first literature review on SC in Spain was performed by Marín, Dujo, and Horcajo.[18] SC was introduced in Spain through a modification of Spanish Civil Law 15/2005. Marín et al. performed a qualitative analysis of the Spanish Supreme Court's jurisprudence from 2005 to 2015 to compare the empirical results of the effects of SC on children to the judges' decisions.[19]

The study examined 33 case studies, of which 20 legal decisions granted SC and 13 did not. One main conclusion is the impossibility of determining which type of custody (sole or shared) is best for children because the outcome depends on other variables. The main variables in this study were educational style and inter-parental communication, quality of parent–child relations, stage of minor's evolution, overnight stay, and conflict level.

Ruiz-Callado and Ruiz measured family ties.[20] Their working hypothesis was that minors in JC had similar family ties in the mother's and the father's home.

This descriptive cross-sectional study was performed on cases in the Family Courts of Alicante (Valencian Community, Spain). Data were collected from January 1, 2013 to December 31, 2017. The researchers interviewed 115 minors whose parents were divorced and for whom the custody decision was controversial, thus analyzing SC in a conflictual context. One important conclusion is that stepfamilies and grandparents play a decisive role for children in such conflictual situations.

Effects on family institution and on parents

For Rodríguez-Domínguez, Jarne, and Carbonell, Spanish jurisprudence grants custody and child custody giving top priority to the BIC.[21] This study analyzed seven courts in the city of Barcelona from 2007 to 2013. It illustrates how the concept used leads to a distinction between the interest of the children and children's wellbeing. Homogenization of concepts is one of the main challenges in the SP literature in Spain. The study's major finding is that the courts increasingly favor JC and that sole custody in favor of mothers decreased during the study period.

Solsona and Spijker's large-scale quantitative analysis compared prevalence of JPC and its primary determinants in Catalonia and the rest of Europe.[22] The data analyzed were microdata on divorce decrees issued from 2007 to 2012. This study also discusses legal and behavioral aspects of these new custody arrangements regulating terms for sharing parenting responsibilities.

The database used was that of the Spanish National Statistics Institute (INE), which signed an agreement with the General Council of the Judiciary on February 14, 1995 to publish justice statistics. The main conclusions are, first, that the 2010 Civil Code of Catalonia led to trends in JPC in Catalonia that differ from (that is, they are more frequent than) those in the rest of Spain. During this period, only Belgium, Denmark, and Sweden had higher rates of JPC within Europe. Another impact of Catalonia's Civil Code was to reduce gender inequalities in the family context.

For Ruiz-Callado and Ruiz, the family model has changed in response to the evolution and transformation of society.[23] Social transformations changing families' structure, composition, and dynamics have impacted divorce legislation. Using a sample from 170 court filings in Alicante's Family Courts, the authors identify the main variables differentiating between families in SC versus sole custody. Two main models emerge: negotiating families (primarily JC) and traditional families (more likely to have sole custody). The main variables analyzed were education level, parents' work activities, sharing of household chores, and childcare.

Although analysis at the province level is valuable, the literature significantly lacks studies comparing different family jurisdictions.

Recently, Solsona, Ajenjo, Brullet, and Gómez-Casillas analyzed JC and its effects on families and gender equality.[24] Some interesting conclusions are that JC is an emerging paradigm (20% of sentences analyzed, 30% of mutual agreement proceedings) and that the dominant paradigm is still mother's sole custody (63% of all sentences, 82% in conflictual proceedings). The authors identify a figure of the absent father and a residual father's sole custody. JC shows a clear pattern of equal distribution of time and expenses.[25]

Solsona and Ajenjo analyze 5894 sentences issued by Barcelona's Family Courts in 2014 and include new variables, such as family income.[26] Higher family income correlates with higher percentage of SC (42%); lower-income families represent only 24% of SC cases. Finally, SC means equality for parents, as children spend comparable amounts of time with each parent. As conflict between parents can increase in cases of indiscriminate attribution of SC, courts should be very careful in adjudicating JC.

Effects on children and parents

Ruiz-Callado and Alcázar analyze children's preferences on how parents and caregivers can best meet their needs.[27] The authors obtained case studies (136 judicial records) from Family Court 2014–2016. The results show that mothers were in greater demand than fathers but that fathers played an active role in children's play and safety needs. Children's preferences were for SC and depended more on child's gender than on age. Age and gender are interesting variables in analyzing children's preferences.

Although González and Viitanen's work on effects of divorce legalization on children's long-term well-being across Europe does not focus specifically on SP, it is valuable to include here because it highlights the importance of longitudinal analysis of children's wellbeing.[28] The authors compare adult outcomes of cohorts of children raised when divorce was banned to cohorts raised after divorce was legalized. The main result is that women who grew up under legal divorce have lower earnings and income and worse health as adults than women who grew up when divorce was illegal. These negative effects are not found for men.

Effects on parents, children, and family

Flaquer, Escobedo, Alsina, and Moreno perform comprehensive analysis of factors contributing to the growth of SR in Spain and variations in children's life satisfaction levels in diverse family arrangements, focusing especially on SR.[29]

The authors use two databases, the Spanish Statistics of Divorce (2007–2015) and the HBSC survey for Spain in 2014. Their main conclusion is that egalitarianism in divorce proceedings affects the progress of SR in Spain. The authors measured this variable by rates of mutual agreement, joint filing, and payment of child maintenance by both parents resulting from increased gender equality. Their main results indicate that children from SR arrangements show better life satisfaction outcomes than children from single-parent families but that these outcomes are still much lower than those for children from intact families.

Although SR is an interesting term, the concept differs from SC or JC, making comparison problematic.

Discussion

Nearly all publications analyzed demonstrate either positive or general effects of SP or JC. For Marin, Dujo, and Horcajo, however, one cannot conclude that SC is more in the BIC than is sole custody.[30] Very few studies conclude that JC has negative effects. Flaquer, Escobedo, Alsina, and Moreno examine variations in child life satisfaction levels but not negative effects.[31] Studies also fail to provide full analysis of the positive effects on children. For example, Ruiz-Callado and Alcázar, and Ruiz-Callado and Ruiz focus on the roles of mothers, fathers, and families.[32] We believe the literature significantly lacks studies on children's wellbeing in SP. Studies of SC should focus on positive, negative, and general effects on children's wellbeing.

The literature also contains very few empirical studies (qualitative or quantitative), possibly due to lack of databases. Furthermore, most empirical studies to date focus on the province or autonomous community. Very few studies compare autonomous communities or make international comparisons (Solson and Spijker compare Catalonia to Spain and other European countries).[33] Many studies focus on a single province, such as Barcelona or Alicante.

The samples, populations, and years of analysis are also heterogeneous and limited, making it difficult to compare and generalize from studies. As the main databases used are the INE and information from Family Courts, we conclude that Spain has very few databases on this important issue.

Following Smyth,[34] we identify significant research gaps. The SP literature presents significant challenges. First, scholarly conclusions are based on results from small nonprobability samples that focus on fathers' points of view. Subjective use of measures is also concerning in Spanish publications.

When measuring the effects of SP on children's wellbeing, the impact of the prior separation and divorce processes should be taken into account, yet the publications analyzed do not do so. Given such omissions, how much of what researchers claim to measure is a consequence of SP versus of the divorce or separation process? How can these different effects be measured? How can we eliminate the influence of separation or divorce? Can this impact be eliminated? Should it be? The empirical studies analyzed do not address these questions properly.

Beyond these concerns, we find multiple warnings for future studies. First, the literature needs empirical studies that enable researchers to contrast positive effects of SP and BIC, as risks and benefits are not yet clear. Although existing empirical studies in international contexts suggest that JPC arrangements have positive effects on the wellbeing of parents and children, the concept, methodology, and contexts of these studies are very heterogeneous.[35]

Second, it is crucial when reviewing cases to identify whether SP family members behave as co-responsible carers and achieve the main goal, the BIC.

Finally, we need studies that analyze different socio-economic family scenarios to provide knowledge of the real diversity of family opportunities from which to choose and obtain SC.

Our review also identifies a clear need for empirical studies on the perverse effects of SP laws. For example, do any parents seek goals against the BIC, such as parents who are not paying the required alimony or child support or parents interested in using the family dwelling? Second, it is important to study the reproduction of social inequalities. Which social groups are marginalized due to SP? Third, no studies assess whether the law is applied arbitrarily due to legal inaccuracy. Finally, research suffers from significant lack of studies on institutional and organizational practice, and of multidisciplinary teams, coordination, human resources, interdepartmental communication, and time dedicated to evaluating cases.

Although the few empirical studies on SC and children's wellbeing in Spain have been used to guide policies and practice, they constitute a highly problematic foundation for policy and practice, as the issues are extremely complex. We must encourage more empirical and longitudinal analysis; Spain does not currently follow up on SP and children's wellbeing and thus lacks related data. Further, very few empirical studies distinguish cooperative arrangements from those developed and maintained in conflictual environments.

JPC's impact on children has received more discussion than the equally important effects of JPC on separated/divorced parents.[36] Separated/divorced parents are more likely to experience maladjustment in different areas of life.[37] JPC can mitigate these negative outcomes for parents. Since parents' wellbeing impacts children's wellbeing directly and indirectly,[38] studies of JPC's impact on children's outcomes should include parents' wellbeing. We would even argue that understanding children's wellbeing requires more research on grandparents.

Some research is now focusing on grandparental childcare. In countries like Spain, where grandparents provide substantial amounts of care, analyzing this issue is important to providing the best care to children. Žilinčíková and Kreidl analyze the "effect of grandparental divorce on odds of providing grandparental childcare and variation of this effect across countries using data collected 2004–2011 in 18 European countries as part of the SHARE project".[39] Their main conclusion is that being divorced significantly reduced the odds of participants having provided grandparental childcare in the past 12 months and their odds of having provided intensive childcare (at least once a week). The effect of divorce varies significantly, however, across countries.

Children's wellbeing also differs significantly depending on whether SP or JC is mandated by the court, decided through mediation, or agreed upon by parents without involvement of mediators or the court. Few studies focus on these issues.

Finally, McIntosh proposes *therapeutic mediation* for post-separation parenting disputes, implementing two forms of mediation: child-focused intervention that encourages parents to consider their children's needs (without children's direct involvement) and child-inclusive intervention.[40] Children are interviewed by a specialist, who constructs a picture of the child's world and concerns and conveys that picture carefully to parents as part of the mediation process.

Children's point of view is absent in Spanish publications, with the exception of a study by Fariña, Seijo, Arce, and Vazquez, who propose "therapeutic justice", with very interesting results.[41] Yet this issue raises many questions, including how to achieve such therapeutic justice in a context of limited resources. Therapeutic justice implies dissolving marriages in a way that enables parents' to assume positive joint responsibility while focusing on children's wellbeing. At present, implementing such an initiative remains only a very remote possibility in Spain.

Conclusions

Our study highlights the need for consensus on concepts (JPC, SP, place of residence, SR, shared time arrangements, BIC, children's wellbeing, etc.) and methodologies (sample size, geographical scope of analysis, unit of analysis [e.g., separated, divorced, unmarried parents], age and gender of children, conflict or lack of conflict between parents).

The literature also needs better objective and subjective indicators and indexes for data analysis. Our study finds a lack of surveys and databases. Solsona and Spijker stress the limitations of the current data, which omit information on parental shared time plans and how the plans are applied.[42] The literature also shows a significant lack of international comparisons.

One important research challenge on SP and children's wellbeing in Spain is lack of follow-up. To obtain in-depth knowledge of how SC is actually applied, researchers and social scientists must follow children's wellbeing over long time periods. A major challenge to longitudinal analyses in Spain is lack of databases.

Another serious limitation in SP research is the difficulty of determining whether families comply with the agreements. Flaquer notes that Spain has no administrative agency in charge of supervising smooth functioning of the child maintenance system, monitoring payment of allowances, and enforcing compliance.[43] This is a very important issue when addressing children's wellbeing.

What does this literature review add to the existing literature? As a critical review of the most recent empirical studies (2015–2019) in Spain, our study includes new studies not considered in previous reviews of the national or international context. It provides a comprehensive overview of the state of the discussion and the gaps in empirical studies of the effects of SP and JPC on children's wellbeing in Spain.

Finally, we highlight that this study summarizes the arguments and empirical results from a crucial point of view—that of the effects of SP and JPC on the wellbeing of both children and parents.

Notes

1 Colin Creighton, "The rise and decline of the 'male breadwinner family' in Britain," *Cambridge Journal of Economics* 23, no. 5 (1999): 519–541; Rosemary Crompton, *Restructuring gender relations and employment: The decline of the male breadwinner* (Oxford: Oxford University Press, 1999); Lluis Flaquer, "Factors underlying the growth of shared parenting after divorce in Spain" (Working Paper presented at the International Conference on Shared Parenting, Strasbourg, November 22–23, 2018); Jane Lewis, "The Decline of the Male Breadwinner Model: Implications for Work and Care," *Social Politics: International Studies in Gender, State & Society* 8, no. 2 (2001): 152–169.
2 Abraham H. Maslow, *Motivation and Personality* (New York: Harper, 1954).
3 Ronald Inglehart, "The silent revolution in Europe: Intergenerational change in post-industrial societies," *American Political Science Review* 65, no. 4 (1971): 991–1017.

4 Ron J. Lesthaeghe, "The unfolding story of the Second Demographic Transition," *Population and Development Review* 36, no. 2 (2010): 211–251.
5 Pau Miret and Anna María Cabré, "Pautas Recientes en la Formación Familiar en España: Constitución de la Pareja y Fecundidad," *Papeles de Economía Española* 104 (2005): 17–36.
6 Frances Goldscheider, Eva Bernhardt and Trude Lappegård, "The gender revolution: A framework for understanding changing family and demographic behavior," *Population and Development Review* 41, no. 2 (2015): 207–239; Lesthaeghe, "Unfolding."
7 Creighton, "Rise and Decline;" Crompton, *Restructuring gender*; Flaquer, "Factors;" Lewis, "Decline."
8 Michael E. Lamb, "The history of research on father involvement: An overview," *Marriage & Family Review* 29, no. 2–3 (2000): 23–42.
9 Sara McLanahan and Christine Percheski, "Family structure and the reproduction of inequality," *Annual Review of Sociology* 34, no. 1 (2008): 257–276; Robert D. Putnam, *Our kids: The American Dream in crisis* (New York: Simon & Schuster, 2015).
10 Judy Cashmore et al., "Shared care parenting arrangements since the 2006 family law reforms," Report for: Australian Government, Attorney-General's Department (Sydney, 2010), 27 July 2020. Retrieved from www.arts.unsw.edu.au/sites/default/files/documents/2_AG_Shared_Care.pdf; Juliana M. Sobolewski and Paul R. Amato, "Parents' discord and divorce, parent–child relationships and subjective well-being in early adulthood: Is feeling close to two parents always better than feeling close to one?," *Social Forces* 85, no. 3 (2007): 1105–1124; Lluis Flaquer, Anna Escobedo, Anna Garrido Alsina and Carmen Moreno. "Gender equality, child well-being and shared residence in Spain," in *Llibre de resums de les sessions dels Grups de treball: VII Congrés Català de Sociologia i V Congrés Català de Joves Sociòlegs/Sociòlogues* (Barcelona: Associació Catalana de Sociologia, 2017), 95–96.
11 Wilma Bakker and Clara H. Mulder, "Characteristics of post-separation families in the Netherlands: Shared residence versus resident mother arrangements," *GeoJournal* 78, no. 5 (2013): 851–866; Emma Fransson et al., "The living conditions of children with shared residence: The Swedish example," *Child Indicators Research* 11, no. 3 (2018): 861–883.
12 Bruce Smyth, "A 5-year retrospective of post-separation shared care research in Australia," *Journal of Family Studies* 15, no. 1 (2009): 36–59.
13 Marta Marín, Víctor Dujo and Pedro José Horcajo, "Estudio Comparativo de las Decisiones de los Magistrados del Tribunal Supremo Español y los Resultados de Estudios Empíricos sobre las Implicaciones Psicológicas en Menores en Situación de Guarda y Custodia Compartida," *Anuario de Psicología Jurídica* 27, no. 1 (2017): 115–125.
14 Daniel R. Meyer, María Cancian and Steven T. Cook. "The growth in shared custody in the United States: Patterns and implications," *Family Court Review* 55, no. 4 (2017): 500–512.
15 Francisca Fariña et al., "Custodia Compartida, Corresponsabilidad Parental y Justicia Terapéutica como Nuevo Paradigma," *Anuario de Psicología Jurídica* 27, no. 1 (2017): 107–113, https://doi.org/10.1016/j.apj.2016.11.001; Francisca Fariña et al., "Joint Custody, Parental Co-Responsibility, and Therapeutic Jurisprudence as a New Paradigm," *Anuario de Psicología Jurídica* 27, no. 1 (2017): 107–113.
16 American Law Institute, *Principles of the law of family dissolution: Analysis and recommendations* (Newark, NJ: Matthew Bender, 2002); María Cancian et al., "Who gets custody now? Dramatic changes in children's living arrangements after divorce," *Demography* 51, no. 4 (2014): 1381–1396.
17 Robin Whittemore and Kathleen Knafl, "The integrative review: Updated methodology," *Journal of Advanced Nursing* 52, no. 5 (2005): 546–553.
18 Marín et al., "Estudio Comparativo."
19 Ibid.
20 Raúl Ruiz-Callado and Rafael A. Ruiz, "Propiedades Sociométricas del Cuestionario de Arraigo Familiar en Supuestos de Custodia Compartida Disputada," *Zerbitzuan: Gizarte zerbitzuetarako aldizkaria = Revista de Servicios Sociales* 66 (2018): 21–32.

21. Carlos Rodríguez-Domínguez, Adolfo Jarne and Xavier Carbonell, "Análisis de las Atribuciones de Guarda y Custodia de Menores en las Sentencias Judiciales," *Acción Psicológica* 12, no. 1 (2015): 1–10.
22. Montse Solsona and Jeroen Spijker, "Effects of the 2010 Civil Code on trends in joint physical custody in Catalonia: A comparison with the rest of Spain," *Population* 71, no. 2 (2016): 297–323.
23. Raúl Ruiz-Callado and Rafael A. Ruiz, "Custodia Compartida y Familias Negociadoras: Perfil Socio-Demográfico," *Revista de Ciencias Sociales* 23, no. 3 (2017): 28–38.
24. Montse Solsona et al., *Custodia Compartida Pacto de Pareja? Equidad de Género?* (Barcelona: Icari, 2020).
25. Montse Solsona and Marc Ajenjo, "La Custodia Compartida: Un Paso Más hacia la Igualdad de Género?," *Perspectives Demogràfiques* 8 (2017): 1–4.
26. Ibid.
27. Raúl Ruiz-Callado and Rafael Alcázar, "Las Preferencias Infantiles en la Evaluación de la Custodia Compartida: Una Perspectiva Sociológica," *OBETS. Revista de Ciencias Sociales* 14, no. 1 (2019): 207–229.
28. González and Viitanen, "Long-term."
29. Flaquer et al., "Gender Equality."
30. Marín et al., "Estudio Comparativo."
31. Flaquer et al., "Gender equality."
32. Ruiz-Callado and Alcázar, "Preferencias;" Ruiz-Callado and Ruiz, "Propiedades."
33. Solsona and Spijker, "Effects."
34. Smyth, "A 5-year retrospective."
35. Anja Steinbach, "Children's and parents' well-being in joint physical custody: A literature review," *Family Process* 58, no. 2 (2019): 353–369.
36. Paul R. Amato, "The consequences of divorce for adults and children," *Journal of Marriage and Family* 62, no. 4 (2000): 1269–1287.
37. Ibid.; Sanford L. Braver, Jenessa R. Shapiro and Matthew R. Goodman, "Consequences of divorce for parents," in *Handbook of divorce and relationship dissolution*, edited by Mark A. Fine and John H. Harvey (Mahwah, NJ: Lawrence Erlbaum, 2006), 313–337.
38. Harris-Short, "Resisting the march."
39. Zuzana Žilinčíková and Martin Kreidl, "Grandparenting after divorce: Variations across countries," *Advances in Life Course Research* 38 (2018): 61–71.
40. Jennifer McIntosh, "Child inclusion as a principle and as evidence-based practice: Applications to family law services and related sectors," Australian Institute of Family Studies, 27 July 2020. Retrieved from https://aifs.gov.au/cfca/publications/child-inclusion-principle-and-evidence-based-practic/section-1-mandate-child-inclusion.
41. Fariña et al., "Joint custody."
42. Solsona and Spijker, "Effects."
43. Flaquer, "Factors."

References

Amato, P. R. 2000. The consequences of divorce for adults and children. *Journal of Marriage and Family* 62, no. 4 (November): 1269–1287.

American Law Institute. 2002. *Principles of the law of family dissolution: Analysis and recommendations.* Newark, NJ: Matthew Bender.

Bakker, W., and C. H. Mulder. 2013. Characteristics of post-separation families in the Netherlands: Shared residence versus resident mother arrangements. *GeoJournal* 78, no. 5 (October): 851–866.

Braver, S. L., J. R. Shapiro, and M. R. Goodman. 2006. Consequences of divorce for parents. In *Handbook of divorce and relationship dissolution*, ed. M. A. Fine, and J. H. Harvey, 313–337. Mahwah, NJ: Lawrence Erlbaum.

Cancian, M., D. R. Meyer, P. R. Brown, and S. T. Cook. 2014. Who gets custody now? Dramatic changes in children's living arrangements after divorce. *Demography* 51, no. 4 (May), 1381–1396.

Cashmore, J., P. Parkinson, R. Weston et al. 2010. Shared care parenting arrangements since the 2006 family law reforms: Report for: Australian Government, Attorney-General's Department. Retrieved from www.arts.unsw.edu.au/sites/default/files/documents/2_AG_Shared_Care.pdf.

Creighton, C. 1999. The rise and decline of the "male breadwinner family" in Britain. *Cambridge Journal of Economics* 23, no. 5 (September): 519–541.

Crompton, R. 1999. *Restructuring gender relations and employment: The decline of the male breadwinner*. Oxford: Oxford University Press.

Fariña, F., D. Seijo, R. Arce, and M. J. Vázquez. 2017. Custodia compartida, corresponsabilidad parental y justicia terapéutica como nuevo paradigma. *Anuario de Psicología Jurídica* 27, no. 1: 107–113.

Fariña, F., D. Seijo, R. Arce, and M. J. Vazquez. 2017. Joint custody, parental co-responsibility, and therapeutic jurisprudence as a new paradigm. *Anuario de Psicología Jurídica* 27, no. 1: 107–113.

Flaquer, L., A. Escobedo, A. G. Alsina, and C. Moreno. 2017. Gender equality, child well-being and shared residence in Spain. In *Llibre de resums de les sessions dels Grups de treball.: VII Congrés Català de Sociologia i V Congrés Català de Joves Sociòlegs/Sociòlogues*, 95–96. Barcelona: Associació Catalana de Sociologia.

Flaquer, L. I. 2018. Factors underlying the growth of shared parenting after divorce in Spain. Working paper presented at the International Conference on Shared Parenting, Strasbourg, November 22–23.

Fransson, E., S. B. Låftman, V. Östberg, A. Hjern, and M. Bergström. 2018. The living conditions of children with shared residence: The Swedish example. *Child Indicators Research* 11, no. 3, 861–883.

Goldscheider, F., E. Bernhardt, and T. Lappegård. 2015. The gender revolution: A framework for understanding changing family and demographic behavior. *Population and Development Review* 41, no. 2 (June): 207–239.

González, L., and T. Viitanen. 2018. The long-term effects of legalizing divorce on children. *Oxford Bulletin of Economics and Statistics* 80, no. 2 (June): 327–357.

Harris-Short, S. 2010. Resisting the march towards 50/50 shared residence: Rights, welfare and equality in post-separation families. *Journal of Social Welfare & Family Law* 32, no. 3 (October): 257–274.

Inglehart, R. 1971. The silent revolution in Europe: Intergenerational change in post-industrial societies. *American Political Science Review* 65, no. 4 (December), 991–1017.

Lamb, M. E. 2000. The history of research on father involvement: An overview. *Marriage & Family Review* 29, no. 2–3 (October): 23–42.

Lesthaeghe, R. 2010. The unfolding story of the second demographic transition. *Population and Development Review* 36, no. 2 (June): 211–251.

Lewis, J. 2001. The decline of the male breadwinner model: Implications for work and care. *Social Politics: International Studies in Gender, State & Society* 8, no. 2 (Summer): 152–169.

Marín, M., V. Dujo, and P. J. Horcajo. 2017. Estudio comparativo de las decisiones de los magistrados del Tribunal Supremo español y los resultados de estudios empíricos sobre las implicaciones psicológicas en menores en situación de guarda y custodia compartida. *Anuario de Psicología Jurídica* 27, no. 1: 115–125.

Maslow, A. H. 1954. *Motivation and personality*. New York: Harper.

McIntosh, J. 2007. Child inclusion as a principle and as evidence-based practice: Applications to family law services and related sectors. Australian Institute of Family Studies. Retrieved from https://aifs.gov.au/cfca/publications/child-inclusion-principle-and-evidence-based-practic/section-1-mandate-child-inclusion.

McLanahan, S., and C. Percheski. 2008. Family structure and the reproduction of inequality. *Annual Review of Sociology* 34, no. 1 (August): 257–276.

Meyer, D. R., M. Cancian, and S. T. Cook. 2017. The growth in shared custody in the United States: Patterns and implications. *Family Court Review* 55, no. 4 (October): 500–512.

Miret, P., and A. Cabré. 2005. Pautas recientes en la formación familiar en España: Constitución de la pareja y fecundidad. *Papeles de Economía Española* 104: 17–36.

Putnam, R. D. 2015. *Our kids: The American Dream in crisis*. New York: Simon & Schuster.

Rodríguez-Domínguez, C., A. Jarne, and X. Carbonell. 2015. Análisis de las atribuciones de guarda y custodia de menores en las sentencias judiciales. *Acción Psicológica* 12, no. 1: 1–10.

Ruiz-Callado, R., and R. Alcázar. 2019. Las preferencias infantiles en la evaluación de la custodia compartida: Una perspectiva sociológica. *OBETS. Revista de Ciencias Sociales* 14, no. 1: 207–229.

Ruiz-Callado, R., and R. A. Ruiz. 2017. Custodia compartida y familias negociadoras: Perfil socio-demográfico. *Revista de Ciencias Sociales* 23, no. 3: 28–38.

Ruiz-Callado, R., and R. A. Ruiz. 2018. Propiedades sociométricas del cuestionario de arraigo familiar en supuestos de custodia compartida disputada. *Zerbitzuan: Gizarte zerbitzuetarako aldizkaria = Revista de Servicios Sociales* 66: 21–32.

Smyth, B. 2009. A 5-year retrospective of post-separation shared care research in Australia. *Journal of Family Studies* 15, no. 1 (December): 36–59.

Sobolewski, J. M., and P. R. Amato. 2007. Parents' discord and divorce, parent–child relationships and subjective well-being in early adulthood: Is feeling close to two parents always better than feeling close to one? *Social Forces* 85, no. 3 (March): 1105–1124.

Solsona, M., and M. Ajenjo. 2017. La custodia compartida: ¿Un paso más hacia la igualdad de género? *Perspectives Demogràfiques* 8 (October): 1–4.

Solsona, M., M. Ajenjo, C. Brullet, and A. Gómez-Casillas. 2020. *Custodia compartida ¿Pacto de pareja? ¿Equidad de género?* Barcelona: Editorial Icaria.

Solsona, M., and J. Spijker. 2016. Effects of the 2010 Civil Code on trends in joint physical custody in Catalonia: A comparison with the rest of Spain. *Population* 71, no. 2 (September): 297–323.

Steinbach, A. 2019. Children's and parents' well-being in joint physical custody: A literature review. *Family Process* 58, no. 2 (June): 353–369.

Whittemore, R., and K. Knafl. 2005. The integrative review: Updated methodology. *Journal of Advanced Nursing* 52, no. 5 (November): 546–553.

Žilinčíková, Z., and M. Kreidl. 2018. Grandparenting after divorce: Variations across countries. *Advances in Life Course Research* 38 (December): 61–71.

14
FACTORS THAT AFFECT JUDICIAL DECISIONS IN RELOCATION CASES

Bridging the gap between the empirical evidence and socio-legal practice

Yoav Mazeh

Introduction

One of the most difficult situations in post-separation litigation arises when a parent applies to relocate with the children to a distant location. Allowing relocation would separate the child from the parent staying behind; disallowing it would either separate the child from the relocating parent or prevent the parent from choosing the desired place to live. In this chapter I consider the factors that affect judicial decisions in relocation cases. I focus on Israeli case law, but the findings may reflect phenomena that are present in other jurisdictions as well.

Relocation problems are usually severe because relocation rules out ordinary parenting, where the children spend time with both parents on a weekly basis. Studies have repeatedly found that it is important for children to be brought up by both parents and to have a full and meaningful relationship with each one.[1] A full and meaningful relationship means that the children spend a significant part of the time with each parent on a regular basis, including overnight.[2] Experts have concluded that, in divorce and separation cases, the goal should be an arrangement in which the children spend a considerable part of the time with each parent, preferably in a shared parenting scheme.[3]

The study conducted by Kelly and Lamb[4] found that children must see each parent at frequent intervals and should not be detached from a parent for more days than the number of years of their age (for example, a three-year-old child should not be separated from either parent for longer than three consecutive days).

If a parent relocates, joint parenthood clearly becomes inapplicable. Therefore, a parent's decision to relocate denies the children their fundamental right to benefit from the meaningful parenting of both parents and forces a bad choice on the parents, with harmful consequences for the children.[5] Visits and electronic communication are not proper substitutes for joint parenthood.[6]

The normative question

What should affect the decisions of the court in relocation cases? In theory, the primary relevant factor is *the child's best interest*. But, in fact, this is a hollow notion used by the courts to justify a decision they have reached based on other grounds. In itself, the best interest of the child is not instructive or informative because it does not contain any prescriptive parameters for when to allow relocation and when not. I therefore put forward a number of criteria to determine relocation cases. The following criteria are not the only ones that need to be considered in deciding the question of relocation but I suggest that they should be given primary consideration. After reviewing the suggested criteria, I will examine whether Israeli jurisprudence considers these criteria in practice.

Quality of parenting

The first criterion that should be considered is the quality of parenting of each of the parents.[7] Parental qualities must be evaluated based on the attentiveness of the parents, their responsiveness to the child's needs, their ability to demonstrate parental authority, etc.

Level of parental involvement

The second criterion concerns the level of parental involvement of each of the parents.[8] Although parents with a limited level of involvement can also argue against the relocation of their children, parents who have been highly involved stand on firmer ground in their opposition to the relocation of the children.[9]

Past interference of applying parent in relationship of children with other parent

A third criterion that must be considered is whether the applying parent had tried in the past to raise obstacles to the relationship of the children with the other parent.[10] A clean history of the applying parent must be a *sine qua non* condition for approving a relocation application.

Allowing relocation with the children provides the relocating parent with excessive power over the children's relationship with the other parent.[11] It is therefore difficult to see how a court would allow a parent to relocate with a child to a distant location, at times to a different jurisdiction, where enforcement of visitation orders is extremely difficult, after the applying parent has already demonstrated that he or she does not adhere to judicial decisions in this matter.

Child's will

A fourth criterion is the child's will.[12] This should be considered with caution, but when there is a clear indication of the child's will, it should be taken into account.

Parental agreements

The fifth criterion that must be considered is whether the parents had a prior agreement with respect to prospective relocation.[13] If the parents agreed to enable or to restrict prospective relocation, the agreement should be given appropriate weight.

Cause of relocation

The sixth criterion to be considered in relocation applications is the cause of relocation.[14] Although some courts argue that the cause of relocation should not be a factor in granting relocation applications,[15] it is difficult to accept such an argument. Should the court equate an application for relocation in which the applicant parent's goal is to distance the stay-behind parent from the children[16] with one undertaken to meet a child's medical need in a distant location?

It is necessary to ask whether the cause of relocation is related to the children or is it parent-focused and contrary to the children's needs. If it is parent-focused, is it essential for the parent (such as a medical need) or something the parent could have avoided?

The cause of relocation is particularly important because it provides an insight into the level of commitment that the applying parent has to the children. If a parent is willing to relocate for reasons of self-pursuit, irrespective of the damage the relocation inflicts on the child, it must be asked whether this is the appropriate parent to look after the children.

Harm to the children

The seventh criterion is the harm to the children.[17] We have seen that all relocations cause harm to the children because they separate them from one of their parents. But the question is whether there are additional factors that exacerbate the harm to the children.

Custody

The last factor that needs to be addressed is custody. The claim I make is that custody should not be considered as a criterion for deciding relocation applications. At best, custody is an inaccurate proxy for the substantive criteria discussed above. But it is not a parameter in itself. Moreover, according to Israeli law, custody does not indicate the level of attachment of the child to each parent[18] or the extent of parenting time that each parent spends with the child.[19] It does not even provide the custodial parent with decision-making authority. Thus, instead of relying on custody as a proxy for the substantive parameters, courts should consider the significant parameters themselves, described in criteria 1 to 7 above.

Israeli case law

We now turn to consider the implementation of these criteria in Israeli jurisprudence. I conducted a thorough examination of Israeli case law in the matter of parental relocation in a separate study. For the purpose of the present discussion I examine three milestone cases that came before the Israeli Supreme Court, which have affected many other cases, as well as Israeli law in general in this matter.

LCA 4575/00 Jane Doe v. John Doe (8 January 2001)

The couple in this case had signed a divorce agreement when their baby was eleven months old. According to the agreement, the baby would spend three weekdays with the mother and two weekdays with the father, with weekends and holidays divided equally, amounting to approximately a 55:45% division.[20] The agreement included an overseas clause, which stated that, in case one of the parents goes abroad, the child stays in Israel with the other parent. It was also agreed that the mother would have custody.

Three months later, however, the mother applied to the Family Court for permission to relocate with the child to England. The court referred the parties to an evaluator who found that both parents had the same parenting abilities. She also observed, however, that there was a serious risk that the mother would alienate the child from the father.

Nevertheless, she decided to base her recommendation on the tender age presumption. This presumption, which was legislated in Israel in 1962, states that courts ought to determine issues relating to children according to their best interest, "as long as children under the age of six shall reside with their mother unless there are special reasons to order otherwise."[21] Setting aside all substantive considerations, based on the tender age presumption and on her view that scientific studies show that children of young age are more attached to their mothers, she recommended that the mother have custody over the child and be allowed to relocate with him to England.

The Family Court accepted these recommendations and allowed the mother to relocate with the child, ruling that the father shall have visitation rights of one weekend per month with the child.[22] Both parents appealed this judgment. The father appealed against the decision allowing the mother and the child to relocate, and the mother appealed against the decision to give the father visitation rights of a weekend per month, which in her view was too much.

During the appeal, however, the status quo was to be maintained, so that the mother could not take the child to England and the 55:45% parenting time arrangement was to be continued. But the mother had not waited for the District Court decision and relocated alone to England, leaving the child with the father in Israel.

In its judgment, the District Court reversed the ruling of the Family Court.[23] The court reviewed the literature about the importance of both parents for the development of the child,[24] it examined the mother's overall attitude, including her attempt to detach the child from the father and her decision to relocate without the child. The court concluded that the mother was indifferent to the child and to his needs and was not suitable to take care of him, and that therefore the child should remain in Israel and be looked after by his father.

The mother appealed to the Supreme Court, and by the time this court reached a decision the child was over four and a half years old. In its judgment, the Supreme Court allowed the mother to relocate,[25] disregarding practically all the normative criteria we have discussed above.

1. The court ignored the fact that, at the initial stage of the dispute, the evaluator considered both parents as having equal *parenting qualities*. Since that time, the mother has left for England, leaving the child with his father and pursuing her own life.
2. The court was also not concerned by the fact that, at the outset, almost four years before the Supreme Court hearing, the *level of parental involvement* was nearly equal. Since that time, the mother had left for England and the child was for all practical purposes left with the father.
3. More importantly, the mother clearly tried to *interfere in the child's relationship with the father*. Not only did she apply to relocate three months after they signed the agreement, after being granted permission by the Family Court to relocate with the child she appealed to the District Court claiming that a weekend per month was more than the father ought to spend with the child. The mother's behaviour confirmed the evaluator's fear that the mother tried to alienate the child from his father. But this did not have any effect on the judgment of the court.
4. In this case the child did not express any preference and therefore this criterion was inapplicable to the matter.
5. A significant factor in this case should have been the *agreement between the parents*, which stated explicitly that if one of them goes abroad, the child remains in Israel with the other parent. This fact also proved insignificant in the opinion of the court.
6. Most important, the court noted explicitly that the cause or need for relocation was irrelevant to the application.

> The question of need to relocate is altogether irrelevant ... This is the case except if it is apparent from the parent's behaviour that he does not consider the best interest of the child and is focused on his interest alone, in which case it is not the child's best interest to live with this parent in any case.[26]

This particular case started because the mother, in her behaviour, did not "consider the interest of the child and focused on her interest alone." She had applied to relocate shortly after signing the agreement that gave the father broad parenting time and stated that the child should not leave the country. Having gained the right to relocate, she applied to reduce the visitation rights of the father to less than a weekend per month. And when she had to postpone the relocation until the decision of the District Court, she left the child in Israel and moved to England without him.

By the time the case had reached the Supreme Court, the mother had already remarried and had another daughter in England. But the question is whether the mother's behaviour reflected a lack of concern for her son. Putting herself in a situation where she had no choice but to relocate to England indicates such lack of concern, which reinforces the lack of concern that she had displayed earlier, even before her second child was born and the new situation was created.

The Supreme Court, however, did not find that these aspects of her behaviour raised a question about whether she might not consider the interest of the child, but only her own. The court's comment that it was not in the child's interest to be with a parent who did not consider his wellbeing turned out to be lip service, and the jurisprudence deriving from the judgment, as was later demonstrated by interpretations in subsequent case law, is that the cause for relocation is irrelevant.[27]

7. Finally, instead of evaluating the harm of the relocation for the child himself, the court created an *enmeshment between the mother and the child*, claiming that the best way to prevent harm to the child was to enable the mother to be happy. A child could not be happy if his mother was unhappy. Therefore, if the mother is not permitted to relocate to wherever she pleases, her frustration will be absorbed by the children, which inevitably harms them.[28]

Psychologists have repeatedly emphasized the need to differentiate between the parent's needs and those of the child, in the context of divorce.[29] Parenthood is about separating the needs of the child from the needs of the parent and providing for the child's needs, even when it comes at the expense of the parent's needs.

The principle of enmeshment, put forth by the court in 4575/00, held exactly the opposite. Uniting the happiness of a child with that of the parent means that there is no need to separate between the needs of the parent and those of the child.

Custody as the underlying premise of the judgment

The Supreme Court makes it clear that it was determined to allow the mother to relocate with the child. In doing so, the court relied on two main arguments relating to custody. The first is the tender age presumption and the view that contemporary studies show that children of a young age are in greater need of their mothers than they are of their fathers, even if the father is actively involved. The court relied on an article by Klaff, "The tender years doctrine: A defence,"[30] which was the only study to which the court referred in this respect. But as the title of the article clearly indicates, it was written in response to other studies that had challenged the scientific and constitutional validity of the tender years doctrine.[31] These challenges, to which Klaff was merely responding, were not mentioned in any way in the court's judgment, and neither were the various studies that have been published for nearly two decades following Klaff, which have repeatedly reported findings that contradict Klaff's argument.[32]

The second argument of the court was that once it was established that the mother should be the custodian, the outcome of the trial was already determined because, as the court put it, "the right of the custodial parent to relocate abroad is undisputable."[33] In this judgment the court failed to consider any of the normative criteria discussed above. Instead, it clung to custody, which is not indicative of any parenting qualities, and provided extreme rights to the parent holding this title, irrespective of the effect of this decision on the child.

SCivA 9201/08 John Doe *v.* Jane Doe *(5 April 2009)*

The second case I want to consider is from 2009. In this case, an Israeli father and a German mother lived in Israel. The father was highly involved in bringing up their child, and especially so in light of the mother's frequent absences due to her job as a flight attendant for Lufthansa. When the child was a year and a half old, the mother abducted him to Germany and prevented the father from having any contact with the child, including instances when the father had gone to Germany to see the child after having coordinated the visit with the mother.

Under the Hague Convention, the German court held that the mother had abducted the child, that the parents had joint custody over the child, and that the mother must return the child to Israel. Consequently, with the intervention of the welfare authorities and of the police, the child was returned to Israel seven months after his abduction. During this entire period, the mother refused to let the father have any contact with the child.

After the child was returned to Israel, the mother filed an application with the Israeli court to relocate with the child to Germany. While the Family Court allowed the mother to move to Germany for one year,[34] the father's appeal to the District Court was accepted by this court.[35] The District Court referred to studies on the needs of children, which were summarized in the Rotlevi Report,[36] and accepted the evaluator's recommendation that the child should remain in Israel. But the mother appealed to the Supreme Court, which referred the parties to another evaluation by the same evaluator. In her report to the Supreme Court, the evaluator emphasized what she had stated in her previous evaluation. The child was already seven and a half years old. Except for the period of the abduction, the child had spent his entire life in Israel, in day-to-day involvement with his father. He was happy and connected to Israel, both emotionally and socially. His relationship with his father was very significant. The child himself expressed his wish to remain in Israel. He was greatly perturbed by the possibility of relocation, among other things because he would have to stay with his grandmother during his mother's regular absences. Based on these findings and on other observations, the evaluator concluded that relocation would be harmful and traumatic for the child, and recommended that the child remain in Israel.

Nevertheless, the Supreme Court allowed the relocation.[37] The court ascribed no weight to the fact that the *father had been highly involved* in bringing up the child, and that he was able to look after him extensively, while the mother has been working, and would continue to be absent for a significant part of the time. More importantly, the court chose to ignore the *history of the mother* and the fact that she had abducted the child, had prevented all contact of the father with the child, and had returned the child to Israel only after the intervention of the German welfare and police authorities. As was pointed out in the court, the mother continued to violate some of the instructions of the court, even during litigation in the Israeli courts.[38]

The court also ignored the fact that the child, who was seven and a half years old, expressed his will very clearly, and that the evaluator had explained the *trauma and the harm* that would be caused to the child as a result of the relocation. Instead, and without any reference to any study with respect to the wellbeing of children, the court chose to follow the *enmeshment principle* reflected in case law, and stated numerous times in the judgment that if the mother remained in Israel she would be frustrated and unhappy and so would the child. In the words of the court, there is a "necessary symbiosis in the relations of the minor and the mother."[39]

RFMA 1858/14 John Doe *v.* Jane Doe *(3 April 2014)*

The final case I want to discuss is a recent one, from 2014, involving a couple living in Nazareth. The mother was extremely dedicated to her work but would not attend to the child, even when she was at home. It appears from the evaluations in the case that the mother had a problematic, if not dysfunctional, personality. These difficulties were demonstrated, among others, by her treatment of her daughter from a previous marriage, whom she had neglected. The daughter was abusing alcohol at the age of thirteen, for which she was hospitalized. As a result, the mother placed her daughter in a boarding school.

The mother's lack of attentiveness to her children also characterized her attitude to her child from the current relationship and she was routinely away for significant periods of time shortly after he was born, including four nights per week, when she would sleep at her mother's, who lived in the suburbs of Tel-Aviv. By contrast, the father was highly dedicated to the child and had been the one who looked after the baby from birth.

When the couple separated, the baby was six months old. The arrangement was that the father would look after the child every day, and on the days on which the mother would have the child, she would pick him up from the father at 8 p.m. and return him the following morning. This arrangement had been recommended by the welfare officers who were involved in the case, was approved by the court, and was followed for over a year and a half.

When the child was two years old, the mother abducted him and moved to the outskirts of Tel-Aviv (115 km from their former place of residence). The father applied to the Family Court and the court issued an order against the relocation.[40] The mother's appeal to the District Court was denied but the District Court accepted her plea and permitted her to move to Haifa (which is 40 km and 40 minutes away from Nazareth).[41]

Shortly after she moved to Haifa, the mother violated the court order again and moved back to the Tel-Aviv area. The father initiated proceedings against the move but, realizing that the outcome of these proceedings might be that the mother would disconnect from the child, he agreed to the following compromise: the mother would remain in the Tel-Aviv area, the child would stay with each parent for intervals of one week at a time, and when the child reached the age of four, the issue would be reevaluated.

Approximately a year later, when the child reached the age of four, the Family Court appointed an expert for evaluation.[42] The evaluator found that the father had better parenting qualities and that the mother's personality involved risks for the development of the child. He observed that the father's availability to the child was significantly better than that of the mother (who continued to be absent in the afternoon and returned home only around 8 p.m.) and that the child was much more connected emotionally to the father than he was to the mother. Moreover, the child showed symptoms of Hailey–Hailey disease, which required him to live away from beach areas where it is hot and humid, and the mother lived by the sea, in the Tel-Aviv area. Based on these observations, the evaluator recommended that the father had custody of the child and that the mother visited the child once a week in the middle of the week, and had the child for three weekends per month.

The Family Court considered the numerous studies pointing to the role of the father in the development of children,[43] referred at length to the facts of the case, and accepted the recommendations of the evaluator, effective immediately.[44]

The mother appealed to the District Court, which relied on Klaff's article of 1982 and granted custody to her, but without changing the parenting time arrangement approved by the Family Court until the decision of the Supreme Court in the matter.[45] By the time the case reached the Supreme Court, the child was already five years old. It was clear that his primary caregiver had been the father, who was extremely dedicated to the child. On the other hand, when the child was the mother's responsibility, she would place him in daycare, after which he would be looked after by an aunt or the grandmother, rarely by the mother herself. She was barely present, not to mention attentive, even on the days that were her parenting time.

Applying the normative criteria described above would have led to the following conclusion: (a) the *quality of the father's parenting* was significantly better than that of the mother; (b) the father's *level of involvement was markedly higher than the mother's*; (c) the mother had repeatedly *violated court orders*, abducting the child and changing her place of residence contrary to court orders; (d) the *child's will* was to live with his father; (e) the mother had not shown any significant or just *cause* for the relocation; (f) there was risk of dermatologic *harm* to the child as a result of the move to the Tel-Aviv area, but the mother, who is a dermatologist, showed no concern for the needs of the child, only for her own needs. Even according to the judgment in 4575/00, in 2001, "if it is apparent from the parent's behavior that he does not consider the best interest of the child and is focused on his interest alone … it is not in the child's best interest to live with this parent in any case."[46]

The Supreme Court ignored all of the above.[47] It made no reference to any study concerning the wellbeing of children. Instead, it relied on the tender age presumption. We have seen that, according to section 25 of the 1962 Legal Capacity and Guardianship Act, courts must determine issues relating to children based on the best interest of the children, "as long as children under the age of six shall reside with their mother unless there are special reasons to order otherwise."[48] The court held that it was bound by section 25 of the Act, that in this case the child must be with the mother and that relocation was permitted.

The argument of the court that it is bound by the Act and the tender age presumption is implausible. The tender age presumption is not a conclusive instruction. As clearly indicated by its name, it is merely a presumption, a default rule that applies only "if there are no special reasons to order otherwise." If the parents' qualities and all other factors are equal, the presumption indicates a preference for the mother.

But as we have seen above, in this case the quality of parenting, the level of parental involvement, the history of violations, the will of the child, the lack of just cause for relocation, and the risk of harm to the child all clearly indicated that the father was the parent who was more attentive to the needs of the child. These are precisely the "special reasons to order otherwise" that are mentioned in the Act, instructing the courts *not* to apply the default rule of the presumption but rather to assign the more capable parent to care for the child. Thus, contrary to the statement of the court that its decision was dictated by legislation in the matter, in practice its decision was contrary to the instructions of the Act.

Moreover, the court did not simply *use* the tender age presumption; it strengthened this gender-biased rule by holding that in order to diverge from it one must provide the court with "robust evidence" for the "special reasons to order otherwise." But the requirement for robust evidence is clearly not present in the Act, and has been introduced by the court without any reference or support on this matter.

In other contexts, the Supreme Court had stressed numerous times that gender-based discrimination is unconstitutional, and that in instances where such discrimination is implied by legislation, the courts are obliged to interpret the legislation in a way that is non-discriminatory.[49] But in this context, the decision of the court to introduce a requirement for robust evidence resulted in an interpretation of the tender age presumption in a way that is not only unsupported, but also bolsters the discrimination rather than minimizes it.

More importantly, instead of placing the needs of children above all else, the court chose to use a presumption that is both gender-biased and not focused on the children as the highest, indeed the sole criterion, for determining the question of relocation for children under the age of six.

Conclusions

We have seen the gap between the normative criteria that should determine the issue of the relocation of children of divorced parents and the legal practice of the courts in this matter. The normative criteria, which are supported by the literature, focus on the children and their needs. The literature emphasizes the need to separate the interests of the parent from the needs of the children. It does not accept the right of the parent to relocate, or the axiom that the children's best interest is to remain with the custodial parent, without regard to the history of the parent's conduct, where and how far the parent wishes to relocate, and whether the parent wishes to take along the children.

By contrast, the courts hardly pay any attention to the normative criteria. In the 2001 case, for example, the Supreme Court held that the cause for relocation was irrelevant, which precluded a discussion of whether the relocating parent was attentive to the needs of the child or whether the parent was entirely self-focused and oblivious to the damage being caused to the child by separating him from the other parent.

In the 2008 case, the court was not concerned with the fact that the mother had abducted the child and had done everything she could to prevent a relationship between the father and the child. The 2014 case followed along the same lines and added that the fact that the father had been the primary caregiver and the parent to which the child was attached was immaterial.

These judgments, and many others, exhibit a two-steps paradigm. First, the courts decide that the mother should have custody, either because of the tender age presumption or for any other reason. Second, following this decision, they justify the mother's application to relocate either by the rhetoric of the custodial parent's right[50] or by using the enmeshment principle, according to which the child is not happy if the mother is not happy.[51]

Instead of broadcasting to the public that parents need to differentiate between their own aspirations and the needs of their children, and that they should place the needs of the children first, the courts imply that the custodial parent's desires and the children's needs are one, and that whatever the parent wants for herself or himself, inherently becomes what is good for the children.

As noted above, the rulings of 2001 and 2008 have been extremely influential in Israeli case law,[52] and I sadly predict that the 2014 ruling will have the same effect. Although the legal system has accepted decades ago that the upmost consideration should be the protection of the needs of the children,[53] in practice, the needs of the children are swept aside in favour of other doctrines and principles.

The contrast between the judicial practice, on one hand, and the literature and empirical evidence regarding the needs of the children, on the other, reflects the fact that too often the conceptual frameworks of the decision makers have been shaped decades ago, and are based more on unfounded intuitions than on scientific data. It is not a coincidence that the problematic judgments we have reviewed here did not refer to any study that examined the wellbeing of children, except for a 1982 article, which was taken out of context. This is not to say that the literature in this respect is entirely one sided. But it seems to me that the judges, who by profession are lawyers and not developmental psychologists, have not been informed of the vast evidence on the role that both parents play in the development and wellbeing of children. More informed judges, who are aware of the literature on this topic, have reached different decisions. Sadly, these judges tend to serve in the lower instances and their rulings are often reversed by judges of the higher instances, who are not as familiar with the extensive literature in this matter.

The fact that senior judges and many other officials are not exposed to the growing literature and empirical evidence in this area prevents the integration of the scientific observations about the children's need for joint parenthood into the socio-legal practice and their implementation in the judicial field.

Notes

1 E. Mavis Hetherington & Joan Kelly, *For better or for worse: Divorce reconsidered* (London: W. W. Norton, 2003); Paul R. Amato, The consequences of divorce for adults and children, *Journal of Marriage and Family* 62, 1269 (2000); Sanford L. Braver & Diane O'Connell, *Divorced dads: Shattering the myths* (London: Putnam, 1998).
2 Richard A. Warshak, Social science and parenting plans for young children: A consensus report, *Psychology, Public Policy, and Law* 20, 46 (2014); Irwin N. Sandler et al., Relations of parenting quality, interparental conflict, and overnights with mental health problems of children in divorcing families with high legal conflict, *Journal of Family Psychology* 27, 915 (2013); William V. Fabricius et al., Parenting time, parent conflict, parent–child relationships, and children's physical health, in K. Kuehnle & Leslie Drozd (eds), *Parenting plan evaluations: Applied research for the family court* (New York: Oxford University Press, 2012); Eleanor E Maccoby et al., Postdivorce roles of mothers and fathers in the lives of their children, *Journal of Family Psychology* 7, 24 (1993).
3 Joan B. Kelly, Risk and protective factors associated with child and adolescent adjustment following separation and divorce: Social science applications, in Kathryn Kuehnle & Leslie Drozd (eds), *Parenting plan evaluations: Applied research for the family court* (New York: Oxford University Press, 2012); William V. Fabricius, et al., Custody and parenting time: Links to family relationships and well-being after divorce, in Michael E. Lamb (ed.), *The role of the father in child development*, 5th ed. (Chichester: Wiley 2020); Robert Bauserman, Child adjustment in joint-custody versus sole-custody arrangements: A meta-analytic review, *Journal of Family Psychology* 16, 91 (2002); Richard A. Warshak, Social science and children's best interest in relocation cases: Burgess revisited, *Family Law Quarterly* 34, 83 (2000).
4 Joan B. Kelly & Michael E. Lamb, Using child development research to make appropriate custody and access decisions, *Family and Conciliation Courts Review* 38, 297 (2000).
5 Sanford L. Braver et al., Relocation of children after divorce and children's best interests: New evidence and legal considerations, *Journal of Family Psychology* 17, 206 (2003), 219; E. Mavis Hetherington & Margaret Stanley-Hagan, The adjustment of children with divorced parents: A risk and resiliency perspective, *Journal of Child Psychology and Psychiatry* 40, 129 (1999); C. Jack Tucker et al., "Moving on": Residential mobility and children's school lives, *Sociology of Education* 71, 111 (1998); Merril Sobie, Whatever happened to the "best interests" analysis in New York relocation cases? A response, *Pace Law Review* 15, 685 (1995).
6 Elisabeth Bach-Van Horn, Family law in the twenty-first century: Virtual visitation – are webcams being used as an excuse to allow relocation?, *Journal of the American Academy of Matrimonial Lawyers* 21, 171 (2008) at 172:

> The internet can be an instrument for a "face-to-face" encounter between parent and child, but video conferencing with one's child, just like a telephone call, should be used as a supplement to, not a replacement for, in-person visits and communication. Children crave warm hugs from both of their parents before going to bed, enjoy feeling their hair being ruffled by a loving hand while they do their homework, and relish in receiving a "high-five" after a well-played sports match.

See also: *Marshall v. Marshall*, 814 A.2d 1226 (Pa. Super. Ct. 2002); *Graham v. Graham*, 794 A.2d 912 (Pa. Super. Ct. 2002); *Nighswander v. Sudick*, 2000 LEXIS 192 (Conn. Super. 2000).

7 Joan B. Kelly & Michael E. Lamb, Developmental issues in relocation cases involving young children: When, whether, and how?, *Journal of Family Psychology* 17, 193 (2003); Ambika Krishnakumar & Cheryl Buehler, Interparental conflict and parenting behaviors: A meta-analytic review, *Family Relations* 49, 25 (2000); Richard A. Gardner, The Burgess decision and the Wallerstein brief, *Journal of the American Academy of Psychiatry and the Law* 26, 425 (1998); *Hardin v. Hardin*, 618 S.E.2d 169 (Ga. Ct. App. 2005).
8 William G. Austin, Relocation, research, and forensic evaluation: Part Ii: Research in support of the relocation risk assessment model, *Family Court Review* 46, 347 (2008); Judith Wallerstein & Joan B. Kelly, *Surviving the breakup: How children and parents cope with divorce* (New York: Basic Books, 1980), 149; *Brennan v. Brennan*, 857 A.2d 927 (Conn. App. Ct. 2004); *Classick v. Classick*, 155 S.W.3d 842 (Mo. Ct. App. 2005).
9 Sanford L. Braver et al., A longitudinal study of noncustodial parents: Parents without children, *Journal of Family Psychology* 7, 9 (1993); David L. Chambers, Rethinking the substantive rules for custody disputes in divorce, *Michigan Law Review* 83, 477 (1984).
10 William G. Austin, Relocation, research, and forensic evaluation: Part Ii: Research in support of the relocation risk assessment model, *Family Court Review* 46, 347 (2008); D. A. Rollie Thompson, A celebration of Canadian family law and dispute resolution: Movin' on: parental relocation in Canada, *Journal of Child Custody* 42, 398 (2004); Richard A. Warshak, Bringing sense to parental alienation: A look at the disputes and the evidence, *Family Law Quarterly* 37, 273 (2003); In re T.M., 831 N.E.2d 526 (Ohio App. 2005).
11 See Richard A. Warshak, Social science and parenting plans for young children: A Consensus report, *Psychology, Public Policy, and Law* 20, 46 (2014), 58: "The relocation of a parent with the child away from the other parent alters the range of feasible parenting plans and magnifies a parent's ability to effectively exclude and erase the nonmoving parent from the child's life."
12 Megan Gollop & Nicola J. Taylor, New Zealand children and young people's perspectives on relocation following parental separation, *Law and Childhood Studies: Current Legal Issues* 14, 219 (2012); Joan B. Kelly, Developing beneficial parenting plan models for children following separation and divorce, *Journal of the American Academy of Matrimonial Lawyers* 19, 101 (2005); Carol Smart, From children's shoes to children's voices, *Family Court Review* 40, 307 (2002); *Becker v. Becker*, 745 S.W.2d 229 (Mo. App. 1987).
13 *Lenz v. Lenz*, 40 S.W.3d 111 (Tex. Ct. App. 2000); *Tomasko v. Dubuc*, 761 A.2d 407 (N.H. 2000).
14 D. A. Rollie Thompson, A celebration of Canadian family law and dispute resolution; Richard A. Warshak, Social science and children's best interest in relocation cases; *Delgado v. Nazario*, 677 N.Y.S.2d 336 (App. Div. N.Y. 1998); *Cassady v. Signorelli*, 56 Cal. Rptr. 2d 545 (Cal. App. 1st Dist. 1996).
15 In re Marriage of Burgess, 13 Cal. 4th 25 (Cal. 1996); *Gordon v. Goertz*, 2 S.C.R. 27 (Can. 1996); In re Marriage of LaMusga, 32 Cal.4th 1072 (Cal. 2004).
16 *Russenberger v. Russenberger*, 669 So. 2d 1044 (Fla. 1996); *Stout v. Stout*, 1997 ND 61, 560 N.W.2d 903 (ND Supreme Court 1997); *Auge v. Auge*, 334 N.W.2d 393 (Minn. 1983); *Bodne v. Bodne*, 588 S.E.2d 728 (Ga. 2003); *Jones v. Jones*, 903 S.W.2d 277 (Mo. App. Ct. 1995); *Tishmack v. Tishmack*, 611 N.W.2d 204 (N.D. 2000).
17 Janet Leach Richards, Resolving relocation issues pursuant to the Ali Family Dissolution Principles: Are children better protected?, *Brigham Young University Law Review* 1105 (2001); William G. Austin, Relocation law and the threshold of harm: Integrating legal and behavioral perspectives, *Family Law Quarterly* 34, 63 (2000); Joan G. Wexler, Rethinking the modification of child custody decrees, *Yale Law Journal* 94, 757 (1985).
18 M. Frishtik & Z. Yagelnic, Factors affecting Israeli family courts' decisions concerning child custody, *Society and Welfare* 27, 9 (2007).
19 Yoav Mazeh, "Children's custody": A substantive term or a hollow notion?, *Bar-Ilan Law Review (Mechkarey Mishpat)* 29, 207 (2013).
20 Holidays and school vacations in Israel amount to roughly three months a year. The calculation is therefore: $(6/14*0.75) + (7/7*0.25) = 0.45$ (six days out of fourteen that the child

spends with the father regularly, for 75% of the year, plus half of the time during holidays and school vacations, which accounts for 25% of the year. This adds up to approximately 45% that the child spends with the father and 55% with the mother).
21 Section 25 of the Legal Capacity and Guardianship Act (1962).
22 FMC 6173/95 *Jane Doe v. John Doe* (Ramat Gan 5.1.1999).
23 FMA 1125/99 *D.L. v. C.Z.* (Tel Aviv-Jaffa 28.5.2000).
24 Dan Schnitt, The tender years doctrine in solving child's custody disputes, *Tel-Aviv Law Review (Iyunei Mishpat)* 19, 185 (1994); E. A. Berlin, Relocation: No common ground, *Family Advocate* 3, 7 (1989); A. H. Shaki, Main characteristics of the law of child custody in Israel, *Tel Aviv Law Review (Iyunei Mishpat)* 10, 5 (1984).
25 LCA 4575/00 *Jane Doe v. John Doe* (8.1.2001).
26 LCA 4575/00 *Jane Doe v. John Doe* (8.1.2001), para. 13.
27 For subsequent cases that followed this ratio, see RFMA 9358/04 *Jane Doe v. John Doe* (2.5.2005); RFMA 27/06 *John Doe v. Jane Doe* (1.5.2006); FMC 85795/01 *A.T.L. v. Z.B.* (Tel Aviv-Jaffa 22.11.2006); FMC 52121/05 *T.B.Y v. A.B.Y.* (Tel Aviv-Jaffa 26.7.2009); FMC 23903/06 *H.L. v. H.G.* (Jerusalem 11.10.2009); FMC 10428–03–10 *Jane Doe v. John Doe* (Krayot 22.5.2013).
28 *Winn v. Winn*, 593 N.W.2d 662 (Mich. Ct. App. 2000); *Bjornson v. Creighton*, 221 D.L.R. 4th 489 (Ont. C.A. 2002); *Frieze v. Frieze*, 692 N.W.2d 912 (N.D. 2005).
29 Margaret S. Mahler, Symbiosis and individuation: The psychological birth of the human infant, *Psychoanalytic Study of the Child* 29, 89 (1974); H. D. Grotevant & C. R. Cooper, Individuation in family relationships, *Human Development* 29, 82 (1986); Marjolein L. de Jong, Attachment, individuation, and risk of suicide in late adolescence, *Journal of Youth and Adolescence* 21, 357 (1992).
30 R. L. Klaff, The tender years doctrine: A defence, *California Law Review* 70, 335 (1982), cited at LCA 4575/00 *Jane Doe v. John Doe* (8.1.2001), para. 12.
31 Allan Roth, The tender years presumption in child custody disputes, *Journal of Family Law* 15, 423 (1976); Henry H. Foster & Doris Jonas Freed, Life with father, *Family Law Quarterly* 11, 321 (1977); *Devine v. Devine*, 398 So. 2d 686 (Ala. 1981); *King v. Vancil*, 34 Ill. App. 3d 831, 341 N.E.2d 65 (1975).
32 Joan B. Kelly & Michael E. Lamb, Using child development research to make appropriate custody and access decisions, *Family and Conciliation Courts Review* 38, 297 (2000); Paul R. Amato & Joan G. Gilbreth, Nonresident fathers and children's well-being: A meta-analysis, *Journal of Marriage and the Family* 61, 557 (1999); E. Mavis Hetherington et al., What matters? What does not? Five perspectives on the association between marital transitions and children's adjustment, *American Psychologist* 53, 167 (1998); Michael E. Lamb, The development of infant–father attachments, in Michael E. Lamb (ed.), *The role of the father in child development*, 3rd ed. (Chichester: Wiley, 1997); Sanford L. Braver et al., A longitudinal study of noncustodial parents: Parents without children, *Journal of Family Psychology* 7, 9 (1993).
33 LCA 4575/00 *Jane Doe v. John Doe* (8.1.2001), para. 13.
34 FMC 6173/95 *Jane Doe v. John Doe* (Ramat Gan 5.1.1999).
35 FMA 1273/06 *John Doe v. Jane Doe* (Tel Aviv-Jaffa 23.10.2007).
36 Report of the Committee for the Examination of Basic Principles with Respect to Children and the Law, and Their Implementation in Legislation. (2003), general section, 127–166.
37 RFMA 10060/07 *Jane Doe v. John Doe* (2.10.2008).
38 SCivA 9201/08 *John Doe v. Jane Doe* (5.4.2009), at para. 8 of J. Rubinstein's opinion.
39 RFMA 10060/07 *Jane Doe v. John Doe* (2.10.2008), para. 8 of J. Rubinstein's opinion.
40 FMC 24310–12–09 *M.S v. A.K.* (Tiberias 26.6.2011).
41 LFA 45267–06–11 *Jane Doe v. John Doe* (Nazareth 4.7.2011).
42 FMC 23494–01–10 *A.K. v. M.S.* (Tiberias 29.8.2013).
43 Joan B. Kelly & Michael E. Lamb, Using child development research to make appropriate custody and access decisions, *Family and Conciliation Courts Review* 38, 297 (2000);

Lamb, *The role of the father in child development*; Warshak, Social science and children's best interest in relocation cases; Donald Woods Winnicott, *Through pediatrics to psychoanalysis* (London: Routledge, 1978).
44 FMC 23494–01–10 *A.K.* v. *M.S.* (Tiberias 29.8.2013).
45 FMA 38844–10–13 *Jane Doe* v. *John Doe* (Nazareth District Court 10.2.2014).
46 LCA 4575/00 *Jane Doe* v. *John Doe* (8.1.2001), paragraph 13.
47 RFMA 1858/14 *John Doe* v. *Jane Doe* (3.4.2014).
48 Section 25 of the Legal Capacity and Guardianship Act (1962).
49 Yehiel S. Kaplan, Family law in an era of a new policy: From legislation by court to comprehensive and detailed, planned legislation, *Haifa Law Review* 6, 259 (2011), 303; Aharon Barak, Constitutional Interpretation § III (1994), 562–563; MisCrimR 4072/12 *Jane Doe* v. *Great Rabanical Court* (7.4.2013); HJC 6650/04 *Jane Doe* v. *Netanya Rabanical Court*, 61(1) IsrSC 581 (2006), 602; SCrimA 2316/95 *Ganimat* v. *State of Israel*, 49(4) IsrSC 589 (1995).
50 SCivA 9201/08 *John Doe* v. *Jane Doe* (5.4.2009); FMC 4212–12–09 *Jane Doe* v. *John Doe* (Krayot 9.7.2010); RFMA 4028/12 *John doe* v. *Jane Doe* (10.7.2012); RFMA 1858/14 *John Doe* v. *Jane Doe* (3.4.2014).
51 RFMA 10060/07 *Jane Doe* v. *John Doe* (2.10.2008); SCivA 9201/08 *John Doe* v. *Jane Doe* (5.4.2009); FMC 4212–12–09 *Jane Doe* v. *John Doe* (Krayot 9.7.2010); RFMA 4028/12 *John Doe* v. *Jane Doe* (10.7.2012); FMA 35652–07–12 *A.B.H.* v. *M.B.H* (Jerusalem 9.12.2012); RFMA 1858/14 *John Doe* v. *Jane Doe* (3.4.2014); *Winn* v. *Winn*, 593 N.W.2d 662 (Mich. Ct. App. 2000); *Bjornson* v. *Creighton*, 221 D.L.R. 4th 489 (Ont. C.A. 2002); *Frieze* v. *Frieze*, 692 N.W.2d 912 (N.D. 2005).
52 See, for example, SCivA 9201/08 *John Doe* v. *Jane Doe* (5.4.2009); FMC 35320–11–10 *A.A.* v. *Z.A.* (Beersheba 19.6.2011); FMC 30890–03–12 *A.B.Y.* v. *A.B.* (Kfar Saba 30.4.2013); RFMA 1858/14 *John Doe* v. *Jane Doe* (3.4.2014).
53 See, for example, sections 17, 22, 24, 25, 28A, 28B of the Legal Capacity and Guardianship Act (1962), as well as LCA 209/54 *Steiner* v. *Attorney General of Israel*, 9 IsrSC 241 (1955), 251.

15
SHARED PARENTING VERSUS RELOCATION DISPUTES[1]

María Dolores Cano Hurtado

The right to family relations

Problems related to exercising the right to family relations in cases of marital breakdown

The legal relationship between parents and children is made up of a set of both financial and personal obligations and responsibilities, which are obviously accentuated while the children are minors. Therefore, as a result of this relationship, a series of rights and duties arise that must always be exercised and performed in the best interests of the children.

Article 39 of the Spanish Constitution appears in Chapter III of Title I that establishes the Governing Principles of Economic and Social Policy. The article states that:

1. The public authorities shall ensure the social, economic and legal protection of the family.
2. The public authorities shall also ensure the full protection of children, who are equal before the law, irrespective of their parentage and the marital status of the mother. The law shall provide for the investigation of paternity.
3. Parents must provide all forms of assistance to their children, whether born in or outside marital wedlock, while they are still under age and in all other cases provided for by law.
4. Children shall enjoy the protection afforded in the international agreements that safeguard their rights.

Therefore, the rule does not specify the content of the duty of the parents to care for their children; rather, it adopts a generic formula: *all forms of assistance*, correctly remitting to an ordinary law to define the content.[2] This law is the Spanish

Civil Code. In response to the constitutional requirement, the Spanish Civil Code established a new structure of parent–child relations through Law 11/1981, of 13 May 1981, on the Amendment of the Civil Code in relation to Parentage, Parental Authority and the Marital Financial Regime. Specifically, Article 154 of the Spanish Civil Code, amended by Law 26/2015, of July 282015, on the Amendment of the System of Protection of Children and Adolescents, states that:

> Non-emancipated children shall be under parental authority.
>
> Parental authority, as well as parental liability, shall be exercised at all times to the benefit of the children, according to their personality and with respect for their physical and mental integrity.
>
> This authority comprises the following duties and powers:
>
> 1. To ensure they are accompanied and to feed, educate and provide them with an integrated upbringing.
> 2. To represent them and to manage their property.
>
> If the child is sufficiently mature, he/she should always be heard before adopting decisions that affect him/her.
>
> In exercising their powers, the parents may request the assistance of the authorities.

The amendment converted parental authority into parental responsibility that must always be exercised to the benefit of the children, according to their personality and with respect for their physical and psychological integrity.

Accordingly, as stated in Article 110 of the Spanish Civil Code, even if they do not have parental authority, the father and mother are obliged to care for their underage children and support them. Therefore, parent–child relationships produce a series of rights-duties that must always be exercised in the best interests of the child.

At a European level, the Principles of European Family Law, drafted by the European Commission on Family Law (CEFL), were supplemented by the Principles on Parental Responsibilities. In accordance with international and European instruments, the CEFL opted for a broad concept of parental responsibility consisting of a collection of rights and duties relating to the care of the child's personal integrity and property. Concepts such as guardianship and custody that are still used in national systems have been abandoned. The CEFL's concept of parental responsibilities applies to children from the moment they are born until they reach adulthood. A difference has been recognised between young and adolescent children, although the indication of an age limit was intentionally avoided. It not only depends on the child's age, but also on his/her degree of maturity as to whether his/her opinion should be taken into account.[3]

Terminology is not consistent across Europe: for example, in English and Welsh law, the Hague Conference on Private International Law and the European Commission, the term used is "parental responsibility"; however, in Scottish law and the Council of Europe, the plural form is used, "parental responsibilities". The CEFL opted for the latter, despite the fact that some languages (such as French and German) cannot accommodate this form. The reason for preferring the term "parental responsibilities" was that it more clearly expresses the idea that it is comprised not only of one set of rights and duties, but rather of many different rights and duties. It could be argued that the plural form also permits a more flexible approach, particularly when attributing such rights and duties to persons other than the parents.[4]

One of these rights is the right to family relations.[5] When the parents live together with their children, the relationships between them take place naturally within the framework of their daily coexistence and the emotional ties that evolve.[6]

The problem arises when there is a marital breakdown and mainly when sole custody is granted to one of the parents.[7] The breakdown of relations between the parents must not lead to the breakdown of relations with their children, who must remain as far as possible unaffected by the situation. Obviously, when a marital breakdown occurs, a new situation arises in which one of the parents leaves the child's everyday life. The situation can even produce a feeling of loss. It is evident that a new framework of interpersonal relations will develop. From an emotional point of view, the breakdown of the parents' marriage normally has a negative impact on the children, the duration of which will depend fundamentally on how the parents manage this overall situation, both at the time of communicating their decision and throughout the process.[8]

Although the parents are granted a certain degree of autonomy in deciding how to manage their relationships with their children after the marital breakdown, everything is subject to comprehensive judicial control regulated by *ius cogens* rules that enable the courts to take any measures they deem necessary to protect the best interests of the child.

In addition, the right to family relations is reciprocal. As far as the children are concerned, it is configured as a right, as they need to relate to their parents to receive care, education and affection and to enjoy their company by sharing everyday things in life. In short, children require *all forms of assistance* necessary for their personal and emotional development.[9] On the other hand, as far as the parents are concerned, family relations are more of a right-duty.

At an international level, we also find different legal instruments that recognise this right to family relations. These instruments include Article 9.3 of the Convention on the Rights of the Child, adopted by the United Nations General Assembly on 20 November 1989 (ratified on 30 November 1990) and Article 14 of the European Charter of the Rights of the Child (adopted by the European Parliament in its resolution dated 18 July 1992). In addition, Article 24.3 of the Charter of Fundamental Rights of the European Union, signed in Strasbourg on 12 December 2007, and, finally, Article 8 of the Convention for the Protection of Human Rights and Fundamental Freedoms, signed in Rome on 4 November 1950 and ratified by Spain, regulate the right to respect for private and family life.

Therefore, we observe that the right to family relations between parents and children is essential and, in cases of marital breakdown, it is necessary to structure how it is exercised in the best possible way from that moment on.

At present, new technologies allow communications (a term that we consider included in the right to family relations, but with less content) by telephone, video conference, etc. However, there is no doubt that direct physical contact and affection are irreplaceable and necessary, especially in the case of minors, who need the presence of their parents for their emotional and affective development.[10]

Consequently, a change of address from the custodian parent's home creates a severe interference in the right to family relations because, often, the change makes it impossible to continue as before, and implies the risk of the parent becoming a stranger to the child in a short period of time.

Shared parenting: The best option for exercising the right to family relations

As indicated above, the breakdown of a marriage does not mean the breakdown of the parents' relationships with their children. These relationships must remain as far as possible unaffected by the situation and protected from harm. All decisions must always take into account the best interests of the child, which prevail over the personal interests of the parents. It is necessary to ensure that the fundamental rights of the child are protected as a priority and prevail over those of the other parties involved. The best interests of the child are a basic rule that should inspire the acts of individuals and the public authorities. The courts are obliged to decide on the basis of this principle, which must prevail over any other.

The Spanish Supreme Court has declared that joint custody is the most appropriate system to promote the right to family relations.[11] However, joint custody requires a relationship of mutual respect between the parents, adhering to attitudes and behaviour that benefit the child. The aim is that the emotional development of the child is not impaired. Despite the breakdown of emotional relations between the parents, the objective is to maintain a family structure that allows for the balanced growth of the child's. Furthermore, joint custody enables optimum performance of parental responsibility and the tasks that entails.

Therefore, what is actually intended is for the joint custody regime to approximate the coexistence model that existed before the marriage breakdown. Joint custody allows parents to guarantee the possibility of exercising their rights and obligations inherent to parental responsibility and to participate on equal terms in the development and growth of their children, which is also beneficial for them.[12]

The Spanish Supreme Court has established the following benefits of joint custody[13]:

(a) The integration of minors with both parents is encouraged. Imbalances in time spent with each parent are avoided.
(b) The feeling of loss is avoided.
(c) The suitability of the parents is not questioned.
(d) The cooperation of parents is encouraged, in the interests of their children.

However, even if a joint custody regime is adopted, there will still be an impact on the right to family relations because the structure of the family changes. Parents no longer live together with their children and have a common life project. There will also be a change in the relationships, as other people may be incorporated into the family (for example, a parent's new partner).

Change of residence by a parent

Article 19 of the Spanish Constitution states that:

> Spaniards have the right to choose their place of residence freely, and to move about freely within the national territory. Likewise, they have the right to freely enter and leave Spain subject to the conditions to be laid down by the law. This right may not be restricted for political or ideological reasons.[14]

From a European Union perspective, the right to move freely is linked to the status of a European citizen according to Directive 2004/38/EC of the European Parliament and of the Council of 29 April 2004, on the right of citizens of the Union and their family members to move and reside freely within the territory of the Member States (*Official Journal of the European Union* L158, 30 April 2004).

Use of the family home is determined by mutual agreement between the spouses and, in the event of disagreement, the court will decide on the basis of the interests of the family, as regulated in Article 70 of the Spanish Civil Code. When the family remains united in a harmonious environment, there will be no problem in reaching a decision that best meets the interests of all its members, changing address as often as they see fit, either in or outside national territory.

However, the problem arises when the marriage breaks down. In such cases, the type of custody of the children is determined by mutual agreement or a court decision: joint custody or sole custody. In either case, the home at which the children will live after the breakdown will have to be determined.[15]

The problem arises from the fact that, in these situations, three interests collide. First, the interest of the parent with custody of the child and, of course, the right to free movement by establishing his/her residence wherever considered best; second, the interest of the other parent to continue relations with his/her child – a change of residence may harm the relationship if the child moves far away; third, the best interests of the child, who has the right to have a relationship with both parents.

Nowadays, marriages between people from different national and international geographic locations are very common.[16] When a relationship breaks down, it is often the case that one or both partners return to where they grew up so as to access emotional and financial support from their family. A change of address can also occur for professional reasons (transfer, new job offer), affective reasons and, of course, no reason at all.[17]

Accordingly, if the parent with custody of the child decides to change his or her place of residence, the decision will have a direct impact on the child's place of residence. This change of address may lead to a substantial change in the measures adopted after the end of the marriage.

There is no doubt that change of address is a very complex issue, the solution of which, in most cases, will affect the right to family relations that has been exercised until such time. A change of residence of the parent with custody also obviously generates a change in residence of the child under his or her custody.[18] Be it in national territory or, much more so, overseas, this change could damage the right to family relations and even destroy it. For example, the right to family relations could disappear when the child moves far away. In this case, the visits may be scarce due to the high cost of travel and the impossibility of assuming such an expense in the case of limited financial resources. As we indicate below, this change of residence could make joint custody unfeasible.[19]

An important issue to consider in relation to custody is when the change of residence is the result of a decision taken unilaterally by one of the parents. The change of the minor's residence, away from that established in the custody, separation or divorce decision, due to a unilateral decision taken by the parent with custody may pose a problem in allowing the other parent to exercise his/her parental duties. If the decision to change address is understood as part of parental authority, it should be adopted by agreement or established by a court.

The decision to change address cannot be adopted unilaterally.[20] This change can be made lawfully only if both parents agree. The decision therefore requires the express or tacit consent of the other parent. If the change of residence is not agreed, a court will have to intervene.[21]

Effects of a change of residence in a joint custody system

Proximity of the parents' homes: "Conditio sine qua non"

The joint custody system must be applied whenever the necessary requirements are met. This is the system that best protects the child and his/her interests by ensuring his/her emotional stability and comprehensive education. Joint custody is the system that comes closest to the existing form of coexistence prior to the marriage break down. It guarantees the parental responsibility of both parents on equal terms.

Of course, apart from other issues to be considered, the best interests of the child will always be taken into account in a decision to adopt the joint custody system. Nevertheless, one of the essential requirements of a joint custody decision is the proximity of the parent's addresses, as a *conditio sine qua non*. The distance from the parents' homes, which makes frequent movement of the children difficult or impossible, is incompatible with joint custody.

Therefore, when a parent changes his/her residence, the decision has an effect on the joint custody system. This change may even prevent the maintenance of joint custody, when the addresses are far apart. The question that arises is what parameters need to be assessed to determine proximity. The distance between homes must enable joint custody to be compatible with the child's welfare. It is possible to maintain joint custody with homes in different, but nearby, locations but, if one parent moves far away, it will be a major obstacle to maintaining such an arrangement.[22]

The question we could ask ourselves is: What is the maximum geographical distance that would make joint custody remain workable? There is no general rule; the courts provide an ad hoc solution based on the particulars of the case. However, if we examine the rulings by Provincial Courts and by the Spanish Supreme Court, we observe a consistent criterion. The courts effectively provide for approximately 30 minutes by car between the parents' homes (or between the parents' homes and the school – the distance to the school thus being equidistant) in order to establish joint custody. The courts consider that, in large cities such as Madrid and Barcelona, 30 minutes' drive between the home and school is not unusual.

In the Judgment of the Provincial Court of Alicante (Section 9) 64/2014, of 12 February 2014, joint custody was established in a case in which the father had stayed in the family home and the mother had established her new residence in a town 20 km away. Again, in the Judgment of the Provincial Court of Alicante (Section 9) 180/2014, of 4 April 2014, joint custody was established as the parents' homes were only about 25 minutes away by car. The court claimed that, at a distance of more than about 30 minutes by car, joint custody could not be maintained. Along the same lines, in the Judgment of the Provincial Court of Badajoz (Section 2) 222/2019, of 21 May 2019, custody was confirmed on the basis that the determining factor is not the distance between the parents' homes (21 km) but rather the time it takes to travel between them (20 minutes). If different criteria were maintained, no joint custody could be applied in large cities, where travel usually takes longer.

The Spanish Supreme Court applies the same criteria. In its Judgment (Civil Chamber, Section 1) 110/2017, of 17 February 2017, joint custody was established because the distance between the parents' homes was only 20 km. In Judgment (Civil Chamber, Section 1) 370/2017, of 9 June 2017, joint custody was granted because, although the parents' homes were 43 minutes away by car, the school was halfway.

Therefore, as shown, case law encourages joint custody, even in cases in which the parents live in different towns. The limit is approximately 30 minutes by car between both towns or based on the location of the child's school as a reference. Of course, other criteria will always be taken into account in the best interests of the child. The solution is ad hoc. The problem arises when a parent's change of residence makes it impossible to maintain joint custody as a result of the distance.

Relocation disputes and shared parenting

As observed above, to be able to maintain a system of joint custody, the proximity of the parents' homes is a requirement. The problem arises when one of the parents' wishes to move to a distant location that makes joint custody impracticable. In such cases, one of the parents will necessarily have to be granted custody. In the absence of an agreement between the parents, the court will decide.[23]

Changing a child's place of residence in situations in which the parents cease to live together is one of the most important and difficult decisions that can be taken in the child's life and the family itself.[24] Authorisation of a change of residence brings about a substantial change in the child's life. A different home may imply a change of school, friends, social relations and sometimes even language and customs. In addition, of course, it will necessarily lead to a change in relations with the parent without custody and other family members.

The question to be asked in the absence of agreement is what criteria will the court use to authorise or deny a change of address? Case law shows that court authorisation is exclusively based on the benefit to and interests of the child, which take priority over the right of the custodian parent to freely choose his/her residence (Article 19 of the Spanish Constitution).

This benefit to and best interests of the child must be determined, irrespective of the interests of the parents, according to the particular case and all the surrounding circumstances. The court may therefore consider it best to authorise the change of address. In other situations, however, the court may consider it best for the child to stay at home and grant custody to the parent who is not moving. In any event, the principle of proportionality must always be applied in decisions based on the protection of the child's best interests. The court's decision must strike a balance in order to maintain the relationship of the child with both parents. Nevertheless, these relationships will never be the same as they were before the marital crisis occurred.

The Spanish Constitutional Court, in its Judgment of 1 February 2016, stated that the criterion governing the decision to be taken in each case by the court, in the light of the specific circumstances of the case, must necessarily be that of the overriding interest of the child (STC 16/2016, *Recurso de Amparo* 2937/2015). The Judgment states that the grounds for decisions shall be considered in breach of the Constitution if the principle of the child's best interests is not taken fully into account.

This principle is applied to the following obligations of judicial bodies:

1. To reach a weighted judgment.
2. The weighted judgment to be expressly stated in the ruling.
3. To identify the rights and property of all parties, in order to measure the need and proportionality of the measure adopted.

The measures taken are very important and will affect the child's life for many years to come. For this reason, minors have a fundamental right to intervene in the process, to be heard, depending on their age and degree of maturity.[25]

In reaching its decision, the court must assess different parameters simultaneously but will always base its decision on the best interests of the child. This process is not easy, and is the cause of international concern. The International Judicial Conference on Cross-border Family Relocation, held 23–25 March 2010 in Washington was devoted exclusively to this issue. Experts in the field took part and the conference concluded with an important declaration and adopted a number of measures recommending a set of common criteria to states to resolve relocation disputes.[26]

At a European level, the issue was also addressed in the Principles of European Family Law on Parental Responsibility, drawn up by the Commission for European Family Law (Principle 3:21 Relocation).[27]

The following are rulings of the Spanish Supreme Court in resolving the problem of relocation disputes:

1. Judgment of the Spanish Supreme Court (Civil Chamber, Section 1), 4/2018, of 10 January 2018:
   After the divorce, the mother returned to her family's place of origin in Rentería (the Basque Country). The location was more than 1,000 km. from the other parent, who resided in Jerez de la Frontera (Andalucía). The Provincial Court of Guipúzcoa confirmed shared custody for periods of three weeks, based on the findings of the psychosocial report. This situation would be reviewed when the child reached the compulsory school age. However, the Supreme Court argued that the best interests of the child had not been taken into account, as the distance between the homes made it impossible to maintain a system of joint custody. The Supreme Court granted sole custody to the mother on psychological grounds.
2. Judgment of the Spanish Supreme Court (Civil Chamber, Section 1) 229/2018, of 18 April 2018:
   Marriage between a Spanish father and Japanese mother. After the divorce, the mother returned to Japan and was granted sole custody of the children. The family had lived for long periods of time in Japan before the divorce. The father requested joint custody for periods of one year, coinciding with the school year. He proposed the schooling of the children at a Japanese school in Madrid, while they were living in Spain. The Supreme Court considered that joint custody was impossible, due to the high emotional cost and the harm that such a solution would cause to the children's development.
3. Judgment of the Spanish Supreme Court (Civil Chamber, Section 1) 58/2020, of 28 January 2020:
   Marriage between two women living in Madrid. One of the parents lost her job and unilaterally transferred her residence and that of her child to Alicante, her hometown, to be with her parents. The new address was 400 km away. Both the Judge of First Instance and the Provincial High Court of Madrid ruled joint custody in turns by alternating the child's residence on an annual basis, according to the school calendar. The Supreme Court considered that the best interests of the child were not achieved under the system of joint custody. Indeed, Supreme Court doctrine establishes that joint custody cannot be applied in cases of the existence of a long distance between the parents' homes because it would harm the best interests of the child (STS 4/2018, of 20 January 2018 (RJ 2018, 61); STS 229/2018, of 18 April 2018 (RJ 2018, 2177). On these grounds, the Supreme Court granted sole custody to one of the parents. The court's dilemma was determining which of the parents should have sole custody. The Supreme Court based its decision on the psychosocial report and granted sole custody to the parent who unilaterally decided to change the child's residence because she was the main carer of the child. This decision may seem surprising, however the Supreme Court stated that, although the change of habitual residence was objectionable, it would not result in detriment to the child's best interests.

Conclusion

A decision to change address cannot be adopted unilaterally. If the change is not consensual, judicial intervention will be required. The Spanish Supreme Court rules out the application of joint custody when there is a large distance between the parents' homes. The choice of parent to be granted sole custody is based primarily on the expert psychologist's report, which will take into account the age of the child, the place of residence, the relationship with the parent and other family members while respecting the principle of the best interests of the child.

Notes

1 This chapter is part of the Research Project "Derechos y garantías de las personas vulnerables en el Estado de bienestar" (UMA18-FEDERJA-175), supported by the aids to R+D+I projects in the framework of the ERDF Operational Programme 2014–2020, in the 2018 call, Octavio García Pérez and Carmen Sánchez Hernández being the main researchers. It is also part of the project "Inmigración y Derecho: retos actuales desde un enfoque interdisciplinar" (PPIT.UMA.B1.2018/04), of the University of Malaga. Main researcher: Carmen Rocío Fernández Díaz. Email: elenaavileshernandez@uma.es.
2 Espín Cánovas. Comentario al artículo 39 de la Constitución. In *Comentarios a la Constitución de 1978* (dir. Oscar Alzaga Villaamil), Tomo IV (artículos 39 a 55). Madrid, Edersa, http://vlex.com/vid/articulo-39-proteccion-familia-331395 1997; p. 13.
3 Boele-Woelki Katharina and Martiny Dieter. The Commission on European Family Law (CEFL) and its principles of European family law regarding parental responsibilities. *ERA Forum*, 2007; 8: 125–143, 127.
4 Scherpe Jens M. Establishing and ending parental responsibility: A comparative view. In *Responsible parents and parental responsibility* (edited by R. Probert, S. Gilmore and J. Herring). Oxford: Hart Publishing, 2009; 43–62, 45.
5 Acuña San Martín. *Derecho de relación entre los hijos y el progenitor no custodio tras el divorcio.* Madrid, Dykinson S.L.; 2015, 60–61.
6 Beyebach. La repercusión sobre el menor de los procesos de ruptura matrimonial: aspectos emocionales y relacionales. *Cuadernos de Derecho Judicial*, 2009; 2: 295–317. 298.
7 Suárez Herranz. El derecho del hijo a relacionarse con sus padres. *Revista de Derecho de Extremadura*, 2008; 2: 159–170, 164.
8 Beyebach. *Op. cit.*, p. 298; Cortés Arboleda. Adaptación psicológica de los hijos al divorcio de los padres. In *Separación y Divorcio: interferencias parentales* (coord. Francisca Fariña, Ramón Arce, Mercedes Novo y Dolores Seijo). Santiago de Compostela, NINO Centro de Impresión Digital, www.usc.es/export9/sites/webinstitucional/gl/servizos/uforense/descargas/Separacixn_y_Divorcio._Interferencias_parentales.pdf, 2010; 57–76, 58.
9 Pérez Vallejo. Relaciones familiares de los abuelos con los nietos (A propósito de la Ley 42/2003, de 21 de noviembre de Modificación del CC y la de la LEC). In *Libro homenaje al profesor Manuel Albaladejo García*, (coord. J. M. González Porras, F.P. Méndez González). Murcia, Colegio de Registradores de la Propiedad y Mercantiles de España. Servicio de Publicaciones de la Universidad de Murcia; 2004; 3809–3838, 3834.
10 Iglesias Martín. El derecho de custodia y comunicación de los menores en las crisis matrimoniales. Especial referencia en las situaciones de custodia compartida. *Revista Doctrinal Aranzadi Civil-Mercantil*, Parte Doctrina, BIB 2018\10234, 2018; 7: 1–17, 14.
11 *Vid. Guía de criterios de actuación judicial en materia de custodia compartida Consejo General del Poder Judicial (CGPJ)*, adopted on 25 June 2020.
12 Berrocal Lanzarot. Cuestiones controvertidas e implicaciones prácticas en torno a la guarda y custodia compartida. *Revista Crítica de Derecho Inmobiliario*, 2016; 756: 2204-2245, 2210.
13 STS 166/2016, 17th March; STS 526/2016, 12th September; STS 413/2017, 27 June.

14 Belda Pérez-Pedrero. Los derechos a la libre elección de residencia y al libre desplazamiento. *Parlamento y Constitución*. Anuario, 1997; 1: 241–266, 242.
15 *Vid.* Nevado Montero. El cambio de domicilio unilateral por el progenitor custodio. *La Ley Derecho de Familia*, 2017; 16: 1–13.
16 *Vid.* Cano Hurtado. Interferencias en el ejercicio del derecho de relación paterno-filial por cambio de domicilio del progenitor custodio. In *Estudio multidisciplinar sobre interferencias parentales*. Ana Mª Pérez Vallejo (Editora) y Mª Paz Antón Moreno (Coord.). Madrid, Dykinson S.L., 2019; 19–46.
17 Arch Marín, Fábregas Balcells, Viñas Maestre. Solicitud de traslado de menores en situaciones de ruptura familiar: aspectos y criterios para su adecuada valoración. *Revista de Derecho de Familia*. Artículos Doctrinales, 80, julio-septiembre, versión electrónica, 2018.
18 Díaz Martínez. La determinación del lugar de residencia del menor como conflicto en el ejercicio conjunto de la patria potestad por progenitores no convivientes. *Revista Doctrinal Aranzadi Civil-Mercantil*. Parte Jurisprudencia Comentarios, BIB 2012\3483, 2013; 9:1–10.
19 Forcada Miranda. La nueva regulación de la custodia en la Ley 2/2010, de 26 de mayo, de igualdad en las relaciones familiares ante la ruptura de la convivencia de los padres: custodia compartida, autoridad familiar, responsabilidad parental, traslado y sustracción de menores. In *Actas del Vigésimo Encuentro del Foro de Derecho Aragonés*, Zaragoza, www.eljusticiadearagon.com/gestor/ficheros/_n005340_Sesion%20III.pdf, 2010; 177–215, 192.
20 Rodríguez Escudero. La responsabilidad parental y el cambio de domicilio del menor por el progenitor custodio (Aportaciones de la sentencia del TS de 26 de octubre de 2012). *Revista Crítica de Derecho Inmobiliario,* 2014; 746: 2893–2926, 2895.
21 Aguilera Rull. Comentario al a la Sentencia de 20 de octubre de 2014 (RJ 2014, 5376). Cambio de domicilio del menor por el progenitor custodio. *Revista Cuadernos Civitas de Jurisprudencia Civil*, 98, mayo-agosto, versión electrónica, 2015.
22 *Vid.* Álvarez Olalla. Última jurisprudencia del TS en materia de custodia compartida. *Revista Doctrinal Aranzadi Civil-Mercantil*. Parte Jurisprudencia Comentarios, BIB 2018\6537, 2018; 3: 1–10.
23 González Beilfuss. El traslado lícito de menores: las denominadas *Relocation Disputes"*, *Revista Española de Derecho Internacional*. Vol. LXII/2, 2010; 51–75, 53.
24 Carreras Marañas. El cambio de domicilio del progenitor custodio. Problemas sustantivos y procesales. In *Jurisdicción de Familia XX años (Asociación Española de Abogados de Familia)*. Madrid, Dykinson S.L., 2013; 189–248, 201.
25 *Vid.* De La Iglesia Monje. El derecho a ser escuchado y la madurez del menor: su protección judicial en la esfera familiar. *Revista Crítica de Derecho Inmobiliario*, 2017; 759: 345–369.
26 http://catedradip1laplata.com/images/DECLARACI%C3%93N_DE_WASHINGTON_SOBRE_REUBICACI%C3%93N_INTERNACIONAL_DE_NI%C3%91OS.pdf.
27 These principles: www.ceflonline.net/wp-content/uploads/Principles-PR-English.pdf.

References

Acuña San Martín. *Derecho de relación entre los hijos y el progenitor no custodio tras el divorcio*. Madrid, Dykinson S.L.; 2015, 60–61.
Aguilera Rull. Comentario a la Sentencia de 20 de octubre de 2014 (RJ 2014, 5376). Cambio de domicilio del menor por el progenitor custodio. *Revista Cuadernos Civitas de Jurisprudencia Civil*, 98, mayo-agosto, versión electrónica, 2015.
Álvarez Olalla. Última jurisprudencia del TS en materia de custodia compartida. *Revista Doctrinal Aranzadi Civil-Mercantil*. Parte Jurisprudencia Comentarios, BIB 2018\6537, 2018; 3: 1–10.
Arch Marín, Fábregas Balcells, Viñas Maestre. Solicitud de traslado de menores en situaciones de ruptura familiar: aspectos y criterios para su adecuada valoración. *Revista de Derecho de Familia*. Artículos Doctrinales, 80, julio-septiembre, versión electrónica, 2018.
Belda Pérez-Pedrero. Los derechos a la libre elección de residencia y al libre desplazamiento. *Parlamento y Constitución*. Anuario, 1997; 1: 241–266.

Berrocal Lanzarot. Cuestiones controvertidas e implicaciones prácticas en torno a la guarda y custodia compartida. *Revista Crítica de Derecho Inmobiliario*, 2016; 756: 2204–2245, 2210.

Beyebach. La repercusión sobre el menor de los procesos de ruptura matrimonial: aspectos emocionales y relacionales. *Cuadernos de Derecho Judicial*, 2009; 2: 295–317.

Boele-Woelki Katharina and Martiny Dieter. The Commission on European Family Law (CEFL) and its principles of European family law regarding parental responsibilities. *ERA Forum*, 2007; 8: 125–143.

Cano Hurtado. Interferencias en el ejercicio del derecho de relación paterno-filial por cambio de domicilio del progenitor custodio. In *Estudio multidisciplinar sobre interferencias parentales*. Ana Mª Pérez Vallejo (Editora) y Mª Paz Antón Moreno (Coord.). Madrid, Dykinson S.L., 2019; 19–46.

Carreras Marañas. El cambio de domicilio del progenitor custodio. Problemas sustantivos y procesales. In *Jurisdicción de Familia XX años (Asociación Española de Abogados de Familia)*. Madrid, Dykinson S.L., 2013; 189–248.

De La Iglesia Monje. El derecho a ser escuchado y la madurez del menor: su protección judicial en la esfera familiar. *Revista Crítica de Derecho Inmobiliario*, 2017; 759: 345–369.

Díaz Martínez. La determinación del lugar de residencia del menor como conflicto en el ejercicio conjunto de la patria potestad por progenitores no convivientes. *Revista Doctrinal Aranzadi Civil-Mercantil*. Parte Jurisprudencia Comentarios, BIB 2012\3483, 2013; 9: 1–10.

Espín Cánovas. Comentario al artículo 39 de la Constitución. In *Comentarios a la Constitución de 1978 (dir. Oscar Alzaga Villaamil)*, Tomo IV (artículos 39 a 55). Madrid, Edersa, http://vlex.com/vid/articulo-39-proteccion-familia-331395 1997.

Forcada Miranda. La nueva regulación de la custodia en la Ley 2/2010, de 26 de mayo, de igualdad en las relaciones familiares ante la ruptura de la convivencia de los padres: custodia compartida, autoridad familiar, responsabilidad parental, traslado y sustracción de menores. *Actas del Vigésimo Encuentro del Foro de Derecho Aragonés*, Zaragoza, www.eljusticiadearagon.com/gestor/ficheros/_n005340_Sesion%20III.pdf, 2010; 177–215.

González Beilfuss. El traslado lícito de menores: las denominadas *Relocation Disputes*, *Revista Española de Derecho Internacional*. Vol. LXII/2, 2010; 51–75.

Iglesias Martín. El derecho de custodia y comunicación de los menores en las crisis matrimoniales. Especial referencia en las situaciones de custodia compartida. *Revista Doctrinal Aranzadi Civil-Mercantil*, Parte Doctrina, BIB 2018\10234, 2018; 7: 1–17.

Nevado Montero. El cambio de domicilio unilateral por el progenitor custodio. *La Ley Derecho de Familia*, 2017; 16: 1–13.

Pérez Vallejo. Relaciones familiares de los abuelos con los nietos (A propósito de la Ley 42/2003, de 21 de noviembre de Modificación del CC y la de la LEC). In *Libro homenaje al profesor Manuel Albaladejo García*, (coord. J. M. González Porras, F.P. Méndez González). Murcia, Colegio de Registradores de la Propiedad y Mercantiles de España. Servicio de Publicaciones de la Universidad de Murcia; 2004; 3809–3838.

Rodríguez Escudero. La responsabilidad parental y el cambio de domicilio del menor por el progenitor custodio (Aportaciones de la sentencia del TS de 26 de octubre de 2012). *Revista Crítica de Derecho Inmobiliario*, 2014; 746: 2893–2926.

Scherpe. Establishing and ending parental responsibility: A comparative view. In *Responsible Parents and Parental Responsibility* (Edited by R. Probert, S. Gilmore, J. Herring). Hart Publishing, Oxford and Portland, Oregon, 2009; 43–62.

Suárez Herranz. El derecho del hijo a relacionarse con sus padres. *Revista de Derecho de Extremadura*, 2008; 2: 159–170.

16
SHARED PARENTING AND FINANCIAL INTERESTS

Jesús Martín Fuster

Shared parenting and its interest in relation to the payment of maintenance

We will first make a brief reference to the considerations that led the Supreme Court to establish shared parenting as the preferred system. These considerations are decisive in determining the extent to which the financial interests of the parents affect the granting of shared parenting.[1]

Supreme Court Judgment (STS) 496/2011, of 7 July 2011, initiated the case law, by stating that:

> The interpretation of Articles 92, 5, 6 and 7 of the Civil Code (Cc) must be based on the interests of the minors affected by the measure to be taken, which will take place when any of the above criteria are met. The wording of this article does not allow the conclusion that it is an exceptional measure, but should rather be considered as normal. This enables children to exercise their right to maintain relations with both parents, even in crisis situations, provided and whenever it is possible.

This interpretation was consolidated in Supreme Court (SC) case law and is also supported by Constitutional Court Judgment (STC) 185/2012, of 17 October 2012, which declared the provision contained in Article 92.8 Cc as unconstitutional and null and void. The provision required a "favourable" report from the Public Prosecutor's Office in order to grant shared parenting which, in many cases, led to its eventual rejection.

As Pérez Martín points out,[2] even if indirectly, the regional legislation that openly opted for shared parenting as the preferred option has had an influence.

The SC has repeatedly established the advantages of shared parenting, as shown in Supreme Court Judgment (STS) 442/2017, of 13 July, which states that:

With the system of shared parenting, according to the judgments of 25 November 2013, 9 September and 17 November 2015, among others:

a) The integration of minors with both parents is encouraged.
b) A sense of loss is avoided.
c) The suitability of the parents is not questioned.
d) The cooperation of the parents is encouraged, in the interests of their children.

Therefore, there is no point questioning the objective good intentions of the system in light of the court's constant and consistent doctrine and the substantial change resulting from Constitutional Court case law (STC 185/2012, of 17 October 2012).

The court refers to the objective 'good intentions' of the system as ideal in the relations between the children and their parents and in view of the benefits mentioned above.

The system of shared parenting was incorporated into the Civil Code by Law 15/2005, of 8 July 2005, although as an exception, which has since been corrected by case law.[3] The system was not accompanied by a specific mention or regulation of the maintenance to be paid in cases of shared parenting, which has been criticised by legal doctrine.[4]

As a result, it has traditionally been understood that in shared parenting, given that the children spend a comparable amount of time with both parents, neither parent has to pay maintenance to the other. The parents pay their own maintenance costs and 50% of the ordinary and extraordinary expenses.

This meant that many parents were interested in shared parenting in order to avoid paying maintenance to the other parent, even if it was in the child's best interests. Conversely, others were interested in applying for individual custody in order to receive maintenance from the other parent and, if the family home was at stake, to have it granted to the children.

There is no doubt that the granting of one or another form of custody conditions the maintenance and use of the family home.[5] This self-interest in shared parenting may therefore not be in the best interests of the child. In such cases, the suitability of the shared parenting system should be reconsidered.

To avoid these situations,[6] the Supreme Court established case law, with STS 55/2016, of 11 February 2016, which it has repeatedly applied in its judgments. In this particular case, the appellant claimed that the maintenance allowance was not inappropriate under a shared parenting system in which both parents pay their own costs during the time they have custody of the children.

The court ruled that maintenance was payable by the father, as the mother had no income of her own, but limited the allowance to a term of two years, which it considered sufficient for the mother to be able to find work. Based on these facts, the SC ruled as follows:

> This Court must declare that shared parenting does not mean an exemption from paying maintenance when there is disproportion between the income

of the spouses, as in the case at hand, given that the mother does not receive a salary or any income whatsoever (Art. 146 Cc) and the amount of the maintenance must be proportional to the needs of the person receiving it, but also to the wealth or means of the person providing it.

The court therefore highlights the principle of proportionality of maintenance, not only with regard to those who need it, but also to those who provide it, by applying the provisions of Article 145, 146 Cc relating to the duty of family support. Strictly speaking, these articles do not constitute the legal basis for the duty to provide child support[7] – that would derive from parentage pursuant to Articles 110, 111 and 154 of the Constitution[8] but are used by the courts as a distribution criterion in the absence of specific regulations on shared parenting. The idea is that the child should have a similar and adequate standard of living at all times, without a drastic change or a notable difference between the parents but avoiding a situation of luxury.[8]

The SC's decision relating to the time limit is also important:

> The Court commits an error, which is corrected by the Provincial Court, when it establishes a time limit on the receipt of maintenance for two years, as the children's fate cannot be left up to whether or not the mother can find work.
>
> This time limit makes sense in compensatory maintenance, as an incentive to find work, but has no place in child support and is prohibited by Article 152 of the Civil Code.

The SC considers that there cannot be a time limit, as the interests of minors are at stake and such interests cannot be harmed. However, the issue arises, particularly when the maintenance allowance paid by the other parent is substantial, as to whether it can also be an incentive for the mother not to seek employment. If she finds a job and receives income, it would be possible to modify the measure as the circumstances have changed, as the SC itself states later in the decision. In this way, even if the interests of the children are taken into account, it may be the mother's financial self-interest that prevents her from seeking employment, at the expense of the financial effort made by the father.

Even so, in this Supreme Court Judgment, which served as a reference for later cases, this solution appeared reasonable in light of the mother's total lack of income. However, the criterion has also been used in cases in which, although both parents received income, it was disproportionate. Other factors also existed, such as the length of stay with each parent and other expenses attributed to them that were also taken into account. Amongst the most recent judgments is STS 50/2019, of 17 January 2019:

> The system of shared parenting does not entail an equal distribution of time, but aims at a distribution that is as fair as possible and tempered by the parents' different working hours.... The court of appeal considered articles 145, 146 and 151 of the Civil Code and related articles, given that it took

into account the parents' salaries, the time spent with each and that the court had assigned expenses that were not strictly considered as maintenance to the mother.

Accordingly, the SC considered that other factors had to be taken into account, such as the other costs conventionally attributed to the parents and the length of stay, as also claimed by the public prosecutor in the case.

However, maintenance is not established in all cases, given that this "disproportion" or difference must be proven. STS 348/2018, of 7 June 2018, denied a maintenance allowance payable by the father because "in the case at hand, not only is it not proven that the difference in income between the two parents is disproportionate, but it is also the father that pays the traveling expenses to facilitate compliance with the system".

In relation to this assessment of maintenance in shared parenting systems, it is worth mentioning the Judgment by the Provincial Court (SAP) of Cáceres 527/2019, of 26 September 2019. In this case, after admitting the possibility of a maintenance allowance in shared parenting when it is proven that there is a difference between the parents' financial capacity, the court takes into account the difficulty and instability of the mother's employment to impose the payment of maintenance by the father. It points out that "it is also a well-known fact that women generally suffer from disadvantages at work compared to men, both in terms of job opportunities and pay". Furthermore, in reply to the father's allegations that the mother earns income outside the standard job market, the court pointed out that this does not mean higher remuneration, but rather a loss of entitlement that could materialise in a loss of benefits and assistance. Finally, it considered that they did not have a similar financial capacity due to the fact that the father has to pay rent and the mother has a house due to the generosity of her parents.

This flexibility of the criteria in establishing the payment of maintenance is therefore worthy of mention. We consider it fair to not only take into account actual income, but also the general financial capacity or capacity to generate revenue, which therefore facilitates a more realistic and long-lasting solution. However, we also consider it appropriate to assess all of the circumstances with caution and at least question whether being a woman means fewer opportunities and lower pay, as well as the consideration of the "unofficial" income that may be received – if it can be proven to some extent – and the fact that the marital breakdown means that one of the parents has to pay rent; an issue that undoubtedly affects his/her financial capacity.

Application for a change to shared parenting and the financial interests of the parties

One of the problems that occurs in practice is the change from individual custody to shared parenting when, in fact, a very similar system to shared parenting already exists. This again leads to problems of a financial nature for the parents, given that individual custody provides for the payment of maintenance that is jeopardised when shared parenting is requested.

In certain cases, the simple passing of time after a marital breakdown makes the relations between the parents less tense than at the beginning and results in more flexibility and time spent with the parent without custody. This occurs in certain cases without being due to financial reasons. Although the subsequent application for shared parenting by the parent without custody and the elimination of maintenance will again generate conflict.

This occurred in the case subject to STS 658/2015, of 17 November 2015. The mother had been granted custody of her daughter but, over time, the visiting rights and stay became more flexible as the relations between the daughter and her father were good. The problem arose when the father filed for a change in the system to one of shared parenting and the elimination of maintenance. This resulted in the mother requesting exact compliance with the visiting rights established in the agreement by means of a claim for enforcement. In this case, it appears evident that there was already a flexible visiting rights and stay system in place that did not vary much in practice. However, the mother was receiving a maintenance payment of 450 euros and the use of the home, which would be eliminated with shared parenting. This was possibly the main reason for the dispute after the request for the change of system, by claiming the return to the strict regime established in the agreement. The SC in this case ended up granting shared parenting and establishing equal payment of the costs.

A similar situation occurred in the Balearic Islands SAP 286/2011, of 6 September 2011, which highlighted the personal and financial interests of the mother, who was reluctant to accept the change to shared parenting. As in the previous case, a change in circumstances had occurred over time, with the consent of the mother, who subsequently opposed shared parenting. The Provincial Court considered that:

> She is contradicting her own acts in order to attempt to avoid, in her own interests, the formalization of a situation that had naturally taken place with the child. The appellant has even accused the father of trying to avoid the payment of maintenance. However, she did not realise that the establishing of shared parenting only made the de facto relationship to which appellant herself had agreed subject to the rule of law. Her refusal to accept this natural consequence is evidence of the personal interest she accuses the other party of having, namely the loss of the maintenance allowance that was inherent to individual custody.

The situation is similar to that of STS 124/2019, of 26 February 2019, in which, although custody had been granted to the mother by mutual consent when the child was one year old, over time the visiting and stay arrangements with the father had been extended. In this case, based on the previous STS, shared parenting was also granted and the maintenance allowance eliminated, with each parent paying the child's costs while he stayed with them and the rest in equal shares. It was also supported by the change in case law and the fact that although the child had adapted to single-parent custody, this cannot be used as grounds to deny a change to shared parenting.

More uncertainty exists in cases in which the individual custody of a parent is established from the beginning, but with a flexible visiting and stay regime similar to that of shared parenting. It is therefore worth considering whether or not, in such cases, it is possible to change the nomenclature and, if necessary, the maintenance arrangement.

In STS 564/2017, of 17 October 2017, the father filed for shared parenting, given that the time spent with each parent was the same, in addition to the abolition of the maintenance allowance. The SC refused to change the "name", because

> the visiting arrangements do not vary, given that the appellant intends to maintain the same amount of time with the children as that achieved in the last amendment of the system. It therefore follows that there is no material change in circumstances to justify the appellant's claim.
> *(Articles 90 f and 92 of the Civil Code)*

Neither did the court eliminate the maintenance, considering that the equal stay at the family home did not justify exemption from paying maintenance, when there is a disproportion between the incomes of both parents, as in this case.

However, a different solution was reached in STS 490/2019, of 24 September 2019:

> There is evidence that the time spent by the child with each parent is practically the same, as mutually agreed, meaning that the adoption of a system of shared parenting would not extend such time, in practice. Therefore, the child's interests would not be affected and the alleged lack of communication between the parents would be irrelevant, given that they have been able to manage a situation of equal time with their child.
> *Judgment 658/2015, of 17 November 2015 (RJ 2015, 5392)*

Despite this identical situation, taking into account the time that had elapsed with respect to the age of the minor – from two to ten – and the change in the SC case law, the court considered the name change to be appropriate. It also considered that the maintenance payments should be abolished, due to the similarity of the parents' professions and income.

It is also important that the court refers to the fact that "the child's interests would not be affected". This is because the SC often stresses that it is not a third instance and that it only acts in the interests of the minor – STS 32/2019, of 17 January 2019. However, although it is acknowledged that the child's interests were not affected in this case, it revoked the Provincial Court judgment and changed the custody regime and maintenance, which is clearly intended to protect the financial interests of the parent previously without custody, rather than the child. However, despite this, we consider the judgment to be correct, as the personal and financial interests of the parents cannot be overlooked in terms of establishing justice, when the interests of the child are not affected in any way. In other words, if the child's interests are protected, the interests of the parents must also be ensured or, as the SC points out in its Judgment

641/2018, of 20 November 2018, "the interests of the children cannot be absolutely dissociated from those of their parents, when it is possible to reconcile them".

It therefore appears clear that even though individual custody is established, if the stay and visiting rights of the parent without custody are increased and made more flexible, becoming a de facto shared parenting system, there is nothing to prevent the legal system from being changed to one of shared parenting. This may lead to the elimination or reduction of the originally established maintenance allowance when the situation originally taken into account changes. In such cases, if the time spent by the parent without custody with the child under a shared parenting system increases and the respective incomes of the parents change, the situation should be updated, even if this leads to a situation of conflict, as we have seen.

Nevertheless, it is true that, in order for shared parenting to be granted, the SC has required the absence of serious conflict between the parents, to ensure

> a relationship of mutual respect that allows the adoption of attitudes and conduct that benefit the child and do not disturb his/her emotional development, despite the emotional breakdown of the parents, as well as to maintain a reference family framework that supports the harmonious development of the child's personality.
> *(STS 619/2014, of 30 October 2014)*

However, this does not mean that in disputes, which are mainly due to financial issues as we have seen, a system of shared parenting will be denied by making it easier for the parent with custody to prevent the establishing of shared parenting. The SC has established that, instead of a seamless agreement, what is required is a reasonable and efficient attitude towards the development of the child – STS 96/2015, of 16 February 2015. Therefore, the existence of misunderstandings, which are typical in a marital crisis, will not rule out this type of custody and care, unless they significantly affect the children in a negative way.

It can also be observed that the above-mentioned cases show an inclination towards granting shared parenting, making it the preferred system and even considering the change in case law itself as a "certain change" of the circumstances that enable the move to shared parenting, as held in some of its judgments – STS 758/2013, of 25 November 2013, STS 553/2016, of 20 September 2016, STS 490/2019, of 24 September 2019, without petrifying the previous situation, STS 11/2018, of 11 January 2018, STS 654/2018, of 20 November 2018. However, in other cases, it appears to reject this criteria as proof of the existence of the required certain change. It even demands proof of the change, as well as the fact that the move to a different system benefits the child, on the grounds that the existing regime had been working normally and without dispute – as in STS 122/2019, of 26 February 2019, and STS 31/2019, of 17 January 2019.[9]

Are financial interests reproachable?

As to whether it is possible to file for shared parenting on personal and financial grounds with changes in the payment of maintenance or use of the home, STS

391/2015, of 15 July 2015, deals directly with the issue. The father requested shared parenting, claiming the difficulty in paying the agreed maintenance allowance of EUR 240, which he would not have to pay in shared parenting; thus meaning that the use of the family home already granted to the child and the mother would be rendered null and void.

In this case, the Court harshly criticised this attitude, considering it as "totally inadmissible to use shared parenting to avoid paying maintenance and deprive the children and custodial parent of the use of the family home". The SC revoked the judgment and granted shared parenting on the grounds of the child's interests and the capacity of the parents to take such action. The court was asked whether the child's interests could have been impaired by the claims made by the father, to which it replied:

> The answer must be no, given that even assuming that it is in the parent's interests, what has to be determined is whether or not the intended system is in the child's interests, which has been proven. Furthermore, the fact that it is more beneficial for the father to comply with his maintenance obligation at his home is not a false interest if the circumstances so permit, as they do in this case, also because it is established by legislators in Article 149 CC, which regulates "family support".

The different interpretation of the father's interests is obvious. While the Provincial Court considers it inadmissible and reproachable, the Supreme Court merely questions whether the father's interests harm the child, considering that they do not, and even considering the benefits of shared parenting as positive. Therefore, according to this judgment, in deciding whether shared parenting is appropriate, it must be determined whether the request is convenient for the child, without considering the fact that there may be financial interests at stake that are in some way affected by the decision.

We examined other cases of lower court case law, which provide for different solutions:

A different solution to that adopted by the SC can be found in the SAP 138/2016, of 1 April 2016, which states that:

> It is clear that the intention of the plaintiff is to resolve certain alleged financial difficulties by obtaining shared parenting and stop paying maintenance. As he claimed during the trial, he can afford food and clothing but not the maintenance payment, despite having given preference over his daughter's maintenance to payment of the mortgage on his home and a personal loan, the need and origin of which are not recorded in the proceedings. Accordingly, the claim for shared parenting cannot be upheld, which must not be used to resolve of the parents' difficulties, but rather in the best interests of the child.

The court therefore focused on the fact that the intention was not to pay maintenance in exchange for shared parenting, even if the claimant could prove difficulties in doing so. The court decided to focus on this issue, without addressing the benefits for the child or the strengthening of relations, which should have been the case.

These financial reasons and requirements between the parties are taken into account by the courts in their decisions, as in the Lleida SAP 524/2016, of 12 December 2106, in which the court states that:

> what cannot be overlooked is that just before the trial, he claimed equal rights as a parent against the mother. This would have lead to the granting of shared parenting by the courts, unless the mother previously agreed to reduce the maintenance in reasonable terms, in which case the dispute would be resolved. This form of instrumental use of the children and the process is unacceptable. Furthermore, it shows that the same person legally requesting shared parenting by claiming it as the preferred legal and case law system, is considering out of court that it is better for the children to remain in the mother's care (albeit with the reduction in the maintenance).

We also come across decisions that do not consider claims of financial interest to be relevant. In the case subject to Jaén SAP 542/2018, of 23 May 2018, in response to such allegations by the mother, the court considered that:

> if it is Mr. Carlos Miguel's intention not to pay maintenance for his daughter, Ms. Agustina overlooks the fact that under the shared parenting system, the father will have to pay half of all the expenses generated by the child. This new system will therefore not produce any savings; quite the contrary, living with the child may generate more costs than the maintenance he was paying.

And also Judgment 47/2015, of 28 July 2015, by the Court of Violence against Women No. 3 of Barcelona, in which such interests are not taken into account:

> In fact, according to the statements of the parties, as the technical team observes, it is clear that financial interests underlie this process of applying for shared parenting in the case of the father and the request for individual custody by the mother. This all basically relates to the use of the home owned by both parents and the maintenance allowance paid by the father under single-parent custody. Obviously, from a judicial point of view, the financial interests of the parties are not taken into account to determine the form of custody. Given the ongoing situation of the marriage and the current circumstances, as well as the working hours of the parties, custody should be maintained by the mother, however with an extension of the father's visiting rights.

As we have observed, the different cases and possible scenarios are practically infinite. It is difficult to provide a clear and accurate solution in cases in which there is an obvious financial interest and a decision is required that affects the personal lives and conditions of those involved. Nevertheless, despite the harsh approach taken in certain judgments, as shown above, the position held by the SC in its above-mentioned Judgment 391/2015, of 15 July 2015, can be understood and, at least, serve as a starting point. In other words, the possibility of shared parenting being granted should not be ruled out simply because there is a financial interest, as the parent will still be fulfilling his or her parental duties. We should not overlook the fact, as the SC has pointed out, that the regulations relating to the interests of minors are rules of public order and must necessarily be observed by judges and courts in the decisions concerning them – STS 348/2018, of 7 June 2018. We should also recall that, "shared parenting or another alternative system is not a reward nor punishment of the parents, but rather the most appropriate system adopted, provided it is compatible with the interests of the minor, without this necessarily entailing any reward or reproach" (STS 561/2018, of 10 October 2018).

Therefore, if shared parenting is the ideal and preferred system, assuming there is an improvement in the child's interests, any request for a change in such measure should initially be considered as positive, unless there are valid reasons to believe that it is detrimental to the child. If proven that the reasons are purely financial, without the father being suitable to exercise custody, it should be refused, as in the case subject to Madrid SAP 224/2019, of 12 March 2018. The court pointed out that the father suffered from "personality imbalances such as impulsiveness, a tendency towards narcissism, lack of respect for others and obsessive features". This also occurs in cases in which the father has totally neglected his child,[10] as in the case subject to Alicante SAP 482/2011, of 2 October 2011, in which the father was disinterested in the child, did not pay the maintenance nor visited the child, thus showing a lack of ability to exercise shared parenting.

However, as we have observed, all these cases must be analysed in detail by the court and all the circumstances of the case taken into account, without it being possible to draw hasty conclusions. Accordingly, if the father has difficulties in paying maintenance and considers it convenient in his interests to have shared parenting, provided he has a good relationship with his child, if shared parenting can have positive effects for both, it should not automatically be ruled out. Even in cases of unpaid maintenance, it should not be ruled out automatically. This was also the conclusion reached in the case subject to La Rioja SAP 43/2018, of 9 February, in which, despite the claim by the mother of the false and financial interests of the father, the court considered that such claim was not proven, without the existence of outstanding maintenance necessarily constituting a financial interest and not the desire to spend more time with his son, concluding that:

> If the appellant's claims were upheld, nobody in debt could ever claim shared parenting, as there could always be a suspicion that they were doing so in order to avoid having to pay maintenance. This is not the case, because shared parenting does not exonerate the parents of their duty to provide for the needs of the children under their care.

For all these reasons, we believe that the mere existence of a financial interest on the part of one of the parents should not be an obstacle to the granting of shared parenting. This would include an exception in cases in which the parent without custody is not considered suitable, such as manifest neglect of the child or any other situation that results in detriment to the child.

Notes

1. The laws and judgments included in this chapter refer to Spanish legislation and courts. We will focus on the study of Spanish case law, without prejudice to the fact that the arguments and conclusions may be used for other legal systems.
2. Pérez Martín, AJ. Modificación de medidas. *Revista de Derecho de Familia.* N°77/2017 parte Artículos doctrinales. Aranzadi. 2017. 31–57.
3. In contrast to other legal systems, such as the Italian one, where in Article 337 it is recognised that the judge must give priority to the fact that the children are in the care of both parents, unless this is contrary to the interests of the child.
4. Sainz-Cantero Caparrós, MB and Pérez Vallejo, AM. *Protección de la Infancia y marco jurídico de la Coparentalidad tras la Crisis Familiar.* Valencia. Tirant. 2018.
5. Pérez-Salazar Resano, M. La pensión de alimentos en los supuestos de custodia compartida. *Abogados de Familia,* N° 64, Sección Tribuna Abierta. Editorial LA LEY. 2012
6. Anguita Ríos, R.M. Prestaciones alimenticias y asistencia familiar. La pensión de alimentos en los supuestos de custodia compartida. In *Ordenación económica del matrimonio y de la crisis de pareja.* Coord. Cervilla Garzón, MD and Lasarte Álvarez. Tirant. 2018.
7. Costas Rodal, L. Custodia compartida y prestaciones alimenticias cuando hay desproporción en los ingresos de los progenitores. Comentario a la STS de 11 de febrero de 2016. *Revista Doctrinal Aranzadi Civil-Mercantil* num.5/2016 parte Jurisprudencia. Comentarios. Aranzadi. 2016. 157–166.
8. Moreno-Torres Herrera, ML. *Las obligaciones de mantenimiento entre familiares.* Dykinson. 2013.
9. Álvarez Olalla, M.P. Modificación de medidas y custodia compartida. *Revista Cuadernos Civitas de Jurisprudencia Civil* num.110/2019 parte Sentencias, Resoluciones, Comentarios. Pamplona. Civitas, SA. 2019. 305–316.
10. Achón Bruñén, M.J. Pensión de alimentos y uso de la vivienda en caso de custodia compartida. *Práctica de tribunales: revista de derecho procesal civil y mercantil,* N°134. La Ley 11406/2018. 2018.

References

Achón Bruñén, MJ. "Pensión de alimentos y uso de la vivienda en caso de custodia compartida". *Editorial La Ley* 11406/2018 (La Ley, 2018).
Álvarez Olalla, MP. "Última jurisprudencia del TS en materia de Custodia Compartida". *Revista Doctrinal Aranzadi Civil-Mercantil num.3/2018 parte Jurisprudencia.* Comentarios (Aranzadi, 2019).
Álvarez Olalla, MP. "Modificación de medidas y custodia compartida". *Revista Cuadernos Civitas de Jurisprudencia Civil num.110/2019 parte Sentencias,* Resoluciones, Comentarios. Pamplona (Civitas, SA, 2019).
Anguita Ríos, RM. "Prestaciones alimenticias y asistencia familiar. La pensión de alimentos en los supuestos de custodia compartida" In *Ordenación económica del matrimonio y de la crisis de pareja.* Coord. Cervilla Garzón, MD and Lasarte Álvarez (Tirant, 2018).
Costas Rodal, L. "Custodia compartida y prestaciones alimenticias cuando hay desproporción en los ingresos de los progenitores. Comentario a la STS de 11 de febrero de 2016". *Revista Doctrinal Aranzadi Civil-Mercantil num.5/2016 parte Jurisprudencia.* Comentarios (Aranzadi, 2016).
Moreno-Torres Herrera, ML. *Las obligaciones de mantenimiento entre familiares* (Dykinson, 2013).

Moreno-Torres Herrera, ML. "La regulación de la ruptura del matrimonio y de las parejas de hecho". *InDret 4/2015*. Octubre (Indret, 2015).
Pérez Martín, AJ. "Modificación de medidas". *Revista de Derecho de Familia num. 77/2017 parte Artículos doctrinales* (Aranzadi, 2017).
Pérez-Salazar Resano, M. "La guarda y custodia compartida y su incidencia en la pensión alimenticia". *Diario LA LEY,* núm. 7206, de junio de 2010 (La Ley, 2010).
Pérez-Salazar Resano, M. "La pensión de alimentos en los supuestos de custodia compartida". *LA LEY 4094/2012.* (La Ley, 2012)
Sainz-Cantero Caparrós, MB and Pérez Vallejo, AM. *Protección de la Infancia y marco jurídico de la Coparentalidad tras la Crisis Familiar.* Valencia (Tirant, 2018).
Torres Perea, José Manuel de, "Custodia compartida: Una alternativa exigida por la nueva realidad social" *Indret: Revista para el Análisis del Derecho*, ISSN-e 1698–739X, N°. 4, 2011, 61 págs (Indret, 2011).

17
HAVING ADDITIONAL CHILDREN
Should the state regulate family relations?

Yoav Mazeh

Introduction

The right to have children is regarded by many as fundamental,[1] certainly in the context of family law. This is so both with regard to the right to become parents, i.e., the right to have one's first child, and with respect to the freedom to decide how many children one has.[2]

The right of parenthood, however, is not unlimited, and in some circumstances can be restricted by the state. Abusing parents, for example, can lose custody of their children, who are then transferred by the state to foster care. Although these parents are not denied the right to procreate, they are denied the right to raise their children because exercising this right would violate the children's right to be unharmed. Likewise, people who are unable to conceive naturally are often subject to various types of state regulation regarding, for example, fertility treatments[3] and adoption.[4] These highly contested issues are not discussed in this chapter. Our topic is the autonomy of parents to decide how many children they have, and whether the state ought to intervene in this decision or in parental decisions about the distribution of their resources among their children.

The starting point of this discussion is the fact that having more than one child affects the financial wellbeing of previous children. When parental resources are limited, as they usually are, having another child almost inevitably reduces resources available to previous children. Here, we consider the legal treatment of this matter; in other words, whether the decision to have more children is considered to be an element of parents' autonomy or is subject to state regulation. This question is considered with respect to three types of family: intact families, divorced or separated families in which the parent who considers having additional children is custodial, and divorced or separated families in which the parent is non-custodial. We show that these three types of family are treated differently by the law, and raise fundamental questions about this differentiation.

Right to have additional children in intact families

In intact families, it is clear that parents have the right to determine the number of children they wish to have. The state is not entitled to intervene in the parental decision about how many children to have or in parental discretion on how to allocate resources among the children. The one-child policy in China, whereby the state restricted parents to having no more than one child, has been criticized as a violation of a fundamental human right.[5]

Nevertheless, having additional children affects previous children. When a family with given resources has additional children, fewer resources are available for each child. At times, having additional children can mean that the previous children must give up certain privileges or standards to which they have become accustomed, such as private schooling and extracurricular activities, and experience reduced standards of accommodation, either by having a sibling share their bedroom or, in more extreme cases, the family moving to a less prosperous environment. It remains clear that, at least in the Western world, the state has no right to intervene in the parental decision on how many children to have or the manner in which they distribute their resources among their various children.

Families of the custodial parent

Custodial parents in divorced and separated families have the same autonomy as parents in intact families in determining the number of children to have, irrespective of the effect this may have on the standard of living of previous children. When custodial parents choose to have additional children in a new relationship, there is no requirement that resources they have been providing to their previous children not be reduced. This reduction is automatic, because if the income of the custodial parent does not increase significantly, and if the other parent of the subsequent children does not support these children entirely out of his or her resources, the birth of any subsequent children means that the custodial parent can provide less to the previous children. Nevertheless, this decision is entirely within the custodial parent's discretion and autonomy, and is not considered a violation of the parental responsibility of that parent to previous children.

This point is demonstrated in *Grebin v. Grebin*.[6] In this case, a couple with one child divorced, and the father was required to pay $348 a month as child support in addition to health and dental insurance. The father later remarried and had two children with his new wife, who also had a daughter from her previous relationship. On this basis, he applied to modify the child support he was paying. In opposing this claim, the mother argued, among other things, that she too had remarried, had a stepchild and was expecting an additional baby. In other words, the mother's claim was that, because she was distributing her income between her previous biological child, her stepchild and expected baby, she also had fewer resources to provide to her previous biological child, and therefore the court ought not to allow the reduction of the child support. This proposition was approved by the court. It follows, that according to the court, despite the fact that the father also had additional children, he was not allowed to reduce his support of the previous child, whereas the mother was entitled to reduce her support of the joint child.

Families of the non-custodial parent

Unlike parents in intact families and custodial parents, parents who do not have custody over their children are not allowed to reduce what they provide to each child if they decide to have additional children or to share the distribution of their resources with non-biological children.

Practically all legal systems have had to deal with the question of whether a later relationship or the remarriage of the payor of child support, usually the non-custodial father, and the birth of children from this relationship, justifies the reduction of child support and, if so, in which way. In all legal systems, when dealing with non-custodial parents, the distribution of resources among previous and subsequent children is regulated by the state.

In Nebraska,[7] Florida[8] and Connecticut,[9] for example, the fact that the payor of child support has children from a second family can be used "as a shield to defend against an increased support obligation, but not as a sword to decrease an existing order, absent exigent circumstances."[10] Other jurisdictions, such as New Jersey[11] and Texas,[12] as well as the Canadian Federal Child Support Guidelines,[13] state that subsequent children of the payor can be grounds for the reduction of child support.[14]

In practice, however, the general rule in most jurisdictions remains that non-custodial parents cannot reduce the level of resources they provide to their previous children owing to the birth of additional children. Various studies have noted that, even if the law explicitly accounts for subsequent children, and instructs the courts to consider such children and amend the child support accordingly, in practice the courts tend to ignore this circumstance and refuse to reduce child support.[15]

The normative question

Why are parents in intact families and custodial parents allowed to reduce the level of support they provide to their children as a result of their decision to have additional children but non-custodial parents are not? This question may be seen as part of a broader one: why do parents in intact and custodial families have much greater autonomy with regard to their financial responsibilities toward their children than do non-custodial parents? The broader question requires a sweeping discussion, which we conduct in a separate study. Here, we focus on the question of the right to have additional children and to adjust financial support of previous children accordingly.

Several arguments are made against modifying child support paid by non-custodial parents as a result of these parents having had additional children.

Child support is insufficient in the first place, and the custodial home is disadvantaged

The first argument is that child support payments are too low in the first place and they disadvantage the children who do not live with the payor of the child support.[16]

According to this argument, reducing child support because of subsequent children of the payor would further disadvantage the previous children, who usually enjoy a lower standard of living than the father's home even without the reduction of child support.[17]

Whether payors of child support are economically better off than the payees, and whether child support in general is too low, are serious questions that require separate studies. In Israel, for example, this is not the case, and mathematical analysis of child support cases demonstrates that the custodial mother's household is significantly better off than that of the non-custodial father.[18] If in some legal systems child support formulas provide too little, child support formulas should be reexamined. But this question is different from the one we address here, which is not the level of child support in general but the fact that subsequent children of child support payors have their own needs that affect the financial abilities of the payors, which requires the adjustment of child support.

Including the second wife's income in the calculation

Another argument is that a decision on reducing child support payments because of the payor's subsequent children must take into account the income of the other parent (the co-parent) of these children. If the father asks to reduce his child support payments because of children from his second marriage, the second wife's income must also be included in the calculation of the resources available to these children.[19] This is not to say that the step-parent's income is relevant to child support, which is a separate question.[20] The argument is that, if a payor of child support has subsequent children with another spouse, the spouse's income is relevant to the needs of their joint children. This is certainly true. The co-parent's income is clearly relevant to the needs of the joint biological children. But the conclusion ought not to be that, because the co-parent has an income, there is no justification for modifying the child support. Rather, child support should be recalculated in the case of subsequent children, but the co-parent's income must be taken into account in the recalculation.[21]

Incentive to have more children

Yet another argument being made is that allowing parents to reduce their child support as a result of having additional children gives payors of child support an incentive to have more children merely in order to reduce their child support liability.[22] Such a notion raises several issues. First is whether ordinary parents would indeed have additional children merely in order to reduce the support they are providing to their previous children. In extreme cases it is possible to envision such behavior, but this seems a highly unlikely phenomenon in society at large.

Second, even when dealing with parents who do not value in any way the fact that the child support they are paying is going to their children, it is highly unlikely that parents would have additional children merely to receive a reduction in their child support if that reduction is insignificant relative to the real costs of raising an extra child.[23]

Note that some of the advocates who argue that reducing child support because of subsequent children would lead payors of child support to have additional children, also argue that current child support rates do not cover the real costs of raising children.[24] If the initial child support does not cover the real costs of raising children, why then would a discount on part of it lead manipulative parents to have additional children?

Third, given that some jurisdictions grant a child support credit for subsequent children,[25] it makes sense to compare the birth rate of subsequent children in jurisdictions that do and do not grant such a credit. Moreover, because various jurisdictions also provide child support credit to custodial parents who have subsequent children,[26] it also makes sense to examine whether there is a difference in the effect of this credit on the motivation of custodial and non-custodial parents to have additional children.

Nondisclaimable duty

The fundamental argument against reducing child support in this context seems to be the claim that parents' liability for child support is a strict liability.[27] According to this view, parents may not reduce their liability toward their children by voluntarily choosing to have additional children. As Martha Minow put it, child support is a "nondisclaimable duty that should not be altered by activities chosen by the obligor."[28] A parent's liability for child support is at times equated with any other financial obligation, for example a mortgage, which should not be affected by subsequent voluntary undertakings of the obligor.[29]

To evaluate this argument, this chapter considers two perspectives. The first is horizontal, in which the interests of the previous children are not considered in relation to the interests of their parents but in relation to those of subsequent children. The question here is not necessarily limited to cases of divorce or to cases in which a parent is liable for child support. Rather, the question is broadly whether firstborn children have the right not to have their standard of living reduced owing to the birth of siblings.

The second perspective is vertical, and weighs the interests of children in relation to those of their parents. Specifically, the question is whether the interest of children not to have their standard of living reduced has preference over their parents' right, or even liberty, to have additional children and to provide equally for these (even if doing so means a reduction in the level of support that the parents had provided to their previous children until that point). Each of these perspectives must be considered with respect to the three forms of family: intact, custodial parent and non-custodial parent.

Horizontal balance

As shown above, in intact families, it is obvious that firstborn and other older children have no right not to have their standard of living reduced as a result of their parents' subsequent children.[30] The same is true with regard to children living with a custodial parent. Children, in general, do not have a right to any sort of preference over their parents' subsequent children. Such a right is completely unfounded.

Moreover, a law that would grant such preference to previous children and hold that their parents must continue to provide the same level of resources for them despite their subsequent children would be unconstitutional because it would discriminate against the subsequent children, placing them at a severe disadvantage relative to the previous children and making them eligible only for the remains of the parents' resources, after they have provided for the previous children.[31]

Vertical balance

We have seen that, in intact families, the parents' right to have additional children and to distribute their resources to all of their children according to their discretion overrides the interest of an existing child not to have his or her standard of living reduced. The same is true with respect to custodial parents, where it is undisputed that the parents are entitled to have additional children even if this were to reduce the level of resources they would provide to their previous children. The theories mentioned above regarding the nondisclaimable duty of parents and the analogy to a first mortgage do not apply to parents in intact families and to custodial parents. Why should this be different with regard to non-custodial parents? If older children have no horizontal superiority over their younger siblings, and if the parents' right to have additional children overrides the children's interest to not have their standard of living reduced, why should this change when dealing with non-custodial parents who wish to reduce their child support in light of their subsequent children?

Conclusion

The literature dealing with child support justifies state intervention in the parents' autonomy with regard to their property in that the parents' obligation to the financial wellbeing of their children overrides their proprietary rights and autonomy in this context.[32] If the issue concerns the parents' liberty to use their property for their leisure or for any other purpose and the child's interest to be cared for financially, it is the child's interest that takes preference, at least up to the standards of support that have been regulated by the state.

However, the issue raised in this chapter is fundamentally different and comprises two questions of principle: (1) whether older children have superiority over subsequent children of their parents, and (2) whether children's interest in not having their standard of living reduced can override their parents' right to have additional children and to share their resources with their subsequent children. We have seen that these questions receive diametrically opposite answers when addressing intact families and custodian parents, on the one hand, and non-custodians, on the other. We argue that this distinction is unjustified and discriminatory.

The chapter does not propose a formula for dealing with child support in this context. Practical formulas must be examined in light of the overall system within which they are being considered. The objective, here, is to challenge the current paradigm and to encourage a debate around the inconsistent legal treatment of fundamental questions such as the superiority of rights of older siblings, parental liberty to have additional children and to support them according to their own discretion, and the freedom of family relations from state regulation.

Notes

1 *Skinner v. State of Oklahoma ex rel. Williamson*, 316 U.S. 535 (1942(; Lynn P. Freedman and Stephen L. Isaacs, Human rights and reproductive choice, *Studies in Family Planning* 24, 18 (1993).
2 Ibid.
3 Kimberly M. Mutcherson, The fertility industry, anti-discrimination, and parents with disabilities, *Law & Ineq.* 27, 311 (2009); Jim Hawkins, Financing fertility, *Harv. J. Legis.* 47, 115 (2010).
4 W. Bradford Wilcox and Robin Fretwell Wilson, Reforming parentage laws: Bringing up baby: adoption, marriage, and the best interests of the child, *Wm. & Mary Bill Rts. J.* 14, 883 (2006).
5 United Nations, Final Act of the International Conference on Human Rights at 18, Un Doc. A/Conf.32/41, Un Sales No. E.68.Xiv.2 (1968); Betsy Hartmann, *Reproductive rights and wrongs: The global politics of population control and contraceptive choice* (New York: Harper & Row, 1987); John Cleland and W. Parker Mauldin, *The promotion of family planning by financial payments: The case of Bangladesh*, Research Division Working Paper No. 13 (New York: The Population Council, 1990); *Human rights briefs: Women in China* , (Ottawa: Immigration and Refugee Board, 1993); Ellen Keng, Population control through the one-child policy in China: Its effects on women, *Women's Rts. L. Rep.* 18, 205 (1997).
6 *Grebin v. Grebin*, No. A-09–131, LEXIS 214 (Neb. App. 2009).
7 Neb. Ct. R., Child Support Guidelines 4–220 (2008).
8 Fla. Stat. § 61.30(12) (2008).
9 Conn. Agencies Regs. § 46b-215a-3 (2005).
10 Susan Paikin, Periodic review and adjustment: Modification and the Family Support Act of 1988, *Del. Law* 36 (1993), cited in Misti N. Nelc, Inequitable distribution: The effect of Minnesota's child support guidelines on prior and subsequent children, *Law & Ineq.* 17, 97, 109 (1999).
11 N.J. Ct. R. 5:1–:8 App. Ix-A.
12 Texas Fam. Code § 154.12.
13 Federal Child Support Guidelines SOR/97–175, Section 10 (2).
14 Paula Woodland Faerber, Empirical study: A guide to the guidelines: A longitudinal study of child support guidelines in the United States, *J. L. Fam. Stud.* 1, 151 (1999).
15 See, for example, Nelc, 111–113; Deborah H. Bell, Child support orders: The federal–state partnership, *Miss. L.J.* 69, 597, 624 (1999); D. A. Rollie Thompson, The second family conundrum in child support, *Rev. Can. D. Fam.* 18, 227, 234–246 (2001).
16 J. Thomas Oldham, *Preface* in Child Support: The Next Frontier ix, ix-xiii (J. Thomas Oldham & Marygold S. Melli eds., 2000); Martha Garrison, The goals and limits of child support policy, in J. Thomas Oldham & Marygold S. Melli (eds), *Child support: The next frontier* (Ann Arbor, MI: University of Michigan Press, 2000, 16–31); Tonya L. Brito, Fathers behind bars: Rethinking child support policy toward low-income noncustodial fathers and their families, *J. Gender Race & Just.* 15, 617, 627 (2012), stating that "Nearly half of all single mothers and their children lived in poverty."

17 Marianne Takas, Improving child support guidelines: Can simple formulas address complex families? *Fam. L.Q.* 26, 171, 177–178 (1992); Margorie Engel, Pockets of poverty: The second wives club – examining the financial insecurity of women in remarriages, *Wm. & Mary J. Women & L.* 5, 309, 313 (1999); Nelc, 97: "The creation of these 'multiple families' has various repercussions, such as the increased rate of poverty existing in single-parent households and the increased poverty of children and women."

18 See, for example, RFMA 5750/03 *Ochana v. Ochana* (Israel's Supreme Court, 8.6.05), whereby, after the child support had been paid, the mother's household had approximately NIS 8,475 a month and the father's household NIS 825; in the case of FMA 1099/06 *John Doe v. Jane Doe* (District Court, Jerusalem, 10.4.07), the mother's household had approximately NIS 11,800 a month and the father's household NIS 4400, despite the fact that the mother was practically living alone and the father was remarried, had two babies from his second marriage, and the two children from the first marriage were residing at his residence most of the time.

19 Thompson, 242–244; Marianne Takas, Addressing subsequent families in child support guidelines, in Margaret Campbell Haynes (ed.), *Child support guidelines: The next generation* (Washington, DC: Office of Child Support Enforcement, 1994).

20 For a discussion of the income of step-parents, see: Katherine Shaw Spaht, The two "ICS" of the 2001 Louisiana child support guidelines: Economics and politics, *La. L. Rev.* 62, 709 (2002); Clayton P. Kawski, Stepping in(come): Evaluating the inherent inconsistency of Illinois's trend toward consideration of new spouse income in child support modification, *N. Ill. U. L. Rev.* 27, 247 (2007); Melanie B. Jacobs, More parents, more money: Reflections on the financial implications of multiple parentage, *Cardozo J.L. & Gender* 16, 217 (2010).

21 Thompson, 242–244.

22 Carol S. Bruch, Developing standards for child support payments: A critique of current practice, *U.C. Davis L. Rev.* 16, 61 (1982); Martha Minow, How should we think about child support obligations?, in Irwin Garfinkel, Sara S. McLanahan, Daniel R. Meyer & Judith A. Seltzer (eds), *Fathers under fire: The revolution in child support enforcement* (London: Russell Sage Foundation, 2001, 309); Adrienne Jennings Lockie, Multiple families, multiple goals, multiple failures: the need for "limited equalization" as a theory of child support, *Harv. J.L. & Gender* 32, 140 (2009).

23 Jo Michelle Beld, A Minnesota comparative family law symposium: Improving child support guidelines in Minnesota: The "shared responsibility" model for the determination of child support, *Wm. Mitchell L. Rev.* 28, 791 (2001); Ira Mark Ellman, Fudging Failure: The economic analysis used to construct child support guidelines, *U. Chi. Legal F.* 167 (2004); Stephen K. Erickson, If they can do parenting plans, they can do child support plans, *Wm. Mitchell L. Rev.* 33, 827 (2007).

24 Cf, for example, Lockie, 133–136, 140–141.

25 Miss. Code Ann. § 43–19–101(3)(d) (2013); N.D. Admin. Code 75–02–04.1–06.1 (4A)(a)(2)(2013).

26 Md. Family Law Code Ann. § 12–202 (a)(2)(iii)(2) (2013); *Graham v. Adams*, 608 N.E.2d 614, 617 (Ill. Ct. App. 1993); *In re Marriage of Starke*, 939 P.2d 46 (Or. Ct. App. 1997).

27 Thomas P. Malone, Modification lives: Guidelines don't mean an end to changing circumstances, *Fam. Advoc.* 10, 44 (1988); Judith Mitchell Billings, From guesswork to guidelines: The the adoption of uniform child support guidelines in Utah, *Utah L. Rev.* 902 (1989); Rebecca Burton Garland, Second children second best? Equal protection for successive families under state child support guidelines, *Hastings Const. L.Q.* 18, 885 (1991); Shaw Spaht, 709; Morgan, 3.

28 Minow, 320, cited also in Lockie, 141.

29 Malone, 43; Nelc at108; Garland, 887; Lockie, 141; The Florida Senate Interim Report 2010–210 October 2009: Committee on Children, Families, and Elder Affairs: Review Of Child Support Guidelines, retrieved from http://archive.flsenate.gov/data/publications/2010/Senate/reports/interim_reports/pdf/2010–210cf.pdf.

30 Note, however, that according to Biblical law, firstborn children had a right to a double share in the inheritance of their father: Deuteronomy 21:17. This privilege, however, was granted only to firstborn sons, not to daughters, it did not provide a preference with respect to child support, and did not provide any privilege to secondborn children over thirdborn, etc.
31 Christopher L. Blakesley, Louisiana family law, *Louisiana Law Review* 52, 607 (1992), 608; Taylor Gay, All in the family: Examining Louisiana's faulty birth order based discrimination, *La. L. Rev.* 73, 295, 296 (2012); Nelc, 113; *Martinez* v. *Martinez*, 660 A.2d 13 (N.J. Super. Ct. Ch. Div. 1995); Malone, 45; Garland, 881, 884; Harry D. Krause, Child support enforcement: Legislative tasks for the early 1980s, *Fam. L.Q.* 15, 349, 357 (1982); Victoria M. Ho, Support for second families: Stretching financial resources to cover multiple families, *Fam. Advoc.* 16, 40, 42–43 (1993).
32 Oldham, J Thomas & Melli, Marygold Shire, *Child support: The next frontier* (Ann Arbor, MI: University of Michigan Press, 2000); Ira Mark Ellman & Tara O'Toole Ellman, The theory of child support, *Harv. J. Legis.* 45, 107 (2008); Douglas W. Allen & Margaret F. Brinig, Child support guidelines: The good, the bad, and the ugly, *Fam. L.Q.* 45, 135 (2011).

PART III

Shared parenting and parental alienation

18
SHARED PARENTING AS PREVENTIVE OF PARENTAL ALIENATION

Edward Kruk

Definition and impact

Parental alienating behaviours are strategies used to damage or destroy the relationship between a child and a targeted parent, in which children are forced to distance themselves from one parent by another parent. The outcome of parental alienating behaviours is called parental alienation; it is a psychological condition in which children ally themselves strongly with the alienating parent, and reject a relationship with the alienated parent, often to the point of developing extreme feelings of hostility, without legitimate justification (Harman, Kruk & Hines, 2018).

There are two core elements of parental alienation as a form of parent–child estrangement that is not the result of abuse or neglect by the distanced parent. First, an alienating parent diminishes or destroys the relationship between a child and the (targeted) parent; second, the child distances him or herself either temporarily or permanently from the targeted parent (Kruk, 2019). This definition corresponds to the definition of child maltreatment as the commission and omission of acts resulting in harm to a child (Krug, Dahlberg, Mercy, Zwi & Lozano, 2002). In the case of parental alienation, the behaviour of the disruptive parent is intended to destroy a primary attachment, and the negative impact on the child (and the targeted parent) is significant (Drozd & Oleson, 2004).

Research findings consistently show that child maltreatment is associated with adverse consequences for children's health and psychosocial well-being and such impacts tend to persist into adulthood (Luke & Banerjee, 2013; Norman et al., 2012). Similarly, research on parental alienation has enumerated a range of devastating consequences for children and targeted parents, particularly when the previous relationship was characterized by a close and loving parent–child attachment. These consequences are discussed below.

Parental alienation is a pathological condition, as there is no history of abuse or violence by the alienated parent, yet children are robbed of the love and care of that parent and extended family in their lives. Also, hatred is not an emotion that comes naturally to a child; it has to be taught. A parent who would teach a child to hate or fear the other parent represents a grave and persistent danger to the mental and emotional health of that child. The adversarial family law system is very much complicit in the process of parental alienation, as it forces parents into a battle over their children, which involves denigrating each other as parents to the maximum degree possible, and reduces the likelihood of an amicable settlement of parenting-related disagreements and conflicts.

The prevalence of parental alienation is much higher than is commonly assumed. Recent research, using nationally representative online survey panels from the United States, found that up to 13% of parents in the United States feel they are being alienated from a child by another parent. This means that an estimated 10.5 million American parents are the targets of parental alienation behaviours and are not reciprocating these in kind, and over 3.8 million children in the United States are estimated to be moderately to severely alienated from a parent who is not engaging in parental alienation behaviours themselves. With regards to mental health impact, fully half of parents who have been alienated from their child have considered committing suicide within the last year (Harman & Biringen, 2016).

Yet professional misunderstanding and even denial of the concept of parental alienation remains an issue of concern. International bodies have been slow to recognize parental alienation as a serious mental health problem and social problem, and a form of emotional child abuse. The identification of parental alienation has posed serious challenges for mental health and legal practitioners (Kruk, 2019; Poustie, Matthewson and Balmer, 2018).

For professional service providers trained in this distinct form of child maltreatment, a comprehensive assessment of family dynamics will expose parental alienation. First and foremost is the pathological behaviour of the alienating parent. Parental alienation involves a set of abusive strategies on the part of a parent to foster the child's rejection of the other parent. Research on the abusive strategies of alienating parents is considerable, and there are several typologies detailing the specific behaviours and actions of alienating parents, from badmouthing the parent to cutting off all contact between parent and child. One well-known typology is Baker and Darnell's (2006) *Seventeen Strategies of Alienating Parents* (see Table 18.1). This typology describes the full gravity of parental alienation, from mild to severe.

More recently, Kruk (2018) developed a typology based on research on more severe forms of alienation, where the result is complete loss of contact between child and target parent (see Table 18.2).

The second element of parental alienation is the pathological effect on the child and alienated parent. Parental alienation represents a serious and significant form of harm and poses a serious threat to the well-being of both targeted parent and child. For the child, in particular, parental alienation is a significant mental disturbance, in which the child's psychological and physical well-being is seriously compromised (Balmer, Matthewson & Haines, 2018).

Table 18.1 Seventeen strategies of alienating parents

1. Badmouthing: The target parent is portrayed as unloving, unsafe, and unavailable. Flaws are exaggerated or manufactured. Such statements are made frequently, intensely, and with great sincerity.
2. Limiting contact: The target parent has few opportunities to counter the badmouthing message.
3. Interfering with communication: Phones are not answered, e-mail messages are blocked, and messages are not forwarded.
4. Interfering with symbolic communication: Thinking about, talking about, and looking at pictures of a parent are prohibited. The alienating parent creates an environment in which the child does not feel free to engage in these activities. The child's mind and heart are preoccupied with the alienating parent and there is no room left for the child's thoughts and feelings about the target parent.
5. Withdrawal of love: What angers the alienating parent most is the child's love and affection for the target parent. Thus, the child must relinquish the love of the other. The child lives in fear of losing the alienating parent's love and approval.
6. Telling the child that the target parent is dangerous: Stories might be told about ways in which the target parent has tried to harm the child.
7. Forcing child to choose: The alienating parent will compel the child away from the target parent by scheduling competing activities and promising valued items and privileges.
8. Telling the child that the target parent does not love him or her: The alienating parent will foster the belief in the child that he or she is being rejected by the target parent and distort every situation to make it appear as if that is the case.
9. Confiding in the child: The alienating parent will involve the child in discussions about legal matters and share with the child personal and private information about the target parent. The alienating parent will portray him or herself as the victim of the target parent, inducing the child to feel pity for and protective of the alienating parent, and anger and hurt toward the target parent. The confidences are shared in such a way as to flatter the child and appeal to his or her desire to be trusted and involved in adult matters.
10. Forcing child to reject the target parent: Alienating parents create situations in which the child actively rejects the target parent, such as calling the target parent to cancel upcoming parenting time or requesting that the target parent not attend an important school or athletic event. Further, once a child has hurt a parent, the alienation will become entrenched as the child justifies his or her behaviour by devaluing the target parent.
11. Asking the child to spy on the target parent: Once a child betrays a parent by spying on them, he or she will likely feel guilty and uncomfortable being around that parent, thus furthering the alienation.
12. Asking the child to keep secrets from the target parent: The alienating parent will ask or hint that certain information should be withheld from the target parent in order to protect the child's interests. Like spying, keeping secrets creates psychological distance between the target parent and the child.

(continued)

Table 18.1 Cont.

13. Referring to the target parent by first name: Rather than saying "Mummy/Daddy" or "Your mummy/Your daddy", the alienating parent will use the first name of the target parent when talking about that parent to the child. This may result in the child referring to the target parent by first name as well. The message to the child is that the target parent is no longer someone whom the alienating parent respects as an authority figure for the child and no longer someone who has a special bond with the child. By referring to the target parent by first name, the alienating parent is demoting that parent to the level of a peer or neighbour.
14. Referring to a step-parent as "Mum/Dad" and encouraging child to do the same: The alienating parent will refer to that parent as the mother/father to the child and create the expectation that the child will do so as well.
15. Withholding medical, academic, and other important information from target parent/ keeping target parent's name off medical, academic, and other relevant documents: The target parent will be at a decided disadvantage in terms of accessing information, forging relationships, being contacted in emergencies, being invited to participate, being provided with changes in schedules/locations, and so forth. This marginalizes the target parent in the eyes of the child and important adults in his or her life. They also make it considerably more difficult for the target parent to be an active and involved parent.
16. Changing child's name to remove association with target parent: The target parent may feel that the name change represents a rejection of him or her and will experience hurt, sadness, and frustration.
17. Cultivating dependency/undermining the authority of the target parent: An alienating parent develops dependency in their child rather than helps him or her to develop self- sufficiency, critical thinking, autonomy, and independence. At the same time, they will undermine the authority of the target parent in order to ensure that the child is loyal to only one parent.

Source: Baker and Darnell, 2006

The impact of parental alienation on children is profound:

- First, self-hatred is particularly disturbing. Teaching hatred of a parent is tantamount to instilling self-hatred in the child. Children internalize the hatred targeted toward the alienated parent, are led to believe that the alienated parent did not love or want them, and experience severe guilt related to betraying the alienated parent. Their self-hatred and depression are rooted in feelings of being unloved by one of their parents, and from separation from that parent, while being denied the opportunity to mourn the loss of the parent or even talk about the parent (Baker, 2005, 2010; Warshak, 2015).
- Second, alienated children exhibit severe psychosocial disturbances. Social skills are largely lacking in alienated children. These disturbances include disrupted social-emotional development, lack of trust in relationships, social anxiety, and social isolation. They have poor relationships with both of their parents. As adults, they tend to enter partnerships earlier, are more likely to divorce or dissolve their

Table 18.2 Indicators of extreme parental alienation as child abuse: Characteristics of the alienating parent

1.	Seizing the child by force.
2.	A belief in one's entitlement as the primary or sole parental figure in the child's life, and lack of validation or recognition of the salience of the other parent as a parent.
3.	Insensitivity to and disregard for the impact of one's behaviour on one's child; lack of regard for and attunement to child's needs. Willingness to engage in conflict in front of the child. Lack of emotional depth and emotional responsiveness in relationship with one's child. Parentification of the child.
4.	Overt or covert obsession with the other parent, and with hurting the other parent, to the extent that the obsession prevails over one's parental responsibilities.
5.	Willingness and enthusiasm to engage in adversarial combat, and skill in the adversarial arena.
6.	Refusal to communicate or to engage in a negotiation process.
7.	Refusal to accept responsibility for one's own contribution to the problem situation or conflict.
8.	Readiness to accuse the other party of wrongdoing.
9.	Lack of guilt or remorse for one's behaviour.
10.	Exaggeration and dishonesty; an attitude of "the end justifies the means."
11.	Badmouthing of the other parent in front of the child, or avoiding any mention of the other parent in an attempt to erase that parent from the child's memory.
12.	Monitoring and questioning the child in regard to his or her relationship with the other parent.

Source: Kruk, 2018

cohabiting unions, are more likely to have children outside any partnership, and are more likely to become alienated from their own children (Baker, 2005, 2010; Ben-Ami & Baker, 2012; Friedlander & Walters, 2010; Godbout & Parent, 2008).

- Third, life skills are lacking in alienated children. Low self-sufficiency, lack of autonomy, and a lingering dependence on the alienating parent are characteristics of alienated children. This is manifested in ways such as: adultification (the alienating parent treating the child as an adult); parentification (the child taking responsibility for the parent, a reversal of roles); and infantilization (the child is rendered incompetent and incapable of the life tasks of adulthood) (Garber, 2011).
- Fourth, alienated children are more likely to underperform in school and are less likely to attain academic and professional qualifications in adulthood. They are more likely to experience unemployment and have low incomes (Kruk, 2019).
- Fifth, alienated children experience difficulties in controlling their impulses, and struggle with mental health and addiction issues. Parents report that alienated children are more likely to smoke, drink alcohol, abuse drugs, as well as succumb to behavioural addictions, and are more likely to be promiscuous, foregoing contraception and becoming teenage parents (Kruk, 2019).

In the identification of parental alienation, it is important to note that most children who reject their parents for reasons related to actual abuse, neglect, or disinterest by the parent have feelings of ambivalence. On the one hand, they display anger; on the other, they want things to be better. Alienated children express little or no ambivalence. Things are polarized, black and white. They state vehemently but matter-of-factly that they want nothing to do with the parent. They usually display a lack of emotion in relating this information (Clawar & Rivlin, 2013; Gottlieb, 2012).

In regard to paternal alienation, which has been more of a focus of research than maternal alienation, McLanahan, Tach and Schneider (2013) led a joint Princeton–UC Berkeley–Cornell University study on the causal effects of father absence, which concluded that research in this area is extremely robust: children's physical and mental health problems are not only correlated with the parental alienation of fathers, they are caused by the alienation and absence of fathers. Kruk's (2010) study of maternal alienation and comparative analysis of the impact of paternal and maternal alienation (Kruk, 2015) found that, from the perspective of parents themselves, alienation of children leads directly to a broad range of devastating impacts on children.

Legal and mental health interventions

Multiple forms of legal and mental health interventions have been developed and implemented to address the problem of the alienation of parents from their children's lives after parental separation. Three systems or forms of intervention have been the focus of evaluation research.

1. First are therapeutic interventions in cases of parental alienation: family reunification programs and therapeutic services for alienated parents and their children. Children show the best adjustment to the separation of their parents when they maintain active and meaningful relationships with both of their parents; children need both parents actively engaged in their lives on a routine, day-to-day basis. In parental alienation situations, it is vital to restore children's relationships with alienated parents in a timely and considered manner. Reunification efforts should be undertaken with service providers with specialized expertise in parental alienation reunification. Further, the trauma of alienation is severe, and therapeutic services for individual victims of alienation are urgently needed for successful reunification.

   In addition to family reunification, divorce education programs, therapeutic family mediation, post-divorce family therapy, and parental coordination and coaching services are other ways to address the issue of parental alienation.

   In regard to therapeutic practice with alienated children, a number of best practice guidelines have been proposed. First, children's stated wishes regarding parental residence and contact in contested residence cases should be considered, but they should not be determinative in cases of parental alienation. Children do not have the cognitive maturity or capacity to make an informed decision about whether or not to have a relationship with a parent, can be unduly influenced by emotional manipulation to act against their own best interests, and should not be placed in the middle of loyalty conflicts. Second, without a child having permission to change, the child will be conflicted. The alienating parent needs to be involved in treatment and held accountable. The child should not be intimidated or manipulated by the alienating parent.

The child should be helped to develop critical thinking skills in order to enhance his or her ability to resist the pressure of that parent to choose sides. Therapists are advised to not ally with the child against the targeted parent. The targeted parent and child's relationship with that parent must be validated for the child. The therapist can be a role model who values and respects the targeted parent in order to counter the ongoing message that this parent is inadequate and someone to be discarded.

Intervention with children exposed to parental alienation is a sensitive matter. Alienated children seem to have a secret wish for someone to help them reconnect with the parent they claim to hate; despite strongly held positions of alignment, alienated children want nothing more than to be given permission and freedom to love and be loved by both parents. Research has shown that many alienated children can transform quickly from refusing or stanchly resisting the rejected parent to being able to show and receive love from that parent, followed by an equally swift shift back to the alienated position when back in the orbit of the alienating parent.

The research and clinical literature on recovery from cults offers useful ideas for therapists working with adult children affected by parental alienation in childhood. For example, the way in which a person leaves a cult has ramifications for the recovery process. Cult members can walk away from a cult, be cast out from a cult, or be counseled out of a cult. Those who walk away (come to the realization on their own that the cult is not healthy for them) and those who are counseled out (those who are exposed to a deliberate experience designed to instigate the desire to leave) tend to fare better than those who are cast out (those who are rejected from the cult for failing to meet its regulations and strictures) (Clawar & Rivlin, 2013). Regardless of how a cult is abandoned, freeing the children from the toxic influence of an alienating parent is only the beginning of the recovery process. Considerable time and effort are required in therapy to process the experience and undo the negative messages from the parent that have become incorporated into the self. The same may be true of adult children who have experienced parental alienation.

Guidelines for professional practice with alienated parents, who are similarly affected to children, have also been developed. Alienated parents often present initially as anxious, agitated, angry, and afraid. Having sustained severe psychological and emotional trauma, they are in crisis mode and will therefore often make a poor first impression. In contrast, alienating parents make an excellent first impression, presenting as cool, calm, rational, and convincing.

The trauma of parental alienation is a form of psychological domestic violence against the alienated target parent. The target parent is being made to experience the psychological abuse, suffering, and victimization that were part of the childhood experience of the alienating parent. For the targeted parent, parental alienation represents a complex trauma of profound magnitude. The suffering of alienated parents is deep and unending, and tied to constant worry about the well-being of their children, and their inability to protect their children, who they know to be vulnerable.

A primary role of the therapist is to help the parent become educated about parental alienation (for example, what are primary behaviours that turn a child against the other parent and what are the behavioural manifestations of an alienated child) and the dynamics behind alienation. Another key role is the ongoing validation of the alienated parent's parental identity. This is very important, as the parental identity is central to these parents' definition of themselves, yet at every turn their role as parents is undermined. And, finally, support in dealing with the pain and suffering associated with parental alienation, and self-care are essential. In their suffering, alienated parents must strive to achieve the triumph of light over the darkness of trauma, find a way out of the trauma experience being inflicted upon them, and begin recovery of their psychological health and balance. They must strive to free themselves from the imposed trauma experience, to find and keep their own emotional and psychological health within the immense emotional trauma of grief and loss.

Another challenge for alienated parents is to maintain the high road while not becoming overly passive or reactive. An important message to parents is, simply, to never give up their quest for reunification with their alienated children, and, in the face of hostility and rejection from their children, to respond with loving compassion and emotional availability, and project a sense of absolute safety. Patience and hope, unconditional love, being there for one's child, is the best response parents can provide for their children, notwithstanding the sad truth that this may be insufficient to effect reunification.

Finally, wherever possible, alienated parents should try to expose their children to people who regard them, as parents, with honour and respect, to let the children see that their negative opinion, the opinion of the alienating parent, is not shared by the rest of the world. This type of experience will leave a stronger impression than anything the alienated parent can say on his or her own behalf.

2. The second system of intervention is professional recognition of parental alienation as a serious form of individual child abuse, the recognition that parental alienation is a form of family violence and child maltreatment, as it is the result of actions by an individual parent that represent a significant form of harm to children. Recognizing parental alienation as a form of emotional child abuse, linked to child neglect and to physical and sexual abuse, clearly makes it, above all else, a child protection concern. This may involve child removal from the abusive parent or, in most cases, family support services aimed at educating the parent about the effects and unacceptability of alienation, and affecting a reunification process between the child and targeted parent.
3. The third system of intervention is the effective legal enforcement of shared parenting orders, and the legal consequences for parents who withhold children from the other parent. Enforcement is needed to ensure compliance with shared parenting orders, as well as consequences for engaging in parental

alienation behaviours. Enforcement is perhaps the most contentious intervention, as markedly different legal approaches to addressing parental alienation have been suggested by professionals, ranging from incarceration to custody reversal to family therapy to leaving the situation alone.

Some argue that continued exposure to the alienating parent will be counterproductive to reunification efforts; others suggest that using alienation from a parent to punish or deter alienation seems counterintuitive. However, the most recent research indicates that therapeutic interventions in most situations of parental alienation are the most effective when there are strong legal sanctions for noncompliance with shared parenting orders, and there is an emerging consensus among alienation specialists that awarding primary parental responsibility to the targeted parent when parental alienation is severe is an important step in ameliorating parental alienation.

Prevention: The feasibility of a rebuttable legal presumption of shared parenting as the foundation of family law

As far as prevention of parental alienation is concerned, the main focus of this chapter, what is urgently needed is fundamental reform of the family law system, and establishing shared parenting as the foundation of family law.

Parental alienation thrives in an advanced "winner-takes-all" legal system wherein parents are forced to denigrate the other, and in situations where one parent has been legally granted exclusive care and control of the children. Legal systems that remove a parent from a child's life by means of sole custody or primary residence orders are not only contributing to parental alienation, they are also engaging in parental alienation and a form of collective child abuse.

Parental alienation is first and foremost a systemic problem, and just as parental alienation thrives in legal jurisdictions with an adversarial and discretionary approach to child custody determination, parental alienation is least likely to occur in jurisdictions that have legislated shared parenting as the foundation of family law (Giancarlo & Rottman, 2015).

A strong case has been made for legal presumption of shared parenting responsibility (Fabricius, 2020; Kruk, 2013), rebuttable in cases where it is established that a child is in need of protection by means of a child welfare investigation (Fidler & Bala, 2020; Jaffe et al., 2008). This includes cases of family violence and child abuse, but not merely high conflict cases. Shared parenting is a protective factor for children in high conflict cases, and there are effective ways to reduce parental conflict or to establish shared parenting arrangements in which children are shielded from conflict. Parental conflict levels go up in sole custody and primary residence arrangements and go down in shared parenting agreements. And the risk of first-time family violence is much higher where parental relationships are threatened within the adversarial "winner-takes-all" context.

Shared parenting as the cornerstone of family law is a child-focused approach that emphasizes children's needs and parental responsibilities, and reduces the harms attendant to divorce for children and family members. Such a "responsibility-to-needs" framework, which focuses on children's needs, parental responsibility to meet those needs, and the responsibilities of social institutions to support parents in the fulfillment of their parental responsibilities, is gradually supplanting a rights-based approach to child custody across the globe. At the same time, it is recognized that any new approach to parenting after separation must also address the needs of parents; although children's needs are distinct from those of their parents, they are inextricably linked. Mothers and fathers who are satisfied with their parenting arrangements are less conflicted, and reduced conflict is associated with children's well-being. New legislation thus needs to take on board the concerns of both feminist and fathers' advocacy groups, including feminist concerns regarding family violence, recognizing primary caregiving, and inequities associated with awarding legal joint custody without a corresponding responsibility for child care involvement, as well as fathers' concerns about their disenfranchisement from children's lives, the importance of parent–child attachment, combating parental alienation, and access enforcement (Kruk, 2013).

Cosmetic reforms to family law produce limited results in terms of meaningful family justice. These include changing the language of divorce, and shared parenting legislation that retains judicial discretion where child safety and well-being is not at issue. The latter has resulted in only a small proportion of disputed cases being awarded shared parenting within a continuing adversarial framework. A true shared parenting presumption would ensure determinacy and consistency in decision making, and remove judicial discretion in areas in which judges have little or no expertise (Kruk, 2013).

The following shared parenting presumption model was developed with these concerns in mind, and is unique in several respects. First, it is a child-focused framework that takes on board the primary concerns of both feminist and fathers' groups. Second, it merges a rebuttable legal presumption of shared parenting responsibility with a rebuttable presumption against shared parenting in cases of family violence and child abuse. Third, it addresses the issue of discrimination against children of divorce on the basis of parental status, as it adopts a "child in need of protection" criterion rather than the indeterminate "best interests" standard to removal of a parent from the life of a child. The presumption minimizes the subjectivity of the best interest standard while at the same time taking into account the individual and unique circumstances of children and families.

A rebuttable presumption of shared parenting responsibility in contested child cases is defined as children spending equal amounts of time in each parent's household. The presumption involves a four-stage legal process, as follows:

1. Establish a legal requirement that parents develop a parenting plan before any court hearing on child-related living arrangements. The role of the court would be to legally sanction negotiated parenting plans or agreements, whether primary, shared, or equal-time parenting. Parents would retain the option of developing the plan jointly through negotiation, legal negotiation, or family mediation; family mediation and family support services would be focused on assisting parents in the development of the plan. Parental autonomy and self-determination in regard to post-divorce parenting arrangements would thus be the cornerstone of family law.

2. Establish a legal requirement that, in cases where parents cannot arrive at a negotiated agreement, existing parent–child relationships will continue after separation, in proportion to existing arrangements; that is, in cases of dispute regarding post-divorce parenting arrangements, an "approximation rule" would be applied by the court. The relative proportion of time that children will spend with each parent after divorce will closely approximate the relative proportion of time each parent spent performing child caregiving functions before divorce. Children's needs regarding maintaining relationships with each parent, and stability and continuity in regard to their routines and living arrangements, would thus be addressed; and parents' needs for a fair, gender-neutral criterion would also be accommodated. The approximation standard, drafted by Bartlett (2014) for the American Law Institute, incorporates both feminist concerns regarding the primary caregiving role of mothers (Brinig, 2001) and fathers' concerns regarding the maintenance of meaningful relationships with children after divorce. Given the gender convergence in regard to division of childcare tasks and the emerging norm of shared parental responsibility for childcare in two-parent families, such an "approximation" criterion would translate to roughly equal time apportionment in most high conflict cases.
3. Legislate a rebuttable legal presumption of shared parenting time in cases where both parents were primary caregivers before divorce, and are in dispute over the relative proportion of time each parent should spend in the company of their children. A preoccupation with the amount of time spent with each parent is the Achilles' heel of the "approximation" standard, and tracking parental time devoted to children's care before divorce is a dauntingly complex task (Lamb, 2007). When parents dispute each other's estimates of past time devoted to childcare, with "mathematizing time" a focus of conflict, in the interests of shielding children from ongoing conflict, an equal parenting time division would apply.
4. Legislate a rebuttable legal presumption against shared parenting in cases where it is established that a child is in need of protection from a parent or parents. This presumption would develop clear and consistent guidelines for the determination of children's living arrangements in family violence and child maltreatment cases, consistent with those for children in two-parent families, with the safety of children the paramount consideration. For some families, divorce will solve the problems that contributed to the violence; for others, the risk of maltreatment will be ongoing. This presumption does not equate to a "presumption of *no contact* between the perpetrator and child in *all* cases where domestic violence is *alleged*" (Jaffe et al., 2003, emphasis added); as in current practice, courts would make protective orders only when allegations are substantiated. As family violence and spousal abuse are criminal matters, they must be recognized as such in criminal law, and adjudicated after thorough child welfare investigation (Chisolm, 2009).

This legal framework will serve as a bulwark against parental alienation, as parental alienation itself is a serious form of child maltreatment that warrants a child welfare investigation. However, a legal presumption of shared parenting responsibility would only be the first of four pillars of family law reform directed toward addressing the problem of parental alienation, and providing for optimal outcomes for children and families. The remaining three pillars are equally vital to the success of shared parenting arrangements, and are comprised of treatment, prevention, and enforcement. In regard to treatment, non-violent high-conflict couples can be helped via effective therapeutic interventions such as divorce education, family therapy, family mediation, and parenting coordination, to achieve less conflictual, if not amicable, parenting arrangements. As the dust settles after separation and neither parent is threatened by the possible loss of their children via a sole custody or primary residence order, it may be expected that parental conflict levels will naturally decline with the passage of time, as parents quickly learn to separate their former spousal hostilities from their ongoing parenting responsibilities. Some parents will enter into a co-operative co-parenting routine, while others will fare better within a parallel parenting approach, in which their contact with each other is limited. Others will require support or specialized intervention to shield their children from their ongoing conflict. Children's needs for protection from parental conflict must be addressed within any post-divorce parenting arrangement, and a full range of supports must be made available, especially to parents in high conflict situations. Within these programs, children's needs and well-being become a means of connecting the parents in a positive manner at a time when conflict has divided them.

In regard to prevention, shared parenting education within the high school system, in marriage preparation courses, and upon divorce is an essential component of a more comprehensive program of parent education and support. Public education about various models of shared parenting is especially important, including models for high conflict couples. Such programs are well established in numerous jurisdictions, with an emphasis on including parents who have not traditionally been engaged by parenting support programs and services. Shared parenting education should also involve the judicial and legal professions, as the extent to which family law reform can bring about a desired result will depend largely on the attitudes of the judiciary as well as legal practitioners. Assumptions about shared parenting being unworkable in cases of disputed custody, and sole custody being in children's best interests in contested cases, should be challenged, and stereotypes about parents in conflict addressed. Training mental health professionals in intervention techniques in cases of parental alienation is another challenge, as is garnering public and political attention and support to deal effectively with the social problems of fatherlessness, parental alienation, and diminished parental involvement in children's lives after divorce. These problems need to be made more visible, and constructive solutions advanced.

Finally, the enforcement pillar addresses the question of violence and abuse in family relationships, and enables sanctions to be imposed when there is non-compliance or repeated breaches of shared parenting orders. When enforcement measures are necessary to ensure compliance, solutions may involve temporary reduction of parenting time, with a requirement that a parent comply with "make-up" contact if contact has been missed through a breach of an order (Templer, Matthewson, Haines & Cox, 2016).

Conclusion

The present state of knowledge on parental alienation has advanced with an explosion of research over the past decade, with over 1,200 research and clinical studies reported in scientific and professional journals, books, and book chapters (Vanderbilt University Medical Center, 2017).

The research is robust in regard to definition and characteristics of parental alienation, incidence and prevalence rates, and strategies and behaviours of alienating parents, and the effects of parental alienation on child well-being. These clearly point to the phenomenon of parental alienation as a serious but misunderstood and neglected form of emotional child abuse and family violence (Kruk, 2019).

Several challenges exist to overcoming professional and political misunderstanding of parental alienation and the forced separation of loving parents from their children, and political inaction on the issue. A multi-faceted approach to prevention and intervention is required. Four approaches in particular – fundamental reform of the family law system, and establishing shared parenting as the foundation of family law; professional recognition of parental alienation as a serious form of child abuse, and corresponding intervention of child protection authorities; provision of effective treatment programs and services by trained service providers, including reunification services and prevention programs; and effective legal enforcement of shared parenting orders, and legal consequences for parents who withhold children from the other parent – provide a framework in that regard, and represent a call to action for alienated parents and their children.

Alienating parents' denial of responsibility for their children's rejection of the other parent continues to find support among advocates who reject the concept of parental alienation. Their position is that parental alienation is a legal strategy used by abusive parents to deflect blame for their children's fear and hatred of them. They claim that children who reject parents always have valid reasons and all "hated parents" have no one to blame for their suffering but themselves. And yet, among legal and mental health specialists in the area of high conflict divorce, there seems to be very little controversy about parental alienation. For example, a survey taken at the Association of Family and Conciliation Courts' annual (2014) conference reported 98% agreement "in support of the basic tenet of parental alienation: children can be manipulated by one parent to reject the other parent who does not deserve to be rejected." There is an emerging consensus that parental alienation is a serious issue for children and families. This includes a large body of research validating the existence of parental alienation, along with thousands of adults who attest to having suffered this experience as children, and other parents who are currently traumatized, watching helplessly as their relationships with their children are being destroyed.

In regard to parental alienation, the system is the problem; the roots of parental alienation lie mainly in the adversarial nature of family law structures. Parents are set up to fight in an effort to win residence or custody of their children, and the system rewards those skilled in adversarial combat. Parents win their case by disparaging the other parent, engaging in alienating behaviour, which is encouraged in an adversarial arena. Once they obtain their court order, residential parents are placed in a position to exercise their revenge with impunity, confident that non-resident parents have little or no rights. Thus, the removal of a fit and loving parent via a legal primary residence order is in itself a form of parental alienation, as children are robbed of their parents' routine care and nurture, as well as that of their extended family.

Shared parenting, on the other hand, reduces the risk and incidence of parental alienation, because children continue to maintain meaningful routine relationships with both of their parents, and are thus less susceptible to the toxic influence of an alienating parent. At the same time, with shared parenting, parents are not threatened by the potential loss of their children, and are less likely to denigrate the other parent in an effort to bolster their own sense of parental identity and obtain a sole residence order.

Shared parenting is not a panacea for the elimination of parental alienation. But as a legal reform it offers children and families the best chance of doing so. A shared parental responsibility presumption is based on the assumption that it is the responsibility of legal and mental health professionals to support parents in the fulfillment of their parental responsibility to meet children's needs. In no other arena is this more vital than in regard to the best interests of children of separated and divorced parents.

References

Baker, A. J. L. (2005). The long-term effects of parental alienation: A qualitative research study. *American Journal of Family Therapy, 33*, 289–302.

Baker, A. J. L. (2010) Adult recall of parental alienation in a community sample: Prevalence and associations with psychological maltreatment. *Journal of Divorce & Remarriage, 51*, 16–35.

Baker, A. J. L. & Darnell, D. (2006). Behaviors and strategies employed in parental alienation. *Journal of Divorce & Remarriage, 45*, 97–124.

Balmer, S., Matthewson, S. & Haines, J. (2018). Parental alienation: Targeted parent perspective. *Australian Journal of Psychology, 70*, 91–99.

Bartlett, K. T. (2014). Prioritizing past caretaking in child-custody decision-making. *Law and Contemporary Problems, 77*(1), 29–67.

Ben-Ami, N., & Baker, A. J. L. (2012) The long-term correlates of childhood exposure to parental alienation on adult self-sufficiency and well-being. *American Journal of Family Therapy, 40*, 169–183.

Brinig, M. (2001). Feminism and child custody under Chapter Two of the American Law Institute's Principles of the Law of Family Dissolution. *Duke Journal of Gender, Law, and Policy, 8*, 310–321.

Chisolm, R. (2009). *Family courts violence review*. Canberra: Department of the Attorney General.

Clawar, S. S., & Rivlin, B. V. (2013). *Children held hostage: Identifying brainwashed children, presenting a case, and crafting solutions*. Chicago, IL: American Bar Association.

Drozd, L. M., & Olesen, N. W. (2004). Is it abuse, alienation, and/or estrangement? A decision tree. *Journal of Child Custody, 1*(3), 65–106.

Fabricius, W. V. (2020). Equal parenting time: The case for a legal presumption. In J. G. Dwyer (ed.), *The Oxford handbook of children and the law*. Oxford: Oxford University Press.

Fidler, B. J., & Bala, N. (2020). Concepts, controversies and conundrums of "alienation:" Lessons learned in a decade and reflections on challenges ahead. *Family Court Review, 58*(2), 576–603.

Friedlander, S., & Walters, M. G. (2010). When a child rejects a parent: Tailoring the intervention to fit the problem. *Family Court Review, 48*, 98–111.

Garber, B. (2011) Parental alienation and the dynamics of the enmeshed parent–child dyad: Adultification, parentification, and infantilization. *Family Court Review, 49*, 322–335.

Giancarlo, C., & Rottman, K. (2015). Kids come last: The effect of family law involvement in parental alienation. *International Journal of Interdisciplinary Social Sciences*, *9*, 27–42.

Godbout, E., & Parent, C. (2008). The life paths and lived experiences of adults who have experienced parental alienation: A retrospective study. *Journal of Divorce & Remarriage*, *53*, 34–54.

Gottlieb, L. J. (2012). *The Parental Alienation Syndrome: A family therapy and collaborative system approach to amelioration.* Springfield, IL: Charles C Thomas Publisher.

Harman, J., & Biringen, Z. (2016) Prevalence of parental alienation drawn from a representative poll. *Children and Youth Services Review*, *66*, 62–66.

Harman, J., Kruk, E., & Hines, D. (2018). Parental alienating behaviors: An unacknowledged form of family violence. *Psychological Bulletin*, *144*(12), 1275–1299.

Jaffe, P. G., Johnston, J. R., Crooks, C. V., & Bala, N. (2008). Custody disputes involving allegations of domestic violence: Toward a differentiated approach to parenting plans. *Family Court Review*, *46*(3), 500–522.

Jaffe, P., Lemon, N., & Poisson, S. E. (2003). *Child custody and domestic violence: A call for safety and accountability.* Thousand Oaks, CA: Sage.

Krug, E. G., Dahlberg, L. L., Mercy, J. A., Zwi, A., & Lozano, R. (2002). *World report on violence and health.* Geneva: World Health Organization.

Kruk, E. (2010). Collateral damage: The lived experiences of divorced mothers without custody. *Journal of Divorce & Remarriage*, *51*(8), 526–543.

Kruk, E. (2013). *The equal parent presumption.* Montreal: McGill-Queen's University Press.

Kruk, E. (2015). The lived experiences of non-residential parents in Canada: A comparison of mothers and fathers. *International Journal for Family Research and Policy*, *1*(1), 80–95.

Kruk, E. (2018). The perspectives and needs of parents experiencing severe parental alienation: A qualitative study examining parent–child contact loss. Paper presented at the 2018 Conference of the International Association for Relationship Research, Fort Collins, CO, July.

Kruk, E. (2019). Parental alienation as a form of emotional child abuse: Current state of knowledge and future directions for research. *Family Science Review*, *22*(4), 141–164.

Lamb, M. E. (2007). The approximation rule: Another proposed reform that misses the target. *American Journal of Family Therapy*, *1*(2), 135–136.

Luke, N., & Banerjee, R. (2013). Differentiated associations between childhood maltreatment experiences and social understanding: A meta-analysis and systematic review. *Developmental Review*, *33*, 1–28.

McLanahan, S., Tach, L., & Schneider, D. (2013). The causal effects of father absence. *Annual Review of Sociology*, *39*, 399–427.

Norman, R. E., Byambaa, M., De, R., Butchart, A., Scott, J., & Vos, T. (2012). The long-term health consequences of child physical abuse, emotional abuse, and neglect: A systematic review and meta-analysis. *PLoS Medicine*, *9*.

Poustie, C., Matthewson, M., & Balmer, S. (2018). The forgotten parent: The targeted parent perspective of parental alienation. *Journal of Family Issues*, *70*, 91–99.

Templer, K., Matthewson, M., Haines, J., & Cox, G. (2016). Recommendations for best practice in response to parental alienation: Findings from a systematic review. *Journal of Family Therapy*, *39*(1), 103–122.

Vanderbilt University Medical Center (2017). *Parental Alienation Database.* Center for Knowledge Management. Retrieved from www.mc.vanderbilt.edu/pasg/.

Warshak, R. A. (2015). Parental alienation: Overview, management, intervention and practice tips. *Journal of the American Academy of Matrimonial Lawyers,* 28: 181–248.

19
SHARED PARENTING AND POLITICS
Background of equal opportunities in the German context

Jorge Guerra González

Introduction[1]

Shared parenting (SP) or joint physical custody (JPC)[2] after parental separation is not the standard for childcare after parent separation in Germany or worldwide. Nevertheless, both Germany and the world are progressing steadily in this direction. Many promising steps have been taken, though at a slower pace than might be expected. I will try to explore the reasons for this. Analysis will concentrate on the political field and on only one country, Germany, in order to better understand at least one context in the necessary depth. It should then be possible to decide if conditions and conclusions may be applicable to other contexts, circumstances or legal systems.

The political situation in Germany

Germany is presently ruled by the so-called 'Great Coalition' (CDU/CSU and SPD).

In order to situate its parties in the political space we can use a coordinate system (X-axis: left and right; Y-axis: progressive and conservative). Positions are by no means to be used axiologically: up-down, left-right hides no ethical or legal value. Their function is limited to describing an ontological function. *Progressive* will refer to parties that are for (sustainable) change, social equality or social justice, whereas *conservative* will refer to those parties that aim mainly at stability, social cohesion or traditional values. *Left* will refer to parties that favour protecting the workforce in the economic context whereas *right* will refer to those that favour the support of capital structures.

This scheme is simple and perhaps could be considered obsolete but its intention is simply to give an approximate impression of the present German political scene.

According to the scheme, the SPD could be classified as a rather progressive and moderate left-wing party, while the CDU (and the CSU) would be classified as a conservative and moderate right-wing party.

Other important political actors in Germany are:

- *Die Linke* (The Left): Left wing to far-left. We could assume that this party would score highest at progressivism on the list.
- *Die Grünen* (The Greens): Left and progressive with a focus on environmental issues.
- *FDP*: Liberal party; center-right, or clearly right according to the definition used; perhaps more conservative than progressive – or at a half-way point between them.
- *AfD*: Right wing to far right, the most conservative of the list. Newly created (2013), at present with representation in every parliament (at *Länder* or Federal level).

German political parties and shared parenting

In Germany, the context favouring SP has been influenced by three notable events:

1. The publication of *Shared Parenting: Psychology–Law–Practice: Alternate parental childcare after separation and divorce*, by Professor Hildegund Sünderhauf in 2013.[3]
2. The decision of the German Supreme Court (BGH) of 15 June 2016 that enabled German Courts to potentially implement SP even if a parent opposes. This possibility is subject to several strict conditions though (see below). Before this decision, every parent had a de facto veto right on SP.
3. The FDP Parliamentary Motion (13.03.18) in 2018 to consider SP as the legal standard in case of parental separation.

Assuming that SP facilitates children spending equal or very similar time with both parents after their separation, this modern approach would be considered progressive and would imply some advantages:

For children:

- It correlates with the healthiest psychological development for children after their parents' separation/divorce;[4]
- The equal parental positions would diminish parental conflict, which would offer children a healthier, more positive environment.

For parents:

- SP would result in a similar legal position (de facto), mainly if it is combined with JLC. Both parents would receive a similar chance to shape their children and be their models of conduct;
- Both parents can pursue their goals beyond the family – personal, political/working career – under the same, or very similar, conditions.

For society:

- The equal position of men and women after divorce/separation would result in a less profound differentiation of men and women beyond traditional gender roles;
- Similar opportunities and responsibilities for men and women at any level despite parenthood would result in a society that would be more equal and just (equivalent salaries, reduction or removal of any gender gap, comparable access conditions to any societal post, etc.).

With these thoughts in mind, logical thinking would suggest that progressive parties would advocate for SP, whereas conservative parties would be resistant to it. This first supposition is however incorrect. The political placement is exactly the opposite in Germany: the more progressive a party is, the more engaged their support of social justice and equality between man and woman, the less the party will support SP. The opposite is also partially true:

- FDP was the primary advocate for the motion above for SP as a general rule;
- AfD pled for equal consideration between the so-called residence model and SP.[5]
- Die Linke are against SP as a general rule.[6] They proposed a new motion (13.03.2018).
- Die Grünen have a similar position to Die Linke. No legal model should be preferred.[7]
- SPD showed openness for SP in a position paper of 2017 – it pled for the establishment of a legal basis for SP in Germany. After the motion of the FDP, they moved somewhat to the positions of Die Linke, and similar to those of the BGH Court Decision 2017; that is, SP would be fine, but subject to the BGH conditions and should not be applied as a general rule.[8]
- CDU's position would be at least recognisable according to its political frame. It is similar to that of SPD (that is, no rule on SP as it could lead to more parental conflicts that would harm the children).[9]

Summary and comments

1. The most (far) left-oriented parties among those considered (Die Linke and Die Grünen) are the most progressive ones concerning social justice, and show the highest opposition to SP. They advocate that the current legal framework should be left as it is. Parents should choose the post-separation system that best suits their family. Children and their best interest must be paramount. In this regard: the financial protection of the parents should be guaranteed; good parental communication or a low level of parental conflict should be present; the family childcare scheme before separation, as well as secure attachments, should be relevant, as well as the absence of domestic violence and physical proximity of both parents' homes.

2. This situation is analogous to another one in Germany some ten years ago:[10]
    - Until 1998 mothers who were not married to the father of the children had sole custody granted to them.
    - After 1998 mothers could decide if they wanted to share child custody with the fathers or not. No foundation for their decision was necessary, no consequences were derived from their choice (§ 1626a BGB – *old version*).
    - A father successfully took legal action against Germany for discrimination before the European Court of Human Rights (ECHR) 03.12.2009, 22028/04: *Zaunegger v. Germany*. The ECHR saw no reason for discrimination between a father married to the mother, a father not married to the mother, or between fathers and mothers.
    - The German Constitutional Court (BVerfGE 21.07.2010–1 BvR 420/09) confirmed the discrimination but made no large changes towards equality between those fathers and between mothers and fathers, it did not exclude it though. It left the parliament to formulate the necessary legal change.
    - The parliamentary debate was a discussion with apparently 'changed' colours: traditional parties arguing for parental equality in family issues, progressive parties defending the unequal status quo.
    - As a result, the legal advance was very minimal: a mother not married to the father maintained the sole custody of the children (§ 1626a III BGB). However, if those mothers now deny the JLC to the applicant fathers, they have to justify their position in the best interest of the child (§ 1626a II BGB).
3. Examining the German law it is true that no major legal change would really be necessary *to facilitate support of SP*. If you assume that parents have a natural right and duty to their children (Art. 6 II GG); that the constitution makes no difference between fathers and mothers in this regard (Art. 3 GG); that children have a fundamental right to their upbringing by their parents;[11] that duties, responsibilities and contact allow no distinction between mothers and fathers (§§ 1626, 1684 BGB), SP seems to be the logical result of German law – at least de iure.

    The only exception to an equal treatment would be that of § 1626a BGB – an exception that was not sustained by the ECHR.
4. Consequently, we have a society in pursuit of equality and equal opportunities aiming at a detachment from tradition concerning key areas such as politics, labour and economics. However, in the area of the family, society not only accepts traditional family roles but firmly rejects these traditional roles being questioned or modified – primarily by those parties that fuelled the change above.
5. Other associations or interest groups that could have something to say about SP are not included in this document since their perspectives are consistent with those already mentioned – they reflect the same apparent contradiction explained: the more progressive, the less support for SP or vice versa.

Clarifying the contradiction

Assumptions

In order to understand people's actions we may assume:

(a) *People act exclusively as a consequence of emotions*

People act for security (to assure what they have) or for freedom (as a result of feeling secure by having their own needs satisfied or at least under control). If you prefer, they (we) act for fear (to avoid something) or for love (to be able to give something because of the feeling of freedom). They are all emotions. Hence there are no 'rational' actions or decisions. If you want to know what is behind somebody's actions, just look to his or her emotions.

The only rationality is to be sought when we weigh the emotions behind different action options ... and opt for the emotion behind the action that matters more to us.

(b) *People want to do good*

It is not just that we all as a child wanted to be Cinderella (and not the stepmother), or Robin Hood (and not Captain Hook) in the sense that our heroes and heroines (Vicky the Vikinger, Asterix, Pippi Longstocking, etc.) were good people that we would like to be.

Indeed, we need to think that we are good, logical or reasonable for our psychological balance and self-esteem and that we act correspondingly. If not (e.g. cognitive dissonance: to smoke even if we know it is unhealthy) we will have to spend energy in solving the discrepancy so as to keep thinking of ourselves as good, logical or reasonable.

So, there would be no evil but fear ('good' people do wrong things owing to ignorance, weakness, cowardice, etc.), or mental disorder (they can't help doing wrong things – e.g. perception disorders, psychological pathology).

(c) *People act logically*

This is perhaps implied with the assumptions above, but it could be mentioned specifically. Acting (that is, to perform or to omit anything consciously) is always logical and consistent towards the emotion or emotions that lie behind it. So, according to their own circumstances everyone acts logically, even if we do not understand their logic at first.

This means: if there is an apparent contradiction between progressive parties and the rejection of progressive issues such as SP or between its acceptance by conservative parties, it is just a question of accurate analysis to resolve it. There will be emotions supporting these changes, and for the corresponding subjects this attitude will be correct and justifiable.

Left-sided political parties and their traditional positions

It is not possible here to give an in-depth analysis of why, in the context of family issues, political parties tend to behave contrary to expectation – or to have lost their political compass.

For this reason, only the attitude of the left-sided political parties towards the progressive SP will be analysed. The sense of its manifest and simple rejection (at least de facto) compared to the pursuit of their progressive goals is a priori the most difficult to understand.

Conservative parties show more discrepancies between them regarding SP; perhaps they act for political opportunity, to occupy the abandoned political field of the progressive parties. Center or right-leaning parties in Germany have assimilated and are open to other family approaches than the husband earning money and the economically-dependent wife who raises the children and takes care of the household. Support for such images, if at all existent, is irrelevant in the German political landscape. Moreover, the working/social/political development of everyone – or the avoidance of potential economic power losses when productive resources are not optimised (e.g. women as housewives) – has been assumed nowadays by all political agendas.

Die Linke

Some of their ideas that are relevant directly or indirectly to SP will be mentioned. Only updated official positions to the respective issues will be referred to, or of persons acting as speakers.

- Die Linke's view on the equal position of men and women could be seen as the cutting edge of politics at present and indicates that it is still possible and necessary to go further. The next goals include: higher valuing of social work, no tax treatment differences between spouses, equal conditions of men and women in occupational and care work, etc.[12]
- Die Linke is in favour of the introduction of obligatory women participation quota in social and political decision panels.[13]

Die Grünen

Their positions are quite similar to those of Die Linke:

- Equal treatment of men and women in comparable terms to those of Die Linke, but seemingly also considering men in their proposals.[14]
- A practical equality between men and women has been the reality in the Green party for a very long time: in 1986 they introduced a 50% quota for women in all the party committees, panels or boards, and they still work towards this goal[15] (s. Fn 13).

Time for answers

With summary descriptions of Die Linke and Die Grünen in mind, it seems illogical that they do not support actively – rather reject de facto – SP, even if the goals of each party and the results of SP are perfectly compatible and the fact that no parental childcare model is closer to those goals.

It is assumed above that there is no acting without its own emotional logic. So it is time to look for the latent logic behind the enigma. Three explanations are proposed:

Progressive parties require additional support

The simplest explanation is that the contradiction between the progressive goals (equal opportunity, pay, and allocation of managerial positions, etc.) and rejection of SP as a rule is due to lack of information. Progressive parties were just not sufficiently aware that SP would help in reaching their goals and solving related problems, and hence perhaps making other corrective proposals redundant or unnecessary. Since SP would mean that more mothers were able to follow their personal ambitions at any level: social, political, economic – under exactly the same conditions as fathers – fathers and mothers would share the upbringing of their children with the same duties and responsibilities.

Conversely, not supporting SP implies that more men will be freer to follow their professional careers (maybe against their wish at court), earning more and occupying higher professional positions, and more women (maybe conforming to their wish at court) will be dependent on those fathers' child support and alimony and earn less – they would have less time and energy for their career, have lower job positions and receive a poorer pension later.

So, logically, it is just a matter of time until these parties notice this incongruence and start to support SP. In this case it is necessary to make a supplementary effort to bring the message also to those places where they are most needed. Indeed, we all want social justice. It is simply fair to grant everyone the same development opportunities. As correctly stated:

> We want that girls and women equally as boys and men live as they want. They should develop their potential and overcome their boundaries. ... Women and men should live as equals and as partners.[16]

Progressive parties act conservative I: They defend their own inertia and/or try to prevent future possible drawbacks

In this case, progressive parties would be aware of the advantages that SP would offer in order to obtain their social objectives, but their inertia is unilateral. They are used to supporting women in their fight for equality: either to equalize the power position of men where they are disadvantaged or to maintain the power position in the few areas where they have been traditionally privileged (e.g. family issues).

It is possible to arrive at this conclusion by following the arguments against SP from Die Linke or Die Grünen, mainly their claim is that the legal situation (that is, how law is being interpreted) should not change. Because if it does not change we obtain the following picture:

- There are no official statistics about JPC at German family courts, so it is not possible to say how many SPs have been decided to date. However, there cannot be many, despite the Supreme Court Decision, because preconditions exist including that good communication between the parents must exist and this could be complicated in the German Court Procedures, which primarily have an adversarial orientation. In addition: Parents who do communicate properly and have their children and their wellbeing in focus would rather not let courts decide for them.

  Die Linke and Die Grünen additionally claim that they look at the parental child caring model before separation and the binding of the children as a basis to see if SP is appropriate. However, in reality, this basis would be mainly traditional and as such unbalanced. In principle, there will be parental cooperation, but mothers would carry the main part of childcare – as part of a normal, voluntary common decision. The reasons could be diverse: from biological (especially by very young children: breastfeeding and maybe hormonal–oxytocin), to customary, or economic (typically, prior to divorce, the father was the primary source of income in the family).

- So if SP has to be ruled out for the reasons above, German Family Courts will have to decide on the physical parental model after separation.

  The only option offered, provided that there is no proven domestic violence, that both parents want to be part of their children's lives and live relatively close to each other in the aftermath, would be the so-called 'residence model': One parent would offer the 'primary place of residence' (*lebensmittelpunkt*) and be primarily responsible for the rearing of the children; the other parent would be responsible for the financial support (child support). In those cases (without official statistics), it is estimated that in between 80–90% of cases the mother would play the first role, and the father the second role. The only statistics currently available partially confirm this approach.[17]

- So, if things are left in their current state, thousands of '*alleinerziehende*' (single parents) will be produced, mothers (mostly) and fathers, as such is the legal approach on single parenting.[18] This does not mean a father or a mother who was abandoned with the common children by the other parent; *alleinerziehend* is any adult person that raises the children *without any other adult in the home*. This approach is not reliant upon questions of custody (§§ 1626 ff BGB). It depends upon the traditional legal system that one parent raises the children and the other provides financial support for them.

  So – on condition that the mother or the father that offers the *lebensmittelpunkt* is not married again and lives at home with the new spouse – every family court decision on Legal Custody engenders *alleinerziehende* (irrespective of whether the financing parent additionally takes care of the children for 5% or 45% of the time). One parent has to be the rearing parent entitled to child support and officially a single parent, the other has to be the visiting and financing parent. The only exception – in principle, see below – would be: *Wechselmodell* (SP).

  It is interesting to note that child support in Germany is calculated according to the same premise. Only with a *Wechselmodell*, and provided that the child raising parent does not earn much more than the other,[19] the visiting parent has to pay child support. Normally, this is irrespective of the amount of time or costs – which with a division of caring time between 40–60% should be similar to those of the child raising parent - who would receive child support from the financing one nevertheless. This financial aspect may make the 'visiting' more difficult for that parent, so that the residence model could tend to generate single parents *stricto sensu*.

This is often the case: '*Alleinerziehende*' need financial support/protection (they have a poverty risk four times higher than other partner-families with children).[20] So, it is the goal of progressive parties to increase their protection and to facilitate the compatibility of family and work.

- If everything remains like this there will be mothers who, due to the continuation of the unbalanced model before separation, have an even more complicated access to, for example, the labour market than they would have had with SP once the children grow up. At the same time, fathers will continue the inequality model and earn more, reaching, for example, even higher professional seniority.

According to this inertia hypothesis, the approach of Die Linke and Die Grünen, not to pursue gender equality in every social field, would guarantee only mothers a freedom of choice (e.g. if they want SP, they should have it, if not, they will have the main responsibility on the children to decide upon them). There are some insights that support this approach:

- It would be relevant to their attitude on abortion: Die Grünen maintain that the decision on giving birth to the child or not only concerns pregnant women and that any obstacles to its practical implementation should be removed.[21] Die Linke considers that the foetus is part of the body of the mother, so she should freely make this decision. Abortion should therefore be free in Germany and a right of every pregnant woman, i.e., not a crime.[22]

  However, that approach would be dissonant with the rejection of SP by both parties for reasons related to the well-being of the child. It would be a genuine challenge to explain that the birth of the child would mark the line between a 'body part' without rights and 'child entitled to the protection of his/her best-interests'.
- Gender equality movements have not traditionally pursued equality in all fields (e.g. family) or areas. For example, duties such as military or alternative service in Germany remained obligatory only for men; women were allowed to voluntarily serve the community or join the army at any time if they chose to do so.

The attitude of these parties could be understandable if their goal was to accumulate power as a kind of bargaining chip or strategy to prevent possible future drawbacks that could damage achievements made thus far. However, the problem could be that expanding power over certain limits of justice could precisely cause the drawbacks (see below).

Progressive parties act conservative II: They defend the consolidated structure

To understand this hypothesis the arguments could be followed further: If the foundation is not equal (SP), the superstructure cannot be even. If an institution, for instance, pursues contradictory goals synchronically and with the same effort, the likely result would be that it would not obtain any of the goals—which will make its existence necessary until this contradiction is solved.

This premise would also conform to Max Weber's bureaucratic theory of management.[23] According to this theory, bureaucracies that were once established to attain certain beneficial objectives and make organisational work more efficient tend in time to be inefficient, and to expand progressively in size and power. Some aspects could support this assumption:

- In order to pursue and consolidate equal positions for men and women it was crucial to build a protective structure. Imagine Germany at the time of the introduction of Art. 3 in its Grundgesetz (GG – Constitution, Fundamental Act) in 1949: Unmarried mothers could lose their children before the State, women were not allow to work or to buy homes, for example, without male permission (initially permission from their fathers, subsequently from their husbands), etc. This situation is inconceivable nowadays – thanks to the accomplishments of the revised structure, which had to grow steadily for those reasons.

  Because of its success the equality problem in society is very different now but the structure remains.

  Now it is (very) powerful and influential – probably more than ever: its concerns can no longer be ignored in the whole political spectrum.
- This structure would have had enough power or logistical possibilities to change family law and make it more equal, as it did with the achievements in equality at any other political level. However it did not. To my knowledge there have never been demonstrations for equal treatment in front of Family Courts (undoubtedly the most traditional institution in Germany), nor have corresponding political claims been made. Indeed, Family Courts are the ones that produce the most unbalanced results in Germany. In case of conflict at court the children – as we saw – will be mainly granted to the mother; the father will have to provide their financial support. As the divorce rate in Germany is 40–50%,[24] what Family Courts decide will affect essentially the lives of thousands (in total millions) of fathers, mothers and children.
- To my knowledge, no custody quota designed to free women from family and children for their self-development was ever seriously demanded. It is possible to compare this attitude with the parallel in other political areas. In this sense it would have to be noted that SP would be the result of a quota introduction in family issues.
- Under these premises, if the present legal system is left as it is, the basement and hence superstructure will be oblique and as long as the superstructure is askew, the existence of that structure is at least partially justified.

SP could contribute to solving some essential problems in our societies. It is possible to imagine men and women having equal opportunity to pursue professional advancement as well as raising their children. It could mean more equality in salaries, opportunities and responsibilities. This is exactly the structure that most people want and have fought for in their societies.

However, SP could also be perceived as a threat to undermine the foundation of this structure. If the foundations of the structure were even, the structure itself would be more stable and thus might require less effort to produce equitable solutions.

Conclusions

There is a deep inconsistency between progressive approaches and attitudes towards SP. This is surprising as SP would be a streamlined approach to achieving equality more easily for society and all its members, in which parental separation has become common and affects hundreds of thousands of couples and children. No other model guarantees children the opportunity to maximize the benefit from both parents after parent separation, for both parents to enjoy equally parenthood and leave an imprint on their offspring while pursuing other personal and professional goals (working, political, social, creative career, etc.).

This ideal approach does not require it be mandated without exception. An appropriate distance between the parent's homes, a specified age of the children, the agreement of both parents to take this responsibility and the absence of any confirmed domestic violence should certainly be required conditions for the implementation of SP. Certainly, any difficulties or disadvantages for parents and especially children associated with SP should be prevented or removed. SP should become the rule rather than the exception if we accept the premises of the society in which we are living.

However, this is not the case. SP is officially not the preferred approach and unofficially is not supported by precisely those that defined society as it is now – the progressive parties. Their attitude, 'It's better if we do nothing and leave everything as it is' does not make sense according to their own logic. Contrast this with their attitude towards attaining equality in other societal areas through positive discrimination (quota). Here, conversely, they have mobilised powerful resources to change things, precisely because the previous situation/model was not fair. If SP were their preference, it could certainly pave the way to equal opportunities for men and women at all levels.

Paradoxically, SP finds its allies in the traditional parties, those that in theory support families to conform to more conventional structures.

Presuming at worst political calculation under the paradoxical position of traditional parties (to reach certain voters that the progressive parties have abandoned), it is necessary to find the rationale of those with a liberal outlook. This chapter offers three possible explanations for this logical shift; whether these are plausible or not is arguable.

If any of these explanations are correct, then it would be time to reflect. Collaboratively.

Concerning SP:

- Society is not based upon factions of men against women, both supported by respective pressure groups. This would not only be useless – we are part of the same story: born of a mother and a father in families with men and women – it would create unnecessary tensions. Moreover it is impracticable because there is no clear 'front line': supporting mothers but diminishing daughters, sisters, grandmothers, aunts, etc.
- As discussed previously, SP is rejected also because of financial reasons but no other model would produce more equal foundations and opportunities for both parents.

    Besides, if SP is the model that could equal different earning starting positions, current jurisprudence (s. fn 17) would ensure fair and corresponding child support for the most disadvantaged parent – despite equal childcare – if applicable.
- That children need and have access to both parents is standard knowledge in developmental psychology. This knowledge has been specifically confirmed by science, especially in countries that have introduced SP as the rule after parent separation. According to this knowledge, SP is the best care model for those children as their psychological health is comparable to those of intact families (s. Fn 3).

As advocated in mediation, it is better to solve common problems collaboratively, rather than based on rivalry, accusations, blaming or domination. It is not possible to constitute a partnership any other way. Discussion, patience and confidence are key to harmonious cohabitation.

Whether we like it or not, we belong together. The sooner we understand this and pull together, the better. If necessary, we should fight together against any kind of injustice. This struggle should also not tolerate any attack on the position achieved with an immense effort by women (and some men) over decades, or centuries.

To pursue justice unilaterally is lobbying and not justice. The pursuit of justice must include and concern everyone, and not on the basis of categorisation.

Otherwise, this will promote the formation of an opposing lobby – as is currently the case, supporting the other side of politics and beginning to establish itself quickly.

It was certainly not the case that social justice reached every person in the past – and whenever somebody takes too much liberty it is always at the cost of other society members. It was once like this with slaves, foreigners, children and, of course, women paying the price. Now is not time for retaliation, but to do things better.

Society reaps what it sows. The arguments are not about men versus women or vice versa, nor are they about diminishing women's achievements or reducing their protections. They are about implementing justice for everyone, protecting our children and giving them the best possible and equal prospects.

If you let fear drive your actions in an effort to prevent progress or to hold on to power, you may be facilitating what you are trying to avoid. Integrate justice in your objectives, without distinction, and negative results will be avoided.

It is time to think differently: not only with the mind, but also with the heart. If we could just listen to each other with our hearts and minds, two miracles will occur: we will still perceive differences, but they will no longer have any importance for us. *And* we will also be able to recognise ourselves in others, so conflict will vanish or at least lose its destructive potential, thus potentially removing glass ceilings. So – three miracles – we will be able to break the spell and make ourselves and others free.

We can do it. We should do it. Let us do it.

Notes

1 The author thanks Susan Lynn Gelber for her competent and reliable English review, and Judge Marie-France Carlier for her constructive and insightful feedback.
2 Joint legal custody (JLC) refers to the person or persons who are allowed to have rights over and responsibilities for children. In this regard, they are allowed to take decisions on their behalf.
  Joint physical custody (SP) relates to persons who may have access to children on a regular basis.
3 Hildegund Sünderhauf (2013). *Shared parenting: Psychology–law–practice: Alternate parental childcare after separation and divorce.* Berlin: Springer.
4 See, for example, Bastaits and Pasteels (2019), Braver et al. (2018), Nielsen (2018), Steinbach (2018), Fransson, et al. (2016), Baude et al. (2016), Bergström, et al. (2013, 2014, 2015) and Bauserman (2002).
5 https://afdkompakt.de/2019/02/14/mehr-flexibilitaet-beim-umgangsrecht-hilft-kindern-getrennt-lebender-eltern/.
6 www.linksfraktion.de/themen/a-z/detailansicht/wechselmodell/.
7 www.gruene-bundestag.de/themen/familie/wechselmodell-ermoeglichen-aber-nicht-privilegieren.
8 www.spdfraktion.de/themen/wechselmodell-je-haelfte-mama-papa-wohnen; FamFR 18.3.2018: 'Bundestag diskutierte Wechselmodell'.
9 www.cducsu.de/presse/pressemitteilungen/wechselmodell-nicht-gesetzlich-verordnen-sondern-im-alltag-staerken.
10 Guerra (2012).
11 BVerfGE 03.02.2017; Arts 1 and 2 GG.
12 www.linksfraktion.de/presse/pressemitteilungen/detail/gleichstellungsstrategie-der-bundesregierung-setzt-zu-wenig-konkrete-massstaebe/.
13 www.die-linke.de/start/presse/detail/frauenquote-in-aufsichtsraeten/.
14 www.gruene-bundestag.de/themen/frauen.
15 www.bpb.de/geschichte/deutsche-geschichte/frauenwahlrecht/279359/die-frauenquote-bei-den-gruenen.
16 https://www.gruene-bundestag.de/themen/frauen.
17 Statistisches Bundesamt, 2020. For 2019, when Family Courts transferred legal custody to a single parent: to the mother 885, to the father 96. If the parents were not married to each other: 4404 and 1862, respectively.
18 § 21 III SGB II.
19 BGH FamRZ 1998, 286; FamRZ 1991, 182; FamRZ 1984, 39. No child support will be due if the parent raising the children earns three times more than the visiting parent (BGH FamRZ 2013, 1558; FamRZ 1984, 39).

20 www.gruene-bundestag.de/themen/familie/bessere-bedingungen-fuer-alleinerziehende-schaffen.
21 https://gruene.berlin/b%C3%BCndnis-90die-gr%C3%BCnen/schwangerschaftsabbruch-nur-frauen-selbst-k%C3%B6nnen-die-entscheidung-treffen; comp. https://www.n-tv.de/politik/Jobs-fuer-Arzte-nur-bei-Ja-zu-Abtreibung-article21905937.html.
22 www.linksfraktion.de/themen/a-z/detailansicht/schwangerschaftsabbruch/.
23 Weber (1947); Mommsen (2004).
24 They affect 150000–200.000 couples every year and 120.000–170.000 children every year (www.destatis.de/DE/ Themen/Gesellschaft-Umwelt/Bevoelkerung/Eheschliessungen-Ehescheidungen-Lebenspartnerschaften/Tabellen/ehescheidungen-kinder.html). Only married couples and their children are counted in official statistics.

References

Bastaits, K. and Pasteels, I. (2019) Is joint physical custody in the best interests of the child? Parent–child relationships and custodial arrangements. *Journal of Social and Personal Relationships*. DOI: 10.1177/0265407519838071.

Baude, A. et al. (2016) Child adjustment in joint physical custody versus sole custody: A meta-analytic review. *Journal of Divorce & Remarriage* 57(5), 338–360.

Bauserman, R. (2002) Child adjustment in joint-custody versus sole-custody arrangements: A meta-analytic review. *Journal of Family Psychology* 16(1), 91–102.

Bergström, M. et al. (2013) Living in two homes: A Swedish national survey of wellbeing in 12 and 15 year olds with joint physical custody. *BMC Public Health* 13, 868.

Bergström, M. et al. (2014) Mental health in Swedish children living in joint physical custody and their parents' life satisfaction: A cross-sectional study, *Scandinavian Journal of Psychology* 55(5), 433–439.

Bergström, M. et al. (2015) Fifty moves a year: Is there an association between joint physical custody and psychosomatic problems in children? *Journal of Epidemiology and Community Health* 69(8), 769–774.

Braver, S. et al. (2018) Shared parenting after parental separation: The views of 12 experts. *Journal of Divorce & Remarriage* 59(5), 372–287.

Fransson, E. et al. (2016) Psychological complaints among children in joint physical custody and other family types: Considering parental factors. *Scandinavian Journal of Public Health* 44(2), 177–183.

Guerra, J. (2012) Sorgefall Familienrecht, LIT, Münster, 21 ff.

Mommsen, W.J. (2004) *Max Weber und die deutsche Politik 1890–1920*. 3. Aufl., Tübingen, S. 180 ff.

Nielsen, L. (2018) Preface to the Special Issue. Shared physical custody: Recent research, advances, and applications. *Journal of Divorce & Remarriage* 59(4), 237–246.

Steinbach, A. (2018) Children's and parents' well-being in joint physical custody: A literature review. *Family Process* 10(10), 1–20.

Weber, M. (1947) *Wirtschaft und Gesellschaft*, 3. Aufl. 1947, 5. Aufl., Tübingen 1972.

20
CHILD SEXUAL ABUSE, PARENTAL ALIENATION SYNDROME AND CUSTODY

Margarita Ortiz-Tallo and Marta Ferragut

Introduction

When there are children, separations and divorces often pose significant problems in families. All professionals agree that the main objective is the well-being of the children. However, this task is not always easy to perform.

As psychology professionals currently focused on the prevention of sexual abuse in childhood, we have encountered enormously impactful cases that have included combinations of such sensitive and controversial elements as: sexual abuse by the father, parental alienation syndrome caused by the mother, and children with diverse and complex symptomatology providing clear evidence of their tremendous suffering.

Of these three elements, the two perpetrated by adults (sexual abuse and parental alienation) can both be the subject of controversy and classified as 'presumed', depending on the complexity of the case. However, in the third, which affects the most vulnerable members of the family, the children, the victims, the evidence is usually indisputable, and there can be a variety of symptoms. In this chapter we focus on and analyse one symptom in particular, the refusal to visit or be with one of the parents (usually the father), when there is an accusation of abuse from the other parent, which can indicate either sexual abuse by the rejected parent or manipulation or interference by the other parent. Of course, what is important in custody cases is the expert opinion of a forensic psychologist as to evidence of sexual abuse, manipulation or interference.

We have focused on custody in relation to traditional families, father–mother–child, since we have neither found research on nor custody references to same-sex couple cases. We assume that in the future there will be increasing amounts of published research and custody references in various countries relating to such cases.

In this chapter we present some key ideas related to child sexual abuse and parental alienation syndrome, and their bearing on custody in separation or divorce proceedings. Testimony from adult women who have consented to sharing relevant parts of their experiences is included, and finally some conclusions are presented.

Child sexual abuse (CSA)

The World Health Organization (WHO) defines child sexual abuse (CSA) as 'the involvement of a child in sexual activity that he or she does not fully comprehend and is unable to give informed consent to, or for which the child is not developmentally prepared, or else that violates the laws or social taboos of society'.[1,2] This sexual activity is aimed at meeting the needs of the abuser, CSA being one of the most serious types of mistreatment of children.[3,4]

CSA includes different types of adult behaviour that may involve forms of contactless sexual abuse, such as harassment, threats or forced exposure to pornography, and also behaviours involving physical contact, including complete sexual acts or abusive sexual touching.[5] As several authors emphasise, child sexual abuse frequently leaves no physical evidence or the evidence is fleeting.[6,7,8]

Prevalence data suggests that CSA is a problem that affects all social and educational strata and is usually perpetrated by someone close to the child whom they trust and love. UNICEF[9] estimates that about 85 per cent of cases occur in the family context. It is a very difficult problem to bring to light because of the sense of shame felt by the victims and because some victims do not recognise these experiences as CSA until adulthood. Only 30 per cent of victims disclose the abuse while young.[10,11]

Due to this complex and hidden problem, misinformation and even myths remain in circulation. Specifically, there is a belief in legal circles that children can invent the story of abuse.[12,13,14] However, scientific data demonstrates that false allegations of CSA are found in only 2 per cent of the complaints heard in court.[15,16]

Parental alienation syndrome (PAS)

Richard A. Gardner is the author who first defined parental alienation syndrome (PAS), in 1985. The most recent definition states that:

> Its primary manifestation is the child campaign of denigration against a parent, a campaign that has no justification against a good, loving parent. It results in a combination of a programming (brainwashing) parent's indoctrination and the child's own contribution to the vilification of the target parent.

Gardner considers PAS to be

> a subtype of Parental Alienation (PA), which is the general term covering any situation in which a child can be alienated from a parent (physical abuse, verbal abuse, emotional abuse, mental abuse, abandonment and neglect). PAS is the subtype that is caused by a parent systematically programming the child against the other parent.[17]

This concept has generated much controversy from the beginning, as the syndrome is only diagnosed in cases of contested divorces and separations and used in disputes concerning custody of the children. The debate continues among researchers and professionals regarding utilising the concept of PAS. Some authors argue that the concept is useful for identifying why children express hostility toward or fear of one parent, usually the father.[18] Another important part of the scientific community considers that the application of PAS in court is clearly based on gender discrimination, because it is usually the mother who is found to be causing the alienation, thus discriminating against women. PAS has even been called the Malicious Mother Syndrome. In line with this research there is evidence that the syndrome causes a potential gender bias against women in family courts.[19] For this reason, it has been considered essential to include the gender perspective in this analysis.

It could be that the best interests being considered when PAS is diagnosed are those of the parents and not those of the minor, whose best interests should be paramount. In this sense, PAS could also be used by a parent to obtain child custody.[20]

PAS precludes the child being heard in court and assumes that they cannot freely manifest what they really feel or think. Therefore, the child's opinion is not considered credible. In this sense, Gardner argues, considered objectively, the child contributes subjectively to the vilification of the father.[21] However, children can be as accurate as adults when asked to relate something. There can be reasonable alternative explanations for the behaviour of the child and parent that have nothing to do with parental alienation when the child has a preference for one of the parents (usually the mother). Some examples are the child feeling closer to one parent, being reluctant to leave the parent they think needs their emotional support or feeling more comfortable with the relationship style of one of the parents.[22]

Some authors emphasise that PAS has not been recognised by the American Psychiatric Association (APA) in any editions of the *Diagnostic and Statistical Manual of Mental Disorders (DSM)*, and the World Health Organization has not included it in the *International Classification of Diseases (ICD)*. So, in many areas and for many professionals, the use of PAS is a biased interpretation of reality based on stereotypes and prejudices rather than on the best interests of the child.

Internationally, differences exist between countries in relation to the use of PAS in custody proceedings – some examples follow. Some countries such as Brazil recognise PAS as a factor in custody decisions and transfer custody to the non-alienating parent. Many states in the United States have not formally recognised the syndrome in relation to custody, although parental hostility can be a factor taken into account in judicial decisions.[23] In Mexico, rather than PAS, the focus is on alienating behaviours in parents, which need to be evaluated to verify whether and to what extent the psycho-emotional development of the minors involved in these disputes is affected. A psychological evaluation of the whole family is necessary in order to identify the role being played by each member; that is, one will be the alienating parent, another the alienated parent and the minor is the intermediary.[24] In France, in 2018, the Ministry of Families prohibited the use of PAS.[25] In Spain, the General Council of the Judiciary discouraged use of the syndrome,[26] while many specialists, similar to those in Mexico, argue that some parents do demonstrate alienating behaviours and it is thus essential to evaluate the entire family system and its dynamic. In the UK, the Children and Family Court Advisory and Support Service (Cafcass) recognises parental alienation to be the case when

> a child's resistance or hostility towards one parent is not justified and is the result of psychological manipulation by the other parent. It is one of a number of reasons why a child may reject or resist spending time with one parent post-separation. All potential risk factors, such as domestic abuse, must be adequately and safely considered, reduced or resolved before assessing the other case factors or reasons.[27]

PAS needs to be reviewed thoroughly to guide judges and courts in resolving the cases in which it has been used. Complaints of parental alienation arise during the proceedings in which custody of children is discussed, so making such a controversial diagnosis requires the utmost caution, since only in this way will the best interests of the child be met.

Custody

The Leadership Council on Child Abuse and Interpersonal Violence (2008),[28] using empirical data, estimates that 58,000 children a year are placed in the custody of an adult who abuses them. The Save the Children Report on Child Sexual Abuse,[29] described the underprotection of minors and revealed the reality of many mothers who were denied custody as a result of reporting sexual abuse of minors by the father; custody was then granted to the father accused of the abuse.

Sillberg and Dallam[30] present research from 27 custody cases in the United States. In all cases, the mother and children alleged sexual abuse by the father. The average length of time these children spent in the court ordered custody of their fathers was 3.2 years. In all cases, sole custody or shared custody between the parents was granted. The results reveal that the courts initially suspected that the mothers had alienated the fathers. Subsequently, mental health professionals with expertise in child abuse were able to demonstrate that the sexual abuse had taken place and continued in 88 per cent of cases.

According to Martín González,[31] for an abusive parent, the best defence could be an allegation of PAS. Then, any action taken by the other parent (usually the mother) will be considered in relation to the syndrome and, consequently, the parent (usually the mother) may lose custody of the child, which is then granted to the allegedly abusive parent (usually the father).

Other authors consider that, when evaluating minors who report having been sexually abused by the father, it is necessary to be very cautious. In certain cases, they think the mother may have caused parental alienation. An article by Lowestein[32] discusses the CSA assessment process and the types of evidence that point to true versus false allegations, especially when serious hostility exists between the parents. He considers that it is important to prevent and detect CSA but, equally, that the levelling of false sexual allegations must not be allowed. In Mexico, where custody is usually granted exclusively to women, López Orozco[33] notes that, in her experience, the levels of violence witnessed in alienation cases arise from threats and false accusations. Many cases even result in criminal allegations of sexual assault against non-custodial parents to destroy their children's relationship with them. Minor non-existent medical conditions may also be invented that involve daily visits to health facilities, ingestion of medicines and treatment that can affect the child's health and even cause death.

In clinical experience, when there is an accusation of abuse, in most cases the accusing parent honestly believes that their child is experiencing sexual abuse; however, there is no clear evidence that can prove or disprove the allegation. These are very complex and distressing cases for the parents, children and professionals involved.[34] A mother convinced that her child has been abused by their father or someone from the father's family is under considerable stress, which can lead to instability and psychological distress that will result in her not wanting her child to visit the father. In addition, the mother often faces the child's disclosure, divorce and a complex judicial process simultaneously.[35]

When custody must be awarded and an allegation of sexual abuse has been made, obtaining an expert evaluation is vital, as is listening appropriately to the child's version of events because, for some researchers, a child's credibility increases in cases of sexual abuse.[36]

Testimonies

The following extracts are taken from the case histories of psychotherapy patients and reproduced with their permission. Most of them are women who, convinced that their child had been abused by their father, reported the abuse. The last one is an adult woman who was abused by her father as a child. We present testimonies from mothers because, in our experience as clinical psychologists, it is habitually the mothers who seek psychological help.

Mother

> I have two children, a boy who is nearly 10 and a girl of 7, who have both been sexually abused by their own father because neither I nor the professionals (who my children have been able to talk to openly) questioned his version of events or took into account the physical and emotional consequences they were suffering and still suffer. In the eyes of the law, however, the sexual abuse will only ever be an allegation.

Mother

> My children were 4 and 6 years old when they told me in their own words the gross things their own father was doing to them. They told me their biggest secret which I feel I should have known because their behaviour was screaming it out at me. You have to put yourself in my shoes to understand

what I'm talking about. It never enters your head that something like this can happen in your own house and that your own husband can do such monstrous things, and this tortures me to this day; it wounds my soul, and the shame haunts us even though we know that we are not the ones who should feel ashamed.

Mother

My children are suffering as a result of wanting to force the union of ties that are completely broken, and we should not forget that children have feelings and can express themselves, but the reality in my experience is that their words and behaviour have no legal value. Put yourself in their shoes for a moment. How would you feel if you were forced to be in a room with the person who had sexually abused you? And what if it was your mother who took you there, even if you begged her not to?

Mother

I feel trapped and ignored at an institutional level. I would never have reported what was going on in my house if I'd known what would happen next. He would certainly have found another victim and left us as he did his previous partner, leaving behind a son he never took responsibility for. Legally, the accused has the presumption of innocence until proved guilty and the accuser is in the spotlight, being judged or prejudged. Nobody can imagine the terrible pain, the crushing impotency of not being able to do more than I'm doing, and the deep pain and anger I feel at not being able to give my children back their innocence and their childhood.

Mother

I lost custody of my two children after reporting sexual abuse by their father: my 4 year old son has gone to live with his father; my 7 year old daughter, who had a very bad relationship with him, supposedly because she has Parental Alienation Syndrome caused by me, was sent to a Juvenile Centre to live, and I am not allowed to visit her until she recovers from the syndrome they say I caused. No one can imagine the rage, pain and helplessness I feel.

A patient talks about living with her father as a child

He was an evil spirit disguised as a golden boy, a Harry Potter dementor. Charming, witty, handsome, intelligent, cruel, manipulative, cunning, evil and perverted. He robbed me of my childhood and innocence, my peace of mind and my security. In return he left me an infinite sadness, a feeling of deep despair, and truly awful flashbacks which continued to haunt me as an adult. It is my firm belief that if I and my brothers and sisters had been removed from so toxic a home, preyed on by my father and sacrificed by my mother on the altar of respectability, we would have suffered infinitely less as children and adults.

Conclusions

Making custody decisions when cases involve allegations of child sexual abuse and parental alienation is a delicate and complex process. All professionals should act with caution and sensitivity. From the framework presented in the chapter, the following conclusions can be drawn and suggestions made:

1. Child safety should be the priority of custody and parenting adjudications. Children's experiences will influence the rest of their lives, and family litigation can result in important physical and psychological consequences for children. They are the most vulnerable participants in the custody process and must be protected.
2. The professionals involved in custody decisions must have expertise in child sexual abuse when an allegation is made by a parent or a child reveals such. Accurate knowledge and treatment at this juncture facilitates the custody process and ensures the problem is treated from an integrative perspective that considers all aspects of the issue, helps to clarify the situation and makes the child feel safe.
3. Child sexual abuse frequently leaves no physical evidence, or the evidence is fleeting. This is a very difficult experience to prove and sometimes the child's disclosure is the sole main evidence. When a child dares to talk about this situation, how adults react is vital in terms of the child's recovery.
4. Parental alienation syndrome, a diagnosis usually said to be caused by the mother, should not be used as a defence when a child is possibly being sexually abused. Child Sexual Abuse should be evaluated separately in order to assess the real possibility and to ensure the well-being of the child.
5. When a child makes a disclosure that could indicate sexual abuse, an evaluation should be conducted as quickly as possible and professional assistance given. The child needs to be reassured and made to feel as safe as possible during the investigation process.
6. Custody is a very important issue and has a profound influence on the well-being of children. We professionals who work with families as they experience the custody process, the results of which have huge consequences for the children's lives, should be very cautious and take into account all the information available to us.

Notes

1 World Health Organization. *Report of the consultation on child abuse prevention*. Geneva: World Health Organization; 1999.
2 World Health Organization. *Guidelines for medicolegal care for victims of sexual violence*. Geneva: World Health Organization; 2003.

3 Ferragut M, Rueda P, Cerezo MV, Ortiz-Tallo M. What do we know about child sexual abuse? Myths and Truths in Spain. *Journal of Interpersonal Violence* 2020. Retrieved from https://pubmed.ncbi.nlm.nih.gov/32394792/.
4 Lameiras M, Carrera MV, Failde JM. Abusos sexuales a menores: estado de la cuestión a nivel nacional e internacional [Sexual abuse in minors: current status in national and international level]. *Revista d'Estudis de la Violència* 2008; 6: 1–23.
5 Murray LK, Nguyen A, Cohen JA. Child sexual abuse. *Child and Adolescent Psychiatric Clinics of North America* 2015; 23: 321–337.
6 Adams JA, Harper K, Knudson S, Revilla J. Examination findings in legally confirmed child sexual abuse: It's normal to be normal. *Pediatrics* 2003; 94(3): 310–317.
7 Christian CW, Lavelle JM, De Jong AR, Loiselle J, Brenner L, Joffe M. Forensic evidence findings in prepubertal victims of sexual assault. *Pediatrics* 2000; 106: 100–104.
8 Faller KC. The child sexual abuse disclosure controversy: New perspectives on an abiding problem. *Child Abuse & Neglect* 2020; 99: 104285.
9 UNICEF. *A familiar face: Violence in the lives of children and adolescents*. New York: UNICEF; 2017.
10 London K, Bruck M, Ceci S, Shuman D. Disclosure of child sexual abuse: What does the research tell us about the ways that children tell? *Psychology, Public Policy, and Law* 2003; 11: 194–226.
11 Ullman SE. Relationship to perpetrator, disclosure, social reactions, and PTSD symptoms in child sexual abuse survivors. *Journal of Child Sexual Abuse* 2007; 16: 19–36.
12 Brown T, Frederico M, Hewitt L, Sheehan R. The child abuse and divorce myth. *Child Abuse Review* 2001; 10: 113–124.
13 Collings ST. Development, reliability, and validity of the Child Sexual Abuse Myth Scale. *Journal of Interpersonal Violence* 1997; 12: 665–674.
14 Cromer LDM, Goldsmith RE. Child sexual abuse myths: Attitudes, beliefs, and individual differences. *Journal of Child Sexual Abuse* 2010; 19(6): 618–647.
15 Oates RK, Jones DP, Denson D, Sirotnak A, Gary N, Krugman RD. Erroneous concerns about child sexual abuse. *Child Abuse & Neglect* 2000; 24: 149–157.
16 Trocmé N, Tourigny M, MacLaurin B, Fallon B. Major findings from the Canadian incidence study of reported child abuse and neglect. *Child Abuse & Neglect* 2003; 27: 142–439.
17 Gardner R, Sauber RS, Lorandos D. *The International Handbook of Parental Alienation Syndrome: Conceptual, Clinical and Legal Considerations*. Springfield, IL: Charles C. Thomas Publisher, Ltd; 2006.
18 Kelly JB, Johnston J. The alienated child: A reformulation of Parental Alienation Syndrome. *Family Court Review* 2001; 39(3): 249–266.
19 Priolo-Filho S, Goldfarb D, Shesttows D, Sampana J, Williams LCA, Goddman LCS. Judgements regarding parental alienation when parental hostility or child sexual abuse is alleged. *Journal of Child Custody* 2019; 15(4): 302–329.
20 Asociación de Mujeres Juezas. *Conclusiones de la jornada análisis multidisciplinar del denominado síndrome de alienación parental*, celebrada en Madrid, 07/02/2020.
21 Gardner R, Sauber RS, Lorandos D. *The International Handbook of Parental Alienation Syndrome: Conceptual, Clinical and Legal Considerations*. Springfield, IL: Charles C. Thomas Publisher, Ltd; 2006.
22 Warshack RA. When evaluators get it wrong: False positive and parental alienation. *Psychology, Public Policy, and Law* 2019; 26(1): 54–68.
23 Priolo-Filho S, Goldfarb D, Shesttows D, Sampana J, Williams LCA, Goddman LCS. Judgements regarding parental alienation when parental hostility or child sexual abuse is alleged. *Journal of Child Custody* 2019; 15(4): 302–329.
24 López Orozco RE. *Psicología Forense de la teoría a la práctica*. Editorial Vesalius México; 2020.
25 Asociación de Mujeres Juezas. *Conclusiones de la jornada análisis multidisciplinar del denominado síndrome de alienación parental*, celebrada en Madrid, 07/02/2020.
26 Giménez I, López de la Usada M, Nadal C, Alcántara JJ, Peral MC, Andrés S, Poyatos G. Coordinador Parental. Análisis multidisciplinar [Parental coordinator: Multidisciplinary analysis]. Lefebvre; 2020.

27 Children and Family Court Advisory and Support Service (Cafcass). Parental alienation. 2017. Retrieved from www.cafcass.gov.uk/grown-ups/parents-and-carers/divorce-and-separation/parental-alienation/.
28 Leadership Council on Child Abuse and Interpersonal Violence. *How many children are court-ordered into unsupervised contact with an abusive parent after divorce?* 2008. Retrieved from www.leadershipcouncil.org/1/med/PR3.html.
29 Save the Children. *La justicia Española frente al abuso sexual infantil en el entorno familiar [Spanish justice against child sexual abuse in the family environment].* 2012. Retrieved from www.savethechildren.es/sites/default/files/imce/docs/informe_justicia_esp_abuso_sexual_infantil_vok-2.pdf.
30 Silberg J, Dallam S. Abusers gaining custody in family courts: A case series of overturned decisions. *Journal of Child Custody* 2019; 16(2): 140–169.
31 Asociación de Mujeres Juezas. *Conclusiones de la jornada análisis multidisciplinar del denominado síndrome de alienación parental*, celebrada en Madrid, 07/02/2020.
32 Lowestein LF. Child contact disputes between parents and allegations of sex abuse: What does the research say? *Journal of Divorce & Remarriage* 2012; 53: 194–203.
33 López Orozco RE. *Psicología Forense de la teoría a la práctica*. Editorial Vesalius México; 2020.
34 Bala NMC, Mitnick M, Trocmé N, Houston C. Sexual abuse allegations and parental allegations: Smokecreen or fire? *Journal of Family Studies* 2007; 13(1): 26–56.
35 Cyr M, Frappier JY, Hébert M, Tourigny M, McDuff P, Turcotte ME. Impact of child sexual abuse disclosure on the health of nonoffending parents: A longitudinal perspective. *Journal of Child Custody* 2018; 15(2): 147–167.
36 Masip J, Garrido E, Herrero C. El Análisis de Contenido Basado en Criterios (CBCA) [The criteria-based content analysis]. *Revista Iberoamericana de Diagnóstico y Evaluación Psicológica* 2003; 15(1): 75–92.

References

Ferragut M, Rueda P, Cerezo MV, Ortiz-Tallo M. What do we know about child sexual abuse? Myths and truths in Spain. *Journal of Interpersonal Violence* 2020. Retrieved from https://pubmed.ncbi.nlm.nih.gov/32394792/

López Orozco RE. Psicología Forense de la teoría a la práctica. 2020. Editorial Vesalius México.

López Sánchez F. Mitos viejos y nuevos sobre sexualidad. El rol de la educación sexual. 2020. Pirámide España.

UNICEF. *A familiar face: Violence in the lives of children and adolescents.* New York: UNICEF; 2017.

World Health Organization. *Guidelines for medicolegal care for victims of sexual violence.* Geneva: World Health organization; 2003.

21
PARENTAL ALIENATION SYNDROME AND THE 'FRIENDLY PARENT' CONCEPT AS EXAMPLES OF PERVERSION OF THE SYSTEM

Carmen R. Iglesias Martín

Introduction[1]

One of the greatest threats in our society is the violence that takes place within the family. All members of the family unit (partners, children and the environment in which they live can also be included) are potential victims of tension, aggression and abuse. All can experience violation of their basic constitutional rights: life, freedom, personal security, physical and psychological integrity; the right to not be subjected to torture, inhumane or degrading treatment; the right to equality within the family; the right to the protection of personal dignity.[2]

Minors are particularly vulnerable when violence occurs within the family because the perpetrators are also those who must speak for them. For this reason, the protection granted to minors by public authorities must be thorough and comprehensive.[3]

International agencies are increasingly aware of and denouncing domestic violence; that is, the gender-based violence that occurs in the *domus*, the house. Article 19 of the Convention on the Rights of the Child, of 20 November 1989, concerning violence in general, establishes that States are required to take measures 'to protect the child against any form of physical or mental harm or abuse, neglect or negligent treatment, ill-treatment or exploitation, including sexual abuse'.[4] In addition, Council of Europe Resolution 1714 (2010) stated that:

> witnessing violence against the mother is a form of psychological abuse against children with very serious potential consequences and, therefore, children in this situation require more specific action. They are often not

recognized as victims of the psychological impact they experience, or as potential future victims, nor as elements of a chain of reproduction of violence.[5]

This awareness has made it possible for a wide range of laws to be drafted on a national level with the aim of protecting victims of domestic violence. But the peculiarities that family relationships usually present, along with the lack of complaints filed in many cases, implies that violence within the family often remains hidden. Therefore, the measures taken for the protection and comprehensive training of minors are not always effective; in some cases, because the violence has not been verified and, in others, because neither the administration nor the justice system have evaluated the risks adequately.[6]

Protection of the child

In the civil law field, the issues of greatest interest concerning protection of the child in cases of marital crisis are: parental authority, custody and visiting rights.[7] These are all public order issues and thus require the intervention of the Public Prosecutor's Office and judicial approval. In such cases, accusations of violence must be analysed with extreme caution: in child–parent relationships there are many rights and interests at stake but the best interests of the child must always prevail. Judicial investigation of each case must occur and the judge must assess the known facts concerning the violence, together with the possible risks those involved face and the impact these will have on the custody regime chosen for the child.[8] Thus, Article 65 of LO 1/2004, Comprehensive Protection Measures against Gender-Based Violence, of 28 December,[9] states that, 'The Judge may suspend the accused of gender-based violence the exercise of parental authority or custody and care over the minor children to which he refers.'[10]

In cases where violence by a parent is judicially accredited, any type of custody – individual or shared – should be automatically removed given that the effects of this criminal phenomenon on minors can be irreparable if extended over time. Children are already vulnerable in their own right, let alone those who are victims of violence; these children become increasingly fragile as a result of experiencing violence at the hands of those who should care for them and provide a sense of stability and safety. Such children require the protection provided by the legal system; protection that must be comprehensive and that transcends the personal sphere of the victim and extends to the whole family.[11] Hence, criminal and civil issues are involved. For example, on the one hand, a parent's refusal to leave the family home and termination or suspension of communication are criminal matters; on the other hand, exercise of parental authority, such as in the form of custody or communication and residence regime, is a civil matter, as proclaimed by Article 544 ter LEC[12]: 'any other provision deemed appropriate in order to remove the child from danger or to prevent harm under Article 158 CC'.[13] The effectiveness of these measures requires maximum institutional collaboration and involves different public administrations, the judiciary and groups of professionals and victims.[14]

Undoubtedly, this is an issue on which the judge must take all possible precautions. It is clear that the judicial investigation of each case will be decisive in order for the solution to be fair and avoid irremediable consequences, both for the case in which violence is proven and for that in which it is not.[15] To this end, the judge should have all means at their disposal with which to assess the extent of the criminal acts, the risks they may generate and their impact. For example, when there is suspected abuse or violence, parental visits in child contact centres will need to be conducted in a protective manner, with the permanent presence or supervision of professionals.[16] Such visits should be used to observe how the child and parent interact, in order to determine the truth or falsehood of the reported mistreatment or abuse.[17]

Analysis of assumptions

In the 1980s, psychiatrist Richard A. Gardner coined the term parental alienation syndrome to refer to a change in the behaviour of minors toward one parent during custody disputes in contested divorces. He stated that this parental alienation is caused predominantly by the mother as a result of her dislike of the father.[18]

Those who supported this theory saw, in certain behaviours, a willingness to alienate one parent from the child. For example, making decisions alone when parental authority is shared, concealing important information affecting minors, obstruction of the right to visit, obstacles to all forms of contact and making false allegations of abuse. In short, more or less subtle attitudes that encourage the child to favour the alienating parent (the mother), causing the rejection of and aversion and opposition to visiting the alienated parent (the father) or his extended family, based on irrational reasons and suspicion inculcated by the alienating parent.[19]

Undoubtedly, there are parents (mothers and fathers) who use minors for their own purposes and denigrate the other parent. But as noted, 'the fact that in separation and divorce proceedings the minors are used against the other parent is a type of child abuse, which is indeed quite usual, no matter who carries it out.'[20]

A number of studies show that only a small number of false complaints are made.[21] For example, in SAP Castellón 69/2015, of 23 June,[22] reference is made to one parent accusing the other of sexual abuse, which the court ultimately dismisses as false. It states that there are indications of the minors' testimony having been manipulated by a third party, but that it was not possible to prove that it was produced by the mother. However, the absence of the intention to cause harm by the mother is demonstrated, when, having dismissed the criminal case, progressive visits to the father are permitted. The judgement orders progressive visits between the father and daughters aimed at the establishment of shared custody.

When this theory was analysed, it was almost unanimously rejected in papers published in academic psychology and psychiatry journals. They concluded that there was no scientific basis to this theory because the child's rejection of the father may have multiple causes, usually related to the rejected parent himself.[23] Parental alienation syndrome has not been recognised by any professional or scientific association and has been rejected in the WHO's ICD-10.[24] Moreover, the Spanish Association of Neuropsychiatry states that 'parental alienation syndrome as invented by Gardner has no scientific basis and can lead to serious risks in its application in the courts of justice'. Further, it states: that:

> Parental alienation syndrome has provided violent parents with a powerful threat to the couple's desires to leave the relationship. This can lead to even greater helplessness in children subjected to conditions of violence and abuse, who cannot understand the silence of a parent who is silent for fear of such a syndrome.... From this scientific association we believe that the judicial system should review the use of parental alienation syndrome and its measures, which under the claim of therapeutics can only generate psychic harm and perversion of the use of science.[25]

In SAP Vizcaya 256/2008, 27th March,[26] it is stated that:

> more and more professionals in psychology and psychiatry value the formulation of the syndrome more as a form of violence against women, and they remind us that science tells us that the most likely reason for a child to reject a parent is the behaviour of that parent.

However, until parental alienation syndrome was discredited, numerous court judgments were issued on the basis of its existence.[27] Such judgments are usually found in Courts of First Instance and Appeal, finding that rejection of fathers by minors is the result of the conflict of loyalty to which they are subjected. In these conflicts, the child usually chooses the parent to whom he or she feels the greatest attachment; that is, the mother who has contrived to alienate the father.[28]

The most scrutinised of these judgments is SJPII No. 4 of Manresa, of 4 June 2007.[29] Here, the judge

> accepts the position of the expert who acknowledges that the girl suffers from parental alienation syndrome. The best measure to solve the situation was the transfer of custody (from mother to father), rather than suspending visits with the father until the phobia disappeared, as advised by some of the experts consulted.

The novelty of this sentence, therefore, was granting custody to the father. The mother appealed and refused to comply with the ruling until the issue was resolved. It is considered that the evidence upon which the ruling was based was flawed, given that only 'proof' supplied by the father was taken into account and expert reports opposing the existence of parental alienation syndrome were dismissed because the judge did not agree with them. In addition, the court ordered that the daughter be separated from her mother for a period of six months, which is clearly excessive and harmful to the mother–daughter relationship. This judgement, on the basis of lack of evidence, ignored the suspicion that the man was violent to the woman and, instead, accepted a theory with no solid scientific basis.[30]

At this time, use of parental alienation syndrome was widely used as a procedural weapon to disguise men's violence to women and children.[31]

When the mother appealed against the judgment of the JPI of Manresa, AP Barcelona No. 18, it was found that there was 'not sufficient justification to take such a drastic measure as depriving the mother of seeing and maintaining any contact with the daughter for six months, since although there has been a negligent act on the part of the mother, the mother is being punished with unusual harshness' (Judgement 272/2008, of 17 April[32]). This judgment granted custody to the father but ordered immediate re-establishment of contact between mother and daughter.

This judgment is also an example of the irreparable effects that can result from some resolutions. The child in this case spent nearly ten months being unable to see or maintain contact with her mother or maternal family. It was, of course, a resolution in which at no time was the interest of the child taken into account, with the added aggravation of embracing a theory that had only succeeded in jeopardising the development of the child's personality and blaming the victims. Let us not forget that the theory of parental alienation syndrome was created to be used only against mothers who report sexual abuse or abuse of children and, although some argued that it is a gender-neutral theory, it is almost unheard of for a court to recognise or punish the father for alienating behaviour.[33]

The European Court of Human Rights (ECHR) also used parental alienation syndrome repeatedly. In the judgment of the ECHR (Section 4a) on *Bordeianu v. Moldova*, of 11 January 2011,[34] it stated that 'the enforcement of the judgement in question turned out to be a very delicate process due to the parental alienation syndrome suffered by the girl'.[35]

When the theory was called into question, it was the Ministry of Health, Social Policy and Equality itself, which, in 2010, set up a Commission to investigate the alleged parental alienation syndrome. In its report, given the risks involved in incorporating this theory in judicial decisions, it warns all professionals who may intervene in these matters that: 'they should have sufficient training to enable them to understand and detect the construction of the parental alienation syndrome in order to avoid its spread'.[36] Previously, the syndrome having been introduced many years earlier in the United States, the American Association of Judges had warned judges to investigate further with 'children who appear to be alienated by a parent as they may have legitimate and substantial reasons to be angry, distrustful, and afraid. The possibility should be explored, before accusing a parent of inducing such alienation' and insisted that, when they encounter an accusation of alienation of a child by the partner, they should check for domestic violence, as it is an important indicator. The association continues to warn judges to investigate cases thoroughly because 'investigations show that abusers are able to convince the authorities that the woman victim is not adequate or does not deserve sole custody of their children in almost 70% of the cases at issue'.[37]

Nowadays, it is rare to find judgments that mention parental alienation syndrome. It is, however, still mentioned sporadically even if to deny that it is relevant for the case in view of the results of expert reports, but not because it is considered an inadmissible theory, such as in the Judgment of the Spanish Supreme Court, of 16 March (hereinafter, STS 162/2016).[38] In it, the Supreme Court (hereafter, TS) states that the judge of First Instance committed no error concerning the failure to record the circumstances relied upon by the actor to justify the amendment of measures. After examining the expert's report, it coincides with the judgment of the court of appeal that the parental alienation syndrome does not exist in the minors, and the assessments coincide with those made in the previous proceedings. Neither the mother's job instability nor the alleged prejudices of the children have been proven.

Another element of this decision that was quite predictable was the 'friendly parent', which in Spanish means the positive evaluation, in the resolutions, of the friendliest parent, the one with a friendly or collaborative attitude. In principle, this concept fell within the context of the reasonable resolution of child custody disputes whereby courts had to take into account the attitude of the most cooperative parent, the one who did not speak ill of the other, in order to favour him or her when awarding custody.

Like the previous theory, it was beginning to be applied in the US in a somewhat routine manner until the US courts themselves realised that it clashed with the problem of domestic violence and its application in determining custody in such cases would thus be unwise.[39] Custody and visitation rights should not be applied as a reward or punishment (or rather penalty)[40] for the behaviour of parents and 'granting custody to the friendly parent is often done more to punish the other parent than to meet the needs of minors'.[41]

In Spain, judgments, especially in recent years, repeat over and over again the following statement:

> shared custody is not a reward or punishment to the parent who has best behaved during the marriage crisis, but in a complex decision, which must take into account the already stated open criteria that defines what is truly important when establishing the best interests of the child.[42]

This theory, which is as contradictory and perverse as parental alienation theory, makes parents who refuse to accept shared custody on the grounds that it would be too problematic appear to be non-friendly and uncooperative. It pays no attention to possible abuse or violence in the family. If this problem is not thoroughly investigated, a serious mistake will be made and, using a situation of dominance, in a biased and tendentious way, the abusing but apparently collaborative parent will manage to convince us otherwise.

Particular attention must be paid in cases of violence to three versions of events: first, an attempt to state that the violence that has occurred is reciprocal; second, an attempt to state that isolated or unique episodes of violence have occurred; third, an attempt to trivialise the violence, describing it as small acts of antagonism, reckless behaviour, etc.[43] We do not doubt that, in some cases, these statements are true; however, the vast majority are not – and all are fairly common strategies used in defence of violent behaviour.

Some examples of contradictory situations that using the friendly parent criterion can lead to are given below.[44] If one parent refuses to share custody because they believe they have no reason to do so, but the court considers that it is in the child's best interest to have contact with both parents, the refusing parent may be viewed as hostile. The reasons why it is not possible for the other parent to share custody should by analysed in such a situation. Another contradiction that may occur is when the abused parent, who has not filed a complaint, tends to prevent contact of minors with the abuser. Here, it is also necessary to examine the reasons for their insistence on preventing contact with the other parent before classifying them as hostile. Taking the existence of hostile parents for granted could lead us to make irreversible errors, whereas in-depth analysis of each assumption could avoid this situation.

Conclusion

Echoing studies in comparative law, here we acknowledge that both parental alienation syndrome and 'friendly parent' theory have been used preeminently in abusive situations and ultimately blame the victim. This knowledge should prevent us using either to inform decisions made to resolve child custody disputes.[45]

Notes

1 All laws and judgments referred to are according to Spanish laws and courts.
2 Montalbán Huertas, I. et al., 'Cuestiones y propuestas mas relevantes suscitadas en el I Encuentro de Violencia Doméstica', *Encuentros s aobre Violencia Doméstica*, CGPJ, Madrid, 2004, p. 28. Retrieved from www.poderjudicial.es/.
3 In 2015, 27,624 women victims of gender-based violence were registered in Spain under protective orders, according to the National Statistical Institute (INE). The total precautionary measures issued and recorded in the register in matters of gender-based violence during the same year was 84,594, 1.7% more than the previous year. The most common measures were a ban on approaching the victim (36.1% of the total) and prohibition of communicating with the victim (34.3%). Most deaths occur when an aggressor, having been convicted of violence, leaves prison and, skipping the protective order, reaches the victim. It is reported that lack of resources means that is not possible for each victim to be protected by a police officer, thus on many occasions women are in danger (see www.ine.es/).
4 Equally interesting is the finding from a recent United Nations study on violence against children and adolescents:

> Violence can have serious consequences for the development of children. In extreme cases it results in serious injury or even death. However, it can also affect a child's health, learning ability, or even willingness to go to school. Violence can cause the child to flee their homes, exposing them to more danger. Violence also destroys children's self-esteem and can make it impossible for them to be good parents in the future. Children who have experienced violence are more likely to suffer from depression and suicide as adults.
>
> *(www.unicef.org/spanish/protection/index_violence.html)*

It is striking that 'can' is used when speaking of the very serious consequences of violence, in every sense, for the child. We believe that such damage is a reality not a possibility for those who are immersed in such violence.
5 This resolution is reflected by the CGPJ in *Analysis of the care of children of women victims of gender-based violence* (2010), which identifies that, as well as the woman, 'Children are

victims of the gender-based violence against their mothers, and are victims, in all cases, of psychological violence, and sometimes also direct physical violence', which will lead to 'serious consequences in their development' (www.aulaviolenciadegeneroenlocal.es/consejosescolares/archivos/No_hay_una_sola_victima.pdf).

6 Iglesias Martín, C. R., 'La guarda y custodia de los menores en los supuestos de violencia doméstica', *RDP nov-dic 2018*, Ed. Reus, p. 87 ff.

7 Iglesias Martín, C. R. (2019). *La custodia compartida. Hacia una corresponsabilidad parental en plano de igualdad*. Ed. Tirant lo Blanch. Valencia.

8 Águeda Rodríguez, R. M., *La guarda compartida y el interés superior del menor. Supuestos de exclusión*, Ed. HISPALEX, Sevilla, 2016, p. 306. It goes on to establish that:

> controls and precautions must be increased in cases of domestic violence, we are aware that the judicial system is insufficient and final decisions are prolonged in excess, in such a way that precautionary measures (protection order and interim measures) reach unbearable levels. Judicial and extrajudicial control systems need to be increased and improved.
>
> *(p. 326)*

9 LO is the abbreviation for organic law.

10 As amended by LO 8/2015, of 22 July, protection of children and adolescents.

11 Guilarte Martín-Calero, C., 'La protección civil de los menores víctimas de la violencia de género', *La Ley Derecho de Familia*, 17 noviembre 2014, Ed. La Ley 8307/2014, p. 3 ff.

12 LEC is the abbreviation for the Civil Procedure Act.

13 CC is the abbreviation for Civil Code.

14 Iglesia Monje, M. I., de la, 'Ley orgánica de modificación del sistema de protección a la infancia y a la adolescencia: las garantías de una protección uniforme a los menores más vulnerables en base a su supremo interés', Diario La Ley, n° 8590, 24 julio 2015, Ed. La Ley 5021/2015, p. 5 ff.

15 For example, SAP Murcia 57/2001, of 2 March (AC 2001/1243), which granted visitation rights to the father, who had murdered the mother's partner in the presence of his child, despite the child expressing his desire to have no contact with the father, can be considered extremely unfortunate. And in the judgement of JPI No. 4 of Vinaroz, of 16 May 2011, AC 2011/1409, the parent was charged with a felony from which she was later acquitted, during which time she ceased to have contact with her children. Once the acquittal was obtained, it was requested that her visitation rights be resumed gradually, leading, possibly over time, to shared custody. In both cases, the damage caused to the minors involved may be irreparable. In the first case, because being an eyewitness to a murder committed by your father is something that marks you for life; in the second case, because the mother's period of separation from her children (before being acquitted) is time that can never be recovered.

16 González del Pozo, J. P. et al., 'La ejecución forzosa de obligaciones de hacer y entregar cosa determinada en los procesos de familia y menores', *Jurisdicción de familia: especialización… Ejecución de resoluciones y custodia compartida*, CGPJ, Estudios de Derecho Judicial 147, 2008, p. 114 ff.

17 An example of child contact centre follow-up is given to us by SAP Guipúzcoa 100/2016, of 9 May (SRB 2016/188715), which notes that the situation has improved. The collections from and deliveries to the child contact centre resulted in a favourable report for all. And while the minor may find the change in circumstance inconvenient, and the father still needs to make an effort to change certain attitudes, it is no longer considered necessary for the child contact centre to be involved and the child can be picked up from home or school.

18 Gardner, R. A., *Family evaluation in child custody mediation, arbitration, and litigation*. Cresskill, NJ: Creative Therapeutics, 1989. Following his study on conflicting or destructive divorce cases, Gardner stated that parental alienation syndrome is

an alteration that arises almost exclusively during disputes over the custody of a child: the first manifestation is a campaign of denigration against a parent by the children, a campaign that has no justification. This phenomenon is the result of the combination of a programming (brainwashing) of a parent and in which the child contributes with his own contributions, aimed at the parent who is subjected to the alienation. When it appears in the context of actual parental abuse or neglect, the child's animosity may be justified so Parental Alienation Syndrome would not apply to explain the child's hostility.

19 Serrano Castro, F. de A., *Relaciones paterno filiales*, p. 158 ff.
20 Montero Gómez, A., 'Síndrome de alienación patriarcal', *El Correo*, 30 junio 2007, adds that, 'it is not necessary to call it parental alienation syndrome or the malicious mother, unless what is intended is to plant a suspicious label taking for granted the conduct of women in the processes of dissolution of marriage'. Retrieved from www.mujeresenred.net/spip.php?article1090.
21 According to the 2014 State Attorney General's Report, false complaints constitute only 0.010% of allegations of ill-treatment. In addition, of 500 sentences studied, only 0.4% agreed to be deducted from the testimony against women. See: www.eldiario.es/sociedad/CGPJ-libertad-vigilada-supuesto-denuncia_0_495550715.html; www.ine.es/; www.fiscal.es/fiscal/PA_WebApp_SGNTJ_NFIS/.../MEMFIS14.pdf.
22 Judgment of Castellón Court (JUR 2015/233268).
23 Barea Payueta, C., *Justicia patriarcal. Violencia de género y custodia*, Ed. CBP, diciembre 2013, p. 44.
24 ICD-10 is the World Health Organization's *International Classification of Diseases*.
25 Escudero, A., 'Ciencia y pseudociencia en salud mental: el 'síndrome de alienación parental'. La apariencia científica como justificación para su uso en litigios para la custodia de los hijos' (editorial) y 'Lógica del síndrome de alienación parental de Gardner (SAP): 'terapia de la amenaza', *Revista Española de Neuropsiquiatría*, vol. 28, n° 102, año XXVIII, fascículo 2, 2008, pp. 265–266, y p.e 307 ff. The author argues that:

> the risk of change of custody in the face of a possible diagnosis of parental alienation syndrome, especially in women victims of gender-based violence, constitutes a potential deterrent against the reporting of suspicion or evidence of ill-treatment and abuse. ... At the risk of being taken away from her children, the mother is forced to increase the lack of protection of her children to the abuser; the abuser being able to carry out this threat is an effective form of deterrence ... the largest paradox of SAP is that it helps to generate the conditions of a second SAP, only now in reverse, against the parent identified as an alienating parent and against the child, but this time legalized.
>
> *(www.revistaaen.es/index.php/aen/issue/archive)*

26 Judgment of Vizcaya Court (JUR 2008/130045).
27 Gaffal, M., 'Parental alienation in divorce judgements', *InDret 4*, Barcelona, octubre 2012: 'According to the judgements of appeal studied in this article the measures taken were effective and served as a treta to the alienating parent not to exacerbate the problem.' For example, SAP Madrid, of 19 October 2007, JUR 2008/906; SAP Cadiz, of 5 September 2007, JUR 2008/60961; SAP Toledo, of 23 March 2011, JUR 2011/189719. The latter states that there is a clear contradiction between what is said and proven:

> The first thing that is noted in the sentence is a clear contradiction. Having stated as a proven fact that the child claimed that she did not want to go with her father because her mother had told her so, and to rightly estimate that this constitutes serious behaviour on behalf of the mother, however, she later states that that circumstance 'if true is not properly established', and states that there is no expert evidence that the child does not suffer from what has been called parental alienation syndrome. It is

apparent that such a way of thinking, declaring something proven only to then state that it is not, leads to difficulties in determining whether the fact is actually proven or not, something, which in this case, is essential.
28 Ureña Martínez, M., *Malos tratos a menores en el Ámbito Familiar* ... op cit., pp. 85–105. I would like to highlight the detailed jurisprudence, carried out by the author, of the sentences of the time, some contrary to the admission of parental alienation syndrome and others that, in contrast, do admit it (including those that maintain the existing situation and those that change custody and care).
29 Judgment of Primary Court of Manresa (JUR 2007/209316).
30 Alascio Carrasco, L., 'El síndrome de alienación parental. A propósito de la SJPI n° 4 de Manresa, de 14 de junio de 2007', *InDret 1/2008*, Barcelona, p. 5.
31 Montero Gómez, A., 'Síndrome de alienación patriarcal', *op. cit.* Retrieved from www.mujeresenred.net/spip.php?article1090.
32 (AC 2008/1056).
33 Meier, J. S., Domestic violence, child custody, and child protection: understanding judicial resistance and imaging the solutions. *Journal of Gender, Social Policy and the Law*, 11(2), 658–726. Retrieved from www.digitalcommons.wcl.american.edu/jgspl.
34 (JUR 2011/2703).
35 Ortega Domenech, J., 'Luces y sombras de la guarda y custodia compartida a propósito de la nueva legislación aragonesa' ... *op. cit.*, pp. 1477, 1478.
36 Report adopted by the State Observatory on Violence on Women at its meeting on 13 July 2010. Retrieved from www.violenciagenero.msssi.gob.es/violenciaEnCifras/observatorio/gruposTrabajo/docs/ALIENACIONPARENTAL_cap2_lib7.pdf.
From this time is the SAP Málaga 609/2010, of 19 November, JUR 2011/271755, in which it is stated that: 'this Chamber shares the profound scientific doubts that exist about the reality of this syndrome, and, where appropriate, its causes, consequences and solutions'; even so, the judgment still states that it will not judge the existence of the syndrome because it cannot be the subject of judicial resolution; even if it actually exists, which is not the case because, according to the evidence gained by the psychologist, the daughter has very clear ideas about the conflict that exists between her parents. 'Shared custody and care is not feasible, as it would be opposed to Article 92.5 and not in No. 8 of the CC.' Let us remember that the favourable report of the Public Prosecutor's Office was still mandatory at this time.
37 National Council of Juvenile and Family Court Judges, *Domestic violence and the courtroom understanding the problem ... knowing the victim*. Retrieved from www.futureswithoutviolence.org/userfiles/file/Judicial/FinalCourt_Guidelines.pdf.
   Rivera Rangland, E. and Fields, H., *Síndrome de alienación parental: lo que los profesionales necesitan saber*, Vol. 16, n° 6, 2003. Retrieved from www.ndaa-apri.org/apri/index.html.
   Similarly, these authors talk about the guidance of the American Tax Research Institute, which states that:

> Parental Alienation Syndrome is an unproven theory that can threaten the integrity of the criminal system and the safety of abused children. Prosecutors should train on the syndrome and be prepared to argue against its admission to the courts ... the more judges refuse to admit the syndrome as evidence, the more protection will have been achieved in our judicial system for victims of abuse.

They continue to talk about the syndrome presuming that there is a high rate of false allegations, but research shows that this is not the case. In particular, in Spain, the Observatory against Gender and Domestic Violence of the Judiciary states that only 0.4% of complaints are false and, in the report of the State Attorney General's Office, it is reduced to 0.010%. It is a clear prejudice that assumes that women resort more often than men to false allegations of mistreatment in custody proceedings.
38 STS is the abbreviation for Judgment of the Spanish Supreme Court (Law Report 2016/1137).

39 Dore, M. K., 'The friendly parent' concept: A flawed factor for child custody. *Loyola Journal of Public Interest Law*, 6, 45. The author refers to a very descriptive US sentence, the *Ford v. Ford* case, which clearly demonstrates the damage this concept can cause. In this case, it encourages the creation of a conflicting situation that apparently makes one parent seem uncooperative, even as an alienating parent. The assumption is this: the father manipulates the facts to prove that the mother is preventing his visits. Once separated he proposes a change: he will keep her car and leave her his, which he knows will be repossessed; the mother, knowing nothing about this, accepts. And the day before the mother has to take the child to her father, the seize occurs. Because the mother has no way of taking the child, she calls the father to come to her house to pick them up. And so, he does. He shows up at the mother's house with several people and a video camera, stating that the mother is preventing his visits, and the recording is to prove it. Retrieved from www.margaretdore.com/ch_custody.htm.
40 The preferred Spanish translation is to use *penalise* rather than *punish*, as punish implies physical correction, which is not the case.
41 Mason, M. A., *The custody wars: why children are losing the legal battle and what we can do about it*. New York: Perseus, 1999.
42 For example, Judgements of Spanish Supreme Court: STS 4165/2015, of 14 October; STS 4084/2015, of 9 October; STS 3214/2015, of 17 July; STS 615/2015, of 16 February; STS 258/2015, of 16 February; STS 4084/2014, of 22 October; STS 4240/2014, of 16 October; STS 2650/2014, of 2 July; STS 5710/2013, of 25 November; STS 2246/2013, of 29 April; STS 8030/2012, of 10 December; STS 3793/2012, of 25 May; STS 1845/2012, of 9 March; STS 628/2012, of 10 January; STS 5873/2011, of 3 October; STS 4824/2011, of 7 July; STS 4861/2010, of 1 October; STS 963/2010, of 11 March; STS 5969/2009, of 8 October, among many others, constantly quoted by our audiences.
43 Barea Payueta, C., *Justicia patriarcal. Violencia de género y custodia ... op. cit.*, p. 148.
44 Dore, 'The friendly parent' concept, p. 47. All these paradoxes described by the author are very interesting and illustrative of what can be produced.
Another curious incident is the one described in Belz, J. Live with consequences: Custody issues, like divorce, are too complicated for our courts. *World Magazine*, 21 septiembre 2002. It talks about situations that can occur with new partners of parents. It describes the assumption of the stepfather that whatever he does is wrong. From the point of view of the father, if, while the stepfather lives with the minors, he is very demanding and strict, he is a bad stepfather; if, in contrast, he is kind, he does so as an alienating parent of the minors, to turn them against their father.
45 Dalton, K., When paradigms collide: Protecting battered parents and their children in the family court system. *Fam & Concil. Ctx. Rev.* 37, 273, 277 (1999). Dalton states: 'Judges confusing abuse and conflict may ... conclude that the parents who oppose shared parenting are acting vindictively and subordinating the interest of children to their own.'

References

Alascio Carrasco, L., 'El síndrome de alienación parental. A propósito de la SJPI n° 4 de Manresa, de 14 de junio de 2007', *InDret 1/2008*, Barcelona.
Beltz, J. 'Live with consequences: custody issues, like divorce, are too complicated for our courts', *World Magazine*, 21 septiembre 2002.
Dalton, K., 'When paradigms collide: Protecting battered parents and their children in the family court system', *Fam & Concil. Ctx. Rev.* 37, 273, 277 (1999).
Dore, M. K., 'The friendly parent' concept: A flawed factor for child custody', *Loyola Journal of Public Interest Law*, 6, 41–56 (2001).
Escudero, A., 'Ciencia y pseudociencia en salud mental: el 'síndrome de alienación parental'. La apariencia científica como justificación para su uso en litigios para la custodia de los hijos'

(editorial) y 'Lógica del síndrome de alienación parental de Gardner (SAP): 'terapia de la amenaza', *Revista Española de Neuropsiquiatría,* vol. 28, n° 102, año XXVIII, fascículo 2, 2008.

Gaffal, M., 'Parental alienation in divorce judgments', *InDret* 4, 2012, Barcelona. Retrieved from https://papers.ssrn.com/sol3/papers.cfm?abstract_id=2182523.

Gardner, R. A., *Family evaluation in child custody mediation, arbitration, and litigation.* Cresskill, NJ: Creative Therapeutics, 1989.

Guilarte Martín-Calero, C., 'La protección civil de los menores, víctimas de la violencia de género', *La Ley Derecho de Familia,* 17 noviembre 2014, Ed. La Ley 8307/2014.

Iglesia Monje, M. I., de la, 'Ley orgánica de modificación del sistema de protección a la infancia y a la adolescencia: las garantías de una protección uniforme a los menores más vulnerables en base a su supremo interés', Diario La Ley, n° 8590, 24 julio 2015, Ed. La Ley 5021/2015.

Iglesias, C. R. (2019). *La custodia compartida. Hacia una corresponsabilidad parental en plano de igualdad.* Ed. Tirant lo Blanch. Valencia.

Mason, M. A., *The custody wars: Why children are losing the legal battle and what we can do about it.* New York: Perseus, 1999.

Meier, J. S., Domestic violence, child custody, and child protection: Understanding judicial resistance and imaging the solutions. *Journal of Gender, Social Policy and the Law*, 11(2), 2003. Retrieved from https://digitalcommons.wcl.american.edu/jgspl/vol11/iss2/18/.

Rivera Rangland, E. and Fields, H., *Síndrome de alienación parental: lo que los profesionales necesitan saber,* Vol. 16, n° 6, 2003. www.ndaa-apri.org/apri/index.html.

22
COMPENSATION FOR "PARENTAL ALIENATION"
Analysis of ECtHR Judgement 23641/17

Hildegund Sünderhauf-Kravets and Martin Widrig

Introduction

In October 2019, the European Court of Human Rights (ECtHR) unanimously obliged the Republic of Moldova to pay compensation to a mother because it had failed in its duty to protect her right to respect for private and family life, mentioned in Article 8 of the European Convention on Human Rights (ECtHR 23641/17, of 29 October 2019 (*Pisică* v. *Republic of Moldova*), §§ 85, 89, 90; the following numbers and paragraphs refer to this decision). The reason for this ruling was that the Moldovan institutions did not make enough effort to prevent the alienation of three sons from their mother and protect them from alienating behavior by their father. The ECtHR used in its judgement the term "alienation" (§§ 70, 71 and 79), asserted that there were "clear signs that the children had been psychologically alienated from their mother" (§ 79) and described the father's actions that lead to this alienation as "emotional abuse" (§ 71). In this chapter we distinguish between "estrangement" and "alienation"; the terms and definitions used are based on the work of Kelly and Johnston.[1]

- *Estrangement* describes a situation in which the antipathy/refusal of a child toward a parent is largely caused by the parent's behavior or objective circumstances in the parent–child relationship.
- *Alienation* describes a constellation in which the antipathy/refusal of a child toward a parent is significantly caused by the behavior of another person (often the other parent).

The compensation (€12,000, including interest, plus a refund of €2,000 in legal expenses) is a lot of money in Moldova and is the equivalent of four years' income.[2] The judgement is final.

After presenting the relevant facts pertaining to this legislation, we summarize the ECtHR judgement, analyze it, offer some findings and then provide our conclusions.

History of the family and the legislative process

We summarize in this section the history of the family involved in *Pisică* v. *Republic of Moldova* and the various developments in the legislative process.

Divorce and custody proceedings

The applicant is the mother of three sons (§ 5). In 2002, she married P. and gave birth to a son the following year. The parents were divorced in 2006; the mother was granted custody of the child (§ 8). In the same year, the parents reunited, lived together and conceived twin sons, who were born the following year (§ 9).

First custody proceeding

According to the applicant, the father started being aggressive towards her in 2012; mother and children left the family home (§ 10). By the end of July 2013, the father had taken the twins to his house (§ 11). The mother went to court to gain custody of her two sons. She asked the court to hurry because she felt that the father would manipulate the children and turn them against her (§ 12). She mentioned this to the police and the Department for Social Assistance and Family Protection (DSAFP) and complained about limited contact with her children (§§ 12, 13).

Ignored protection order

At the beginning of September 2013, P. returned the children to their mother (§ 14). A few days later the court set a restraining order that prohibited any contact between the father and his children or their mother for three months (§ 15). In December, the order was extended for another three months (§ 17). The order was not enforced. Disregarding the restraining order, P. contacted his children and took them to his house on several occasions (§ 15). The mother complained about this, in January 2014, at the prosecutor's office, insisting that the order should be enforced. There was no reaction from the authority (§ 18). In a report given to the court on 30 January 2014, the DSAFP wrote that both parents were able and willing to rise the children and "the children loved both parents and wanted to be close to both of them" (§ 19).

Circumvention of contact between mother and children

Between April and August the father took all the three sons to his house and prevented them from having any contact with their mother; the mother complained about this several times to the police and other authorities, telling them that the father was being aggressive to her and threatening to take the children away from her (§§ 20 ff.). In July, she asked the court for another restraining order but without success (§§ 24; 27). The mother's request to accelerate the court's decision concerning custody of the two younger children was rejected (§ 25). In July 2014, the district court refused the request for another protection order. Since in the course of 2014 all judges of the court had been involved in a former decision concerning that case, the case was transferred to another district court (§ 27).

Psychological expertise

A DSAFP report, of 19 November 2014, issued the following conclusion: "the children's psychological state was being seriously affected. Although they had a positive attitude towards both parents earlier, they had radically changed their views after living with their father" (§ 28). The DSAFP recommended a psychological examination of the children and suggested that they should be separated from both parents for one month, and in a placement centre, to assist them appropriately and remove them from parental influence (§ 28).

In December, an expert report was produced, which concluded that:

> the children were being involved in the conflict between the parents; that their initially positive attitude towards both parents had clearly become negative as regards the applicant, as a result of P.'s influence; that depriving the children of contact with their mother was a form of emotional abuse; and that any meeting with their mother would constitute a traumatizing event for the children while they continued to live with their father.
>
> (§ 29)

On January 2015, the DSAFP issued another conclusion, largely reiterating its previous findings (§ 30).

Custody decisions

In February 2015, the district court refused to place the children in a placement centre and granted custody of the two younger boys to the father. The court of appeal reversed this judgement in June 2015 and awarded custody to the mother. This judgement became final when the Supreme Court of Justice rejected an appeal by the father in November 2015 (§ 35).

Despite the court's judgement the father refused to allow any contact between mother and sons. The mother complained without success to the police and asked for psychological help for the boys (§§ 33 f.).

In November, the mother went to the Prosecutor General's Office and stated that, because of the influence of the father, the children were suffering from parental alienation syndrome and the authorities had failed to prevent that occurring. She also asked for criminal proceedings to begin against the father (§ 34).

Enforcement proceedings

On 19 January 2016, the mother submitted a writ of enforcement in respect to the custody judgement of 24 June 2015; the bailiff invited the father to hand over the children voluntarily, but he did not (§ 36). Three weeks later, the bailiff, accompanied by the social welfare office, a psychologist and the mother, went to the father's house and demanded that he hand over the children to their mother. However, the children refused to leave and said they wanted to stay with their father (§ 37). The applicant again complained to several authorities about the failure to reunite her with her children and the alienation that was occurring; she asked for temporary placement of the children in a neutral place (§ 38). Again, nothing happened (§ 40).

In February 2016, the prosecutor´s office initiated a criminal investigation against P. after the applicant's complaint about domestic violence in the form of emotional abuse of the children; the proceeding was still ongoing at the last observation by the ECtHR in 2018 (§ 39).

In December 2016, a new protection order in favour of the mother was issued against P. (§ 41). The following day, the applicant tried to collect the children from school but the attempt failed because of the actions of the school and local authorities: the mayor of the village in which the children lived decided that the children should live with their grandparents (father's parents) for 45 days (§ 42). On 19 December 2016, another attempt to enforce the judgement failed (§ 43).

On 27 January and 3 February 2017, the local police and mayor's office asked the mother to show more interest in the children's psychological state. Because she was unable to get in contact with her children, the mother was accused of refusing to cooperate, which prevented relevant decisions being made (§ 44). On 6 February 2017, a psychologist issued a conclusion concerning the state of mind of the children, who were still living with their father's parents. She found that all three children had been seriously affected by the separation from their father (by the protection order) and that any action intending to build up the relationship with their mother would be premature (§ 45). The children would blame the mother for the "loss" of their father and showed resistance to their mother (§ 45). In March, further failed attempts were made to return the children to their mother's care (§§ 46–49).

During a period of more than three years (from the final judgement in November 2015 to the final investigations by the ECtHR in 2018), no successful measures had been taken to return the boys to their mother's care. When mother and children separated from the father in 2012, the twins were five years old. Until the age of 11, the judicial system, supported by social services and psychologists, was unable to avoid parental alienation and to reunite the boys with their mother, despite several judgements and many enforcement efforts.

The court's assessment

The ECtHR admitted the application (§ 55). In this section we summarize the parties' submissions, the general principles used and their application to the case.

The parties' submissions

The applicant stated that the authorities failed, on the one hand, to enforce the judgement of 24 June 2015, which granted her custody of the two younger children, and, on the other hand, to comply with their positive duty to prevent the alienation of her children (§§ 67 and 56 ff.).

The authorities argued that they had taken all reasonable measures to enforce the judgement of 24 June 2015 and to reunite the mother and her children, pointing out that the obligation to take measures to reunite children and their parents is not absolute. The failure to reunite the family was primarily due to the children's opposition and her own failure to involve sufficiently in the process of rebuilding her relationship with her children, while P. encouraged the children to go with her (§§ 60 ff.).

General principles

In its general assessment the court explained the scope of the right to respect for family life, the meaning of the best interests of the child and the child's views and the particular duties to protect the relationship between parents and their children.

Scope of the right to respect for family life

Article 8 protects individuals primarily from arbitrary actions by public authorities. In addition, there are particular obligations inherent to an "effective respect for family life". With respect to parental contact rights, in principle states have an obligation to take measures with a view to reuniting parents and their children, and to facilitate such reunions, if the interests of the child dictate that everything has to be done to preserve relations with the parents (§ 63).

However, this obligation is not absolute since a reunion between children and parents may not be able to take place immediately and may require preparatory measures. Decisive is whether the domestic authorities have taken all steps, that can reasonably be demanded, to facilitate contact (§ 64).

Child's best interests and children's views

There is broad consensus that, in all decision concerning children, their best interests be paramount. The child's best interests, depending on their nature and seriousness, may override those of their parents. In particular, no parent can be entitled to have measures applied that may harm the child's health and development. However, although we must consider the child's views, those views are not necessarily sufficient to override the interests of the parents, especially their desire to have regular contact with their child. Furthermore, the child's right to express his or her own view is not an unconditional veto power. Other factors must be examined to determine the child's best interests (§ 65).

Duty to exercise particular diligence in cases concerning parent–child relationships

There is a duty to exercise particular diligence in cases concerning a person's relationship with his or her child because of the risk that the mere passage of time may result in de facto determination of the matter (§ 66).

Application of these principles to the present case

It remainsto examine whether the local authorities complied with the obligations deriving from Article 8 (§ 67). To do so, the court considered all relevant elements of the proceedings, not only those of the enforcement phase (§ 68). This section summarizes the relevant considerations of the court.

Authorities' awareness of risks

During the custody proceedings, the mother contacted the authorities nine times between July 2013 and November 2015 and complained about the father's actions. She believed these actions aimed at the alienation of the children from her. She complained in different ways. For this reason, the authorities must have been aware of her complaints. Through these complaints, the authorities were also aware that the children were with their father against the wishes of the mother and that he had the opportunity to influence the children (§ 69).

At a first psychological examination of the children in early 2014, the children were deemed to love both parents equally. At a second examination, in November 2014, the children rejected their mother. Because of the complaints of the mother and the results of the evaluations, which confirmed the veracity of the mother's claims, the authorities must have been aware that the father's actions were seriously threatening the relationship between the children and their mother (§ 69).

Absence of protection

The court notes that, from January to November 2014, there was no psychological follow-up, despite the mother's complaints. In November 2014, the DSAFP recommended separation of the children temporarily from both parents, to provide them with psychological assistance away from the influence of their parent. This recommendation was never followed, although a third report, of December 2014, concluded that the children's alienation from their mother, as a result of the father's actions, constituted an emotional abuse of the children (§ 70).

In the absence of any measures to protect the children, the court concluded that the mother had used all means at her disposal. The judges also considered that, although a protection order had been issued, P. could continue acting with impunity; that when the prosecutor finally initiated a criminal investigation against P., he annulled nine previous decisions refusing to do just that (§ 71); and that the contact schedule, recommended by the DSAFP, which suggested the children alternate stays with both parents, was not respected by P. (§ 72).

Violation of the principle of exceptional diligence

Despite the request of the mother to decide the custody case quickly, and her many complaints, the first-instance court took a year and a half to decide. This contributed to the period during which the mother did not have meaningful contact with her children, while the father was able to alienate the children from her. This delay in deciding the case was contrary to the principle of exceptional diligence in decisions concerning parent–child relationships (§ 73).

Insufficient enforcement of the custody decision

In enforcing the judgement, the authorities did "not remain totally passive" and did take several relevant measures. Notably, the bailiff acted swiftly, but the children's strong opposition frustrated his efforts to enforce the judgement. In February 2016, a criminal investigation was initiated against the father (§ 74).

However, after the first attempt to enforce the judgement, on 9 February 2016, the authorities were apparently inactive. The next measure was taken on 15 December 2016, when a court issued a protection order, barring the father from contacting his children (§ 75).

Failure to review actions of domestic authorities

On 16 December 2016, at the children's school, a second attempt was made to persuade the children to live with their mother. Because of missing information and contact with the people involved, the court could not judge the consequences of the actions by the authorities involved. However, no domestic authority analyzed the situation in order to determine the reasons for the failure to reunite the mother and her children, i.e. whether it was because of the children's refusal to cooperate or, at least partially, because of the actions of those involved (§ 76).

On two further occasions the authorities tried to reunite the mother and her children, but in both cases the children refused to go with her (§ 77).

Lack of evidence for sufficient implication by the authorities

The court accepted that the refusal of the children to live with their mother caused a difficult situation for the authorities, which needed a variety of complex measures to prepare the reunification of the children with the mother and sufficient time. There were serious attempts to find a solution in 2017. However, there was no evidence of such activity in 2016, and the government did not explain this apparent inactivity (§ 78).

Conclusions of the court

The court shared the view that the alienation of the children was a major factor impeding the enforcement of the custody decision of 24 June 2015. The failure of the authorities to react to the mother's complaints and to examine the custody case in an urgent matter "substantially contributed to the eventual difficulties in enforcing" that decision. Furthermore, the authorities made only two attempts to enforce the custody decision in the first year after it was passed. Importantly, in 2016, they did no preparatory psychological work with the family to facilitate the enforcement, despite the clear signs of an alienation of the children from their mother and that complex preparations were necessary to enforce the custody decision (§ 79).

For these reasons, the court found that the domestic authorities "did not act with the exceptional diligence required … or discharge their positive obligations under Article 8 of the Convention". Consequently, there had been a violation of Article 8 of the Convention (§ 80).

Analysis

The following analysis shows the relevance of the judgement of the ECtHR to cases in which a child rejects a parent and professionals establish that this is largely due to the influence of others.

Commitment to "parental alienation"

The ECtHR writes, in its considerations and in the headnote, explicitly about a "from his mother alienated child" (§§ 70, 73, 79 and headnote). Furthermore, the court also mentioned in its considerations in its public media communication (ECtHR press release 368, of 29 October 2019) that the father alienated the children from their mother by his "parental alienation behavior" (§ 73, see also § 69).

The court considers that the alienation of the applicant's children

> was a major factor impeding the enforcement of the judgment of June 24, 2015. Therefore, the authorities' failure to react to the applicant's complaints about alienation and to examine the custody case in an urgent matter must be seen as having substantially contributed to the eventual difficulties in enforcing the judgment mentioned above. Moreover, the authorities made only two attempts to enforce the judgment in the first year of the enforcement proceedings (2016). More importantly, in 2016, they did no preparatory psychological work with the children or their parents to facilitate the enforcement, despite there being clear signs that the children had been psychologically alienated from their mother … and that complex preparations for the enforcement were therefore necessary.
>
> (§ 79)

Hence, the ECtHR acknowledges the phenomena of "alienated children" and that one parent can alienate a child via his or her behavior.

"Parental alienation" is emotional child abuse

The ECtHR refers in its considerations to a psychological report compiled by an expert that concludes that the alienation of the children from their mother was a kind of emotional child abuse (§ 70). Furthermore, the ECtHR considers that there was no further "measure aimed at protecting the children from the ongoing emotional abuse" and that the mother could not do anything more than she actually did (§ 71).

The court referred to the alienation of the children and named it "emotional abuse". By doing so, the ECtHR recognizes parental alienation as a form of emotional child abuse.

Neutral placement and replacement as possible interventions

The ECtHR refers explicitly to the recommendations of the DSAFP to isolate the children temporarily from both parents and to provide them with psychological support in a neutral environment. The ECtHR criticizes the courts' failure to follow this recommendation, even though a second psychological report identified the alienation of the children as a form of emotional child abuse (§ 70).

The court refers to the recommendation of a neutral placement, does not criticize it and emphasizes that the recommendation was never followed. For this reason, it seems that the ECtHR considers a temporary placement in the context of parental alienation a viable intervention to protect children from harm.

Duty to perform exceptional diligence

The ECtHR concludes that the Moldovan authorities worked neither carefully nor quickly enough (§§ 66, 80). The judges emphasize that, in cases concerning a parent's relationship with his or her children, there is a duty to exercise exceptional diligence, "in view of the risk that the passage of time may result in a de facto determination of the matter" (§ 66). The ECtHR acknowledges that, with respect to the enforcement of the custody decision, the authorities were not "totally passive" (§ 74). Nevertheless, they did not react properly. First, they did not take appropriate actions and, second, they waited too long (§§ 75–78). The court mentions that, for more than one year,

> the authorities did not do preparatory psychological work with the children or their parents to facilitate the enforcement, despite there being clear signs that the children had been psychologically alienated from their mother ... and that complex preparations for the enforcement were therefore necessary.
>
> (§ 79)

In addition, for most of 2016, the authorities could not explain why they took no further action (§§ 78, 80).

According to the judgement, authorities must:

1. take the right action, including psychological work with children and parents to prepare reunification
2. act quickly and
3. be able to prove that they have taken all necessary measures that can reasonably be expected.

None of this happened. The ECtHR finds that, "the domestic authorities did not act with the exceptional diligence required of them ... or discharge their positive obligations under Article 8 of the Convention" (§ 80).

Claims of "parental alienation" must be taken seriously

The ECtHR finds that the domestic authorities knew of the mother's complaints and, following the psychological report in (2014), also knew that she was right (§ 69). The court criticized the Moldovan courts for taking eighteen months to decide on the custody issue, although they were aware of the alienation (§ 70). The ECtHR acknowledges a causal connection between the loss of time (due to not listening to the mother's complaints) and the later difficulties in enforcing the court's decision (§ 79). The court acknowledged this, although the mother used the term "parental alienation syndrome" and expressed her fear of alienation (§§ 34, 41). This means that, in general, if someone claims that they are experiencing parental alienation or parental alienation syndrome, they should not simply be ignored. In contrast, such a concern must be taken seriously.

The best interests of the child are more important than the child's expressed will

The ECtHR always attaches great importance to the best interests of children. In its general considerations, the court emphasizes that we must consider the wishes of children in an appropriate way. However, the wish of a child is not a veto without exception. The best interests of a child must still be determined and are more important than the child's expressed will (§ 65).

Findings

Alienated children are already part of a high risk group as a result of parental separation. Alienation and exposure to alienating behavior places an additional strain upon them.[3] Children victims of parental alienation suffer the consequences of this phenomenon even into adulthood. For instance, in a retrospective study conducted by Amy Baker, 70% of participants stated that they have suffered, or continue to suffer, from significant depression, 33% had serious drugs or alcohol problems in their youth, 66% had been divorced at least once themselves, and 50% had a child who was alienated from them by the other parent.[4] Furthermore, most of the participants in that study shared the view that, although they had rejected a parent when they were a child, they had secretly hoped that someone would notice that they didn't mean what they said – a result that complies with that of a study by Clawar and Rivlin, in which 80% of alienated children wished that someone had noticed the alienation and stopped it.[5]

Rejected parents of alienated children also suffer. They too suffer from depression, traumatizing stress-related symptoms, and suicidal ideation. According to the results of two recent studies, with data from different regions in Canada and the US, more than 30% of the participant parents were victims of alienating behavior by the other parent, which clearly exceeds earlier estimations.[6]

Nevertheless, and even though parental alienation is a much studied phenomenon – the Parental Alienation Database of the Vanderbuilt University Medical Center alone contains 1396 scholarly books, book chapters and papers on this topic – many courts and authorities still appear to be taking a passive approach if a child rejects a parent, even when experts recommend an intervention. A possible explanation could be fear of identifying so-called parental alienation syndrome, which is highly disputed. Richard Gardner coined the term in the 1980s and described parental alienation syndrome as being a similar phenomenon to parental alienation. However, as his biggest critic, Carol Bruch distinguished clearly between the two expressions.[7] The American Psychological Association dismisses parental alienation syndrome but recognizes, however, that

> the more generalized concept of parental alienation often is viewed as a legitimate dynamic in many family situations, describing the harm done to a child's security with one caregiver as a result of exposure to another caregiver's unfavorable actions toward or criticism of that person.[8]

Gardner's parental alienation syndrome was heavily criticized,[9] particularly by two independent groups. One group involved the highly respected Joan B. Kelly and Janet R. Johnston, who, in 2001, proposed, as an alternative, the concept of "parental alienation".[10] The other considered itself to be a "defender of abused women and children".[11] Some representatives of the second group also deny the existence of parental alienation and seem to consider alienation claims as:

> fabricated by male perpetrators of intimate partner violence, often also abusive fathers, to exert control over the victimized mother and maintain contact with children, who justifiably resist or refuse contact with them, this being an adaptive and positive coping mechanism.[12]

At the other extreme, some men's rights activists seem to claim that mothers alienate children to seek revenge and others even make "false and malicious allegations of abuse".[13]

Polarized debates continue today. However, significantly, few scientists deny the existence of the phenomena described by parental alienation.[14] In a survey conducted at a family law conference held by the highly respected Association of Family and Conciliation Courts (AFCC) in 2010 concerning parental alienation, of 300 family law professionals 98% answered "yes" to the question: "Do you think that some children are manipulated by one parent to irrationally and unjustifiably reject the other parent?"[15]

Furthermore, even harsh critics parental alienation syndrome consider "alienating behavior" to be a form of child abuse, which requires prompt intervention on the part of the authorities.[16] The change of physical custody or a temporary placement at a neutral location are possible interventions, among others, to protect children from harm.[17] Whether they are appropriate and proportionate must be determined in each particular case. In addition, parental alienation is gender-neutral.[18]

It is undisputed that children may resist contact for different reasons. Various factors may influence this behavior and it may be necessary to determine each one.[19] In consequence, just because a child rejects a parent this does not mean that we can conclude that a child has been subjected to alienating behavior by the other parent or, at the other extreme, abused. However, being indifferent and taking a passive approach when a child rejects a parent may be as harmful for that child as placing him or her with an abusive parent.[20] Loss of contact with a living parent seems to have, independent of the reasons for such contact loss, serious consequences for the well-being of children. These consequences can last for a lifetime and affect those concerned twice as much and three times as long as the death of a parent.[21] For these reasons, we should avoid such losses of contact whenever possible.[22]

In the view of the above, the judgment discussed is important. It neither excludes nor restricts a differentiated approach, as requested by many scholars. What matters is, independent of what the phenomena is being called, that children and parents concerned by parental alienation (or other forms of contact problem) are taken seriously and appropriately assisted.

Conclusions

The ECtHR recognized in this judgement that alienated children and parents who influence their children to respond negatively to the other parent (alienating behavior) exist. By doing so, the court implicitly recognizes parental alienation. The court does not recognize a syndrome! The court considers alienating behavior to be a form of emotional child abuse and requests that when there are indications of such that quick and carefully chosen measures are applied. In addition, we must take parents' fears and concerns seriously, even if they talk about the non-recognized parental alienation syndrome. The burden of proof for sufficient diligence in a particular case lies with the authorities. It is important to take children's wishes seriously; however, we must verify that their expressed wish is compatible with their best interests.

The fact that the ECtHR recognizes parental alienation could contribute to a greater awareness of this problem at in politics, society and practice. Hopefully, it will stimulate necessary research in the field. In addition, this judgement may contribute to the better protection of children and parents because decisions based on authorities' simple "acceptance" of alienation and passive response are incompatible with it. Finally, this recognition of parental alienation may be a cause of satisfaction for millions of children and parents concerned, whose lives have been seriously impaired as a result of this traumatizing behavior.

Notes

1 Kelly and Johnston 2001, p. 251 ff.
2 Average income in Moldova was US$3,900 in 2018 Retrieved from https://data.worldbank.org/indicator/NY.GNP.PCAP.CD?locations=MD&view=chart.
3 Johnston, J. R. 2005. Children of divorce who reject a parent and refuse visitation: Recent research and social policy implications for the alienated child. *Family Law Quarterly* 38: 757–775, p. 771.
4 Baker, A. J. L. 2005. The long-term effects of parental alienation on adult children: A qualitative research study. *American Journal of Family Therapy* 33: 289–302, p. 296 ff.
5 Fidler and Bala 2001, p. 21.
6 Harman et al. "Prevalence of adults who are targets of parental alienation"; Harman, J. J., Leder-Elder. S., and Biringen, Z. 2016. Prevalence of parental alienation drawn from a representative poll. *Children and Youth Services Review* 66: 62–66, p. 65.
7 Gardner, R. 2004. Commentary on Kelly and Johnston's "The alienated child: A reformulation of parental alienation syndrome". *Family Court Review* 39: 611–621, p. 613 f.; Bruch, C. 2001. Parental alienation syndrome and parental alienation: Getting it wrong in child custody cases. *Family Law Quarterly* 35: 527–552, p. 549.
8 American Psychological Association, definition of parental alienation syndrome (PAS). Retrieved from https://dictionary.apa.org/parental-alienation-syndrome.
9 For example, Rand, D. C. 2010. Parental alienation critics and the politics of science. *American Journal of Family Therapy* 39: 48–71. Some scholars claim that even today misinformation regarding parental alienation syndrome is in circulation (see, e.g., Bernet, W. 2020. Parental alienation and misinformation proliferation. *Family Court Review* 50: 293–307).
10 Kelly and Johnston 2001 (n. 1), p. 251 ff.
11 See, e.g., Rand 2010 (n. 9), p. 49.
12 Fidler and Bala 2010 (n. 5) p. 10, referring to Carol Bruch, Jennifer Hoult und Joan Meier; Whitcombe, S. 2013. Psychopathology and the conceptualisation of mental disorder: The debate around the inclusion of parental alienation in DSM-5. *Counselling Psychology Review* 28(3): 6–18, p. 8.
13 Fidler and Bala 2010 (n. 5), p. 10. For relevant background information, see Johnston and Sullivan 2020p. 273 f.
14 Rauscher, T. 2014. Commentary on § 1684 BGB. In *J. von Staudingers Kommentar zum Bürgerlichen Gesetzbuch mit Einführungsgesetz und Nebengesetzen, Buch 4, Familienrecht, §§ 1684–1717 (Elterliche Sorge 3–Umgangsrecht)*, ed. Coester, M., Rauscher, T., and Salgo, L., Berlin, n. 39.
15 Baker, A., Jaffe, P., Bernet, W., and Johnston, J. 2011. *Brief report on parental alienation survey*. AFCC E-News 6/5. Retrieved from www.afccnet.org/Portals/0/PublicDocuments/2011_may.pdf.
16 Johnston, J. R., and Kelly, J. B. 2004. Rejoinder to Gardner's "commentary on Kelly and Johnston's 'The alienated child: A reformulation of parental alienation syndrome'". *Family Court Review* 42: 622–628, p. 626; Saini et al. 2016p. 425.
17 Johnston 2005 (n. 3), p. 760 and 770 f.
18 Kruk 2018p. 142.
19 Johnston and Sullivan 2020 (n. 13), p. 279 ff.
20 Ibid, p. 272.

21 Prinz, A., and Gresser, U. 2015. Macht Kontaktabbruch zu den leiblichen Eltern Kinder krank? *Neue Zeitschrift für Familienrecht*, 989–994, p. 993 f.
22 Ibid, p. 994.

References

Bernet, W. 2020. Parental alienation and misinformation proliferation. *Family Court Review* 50: 293–307.

Fidler, B. J., and Bala, N. 2010. *Children resisting postseparation contact with a parent: Concepts, controversies and conundrums*. *Family Court Review* 48: 10–47.

Harman, J. J., Leder-Elder, S., and Biringen, Z. 2019. *Prevalence of adults who are targets of parental alienation behaviours and their impact*. Children and Youth Services Review 106. Retrieved from https://pasg.info/app/uploads/2019/10/Harman-Jennifer.pdf

Johnston, J. R., and Sullivan, M. J. 2020. *Parental alienation: In search for common ground for a more differentiated theory*. *Family Court Review* 58: 270–292.

Kelly, J. B., and Johnston, J. R. 2001. *The alienated child: A reformulation of parental alienation syndrome*. *Family Court Review* 39: 249–266.

Kruk, E. 2018. *Parental alienation as a form of emotional child abuse: Current state of knowledge and future directions for research*. *Family Science Review* 22: 141–164.

Saini, M., Johnston, J. R., Fidler, B. J., and Bala, N. 2016. Empirical studies of alienation. In L. Drozd, M. Saini, and N. Olesen (eds), *Parenting plan evaluations: Applied research for the family court*, 2nd ed. New York: Oxford University Press, 374–430.

23
THE COOPERATIVE PARENTING TRIANGLE
A tool to help divorced parents

Päivi Hietanen

Introduction: Cooperative parenting allows parents an active role in the child's life

By nature, a child loves both parents and wishes to remain loyal to both of them. A child will feel safe and secure if they can see that their parents are able to work together. This feeling of security helps the child to adapt to the changes to family life brought about by the divorce. The child will not have to choose one parent over the other or take responsibility for the adults' issues or feelings. For the child, what is crucial about the divorce is not the divorce itself; what matters, instead, is the way the parents handle the divorce, as well as what the child's life will be like and what kind of relationship the parents manage to build with one another after the divorce.

Supporting cooperative parenting helps parents to see the significance of the other parent to the child as an important interpersonal relationship after a divorce. Cooperative parenting after a divorce requires the parents to make a conscious decision to prioritise the child and their wellbeing. Parents must strive to find a way to cooperate that allows them to take care of matters concerning the child and to raise and care for the child.

Cooperative parenting is based on three factors: the child's best interests, the parents' attitudes and behaviour towards each other and taking care of everyday matters. Dialogue between the parents plays a key role. Problems that occur in cooperative parenting are often rooted in communication issues. A lack of dialogue and cooperation allows for the formation of negative interpretations of the other parent, which reduces the possibility of cooperation. The child's safe growth and development can be adversely affected if the child becomes the focus of the parents' disputes or acts as a messenger between the parents.

Functional cooperative parenting allows parents to play an active role in their child's development despite going through a divorce. In practice, cooperative parenting means jointly agreed decisions and taking each other into account when dealing with issues that concern the child. Dialogue between the parents plays an important role, as does commitment to parenting and caring for the child. The child's needs will be neglected and their positive development undermined if one parent tries to ally themselves with the child against the other parent, or if the right of access is used as a means of extortion against the other parent.

In a divorce, parents must be supported on the road to appropriate and functional cooperative parenting in order to avoid prolonged custody disputes. The Cooperative Parenting Triangle is a functional tool that can be used when working with divorced parents. The triangle helps the parents to understand their own role and that of their partner, the significance of a functional parenting relationship and the status of the child during the divorce.

The triangle can be used when working with individuals, with couples and in peer support groups to review and discuss cooperative parenting. The Cooperative Parenting Triangle was developed by the Federation of Mother and Child Homes and Shelters in Finland in collaboration with professionals who work with divorced parents and families affected by divorce.

Cooperative parenting: Values, attitudes and everyday life

Terävä and Böök (2019)[1] interviewed social and health care professionals who work with divorced parents. The aim of their study was to investigate the professionals' perspectives on and experiences with cooperative parenting and how to parent cooperatively after a divorce.[2] The study concretised three factors that form the foundation of cooperative parenting after a divorce: values, attitudes and everyday life.

The primary values are the child's right to their parents and the right to a safe everyday life. Parents should be able to examine the choices and solutions that they have made from the perspective of ensuring that the child's best interests and rights are safeguarded. The child has the right to be heard, and attention must be paid to their wishes and opinions when coming up with solutions that affect their life. The child must be told of any solutions and decisions that will affect their life, and these must be discussed with the child.[3]

Attitude refers to the respect shown towards the other parent. Cooperation requires the parents to tolerate one another and to accept each other as a part of their lives, despite the divorce. This also often requires parents to accept that they must deal with disappointment and guilt relating to the divorce crisis and to their own personal growth.

Interaction between the parents and their behaviour towards one another play a key role in everyday life. Functional dialogue and interaction are vital to successful post-divorce cooperative parenting. A lack of functional dialogue or interaction lessens the possibilities for cooperation and weakens the parents' ability to get on and take joint responsibility for matters concerning the child. A complete lack of dialogue or hostile dialogue also makes the parents susceptible to creating their own, sometimes distorted, interpretations of a situation or the other parent's intentions. This can lead to conflict and custody disputes in court.

Appropriate behaviour towards one another creates a foundation for functional cooperative parenting. This requires both parents to be able and willing to make compromises and to be flexible where necessary.[4] Interaction skills can be developed and learnt throughout life. A divorce can be a turning point in life that causes you to examine your own relationships in a new light. In the best-case scenario, a divorce can help you to learn more about yourself and the other parent. It is important to understand that we cannot change another parent, but we can influence our own behaviour, thoughts and attitudes.

Three different style of cooperative parenting

Three different methods of implementing cooperative parenting were observed in interviews with cooperating parents and experiences of cooperative parenting. Parents explained that the help and instructions they received from professionals were significant. With support, the parents were able to move towards functional cooperative parenting.[5]

In *appropriate cooperation*,[6] parents are civil towards one another, but are not friends. The parents inform one another of matters relating to their child, agree on child-rearing matters together, and are also prepared to seek help for their child as necessary. The parents are in contact with one another when required but not on a daily basis. In this model, parents explained that they had to rely on outside help in order to successfully implement cooperative parenting after their divorce. In particular, it was important for them to deal with their own feelings surrounding the divorce.

In the *close cooperation method*,[7] the parents are often in contact with one another. They do not, however, share their personal business with one another; instead, they focus on caring for their child and sharing everyday parenting responsibilities. The parents have realised that the implementation of cooperative parenting requires them to make an effort, and that good cooperative parenting does not spontaneously arise. We can speak of a growth process described as "success through challenges".[8]

In the *seamless cooperative parenting model*,[9] it is usual for ex-spouses to have already worked on a solution for their separation while still in a relationship together. They have sought help for their relationship or family problems. They have discussed their separation and subsequent changes together, and it came as no surprise to either party. In such cases, the cooperative parenting may be seamless, and the parents are often in contact with one another. They describe their relationship as a friendship. The parents help one another with everyday matters and otherwise in life, such as financially.

Cooperative parenting requires a conscious decision

Parents can achieve a good cooperative relationship, despite initial difficulties relating to divorce, if they are given information and support from professionals and if they are allowed time to go through their own divorce process. Early support in the initial phase of a divorce can prevent conflicts from deepening or prolonged custody disputes from arising.

The way in which the divorce takes place can also affect cooperative parenting. If a divorce comes as a surprise, or perhaps infidelity is a factor, this can hinder cooperative parenting due to the adults' own feelings of hurt, shame or rejection. If parents work together on a divorce solution, seek help for any couple or family relationship issues and come together to consider solutions surrounding the child's situation in advance, the chances for good post-divorce cooperative parenting are favourable.[10]

A cooperative relationship does not spontaneously occur and instead demands a conscious decision to work with the other parent to act in the best interests of the child. The emotional connection a parent has with their child, love, attachment and caring all help to put the child first. A parent's empathy and understanding towards the other parent are beneficial to cooperation, as are mutual respect, appreciation and trust.[11]

It is important to remember that there is no single correct model for cooperative parenting, and that each family and set of parents must find the method of cooperative parenting that is suitable for them and their situation.

The Cooperative Parenting Triangle as a tool[12]

The Cooperative Parenting Triangle[13] is meant to be used as a tool while working with parents. The triangle is a simple picture that can help parents to talk about their family situation (see Figure 23.1). It can be used at family mediation meetings or

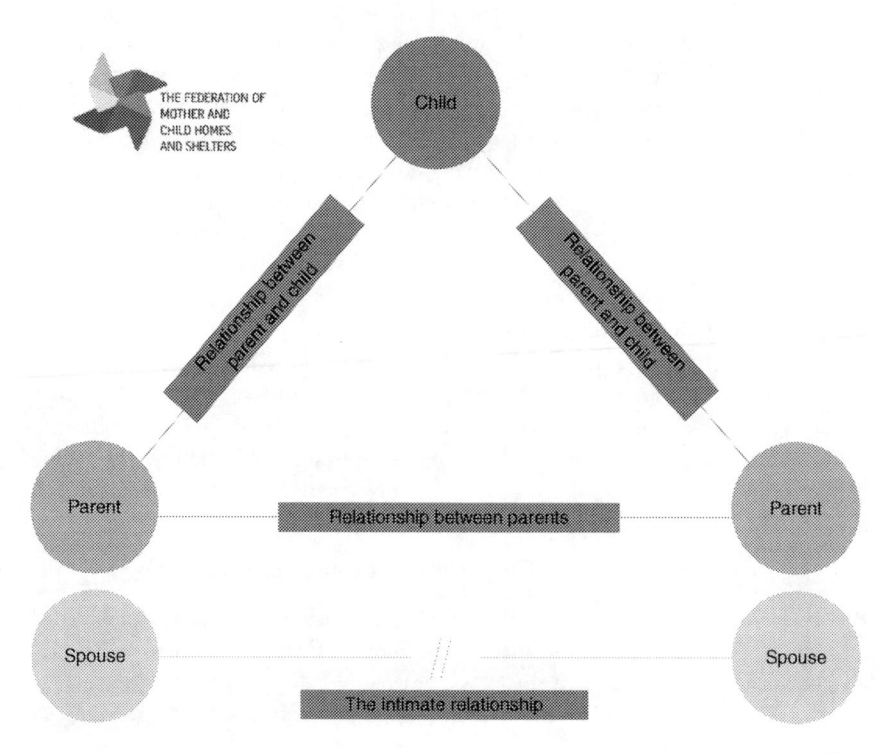

Figure 23.1 The Cooperative Parenting Triangle. A relationship can end – parenthood cannot
Source: The federation of mother and child homes and shelters

when providing information about the divorce and the position of the child between the parents. The triangle can be used as a conversation-starter and for sharing information in individual, couple and group meetings.

The triangle can aid discussions about parenting after a divorce, how parents cope with the other parent, what parents have learnt about parenting after their divorce and what is easy and what is not.

While working with a parent, you can ask about cooperative parenting and their need for support using questions like this:

- What is already working and what is not?
- What could the parent do differently?
- What does it mean for the child if the parental relationship or the parent–child relationship ends?
- Which things are good in the parental relationship at the moment?
- How have the parents shared parenting roles and responsibilities?
- What kind of relationship does each parent have with the child?
- What do the parents appreciate in each other?
- What complicates maintenance of the parent–child relationships?
- Do feelings caused by the end of the parents' intimate relationship affect their parental relationship?

The triangle helps parents to consider their own role as a parent, their relationship to the other parent and their relationship to their child. The triangle helps parents to concentrate on the child's perspective. Through conversation, the parent can be aided in understanding the child's position between the parents, and the importance of the continuity of the child's relationships with regard to the child's growth and development.

When working with parents, it is good to highlight any areas in which the parents are succeeding, along with any concerns. It is important to talk about the parental relationship and how it functions between them. Similarly, it is also important to discuss each parent's relationship with their child. Topics relating to the parent–child relationship can be discussed with the parent, as well as the ways in which a parent can promote the child's wellbeing, ensure the child is heard and create a safe growth environment for the child through their own actions.

Becoming motivated to act in an appropriate and constructive manner towards the other parent is in the best interest of the child. Encouraged by the help of a professional who is detached from the situation, parents can communicate any wishes and expectations they may have with regard to organising matters for their child. It is also good for parents to share their thoughts on what they hope for their child's future, and which things they personally consider important in the parent–child relationship.

Summary: A relationship can end but parenthood cannot

The end of an intimate relationship does not mean the end of a parental relationship. The child forms a separate relationship with each parent. These relationships have a crucial impact on the child's whole life because they are the foundation on which the child will build their self-image and self-esteem.

Maintaining both parent–child relationships and having the parents support each other's parenthood is important for the growth and development of the child. The parents have a shared responsibility for making sure the child receives proper care, nurture and parenting.

It takes a lot of effort, many discussions and flexibility for the parents to make joint custody and cooperative parenting work after a divorce. Cooperative parenting is not easy if there is a lot of tension between the parents or if the parents have great difficulty in discussing matters that concern their child.

It can be very stressful for the child, and may cause serious problems, if the parents fight over their child and find it difficult to cooperate. It is therefore vital that both parents seek help as early as possible for any cooperation problems that they cannot resolve together. The parents should be willing to learn to cooperate with each other.

Knowingly setting the child's welfare as a priority makes cooperative parenting easier. Co-parenting protects the child from the losses and negative effects of a divorce. Parents who engage in co-parenting build a cooperative relationship that is good for their child and works well in their situation. They understand the significance and value to the child of the other parent and try to support and protect this relationship within their resources.

I want to end with these words from a divorced parent whose thoughts about coparenting, after getting help, were as follows:

> Co-parenting after a divorce. It means taking care of the child, together. It means talking to each other, even though you don't always want to. It means compromise, flexibility and openness. Our main aim, as parents, is the welfare of our children. And that is something I sometimes have to remind myself of. It is trust that both parents have the same goal, and that goal is the best interest of the child. It is understanding that our marriage is over, but we must do our best, together, so that our children feel loved.

Facts about Finland

In accordance with the Child Custody and Right of Access Act, parents are jointly responsible for the duties inherent in custody. Parents must contribute towards fostering the relationship between the child and the child's other parent despite a divorce or separation. Parents may not cause detriment to the relationship between the child and the other parent. Parents must also ensure that it is possible to foster other relationships that are important to the child. Parents must consider their child's opinions and views when deciding on matters that affect the child's life.[14]

Together, parents can draw up agreements concerning the child without visiting a child welfare supervisor or obtaining a decision from a court of law. Nevertheless, matters relating to child custody, access, child support and residence are often agreed with a child welfare supervisor present. The task of the child welfare supervisor is to ensure that the agreement made by the parents is in the best interests of the child.

In 2019, a total of 45,181 agreements concerning children were confirmed by child welfare supervisors. Of these, 27,214 concerned child custody, 23,222 concerned the right of access, and 16,040 concerned the residence of the child. The most common form of custody is joint custody. Last year, 93 per cent of agreements resulted in the parents being awarded joint custody, 6 per cent awarded sole custody to the mother and 1 per cent awarded sole custody to the father.[15]

In 2019, a total of 3,300 agreements resulted in alternating residence, wherein the child resides for equal or almost equal amounts of time with both parents.[16] It must be noted, however, that in Finland a child may currently only have one official address. However, alternating residence is more common than the statistics show.[17] From 2020, parents have been able to choose alternating residence as a type of residence after a divorce, meaning that it will be even more important to compile statistics on alternating residence in the future.

Around half of marriages in Finland end in divorce. In 2019, 22,296 marriages and 13,365 divorces were registered.[18] The statistics do not show the numbers of common-law marriages and common-law divorces. Due to the high rate of divorce, and the need for support for the parents and child during a divorce, there has been a desire in both Finland's public sector and in its organisations to actively develop new kinds of divorce service. The aim is to promote parental conciliation and cooperative parenting, and to ensure a safe family life in which the rights of the child are addressed.

Notes

1 Terävä & Böök (2019) Yhteistyövanhemmuus eron jälkeen–mitä miksi miten sivut 11–19. Teoksessa Hietanen & Keinonen & Kettunen (toim.) (2019): Yhteistyövanhemmuuden käsikirja. Ensi- ja turvakotien liitto.
2 www.researchgate.net/publication/327731724_ESFR-conference_abstract_Terava_Johanna_Book_Marja_Leena_Coparenting_after_divorce.
3 Convention on the Rights of the Child, Article 12. Retrieved from www.ohchr.org/en/professionalinterest/pages/crc.aspx.
4 Kääriäinen, Aino (2008): Ero haastaa vanhemmuuden. Lastensuojelun Keskusliitto (Neuvo-projekti).
5 Kauppinen, Nina (2013): Eron jälkeinen selviytyminen ja onnistunut yhteistyö eroperheiden tarinoissa. Turku. Turun yliopisto. Lapsi- ja nuorisososiaalityön ammatillinen lisensiaattitutkimus, sivut 144–146.
Kettunen, Maarita (2019): Vanhempien kokemuksia yhteistyövanhemmuuden rakentamisesta sivut 21–29. Teoksessa Hietanen & Keinonen & Kettunen (toim.) (2019): Yhteistyövanhemmuuden käsikirja. Ensi- ja turvakotien liitto
6 Kauppinen, Nina (2013): Eron jälkeinen selviytyminen ja onnistunut yhteistyö eroperheiden tarinoissa. Turku. Turun yliopisto. Lapsi- ja nuorisososiaalityön ammatillinen lisensiaattitutkimus, sivut 144–146.
7 Kauppinen, Nina (2013): Eron jälkeinen selviytyminen ja onnistunut yhteistyö eroperheiden tarinoissa. Turku. Turun yliopisto. Lapsi- ja nuorisososiaalityön ammatillinen lisensiaattitutkimus, sivut 144–146.
8 Kauppinen, Nina (2013): Eron jälkeinen selviytyminen ja onnistunut yhteistyö eroperheiden tarinoissa. Turku. Turun yliopisto. Lapsi- ja nuorisososiaalityön ammatillinen lisensiaattitutkimus, sivut 144–146.

9 Kauppinen, Nina (2013): Eron jälkeinen selviytyminen ja onnistunut yhteistyö eroperheiden tarinoissa. Turku. Turun yliopisto. Lapsi- ja nuorisososiaalityön ammatillinen lisensiaattitutkimus, sivut 144–146.
10 Kääriäinen, Aino (2008): Ero haastaa vanhemmuuden. Lastensuojelun Keskusliitto (Neuvo-projekti).
11 Kauppinen, Nina (2013): Eron jälkeinen selviytyminen ja onnistunut yhteistyö eroperheiden tarinoissa. Turku. Turun yliopisto. Lapsi- ja nuorisososiaalityön ammatillinen lisensiaattitutkimus, sivut 144–146.
Kettunen, Maarita (2019): Vanhempien kokemuksia yhteistyövanhemmuuden rakentamisesta sivut 21–29. Teoksessa Hietanen & Keinonen & Kettunen (toim.) (2019): Yhteistyövanhemmuuden käsikirja. Ensi- ja turvakotien liitto.
12 https://issuu.com/ensi-jaturvakotienliitto/docs/etl_yhteistyovanhemmuudenkolmio_flyer_en_issuu_270.
13 Hietanen & Niininen (2019): Yhteistyövanhemmuuden kolmio työvälineenä, sivut 39–49. Teoksessa Hietanen & Keinonen & Kettunen (toim.) (2019): Yhteistyövanhemmuuden käsikirja. Ensi- ja turvakotien liitto.
14 www.finlex.fi/en/laki/kaannokset/1983/en19830361.pdf.
15 www.thl.fi/tilastoliite/tilastoraportit/2020/Liitetaulukot/Tr20_20liitetaulukot.pdf.
16 www.thl.fi/tilastoliite/tilastoraportit/2020/Liitetaulukot/Tr20_20liitetaulukot.pdf.
17 www.stat.fi/til/perh/2018/03/perh_2018_03_2019–06–17_tie_001_en.html.
18 www.stat.fi/til/ssaaty/2019/ssaaty_2019_2020–05–08_tie_001_en.html.

PART IV

Alternative dispute resolution on shared parenting and joint parenting plan

24
MANDATORY MEDIATION AND LEGAL PRESUMPTION FOR SHARED PARENTING

Hildegund Sünderhauf-Kravets

A legal presumption of shared parenting can lead to de-escalation in custody disputes after parental separation. This chapter analyses how resolution of custody disputes is connected with the success of (mandatory) mediation.

In the discussion about legal or court-ordered mandatory mediation in Europe we often refer to the positive experiences with mandatory mediation in Australia and other countries. The success of family mediation cannot be taken into consideration without regarding the legal framework about equal or non-equal parental responsibility. This chapter will use the opportunity to suggest an important consideration, which examines the interlinkage of the principle of shared parenting and the likeliness of successful mediation. Firstly, the idea of mandatory mediation will be summarised; secondly, the experiences in Australia, where the legal principle of shared parenting and mediation has been in family law since 2006, will be discussed; and finally, the application of this knowledge to the legal situation in European countries will be considered.

Mandatory mediation
Mediation is not a modern tool in alternative dispute resolution

Since even family professionals are sometimes not entirely sure of what mediation entails, it is important to consider this before addressing the specialist field of *mandatory* mediation. Mediation isn´t modern, it is based on very old human knowledge.[1] One of the oldest sources can be found in the Bible (Book of Mathew):

> 15 Moreover if thy brother shall trespass against thee, go and tell him his fault between thee and him alone: if he shall hear thee, thou hast gained thy brother.

> 16 But if he will not hear thee, then take with thee one or two more, that in the mouth of two or three witnesses every word may be established.
> 17 And if he shall neglect to hear them, tell it unto the church ...[2]

That means, in today's words, that *first* you are asked to solve problems with one another by yourself. *Second,* you may take one or two people to mediate and only if this fails, you should *third* go and tell it to the public authorities (today we would say: bring it to court).

In the 1970s and 1980s mediation become a field of social science and later of legal science. I prefer to refer to the roots of mediation theory, established in the 1980s, especially to Fisher and Ury from the Harvard Negotiation Project.[3] This is because nowadays some 'let's sit down and talk about it nicely' arrangements, are called mediation and unsurprisingly often lead to nothing. These efforts are actually nothing less than a waste of time and money for the parties involved.

Definition of mediation

Mediation is conflict regulation with the support of a neutral third party, the mediator. In family disputes family mediation is a specified field.[4] Mediation is:

- A structured process that leads participants through negotiations.
- Non-repressive assistance to solve conflicts not *for* the parties but *by* the parties themselves.
- A process in which the parties in conflict remain 100% sovereign and responsible for the solution.

Mediation is not conciliation, because the mediator will not give advice or suggest any solutions. Mediation is not arbitration, because the mediator has neither the 'last word' nor any right of decision. Mediation is not facilitation, coaching or counselling, because mediation tries to lead towards a convention and, if possible, to a contract. Mediation is not therapy, because it will not try to cure – the reasons why the conflict partners have difficulties are only interesting in a future-focused perspective; it should not be about the past. Last but not least, mediation should not be something that one goes through quickly to prepare oneself for the next legal step or for going to court – on the contrary, mediation should be the last effort to bury the hatchet.

Preconditions for successful mediation

Mediation can be a very powerful intervention and mediators are sometimes able to solve even serious conflicts. But mediation is no simple fix and there are several important preconditions:

(1) Balance of power between the parties
(2) Legal autonomy to make arrangements
(3) Neutrality of the mediator (personally, structurally and financially)

(4) Transparency of the whole process
(5) Willingness and ability of those in conflict to find a compromise
(6) Legally binding force of the result of negotiations.
(7) 'Mediation is appropriate when an impasse has been reached.'[5]

The fifth precondition implies that mediation is not appropriate in cases of *real* high conflict and not the kind of 'high conflict strategy' that is often found in family conflicts. Courts assume that high conflict is a contraindication for shared parenting as it leads to a strategy for the residential parent – mostly mothers – to create conflict as much as possible in order to prevent shared parenting arrangements.

There is also wide agreement that in cases of (proven) domestic violence and/or child abuse family mediation is not appropriate.[6] Despite this, in California, a study of difficult family mediation cases (including violence and substance abuse) concluded that these difficult cases must not be excluded but that 'these cases place numerous resource demands on family courts, increasing the need for specialized training, post-mediation investigation and evaluation, services in addition to mediation, and additional judicial officer time'.[7]

The seventh precondition above means that as long as one or both parties assume that they will win in court there is unlikely to be a willingness for compromise. This impasse can be reached after a long period of disagreement without a winner or progress. It can be set by law if there is a presumption for shared parenting. The impasse will not be reached as long as one conflict partner assumes that he or she has a gender-based advantage in court.

Voluntary versus mandatory mediation

For a long time the voluntary requirement of participants was a 'dogma'.[8] Voluntariness was set as a precondition that included the possibility to terminate the process by any party at any stage of the mediation process. For example, the German mediation law from 2012 sets voluntariness of the parties at all stages of the process not only as a precondition but as a characteristic for mediation (§§ 1 and 2 MediationsG).

In other countries and in many US states, including California, mandatory mediation before court proceedings is set by law.[9] Family mediation in Australia also overcame this precondition, for the simple reason that mandatory mediation in family conflicts works. It works because of the (good or bad but strong) personal relationship between parents and because of their love for their children. Germany also had the same discussion before family law set mandatory counselling (§ 156 I, 2, 4 FamFG) in 2009. At the time, many counsellors argued that the voluntarily participation of parents in the counselling process was already a precondition. Despite this, mandatory counselling *works* and after 2009, the counsellors changed their approach and parents had to commit, in a preliminary first step, to be willing to cooperate, to join into the process and to then continue the process in this knowledge. It is the same as in mediation: There is a chance to draw in the parents' by building on their love for their children and explaining the eight arguments in favour of parental mediation in child-related disputes.

Eight arguments in favour of mandatory mediation

There are many more individual arguments supporting mandatory mediation in childcare and custody disputes between parents, but those below are evident in almost every case:

(1) *Take responsibility*: Parents must accept their responsibility. They are the experts on their children and it is important that they have the confidence to take responsibility rather than handing this over to a judge who will not know them or their children.

(2) *Communicate*: Most parents do not have legal problems, but socio-emotional problems and difficulties in communication. Mediation can help to create better communication; something that legal proceedings do not do.

(3) *Recognise that win–win options are possible*: In a court case there will probably be a winner and a loser. One of the parents will lose – let the parents consider for a moment that they are the losing parent. How would they feel? How would their relationship with the other parent develop after this decision? How would this affect their relationship with their children? Would they be able to sit next to each other on their children's wedding days or would one parent be abandoned forever? In mediation, parents have the opportunity to find fair regulations that create two winners (or more, if you include the children).

(4) *Remove the lawyers' shackles*: Lawyers may increase the conflict rather than reduce it. Since there are no legal questions at the centre of the conflict, lawyers are probably not needed in the child-related process at all. This would save the parents money and avoid frustration.

(5) *Avoid escalation*: No one wants to end in a custody-battle burnout.[10] De-escalation is also linked with the non-involvement of lawyers.

(6) *Bury the hatchet*: Negotiated arrangements have a higher acceptance and remain more sustainable than court decisions do. After court decisions, the losing parent may go on to seek further opportunities for revenge.

(7) *Provide a positive model*: Children learn from role models. Parents can show their children a positive example of how to resolve disputes in a fair way. Mediation can be a relief not only for parents but also their children.

(8) *Avoid courts*: Mandatory mediation not only reduces the impact of parental disputes on the justice process but can also be faster and cheaper for parents.

Using the arguments above, the mediator must ensure that the parents participate and commit to the process; they can then follow their agenda.

Of course, there will be parents who cannot be part of a mediation process and who are unable to share parenthood after separation. However, one should not let them get away too easily with the argument 'I can't', if the true reason is 'I don't want to'. In a case where a parent or the parents really 'can't', it may be necessary to investigate the parents' psychological states and whether they are able to care for their children at all.[11]

Best alternatives to a negotiated agreement (BATNA)

To evaluate their own situation, parties should know their '*best alternatives to a negotiated agreement*'. The so-called BATNAs are part of the mediation theory of Fisher and Ury[12] from the Harvard Negotiation Project, founded in the early 1980s. If one party assumes that they will win in court, winning, respectively, power and money (that means power over the children, power over the ex-partner and receiving or paying child support), the likelihood of success with mediation is very low. This implies that the legal, social and individual situations of the parties have significant relevance to the possible outcome in the mediation process. Frankly, as long as mothers assume that they will win in court – because of gender; because of the widespread belief that children belong to their mothers more than to their fathers; because of the dogma that continuity in child custody is more important than continuity in parent–child relations – as long as mothers have these advantages, from their perspective there is no reason for negotiating in mediation. They can fight and in most cases they will win. To put it differently: as long as there is no gender equality in courts and no legal presumption of shared parenting in the law, the BATNAs do not support mediation. This is sad for the parents, because mediation has many advantages compared with legal proceedings and this is also the reason why a legal presumption of shared parenting and mandatory mediation belonging together is so important.

Mandatory mediation in Australia

The following sections explain the Australian procedure for resolving family conflict and the work of family relationship centres (FRC) in connection with the 2006 family law reform, which introduced the legal presumption of shared parenting.

Australian family law reform, 2006

The 2006 family law reform in Australia had two interlinked aspects:

(1) *Shared parenting* as a rebuttable presumption in law, as to be usually in the best interest of the child.
(2) *Mandatory mediation*, which means that people are not allowed to claim in family courts without trying to resolve the dispute in mediation beforehand.

The government founded 65 family relationship centres (FRCs) throughout the country as local low-threshold services (where lawyers, psychologists and social workers work in teams).

Work of family relationship centres

The FRCs offer counselling related to separation and divorce, family dispute, parent–child contact, work with grandparents and difficulties in couples' relationships.

Figure 24.1 shows the mediation process offered by FRCs:

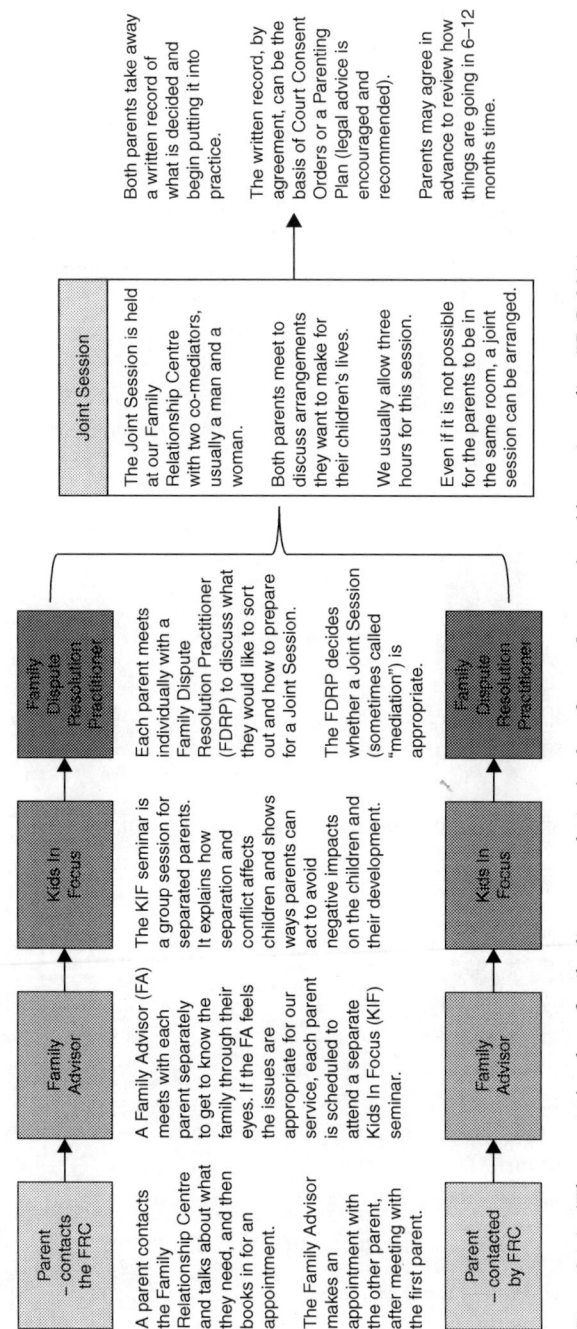

Figure 24.1 'The parents' path to family dispute resolution', taken from a flyer produced by an Australian FRC, 2014

(1) One parent (or both) contacts the FRC.
(2) The family advisor talks to both parents (separately).
(3) Both parents get sent on a 'kids in focus' parenting course.
(4) Both parents talk, on another occasion, to the family dispute resolution practitioner (mediator) and he or she decides whether a joint session is appropriate.
(5) The mediation session takes place, usually as co-mediation (with a male and a female mediator) for up to three hours.
(6) At the end of the session, the parents receive a written record of the results and put them into practice.

Changes in society and the judicial system after 2006

After only a few years there were 32% fewer child-related court proceedings in Australia compared with the time before the law reform. We can find a high acceptance of FRCs in Australian society and also a high social acceptance of shared parenting in general. The number of shared parenting arrangements increased all over the country.[13] The legal presumption for shared parenting is the 'conditio sine qua non' for the rising success of mandatory mediation – particularly in high conflict separation and divorce. Under the well-known childcare models for separated families – in which mostly mothers care for children and fathers pay child support and have occasional visits – mandatory mediation by law (or court-ordered mandatory mediation) will probably not change anything and there will be no de-escalation by mediation.

Legal situation in Europe
Still quite behind

Almost all countries in Europe recognise shared *legal* custody after divorce. Some countries – but not all – have explicit legal regulations for shared parenting. But only a small number of countries have a legal presumption for shared *physical* custody, named shared parenting (Belgium for example). In almost all countries courts still grant physical custody to mothers and visiting times to fathers, instead seeking shared parenting arrangements. Most European countries are unaware of mandatory mediation and only a few recognise voluntary mediation in child-related family disputes.

Council of Europe Resolution no. 2079

In October 2015, the Council of Europe set resolution no. 2079: 'Equality and shared parental responsibility: The role of fathers'.[14] In point 5.5, 'the Assembly calls on Member States to:

- Introduce into their laws the *principle of shared residence* following a separation,
- limiting any exceptions to cases of child abuse or neglect, or domestic violence,

- with the amount of time for which the child lives with each parent being adjusted according to the child's needs and interests ...'

In point 5.9, the Assembly calls on Member States to:

- Encourage and, where appropriate, develop *mediation* within the framework of judicial proceedings in family cases involving children,
- in particular by instituting a court-ordered mandatory information session, in order to make the parents aware that *shared residence* may be an appropriate option in the best interests of the child, and to work towards such a solution,
- by ensuring that mediators receive appropriate training and
- by encouraging multidisciplinary co-operation based on the 'Cochem model'.

It is by purpose rather than accident that the legal presumption for shared parenting and the development of mediation are linked together in the Council of Europe's resolution, because of the interlinkage shown above.

The resolution has lighted the discussion about shared parenting in all countries, but the national legislation is slow and often favours the concerns of particular parties. Unfortunately, the issue of shared parenting is not a particular 'women against men' or 'men against women' concern and nor is shared parenting especially a conservative, liberal or left-wing theme and thus no political party hopes to attract votes on the basis of their approach to this subject. All parties in the discussion are using the 'best interest of the child' argument for their own purposes (and sometimes hide behind it to disguise the real issues of power (over the child and over the ex-partner) and money (especially child support, but also government grants for single parents)). The arguments are sometimes quite amazing, because international scientific psychological studies over three decades have significantly shown that shared parenting – in general – is better for children after parental separation than single parenting.[15]

The European Court of Human Rights (ECtHR) has been expected for many years to make a judgement about the refusal of shared physical custody in several countries on the basis of their possible violation of Article 8 of the European Convention on Human Rights (the right to respect for private and family life); unfortunately, it maintains silence for now.

Conclusion

This chapter reaches the following conclusions:

(1) Under a legal principle of shared parenting, the opportunity to find a shared parenting solution by mediation is much higher than without it.
(2) Mandatory mediation makes no sense if one parent is much more likely (for example, on the basis of gender) to win single physical custody in court than the other.
(3) The best alternatives to negotiated agreements (BATNA) theory clarifies why the legal principle of shared parenting and mandatory mediation are linked together.

(4) Australian experiences prove that a law reform can make a change in society and reduce court proceedings.
(5) Australian experiences also prove that a law reform can reduce the number of court proceedings.
(6) To fulfil the demands of the Council of Europe resolution no. 2079 (2015), European countries need to modify their family law to promote shared parenting and mediation rather than pursuing court orders granting single custody.
(7) A judgement of the ECHR is expected to acknowledge an injury to the right to respect for private and family life (Article 8 of the European Convention on Human Rights) by refusal of the principle of shared parenting by national law and the judicial system.

Notes

1 Wendland, M. (2017). Von Aristoteles über Kohlbergs Stufenlehre zum Harvard-Modell–Zur rechtsphilosophischen Begründung des Mediationsverfahrens. [From Aristotle to Kohlberg's stages of moral development to the Harvard model: The justification of the mediation process in the philosophy of law]. In K. Kriegel-Schmidt (ed.), *Mediation als Wissenschaftszweig. Im Spannungsfeld von Fachexpertise und Interdisziplinarität.* Wiesbaden: SpringerVS, pp. 131–137.
2 The King James Bible, Gospel of Matthew (18:15–17), with reference to the Torah (Deuteronomy 19:15).
3 Fisher R. & Ury, W. (1981). *Getting to yes: Negotiating an agreement without giving in.* New York, Penguin (2012 edition co-authored with B. Patton).
4 Folberg, J., Milne, A. & Salem, P. (2004). *Divorce and family mediation.* New York: Guilford Press.
5 Cormick, G. & Patton, L. (1980). Environmental mediation: Defining the process through experience. In L. M. Laked (ed.), *Environmental mediation: The search for consensus.* Boulder, CO: Westview Press, pp. 76–85.
6 CFCC (11/2002), Domestic violence in court-based child-custody mediation cases in San Francisco, California. Retrieved from www.courts.ca.gov/documents/resupDV99.pdf [25.09.2020]
7 CFCC (03/2003), Difficult cases in California court-based child custody mediation, p. 8. Retrieved from www.courts.ca.gov/documents/resupDiffCases99.pdf?1512086400040
8 Marx, A. (2017). Obligatorische Mediation und das Prinzip der Freiwilligkeit–eine rechtsvergleichende Studie Deutschland–USA [Mandatory mediation and the principle of voluntariness: A comparative study of German and US law]. In K. Kriegel-Schmidt (ed.), *Mediation als Wissenschaftszweig im Spannungsfeld von Fachexpertise und Interdisziplinarität.* Wiesbaden: SpringerVS, p. 449–459; Nelle, A. & Hacke, A. (2001): Obligatorische Mediation: Selbstwiderspruch oder Reforminstrument? [Mandatory mediation: Antagonism or instrument for reformation?] *Zeitschrift für Konfliktmanagement (ZKM),* 2, p. 56 ff.
9 See Marx (2017).
10 Turkat, I. D. (2000). Custody battle burnout. *American Journal of Family Therapy,* 28, pp. 201–215.
11 Turkat, I. D. (2002). Shared parenting dysfunction. *American Journal of Family Therapy,* 30, pp. 385–393.
12 See Fisher and Ury (1981).
13 Parkinson, P. (2008). Keeping in contact: The role of family relationship centers in Australia. *Child & Family Law Quarterly,* 18(2), pp. 157–174; Parkinson, P. (2013). The idea of family relationship centers in Australia. *Family Court Review,* 51(2), pp. 195–213; Moloney, L., Qu,

L., Weston, R. & Hand, K. (2013). Evaluating the work of Australia's family relationship centers: Evidence from the first 5 years. *Family Court Review*, 51, pp. 234–249.

14 Council of Europe (2015). Resolution no. 2079: Equality and shared parental responsibility: The role of fathers. Retrieved from http://assembly.coe.int/nw/xml/XRef/Xref-XML2HTML-EN.asp?fileid=22220.

15 Sünderhauf, H. (2013). *Wechselmodell: Psychologie, Recht, Praxis* [*Shared parenting: Psychology, law, practice*]. Wiesbaden: Springer VS; Nielsen, L. (2020). Joint versus sole physical custody: Which is best for children? *Journal of the American Academy of Matrimonial Lawyers*, 28, pp. 79–139.

25
PARENTING COORDINATION AS AN ALTERNATIVE DISPUTE RESOLUTION SYSTEM IN SPANISH FAMILY LAW

Yolanda De Lucchi López-Tapia

High-conflict family breakdowns: Realities and costs

There is a proven yearly increase in the breakdown of marriages or common-law marriages in which minors or older children with disabilities are involved. Although there is a higher percentage of consensual separations than contentious ones, conflicts persist in a considerable number of cases, especially just after separation, when it comes to enforcing the measures dictated by the court. Despite the existence of a judgment regulating the relationship between parents and children in a separation, the conflict between the parents does not disappear. Instead, it is exacerbated to the point where even petty issues are discussed in courts and endless claims or writs are filed daily; in short, judicializing conflicts. These cases, known as high-conflict post-separation cases, have an extremely negative impact on children.

Furthermore, these conflicts often lack any legal basis. Parents frequently disagree over matters relating to their children's schooling, such as challenging an unauthorized change of school, or over matters related to extra expenses, such as questioning whether a child's orthodontic treatment is really necessary. As regards education, they may not agree on, for instance, the child's need to learn Chinese, or regarding family celebrations there may be disagreement regarding where their child's first communion should be held. These extrajudicial issues must be decided by a judge who is unaware of the family's situation, who does not live with the minor and who has no knowledge of the realities behind the problem. It is well known that conflicts in family law have very different characteristics compared to other legal disputes, since, in this case, the emotional component is extremely high. Therefore, it is much more difficult to obtain a satisfactory and lasting solution for those involved.

For this reason, high-conflict family separations that persist over time, generate elevated social costs. On the one hand, there is an overload in the courts, both in first instance and family courts, as well as those dealing with violence against women. These courts are mired in countless requests to deal with issues regarding the execution of judgments, modifications of measures or voluntary proceedings caused by disagreements over the exercise of parental authority, which place families in an endless cycle of legal disputes.[1]

On the other hand, minors are those who suffer most in the escalation of conflict, as they are involved in constant disputes between their parents and, in many cases, feel coerced into choosing one or the other; in short, they are forced to grow up in a permanently hostile environment, which affects their psycho-evolutionary development.

Inefficiency in the Spanish judicial management of post-separation conflicts

In family matters, the Spanish judicial system has been found to be highly inadequate and ineffective. At the initial stage of the family conflict, when the court is called upon to process the separation or divorce proceedings or deal with the minors involved, the characteristics of these proceedings are based on a contradictory structure, where there is a plaintiff and a defendant, someone who asks and someone who receives,[2] and do not encourage comprehensive management of the conflict. Even though the court has the power to decide ex officio on most matters, certain issues that are important to resolving the conflict may not be dealt with.

Nevertheless, despite the special consideration of these proceedings as instruments of appeasement of family conflicts and not as strictly confrontational,[3] the reality is that the judge must decide on the main criteria for the organization of a family without knowing its structure and without the necessary skills to evaluate the different family dynamics prior to the marital separation.

In a post-separation phase, when the family regime has been established in a court ruling, the procedural enforcement mechanism is used to report a breach of the regime. The enforcement of rulings delivered in family trials is subject to special rules set forth in Article 776 of the LEC (Spanish Civil Procedure Act). However, it is in fact a rather ineffective channel in practice because the procedural rules are not well-designed for this type of conflict. Bringing a claim for enforcement and the subsequent request for compliance always leads to cases of opposition to its enforcement that ends with a court order imposing either coercive fines to force compliance with pecuniary or personal obligations, or the initiation of criminal proceedings for the crime of disobedience to authority, or the modification of visiting arrangements.[4] In all these cases, the procedural mechanisms only exacerbate the conflict between the parents.[5]

The provisions of Article 776 regarding these types of obligation are twofold: paragraph 2 establishes the possibility of extending periodic penalty payments that require compliance with the obligation beyond one year, which is the general rule provided for in Article 709 of the LEC, while paragraph 3 provides for the possibility of sanctioning the non-compliant parent with new custody and visiting arrangements.

The LEC does not foresee how long the imposition of these coercive fines should last in the first case, which, while they are being used to force the parent to fulfil their obligations, are inexorably lengthening the default in the breach.[6] Moreover, this is not about a delay in the payment of debts, but rather the delay in maintaining the personal and emotional ties between the parent and child – ties that lead to adequate and satisfactory management of the conflict. Indeed, the longer it takes to re-establish the visiting arrangements, the harder it will be to restore a healthy relationship between the parent and child.

The second measure provided for Article. 776.3 of the LEC, changes to custody and visiting arrangements,is also ineffective because it is conceived as a punishment to the non-compliant parent. This should be a restrictive measure, since it should not be forgotten that what must prevail is the principle of the best interest of the minor, which may be difficult to reconcile with a restrictive change in the custody and visiting arrangements.[7]

In addition to the intrinsic difficulty of the two measures fulfilling the general objective of normalizing family relationships after the separation, there is the purely procedural obstacle, when the judgment is enforced, of articulating a true declaratory incident in which the reality of the breaches can be proven. This is because the reasons for opposition, as we have previously established, are legally restricted and only the court can allow the application of a relatively broad criterion. In most cases, this means that the solution for the incident does not involve understanding the reality of the problem, but only verifying non-compliance with the judgment.

However, on top of the fact that the procedural mechanism is not ideal for processing a conflict management system, the main difficulty lies in the very nature of the conflicts and in the role that the judge must play in this phase of the family breakdown.

If the judge continues to have absolute power in resolving a conflict, a conflict about which he does not know the grounds and realities, the resolution – which is not a solution – of the first conflict will give way to successive conflicts derived from an imposed decision. This only leads parents to believe that the wrong solution to all their disagreements is the result of the decision of the judge who issued the initial ruling that established the measures governing their current post-separation situation with their children.

It is thus necessary to change the role of the judge, who, as the holder of jurisdictional power, manages the post-separation phase. However, the judge's role should be to supervise the reorganization of family life, using other means of support that may be more effective for the adequate management of the conflicts that originate in this phase. This will be focused on in the following sections.

Faced with the search for legal instruments that can facilitate the management of these post-separation disputes, mediation – due to its more generalized use and its legal regulation – is the first alternative dispute resolution method proposed as an alternative. Mediation in the context of family law was established decades ago as a useful tool in conflict management because it addresses the emotional aspects of a dispute. However, although mediation has proven to be relatively effective in the initial phases of conflict, when the family process has not yet started or once it has begun but a judgment has not yet been handed down, its effectiveness declines sharply when it comes to resolving post-separation conflicts.

This is because mediation should be based essentially on the willingness of the parties to follow a procedure that aims to reach an agreement between them. In post-separation disputes, the starting point is a highly conflictive situation in which the voluntariness component disappears and means that the opposing parties reject mediation.[8] Indeed, the voluntariness component in mediation is already being rethought as an element in its own right[9] and in some European countries the trend has even been reversed and coercive measures are being taken to make couples engage in mediation. However, we must remember that the goal of mediation is to reach an agreement,[10] which by its very nature implies that we cannot force the parties to do so. Moreover, mitigated obligation, that is, the mandatory, informative and exploratory initial session contained in the forthcoming new mediation regulation, is something that family courts have been doing for a long time and that is not proving to be more effective than totally voluntary mediation.

Considering all these factors, it can be seen that, in relation to enforcing judgments, mediation is not the most useful tool. Therefore, it is necessary to resort to other more effective instruments in which the element of voluntariness of the parties is not decisive in the choice of method.

Parenting coordination as a tool to help manage post-separation disputes in Spain

The parenting plan

The divorce agreement is the document produced by the mutual agreement of parents that the LEC (Article 777) and the CC (Civil Code, Articles 81, 82, 83, 86 and 87) require to be submitted in family proceedings by mutual agreement and that the judge must approve, unless they are harmful to the children or seriously harmful to one of the spouses (Article 90.2 CC). In contentious proceedings, although the submission of a divorce agreement with the claim is not required, the parent who files it must include the measures that he or she wishes the judge to adopt, without prejudice to the judge's power to rule ex officio on specific measures contained in Article 91 of the CC.

Prima facie, the divorce agreement is useful for the regulation of the new family structure after the separation, but is insufficient since the minimum content established in Article 90 is not enough to provide for all possible contingencies of the future "family".[11] Hence, despite having issued a judgment that includes the divorce agreement proposed by the parties or the measures the judge has deemed appropriate, it is highly probable that numerous disputes may arise later about situations not contemplated in the agreement itself or in the judgment that includes the measures. Moreover, this implies that before a new conflict arises the parents must go to court to let the judge decide on the matter through any of the previously established channels.

To reduce post-separation conflict, Law 25/2010, of 29 July, of the second book of the Civil Code of Catalonia on individuals and families, has incorporated the obligation to file a parenting plan together with the claim in family proceedings and within the divorce agreement (Article 233–2. 4 a). The parenting plan is a document that specifies the way in which both parents plan to exercise their parental responsibilities. It must specify the commitments they make regarding the custody, care and education of their children. The plan helps parents responsibly organize for themselves the care of their children after the separation and anticipates the criteria for solving the most important problems that affect them. Consequently, when conflicts arise and need to be settled by the judge, the judge can follow the guidelines established in the parenting plan. Thus, Article 233–9, 2 of the Civil Code of Catalonia specifies the content of the plan as follows:

(a) The place or places where the children will normally live. This must include rules determining, at all times, which parent has custody.
(b) The tasks for which each parent must take responsibility regarding the children's daily activities.
(c) The way in which changes to custody should be made and, if applicable, how the costs incurred should be shared.
(d) The arrangements regarding the relationship and communication with the children when a parent is not with them.
(e) The arrangements regarding the stays with each parent during vacation periods and on dates especially important for the children, their parents or family.

Submitting a parenting plans has two great benefits over submitting only a divorce agreement:

- It reduces the possibility of post-separation conflict, insofar as it regulates in detail the possible areas of friction that may arise.
- It allows for anticipating the criteria for the resolution of subsequent disputes when, despite the implementation of a parenting plan, discrepancies arise in the exercise of parental authority.

These two benefits provide a general and primary benefit – the emotional stability of minors and their parents – because they experience less turmoil caused by the eternal conflicts that arise after the break-up.

Parenting coordination as part of the parenting plan

Within the context of the so-called parenting plan, the parenting coordination method also emerges.

Although implementing a parenting plan undoubtedly improves the management of post-separation disputes, in a number of cases supervision of the plan is needed; that is, the therapeutic intervention of an expert who advises, recommends, determines and, in some cases, decides on the undertaking of the parenting plan by the parents. Until now, this supervision has been entrusted to the so-called family meeting points. However, based on the experience of other countries, parenting coordination has recently been introduced in Spain[12] as an "alternative dispute resolution process in which an independent expert helps parents in serious difficulties following their separation or divorce process to implement their parenting plan and to reduce conflict for the benefit of minors".[13]

The implementation of this new role is at a relatively advanced stage and there are already numerous judgments that have ruled on the need for a parenting coordinator. Moreover, the Spanish State and the Autonomous Communities are thinking of applying pilot plans to help in said implementation. However, the fact is that, from a strictly procedural point of view, there are no defined rules that protect parenting coordination, so it may be somewhat dangerous to implement it jurisprudentially.[14] Indeed, the definitions considered for the role of parenting coordinator do not actually establish who this person is and what he or she should do.

Despite that fact that it is not legally part of our civil or procedural legislation (since it is something new in our legal system), the flexibility provided by the rules regulating family law[15] has allowed judicial use of this instrument.[16]

The starting premise when analyzing this emerging role should be that use of the parenting coordination service is not a resource that should be considered as the norm in a family process.[17] It should not be forgotten that the exercise of responsible parenting is the most efficient approach to conflict resolution, and indiscriminate use of parenting coordination services could make parents feel they do not need to assume as much responsibility for managing their family situation. Therefore, the parenting coordinator cannot replace the parents' sense of responsibility because this would achieve a totally pernicious effect. Hence, parenting coordination should be used only in potentially extreme cases,[18] including cases of domestic violence where mediation is prohibited, as provided for in Article 87.5 LOPJ (Organic Law of the Judiciary), when the police risk assessment is non-existent.

The functions of the parenting coordinator are very diverse and can be summarized as follows:

- Interview parents, minors, family members, teachers and psychiatrists or psychologists who care for parents and/or children.
- Assessment of the situation of the minor and his/her family.
- Advise and agree with parents on the appropriate measures to take (schedules, guidelines, and conditions for the normalization of the parent–child relationship).
- Provide professional opinions about the minor and his/her family.
- Inform the court about the agreements the parties have reached as a result of the intervention. In the case of disagreements, make suggestions to the judge about the personal relationships or living arrangements of the minors with the parents that the coordinator considers appropriate.

Procedural issues relating to the implementation of parenting coordination

Apart from the action of the parenting coordinator from a family therapy point of view, from a strictly procedural perspective the functions of the parenting coordinator are not agreed upon at jurisprudential level; that is, how far the parenting coordinator can go to achieve the aforementioned goals of preventing the conflict reaching court and achieving the best solution possible.

Initially, the TSJ (Supreme Court) of Catalonia, in its previously mentioned Judgment 11/2015, limits said intervention to a merely advisory function of the court, that is:

> informing the Court on the agreements reached by the parties with the coordinator's intervention or making proposals that are deemed appropriate regarding the personal relationship or visiting arrangements of the minor with the corresponding parent, so that the Judge can decide appropriately in case of disagreement.

However, some subsequent resolutions of the hearings consider that the coordinator can make binding decisions for the family in specific cases.[19] From the point of view of comparative law, the role of the parenting coordinator exceeds the mere advice of the judge and becomes a decision-making figure in family conflicts, taking as reference the terms and conditions established in the judgment.[20] In the Spanish legal system, determining that the parenting coordinator can make binding decisions for the parties directly affects the principle of exclusivity of the jurisdictional function set forth in Article 117 of the Spanish Constitution. Certainly, it could be conceived as a kind of arbitration in family law matters[21] but to reach this status a legal reform is necessary as it is not enough to have mere legal support for the role. Let us not forget that most matters in family law are not decided according to the will of individuals.

The legal nature of the parenting coordinator role will vary according to the functions assigned to that person. If we are dealing with a professional who, evaluating the needs of the family, provides information and opinions based on their specialized knowledge, in such a way that the judge can assess these opinions and take them into account when making the relevant decisions, the parenting coordinator is a judicial expert – who could even be called upon at the request of one of the parties. However, the role of the parenting coordinator is not limited to providing their specialist opinion in a passive manner; rather, as the previously mentioned Judgment of the High Court of Justice of Catalonia establishes in ruling 11/2015, it can be described as "dynamic action in the execution of a judgement".

If this is the legal nature of the parenting coordinator, another issue would be to determine if this role should be fulfilled by a member of the psychosocial team affiliated to the courts or by a different person, usually a psychologist from the official psychology association who works for the courts as a legal expert. Thus, if the functions of the parenting coordinator exceed those of an expert and cover issues such as decision-making, we are dealing with a figure with a different legal nature. In this case, we would then be speaking of an assistant to the judge in the exercise of jurisdictional power, assisting in the effective implementation of the measures agreed by the judge, with powers to manage the conflict, mediate andredirect the family towards the normalization of the new situation in a peaceful climate that allows the family to accept, within a reasonable time, the new guidelines and be able to self-manage them.

In addition to these issues, there are questions regarding the practical implementation of the role. How is the parenting coordinator appointed? Can the decisions made by the parenting coordinator be "appealed"? What can be done in cases of non-compliance with the decisions made by the parenting coordinator? How long does the intervention of the parenting coordinator last? Who will bear the cost of the parenting coordination?

These are issues that need to be clarified if the role of the parental coordinator is here to stay.

Notes

1 It is estimated that these legal disputes, which represent only 10 percent of families, use 90 percent of judicial resources.
2 As stated by Lauroba Lacasa, E., "The forum does not seem an optimal space to manage family conflicts. Furthermore, not even those who benefit from a family process obtain a high level of satisfaction," in Instrumentos para una gestión constructiva de los conflictos familiares: mediación, derecho colaborativo, arbitraje ¿y…? *Indret Persona y Familia* [*Review on the Analysis of Law*] 4, 2018, p. 5.
3 As stated by the Judgment of the High Court of Justice of Catalonia (STSJ) 11/2015, of 26 February (TOL 4,777,692).
4 The jurisprudence of the ECHR has been forceful when it comes to demanding compliance with Article 8 of the ECHR, which recognizes the right to respect private and family life; and, therefore, respects the right to have real and effective contact with minor children. Vid SSTEDH, of 15 January 2015, rec. n° 62198/11, in *Kuppinger* vs. *Germany*, and SSTEDH, of 17 February 2016, rec. n° 35532/12, in *Bondevalli* vs. *Italy*. In both cases, the United States was sentenced because the actions of its national courts have not guaranteed the right of parents to have effective and real contact with them.
5 As stated by Ortuño Muñoz, the request is often an invitation for the other party to make imputations to the executing party, as in a game of "ping pong". This may create a conflict that leads nowhere. See Ortuño Muñoz, Pascual, "La alta conflictividad en las relaciones paterno o materno-filiales en la ejecución de los procesos de familia". Review in Boletín Violencia de Género. Jueces para la Democracia. February 2019. Retrieved from https://docplayer.es/127309813-Boletin-comision-de-violencia-de-genero-prevencion-de-la-violencia-de-genero-en-las-crisis-de-pareja-coordinador-a-de-parentalidad-editorial.html.
"La alta conflictividad en las relaciones paterno o materno-filiales en la ejecución de los procesos de familia". *Boletín Violencia de Género. Jueces para la Democracia*. February 2019.
6 Ortuño Muñoz, *op. cit.*, p. 3.
7 In this respect, the jurisprudence of the ECHR is categorical, condemning the countries that do not adequately guarantee the right of parents to maintain contact with their minor children, as required by Article 8 of the ECHR, which recognizes the right to respect private and family life. See, for example, STEDH, of 15 January 2015, rec. No. 62198/11, in *Kuppinger* v. *Germany*, and STEDH, of 17 February 2016, rec. n° 35532/12, in *Bondevalli* v. *Italy*. In both cases, countries are condemned because the actions of their national courts have not guaranteed the right of parents to have effective and real contact with their children.
8 As established by Abril Pérez del Campo, C. "the non-directive emphasis of the intervention, in which mediation transfers decision-making capacity over agreements exclusively to individuals who have been in deep conflict for a long time, makes it difficult to contain the mediator's conflict and sometimes generates agreements that have more to do with the emotional response of one of the parents to the breakdown than with real alternative

solutions to the family problem raised", in Parenting coordination. *Jueces para la Democracia [Gender Violence Newsletter]*, February 2019, p. 2.
9 On 11 January 2020, the Council of Ministers approved the Draft Law to Promote Mediation, which establishes the obligation to try a mediation process before going to court in certain types of trial, among which are family trials. Faced with the current mediation model based on its exclusively voluntary nature, the aim is to establish a "mitigated obligation", in the sense that it would be mandatory for the parties to attend an informative mediation session and an exploratory session attempting to resolve the conflict – that may require only one action – and that would occur in the six months prior to the filing of the demand. It does not therefore imply an obligation to undergo a mediation proceeding – that would be contrary to the principle of voluntariness that mediation inspires – but to have been informed of its existence and advantages.
10 Also questioned by Lauroba, p. 12.
11 Article 90 of the Spanish Civil Code establishes the following points as minimum content of the regulatory agreement:

(a) The care of the children subject to the parental authority of both, the exercise of this and, where appropriate, the communication and visiting arrangements of the children with the parent who does not normally live with them.
(b) If it is considered necessary, the visiting and communication arrangements of the grandchildren with their grandparents, always considering their interest.
(c) The allocation of the use of the family home and items.
(d) The contribution to the marriage and maintenance expenses, as well as the bases of updating and guaranteeing them when applicable.
(e) The settlement, when appropriate, of the financial arrangements for the marriage.
(f) The alimony that according to Article 97 is to be paid, where appropriate, to one of the spouses.

12 This figure was first implemented in Canada and the US, from where it has been "imported" into our legal system. *Vid.* D´Abate, D. Parenting coordinator: A new service for high conflict divorcing families. *Intervención OPTSQ* 122, 2005, pp. 1–9.
13 García-Herrera, A. Reestructuración de la familia tras la separación parental: mediación intrajudicial, mediación en el punto de encuentro familiar y coordinación de parentalidad. *InDret [Review on the Analysis of Law]* 2/2016, p. 17.
14 This concern is also expressed by Garcia-Herrera, A. *op.cit.*, p. 24 and Lauroba, E. *op. cit.*, p. 35.
15 The legal framework is broad, always from a general point of view, bearing in mind that there is no precept that defines and establishes the functions that the parental coordination is called on to develop: Universal Convention of the Rights of the Child (arts. 3.1 and 4); 1996 European Convention on the Rights of the Child [art. 6 a)]; Spanish Constitution (art. 39); European Regulation 2201/2003 and Hague Conventions of 1980 and 1996; Civil Code, Organic Law 1/1996, of 15 January, on the Legal Protection of Minors, as amended by the Civil Code and the Civil Procedure Law, which introduced art. 158 CC, Law 14/2010, of 27 May, on the Rights and Opportunities of Children and Adolescents (arts. 38, 39, 81 and 116.3).
16 As established by the STSJ Catalonia 1/2017, of 12 January:

The various laws, both civil substantive … and procedural … are giving judges a wide margin of action ex officio when it comes to taking measures to prevent harm to minors, or to know the real family situation, allowing them to take the most appropriate decisions, based on the best interests of the minor, which must always prevail.

17 Vid SAP Barcelona 71/2018, of 1 February.
18 Ortuño Muñoz, *op. cit.*, p. 7.

19 AAP Barcelona 549/2018, of 5 October; AAP Barcelona 102/2019, 3 May.
20 American Psychological Association. 2012. Guidelines for the practice of parenting coordination de APA. *American Psychologist* 67(1), pp. 63–71.
21 Something that is beginning to be implemented in foreign legal systems. See the study by Lauroba Lacasa, E. *op. cit.*, p. 41 et seq.

26
PIFE – AN INTERVENTION AIMED AT RESTORING THE PARENT–CHILD BOND RUPTURED BY ACUTE SEPARATION CONFLICT OR PARENTAL ALIENATION

Celia Lillo

Introduction

Developed over the past five years in Montreal and inspired by a model of collaborative expertise,[1] the PIFE (Processus d'Intervention Familiale Encadrée) intervention has proven its worth. It is increasingly requested by lawyers representing clients in conflictual divorce disputes in the Superior Court, District of Montreal, Family Division, and by Youth Protection workers applying judicial measures issued by the Court of Quebec, Youth Division (in situations of 'psychological ill treatment' related to the exposure of the child to an acute separation conflict).

The PIFE is a supervised family intervention process that exists and functions within a psycho-judicial framework. It involves a specific type of professional collaboration between a psychologist, lawyers, and a judge, as suggested by some clinicians and researchers specializing in this field.[2]

The PIFE uses language describing the 'risk of a break in the parent–child bond' rather than 'parental alienation'. The process aims to be as unpolarizing as possible by avoiding references to one parent as alienated and the other alienating, speaking instead of a parent who has remained 'closer' and a parent who has been left out or 'distanced'.

The re-establishment of the parent–child relationship within a set timeframe or a given custodial arrangement is not held as a predetermined objective in the PIFE. However, a successful process may result in a renewed parental shared custody arrangement for children who had previously cut all contact with one of the parents.

Clinical cases involving parental alienation formed the basis for my presentation on 'Parental alienation/shared custody: Challenge or ideal solution' at the International Scientific Conference on Best Interest of Child and Shared Parenting, 2–3 December 2019 in Malaga, Spain. Based on results obtained in applying the PIFE in these cases, I was able to show that it is possible to achieve shared custody at the end of a process of restoring the parent–child relationship when conditions outlined in the PIFE are met.[3]

This chapter presents the key principles guiding the PIFE supervised family intervention process[4], and outlines a two-phase path to applying the PIFE's protocol:

1. *Preliminary phase*: consent to a PIFE intervention mandate is granted by all parties and ratified by the Court; an *evaluation* is made to determine if conditions are met for an intervention process to begin.
2. *Intervention phase*: restoring the parent–child relationship, from the first reconnection meeting at the psychologist's office to the first overnight stays with the 'distanced' parent.

We will conclude with observations and findings of PIFE protocol applications from our clinical practice over the past five years in Montréal, Canada.

Key principles guiding the PIFE intervention
Systemic–strategic perspective

The PIFE operates from a systemic–strategic perspective[5] through close interdisciplinary collaboration based on providing both help and support for parental collaboration. Given the context of conflict and the emotional and psychological stakes involved, it also allows for minimal constraint to be exercised by the court, if needed (outlined in the PIFE protocol, p. 7).

Parents are challenged to demonstrate their collaborative efforts step by step through concrete actions, according to their abilities and considering the reality and context experienced by the child. Emphasis is on skills and progress rather than shortcomings, and problems that arise are openly faced with a focus on resolution rather than fault-finding.

This process uses a systemic perspective that considers the complexity of the relational configuration within the family, in contrast to the more limited employment of binary logic (e.g. alienated versus alienating parent).

Early intervention

It is important to act quickly before the rupture of a parent–child link becomes irreversible. Too much time between separation and legal proceedings amplifies parental conflict, increases a child's distress, and jeopardizes an already fragile parent–child bond. A psychosocial assessment for child custody is not a requirement of the PIFE; however, if an assessment is made it may include a recommendation that the PIFE mandate be entrusted to a psychologist.

Optimal parental collaboration

The PIFE focuses on encouraging the cooperation of both parents. Ultimately, it is they who will work out ways to re-establish the parent–child bond, and their commitment to the PIFE process implies a move away from an adversarial mindset toward one of optimal collaboration.

Working alliance with parents

To preserve the intervention's effectiveness, it is essential for the psychologist to develop and maintain an effective alliance with each family member involved.

The psychologist must remain attentive to the risk of forming uneven alliances. Maintaining impartiality is key, as the child's best interests take precedence over all other considerations.

Considering the child's needs

Children need to maintain an optimal relationship with each parent. They need to be free from feeling responsible for parental conflict and custody decisions. Ample research has shown that parental conflict and the breakdown of the parent–child relationship have serious consequences for a child's future development. The repercussions have been documented by research on alienated adult children's experience of parental alienation.

Confidentiality

The psychologist will obtain free and informed consent from each parent on each occasion, specifying the type of information and to whom it will be shared so that they can discuss relevant information in writing or orally with third parties. The psychologist will be mindful to reveal only elements deemed useful to finding solutions and to the evolution of the family situation.

PIFE protocol application path

Preliminary phase

The purpose of this phase is to obtain the agreement of all parties to consent to the intervention mandate, and to have it ratified by the court. An evaluation will follow to verify whether the conditions are in place for the subsequent intervention phase.

Preliminary phase: Mandate and consent

This stage often begins when one of the two lawyers involved in the case requests information. The psychologist will explain the protocol's application and preliminary stages.

This lawyer then informs the other lawyer in the case, who in turn contacts the psychologist to confirm agreement and continue the process.

The psychologist then sends a letter to the lawyers accompanied by a model consent form for the PIFE protocol (14-page document). This letter will propose the following steps:

Conference call between *psychologist and lawyers*:

- To verify lawyers' expectations regarding the objectives pursued in the context of the PIFE.
- To verify lawyers' understanding of the intervention's modalities and rules of operation.

Joint meeting between *psychologist and parents*:

- To outline the terms and conditions of the intervention and to emphasize the need for cooperation and accountability.
- To ensure that the process, rules of operation, and concrete implications for each parent are well-understood.

Meeting between *psychologist, parents and lawyers*:

- To verify that the specifics of the PIFE intervention are well-understood and that all parties agree to adhere to the process.
- To obtain the consent of the parties and their signatures.

This phase ends following the court's certification of the parties' consent to participate in the process.

The consent form for the PIFE protocol includes the following elements:

Preamble: Legal context under which the PIFE will be applied

1. Mandate and objectives
2. Parental collaboration
3. Intervention modalities and stages
4. Interdisciplinary work and parental consent
5. Psychologist intervention: levels
6. Meetings with children
7. Planning of individual and joint meetings
8. Intervention assessments: content and parental consent
9. Need for consistency between interventions
10. Quiz in case of lack of consensual solution or obstacles
11. Possibility of a return to court
12. Testimony before the court
13. Situations in which the process is interrupted
14. Length of term
15. Confidentiality

16. Fees
17. Signatures of parents, with lawyers and psychologist.

An illustrated example of PIFE protocol consent is presented in the Appendix.

Preliminary phase: Evaluation stage

Parents are informed of the purpose and nature of the evaluation process and give their consent prior to signing the PIFE protocol. The intention of the evaluation is not to determine psychological profiles or draw up portraits of parenting skills, but to determine factors that could make positive contributions to the intervention process. The psychologist will meet with both parents together, then hold individual meetings with each parent, followed by individual feedback meetings with each parent, and then a final joint meeting to conclude the evaluation.

The following themes will be explored:

(a) Each parent's real level of motivation to engage in the supervised family intervention process.
(b) Each parent's capacity to mobilize and initiate the changes proposed by the intervention plan and follow specific instructions.
(c) The family and legal context surrounding each parent, which could either increase or reduce parental conflict.
(d) The ability of each parent to define the family situation rationally and realistically, taking into consideration the complexities of the family's dynamic.
(e) The capacity to agree on themes to be worked on that will contribute to a timely parent–child reconnection.
(f) Each parent's capacity to propose new solutions and to focus on the 'here and now', instead of falling into patterns of past blaming.

The evaluation will consider parents' viewpoints regarding the impact of their conflict on the children and their possible need for individualized psychological help.

The psychologist will not meet with the child in the preliminary stage, but instead will encourage parental commitment by empowering parents to take the lead and responsibility for their involvement in the process. The child will see that it is the parents who have decided on the best means for re-establishing the bond, namely, the PIFE family intervention.

Intervention phase: From parent–child reconnection to re-establishing the parent–child bond

The intervention phase can last up to a year depending on the family situation. This phase has three stages: the parent–child reconnection, the re-establishment of the bond, and the rebalancing of weakened parent–child bonds and parental roles.

The steps are interlocking, each incorporating elements from the previous one. They require the psychologist to pay close attention to preparations for each meeting: choosing themes to be addressed and intervention strategies to be deployed. After each meeting, the psychologist must write a summary of the agreed-upon topics and/or recommendations made during the meetings. This document will be sent to the parents for approval before the next meeting.

During each stage of the intervention process the psychologist will meet with the parents together and separately, the child alone and with each parent separately, and sometimes all family members together. The psychologist may also meet with new spouses and/or members of the extended family. If necessary, the psychologist may also meet with lawyers and/or other involved parties (social workers, caregivers, etc.).

Parent–child reconnection process

This process begins with preparation for a first contact. The preparation is carried out over several successive meetings. The main objective of these meetings is to guide everyone in the anticipation and creation of a scenario for a positive first parent–child contact, which will be based upon both their individual memory resources and shared memories from past positive experiences.

Preparing for the first parent–child reconnection

The first step is *meeting both parents together*. The purpose of this meeting is to outline the reconnection process to both parents at the same time. Their initial task will be to work on a potential scenario for the first parent–child meeting that includes small, concrete, and measurable objectives. This will ensure their child's body language, fears, frustrations and resistances are respected. Each parent will reflect on this scenario and share it with the psychologist during subsequent individual meetings. The psychologist will meet with each parent individually first and foster a gradual combining of the scenarios they have developed, so as to avoid it becoming a source of new tension.

The second step is *an individual meeting with the closer parent*. The psychologist will strategically choose to meet with the closer parent first. Because of the impact his or her influence has over the child, this parent is the main driver for change vi-à-vis the objective of re-establishing contact. The closer parent's contribution to the process is therefore crucial. When this parent is asked to list various possible scenarios for resuming contact, resistance and fears are commonly manifested. The psychologist will respond with a focus on helping to allay these fears while offering reassurance that a safe environment will be ensured for the child. The closer parent, now reassured, will work on developing scenarios for the first parent–child reconnection. They will then undertake to prepare the child for his or her first meeting with the psychologist by explaining the psychologist's role and mandate.

The third step is a *one-on-one meeting with the distanced parent*. This meeting will help this parent mentally prepare in two ways. First, the parent will think of ways in which to create a degree of closeness with their child before the first reconnection takes place, for example sending a gift, a photo album or writing a letter. Next, the parent will prepare themself for the actual scenario of this first contact and consider possible sources of apprehension for the child.

The parent will then be led to review behaviours and attitudes that could be misinterpreted or misunderstood by his or her child, and that could be used by the other parent to justify the child's resistance. The psychologist will therefore advise this parent to avoid being too eager about the reconnection meeting with the child and to avoid expressing overly intense feelings. The psychologist will try to make the parent aware that the more eager they are to get closer to the child, the more the child will resist the suggestion. This parent will then be encouraged to adopt a determined but serene attitude during this often very challenging part of the process.

The fourth step is *meeting with the child*. The psychologist will have a first meeting with the child after reflections with both parents on the preparation for the first reconnection meeting are already underway.

The psychologist will begin by informing the child that meetings with the parents have already taken place and that both have consented to this contact. The psychologist will make sure that the child understands the intervention process and everyone's role in it. Depending on the child's maturity level, the psychologist may also inform him or her that, based on their consent, the court has ordered his or her parents to participate in this process with a view to restoring contact between the child and the distanced parent.

Next, the psychologist and the child will explore things he or she likes to do with friends, interests and hobbies, and the child's fondest wishes, hopes and dreams. The psychologist will foster warm and open dialogue by encouraging spontaneity in the child. His or her words will be received in an empathetic manner to encourage the free expression of experiences and emotions related to the family conflict. This will inform the psychologist about the child's negative perceptions regarding the distanced parent.

Even if the psychologist feels that the child's speech is unduly influenced in a negative way by the perceptions of the closer parent, they will nevertheless listen non-judgmentally. In this context, the psychologist will receive the child's possibly denigrating speech towards the distanced parent with empathy and, above all, will not confront the child regarding objective elements of which they have become aware.

The psychologist will find the appropriate moment to bring up the topic of developing possible scenarios for the child's first reconnection with the distanced parent. The photo album and/or letter that this parent has given to the psychologist to give to the child may provide an opening. Children's responses here will vary according to their age, the degree of parental conflict, and the relationship with the closer parent. On some occasions, a child will refuse to look at the photo album and will say that he or she has no pleasant memories shared with that parent. In the face of this type of resistance, the psychologist will try to reassure the child by asking him or her to explain these apprehensions about the distanced parent. The child will be reassured that there will be no possibility of clashes during the meeting since the psychologist will be present throughout. Finally, the psychologist and the child will patiently work out a scenario and context for the reconnection meeting that he or she finds the most reassuring and will eventually need to accept. In the case of a child's extreme resistance, a meeting may be held with the child and the closer parent to explain the meaning of the PIFE intervention and the parents' commitment to collaborate in re-establishing contact.

The fifth step is a *second meeting with both parents*. The parents will agree on the common development of a realistic scenario for the first parent–child reconnection meeting. Each parent will be invited to present a possible scenario, involving an activity that the distanced parent will be able to share with the child. It will be an activity that the child has already enjoyed in the past. Often, the closer parent is best able to advise the other parent about the child's preferred activity. The goal is to rekindle positive relationship experiences from the past. Scenarios will be evaluated, and an agreement reached regarding the choice of activity and the contribution of each person to ensure the activity runs smoothly. The closer parent will commit to preparing the child for the activity with a calm and positive attitude, and the distanced parent will commit to providing the material required. After this meeting, the psychologist will send a letter to the parents confirming their agreement for the reconnection meeting. This letter will include the date, time, location, type of activity, how it will take place, and its duration.

First parent–child reconnection meeting

This first meeting begins with short one-on-one interviews with the child and the distanced parent. The psychologist will first meet with the distanced parent for a few moments to ease their anxiety and remind them to focus on the present activity and to share a pleasant and constructive moment with the child. A few minutes will then be spent with the child so that he or she can express apprehensions and be reassured before meeting the distanced parent who is waiting in an adjacent office. The reconciliation itself will take place gradually in the presence of the psychologist through an activity carefully chosen and planned by both parents in advance, for example building a Lego model, doing crafts, playing a board game, or preparing a small dessert.

Throughout the activity, the child is granted maximum space to allow for his or her initiative, spontaneity, and desire to enjoy the activity to emerge to the fullest degree possible. At some point, the child may begin to enjoy engaging in the activity and begin speaking and initiating a dialogue with the distanced parent. The final product of their activity may be photographed either on the initiative of the distanced parent or at the request of the psychologist. It has been agreed with the parents beforehand that a record will be kept of these meetings together with a photo of their 'creation', which can be used as a link in the reconstruction of their broken bond.

The child's openness to this first reconnection meeting may be expressed in the acceptance of a hug or kiss from the distanced parent at the time of the latter's departure. In the absence of such an initiative (hugging, for example), it will nevertheless be important for the parent to maintain a distance and to respect the child's body language to avoid rushing him or her.

The child will then remain alone with the psychologist, who will debrief with him or her on the activity. The child generally has a positive perception of this first parent–child reconnection. The child can express what he or she liked or liked less and sometimes already has in mind and shares about the type of activity he or she would like to share with this parent in a near future encounter. When the closer parent comes to pick the child up after the activity, however, it may happen that the child will then express ambivalence about the positive assessment he or she had made beforehand. This could suggest that, even though internally there may be some change in the child's attitude and perception towards the distanced parent, the child continues to show his or her previous unconditional loyalty to the closer parent. The psychologist will discuss this observation with the closer parent in a one-on-one meeting (without the child present).

After the first reconnection meeting has been concluded, the psychologist will send a letter to the parents proposing a date in the following days for a meeting to evaluate the impact of this first re-establishment of contact on the child, and to take note of adjustments to be included in the planning of a second reconnection meeting. *This step will be repeated after every subsequent parent–child reconnection meeting.*

Parent–child reconnection process evolution

The process that began with an initial reconnection in the psychologist's office will continue with a series of successive recreational or cultural activities, to be scheduled on a weekly basis, if possible. After a number of meetings at the psychologist's office, the distanced parent and child will start engaging in activities outside the office that may gradually increase in duration. The point of departure and return for the first few shared activities followed by a debriefing will take place at the psychologist's office. Eventually the pick-up and drop-off for these activities may move to the home of the closer parent if both parents and the psychologist observe that the child is motivated and/or looks forward to a future activity with the distanced parent. Pick-up and drop-off at the closer parent's home may then allow the distanced parent and the child the further step forward of being able to share a pleasant moment together in the child's familiar environment.

In a further positive progression of the reconnection process, an agreement may be reached via the psychologist so that the closer parent accepts the presence of the distanced parent in the child's regular activities, for example during the weekly accompaniment of the child to a sports activity. At this stage of the intervention a certain minimum level of trust begins to be restored between the parents and an agreement on more effective means of communication is reached between them. Co-parental meetings are encouraged with the psychologist to re-establish a cooperative dynamic between them and discuss progress. Because of the conflict in the parents' history, the psychologist's presence will remain necessary for some time, to guide them toward fruitful exchanges about their child and to establish more functional co-parenting. The psychologist will use effective intervention strategies to defuse situations of conflict and/or blockages as they arise; however, they will not always be able to do this alone, especially when the closer parent is obstructing. The psychologist will then have to reactivate the alliance with the lawyers so that they can once again encourage the parents to cooperate as fully as possible. At such times, the psychologist must also remind parents of the possible legal consequences of uncollaborative behaviours.

Re-establishing the parent–child bond

Re-establishment of the parent–child bond will gradually take hold as successful outcomes begin to accrue from the activities chosen and jointly planned by the parents and the child with the psychologist's support. The desire to recreate an emotional bond will manifest itself as the child feels more and more confident and secure in the company of the distanced parent, as they start to enjoy meeting and talking together on the phone on a regular basis. The child will gradually spend more time at the distanced parent's home, slowly getting used to the idea of overnight stays with this parent at some point. Getting to the point of a first overnight stay with the distanced parent will require psychological preparation to help the child reclaim spaces (physical and emotional) compromised by the distancing, for example by reoccupying his or her bedroom, not seen since the break-up and possibly believed never to be seen again. With the encouragement of the closer parent, the child will be involved in preparing his or her room together with the distanced parent, choosing a new colour for the walls and new decor, thus marking the beginning of a 'historic' moment in the re-appropriation of a space that he or she had already occupied.

At this stage in the re-establishment of the bond, the psychologist has succeeded in fostering concrete collaboration in both the parents and the child. This will have stimulated the parents' return to a level of mutual trust, particularly in their ability to exercise increasingly effective co-parenting.

Rebalancing parental roles and weakened parent–child bonds

Once parents' mutual trust has begun to rebuild and the emergence of a new parent–child emotional consolidation is palpable, parents with the psychologist's support can more peacefully negotiate a healthier and more balanced redistribution of parental roles, stimulated by a common vision for their child's best interests.

The psychologist will help parents realize a key concept: the more they recognize the value of the other parent in their child's day to day life, the happier the child will become. During the rebalancing process, the child's needs will be increasingly recognized and met by both parents, who will put their strengths to work in a complementary way.

The psychologist's interventions will also aim to sensitize parents to the need for adjustments, to be initiated by both parents and that will help the child be liberated from roles and responsibilities that do not belong to a child, for example protector, confidante, which have been reinforced by the parental conflict.

In addition, parents will accept the idea that it is normal for a child to prefer one parent over the other for practical reasons, such as affinities linked to the child's gender and age, natural affinities or shared interests.

At this stage, parents sometimes reach a spontaneous agreement about the time each will share with their child. This demonstrates parental recognition of the other's role in their child's life and place within the exercise of joint parenthood.

Conclusion

The main findings that have emerged from the PIFE protocol's application in my clinical practice show that the PIFE's effectiveness will be optimal if the following conditions are met:

1. The installation of a psycho-judicial framework prior to intervention via a preliminary phase, where the PIFE protocol is discussed with parents and lawyers and then approved in court. This provides a precise and detailed framework for the course of the intervention as well as its operating rules. The parties know in advance what to expect from the process.
2. Encouragement for parental collaboration and emphasis on the psychologist's role in facilitating each parent's desire for active involvement. The psychologist is able to create an alliance with each parent and prepare the ground for optimal collaboration in cases where previously neither parent was able to agree to give the other a place in the parenting role.
3. An intervention centred on feasible, short-term solutions using a dual approach of offering both support and constraint. This constraint will be manifested through collaborative work with lawyers and in the production of periodic intervention reports.
4. Close collaboration of all professionals involved in an interdisciplinary context where the complementary roles of each are essential. The focus of each professional is on maintaining consistency throughout the various interventions to achieve the same goal: the re-establishment of the parent–child bond and the rebalancing of parental bonds and roles. The family thus receives the same message from all participants in the process and feels the support of a solid and coherent team.

Most of these findings are in line with a research-based pilot project and protocol, called the Parenting Conflict Resolution (PCR), which is intended to reduce parental conflict, improve inter-parental communication, and support or restore the parent–child relationship.[6]

Appendix
Illustrated example of PIFE protocol consent

Preamble

The parents have been separated for five years. Together, they have two 2 children. Several judgments have been rendered since the beginning of their legal proceedings four years ago. The most recent judgment concerning the terms of custody has not been respected. The children cut off all contact with their father six months ago.

1. *Mandate and objectives*: The parents and their lawyers agree to give the psychologist a mandate for family intervention under the PIFE program. The purpose of

this mandate is to support the parents and children in the process of optimally *rebalancing the parent–child relationship that has been damaged by parental conflict, and more specifically to*:

- Facilitate the resumption of contact and re-establish and consolidate the father–child bond.
- Create a place where children can express their experiences, needs, frustrations and requests.
- Free children from parental conflict to allow them to focus on their own needs.

To this end, the psychologist will first meet each parent individually, then possibly both parents together, to create the best conditions and relational context for restoring and consolidating the father–child bond.

2. *Parental collaboration*: Supported by their lawyers, parents agree to actively engage in the reconnection process for as long as it takes to complete. They also agree to ratify this consent to the court.
3. *Methods of intervention*: The psychologist will recommend a systemic-familial type of intervention encouraging parents to seek short-term solutions to gradually restore parent–child contact and avoid further deterioration of the relationship. Prior to executing the mandate, the psychologist will meet with the lawyers and parents to obtain the consent of all parties to the PIFE protocol. Assessment meetings will then be held with the parents together and then separately.
4. *Interdisciplinary work*: The psychologist informs the parents that they will be asked periodically for authorization to gather relevant information from other professionals. Their consent will also be requested for each written and/or oral exchange the psychologist engages in with their lawyers, and for the transmission of relevant information to the judge and lawyers via the intervention reports.
5. *Levels of intervention*: The psychologist will be required to intervene at several points during the process: (1) assessment and analysis of difficulties and possible relational deadlocks; (2) gradual restoration of an action plan with minimum, realistic, and assessable objectives; (3) proposal of ways and means to re-establish parent–child contact with a view to re-establishing the bond; (4) evaluation of the outcome of this attempt at the next interview; (5) encouragement of the transmission of relevant and useful information to the other parent, thereby helping to ensure consistency and continuity in response to the children's needs and in finding solutions; (6) intervention in conflict management and resolution between parents and/or parent–child conflict, separately or jointly; (7) facilitation of coordination and follow up of interventions of the various people involved with the children or parents; (8) reinforcement of parenting skills each parent possesses individually and in common; (9) support in the medium term in the establishment of minimally acceptable and effective communication between the parents.

6. *Meetings with the children*: The psychologist will offer the children a place to talk and will be able to perceive how each one is situated within the parental couple and the wider family system. Subsequently, the psychologist will work together with each child to find the first steps that will allow them to experience minimal contact with their father in the most peaceful way possible and with optimal support from their mother.
7. *Planning of individual and joint meetings*: The psychologist will submit to the parents one month in advance a schedule of foreseeable individual or joint meetings. The parents must confirm their availability as soon as possible or suggest other dates if necessary. However, the frequency and duration of meetings with each parent may be modified as the process of resuming parent–child contact and rebalancing the parent–child relationship evolves.
8. *Intervention assessments*: Following their consent, the parents will be informed via brief progress reports on the outcome of the process. These reports will take stock of each parent's willingness and ability to do what is in their power to contribute to the restoration of the parent–child bond. These assessments will also reflect each child's experiences and needs as we see them in their relational context. The reports will be presented and discussed with each parent and then given to each one. With each parent's consent, these reports can be sent to their lawyers and to the judge.
9. *Need for consistency between interventions*: The psychologist expects to be informed of any familial problem by one or both parents if a decision regarding the restoration of the parent–child relationship is to be made by another professional involved in the family's situation. If this happens, the psychologist will contact the other professionals involved in the PIFE as quickly as possible to ensure the interventions of all parties involved remain as consistent and effective as possible, and to prevent the child from feeling torn by divergent intentions on the part of various professionals.
10. *In the absence of a consensual solution*: At the request of the parents and/or lawyers and if the psychologist finds it relevant to the objective of rebalancing parent–child relationships, they may issue a recommendation, which may be made orally or in writing within a reasonable time and according to the urgency of the situation.
11. *In the event of an obstacle in the process*: The psychologist will proceed with an analysis of the nature and possible causes that may have contributed to blocking the process of re-establishing the relationship. Various hypotheses may be examined, in particular: (1) denial of the problem or non-recognition of the problem; (2) inability of the parent to exercise their influence on or authority over the child; (3) voluntary but possibly justified obstruction; (4) voluntary and unjustified obstruction. Depending on the nature of the obstacle, other interventions may be considered in collaboration with the parents and lawyers to circumvent the difficulties and look at possible solutions.
12. *Possibility of a return to court*: The psychologist may then submit a progress report on the PIFE process and present possible solutions to the judge hearing the case

before they render a decision. Recommendations may be made on whether it is appropriate to continue the PIFE process or move to another type of intervention.
13. *Testimony*: The psychologist may not act as an expert in the event of a dispute between the parents before any court involving the children. The psychologist may not therefore give an opinion on parenting skills and/or make recommendations concerning the type of custody and access applied to the children.
14. *Interruption or termination of process*: It is agreed that the psychologist may terminate the intervention process if either parent refuses to cooperate or fails to act in good faith. If this is the case, a notice of intention will be given to the judge, the parents and their lawyers. A parent can also end the PIFE process by explaining their reasons in writing and after getting advice from their lawyer. In such a case, the parent will be informed that this refusal to cooperate will bring the case back before the judge, who will ensure that the appropriate decisions are made in the best interests of the child.
15. *Term of office*: This mandate may extend over a period of approximately six months from the signature date. Following this period will be an evaluation of objectives achieved and modalities for continuing the process. If necessary, new objectives will be identified.
16. *Confidentiality*: The confidentiality agreement will be presented and reviewed to ensure full comprehension and agreement by all parties.
17. *Fees*: The psychologist's fees will be paid by both parents in accordance with the judgment rendered by the judge.
18. *Signatures of the parties*: The consent will be signed by the parents, their lawyers and the psychologist.
19. *Consent*: A consent form for proceeding to the preliminary evaluation phase will be included in an appendix.

References

(1) Van Dieren, B., De Hemptine, M. & Renchon, J.L. (2011). Le risque de rupture du lien parent-enfant et l'expertise axée sur la collaboration parentale. *Revue Trimestrielle de Droit Familial* 2: 261–298.
(2) Templer, K., Matthewson, M., Haines, J. & Cox, G. (2017). Recommendations for best practice in response to parental alienation: Findings from a systematic review. *Journal of Family Therapy* 39: 103–122.
(3) Lillo, C. (2019). Parental alienation and shared custody: Challenge or ideal situation? Paper presented at the International Scientific Conference on Best interest of Child and Shared Parenting. Malaga, Spain, 2 December.
(4) Van Dieren, B. & Lillo, C. (2016). Expertise collaborative et Processus d'intervention familiale encadrée. In O. Odinetz & R. Broca (eds), *Séparations conflictuelles et aliénation parentale. Enfants en danger*. Lyon, France: Chronique Sociale, 288–303.
(5) Seron, C. & Wittezaele, J.J. (2009). *Aide ou contrôle: l'intervention thérapeutique sous contrainte*, 2nd ed. Bruxelles, Belgique: De Boek.
(6) Cyr, F., Poitras, K. & Godbout, E. (2020). An interdisciplinary case management protocol for child resistance or refusal dynamics. *Family Court Review* 58(2): 560–575.

27
CO-RESPONSIBILITY PLAN AND SHARED PARENTING

Belén Casado Casado

Introduction

Since 2005, when the law was reformed to establish the possibility of shared parenting or physical joint custody of the minor in cases of separation or divorce,[1] this has been and continues to be a highly debated measure, attracting much media coverage, which has caused and continues to cause immense social upheaval. At that time, most were unaware of the possibility that the minor could be cared for by both parents in a more equal way, sharing time and activities and thus strengthening the parent–child relationship so that the child is less affected by the break-up. Shared parenting would allow the minor to maintain a closer relationship with his or her parents even if they no longer live together. The social reality demanded a rule that would take into account the existence of parents more involved in the care of their children and that would rule out the automatic custody of the minor for the mother and the figure of the father as a simple visiting parent.

The 2005 law states, literally, that shared parenting is an exceptional measure. However, this law has been systematically interpreted in an unorthodox way in case law. In fact, it is considered that, when the legal text uses the term "exceptionality", it refers only to the circumstances necessary for shared parenting to be decided, but not to the fact that shared parenting is an exceptional measure. Therefore, in accordance with this interpretation, shared parenting needs to be applied more frequently.

However, we can deduce a certain level of reluctance to adopt shared parenting if we take into consideration certain criteria that are applied in a rigorous way by courts. Among these criteria, two stand out: the child's age and the relationship between parents. These criteria are applied from the perspective of the best interest of the child. In addition, there is a doctrinal debate from which we can deduce that the exceptional nature of shared parenting is still present, at least in an underlying way.

At the end of the first decade of the twentieth century, a new legal concept appeared. We refer to parental co-responsibility. At the same time, a serious economic crisis was taking place in Spain, which lasted almost a decade. These two circumstances helped spur what has been called the "battle for shared parenting". The number of legal claims presented requesting shared parenting of the minor increased, some of them advocating the term "parental responsibility" or "parental co-responsibility". It could even be said that shared parenting became trendy. Similarly, different parliaments in various Spanish autonomous communities passed laws favouring shared parenting.

The principle of parental co-responsibility is introduced at a legal and international level. The International Convention on Children's Rights was one of the first treaties to acknowledge the same as a human right of children and adolescents. European Union Regulatio 1347/2000 defines "parental responsibility" as the rights and obligations conferred upon a natural person or legal entity by virtue of a court decision by operation of law or following an agreement with legal effects, in relation to the person or the assets of a child, and, specifically, custody and visiting rights.

Recommendation No. 5 of the Committee of Ministers of Member States R. 84, of 28 February 1984, states that the responsibilities of parents with regards to children should belong jointly to both parents, adding in Recommendation 10 that if parental responsibilities are exercised jointly by both parents, any decision should be taken by agreement.

The European Convention for the Protection of Human Rights and Fundamental Freedoms, of 22 November 1984, established that spouses enjoy equal rights and responsibilities of a civil nature, including in relations with their children, both in the event of marriage and after its dissolution.

Spanish Organic Law 3/2007, of 22 March 2007, "on effective equality of women and men" has also integrated "paternal co-responsibility" as one of its landmark criteria. This shared parenting arises from the filial bond, which is why, in accordance with Article 92 of this Act, separation, annulment and divorce do not exempt parents from their responsibilities to their children. Furthermore, Article 154 of the CC (Spanish Civil Code), as amended by the second paragraph of Article 8 of Act 26/2015, of 28 July, on the protection of children and adolescents, has introduced into the text a literal reference to "parental authority as parental responsibility".[2]

Shared parenting: Case law analysis

The latest judicial rulings help us to understand the evolution of shared parenting. The need for legal reform is evident.

Current case law refers to shared parenting as a normal and desirable measure, and this "normality" is presented as contrary to exceptional.[3] The application of the principle of the best interests of the child has evolved in response to social reality. However, the text of the law has not changed in the last 15 years, and still considers shared parenting to be an exceptional measure. This legal text is completely overtaken by social reality. Interpretations of this issue on the part of the legal order and case law have evolved likewise.

This evolution has evolved as follows: the non-existence of shared parenting due to its lack of legal acknowledgement; its existence or exceptional acknowledgement, first in case law and then in the law passed in 2005; acknowledgment of the need for some markers or interpretative criteria to define the interest of the minor (age, previous practice of the parents, residence, working hours, etc.); and, finally, a general shared parenting rule. Now, with the reversed burden of proof, it must be demonstrated that it is not advisable for the minor because such shared parenting is always the desirable decision. The age of the minor is not a reliable detail now or the previous behaviour of parents. We say this because, from our case law analysis, it is evident that hearings usually take into account the child's age in cases where they need to affirm that shared parenting is not appropriate because a child, from a very young age, has been exclusively cared for by the mother. However, the High Court understands that circumstances change, for example the child may have been five when the first custody decision was made and is now 12, and a review of measures is thus required if shared parenting is now to be granted.[4] Parents' previous behaviour may now be irrelevant. This implies that shared parenting can be decided in spite of the fact that only one parent has taken care of the child. However, it can be relevant in the case whereby, for example, a parent was not previously in any form of contact with the child or showing any concern about him or her, or living at a great distance from him or her. In the same way, courts consider that bad relations between the parents are not to be taken into account in order to decide shared parenting, given that they can be based on mere distrust or breaches that must be resolved in the best interest of the child; the only exception is in cases described by courts as being of "notorious seriousness".[5]

In those cases where shared parenting is deemed inadvisable, detailed evidence must be produced. This shows that we have gone from one extreme to another: immediate and exclusive custody to the mother in all cases except exceptions to shared parenting always except exceptions.[6]

With regard to the necessary requirements for a modification of measures, the Civil Procedural Law in Spain (*Ley de Enjuiciamiento Civil*) states clearly in Article 775.1 that a substantial alteration of circumstances is necessary, unless, as specified in Article 775.3, there is mutual agreement on the modification; then the procedures provided for in Article 777 LEC will be followed without further ado.

The High Court has cited, for the purpose of modifying custody measures, the change in social attitudes.[7] However, we do not think that this argument can be used as an exclusive criteria because we have observed that other circumstances "favouring" shared parenting were also used, such as the child's older age and a favourable report of the prosecutor. In some cases, we also found that, when shared parenting was deemed appropriate, the previous regime had been sole custody but with broad visiting access, that is, *de facto* shared parenting was being exercised, even though this approach had not actually been legally established. By this we mean that it is difficult for the change in social and scientific opinion argument to be useful on its own if it is not combined with other favourable details that make it advisable in the interest of the minor. The change in social or scientific opinion should only be one favourable criterion in favour of shared parenting taken together with many others in the interest of the minor.

Article 90.3 of the Civil Code in its new wording granted by Law 15/2015, of 2 July, of the Voluntary Jurisdiction, allows the possible modification of measures by declaring:

> 3. The measures that the Judge adopts in the absence of an agreement or those agreed by the spouses judicially, can be modified judicially or by new agreement approved by the Judge, when the new requirements of the children or the change of the circumstances of the spouses require the same. The measures that have been agreed upon before the Judicial Secretary or in a public deed may be modified by a new agreement, subject to the same requirements demanded by this Code.

Therefore, we see how the possibility has been introduced to change the agreement not only on the basis of "substantial alteration of circumstances of the spouses", but also when "the new needs of the children make it advisable". This legal change extends the possible modification of measures by introducing new, less restrictive grounds. For example, there is a tendency in case law to consider that changes in the age of the minor are significant for the purpose of requesting a modification of measures because the minor's circumstances make it advisable, he or she has greater autonomy and is less dependent, etc. But we cannot forget that the fact that the minor had been under the custody of one of the parents (normally the mother) during the first stage of his or her life was a criterion to be taken into account when rejecting shared parenting, since it was understood that the change was not appropriate since the minor had always been cared for by one of the parents since he or she was very young. The criteria seem to be reversed in the quest for the widespread application of shared parenting, either through an *ex novo* process or by seeking shared parenting through a process of modification of measures.

If we understand that the change in the doctrinal trend could in itself lead to the modification of previous measures, the judicial route would be the possibility for any of the parties to cease to comply with what was agreed with judicial endorsement, since a new review or request is possible.

Given that shared parenting is the general rule and a normal and desirable measure, it would be understandable if, today, the judge was able to choose this measure even if neither of the parents requested such custody. However, the Civil Code adheres to the text of the 2005 law, according to which shared parenting cannot be assessed by the ex officio judge. On the contrary, it is a necessary requirement that at least one of the parents requests this measure. A future legal amendment will therefore be necessary to enable the judge to assess shared parenting ex officio.[8] The fact that the parents are not interested in shared parenting does not mean that they are not desirous of caring for their children together. If shared parenting is forced on parents who both desire that one of them has sole custody, it is unclear how they will organise this in practice.

Parental co-responsibility plan

Associated with parental co-responsibility is the so-called "Plan of parental co-responsibility", which lays out how parents are to apportion their care of the child.

This is reflected in some regional legislation. For example, the Catalan legislation refers to a parental plan in its Article 233.9.2.[9] This plan is a mandatory element of the settlement agreement. It details how the parents are to exercise parental responsibility, that is, in terms of custody, care, education, etc. It therefore includes all the powers inherent in the exercise of parental responsibility:

(a) The place or places where the child will normally live. Rules must be included to determine which parent has custody at any given time.
(b) The tasks for which each parent must take responsibility in relation to the child's daily activities.
(c) How changes in custody should be made and, if appropriate, how the costs involved should be shared.
(d) The regime for parent–child relations and communication with one parent whilst the child is with the other parent.
(e) Arrangements for the child to stay with each parent during holiday periods and on dates specially designated for the child, the parents or their family.
(f) The type of education and extra-curricular, educational and leisure activities the child engages in.
(g) How the duty to share all information concerning the education, health and welfare of the child is to be fulfilled.
(h) How decisions concerning change of address and other matters relevant to the child are taken.[10]

This parental plan does not involve the award of any specific custody but is open to any custody and care regime for the child.

The legislation of Aragon refers to a "Family Relations Pact" or "Family Coexistence Pact", and is similar in content to the regulatory agreement in Article 90 CC. The legislation in Navarre (*Derecho Foral*) does not mention a parenting plan because, in a very general way, it establishes the same in Article 3 sections 5 and 6:

> 5. If the judge decides on shared parenting, he or she will establish a regime of cohabitation of each of the parents with the children, adapted to the circumstances of the family situation, which guarantees both parents the exercise of their rights and obligations in a situation of equity.

> 6. If the judge decides on individual custody, he or she will establish a system of communication, stays or visits with the other parent that guarantees the exercise of the powers and duties inherent in the parental authority attributed to him or her in accordance with Law 63 of the Compilation of the Civil Law of Navarre.

Law 7/2015, of 30 June, on family relations in cases of separation or break-up of parents in the Basque Country, uses similar wording in its Articles 9.5 and 9.6.

In the Spanish Preliminary Draft Law on the Exercise of Shared Parental Responsibility and other measures to be adopted after ceasing living together (10–04–2014),[11] the term "parental co-responsibility" is used as a synonym for parental responsibility. This principle is defined as the equitable distribution of the rights and duties that parents must exercise in relation to their children. This principle is also understood as being in favour of the self-regulation of family conflict, which it relates to the right to equality between parents in order to assign adequate shared participation; it also starts from the idea that this family co-responsibility has its origin in the filial bond.

This preliminary draft law establishes that all regulatory agreements must include, as a minimum, a plan of parental co-responsibility with the intention of promoting an agreement, so that the parents themselves organise the responsibilities, coexistence and care of the minor. There is thus freedom of agreement, but the judge intervenes if these agreements are burdensome for the child.

The plan for parental co-responsibility should address the following issues:

(1) How to decide and share all aspects affecting the education, health, welfare, usual residence and other relevant issues for the child.
(2) The fulfilment of the duties concerning custody, care, education and leisure of the child.
(3) The periods of cohabitation with each parent and the correlative regime of stay, relationship and communication with the absent partner.
(4) The place or places of residence of the child, determining which will appear for the purposes of registration, which should preferably coincide with that of the parent with whom, in annual calculation, the child spends most of their time.
(5) The rules for the collection and delivery of the child in changes of custody, or in the exercise of stay, relationship and communication with them.

The parental plan is thus a tool for managing custody, amongst other things. Thus, the key points of the plan cover: distribution of periods of cohabitation in cases of shared parenting and distribution of stays in cases of single-parent custody; the residence or domicile of the minor the manner of exercising parental responsibilities in general; the right to information and decision-making power on matters relating to the minor; general aspects relating to the minor's education, including choice of school, health issues, and religious or ideological issues. It also refers to an obligation of communication between the parents on matters related to the minor in order to satisfy the right to information of both parents.[12]

When the parenting plan refers to the distribution of tasks or responsibilities of each parent in relation to daily life, it refers to shared parenting. The same is true of sections (a), (b) and (c) of the Catalan parental plan. However, this content could appear in any regulatory agreement as a mandatory clause for the parents to detail how parental authority will be exercised and functions shared following their separation. Provision of this clause means that the law will provide the obligatory content for the settlement agreement. The law thus allows for greater precision in the agreement regulating parental responsibilities.

The parenting plan does not necessarily have to concern shared parenting since it is obligatory to govern any system of custody in terms of periods of cohabitation with each parent, in addition to the distribution of holidays, designated days or vacation periods.

Legal acknowledgement of the parenting plan would make both parents aware of how tasks are to be distributed. The plan would also become a mechanism to avoid later conflict; it would reject the previously established idea of the non-custodial parent having little decision-making power, right to information and power to intervene in general in the interest of self-regulation and equality between parents. The parent–child relationship must ensure that emotional ties and responsibilities to the child are maintained after separation or divorce. This is determined by Articles 92.1 and 110 of the Civil Code.

This distribution or division of tasks is based on the interests of the child, but also on the interests of the parents, since it establishes more egalitarian guidelines for the fulfilment of paternal–filial duties. We could even consider that it has much more to do with the interests of the parents by establishing duties, right to information, decision-making power on matters pertaining to the child, such as education, and systems of communication.

In relation to the custody of the child, the parenting plan concerns only the domicile arrangements and distribution of daily activities; everything else is built on the shared exercise of parental authority, of which custody of the child is only one element. Sharing of the child's daily activities is vital in shared parenting.

The fact that this parenting plan has no economic content is very significant. Only the Catalan parental plan talks about sharing the costs of changing the child's domicile; however, everything else it regulates is not directly related to economic distribution. We can affirm that the parental responsibility plan is not used for this purpose if we interpret it as being different to the general agreement for the regulation of matters after the parental break-up, which corresponds more to the term regulatory agreement used in common law. The parental plan will undoubtedly be an integral part of that agreement.

We affirm that the idea of generalised shared parenting should not be linked or related to the idea of a generalised and obligatory parenting plan and we believe that this is what is happening at present. The convenience and equality of sharing parental responsibilities after the break-up, the greater involvement of both parents, and the greater social awareness of the equality of rights and duties in the interest of the minor and in the interest of his or her parents, should not necessarily occur only because there is also an equal sharing of periods of cohabitation with the minor. Shared parenting is based on this more equal sharing of life and daily responsibilities, as the minor would then live with both parents for similar periods of time; it is therefore only part of the plan. However, greater equality and involvement in the exercise of parental responsibilities could be achieved without necessarily establishing shared parenting. Shared parenting would proceed when it is advisable for the minor according to the fulfilment of certain criteria. The parenting plan should become a general instrument except when the situation of the minor makes it inadvisable, for example if one of the parents has psychological problems, is in prison, is the perpetrator of domestic violence or has been deprived of parental authority.

On the other hand, the parenting plan should aim at the equal distribution of responsibilities. However, it is a self-regulating instrument, thus the parties can decide to exercise parental authority in a less equitable way or agree to one parent having exclusive parental authority. In accordance with the provisions of Article 90.2 CC, modifying the parenting plan is permitted unless doing so causes problems for the child. In the case of contentious proceedings, the judge can only ignore the equitable distribution of function if they can justify that this approach is in the best interests of the child.

Since the plan concerns parental management of issues such as the child's health, education, religious activities, etc., it is difficult for the judge to determine how best to allot responsibility when the parents are not in agreement. Here, the judge would base grant decision-making power to one parent on Article 156 CC and the child's opinion on the matter, if he or she was sufficiently mature.

Equality in the distribution of parental responsibilities, as the basis for the parenting plan, would also necessarily entail a proposal for custody or guardianship of the minor that is equal; that is, not short and infrequent stays with the non-custodial parent.[13] It is common for the concepts of the parental co-responsibility plan and shared parenting to be confused. Perhaps this is due to a tendency to idealize shared parenting and understand it as a guarantee of maximum justice and equity. However, in practice this is not always the case.

Conclusions

In recent years, courts have upheld shared parenting claims in most cases because consideration of shared custody is now the rule of general application, with exceptions.

We understand that, with this general rule, the courts are opting *for a rebuttable* presumption of convenience of this measure in the best interest of the child. As a result, courts are no longer considering long-established case law criteria to assess shared parenting. Only if the presumption of shared parenting meets with difficulties or objections are the case law criteria taken into account.

In any case, the 2005 law is still in force, and it literally states that shared parenting is exceptional. This is why it is very doubtful that it can be argued today that shared parenting should be the measure of general application as it is the most beneficial for the minor without applying an interpretation contrary to the law or *contra legem*.

Some recent judgements understand that changes in doctrinal and social opinion can lead to modification of measures; for example, demands for shared parenting are increasing steadily. We are now faced with the same problem referred to above. It is difficult to maintain the generalised nature of shared parenting since the opposite is true. It is therefore even more difficult to argue that the generalised application of shared parenting can serve as a basis for a review of previous judicial pronouncements from the perspective of generality, based exclusively on the change of doctrinal opinion on the matter.

Shared parenting is imposed both as a measure to safeguard the interests of the minor and as a mechanism that indirectly protects the interests of the parents. Generalised shared parenting would only be appropriate when it is intended to safeguard the interests of the minor, which are those that prevail in any case. It is not suitable when the concept of protecting the minor is actually being used to protect the personal interests of the parents, such as their financial arrangements. In actual fact, all child custody decisions – a presumption of shared parenting or otherwise – are directly or indirectly informed by parents' financial circumstances, such as ability to pay maintenance and use of home.

There is also currently a trend towards establishing a more or less equal distribution of the functions involved in the exercise of parental authority. The term parental co-responsibility refers to this.

We believe that the idea of generalised shared parenting is currently being confused with a generalised parenting plan. The convenience of sharing parental responsibilities after the break-up, the idea of equality in sharing, the greater involvement of both parents, the greater social awareness of equal rights and duties in the interest of the minor and in the interest of his or her parents should not necessarily be achieved by a similar distribution of periods of cohabitation with the minor.

The parenting plan should become a widely used instrument for establishing self-regulation and equal sharing of parental responsibilities.

Case law

Judgement of the Spanish Supreme Court, of 8 November 2009
Judgement of the Spanish Supreme Court, of 28 September 2009
Judgement of the Spanish Supreme Court, of 10 March 2010
Judgement of the Spanish Supreme Court, of 11 March 2010
Judgement of the Spanish Supreme Court, of 11 October 2010
Judgement of the Spanish Supreme Court, of 7 July 2011
Judgement of the Spanish Supreme Court, of 9 March 2012
Judgement of the Spanish Supreme Court, of 19 April 2012
Judgement of the Spanish Supreme Court, of 25 May 2012
Judgement of the Spanish Supreme Court, of 9 December of 2012
Judgement of the Spanish Supreme Court, of 10 December 2012
Judgement of the Spanish Supreme Court, of 29 April 2013
Judgement of the Spanish Supreme Court, of 7 June 2013
Judgement of the Spanish Supreme Court, of 19 July 2013
Judgement of the Spanish Supreme Court, of 25 November 2013
Judgement of the Spanish Supreme Court, of 12 December 2013
Judgement of the Spanish Supreme Court, of 25 April 2014
Judgement of the Spanish Supreme Court, of 2 July 2014
Judgement of the Spanish Supreme Court, of 30 October 2014

Judgement of the Spanish Supreme Court, of 16 February 2015
Judgement of the Spanish Supreme Court, of 15 July 2015
Judgement of the Spanish Supreme Court, of 15 October 2015
Judgement of the Spanish Supreme Court, of 11 February 2016
Judgement of the Spanish Supreme Court, of 29 March 2016
Judgement of the Spanish Supreme Court, of 12 April 2016
Judgement of the Spanish Supreme Court, of 3 June 2016
Judgement of the Spanish Supreme Court, of 17 February 2017
Judgement of the Spanish Supreme Court, of 7 March 2017
Judgement of the Spanish Supreme Court, of 13 July 2017
Judgement of the Spanish Supreme Court, of 27 September 2017
Judgement of the Spanish Supreme Court, of 10 January 2018
Judgement of the Spanish Supreme Court, of 4 April 2018
Judgement of the Spanish Supreme Court, of 6 April 2018
Judgement of the Spanish Supreme Court, of 17 January 2019

Notes

1. Lathrop Gómez F. *Custodia compartida de los hijos.* Madrid. Editorial La Ley; 2008: 276.
2. Acuña San Martín M. Corresponsabilidad Parental. El principio de corresponsabilidad parental. *Revista de derecho (Coquimbo)* 2013, retrieved from https://scielo.conicyt.cl/scielo.php?script=sci_arttext&pid=S0718–97532013000200002#n39; Echevarría Guevara K.L. *La guarda y custodia compartida de los hijos. Doctorado Problemática Actual del Derecho de Família*; 2011, retrieved from https://digibug.ugr.es/bitstream/handle/10481/20323/20702863.pdf;jsessionid=10C3E908FA2706CDE7D0255CFD1DE051?sequence=1.
3. Judgements of the Spanish Supreme Court, of 29 April 2013, 25 April 2014, 16 February 2015, 29 March 2016, among others.
4. Judgement of the Spanish Supreme Court, of 12 April 2016.
5. Judgement of the Spanish Supreme Court, of 29 March 2016.
   Aznar Domingo A. Criterios jurisprudenciales que determinan la guarda y custodia compartida. *La custodia compartida: análisis y valoración como método más favorable.* Editorial: Revista de Jurisprudencia El Derecho 1. IV; 2019; Guilarte Martín-Calero C. La custodia compartida alternativa. Un estudio doctrinal y jurisprudencial. INDRET, *Revista para el Análisis del Derecho* 2008, retrieved from www.raco.cat/index.php/InDret/article/view/124245/172218.
6. Quintana Martín V, Introducción: tipos de guarda y custodia. *La guarda y custodia compartida,* Chapter I. Valencia, Tirant Lo Blanch; 2016; La Vanguardia; 2019. Shared parenting increased 11% in 2018, retrieved from www.lavanguardia.com/vida/20191009/47881987653/la-custodia-compartida-aumento-un-11--en-2018.html.
7. Judgements of the Spanish Supreme Court, of 30 October 2014, 29 March 2016, 12 April 2016.
8. De Torres Perea J.M. La custodia compartida. *Practicum Familia.* Madrid, Aranzadi; 2016: 629–659.
9. Giralt Pagé N. El pla de parentalitat. *Economist & Jurist edició Catalunya* 2012; 157: 7; Lauroba Lacasa M.E. Ejercicio de la guarda y responsabilidad parental. La propuesta del código civil catalán. *Revista Jurídica de Catalunya* 2011; 2: 327.
10. Lauroba Lacasa M.E. Los planes de parentalidad en el libro segundo del código civil de Cataluña. *Revista Jurídica de Catalunya* 2012; 4: 906.

11. Mateo Bueno F.F. *El decepcionante Anteproyecto de Ley sobre Corresponsabilidad Parental*; 2015, retrieved from www.mateobuenoabogado.com/el-decepcionante-anteproyecto-de-ley-sobre-la-corresponsabilidad-parental/.
12. Pérez Vallejo A.M, Sainz Cantero Caparrós M.B. Protección de la infancia y marco jurídico de la coparentalidad tras la crisis familiar. *Parentalidad positiva y el plan de coparentalidad*. Chapter VII. Valencia. Editorial Tirant lo Blanch; 2018.
13. Cuatrecasas Cuatrecasas S. *¿Para qué sirve el Plan de Parentalidad? Plan de Parentalidad?*; 2018, retrieved from www.silviacuatrecasas.com/para-que-sirve-el-plan-de-parentalidad-plan-de-parentalidad/.

PART V

Recent evolution of shared parenting in a comparative scenario

28
RECENT DEVELOPMENTS IN SHARED PARENTING IN WESTERN COUNTRIES

José Manuel de Torres Perea

Introduction

In this chapter, we study the recent evolution of shared parenting in different countries located in the West. Keogh, Smyth and Masardo begin their 2018 article on shared parenting by stating: "Shared-parenting appears to be increasingly popular in many Western countries."[1] In addition, they refer to the Council of Europe document "Equality and shared parental responsibility: The role of fathers", which establishes that: "States are called upon to introduce or, as appropriate, make greater use of shared residence arrangements, which are often the best way to preserve contact between children and their parents."[2] The best way to validate this statement is to analyse the social impact of shared parenting in Western countries.

Moreover, the European Court of Human Rights has stated that each State initially has an obligation to take measures with a view to reuniting parents with their children and an obligation to facilitate such reunions, in so far as the interests of the child require that everything must be done to preserve personal relations.[3] This has been interpreted as the existence of a rebuttable presumption in favour of contact between children and parents, as analysed in Chapter 4.

In accordance with this view, we now aim to study the impact of shared parenting in Western countries, in order to check if this alleged development is real. We focus on several European countries: Nordic countries, the UK, the Netherlands, Belgium and Spain, in addition to the United States, Canada and Australia. We offer this study to introduce the final part of this book dedicated to a comparative study of shared parenting in a global scenario.

Shared parenting in Nordic countries

We start by analysing a type of society that is traditionally considered as benchmark of modern society in the Western world. Nordic countries seek to achieve the so-called symmetrical family model. This means the political pursuit of a model in which women and men share paid and unpaid work equally between them.[4] Therefore, the studies show us the existence of a convergence between mother and father time-use patterns in housework, childcare, etc.[5] This trend is also continued after separation, which implies a more open-minded approach to shared parenting than before.[6] In these countries, there are studies that analyse the social evolution of shared parenting that are considered useful tools by lawmakers. For example, Fransson's conclusion in a recent Swedish study was that children with shared residence scored better than children in sole custody in social relations with peers and parents, healthy lifestyles and culture or leisure activities.[7]

We can use the Norwegian experience to draw certain conclusions. According to Kitterød and Wiik, in the 2000s there was a "dramatic increase" in shared residence for children among parents living apart and a related shift away from sole-parent custody, usually the mother[8]; that is, shared parenting increased from 10 to 25% during the first decades of this century.[9] They offer the following key points to understand the impact of shared parenting in Norway. First, shared residence after separation was typically exercised by parents with greater socioeconomic means, who reported low levels of inter-parent conflict. However, they added that, recently, shared residence has become more widespread for other types of Norwegian parents. Second, surveys reveal that more than 80% of parents reported no change in their shared parenting arrangement after separation. Third, the Norwegian government sees encouraging more equal parenting roles among separated parents as an important political ambition.

Currently, a major debate on shared-time parenting is being conducted in Norway. In 2015–2016 it was proposed that shared residence be introduced into the Children's Act as a reference guideline.[10] However, the Ombudsman for Children highlighted that the guiding principle should be to guarantee the best interests of each child, rather than equality between the parents.[11] Consequently, Article 36 of the Children and Parents Act[12] still states that, if the parents do not reach an agreement, the court must decide which of the parents shall have custody of the child. When there are special reasons for doing so, the court may nonetheless decide that both parents shall have custody of the child.

In any case, the government looks likely to promote shared residence as a viable alternative when parents separate. In conclusion, Smyth considers the Norwegian shared-parenting context as fascinating and points out that this model has long been considered the egalitarian ideal for achieving the dual "earner–carer" family model.[13]

Shared parenting in Australia

Another legal system in which there is a link between social studies that provide reliable data on patterns of parenting after separation and legislation is that of Australia. The Australian experience shows how law reforms can raise additional social concerns regarding the interests of the parties involved when the custody of a child is decided after a marital crisis. It also shows how a legal evolution of subsequent changes may lead to a reasonable acceptance or tolerance of the final outcome by the concerned parties. In fact, Australian authors refer to this legal process as a battle and even trench warfare.[14]

The reform of 1995 followed in the steps of those of the English Children Act 1989. The starting point was the sole physical single-parent custody model, with "reasonable" access to the other parent. In the Australian Law Reform Act 1995, the term custody was replaced by residence and access by contact. A significant factor of the reform was the existence of a domestic violence background. No provision was made, however, for the possibility of considering shared parenting to be in the best interests of the child.

With the arrival of the new millennium, there was a trend towards a presumption of equal division of the child's time after divorce, which gained momentum. The hypothesis was that joint custody should be the norm, in order to protect fathers' rights.[15] In fact, it was claimed as a legal presumption in order to establish that parents should share parenting time with their children equally after separation.[16] This trend was heatedly contested by women's groups. According to Boyd, the "responsibility cast upon mothers to ensure contact between children and fathers can be both a burden and a constraint on maternal autonomy".[17] He added that the creation of a pro-contact culture could put mothers and children at risk of suffering violence.[18] These arguments were later opposed by Parkinson in 2011,[19] who stated that marriage is dissolvable but parenthood is not. Moreover, he added that it is a fact that, in the majority of cases, the best interest of the child is served by having both parents involved in his or her life.

In any case, after the parliamentary enquiry of 2003, the Family Law Amendment, the Shared Parental Responsibility-Act, was passed in 2006. This regulation established two primary guiding factors: the "benefit to the child of having a meaningful relationship with both ... parents" and "the need to protect the child from physical or psychological harm, from being subjected or exposed to abuse, neglect or family violence". However, as Parkinson states, the Gordian knot of the reform was the introduction of a presumption of equal sharing of parental responsibility in cases that do not involve violence or abuse.[20]

This legislation was harshly criticized by several scholars. For example, Simone considered that because the new regulation was focused on encouraging each parent to facilitate a close and continuing relationship between the child and the "other parent", women would be deterred from making allegations of family violence.[21] In other words, Australian scholars argued that this primary consideration had the effect of silencing mothers' concerns and the mothers tended not to report violence because they felt that doing so would backfire on them.[22] Following publication of a report by the Australian Institute of Family Studies, an Australian government research body, and other legislative reviews, especially that of the 2010 Australian Law Reform Commission, this regulation was amended by the Australian Family Violence and Other Measures Act 2011. It was alleged that, by then, the benefit of having a meaningful relationship with both parents had been applied as almost an absolute consideration, irrespective of the child having to live within a safe or unsafe family environment.

Fehlberg stated that it was necessary to remedy this legal paradox in order to ensure that, when weighing up the situation, safety was given greater weight.[23] Therefore, it was alleged that it is now perceived that prioritizing the relationship with parents over the safety of the child has a negative impact in cases of violence and abuse. Finally, the amendment of the 2011 Act changed the situation of the child by seeking a balance between the issues at stake. In particular, the primary considerations were modified. In the event of conflict between these two guiding primary factors, the protection of the child from physical or psychological harm, being subjected or exposed to abuse, neglect or family violence, should have greater weight than the child's meaningful relationship with both parents.

Parkinson considers that the reform of 2006 and the amendments of 2011 sent high-level messages to the general public that parental responsibility should be shared, unless there has been a history of family violence or child abuse. He considers that perhaps, for this reason, it was a more common option than it had been before 2006 and that "legislation contributed to an increased awareness and acceptance of shared care arrangements as a viable and 'normal' option for parenting after separation".[24] This legislation also sent a message to ensure the substantial involvement of both parents and, finally, that the courts must act protectively in cases of concern about family violence or child abuse, cases in which the parties cannot act by themselves. His opinion is that the Australian family law system has found a reasonable balance, taking into account the different messages that the law was required to send to a "diverse range of audiences".[25] In any case, the proportion of children in shared parenting has almost doubled from a low figure of 9% in 2002–2003 to 17% in 2014–2015.[26]

Shared parenting in the United States

Experts inform us that there is currently an important decline in mothers being granted sole custody following divorce and a significant increase in shared parenting in the US.[27] Therefore, studying the impact of shared parenting arrangements in the US could provide a guideline to understanding how this option fares in one of the more significant Western countries. In the United States, the movement to introduce joint legal and physical custody (JPC) into legislation started in the late 1970s with claims for fathers' rights.[28] As a result of this movement, it was quickly legally permitted in different states, starting in California in 1980.[29] From then on, each state applied joint custody either as a legal presumption, a legal preference or merely an option, the last being the most common, which is determined in accordance with the best interests of the child.

In the late 1980s, the presumption's zenith,[30] Maccoby and Mnookin conducted a study[31] of 1,000 divorced families in two counties of California, one of the states that adopted JPC as a legal presumption. In 79% of these cases, the court decreed JPC, regardless of whether the parents consented and, in the majority of cases, automatically. The study concluded that, one year after the court order, the expected commitment of both parents to the lives of their children did not exist. In fact, most children finally ended up living with their mothers, while the fathers ceased to become the primary supporters of their children. Therefore, it was clear at the time that there was something wrong with the application of this presumption.

The JPC movement of the 1980s was based on the premise that there was already a change in gender roles in contemporary society. However, it appears that this change was still emerging, as indicated by the Macoby and Mnookin study. Therefore, it was not possible to impose a change in the private preferences of parents by law. It would be necessary to wait until this social change had matured to a sufficient degree to be acceptable to the majority of stakeholders. The situation gave rise to a chorus of criticism from different sectors.[32] Accordingly, this led to the decline of the JPC, as some states withdrew the legal presumption while maintaining it as an option.

The next step took place in 1987 when the regulations of the State of Washington introduced a new concept that soon became global,[33] the adoption of parenting plans. Only in cases of disagreement does the judge decide. These parenting plans are the inevitable consequence of a new era, in which the family is no longer considered as the domain of a primary parent with little room for a subsidiary one. It is a new time in which separation and divorce are no longer exceptions but the norm. Therefore, parenting plans are the best tool for regulating the constant involvement of both parents with their children and allocating custodial responsibilities to both parents.

Nowadays, the social reality of the US is totally different: in the last five decades, births outside of marriage have increased from 18 to 31% and working mothers with young children from 30 to 64.2%.[34] Accordingly, a legal evolution has occurred, from the tender years doctrine, which implied an explicit preference for maternal custody,[35] to a more gender-neutral approach. In fact, shared parenting laws were enacted by nine states in the 1970s, 29 in the 1980s, 10 in the 1990s and only one, Arkansas, in 2003. Finally, two states (Washington and West Virginia) still do not have shared parenting laws.[36] However, the guiding principles have been changed in many states and there is a current trend in favour of more gender-neutral laws.[37] In other cases, the trend is towards presumptive equal-time shared parenting, such as in the case of the statute of Arkansas, revised in 2013. This statute directs courts to maximize a child's time with each parent,[38] the judge being free to interpret the meaning of this legal provision.

In order to offer an analysis of the current situation in the US, we propose that of Meyer, Cancian and Cook on the effect of shared parenting in Wisconsin. The statute of Wisconsin states that "a child is entitled to periods of physical placement with both parents unless, after a hearing, the court finds that physical placement with a parent would endanger the child's physical, mental or emotional health". "Placement" should be interpreted as "custody".[39]

The study encompasses a period of more than 20 years and reaches the following conclusions. There is a rapidly increasing prevalence of shared parenting in all examined groups. Parental characteristics such as income are related to custody outcomes, with the child's characteristics being less relevant. The income differences are related to the effort that blue-collar worker parents must undertake to maintain two homes for their children. In general, there is also an increasing legal and social preference for shared parenting.[40]

In their conclusions, the authors highlight the following implications. First, traditional tax and transfer programmes in the US should be changed to define families that apply shared parenting. Second, courts and professionals should clearly explain the benefits and risks of shared parenting arrangements to parents, bearing in mind that shared parenting can work well or poorly, depending on a number of diverse circumstances. Third, there is no research consensus on the viability of shared custody when there are safety concerns. Fourth, more sophisticated analytical techniques should be developed to answer the important questions raised by shared parenting. These questions can only be answered with data.[41]

Shared parenting in the UK

In English and Welsh law, concern for the welfare of a child after his or her parents' separation began in the 1970s. *M* v. *M* is a well-known case that declared the "right of children of contact with the non-resident parent".[42] As Felicity Kaganas states, later judgements abandoned the language of rights and referred instead to a very strong presumption in favour of contact.[43] This terminology was again changed in Re L family law. The case already highlighted that the welfare principle would make a presumption of contact inadequate, therefore it was suggested that the correct word that should be used was "assumption".[44] Kaganas considers that, in spite of this terminological change, the courts maintained the aforementioned presumption on a *de facto* basis.[45] Both the Children Act 1989 and Scottish Children Act 1995 replaced the term custody with residence and access by contact. It was considered that the word "custody" implied an arrangement whereby legal and physical custody was with a *primary parent* while the secondary parent had only "access".

The 1989 Act was amended by the Children and Families Act 2014. On this occasion, the English lawmakers introduced a presumption of parental involvement. This presumption was adopted in the law of England and Wales after a vigorous debate that lasted more than two decades. The debate discussed the pros and cons of a shared parenting option after marital crisis. As Trinder says, it was focused on four different aspects: welfare, rights, risks and resources.[46]

Kaganas refers to an article of 2010 to explain that, at this point, the courts had assumed that contact with parents was "almost always" in the best interests of the child.[47] However, the global trend in favour of considering shared parenting as the norm experienced serious setbacks as a result of the aforementioned Australian experience. The conclusions of the Family Justice Review were to take into account the results of the evaluation of the application of the Australian Act 2006. However, the English government ignored these conclusions and decided that a legal change should be made to emphasise the importance of children having an ongoing relationship with both parents after family separation but taking into account that a meaningful relationship does not imply an equal division of time.

Finally, subsection 2 of Section 1 of the Children Act 1989 was amended by Section 11 of the 2014 Act, to include the following text:

2A. A court, in the circumstances mentioned in subsection (4a) or (7), is as respects to each parent within subsection (6a) to presume, unless the contrary is shown, that involvement of that parent in the life of the child concerned will further the child's welfare. 2B. In subsection (2A) "involvement" means involvement of some kind, either direct or indirect, but not any particular division of a child's time.

Subsection 6 was also modified:

In subsection (2A) "parent" means parent of the child concerned; and, for the purposes of that subsection, a parent of the child concerned – (a) is within this paragraph in that a parent can be involved in the child's life in a way that does not put the child at risk of suffering harm; and (b) is to be treated as being within paragraph (a) unless there is some evidence before the court in the particular proceedings to suggest that involvement of that parent in the child's life would put the child at risk of suffering harm whatever the form of the involvement.

The strongest criticism is that the introduction of such a presumption would be incompatible with the best interests of the child principle. In fact, the current formulation of Section 1 of the Children Act states that:

When a court determines any question with respect to – (a) the upbringing of a child; or (b) the administration of a child's property or the application of any income arising from it, the child's welfare shall be the court's paramount consideration.

This incompatibility is caused by the need to substantiate the paramount consideration of the child's welfare by close judicial control of the situation of a child in every different case, which would prevent the use of general presumptions. In fact, Sir James Munby, President of the Family Division of the High Court of England and Wales at this time, stated that there cannot be presumptions in a case governed by Section 1 of the Children Act 1989.[48] Moreover, Andrew Bainham considered that the welfare principle required "a court to consider all circumstances bearing on welfare, rather than the basic facts of a presumption simply prevailing in the absence of evidence to the contrary". He considered that the underlying problem was that the presumption may run the risk of subordinating the welfare of the child to the parents' interests.[49]

The interpretation of the new presumption was also the object of intense debate due to its complex wording. Particularly, the application of the exception to the presumption set out in Section 2 in cases in which "there is some evidence before the court in the particular proceedings to suggest that involvement of that parent in the child's life would put the child at risk of suffering harm whatever the form of the involvement". This could prevent direct but not indirect involvement and may place the burden of proof on the respondent to rebut the presumption.[50] Interpretation of the concept "involvement" may be quite difficult. Authors claim that, having parental responsibility for a child, it is difficult to imagine a case in which the applicant could fail to be deemed worthy of involvement with the child.[51]

In any case, well-known doctrine states that the application of this presumption is different from other legal presumptions. In fact, Kaganas deduces from Explanatory Note 728 of Section 11 of the Children Act 2014 that the "court still has discretion despite the operation of the presumption". This means that it could order no contact, even if the presumption is not rebutted. She considers that the presumption is only "one of the factors that the court has to take into account when applying the principle that the child's welfare is paramount".[52]

This approach results from the fact that, in the UK, the best interests of the child principle is considered to be the court's paramount consideration; this is different to the concept included in Article 3 of the United Nations Convention on the Rights of the Child (UNCRC), which states that it is a primary consideration. As seen in Chapter 4, the second interpretation of the best interests of the child could be compatible with a presumption in favour of shared parenting.

In any case, as Smyth points out, the UK's story of shared parenting is somewhat brief because of the lack of data and empirical research. All the debates refer to a data vacuum.[53] This dearth of data makes it very difficult, if not impossible, to establish the number of shared parenting custody arrangements in the UK. Researchers are requesting better data on which to base guidelines offered to lawmakers. In fact, scholars state that legal decisions in the UK appear to be based on data from Australia, which is a risky approach.[54]

Shared parenting in Canada

Another example of lack of data and empirical research is the case of Canada,[55] where the different provinces appear to be introducing shared parenting in very different ways.[56] However, certain conclusions can be drawn based on some data records from official collections and surveys. One conclusion is that, on average, 20% of custody arrangements are on the basis of shared parenting. This arrangement is more common in the provinces where the law has recently been reformed, such as British Colombia,[57] Alberta and Quebec[58]; here, shared parenting now accounts for 30% of custody arrangements.[59] However, as Bala et al. state, there is a lack of reliable data with which to measure the impact of shared parenting after separation. Nevertheless, they conclude from the available studies that, first, that shared parenting is normally the result of a negotiated arrangement and not a court order; second, that shared parenting decisions are directly linked to the parents' previous behaviour, roles and income; and third, that judges prefer to opt for shared parenting when paternal conflict is low and children are younger.[60] Family culture is changing in Canada. In the 1970s the Supreme Court considered that children staying with their mother after separation or divorce was common sense.[61] Today, however, there is an increasing use of shared parenting due to a gradual gender convergence. In fact, scholars refer to "tag-team parenting" as a growing model in which fathers contribute more to child care as a result of women's participation in the labour market. This trend is observed in both intact and separated families.[62]

The decision of the court in *Ladisa* v. *Ladisa*, 2005, is oft quoted as an important precedent. Here, the Supreme Court upheld the decision of the trial judge in favour of joint custody in spite of the opposition of the mother, as it was considered that the parents were able to resolve their disagreements.[63]

However, the tension continues in court cases concerning parenting. The judge must find a balance between two options: to give mothers the power of veto over shared parenting, by declaring that without cooperation, it is not possible or to place the child in the centre of a conflictive environment. This means that, in cases of litigation, a conflict exists between the desire to order joint custody and the risk of doing so.[64]

In this context, attempts to reform the law can be observed. First, by Bill C-22 in 2002, which attempted to promote the involvement of non-custodian parents and was criticised by both fathers' groups due to its lack of ambition, and feminist groups because it did not contemplate the risk of violence. Second, by Bill C-560 in 2013, which proposed the introduction of a presumption to establish that shared parenting, with equal time, would be in the best interests of the child. This proposal was widely opposed by legal professionals.[65]

We finish this section on the impact of shared parenting in Canada by referring to the conclusions of Bala et al. They consider that the presumption of equal parenting time proposed by Bill C-560 is not acceptable, as statistics show that equal time is not the rule in intact families (non-separated ones). Moreover, this option is not supported by social science.[66] Perhaps the main problem is interpreting shared parenting as meaning equal parenting time, which is a big mistake. Shared parenting involves the provision of ongoing contact by a child with both parents, so that both remain involved in his or her life. It does not necessarily imply a sharing of the child's overnight stays between the parents. The child can continue to stay at the home of one of the parent's but have direct and daily contact with the other. Establishing time-sharing arrangements may be useful as a starting point; however, what is really important is creating conditions to ensure that contact between the child and both parents is possible and effective.

Shared parenting in the Netherlands and Belgium

In March 2009, Dutch law was overhauled by the Promotion of Continued Parenting and Proper Divorce Act. This Act sought to encourage equal-time arrangements and states that, when parents have joint legal custody, it means that the child has "the right to equal care and upbringing by both parents". The blatantly obvious problem was how to define the term "right to equal time". The Dutch Supreme Court had the opportunity to specify this right in a negative way. It stated that it does not imply equal-time shared parenting.[67] In fact, some believe that this mentioned right is a legal desire to encourage parents to achieve these type of arrangement.[68]

However, this reform was made without reliable research data. In fact, there is still a significant lack of empirical data at the lawmakers' disposal.[69] Nevertheless, Poortman and van Gaalen make the following observations from the scarce empirical data available. First, the rate of shared parenting has evolved from less than 1% before 1980 to more than 20% in recent years. Second, after the reform of 2009, records show that a fifth of parents who shared parenting changed to a sole custody arrangement, which results in a less stable common residence for the child. Third, "Dutch parents who opt for shared residence appear to be a selective group". Finally, fourth, shared parenting does not appear to produce harmful effects for children or parents. On the contrary, shared residence is positively related to child well-being.[70]

In 2006 a legislative change in Belgium was also produced by the Act of 18 July (Moniteur belge 4 September 2006), the matter being regulated by Article 374 of the Civil Code. According to this Act, in the absence of an agreement between the parents, judges should consider making orders for what is called "alternative child residence".[71] This alternative residence implies that a child spends at least a third (33%) of his or her time with each parent. In addition, Article 374 § 2 al.2 CC states that, when parents cannot reach an agreement on the child's place of residence, equally divided alternating residence must be given initial consideration by the court if either parent requests it. Declerk[72] states that the targets of the reform were: first, to guarantee the bond between children and parents; second, to increase the predictability of judicial decisions; and third, to reduce litigation over matters pertaining to children.[73] Moreover, the Law of 30 July 2013 (Moniteur belge 27 September 2013) encourages parents to resolve their disputes through reconciliation, mediation or other forms of settlement.[74] The conclusion of Vanassche et al. when studying this matter is that Belgium has been a pioneer in legislating for alternating residence, which is considered a model of shared parenting that works well in that country.[75]

Shared parenting in Spain

The case of Spain deserves special attention, as we mentioned in the Introduction to this book. In this country, three different situations affecting shared parenting exist, which has caused different social statistical effects. I refer again to the Introduction, and also Chapter 8 on the situation with Spanish case law.

On the one hand, in most parts of the country, the common Civil Code is directly applied, which considers shared parenting as an exceptional measure in the absence of agreement. However, in two autonomous regions, Aragon and Valencia, the presumption in favour of shared parenting has been applied for some years. In other territories, such as Catalonia, where this presumption has not been introduced, the regional regulations have adopted a more favourable approach to shared parenting. This is interesting if we confront this legal situation with statistical data. The data shows that regions in which a presumption in favour of shared parenting has been introduced or shared parenting is viewed favourably have a greater proportion of shared parenting than other regions in which the Civil Code is directly applied. Sometimes, the proportion of shared parenting in regions with regulations that are favourable to this measure is double that of the proportion of other regions.

On the other hand, since 2009 the Spanish Supreme Court has been developing case law in favour of shared parenting. In fact, in 2013 it issued a precedent-setting judgement on the matter. The Supreme Court departed from the provisions of Article 92.8 of the Civil Code, which considers that, in the absence of agreement, shared parenting can only be adopted in exceptional cases. On the contrary, the High Court stated in this precedent that the best interest of the child requires shared parenting to be considered as the ideal measure that should normally and regularly be adopted when deciding on the custody of a child after the separation of his or her parents.[76] If we analyse the statistical evolution of shared parenting in Spain since then, according to the Spanish National Institute of Statistics, it increased from 10% in 2009 to 37.5% in 2019

Therefore, the legal or judicial introduction of shared parenting presumptions, or measures that benefit it, may have a direct impact on the evolution of parent–child relations, according to the statistics. This may be a useful legislative tool if the data studies and psychological research conclude that shared parenting is generally beneficial for children: a measure that would follow a Western world trend.

Conclusion

We can deduce from this broad approach that, in Western countries, there is a significant increase in the number of shared parenting arrangements following divorce or separation. This evolution is the result of a radical change in our society, in the search for a more equal and co-responsible world.

As a result of this trend, a new debate has arisen on the social and political scene. This debate concerns cases in which parents argue about custody of their children. Experts question whether a rebuttable legal presumption in favour of shared parenting could be established as a starting point. The Australian experience provides insight into the level of belligerence caused by this issue. In fact, after introducing a legal presumption in 2006 of equal sharing of parental responsibility in cases that do not involve violence or abuse, this presumption was repealed in 2011. Perhaps the formulation of the presumption was unfortunate. In any case, it is not normal for violence to occur in every separation or divorce.

In addition, the other argument against this presumption is that it is incompatible with the best interests of the child principle, which is analysed in Chapter 4. In fact, an interpretation of this principle in accordance with Article 3 of the UNCRC provides clarity – in favour of this presumption. The acceptance of this presumption is an open issue that must be the object of thorough research, data analysis and psychological study. In any case, its introduction may have a direct impact on the statistical percentage of shared parenting agreements and decisions.

Finally, we must highlight the fact that the increase in shared parenting in Western countries is indisputable and a sign of maturity of such societies, especially when it is the result of an agreement between the parents.

Notes

1 Elisabeth Keogh, Bruce Smyth and Alexander Masardo (2018). "Law reform for shared-time parenting after separation: Reflections from Australia". Singapore Academy of Law Journal, 30, 518–544.

2 Doc 13870, 14 September 2015. Retrieved from http://assembly.coe.in/nw/xml/XRef/Xref-XML2HTML-EN.asp?fileid=22022&lang=en.
3 See *Hokkanen* v. *Finland*, no. 19823/92, § 55, 23 September 1994; *Ignaccolo-Zenide* v. *Romania*, no. 31679/96, § 94, ECHR 2000-I; *A.V.* v. *Slovenia*, no. 878/13, § 73, 9 April 2019; and *Pisica* v. *Republic of Moldova* (application no. 23641/17), 23641/17, [2019] ECHR 779.
4 Ragni H. Kitterød and T. Lappegård (2012). A typology of work–family arrangements among dual-earner couples in Norway. *Family Relations*, 61, 671–685.
5 Ragni H. Kitterød & M. Rønsen (2014). Jobb og hjem i barnefasen. Nå jobber også far mindre når barna er små. *Søkelys på arbeidslivet*, 33, 23–41, cited by Ragni H. Kitterød & K. Aarskaug Wiik (2017). Shared residence among parents living apart in Norway. *Family Court Review*, 55(4), 556–571.
6 Kitterød & Rønsen (2014), cited by Kitterød and Wiik (2017).
7 Emma Fransson, Sara Brolin. Låftman, Viveca Östberg, Anders Hjern and Malin Bergström (2018). "The living conditions of children in shared residence: The Swedish example". *Child Indicators Research*, 11(3), 861–883. They state that "this was particularly true for economic and material conditions, relations with parents, and health related outcomes, while fewer differences were found regarding school conditions (at least those studied)". Also see Section 2a, Chapter 6 Swedish Act on the Children and Parents Code that came into force on 1 October 1998:

> The best interests of the child shall be the primary consideration in the determination under the provisions of this chapter of all questions concerning custody, residence and contact. In the assessment of what is in the best interests of the child, particular attention shall be paid to the child's need of close and good contact with both parents. The risk of the child being abused, being unlawfully removed or detained, or otherwise suffering harm shall be taken into account.

8 Kitterød and Wiik, "Shared residence among parents living apart in Norway".
9 Ragni Hege Kitterød and T. Lyngstad (2014) "Characteristics of parents with shared residence and father sole custody: Evidence from Norway 2012". Discussion paper 780, Research department, Statistics Norway. Quoted in Kitterød and Wiik, "Shared residence among parents living apart in Norway".
10 Norway Act of 8 April 1981 No. 7 relating to Children and Parents (Children Act). Section 48:

> Decisions on parental responsibility, international relocation, custody and access, and procedure in such matters, shall first and foremost have regard for the best interests of the child. When making such decisions, regard shall be paid to ensuring that the child is not subjected to violence or in any other way treated in such a manner as to impair or endanger his or her physical or mental health.

In July 2016, Section 51 was amended in order to introduce the obligation of parents with children under the age of 16 to attend mediation before bringing an action concerning parental responsibility, custody or access.

11 Kitterød and Wiik, "Shared residence among parents living apart in Norway".
12 Act of 8 April 1981 No. 7 relating to Children and Parents (the Children Act). Last amended in September 2019. Lov 8. april 1981 nr. 7 om barn og foreldre (barnelova).
13 Bruce M. Smyth (2017) "Special issue on shared-time parenting after separation". *Family Court Review*, 55, 494–499.
14 Patrick Parkinson (2018). "Shared physical custody: What can we learn from Australian law reform?" Journal of Divorce & Remarriage, 59, 401–413.
15 Richard Collier and Sally Sheldon (eds) (2006). *Fathers' rights activism and law reform in comparative perspective*. London: Hart Publishing.
16 Parkinson, "Shared physical custody, p. 4.
17 Susan B. Boyd (2010). "Autonomy for mothers? Relational theory and parenting apart". Feminist Legal Studies, 18, 137–158.

18 Juliet Behrens (1996). "Ending the silence but… family violence under the Family Law Reform Act". *Australian Journal of Family Law*, 10, 35–47.
19 Patrick Parkinson (2011). *Family law and the indissolubility of parenthood*. New York: Cambridge University Press.
20 Parkinson, "Shared physical custody", p. 5, stresses that the presumption did not say anything about how time should be allocated between parents, defining "substantial and significant time" as time that is not limited to weekends and holidays.
21 Tracey de Simone (2018). "The friendly parent provisions in Australian family law: How friendly will you need to be?" *Australian Journal of Family Law*, 22, 56–71.
22 Rae Kaspiew, Matthew Gray, Ruth Weston, Lawrie Moloney, Kelly Hand, Lixia Qu (2009). *Evaluation of the 2006 family law reforms*. Melbourne, Australian Institute of Family Studies, Summary, page 12.
23 Belinda Fehlberg (2011). "Legislating for shared time parenting after separation: A research review". International Journal of Law, Policy and the Family, 25(3), 318–337.
24 Parkinson, "Shared physical custody", p. 11.
25 Ibid., pp. 9–11. However, as he says, we can believe too much in law …
26 Bruce M. Smyth and Richard Chisholm (2017). "Shared-time parenting after separation in Australia: Precursors, prevalence and postreform patterns". *Family Court Review*, 55(4), 586–603.
27 Daniel R. Meyer, Maria Cancian and Steven T. Cook (2017). "The growth in shared custody in the United States: Patterns and implications". *Family Court Review*, 55(4), 500–512.
28 Herbert Jacob (1988). Silent revolution: The transformation of divorce law in the United States. Chicago, IL: University of Chicago Press, pp. 136–143.
29 See Article 3080 Cal. Fam. Code.
30 Parkinson, *Family law and the indissolubility of parenthood*, p. 47.
31 Eleanor E. Maccoby and Robert H. Mnookin (1992). *Dividing the child: Social and legal dilemmas of custody*. Cambridge, MA: Havard University Press, p. 107.
32 Elizabeth S. Scott (2000). "Social norms and legal regulation on marriage". *Virginia Law Review*, 86(8), n. 190.
33 Parkinson, *Family law and the indissolubility of parenthood*, p. 48.
34 Meyer et al., "The growth in shared custody in the United States", p. 500.
35 Robert E. Emery (1994). *Renegotiating family relationships: Divorce, child custody, and mediation*. New York: Guilford Press.
36 Martin Halla (2013). "The effect of joint custody on family outcomes". *Journal of the European Economic Association*, 11, 278–315; Meyer et al., "The growth in shared custody in the United States", p. 501.
37 Joan B. Kelly, 2007, "Children's living arrangements following separation and divorce: Insights from empirical and clinical research". *Family Process*, 46, 35–52.
38 See William V. Fabricius, Michael Aaron, Faren R. Akins, John J. Assini and Tracy McElroy (2018). "What happens when there is presumptive 50/50 parenting time? An evaluation of Arizona's new child custody statute". *Journal of Divorce & Remarriage*, 59(5), 414–428; and Chapter 29 in this book.
39 Meyer et al., "The growth in shared custody in the United States", p. 501.
40 Ibid., pp. 508–509.
41 Ibid., p. 509.
42 *M v. M* (Child: Access), 1973, 2 All ER 81 at 85.
43 Felicity Kaganas (2018). "Parental involvement: a discretionary presumption". *Legal Studies*, 38(4), 549–570. She refers to Re M (Contact: Welfare test) 1995, 1 FLR 274 at 281; Re H Minors Access, 1992, 1 FLR 148 at 152; and Re O, Contact: Imposition of Conditions, 1995, 2 FLR 124 at 128.
44 Re L, Contact Domestic Violence, Re V, Contact: Domestic Violence; Re M, Contact: Domestic Violence; Re H, Contact: Domestic Violence, 2002, 2 FLR 334 at 364.
45 Kaganas, "Parental involvement", p. 553.

46 Liz Trinder (2014). "Climate change? The multiple trajectories of shared care law, policy and social practices". *Child and Family Law Quarterly*, 26(1), 30–50.
47 Kaganas, "Parental involvement", p. 554. She refers to the article by S. Harri-Short (2010). "Resisting the march towards 50/50 shared residence: Rights, welfare, and equality in post-separation families". *Journal of Social Welfare and Family Law*, 32(3), 257–274; and Re O, Contact: Imposition of Conditions, 1995, 2 FRL 124 at 128.
48 Munby LJ in Re F, Relocation, 2012, EWCA Civ 1364, 2013, 1 FLR 645, 2013 1 FLR 645, at para. 37
49 Andrew Bainham and Stephen Gilmore (2015), "The English Children and Families Act 2014". Victoria University of Wellington Law Review, 46(3), pp. 627–648, p. 633.
50 Andrew Bainham and Stephen Gilmore (2013). *Children: The Modern Law*, 4th ed. Bristol: Jordan publishing, p. 243; and Stephen Gilmore and Lisa Glennon (2014). *Hayes and Williams' Family Law*, 4th ed. Oxford: Oxford University Press, 482. It is stated that this situation could be especially serious when the respondent may be a victim of domestic abuse, who would be obliged to rebut the presumption.
51 Bainham and Gilmore, "The English Children and Families Act 2014", p. 627.
52 Kaganas, "Parental involvement", p. 557.
53 Smyth, "Special Issue", p. 496.
54 Tina Haux, Stephen McKay and Ruth Cain (2017). "Shared care after separation in the United Kingdom: Limited data, limited practice?". *Family Court Review*, 55(4), pp. 572–583.
55 The Canada Divorce Act was enacted in 1986. Together with this federal regulation, there are different provincial legislations which vary in their content.
56 Smyth, "Special Issue", p. 495.
57 The British Columbia Family Law Act, adopted in 2013, states that parental responsibility implies that each parent exercise their responsibility with "respect to the child in consultation with the child's other parent, unless consultation would be unreasonable or inappropriate in the circumstances". It adds that, in respect to parenting arrangements, it must not be presumed that "the parenting time should be equal among the guardians".
58 In Quebec rules, the Civil Code that was enacted in 1991. Commentators state that in this province there is a strong trend towards shared parenting arrangements. Dominique Goubau (2013). *La garde partagée: vague passangère ou tendance locale*. In Benôit Moore edit, Mélanges Jean Pineasu, Montreal QC, Les Éditions Thérmis, 2003, p. 107.
59 Nicholas Bala, Rachel Birnbaum, Karine Poitras, Michael Saini, Francine Cyr and Shawna LeClair (2017). "Shared parenting in Canada: Increasing use but continued controversy". *Family Court Review*, 55(4), 513–530. Even in the case of Ontario, where there has not been legislative reform, there has been an increase in shared parenting decisions, which "also reveals that there have been changes over parenting arrangements even without legislative reform" (p. 526). Finally, they conclude that in Canada shared parenting arrangements imply a situation in which the child stay which parent at least 40% of the time. (p. 517).
60 Bala et al., "Shared parenting in Canada", p. 514.
61 *Talsky* v. *Talsky*, 1976, 2.S.C.R. 292 (Can).
62 Bala et al., "Shared parenting in Canada", p. 517.
63 *Ladisa* v. *Ladisa*, 2005, 11 R.F.L. (6th) 50 Can. Ont. C.A
64 Rachel Birnbaum, Shely Polak and Nida Sohani (2016). "Shared parenting: Ontario case law and social science research". *Canadian Family Law Quarterly*, 35(139), 130.
65 Bala et al., "Shared parenting in Canada", p. 524.
66 Sharon Moyer (2007). "Child custody arrangements: Their characteristics and outcomes". Department Justice Canada. Retrieved from www.justice.gc.ca/eng/rp-pr/fl-lf/parent/2004_3/pdf/2004_3e.pdf.
67 Masha V. Antokolskaia (2011). "Co-ouderschap in Nederland: Eindelikk duidelijkehied". *Justitiële Verkenningen*, 37(6), pp. 9–19, cited in Anne-Rigt Poortman and Ruben van Gaalen (2017). "Shared residence after separation: A review and new findings from the Netherlands". *Family Court Review*, 55(4), p. 531–544.

68 Nathalie Nikolina (2015)."Divided parents, shared children: Legal aspects of (residencial) co-parenting in England, the Netherlands and Belgium". Dissertation, *Intersentia*, Cambridge, cited in Poortman and van Gaalen, "Shared residence after separation", p. 532.
69 Smyth, "Special issue", p. 496.
70 Poortman and van Gaalen, "Shared residence after separation", p. 540.
71 Smyth, "Special issue", p. 496.
72 Charlotte Declerck, "De verbkifsregeling anno 2015". *Tijdschrift voor Notarissen*, pp. 491–503, cited in Sofie Vanassche, An Katrien Sodermans, Charlotte Declerck and Koen Matthijs (2017). "Alternating residence for children after parental separation: Recent findings from Belgium". *Family Court Review*, 55(4), 545–555.
73 In fact, this type of parenting has increased from 9% in the early 1990s to 37% in 2008.
74 Vanassche et al., "Alternating residence for children after parental separation", p. 553. Even the family court judge can order a referral to the mediation chamber without the consent of the parents involved.
75 Ibid., p. 552.
76 Judgement of the Spanish Supreme Court of April 29, 2013 (RJ\2013\3269). Reporting Judge: José Antonio Seijas Quintana. See José Manuel de Torres Perea (2020). Spanish modern family law through an analysis of eighty landmark decisions, Part 2, Chapter 2. Pamplona: Thomson-Reuters, p. 111.

References

Bala, Nicholas, Birnbaum, Rachel, Poitras, Karine, Saini, Michael, Cyr, Francine and LeClair, Shawna (2017). "Shared parenting in Canada: Increasing use but continued controversy", *Family Court Review*, 55(4), 513–530.
Boyd, Susan B. (2010). "Autonomy for mothers? Relational theory and parenting apart". *Feminist Legal Studies*, 18, 137–158.
Collier, Richard and Sheldon, Sally (eds) (2006). *Fathers' rights activism and law reform in comparative perspective*. London: Hart Publishing.
Jacob, Herbert (1988). *Silent revolution: The transformation of divorce law in the United States*. Chicago, IL: University of Chicago Press.
Kaganas, Felicity (2018). "Parental involvement: A discretionary presumption". *Legal Studies*, 38(4), 549–570.
Kelly, Joan B. (2007). "Children's living arrangements following separation and divorce: Insights from empirical and clinical research". *Family Process*, 46, 35–52.
Keogh, Elisabeth, Smyth, Bruce and Masardo, Alexander (2018). "Law reform for shared-time parenting after separation: Reflections from Australia". *Singapore Academy of Law Journal*, 30, 518–544.
Kitterød, Ragni Hege and Wiik, Kenneth A. (2017). "Shared residence among parents living apart in Norway". *Family Court Review*, 55(4), 556–571.
Meyer, Daniel R., Cancian, Maria and Cook, Steven T. (2017). "The growth in shared custody in the United States: Patterns and implications". *Family Court Review*, 55(4), 500–512.
Parkinson, Patrick (2011). *Family law and the indissolubility of parenthood*. New York: Cambridge University Press.
Parkinson, Patrick (2018). "Shared physical custody: What can we learn from Australian law reform?". *Journal of Divorce & Remarriage*, 59, 401–413.
Torres Perea, José Manuel de (2020). *Spanish modern family law through an analysis of eighty landmark decisions*, Part 2, Chapter 2. Pamplona: Thomson-Reuters.
Vanassche, Sofie, Sodermans, An Katrien, Declerck, Charlotte and Matthijs Koen (2017). "Alternating residence for children after parental separation: Recent findings from Belgium". *Family Court Review*, 55(4), 545–555.

29
WHAT HAPPENS WHEN THERE IS PRESUMPTIVE 50/50 PARENTING TIME?

An evaluation of Arizona's new child custody statute[1]

William V. Fabricius, Michael Aaron, Faren R. Akins, John J. Assini and Tracy McElroy

In January 2013, Arizona became the first state to order that, "Consistent with the child's best interests, the court shall adopt a parenting plan that provides for both parents to share legal decision-making regarding their child and that maximizes their respective parenting time" (Arizona Revised Statutes 25-403.02). The governor's signing statement released to the media on May 9, 2012 stated: "The ultimate goal is to limit one-sided custody decisions and to encourage as much shared parent–child time as possible for the positive development of the child."

The background of this legislation began 10 years prior to its passage, during which time Arizona family law professionals were kept informed about the research findings regarding parenting time by means of presentations at the Domestic Relations Committee (DRC) of the Arizona legislature, at the meetings of the Arizona chapter of the Association of Family and Conciliation Courts. (AFCC), and at various state-wide continuing education sessions. In the interests of full disclosure, author Fabricius presented this research. Initially, there was some skepticism about the findings of benefits to children associated with more shared parenting time up to and including equal parenting time with both parents. However, as research findings accumulated favoring the benefits there was more acceptance of shared parenting time, notably among judges. In October 2008, at a family law judicial conference in Phoenix, Arizona, there were indications of strongly favorable attitudes toward equal parenting time among the 43 judges and commissioners in attendance. In a similar conference in Tucson, Arizona, eighteen months later, in April 2010, 37 judges and commissioners responded individually and anonymously to hypothetical parenting time cases, and they overwhelmingly endorsed awarding equal parenting time in those hypothetical cases.

The public was not generally aware of the favorable judicial attitude toward equal parenting time. A study of a representative sample of Arizona citizens conducted in 2008 (Braver, Ellman, Votruba & Fabricius, 2011) revealed that the public thought that only about one-fourth of judges would order equal parenting time in the same hypothetical cases in which about 90% of the attendees at the judicial conference had said they would order equal parenting time.

In late 2008, Fabricius established and chaired a sub-committee, named the Ad Hoc Custody Workgroup, at the DRC to consider reforms to the child custody statutes. In May 2010, the first bill to come from this committee became law (ARS 25–103 B and C) stating that, "absent evidence to the contrary, it is in a child's best interest to have substantial, frequent, meaningful and continuing parenting time with both parents," and further that, "a court shall apply the provisions of this title in a manner that is consistent with this section." The language appeared to some lawyers to be a rebuttable presumption for shared parenting, even though the statute did not define the words "substantial, frequent, meaningful and continuing." There was little public awareness of this change, though there were anecdotal accounts that some judges announced that they would now be ordering more shared parenting time in accordance with the new 2010 law.

After completing work on the 2010 bill, the Ad Hoc Custody Workgroup was charged with crafting a comprehensive reform of the statutes regarding parenting time and decision-making (ARS 25–403). This work was highly visible to the family law community, with a website (www.dev.azcourts.gov/cscommittees/Ad-Hoc-Custody-Workgroup) and communications maintained by the Administrative Office of the Courts. Membership was open to all interested stakeholders and included judges, attorneys, conciliation court directors, mental health providers, anti-domestic violence advocates, fathers' rights advocates, and lay parents. The bill was completed in February 2012, passed by both houses of the state legislature with only nine dissenting votes in May 2012, and became law in January 2013. From the beginning of this legislative journey in 2008, it had taken 42 months and 48 meetings involving 47 individuals to create both bills. The public was made aware of the impending 2013 enactment of the new law by an *Arizona Republic* newspaper article on June 16, 2012 (http://archive.azcentral.com/news/politics/articles/2012/05/22/20120522child-custody-fathers-rights-battle.html).

The current study presents the findings of an evaluation of the 2013 law. The evaluation was conducted by means of a state-wide survey of the four family law professions: conciliation court staff, judges, mental health providers, and attorneys. The survey assessed each group's impressions and opinions of the impact of the new law and how well it was functioning four years after implementation. The four professional groups have somewhat differing perspectives stemming from the types of clients and the range of issues with which they deal. Conciliation court staff and attorneys see the most parents, followed by judges and then by mental health providers, who see the fewest. In terms of the depth of their interactions with the parents, the ordering is different. Mental health providers have the most in-depth, direct contact with both parents and gain the most insight into both parents' situations. Conciliation court staff also have direct contact with both parents while providing mediation and other services, but on a shorter-term basis than mental health providers. Judges have contact with both parents, but the contact is less direct because it is constrained by the courtroom context, managed by attorneys, and sometimes filtered through the reports of mental health providers. Attorneys have direct, in-depth contact, but mostly with one parent. Thus, we reasoned that by averaging the ratings across the four professions we could obtain a comprehensive perspective on various aspects of the 2013 law that gave equal weight to each of the four overlapping but distinct professional perspectives. We also tested for differences among the groups for any additional insight that could provide.

Method

Procedures

All authors participated in and consulted with each other in developing the survey. The authors included a mental health provider (Akins), an attorney (Aaron), a judge (Assini), and a conciliation court director (McElroy). The survey questions were sent by email to as many professionals as we could locate from each of the four areas of family law practice. Email contact lists came from the Arizona State Bar Association, the Arizona Chapter of the Association of Family and Conciliation Courts, individual county Superior Court mental health provider lists, and personal contacts. The survey was also sent to the presiding judges in all 15 county Superior Courts, with a request to forward the survey to all the judges presiding over family law cases. Survey questions were formatted using a five-point Likert Scale with a "neutral" midpoint. Survey questions were presented to participants through Survey Monkey, an online instrument adaptable for various types of surveys. Data were collected for several weeks in early 2017, with queries sent out on various occasions to encourage as much participation as possible. All procedures were approved by the University Institutional Review Board.

Participants

Mental health practitioners

There were 34 respondents (59% women) from 10 of the 15 counties in Arizona, representing 50% of the total number of the listed county mental health providers. The distribution of their number of years practicing in the family law system in Arizona was as follows: 1–4 years = 12%; 5–10 years = 18%; 10–15 years = 16%; 15+ years = 54%.

Mental health professionals include independently-licensed psychologists, professional counselors, marriage and family therapists, and social workers. Working with high-conflict families involved in the family court system, these professionals provide court-ordered child custody evaluations, dispute resolutions, and services centered on stressful parent–child relationships, co-parenting disputes, and domestic violence. Typically, these professionals have significant contact with their clients involving many hours across weeks, months, or years. Fees, types of services, estimated time needed, and other parameters are typically set by the providers. Agreement to these services is often stipulated by the recipient and then authorized or ordered by the court. In most cases involving assessment services such as psychological evaluations, parenting-time and decision-making evaluations, and limited/focused assessments, the provider may offer service updates or reports to the court. In most cases involving treatment, the information shared between the recipient and the provider remains confidential unless release is ordered by the court.

Attorneys

There were 108 respondents (72% women) from all 15 counties in Arizona, representing 11% of the total number of family law attorneys in the state. The distribution of their number of years practicing in the family law system in Arizona was as follows: 1–4 years = 10%; 5–10 years = 22%; 10–15 years = 12%; 15+ years = 56%.

Attorneys are either solo practitioners or members of small or large law firms. Attorneys can serve their clients in one or more of the following capacities: mediator, parent coordinator, child's attorney, pro tempore settlement judge, collaborative lawyer, and litigator. The attorneys are involved in formal and informal settlement talks, and represent parents at both temporary and final hearings or trials. Some attorneys' cases are uncontested; some are resolved through conciliation court services or mediation; and others are litigated.

Judges

There were 30 respondents from 8 of the 15 counties in Arizona, representing 40% of the total number of potential respondents. Judges were not asked to report the number of years practicing family law in Arizona nor asked their sex because that information could potentially identify them in the smaller counties.

Each county in Arizona has a Superior Court division handling family law cases. Some of the smaller counties have one judge who hears all matters concerning family, civil, criminal, and probate law. The larger counties have up to 25 judges who are on a family law bench "rotation" (usually 3–4 years in length), during which time they only hear family law cases. Judges may or may not have practiced family law as attorneys. When parents disagree about parenting time upon separation and request a hearing for "temporary orders," judges typically spend one to two hours with both parents before making a determination about a parenting time schedule to be in place until a final decree is issued. Arizona is typical in that most parents come to a final agreement on their own or with the advice of attorneys or mediation services, and only a small percentage of cases are decided by a judge after a trial.

Conciliation court staff

There were 37 respondents (76% women) from 7 of the 15 counties in Arizona, representing 82% of the total number of staff in the state conciliation courts. The distribution of their number of years practicing in the family law system in Arizona was as follows: 1–4 years = 36%; 5–10 years = 22%; 10–15 years = 3%; 15+ years = 39%.

Conciliation court staff include mediators, attorneys, conciliators, counselors, and evaluators employed by the court. Most staff employed in these positions are required to have a Master's degree in a social science and/or a law degree, as well as specific training in mediation, domestic violence, child abuse, and family dynamics. Court services are offered at low or at no cost to families and are most often utilized by parents who are not represented by attorneys, but families with attorneys also use these services. Conciliation services may be used to address a variety of issues, including not only disagreement about parenting time but also intractable conflict between parents, Department of Child Safety involvement, and significant safety concerns such as substance abuse, domestic violence, criminal history, and mental health issues. Services such as mediation can be initiated by the parties or by the court, while most other services (custody evaluations, child interviews, parent education, high conflict classes, etc.) are initiated by court order only. The elapsed time from when parties file until they are ordered for services varies by county and by the issues involved, ranging from within two weeks to 60 days. The amount of time spent with the parties or on a particular case also varies and depends on the service. Mediation sessions may last from one to four hours, and most offices see the parties for one or two sessions. On the other hand, in an evaluative service, the children may also be interviewed, and collateral information will be collected, which can result in multiple sessions with the family and in a lengthy report with recommendations to the court, generally within 60–90 days of the parties' first appointment.

Results

Not all groups were asked all questions. Some questions were appropriate for some groups but not others. Tables 29.1 and 29.2 identify in the columns labeled "Groups" which groups were asked each question.

Table 29.1 shows the questions on which there were no significant differences among groups; thus, on these questions, the general perspective reflected a consensus. The first three questions assessed the effectiveness of the law in achieving the intended outcome of encouraging more shared parenting time. The consensus was that the law functioned as a rebuttable presumption for *equal* parenting time. The overall mean rating was 3.83, close to the response scale value of "somewhat agree" (an average of only 17% of respondents "disagreed," and 12% were "neutral"). There was also consensus that the law had led to a "moderate increase" in parenting time with fathers ($M = 4.04$; only 2% felt it had "decreased," and 15% were "neutral"). In response to the question, "What do you think a 'good dad's' chances are of getting equal parenting time if mom wants the children to live with her?" judges and attorneys agreed that it was 75% (41% answered that he had either a 90% or a 100% chance).

Table 29.1 Variables that showed no significant differences among groups

Variable	Groups[a]	Mean[b]	Adjacent scale values	Test of mean differences
Rebuttable presumption of equal parenting time	CC J MH A	3.83	3 = neutral; 4 = somewhat agree	$F(3,192) = 1.64$, $p = 0.187$
Effect on parenting time with fathers	CC J MH A	4.04	4 = moderate increase; 5 = large increase	$F(3,197) = 2.45$, $p = 0.065$
"Good dad's" chances of equal parenting time	J A	0.75	0.70 = 70%; 0.80 = 80%	$t(115) = 1.40$, $p = 0.165$
Legal conflict prior to final decree	CC J MH A	3.17	3 = neutral; 4 = moderate increase	$F(3,198) = 1.58$, $p = 0.195$
Number of court hearings	J A	3.36	3 = neutral; 4 = moderate increase	$t(128) = 0.11$, $p = 0.912$
Number of post-decree filings	J A	3.76	3 = neutral; 4 = moderate increase	$t(128) = 1.59$, $p = 0.115$
Amount of child support ordered	J A	2.73	3 = neutral; 2 = moderate decrease	$t(128) = 0.61$, $p = 0.546$
Deviations from support guidelines	J A	3.06	3 = neutral; 4 = moderate increase	$t(128) = 0.30$, $p = 0.0747$
How fathers evaluate the law	CC J MH A	4.38	4 = somewhat positive; 5 = strongly positive	$F(3,194) = 0.04$, $p = 0.990$
Fathers' financial situations	J A	3.63	3 = neutral; 4 = moderately beneficial	$t(127) = 1.54$, $p = 0.126$

[a] CC = conciliation court staff; J = judges; MH = mental health providers; A = family law attorneys; [b] unweighted means.

The next three questions in Table 29.1 assessed the effects of the law on court proceedings. The consensus was that the law had neither increased nor decreased legal conflict leading up to the final decree (M = 3.13; 37% answered "neutral," and the distribution was symmetrical). Judges and attorneys agreed that the effects on the number of court hearings and post-decree filings were between "neutral" and "moderate increase" (Ms = 3.36 and 3.76, respectively).

Table 29.2 Variables that showed significant differences among groups

Variable	Groups[a]	Mean[b]	Adjacent scale values	Test of mean differences
Overall evaluation of the law	CC J MH A	3.53	3 = neutral; 4 = somewhat positive	$F(3,190) = 5.29$, $p = 0.002$
Effect on children's best interests	CC J MH A	3.40	3 = neutral; 4 = somewhat positive	$F(3,195) = 7.17$, $p = 0.000$
Effect on parent conflict	CC J MH A	2.98	3 = neutral; 2 = somewhat detrimental	$F(3,194) = 4.93$, $p = 0.003$
Allegations of domestic violence	CC J MH A	3.35	3 = neutral; 4 = moderate increase	$F(3,195) = 2.98$, $p = 0.030$
Allegations of child abuse	CC J MH A	3.28	3 = neutral; 4 = moderate increase	$F(3,194) = 2.72$, $p = 0.046$
Allegations of substance abuse	CC J MH A	3.31	3 = neutral; 4 = moderate increase	$F(3,192) = 3.91$, $p = 0.010$
How mothers evaluate the law	CC J MH A	2.34	3 = neutral; 2 = somewhat negative	$F(3,192) = 4.86$, $p = 0.003$
Percentage of mothers feeling "forced"	CC MH	0.52	5 = 50%; 6 = 60%	$t(69) = 2.70$, $p = 0.010$
Mothers' financial situations	J A	2.38	3 = neutral; 2 = moderately detrimental	$t(126) = 2.10$, $p = 0.037$

[a] CC = conciliation court staff; J = judges; MH = mental health providers; A = family law attorneys; [b] unweighted means.

The next two questions asked about child support. Judges and attorneys agreed that the effect of the law on the amount of child support ordered in the final decree was between "neutral" and "moderate decrease" (M = 2.73; 52% answered "neutral"), and that there was no effect on deviations from the child support guidelines (M = 3.06; 84% answered "neutral").

The last two questions in Table 29.1 related to fathers' experiences. The consensus was that fathers evaluated the law between "somewhat positive" and "strongly positive" (M = 4.37; only 2% felt fathers evaluated it as "negative," and 6% felt fathers were "neutral"). Judges and attorneys agreed that the effect of the law on fathers' overall financial situations was between "neutral" and "moderately beneficial" (M = 3.63).

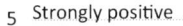

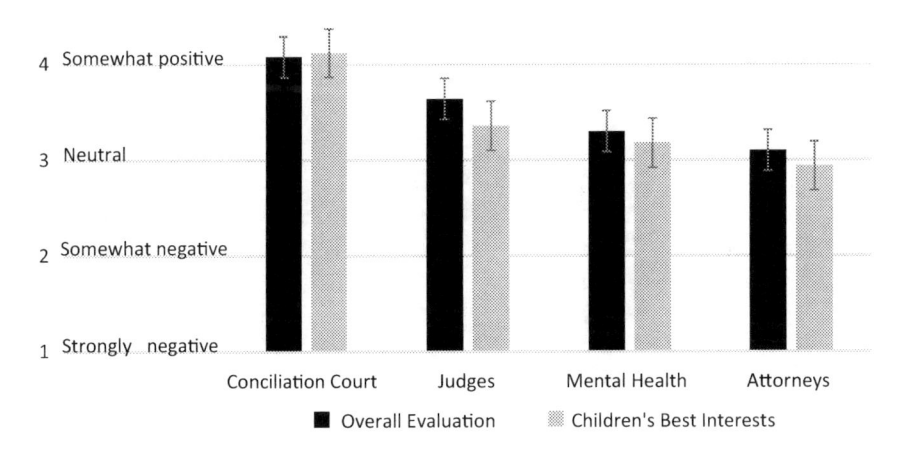

Figure 29.1 Means and standard errors of the ratings of the four groups on overall evaluation of the law and effect on children's best interests. This figure presents the findings of an evaluation of the 2013 law. (Arizona Revised Statutes 25-403.02). This evaluation was conducted through a statewide survey of Arizona, the results of which are discussed in this chapter

Table 29.2 shows the questions on which there were significant differences among groups. The first two questions assessed evaluation of the law, and the general perspective reflected positive overall evaluation (M = 3.53) and beneficial effects on children's best interests (M = 3.40). Figure 29.1 shows the group means. Attorneys and, to a lesser degree, mental health providers were close to "neutral" on both questions; judges were between "neutral" and "somewhat positive;" and conciliation court staff were "somewhat positive." Post-hoc t-tests revealed that conciliation court staff evaluated the law significantly more positively on both questions than mental health providers and attorneys, who did not differ. When we explored the distribution of responses, we discovered that very few (12% or less) of the attorneys and mental health providers answered "neutral." Instead, there were two distinct sub-groups within each group. On both questions, about half of the attorneys answered either "somewhat positive" or "strongly positive," and half answered either "somewhat negative" or "strongly negative." The split among mental health providers was closer to two-thirds positive ratings versus one-third negative ratings. The sub-groups did not differ by sex of respondent. Mental health providers who had practiced family law in Arizona for more years evaluated the law significantly more positively overall ($r = 0.371$, $n = 31$, $p = 0.040$) and marginally more positively in terms of children's best interests ($r = 0.313$, $n = 31$, $p = 0.086$). The sub-groups of attorneys did not differ by number of years in family law in Arizona.

The next question in Table 29.2 referred to parent conflict. The general perspective was that the law had neither increased nor decreased parent conflict (M = 2.98). Figure 29.2 shows the group means. Judges were very close to "neutral" (40% answered "neutral"); conciliation court staff were between "neutral" and "somewhat

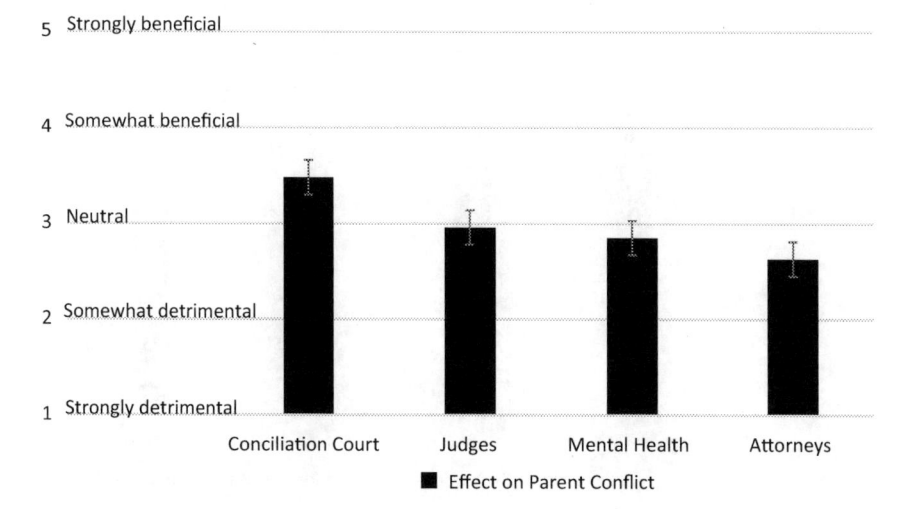

Figure 29.2 Means and standard errors of the ratings of the four groups on effect on parent conflict

beneficial;" and mental health providers and attorneys were between "neutral" and "somewhat detrimental." Post-hoc *t*-tests revealed that conciliation court staff felt that the effect of the law on parent conflict was more beneficial than mental health providers and attorneys, who did not differ.

The next three questions revealed that the general perspective was that the law had led to somewhat more than "neutral" but less than "moderate increase" in allegations of domestic violence (M = 3.35), child abuse (3.28), and substance abuse (M = 3.31). Figure 29.3 shows the group means. On all three variables, conciliation court staff and, to a lesser degree, judges were close to "neutral" (70–80% of individuals in both groups answered "neutral"), while mental health providers and attorneys were between "neutral" and "moderate increase" (45–55% in both groups answered "neutral"). Post-hoc *t*-tests revealed that attorneys felt that there were more allegations of all three types than conciliation court staff.

The last three questions in Table 29.2 referred to mothers' experiences. The general perspective was that mothers evaluated the law between "neutral" and "somewhat negative" (M = 2.34), and post-hoc *t*-tests revealed that attorneys felt that mothers evaluated the law more negatively (M = 1.96) than the other three groups (M = 2.47). The general perspective was that 52% of mothers felt "forced" into accepting less parenting time for themselves (62% for mental health providers and 42% for conciliation court staff). Finally, the general perspective was that the effect of the law on mothers' financial situations was between "neutral" and "moderately detrimental" (M = 2.38), and attorneys felt it was more detrimental (M = 2.19) than judges (M = 2.56).

In addition to assessing whether the respondents' opinions differed among the four professional groups, we explored whether their opinions differed based on the number of years they had worked in family law in Arizona, and by their sex. As noted earlier,

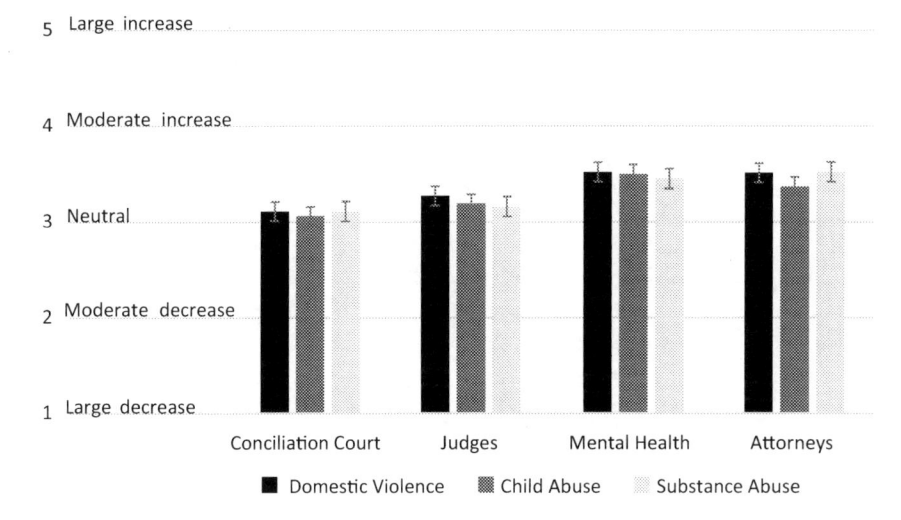

Figure 29.3 Means and standard errors of the ratings of the four groups on allegations of domestic violence, allegations of child abuse, and allegations of substance abuse

judges were not asked these two questions to protect their anonymity. Only three questions were correlated with the number of years in practice: effect on parenting time with fathers ($r = 0.212$, $n = 166$, $p = 0.006$); percent of mothers feeling "forced" ($r = 0.160$, $n = 171$, $p = 0.006$); and effect on parent conflict ($r = 0.212$, $n = 129$, $p = 0.006$). Conciliation court staff, mental health providers, and attorneys who had been in the field longer perceived a greater increase in parenting time with fathers, more mothers feeling "forced" into accepting less parenting time for themselves, and more parent conflict than their colleagues who had come to the field more recently. Only four questions correlated with sex of respondent. The first was allegations of domestic violence ($r = 0.174$, $n = 164$, $p = 0.028$). Female conciliation court staff, mental health providers, and attorneys perceived more allegations of domestic violence. The remaining three questions were asked of only judges and attorneys, and thus the following correlations with sex include only attorneys: number of court hearings ($r = 0.234$, $n = 99$, $p = 0.020$); number of post-decree filings ($r = 0.230$, $n = 98$, $p = 0.002$); and mothers' financial situations ($r = -0.218$, $n = 96$, $p = 0.003$). Female attorneys perceived more hearings and filings and more detrimental effect on mothers' financial situations.

Finally, we tested whether the differences among the groups, shown in Table 29.2, would remain after accounting for number of years in family law in Arizona and respondent sex. We entered these three predictor variables (i.e., professional perspective, years, and sex) simultaneously into regression analyses of the first eight questions in Table 29.2. Mothers' financial situations could not be included in the regression analyses because it was asked of only judges and attorneys, and years and sex were not available for judges. Because the prior *t*-tests generally showed that conciliation court staff differed from mental health providers and attorneys (with judges falling between the court staff and the private professionals), we categorized everyone into one of two groups: public professionals (including only court staff because number of years and sex were not available for judges) and private professionals (including mental health providers and attorneys). Among these three predictor variables, professional perspective correlated significantly with number of years ($r = 0.262, n = 171, p = 0.001$; those in private practice tended to have been in family law in Arizona longer than conciliation court staff.

In each of the regression analyses of the first eight questions in Table 29.2, professional perspective emerged as a significant predictor while controlling for number of years and sex. Consistent with the t-tests in Table 29.2, public professionals evaluated the law more positively, perceived less parent conflict and allegations resulting from the law, and felt that mothers' experiences with the law were more positive than private professionals. In only two regression analyses (i.e., effect on parent conflict, and allegations of domestic violence), did sex of respondent also emerge as an independent predictor while controlling for professional perspective and number of years. Female public and private professionals perceived more parent conflict and allegations of domestic violence than did male professionals. Number of years in family law in Arizona never emerged as an independent predictor.

Discussion

The data reported here come from a state-wide survey about Arizona's 2013 child custody reform, which directed courts, when consistent with children's best interests, to "maximize" children's parenting time with both parents. We received responses from 209 family law professionals in total; these represented 50% of the mental health practitioners in the state, 11% of the attorneys, 40% of the judges, and 82% of the county conciliation court staff. We combined the views of all four groups to obtain a comprehensive perspective on the 2013 statute.

The comprehensive professional perspective revealed that the new law is functioning as a rebuttable presumption of *equal* parenting time; that it has resulted in children having increased parenting time with fathers; and that "good dads" are now virtually assured of being awarded equal parenting time even when mothers want the children to live primarily with them. This is noteworthy because the bill that became law deliberately did not include presumption language or specific amounts of parenting time. Courts were directed only to "maximize" parenting time with both parents, and judges were free to interpret the meaning of "maximize." Nevertheless, most judges have chosen to begin with equal parenting time as the presumed starting point when parents disagree.

The comprehensive professional perspective also revealed that the law is evaluated positively overall and positively in terms of children's best interests. This is noteworthy because in on-going debates in most other state legislatures, arguments that a rebuttable presumption of equal parenting time would constrain judicial latitude in dealing with atypical families and thereby be averse to children's best interests have helped prevent similar legislation from being enacted. The fact that the Arizona law is seen as beneficial to children's best interests suggests that courts continue to exercise latitude when necessary, as intended. The 2013 reforms left largely intact the list of children's best interest factors that courts are required to consider in determining the appropriateness of a parenting time plan.

Concerns are sometimes expressed that laws favoring shared parenting time might lead to increases in parent conflict, and thus it is noteworthy that the comprehensive professional perspective is that the Arizona law has a neutral impact on parent conflict and on legal conflict. This suggests that parents are not litigating more over equal parenting time now than they did before. The number of court hearings and post-decree filings are seen to have increased somewhat, which suggests that some parents have returned to court to seek modifications of their parenting plans under the new law. Allegations of domestic violence, child abuse, and substance abuse are also seen to have increased somewhat. These increases are small, about one-half step in the response scale above "neutral" in each case. The perceived increase in allegations is consistent with the findings of an evaluation of Oregon's 1997 law that legislated child custody and mediation change (Allen & Brinig, 2011).

Another concern is that revising custody laws in ways that encourage more shared parenting time might dramatically reduce child support payments and leave children in worse financial situations. According to the comprehensive professional perspective, child support has decreased somewhat after the 2013 law, but deviations from the child support guidelines have not been affected by the law. Deviations occur when the guidelines do not fit individual families' situations, and Arizona's guidelines already included adjustments for equal parenting time. It is expected that child support should have decreased somewhat, because Arizona adjusts child support awards incrementally in line with parenting time so that even small increases in parenting time result in comparable decreases in child support. Consistent with the fact that most child support is paid by fathers to mothers, the law is seen as somewhat beneficial to fathers' financial situations and as somewhat detrimental to mothers' financial situations.

Finally, the comprehensive professional perspective is that fathers evaluate the law more positively, mothers evaluate it more negatively, and about 50% of mothers feel "forced" to accept less parenting time so that the children can spend more time with their fathers. This view of mothers appears to be at odds with public opinion findings in 2008 in Arizona that showed widespread support for equal parenting time (Braver, Ellman, Votruba & Fabricius, 2011). This discrepancy between mothers' attitudes expressed in surveys and the judgments of professionals working with them could reflect difficulties that become apparent to mothers when facing the prospect of equal parenting time in their specific family situations.

Differences between and within the four professional groups appeared on about half of the questions we asked. Conciliation court staff viewed the law significantly more positively than those in private practice (i.e., mental health providers and attorneys), and these associations with professional perspective were independent of respondent sex and number of years in family law in Arizona. Respondent sex had independent associations with only two of these questions. Females perceived more parent conflict and allegations of domestic violence than males regardless of professional perspective and number of years in family law. This difference could reflect mothers being more comfortable discussing these issues with female professionals.

Mental health providers and attorneys were each split into two distinct sub-groups regarding how they evaluated the law. Only about half of the attorneys and only about one-third of the mental health providers evaluated the law negatively. The mental health providers who evaluated the law more favorably had been in practice longer, but they were not more likely to be male or female. The attorneys who evaluated the law more favorably were neither more likely to have been in practice longer nor more likely to be male or female. Female attorneys did perceive more court hearings and post-decree filings, and more detrimental effects of the law on mothers' financial situations than male attorneys. Mothers might be more comfortable discussing financial situations with female attorneys, but it is hard to understand why both male and female attorneys would not perceive the same increase in court proceedings.

Overall, then, according to Arizona's family law professionals, changing the custody laws in 2013 to be more favorable towards shared parenting increased the amount of parenting time children have with their fathers, and was not followed by an increase in legal or interpersonal conflict between parents, but was followed by small increases in allegations of domestic violence, child abuse, and substance abuse. Most professionals view the law favorably, and feel that it serves the best interests of Arizona's children.

There are two interesting questions about how this family policy change occurred. The first involves the means by which the 2010 and 2013 bills came to be written and voted into law. These legislative processes unfolded over several years with the coordination of a few central actors. This history cannot be presented here due to space limitations but will be the subject of a future paper.

The second interesting question involves how the law came to be interpreted and implemented as a rebuttable presumption for equal parenting time. There was deliberately no mention in the new law of either "equal" parenting time or any percentages of parenting time. Likewise, there was no mention of a "presumption" regarding parenting time. This was done in order to allay concerns that the law would constrain judicial latitude in dealing with atypical families. Nevertheless, since the law change in 2013, most judges have chosen to begin with equal parenting time as the presumed starting point when parents disagree. By 2008, however, at the very beginning of the legislature reform process, judges already held favorable attitudes toward equal parenting time, and their attitudes coincided with broader public opinion favoring equal parenting time not only in Arizona but elsewhere (Fabricius, Sokol, Diaz & Braver, 2012). This underlying cultural endorsement of equal parenting has not led, as far as we can tell, to similar widespread judicial behavior in other states. Arizona judges' implementation of the law as a rebuttable presumption might have been at least partly due to the extensive training they received about the research on parenting time. Awareness that the research showed benefits to children associated with increased parenting time with fathers up to and including equal parenting time with both parents might have given them the reassurance they needed to act on their positive attitudes toward equal parenting time.

An important limitation of this evaluation of the 2013 Arizona law is that it did not include direct assessments of children and parents. The perceptions of professionals who work with these families are not substitutes for data obtained from children about their adjustment, and from parents about parenting time, conflict, violence, abuse, and financial stress. Ideally, such direct assessments should be obtained from randomly selected families who passed through the system before and after the law change. Such a study could provide strong evidence of the causal impact of the law change, but it would be costly. Repeated efforts to obtain funding for such a study of the Arizona law have been unsuccessful, but a similar effort should be made in the next state that passes similar legislation.

A second limitation is that we cannot estimate the degree to which self-selection bias might have influenced the results. This is a concern primarily in the case of the attorneys, because we received responses from only 11% of them. The response rates among the other groups, especially conciliation court staff, were substantially higher and so potential self-selection bias is less of a concern for them.

Note

1 This chapter is a reprint of the one published in the *Journal of Divorce & Remarriage*, 59, 5 (2018), 414–428.

References

Allen, D.W. & Brinig, M.F. (2011). Do joint parenting laws make any difference? *Journal of Empirical Legal Studies*, 8, 2, 304–324.

Braver, S.L., Ellman, I., Votruba, A. & Fabricius, W.V. (2011). Lay judgments about child custody after divorce. *Psychology, Public Policy and Law*, 17, 212–240.

Fabricius, W.V., Sokol, K.R., Diaz, P. & Braver, S.L. (2012). Parenting time, parent conflict, parent–child relationships, and children's physical health. In K. Kuehnle & L. Drozd (eds), *Parenting plan evaluations: Applied research for the family court* (pp. 188–213). New York, NY: Oxford University Press.

30
THE BEST INTERESTS OF THE CHILD AND PARENTAL AUTHORITY IN PHILIPPINE FAMILY LAW

Ryan Jeremiah Donato Quan and
Blesscille V. Guerra-Termulo

Introduction

The granting and determination of who may exercise parental authority over children affects child rights, especially if there is abandonment, neglect, or abuse. Laws provide rules on parental authority stemming from the natural right of parents over the person and property of children. However, even in a situation where the family is intact and parental authority rules are clear, the respect and protection of child rights are not guaranteed. This is where the principle of the best interests of the child comes into play.

The 1987 Philippine Constitution recognizes the family as the foundation of the nation, and the State bears upon itself the obligation not only to strengthen the family but also to promote its development.[1]

This is likewise enshrined in the Family Code of the Philippines, which provides that it is public policy to protect and cherish the family.[2] As a consequence, the law governs family relations, including those between parents and children.[3] Family relations, especially those that affect children, are not left to the discretion of private individuals, even of the parents. And one of the prevailing principles that permeated Philippine law and jurisprudence governing the relationship between parents and children is the principle of the best interests of the child. It bears stressing that, while protection of the family is crucial for a nation, safeguarding the child's best interests is equally important for the future of a nation.

This chapter presents the relevant Philippine laws, jurisprudence, and principles that govern parental authority, one of the rights granted by law to parents or duly appointed guardians. It is divided into four parts. The first section discusses the principle of the best interests of the child in international law and how it is operationalized in the Philippine setting. It then presents the concept of parental authority under the Family Code of the Philippines. The third part focuses on the rules on parental authority applicable to legitimate and illegitimate children, those applied when parents separate, and the application of the Tender Age Rule. This section likewise illustrates the instances when parental authority can be suspended and terminated, highlighting protection of the child's best interests. The chapter concludes with some salient points and observations on the application of the principle of the best interests of the child in Philippine family law and jurisprudence, particularly as regards parental authority.

Best interests of the child

The best interests of the child is a principle that is well-entrenched in the Philippine legal system. As a principle that has been applied and interpreted by the Supreme Court, it has formed part of the law of the land.[4]

The United Nations Convention on the Rights of the Child (UNCRC) states that, "[i]n all actions concerning children, whether undertaken by public or private social welfare institutions, courts of law, administrative authorities or legislative bodies, the best interests of the child shall be a primary consideration".[5] This principle intends to make sure that all the rights of the child guaranteed by the Convention are fully and effectively enjoyed.[6] It also aims for the child's overall development and well-being.[7] According to the UN Committee on the Rights of the Child (CRC Committee), the "best interests of the child" has three dimensions: it is a substantive right, a fundamental and interpretive legal principle, and a rule of procedure.[8] As a substantive right, children have the right to have their best interests be given the highest degree of consideration in all instances when a decision is to be made concerning them.[9] As a fundamental and interpretive legal principle, the interpretation of laws and rules should be done in a way that is congruent to the best interests of the child if there are multiple interpretations possible.[10] And as a rule of procedure, the best interests of the child must be integrated in the decision-making process that affects a child or a group of children in any way.[11] All of these dimensions then need to be considered in any matter concerning children.

In the Philippines, this principle is predominantly used in deciding cases that involve "adoption, guardianship, support, personal status, minors in conflict with the law, and child custody".[12] Consistent with the aims of the UNCRC, courts are required to take into consideration all the pertinent factors that may affect the development and well-being of the child.[13] For instance, in a custody case where the court needs to determine who should be given custody of the child, the courts are required to consider which parent or guardian has the capability to attend to the "physical, educational, social and moral welfare of the children".[14] Among the factors to be considered are material resources and the moral and social situations of each parent; the previous care and devotion shown by each of the parents; their religious background, moral uprightness, home environment and time availability; and the children's emotional and educational needs.[15] This is just one of the examples of how the Supreme Court of the Philippines has articulated the principle of the best interests of the child.

The principle of the best interests of the child forms part of the core of child rights. Considering that issues relating to parental authority affect the rights and welfare of children, this chapter utilizes the best interests principle as a lens for examining the concept and the rules governing parental authority.

Parental authority

Parental authority is one of the areas in Philippine family law where the application of the best interests of the child principle is of utmost importance. The Family Code of the Philippines provides that parental authority and responsibility include "the caring and rearing of [such children] for civic consciousness and efficiency and the development of their moral, mental and physical character and well-being".[16] Parental authority springs from the natural right that parents have over the person and property of their children.[17]

The Philippine Supreme Court has defined parental authority as "a mass of rights and obligations which the law grants to parents for the purpose of the children's physical preservation and development, as well as the cultivation of their intellect and the education of their heart and senses".[18] This definition implies that, in the exercise of parental authority, the welfare of the child is of paramount interest compared with the right of the parents to exercise such authority; consequently, the degree to which parents should exercise their control over the person and the properties of their child is primarily determined by the needs of the latter.[19] Since parental authority is granted by law, parents are not allowed to unilaterally relinquish or convey the same except in the specific instances prescribed by law.[20]

Article 220 of the Family Code enumerates the rights and duties of the parents or guardian exercising parental authority over children:

1. To keep them in their company, to support, educate and instruct them by right precept and good example, and to provide for their upbringing in keeping with their means;
2. To give them love and affection, advice and counsel, companionship and understanding;
3. To provide them with moral and spiritual guidance, inculcate in them honesty, integrity, self-discipline, self-reliance, industry and thrift, stimulate their interest in civic affairs, and inspire in them compliance with the duties of citizenship;
4. To enhance, protect, preserve and maintain their physical and mental health at all times;
5. To furnish them with good and wholesome educational materials, supervise their activities, recreation and association with others, protect them from bad company, and prevent them from acquiring habits detrimental to their health, studies and morals;
6. To represent them in all matters affecting their interests;
7. To demand from them respect and obedience;
8. To impose discipline on them as may be required under the circumstances; and
9. To perform such other duties as are imposed by law upon parents and guardians.[21]

In general, the scope of parental authority and the right to exercise the same depend on the status of the child (i.e. legitimate or illegitimate) and the status of the legal relationship between the parents (i.e. valid marriage, void marriage, or separated). These are discussed in more detail in the following sections.

Rules on parental authority

There are only two classes of children under the Family Code: legitimate children and illegitimate children. The classification of children is determined by law and it can neither be a subject of a compromise nor be assigned through a mere declaration by any person.[22]

Legitimate children are those who are born or conceived during the marriage of their parents.[23] It bears stressing that such a marriage should be valid under the law. On the other hand, illegitimate children are those who are conceived and born outside a valid marriage.[24] Simply put, children who are not conceived and born during a lawful marriage are considered illegitimate. However, there are exceptions to this general rule on illegitimate children. According to the Family Code, the following children are still considered as legitimate: (a) children who are conceived or born before the finality of the decision declaring the marriage of the parents as void because of the psychological incapacity of either party[25]; and (b) children who are born during a subsequent void marriage because of the failure of the parents to comply with the legal requirements on the partition and distribution of the properties involved in a previous marriage.[26]

Legitimate children

In the case of legitimate children, parental authority is jointly exercised by the father and mother.[27] The parents exercise their authority over their common children.[28] If the father and mother disagree in performing their parental authority, the law provides that it will be the decision of the father that will be followed.[29] Professor Melencio S. Sta. Maria, an authority on Persons and Family Law in the Philippines, explains the rationale for the preferential choice of the father, thus:

> The law is designed to provide a mechanism by which the conflicts in the family will be resolved principally by people within the family. Hence, the decision of the mother and the children must defer to the decision of the father.[30]

If the mother desires to contest or overturn the decision of the father, she needs to initiate an action before a court and secure a judicial order.[31] In this regard, the law places the burden on the mother not only to prove that her decision should prevail over the father's but also that this should have the necessary judicia imprimatur. In cases where the mother does not have the means to initiate a court action, it is possible for the rule on the preferential choice of the father to be subject to abuse.

While the rule on the preferential choice of the father makes it easier for parents to decide on the matters relating to their children in times of conflict, it does not seem to always be consistent with the best interests of the child. Being a father does not *per se* guarantee that he would decide according to this principle. The primordial issue is that all decisions must focus on the welfare of the child as the paramount consideration. It should not simply be a matter of expediency by providing a mechanism so the family can operate more efficiently. What is more important is that, even in times of conflict, or especially in times of conflict, both parents should be guided by the principle that places the best interests of the child at the heart of every decision.

On the part of the children, the law requires them to respect and obey their parents while they are still under the latter's authority.[32]

Illegitimate children

Philippine law grants sole parental authority to the mother in the case of illegitimate children.[33]

Professor Sta. Maria argues that there should be an exception to this exclusive right because joint parental authority could still be exercised over the person and property of illegitimate children. First, he contends that since Article 211 of the Family Code mentions that joint parental authority is exercised over the "common children", this should be construed to be applicable to both legitimate and illegitimate children.[34] Second, joint parental authority can be exercised if these concur: (a) there is no question as to who the father is; and (b) the father and mother are living together outside a lawful marriage.[35]

While these arguments would seem to make the provisions of the Family Code regarding the rules on parental authority over illegitimate children more consistent, the Supreme Court has ruled that, despite the fact that there is an admission of paternity by the father, the mother's sole parental authority over an illegitimate child remains.[36] The exception to this rule is when the mother defaults from her rights and obligations.[37] As a consequence, when the father of an illegitimate child admits and recognizes the paternity of the latter, the same does not give rise to the father being granted parental authority.[38] Instead, such admission and recognition "may be a ground for ordering him [the father] to give support" to his illegitimate child.[39]

In view of the foregoing, the mother's right to exercise parental authority over an illegitimate child prevails despite the admission of the father with respect to the paternity of said child.

When parents separate

In the case of parental separation, it is the court that designates the parent to be granted parental authority over the child or children.[40] Generally, the law does not provide any presumption in favor of which parent is to be granted parental authority. In deciding between the mother and the father, all relevant factors will be considered by the court.[41]

If the child involved is older than seven years of age, the court is required to take into account the parent chosen by the child.[42] In the case of *Espiritu* v. *Court of Appeals*,[43] the issue that confronted the court was the rightful custody of the children, both of whom were over seven years of age at the time.[44] In the course of the proceedings, the children stated that, given the choice, they would choose their father to have custody of them.[45] According to the Supreme Court, although children's choice of parent will be taken into account in custody cases, the court will not simply ascribe to such choice.[46] Thus, in instances when the children's choice of parent is considered, the subsequent task of the court is to examine the fitness of that parent.[47] In fact, the court emphasized that, regardless of the age of the child, "the paramount criterion must always be the child's interests".[48] In this case, the court agreed with the children's choice and granted custody in favor of the father. Based on the facts of this case, "the illicit or immoral activities of the mother had already caused emotional disturbances, personality conflicts, and exposure to conflicting moral values …"[49] These findings were supported by the reports of a child psychologist who attended to one of the children.[50] In addition, the mother was also convicted of bigamy.[51] The court further mentioned that, because both children were over seven years of age, they were "thus perfectly capable of making a fairly intelligent choice".[52]

The best interests of the child as a fundamental, interpretive principle and a rule of procedure is evidenced by the manner in which the Supreme Court decides custody cases when parents are separated.

Parents are not the only persons who may be granted parental authority by law. The Family Code grants what is called *substitute parental authority* to a surviving grandparent of the child in case of death, absence, or unsuitability of parents.[53] If the children have several grandparents, the court will also take into account all the relevant factors in deciding which grandparent is most suitable to be granted substitute parental authority.[54] The court shall apply the same principles that it follows when choosing between the child's parents.

The Family Code likewise provides an order of preference that the court may consider in determining who can exercise substitute parental authority. If there are no parents, judicially appointed guardian, or surviving grandparent, substitute parental authority may also be exercised by the oldest brother or sister of the child, if they are over 21 years of age, or by the child's actual custodian.[55] The court determines if these persons are fit and qualified to be granted substitute parental authority. While the tenor of Article 216 of the Family Code seems to be mandatory, the order of preference is not mandatory in determining the person who will be given such authority because the primary consideration is still the best interests of the child.[56]

The designation of the person who can exercise substitute parental authority is significant because they exercise all the rights and obligations enumerated in Articles 209 and 220 of the Family Code, as previously mentioned.

The Tender Age Rule

As mentioned earlier, the Philippines follows the Tender Age Rule, which means no child below seven years of age, considered as tender age, shall be separated from the mother.[57] The rationale for this rule is that the law recognizes that minor children need the loving care of their mothers.[58] The Supreme Court affirms the rationale that "[n]o man can sound the deep sorrows of a mother who is deprived of her child of tender age".[59] Application of the Tender Age Rule is mandatory. This was demonstrated in a case in which the Supreme Court declared void a joint agreement regarding the custody of a child below seven years of age.

In the case of *Dacasin v. Dacasin*,[60] the parents of the child were an American father and a Filipino mother who were divorced in the United States.[61] Subsequently, the parents entered into contract whereby they agreed to have joint custody of the child.[62] They also agreed that any controversy arising from the contract would be exclusively adjudicated in the Philippines.[63] Two years after executing the contract, the father sued the mother before a Philippine court because she had reneged on the contract.[64] The father argued that, contrary to their agreement, the mother had been exercising sole custody of their child.[65]

The Supreme Court ruled that the contract between the parents was void because it was contrary to the law. The court noted two relevant facts pertaining to the date at which the contract was entered into by the parents: the child was of tender age, below seven years of age, and the parents were "no longer married under [US law]" because they were divorced in the US.[66] As a result, Article 213 of the Family Code applies and the sole custody of the child is granted to the mother.[67] Hence, the contract between the parents was clearly in contravention of Philippine law. The court emphasized that the Tender Age Rule provided in Article 213 does not apply to judicial custodial agreements only.[68] The court explained:

> To limit this provision's enforceability to court sanctioned agreements while placing private agreements beyond its reach is to sanction a double standard in custody regulation of children under seven years old of separated parents. This effectively empowers separated parents, by the simple expedient of avoiding the courts, to subvert a legislative policy vesting to the separated mother sole custody of her children under seven years of age ...[69]

Simply put, since the issue of rightful custody of children is governed by law, the provisions of the Family Code relating to said issue, particularly Article 213, encompass private or personal arrangements by any party.

However, there is an exception to the Tender Age Rule. If the court finds compelling reasons to deprive the mother of custody of her child, then the rule will not be applied.[70] This means that, according to the law, the mother, as a general rule, enjoys the presumption of rightful sole custody of her child who is below seven years of age. Anyone who contests this presumption has the burden of proving otherwise by showing "compelling reasons" to take the child away from the mother's custody. In such cases, the courts are then tasked with determining whether there are indeed compelling reasons to deprive the mother of child custody and deciding who is fit to exercise the same.

The Supreme Court has articulated the interpretation and application of the Tender Age Rule in several cases. For example, in the case of *Pablo-Gualberto v. Gualberto V*,[71] the father petitioned for the marriage to be nullified and requested that he be granted custody of their four-year-old child.[72] The mother took the child with her when they separated.[73] During the trial, the father presented evidence that the mother was engaged in a lesbian relationship.[74] At first, the lower court awarded the custody *pendente lite* in favor of the father but eventually reversed its order.[75] Later, the Court of Appeals reversed the order of the lower court and granted the custody *pendente lite* to the father.[76] The mother appealed before the Supreme Court.

In its decision, the Supreme Court emphasized two important points: the best interests of the child as the primary consideration and the rule on tender age or the tender-age presumption. The court explained that the best interests of the child should always be the paramount consideration taking into account "all relevant circumstances that would have a bearing on the children's well-being and development".[77] With respect to the Tender Age Rule, the court reiterated that, to deprive the mother of custody, there must be compelling evidence demonstrating that she is unfit to look after the child.[78] In this case, the court ruled that a mother's sexual preference alone does not amount to the compelling evidence required by law.[79] Instead, the father had to prove that the mother's "moral lapses ... had an adverse effect on the welfare of the child or [had] distracted the offending spouse from exercising proper parental care".[80] Thus, the mere fact that the mother was a lesbian and having relations with another woman could not deprive her of the custody granted to her by the rules. The court likewise mentioned that the mere fact that a mother is a prostitute or is unfaithful does not automatically "render her unfit to have custody of her minor child"; it also stressed that, in cases where custody was not granted to mothers who were unfaithful to their husbands, it was proven that the children's exposure "to the mother's alleged sexual proclivities" had a detrimental effect on their moral and psychological development.[81] This further strengthened the court's decision that sexual preference alone cannot be the sole basis upon which to determine the mother's fitness.[82]

The Supreme Court has found depriving the mother of parental authority justified in cases where there exist "neglect or abandonment, unemployment, immorality, habitual drunkenness, drug addiction, maltreatment of the child, insanity, and affliction with a communicable disease".[83]

In the case of *Unson III v. Navarro*,[84] the Supreme Court deprived the mother of parental authority because she was publicly living with her brother-in-law, the uncle of the child.[85] The court ruled that there is no question as to the "obviously unwholesome" effect that the mother's relationship with her brother-in-law could have on the child's moral and social outlook.[86]

It can be observed from the following decisions of the Supreme Court that, in cases involving children, it is the best interests of the child that is the controlling principle and consideration. While laws and rules are set in place to guide the courts in judicial determination of issues, they are to be interpreted in such a way that the overall welfare of the child is the paramount consideration. As such, the principle of the best interests of the child serves as both a parameter and an end-goal. To achieve this goal, it could be observed from the cases mentioned that the courts must consider the minutest of details surrounding the case and take into account all relevant factors present. While there is a presumption granted by law in favor of the mother, every decision is still determined by the litmus test of the principle of the best interests of the child.

Termination and suspension of parental authority

Parental authority is permanently terminated in the following instances: (1) when the parents die; (2) when the child dies; or (3) when the child reaches the age of majority, i.e. 18 years of age.[87] Aside from these, a person who subjected a child or allowed the child to be subjected to sexual abuse is permanently deprived of parental authority.[88]

The Family Code also provides instances when parental authority may be terminated but the nature of such termination is not permanent. These instances concern situations in which parents are deprived of parental authority, provided that there is "clear, convincing and positive proof" of the necessity for such deprivation.[89] Under the Family Code, parental authority is also terminated when: (1) the child is adopted; (2) a general guardian has been appointed; (3) the child has been declared legally abandoned; (4) a court judgment depriving a party of parental authority has become final; and (5) the person granted parental authority has been declared absent or incapacitated legally.[90] In such cases, parental authority may be restored by virtue of a favorable ruling by a higher court.[91] The courts may also grant parental authority in favor of another party after examination of all relevant circumstances.

Parental authority may also be suspended under the Family Code. The law uses the word "suspension" since the deprivation of parental authority is not permanent. It is possible to revoke the suspension after a judicial determination that the cause of suspension has ended and the party involved would not repeat the same.[92]

When a parent or a person who exercises parental authority has been convicted of a crime that includes the penalty of civil interdiction, parental authority is suspended.[93] Civil interdiction is an accessory penalty imposed in criminal cases that deprives the convicted person of the right to parental authority, guardianship, marital authority, and the right to manage and dispose of his or her property.[94] Parental authority is automatically reinstated once the convicted person has completed the service of the penalty or if he or she has been pardoned or granted amnesty.[95]

The Family Code further enumerates the following instances when the court may suspend parental authority: (1) harsh or cruel treatment of the child; (2) giving of corrupting orders to the child; (3) compelling the child to beg; (4) subjecting the child or allowing the child to be subjected to acts of lasciviousness; and (5) culpable neglect or incompetence.[96]

These rules bolster the idea that the principle of the best interests of the child is an important aspect in allowing parents to continue exercising parental authority over their children, considering that the removal of such authority hinges largely on the effect of phenomena particular to the child. The courts are tasked to decide such cases, applying the best interests of the child principle.

Conclusions

Under the CRC Committee's General Comment, the best interests of the child is a threefold concept: a substantive right, a fundamental and interpretive legal principle, and a rule of procedure. Philippine jurisprudence shows that this threefold concept is applied by the Supreme Court in decisions that involve children, particularly in determining the party to be granted child custody and the right to exercise parental authority. However, it could be observed that the aspect of the child's best interests as a substantive right is not adequately emphasized. While the Family Code explicitly adheres to the principle of the best interests of the child, court decisions have not expressly stated that such a substantive right exists and must be recognized in favor of the child. What the Supreme Court has underscored and demonstrated in its decisions are the two other dimensions: the child's best interests as a legal principle and as a rule of procedure. It seems that the best interests of the child as a substantive right is merely an adjunct of a legal principle or rule of procedure or emerges from the rule of procedure. Another way of looking at this situation is that the best interests of the child is a principle that underlies Philippine family law and is used as a means to protect substantive child rights. It is hoped that, as Philippine jurisprudence evolves and in accordance with the opinion of the UN CRC Committee, the court will at some point recognize the best interests of the child as a substantive right. This will contribute to better protection of children's rights.

Application of the principle of the child's best interests is the cornerstone of every case involving the issues of parental authority and rightful custody. While the letter of the law provides mechanisms and presumptions that guide the courts in dispensing justice in cases involving such issues, the heart of every decision is determined by the child's best interests. There is no question that the principle merely complements the existing provisions of the Family Code; rather, it is deeply entrenched in the understanding, interpretation, and application of that code.

Philippine family law and jurisprudence make the best interests of the child the paramount consideration. Integrating the principle within the Family Code, as observed in Supreme Court cases, demonstrates a recognition that the best interests of the child is a dynamic concept that cannot be boxed by fixed criteria or elements. It can be anticipated that the interpretation and application of the principle will continue to progress depending on the attending circumstances presented before the court.

As may be gleaned from the discussions above, the courts play a crucial role in cases involving parental authority, including child custody cases. The decisions they render must always place the best interests of the child as the paramount consideration. As such, there is a need for continued training on child rights and child sensitivity among judges and court personnel to ensure that the child's rights, welfare, and well-being are protected.

Parental authority, while traditionally viewed as a family law issue, must also be seen as a child rights issue. If the persons granted parental authority do not treat a child properly, the child's overall well-being is affected. Violence, neglect, and other forms of ill-treatment of children, especially at home, which should be a safe place, and committed by parents or guardians who should be the child's protectors, are reprehensible violations of child rights. Protecting children and making sure that they gain the most from their formative years not only secures the future of a nation but also reflects society's true character. As aptly stated by former South African President

Nelson Mandela, "[t]here is no keener revelation of a society's soul than the way in which it treats its children".[97]

Notes

1 The Constitution of the Republic of the Philippines, art. XV, § 1.
2 Family Code of the Philippines (Family Code), Executive Order No. 209, art. 149 (1987).
3 Ibid., arts. 149–50.
4 Act to Ordain and Institute the Civil Code of the Philippines (Civil Code), Republic Act No. 386, art. 8 (1950); "Judicial decisions applying or interpreting the laws or the Constitution shall form part of the legal system of the Philippines."
5 United Nations Convention on the Rights of the Child, art. 3, 1577 U.N.T.S. 3.
6 UN Committee on the Rights of the Child, CRC General Comment No. 14, Sixty-Second Session (2013), U.N. Doc. CRC/C/GC/14 (2013), ¶ 4.
7 Ibid., ¶ 5.
8 Ibid., ¶ 6.
9 Ibid., ¶ 6 (a).
10 Ibid., ¶ 6 (b).
11 Ibid., ¶ 6 (c).
12 *Pablo-Gualberto v. Gualberto*, 461 SCRA 450, 475 (2005).
13 Ibid., p. 476.
14 Ibid.
15 Ibid.
16 Family Code, art. 209.
17 Ibid.
18 *Masbate v. Relucio*, 875 SCRA 25, 39–40 (2018).
19 Ibid., at 47–48.
20 Family Code, art. 211.
21 Ibid., art. 220.
22 *Angeles v. Maglaya*, 469 SCRA 363, 375–76 (2005).
23 Family Code, art. 164.
24 Ibid., art. 165.
25 Ibid., arts. 36 and 54.
26 Ibid., arts. 52 and 53.
27 Family Code, art. 211.
28 Ibid.
29 Ibid.
30 Melencio S. Sta. Maria (2019). *Persons and family relations law*. Manila: Rex Bookstore.
31 Family Code, art. 211.
32 Ibid., art. 211.
33 Ibid., art. 176.
34 Sta. Maria, supra note 30, p. 868.
35 Ibid., p. 869.
36 *Briones v. Miguel*, 440 SCRA 455, 464 (2004).
37 Ibid.
38 *David v. Court of Appeals*, 250 SCRA 82, 86 (1995).
39 Ibid.
40 Family Code, art. 213.
41 Ibid.
42 Ibid.
43 *Espiritu v. Court of Appeals*, 242 SCRA 362 (1995).
44 Ibid., p. 368.
45 Ibid., pp. 368–69 and 372.

46 Ibid., p. 368.
47 Ibid.
48 Ibid., p. 367.
49 Espiritu, 242 SCRA, p. 375.
50 Ibid., pp. 372–73.
51 Ibid., p. 375.
52 Ibid., p. 370.
53 Family Code, art. 214.
54 Ibid.
55 Ibid., art. 216.
56 Masbate, 875 SCRA, pp. 48–49.
57 Family Code, art. 213.
58 Pablo-Gualberto, 461 SCRA, pp. 471–72.
59 Ibid., p. 471.
60 *Dacasin* v. *Dacasin*, 611 SCRA 657 (2010).
61 Ibid., p. 660.
62 Ibid.
63 Ibid.
64 Ibid.
65 Ibid.
66 Dacasin, 611 SCRA, pp. 664–65.
67 Ibid., pp. 665–66.
68 Ibid., pp. 665–67.
69 Ibid., p. 667.
70 Family Code, art. 213.
71 Pablo-Gualberto v. Gualberto V, 461 SCRA 450 (2005).
72 Ibid., p. 457.
73 Ibid., pp. 457–58.
74 Ibid., p. 458.
75 Ibid., p. 459–60.
76 Ibid., p. 461.
77 Pablo-Gualberto, 461 SCRA, pp. 475–76.
78 Ibid., p. 476.
79 Ibid., p. 477.
80 Ibid.
81 Ibid., pp. 477–78.
82 Ibid.
83 Briones, 440 SCRA, p. 465.
84 Unson III v. Navarro, 101 SCRA 183 (1980).
85 Ibid., p. 189.
86 Ibid.
87 Family Code, art. 228.
88 Ibid., art. 232.
89 Sta. Maria, supra note 30, p. 947.
90 Family Code, art. 229.
91 Ibid.
92 Ibid., art. 231.
93 Family Code, art. 230.
94 Act Revising the Penal Code and Other Penal Laws (Revised Penal Code), Act No. 3815, art. 34 (1930).
95 Family Code, art. 230.
96 Ibid., art. 231.
97 Nelson Mandela, retrieved from www.azquotes.com/author/9365-Nelson_Mandela/tag/children.

Acts and court rulings

Act Revising the Penal Code and Other Penal Laws, Act No. 3815 (1930)
Act to Ordain and Institute the Civil Code of the Philippines, Republic Act No. 386 (1950)
Philippine Supreme Court (2005), *Angeles* v. *Maglaya*, 469 SCRA 363
Philippine Supreme Court (2004), *Briones* v. *Miguel*, 440 SCRA 455
Philippine Supreme Court (2010), *Dacasin* v. *Dacasin*, 611 SCRA 657
Philippine Supreme Court (1995), *David* v. *Court of Appeals*, 250 SCRA 82
Philippine Supreme Court (1995), *Espiritu* v. *Court of Appeals*, 242 SCRA 362
Philippine Supreme Court (2018), *Masbate* v. *Relucio*, 875 SCRA 25
Philippine Supreme Court (2005), *Pablo-Gualberto* v. *Gualberto V*, 461 SCRA 450
Philippine Supreme Court (1980), *Unson III v. Navarro, 101 SCRA 183*

31
MEETING THEIR PARENTS
A right always ignored for divorce-affected minors

Fahad Ahmad Siddiqi

Rapid social and economic changes result in conjugal and familial relationships becoming more complex and so too the conditions of their dissolution. As these social changes that affect family life escalate, laws governing family relationships, during and after the marriage, need to be amended. At present, the legal framework for child custody is based on the assumption that custody can be vested with either one of the contesting parties and suitability is determined in a comparative manner. But just as the basis for dissolving marriage has shifted over time as society has progressed, custody must also be thought about differently and a broader framework should be provided within which divorcing parents and children can decide what custodial arrangement works best for them.

While the judiciary has tried to take steps to mitigate this traditional viewpoint, the idea that under certain favourable circumstances the welfare of the minor could also be ensured by simultaneous association with both parents remains ignored. Since there is no inherent contradiction between pursuing the welfare of the minor and the concept of shared parenting/custody, the law needs to provide for this option, provided certain conditions are met.

It is a known fact that a large number of divorce/separation-affected minor children suffer from personality disorders, tendency to misconduct, substance abuse, criminal and antisocial traits, etc. Often, this is simply because non-custodial parents are denied appropriate contact, which then means their children are involved in child custody litigation due to procedural technicalities such as monthly visitation within court premises for a period as little as one or two hours, once or twice a month. Unsurprisingly, child custody litigation is based upon protecting the interests of the minor, with their welfare being the paramount consideration. However, while protecting the welfare of the minor, family courts in Pakistan often place restrictions on the minors' enjoyment of the fundamental right of free access to one's parents, often with no explanation. The General Clauses Act 1897, Section 24-A, establishes that every authority has to pass a speaking order[1] while adjudicating the civil rights of the litigants, and must give valid reasons as to why a fundamental right of the minor to have equal and frequent access to both parents is curtailed and restricted to a mere two-hour visit once or twice a month, to be held within the court premises instead of the home of the non-custodial parent. Neither should the custodial parent (often mothers) be deprived of the complete custody of and access to the minor nor the minor child be deterred and prevented from meeting and seeing their own non-custodial parent – with whom, in the normal situation, they would have free access to and could receive fatherly and motherly love and affection.

Right to fair trial for the determination of one's civil rights is another fundamental right of a non-custodial parent that is often negated. It should be noted here that the concept of fair trial and due process has always been the golden principle of administration of justice but since incorporation of Article 10-A of the Constitution of the Islamic Republic of Pakistan it has become more important that due process should be adopted for conducting a fair trial and an order passed in violation of due process might be considered to be void. The honourable Supreme Court of Pakistan makes it abundantly clear that every family/guardian court is under a constitutional as well as a statutory obligation to assign valid reasons for curtailing the fundamental rights of movement and frequent access of a minor child involved in child custody litigation and that imposing a restriction for an indefinite period that the non-custodial parent, despite being the real father/mother of the minor, will meet with their child/ren for merely two hours twice a month within the court premises is in clear contravention of the citation mentioned above. It is seen that, as a matter of practice, a visitation schedule set out by a guardian/family court while adjudicating an application under the provisions of Section 12 of the Guardian and Wards Act 1890 gives no reason or justification as to why the monthly meeting between the divorce-affected child with their non-custodial parent should be conducted within the court premises and that only for two hours. Irrespective of the fact that the non-custodial father, is considered a Natural Guardian of the minors children under the tenets of Islamic Law. Reliance is placed at 2012 SCMR 1235.

A family court is deemed to be aware of the fact that where the visitation right of a minor is in question, in deciding that question the court must have regard to the minor's welfare as the first and paramount consideration. It may not take into consideration whether, from any other point of view, the father's claim in respect of that visitation is superior to that of the mother or the mother's claim is superior to that of the father. Hence, an order granting visitation rights of the minor allowing them to have better access to their non-custodial parent must not be dealt with on the basis of mere technicalities. The order granting visitation rights of the minor requires due diligence to be practised by the learned family/guardian courts responsible for handling the matter and producing a schedule comprising better interaction with the non-custodial side of the family in order to minimize the negative effects of separation of the minor's parents inter-se.

It needs to be understood that the time has come to give up the archaic mindset adopted since the colonial era, which suggests that allowing a non-custodial parent to have restricted access of a mere two hours once or twice a month to be held within the court premises helps to ensure the welfare of the minor.

Our family justice system is obliged to follow the commands of superior courts while setting out an interim visitation schedule of meetings between a minor child and their non-custodial parent (usually the father). It is the right time for our family justice system at the lowest level to start appreciating that a court's powers with regard to visitation rights and custody of minors and the nature of parental care are not a typical legal matter, and must be undertaken in the way that a wise parent would. 'Welfare' would be better construed in a way that includes all the dominant factors essential in determining the actual welfare of the minor with technicalities of law not adhered to in such cases.[2]

For the first time, guidelines were issued by the honourable Lahore High Court in 2009.[3] This court observed,

> cases pertaining to custody/visitation issues of the minors are not ordinary cases like the breach and enforcement of other civil rights/obligations, such as the property disputes, etc. These cases have their own dimensions, repercussions, and consequences, founded upon the human emotions and sentiments. The resolution and adjudication of this special kind of matters, therefore, should be conceived considered and settled in a different perspective and context, which obviously revolves around the welfare of the minor, but at the same time the natural feelings of the parents cannot be overlooked and ignored;

> A parent loves their child unconditionally and the child shares the same affection towards their parent. In such cases, therefore, there are three main characters in the scenario, a mother, a father, and a child and, in certain cases, the brothers and sisters of the minor, they are all the stakeholders and the emotions and feelings of every one of them should be kept into view while deciding the noted issue, besides the personal law of the minor and the rule about his welfare as mentioned earlier which should be of pivotal consideration.

> Putting together all these factors we can contemplate that neither the mother should be altogether deprived of the complete custody if she has the lawful custody of the minor (until her right of custody terminates on account of some courts' order or otherwise) nor should the father be deterred and prevented to meet and see his own child with whom in normal circumstances, he would have had free access and interaction and could have showered his love and affection if the relationship between the parents was normal; this also is true position vice versa.

> The third important character is the child himself, who under the law of nature should have the privilege of the love and affection of both the parents, which is one of the greatest blessings of the God Almighty, but if for certain reasons, the parents on account of their discord and disparity have fallen apart, the child should not be deprived of having the maximum of what he/she could achieve from either of the parents. And it does not behoove the adversary parties, who may even have hatred towards each

other to claim exclusive possession over the child, as one could demand in the matter of the property dispute, etc.

Besides, it may be clearly understood that the father is the natural and legal guardian and under the Islamic Personal Law, the right of mother to 'Hizanat', in case of a male child, terminates around the age of seven years, (this observation, in no manner, shall be construed of causing any prejudice to either party on the issue of minor's custody), which has nexus and must be kept into view while considering the question of visitation.[4]

It is significant to be observed at this juncture that the Guardian and Wards Act was passed in 1890, almost 130 years ago. The Family Courts Act 1964 was passed by Parliament almost 54/55 years ago but our society is evolving at a rapid pace. Pakistan today is adopting a new ethos and new concepts. In 1964 when the Family Courts Act was passed, Pakistani women may not have been working women but now many women of present-day Pakistan are working and earning their own livelihood. The standards set primarily in 1890 by the colonizers and later in 1964 by the Pakistani parliament cannot be made applicable directly to the litigants of this digital twenty-first century, when many of these litigants live in metropolitan cities like Lahore, Karachi and Islamabad. Therefore the time has come to change our mindset of finding out who is the better parent to adopt a new mindset in order to find out how both parents can behave in a better way; so that the child can have the best from both of them while keeping in view of the observations made by superior courts of Pakistan in multiple judgments like the one expressed by the honourable Lahore High Court to the effect that 'Rights, if any, of the parents are to be given a second place and the child's welfare, will always be the key consideration.[5] The welfare of the minor/child includes, but is not limited to his health, education, physical, mental and psychological well-being as well as his development'. Earlier, the honourable Lahore High Court laid emphasis on the fact that welfare of minors was the prime consideration before the Court.[6] Admittedly, the respondent was the father of the minor and as the natural guardian he had right of his supervision under Islamic Law, therefore on separation of the parents the minor could not be permanently deprived of the love and affection of either of the parents. Similarly, the honourable division bench of the Baluchistan High Court held that neither the father nor the minor could be deprived of the company of each other.[7] The father being a natural guardian was not only required to participate in the upbringing of the minor, but should also develop love, bondage, and affinity with her, to achieve such purpose. The court was to facilitate a congenial, homely and friendly environment and reasonable visitation schedule. The office of the guardian judge or office of Civil Nazir of the court, which lacked proper facilities and arrangements for the said purpose, was neither conducive nor effective and was not comparable to a homely environment. Meeting in court premises could not serve the purpose of the meeting, and it was not in the interest or welfare of the minor to hold a meeting in the court premises. The meeting of the minor with the father, preferably to be held at the residence of the father.

Whereas the honourable Sindh High Court said that the, 'Father and mother both were working parents, therefore, had equal right to have temporary custody of a minor.'[8] The minor daughter was of tender age and she required the love and care of both parents. The father was entitled to spend some time with his daughter at his house during summer vacations. And in the case of *Mst Aliya Fazil* v. *Mirza Farhan Rubbani*, 2013 MLD 1631 Lahore, honourable Lahore High Court observed that, the

> Father could not be denied the minimum right of access to his minor children nor would he be considered an alien enemy qua them. A child would need love, affection, care and attention of mother as well as love, affection, company and guiding hand of father... Depriving father of his right to meet his children would lead to emotional deprivation on both sides.
> *(2013 MLD 1631 Lahore)*

Under the mandate of family jurisprudence and in view of locus parentis capacity, advocates practising in child custody jurisdiction who are setting an interim visitation schedule of meetings for a minor child with his/her non-custodial parent, should understand that it is common practice among couples to use children as pawns in a game of emotional chess. This amounts to irresponsible parenting and can scar children emotionally post-separation. In due course, the parents often move on in their lives and onto another partner; however, children carry the trauma of being manipulated and torn apart emotionally, throughout their lives.

Provisions of the Constitution of the Islamic Republic of Pakistan need to be implemented to the letter and spirit in custody and guardianship proceedings as well, in order to ensure protection of fundamental rights of fair trial, right of privacy and dignity of man.[9] The right of fair trial and other rights of children from broken families and of the non-custodial parents simultaneously, should also be implemented by announcing a reasonable at home minimum standard visitation schedule right from the start of child custody litigation, in a similar manner to that of the fixation of interim maintenance allowance under the provision of Family Courts Act 1964. The minimum at home visitation schedule should be available to all non-custodial parents without discrimination from the very beginning of the trial, at least during the interim stage, and until the final disposal of litigation pending adjudication before the learned guardian/family judges, respectively.

Notes

1 A speaking order means that a judicial order must show that the judge or tribunal has considered all points involved in the case and has decided the case after attending the arguments pro and contra. A judgment is to be based on evidence/material available on the record and the reason in support of the judgment. A speaking order of the court confirms with the provisions of law, that is, it is a concise statement of the case, the points for determination that have been raised or have arisen in that case, decision thereon and the reasons for such a decision.
2 2002 PLD 267 SC.
3 *Mst. Maryam Masood* vs. *Mughisuddin Mirza and Others*, 2009 CLC 1443.
4 https://hi-in.facebook.com/CCLSIP/posts/891972771142921.
5 *Sughran Bibi* vs. *Munawar Akram*, 2019 MLD 2036.
6 *Mst. Ayesha Shahid* vs. *Additional District Judge and Others*, 2018 MLD 1592 Lahore.

7 *Abdul Khaliq* vs. *Ms Mah Noor and Others*, 2018 PLD 44 Quetta.
8 *Imran Butt* vs. *Mehreen Imran*, 2015 CLC 1209 Sindh.
9 Article 10-A of the Constitution of the Islamic Republic of Pakistan, 1973.

Court cases reported by the Superior Courts of Pakistan

2012 SCMR 1235
2002 PLD 26 SC
2009 CLC 1443 Lahore
2019 MLD 2036
2018 MLD 1592 Lahore
2018 PLD 44 Quetta
2015 CLC 1209 Karachi

32

THE BEST INTEREST OF THE CHILD IN THE CASE LAW OF THE SPANISH SUPREME COURT

José Manuel Martín Fuster

Introduction

This chapter will study the best interests of the child concerning shared custody in the current case law of the *Tribunal Supremo* (Spanish Supreme Court, hereinafter, TS). The criteria followed for the determination of this type of custody and what issues arise in practice will be discussed.[1]

We begin by pointing out that the introduction of the principle of the best interests of the child into our system has meant a complete transformation of family law, with the child now being the true protagonist. This has been possible following important *legislative work*, which has resulted in the incorporation of the principle of the best interests of the child in the second article of the *Ley Orgánica de Protección Jurídica del Menor* (Legal Protection of Minors) as a general principle of our legal order and the conversion of this principle into an imperative rule.

Thus, regarding the legal regulation of the best interests of the child in this matter that concerns us, we can find several regulations[2]: the Spanish Civil Code, in Articles 90, 92, 103 and 159; Article 2 of Organic Law (LO) 1/1996, of 15 January, on Legal Protection of Minors; Article 3.1 of the United Nations Convention on the Rights of the Child and Principle 15 of such; and Article 24.2 of the EU Charter of Fundamental Rights.[3]

In accordance with the aforementioned LO 1/1996, on the Legal Protection of Minors, we should highlight that, after the reform introduced by LO 8/2015, of 22 July, Article 2 states:

> 1. Every minor has the right to have *his/her best interest valued and considered as essential in all the actions and decisions* that concern him or her, both in the public and private spheres. In the application of this law and other regulations affecting them, as well as the actions concerning minors adopted

by institutions, public or private, courts, or legislative bodies shall give *priority to their best interests over any other legitimate interests* that may be involved.

The Preamble of LO 8/2015, the reason for this reform and the strengthening of the interest of minors is indicated. It states that the right of the child to have his/her best interests at heart, a fundamental principle in this area, is reinforced, as it is an undefined legal concept that has been subject to various interpretations. In order to adhere to that concept, Article 2 is modified, incorporating both the case law of the Supreme Court as well as the criteria of General Comment No. 14, of 29 May 2013, of the United Nations Committee on the Rights of the Child, regarding the right of the child to have his/her best interests given primary consideration.

This concept is applied in three ways:

1. On the one hand, it is a *substantive right* in the sense that the minor has the right, when a measure that concerns him/her is adopted, to have his/her best interests assessed and, if other interests are involved, that they are also taken into account when reaching a solution.
2. On the other hand, it is a *general principle of an interpretative nature*, so that if a legal provision can be interpreted in more than one way, the interpretation that best meets the interests of the minor must be chosen.
3. Lastly, this principle is a *rule of procedure*.

These three applications have the same purpose: to ensure the complete and effective respect of all the rights of the minor, as well as their integral development.

In this sense, de Torres Perea points out that the rule includes the best interests of the minor in the form of a general clause, giving priority to any other interest that may arise. And it is very likely that, in future resolutions, the interests of the minor will be applied in the search for justice in the specific case as a general clause, capable of neutralizing the application of mandatory rules.[4]

The minor's interest in shared custody

The evolution of the consideration of the minor's interest has also led to a change in the case law of our Supreme Court regarding the granting of shared custody.

With regard to legal regulation, it should be noted that Law 15/2005, of 8 July, amended Article 92 CC by introducing the possibility of establishing shared custody if requested by parents. Thus, Article 92.5 CC points out that shared custody of children will be agreed upon when requested by the parents in the proposed regulatory agreement or when both parents reach this agreement during the course of the procedure. Likewise, Section 8 of this same provision determines that, in exceptional circumstances, even when the assumptions of Article 92.5 CC do not arise, the judge, at the request of one of the parties, together with a report from the Public Prosecutor's Office, may agree to shared custody on the basis that only in this way can the best interests of the child be adequately protected. We see how this interest becomes, in this area too, the central concern when granting custody of the child.

An interesting aspect of this issue is the question of the power of the Court to decide joint custody ex officio. But the reform was so cautious that, in practice, it was a step backwards from the previous doctrine of the Spanish Constitutional Court, which allowed the judge to establish ex officio a shared parenting regime because this model must now be requested.[5]

It should also be noted that there are cases in which joint custody is excluded by law. Thus, according to Article 92.7 CC, when "either of the parents is involved in a criminal proceeding initiated for attempting against the life, liberty, moral integrity or sexual freedom or indemnity of the other spouse or the children who live with both" or in case of "well-founded indications of domestic violence".

Despite this regulation, interpretative doubts and questions have arisen that have been dealt with by the courts, especially the Supreme Court, which has been setting the criteria on the origin of shared custody in the event of disagreement with the parents.

Here, we have to say that the fundamental idea that sustains shared custody is shared parenting, the full equalisation of the responsibilities assumed by both parents in the ordinary tasks of care, attention and education of the children, so that both participate in a balanced manner in the performance of such tasks and responsibilities. The aim is not to divide the time spent with each parent equally; rather, it is to equate the dedication of both parents to their children and to create an effective bond that takes into account what the mother and father can offer them as a woman and a man.[6]

In contrast to current regulation, which seems to conceive of joint custody as something exceptional (Article 92.8 CC), the Supreme Court understands that it should be considered the normal and desirable regime, because it allows the right of the child to relate to both parents, even in crisis situations, whenever this is possible. Furthermore, the Supreme Court emphasises the risk of setting the minor's situation in stone, in the event of establishing sole custody.

Regarding the view of joint custody as an exceptional approach, it is interesting to note how STS 579/2011, of 22 July, interprets it:

> The exceptional nature referred to at the beginning of paragraph 8 must be interpreted, therefore, in relation to paragraph five of the article itself, which allows for shared custody to be agreed upon when requested by both parents or with the agreement of the other. If there is no agreement, Article 92.8 CC does not exclude this possibility, but in this case, the Judge must agree to it on the grounds that only in this way is the best interest of the minor adequately protected.[7] Hence, it is not necessary to specify the meaning of "exceptionality", since it appears clearly that it *refers to the lack of agreement between the spouses on shared custody, not to the specific circumstances to agree on it.*

With regards to the evolution of case law in this matter, we can highlight Judgement 623/2009, of 8 October,[8] where shared custody is now conceived as the general rule for awarding of custody of minors, in the event of a crisis in the marriage or cohabitation of the parents, provided that its application does not result in negative consequences for the "interest of the minor". This is because the protection of this interest requires the maintenance of relations with both parents to be preserved, as far as possible.

Thus, the shared custody system is the closest to the model of cohabitation that existed before the marriage broke up, and it also guarantees parents the possibility of continuing to exercise the rights and duties inherent to parental authority and to participate on equal conditions in the development and growth of their children (Judgement 391/2015, of 15 July; Judgement 22/2018, of 17 January). This conception of shared custody provided the impetus to review current, sole-parent, custody arrangements.

Regarding the criteria for joint custody, the aforementioned STS 623/2009, of 8 October, and STS 257/2013, of 29 April, are decisive in providing the criteria to be applied by the Judgement in 2009.

The 2009 Judgement states that, in matters of shared custody, the Civil Code contains an open clause that obliges the judge to agree to this modality always in the interest of the minor and highlights the difficulty of specifying what this interest consists of in the absence of a list of criteria, as occurs in some legal systems. Therefore, the 2009 Judgement concludes that the following criteria are being used to inform joint custody decisions: the previous practices of parents in their relationships with the minors; the wishes expressed by the minors; the number of children in the family; the fulfilment by the parents of their duties to and mutual respect for each other; the agreements adopted by the parents; the location of their respective addresses; the parents' schedules and activities; the results of the legally required reports; and, in short, anything else that may affect the ability of the minors to live a suitable life in a situation of cohabitation, which must necessarily be more complex than that when the parents were living together.

Judgement STS 257/2013, of 29 April,[9] was influenced by STC 185/2012, of 17 October, which declared the "favorable" subsection of the report of the Public Prosecutor's Office included in Article 92.8 CC to be unconstitutional and void so currently it is exclusively up to the judge or court to verify whether the legal requirements for applying joint custody have been met.

This judgement also declares as case law that interpretation of Articles 92.5 and 92.6 CC must be based on the interest of minors who are going to be affected by the measure to be taken, which will be granted when concurring criteria, such as those described above, are met. Note that the wording of Article 92 does not conclude that joint custody is an exceptional measure; rather, it states that it should be considered *normal and even desirable* because it adheres to the child's right to relate to both parents, even in crisis situations, whenever possible and for as long as possible.[10]

So, in relation to shared custody, we can identify the following criteria:

(a) *Respect between parents*: STS 758/2013, of 25 November 2013, states that a bad relationship between parents cannot prevent the establishment of joint custody, provided that the interests of children are preserved. In the same sense, STS51/2016, of 11 February 2016, highlights "the fact that the parents are not in good harmony is a logical consequence after a decision of marital breakup, since the unusual would be a situation of intimate cohabitation". The existence of misunderstandings, typical of marital crisis, does not prevent per se this custody regime, unless they have a significantly detrimental effect on minors. In order for the tense situation between parents to be a reason for advising against shared custody, it must be deemed worse than is usual during marital crisis (Judgement 433/2016, of 27 June).

(b) *Involvement of parents in childcare during marriage*: This criterion refers to checking whether both parents are involved in the daily tasks of the minors, such as taking them to medical check-ups and school activities and helping with homework. As an example, we find that STS 257/2013, of 29 April, denied shared custody on the basis that, among other reasons, nothing was stated about the fulfilment by the parents of their duties in relation to their children or whether they demonstrated mutual respect in their personal relationship. On the contrary, episodes of a criminal nature and the father's lack of punctuality in arrangements with his daughter were both mentioned.

(c) *Availability of time and access to family support*: As an example we cite the STS of 15 October 2014, which declared that shared custody would not be beneficial for the children because the mother had devoted herself entirely to their care, to the extent of having given up her job. Further, it was found that the daughter experienced conflict with the paternal family, members of which would have to help her father care for her because he had limited time.

(d) *Proximity of parents' homes*: The Supreme Court rejects requests for joint custody if the parents live too far apart on the basis that it can have very damaging and burdensome effects for those involved. Thus, STS of 1 March 2016 denied joint custody because one parent lived in Cadiz and the other in Granada. The ruling points out that such distances make weekly stays infeasible because of the child's school attendance and the disruption to their routines.

(e) *Age of and wishes expressed by minors*: This criterion is closely linked to the principle of the best interests of the minor that governs all family procedures. The STS of 22 October 2014 considered that a child's young age should not exclude joint custody because young children are able to adapt well to changing situations such as alternating parental care and change of domicile. Regarding the wishes of the child, although these are relevant and must be considered, they are not decisive. What the minor wants is not always in his/her best interests. What the child desires is just one more element to bear in mind when deciding on the most suitable custody arrangement (Supreme Court ruling 249/2018, of 25 April).

(f) *Contribution of a parenting plan*: This requirement appeared in the Catalan Civil Code for the first time in 2011. The plan takes into account the needs and availability of both parents so that the arrangements for joint custody can be adapted to them.

(g) *Psychosocial report on the minor*: The psychosocial report of the family unit is another criterion that is taken into account when establishing joint custody. Children over 12 years of age, and younger children who are sufficiently mature, have the right to be heard through the so-called examination test of minors before the judge and public prosecutor. A psychosocial report is prepared for children below the age of 12 to ascertain the best custody arrangement for them (STS 296/2017, of 12 May 2017).

We also highlight that case law seeks to avoid what is known as "the risk of petrification" of relations with the minor. Thus, STS 390/2015, of 26 June, indicates that the interest of the minor prevails and this interest undoubtedly requires a greater commitment and collaboration from their parents in order for these types of situations to be resolved within a framework of family normality. In the case examined in the judgment, the agreement of the parties petrifies the situation of the minor without taking into account the changes that have occurred since then.

Citing STS 616/2014, of 18 November, the fact that the system established in the custody agreement has worked properly is not a reason not to update it. On the contrary, doing so means neglecting the fact that children grow older and their needs may change. Crucially, the situation of the parents may also change. The original non-custodial parent may now be in a position to assume joint custody.

Likewise, it is highlighted that the case law of the TS does not require, when agreeing to joint custody, that the minor must stay with each parent for the same amount of time. Thus, for example, Judgements of 13 November 2018 and 30/2019 of 17 January state: "The shared custody system does not entail an equal distribution of times, but aims at a distribution that is as equitable as possible and tempered with the diversity of the working hours of the parents."

Finally, regarding shared custody as the desirable regime, we have to point out that, in some regional legislation, shared custody has been preferred; specifically, Aragon (Article 80.2 CDF), Valencia (Article 5 of Law 5/2011, later declared unconstitutional and annulled) and the Basque Country (Article 6 of Law 7/2015). However, currently, Aragon (having changed the law), Catalonia and Navarra do not opt for joint custody, so only the Basque Country maintains this approach.[11]

The minor's interest in the modification of measures

In the case of a modification of measures, Article 90.3 CC states that:

> The measures that the Judge adopts in default of agreement or those agreed by the spouses judicially, may be modified judicially or by a new agreement approved by the Judge, when required by the new needs of children or the change of circumstances of the spouses.

In the case of minors, the Supreme Court has established that:

> this wording comes to reflect the jurisprudential position that gave precedence to the interest of the minor in the analysis of issues related to their protection, custody, considering that the new needs of children will not have to be based on a "substantial" change, but true.

Now, do the changes in social reality and jurisprudence have sufficient weight to support the "alteration of circumstances" necessary to grant shared custody? It seems that the Supreme Court considers that the jurisprudential change is per se a substantial variation in circumstances:

> there has been an extraordinary and sustained change in circumstances after the cited case law of the Constitutional Court of which this Chamber has been made, to the point of establishing that the shared custody system must be considered normal and not exceptional.
> *(STS, of 15 July 2015)*

This doctrine would imply the possibility of reviewing single-parent custody previously granted.

Despite the above, the position of the Supreme Court on this matter has not always been homogeneous. Thus, we can find contrary judgements demonstrating that the simple change in case law and social reality does not in itself justify change in custody. Among them, the Judgement of 9 March 2016 in which the court denies the modification of the custody regime, considering that it is not proven that, in a short period of time since exclusive custody was adopted, there have been any circumstance that justify modifying what was agreed by the parents. More recently, in the same vein, it is stated in STS of 25 April 2018:

> The goodness of this regime is not discussed, but if it is possible to adopt it at this time, always for the benefit and interest of the minor, and it is evident that there are no necessary circumstances for it since they are the same that existed when the custody measure was agreed.

In another recent ruling, STS 527/2018, of 25 September, despite the fact that the distance between the parents' residences was not a problem and ignoring the assumptions of Article 92 CC, the Supreme Court decided to maintain the sole custody of the mother. The ruling concluded that both parents were equally trained, both were involved in the education of their children, both maintained irreproachable conduct and, as the contested sentence stated, there were no objective and transcendental causes that advised the modification of the measures agreed between them, not having declared that the father's consent was vitiated.

Here, the arguments used by the TS are striking, as those same arguments could well be used to grant joint custody. And this is because the sentence shows that both parents are equally trained and involved in the education of their children and maintain irreproachable conduct. Following the jurisprudential doctrine that understands that joint custody is the most desirable and reliable approach, we do not understand why, in this case, it was not granted.

But, as we have said, the position of the TS has been vacillating and we can identify sentences that do find in favor of shared custody at appeal because the situation of the parents and children has changed and joint custody is now the prevailing approach. Among the first sentences that follow this line, we find Judgement 390/2015, of 26

June, which finds that, "at the time it was signed it was a certainly uncertain custody regime, as has been demonstrated with the evolution of the doctrine of this room and of society itself". Similar arguments are contained in the Judgement of STS 51/2016, of 20 November 2018.

The lack of homogeneity in appeal judgements is demonstrated by two judgements dated 26 February 2019, which hold different positions.

The judgement resolving appeal 3354/2018 indicated that a change to joint custody had not been shown to benefit the minors involved and also that the existing, sole custody, arrangement was still effective. No psychosocial report on the children was presented to the court, evidence that would have had to be taken into account when deciding on whether to grant joint custody. The judgement rejecting joint custody appears to us contrary to jurisprudential doctrine because it petrifies the situation it wants to avoid in other resolutions; that is, not identifying any problems or difficulties regarding the current custody arrangement that might now favor joint custody.

In the STS of the same day, 26 February 2019, resolving appeal 3386/2018, joint custody was allowed on the basis of changed circumstances over the passage of time and acknowledging the jurisprudential criterion of avoiding the risk of petrification. It stated: "The pass of time and the adaptation of the minor to single-parent custody, cannot serve as an argument to deny his transformation into joint custody."

To conclude on this matter, we would like to briefly discuss a different issue that is raised frequently in court: the case in which one parent (usually the mother) is granted sole custody but the father is granted extensive visiting rights and ordered to pay maintenance. Here, it may transpire that such an arrangement extends to the point where the father is spending almost equal time with the children and then requests that joint custody be considered and maintenance payments amended accordingly.

In these cases, modification of the legal terms of custody from *exclusive custody with extensive visiting rights* to *shared custody* is not usually accepted by case law if no changes in circumstance have occurred and it appears that the reason for desiring joint custody is to address the maintenance payments issue (for example, STS 564/2017, of 17 October).

The truth is that, given the variety of ways in which to exercise shared custody, depending on the circumstances of each family, there should be no problem in agreeing to the modification of the regime, when both parents spend almost equal time with the minor outside of school.

Lastly, we highlight that the last Supreme Court ruling on this matter at the time of writing, STS 490/2019, of 24 September, granted joint custody. In this case it was established that the minor spent almost equal time with both parents, an arrangement adopted by mutual consent, so that changing the custody regime would not affect the minor. Also, the alleged lack of communication between the parents was deemed irrelevant because they had managed to cope with the existing custody regime. However, there were two major changes to take into account when ruling on shared custody: the child was two when the original custody regime was established and was now ten; and the jurisprudential changes that had occurred between the first ruling and the custody appeal. As well as ruling in favor of joint custody in this case, the

Supreme Court also addressed the maintenance issue so that the parents made equal financial contributions to the rearing of their child on the basis of time spent with child and working in similarly paid professions.

A different matter is the modification of maintenance payments on the basis of changing the name of the custody regime. Usually in case of shared custody, if the parents' resources are similar, they each spend the same on the child when he or she stays with them, pay half of school and medical expenses and contribute equally to unexpected expenses. However, the establishment of joint custody, as indicated by the STS of 11 February 2016,

> does not exempt from the payment of maintenance, when there is a disproportion between the income of both spouses, or as in this case, when the parent does not receive any salary (Art. 146 CC) since the amount of maintenance will be proportional to the needs of the recipient, but also to the flow or means of the person who gives them.

Conclusions

We have examined how the Judgement of the Spanish Supreme Court 623/2009, of 8 October, regarding the determination of custody, has established that, in each specific case, the system that best suits the minor and his or her interests must prevail. Shared custody is now the general rule and seen as the most desirable custody regime. The term "exceptional", as used in Article 92 CC, is interpreted in the sense that joint custody is exceptional only if it is not requested jointly by both parents; it is not an exceptional measure.

The purpose of this judgement is to make the custody arrangement as similar as possible to the model of cohabitation that existed before the marriage break-up, thus guaranteeing parents the possibility of continuing to exercise the rights and obligations inherent to parental power or responsibility and to participate on equal terms in the development and growth of their children, an arrangement which also seems most beneficial for them.[12]

Generally, we observe in the case law that when there is no psychosocial report advising against shared custody, the parents do not live great distances from each other and there is no parental conflict, joint custody is likely to be granted. Case law also takes into account changes such as the older age of the child and new social and jurisdictional perspectives on shared custody. Case law also considers the risk of petrification of the minor's situation in that joint custody cannot be rejected on the grounds that the minor has always lived with his or her mother or that, because of his or her young age, the minor needs routine and stability.

However, we have shown that sometimes the Supreme Court does not take a homogeneous approach in its decisions. Indeed, it sometimes requires that a change in circumstances be demonstrated which advises the establishment of joint custody, in addition to changing case law.

Taking into account case law that favors the shared custody model, we considered the following questions. Should it be proven that the shared custody regime is appropriate? Or, in contrast, should it be proven that the shared custody regime does not apply? According to some researchers, the preference for this custody model is unquestionable and therefore "it is not necessary to prove the advisability of shared custody but to prove that in the specific case it does not proceed".[13]

Now, it is understood that, following separation or divorce, shared custody must prevail because it is the general rule according to case law. However, there are cases in which a request is made to modify measures already agreed. In these cases, the law and case law require a "certain change" in circumstances to justify modification of custody arrangements. We have shown that the passage of time and changes in case law have been admitted as just cause for addressing custody arrangements.

A father changing his mind after a few years is not recognised as a "certain" change sufficient to grant joint custody. However, even in this case, joint custody should be given if it would benefit the minor, if the father's situation has changed and he is now able to look after the child and bearing in mind that joint custody is viewed as "desirable" in case law.

For all these reasons, while recognising that awarding joint custody is a complex issue that must be resolved case by case, being given appropriate, clear and homogeneous advice by the courts would ensure better protection of the best interests of the child.

Notes

1 The laws and judgements included in this chapter refer to Spanish legislation and the Spanish courts.
2 Regarding the international sphere, Aznar Domingo highlights the Declaration of the Rights of the Child proclaimed by the United Nations General Assembly in its Resolution 1386, of 20 November 1959, which used for the first time the term "best interests of the child", as being highly relevant. In particular, he notes precept 7, which states that "the best interests of the child must be the guiding principle of those who are responsible for their education and guidance". See A. Aznar Domingo. La custodia compartida: análisis y valoración como método más favorable. *Revista de Jurisprudencia El Derecho*, 1, 2019.
3 There is now a growing trend towards shared custody arrangements in Europe. In her study, Hayden states that the English courts have been able to adapt with much more ease to accepting the shared custody model, whereas the Spanish courts have found this transition more difficult; A. Hayden, Shared custody: A comparative study of the position in Spain and England. *InDret*, 1, 2011.
4 J.M. de Torres Perea, Estudio de la función atribuida al interés del menor como cláusula general por una relevante línea jurisprudencial. *Diario La Ley*, 8737, 2016.
5 J.M. de Torres Perea, Joint custody: An alternative required by the new social reality. *InDret*, 4, 2011.
6 Consejo General de Poder Judicial, *Criterios sobre la modalidad de custodia, Guía de criterios de actuación judicial en materia de custodia compartida*, Ed. Tirant 2020.
7 More controversial is the imposition of shared parenting when the father does not want either shared parenting or sole custody; see Judgement of the Court of Appeals of Cordoba, of 23 January 2018 (JUR\2018\46596).
8 Judgement 623/2009 of, 8 October. Appeal 1471/2006. Speaker: Roca Trías.
9 Judgement 257/2013, of 29 April. Appeal 2525/2011. Speaker: Seijas Quintana.
10 It is said that the approval of a national law with the essential common framework for shared custody models would enhance equal opportunities for families immersed in the

trauma of separation. See A.M. Pérez Vallejo and M.B. Sainz Cantero Caparrós, *El principio de coparentalidad y el derecho de los hijos a relacionarse con sus progenitores, paradigmas de los modernos modelos de custodia*. Ed. Tirant 2018.

11 M. Linacero De La Fuente, Medidas en los procesos de familia en relación a los hijos. *Guarda y custodia, Tratado de Derecho de familia*. Ed. Tirant, 2020.

12 For more information, see M. Garriga Gorina, Continuity as an alternative to joint physical custody: The approximation standard. *InDret*, 3, 2008.

13 I. Pérez Calvo, Custodia exclusiva/ custodia compartida. Custodia compartida en el camino de la corresponsabilidad parental in *Tratado sobre la igualdad jurídica y social de la mujer en el siglo XXI*. Vlex, 2019.

References

Aznar Domingo. La custodia compartida: análisis y valoración como método más favorable. *Revista de Jurisprudencia El Derecho*, 1, 2019.

Eekelaar, J. The role of the best interest principle in decisions affecting children and decisions about children. *International Journal of Children's Rights*, 23, 2015.

Garriga Gorina, M. Continuity as an alternative to joint physical custody: The approximation standard. *InDret*, 3, 2008.

Hayden, A. Shared custody: A comparative study of the position in Spain and England. InDret, 1, 2011.

Linacero De La Fuente, M. Medidas en los procesos de familia en relación a los hijos. *Guarda y custodia, Tratado de Derecho de familia*. Ed. Tirant, 2020.

Pérez Calvo, I. Custodia exclusiva/ custodia compartida. Custodia compartida en el camino de la corresponsabilidad parental in *Tratado sobre la igualdad jurídica y social de la mujer en el siglo XXI*. Fernández González, Vlex. 2019.

Pérez Vallejo, A.M., Sainz Cantero Caparrós, M.B. El principio de coparentalidad y el derecho de los hijos a relacionarse con sus progenitores, paradigmas de los modernos modelos de custodia. Ed. Tirant, 2018.

Torres Perea, J.M. de, Joint custody: An alternative required by the new social reality. *InDret*, 4, 2011.

Torres Perea, J.M. de, Estudio de la función atribuida al interés del menor como cláusula general por una relevante línea jurisprudencial. *Diario La Ley*, 8737, 2016.

33
DIVORCE AND LOSS OF PATERNAL CONTACT
A perspective from Norway

Eivind Meland

When we, a research group with colleagues from Western Norway, first published a research paper on adolescents' experience of divorce, it was rather novel in our country[1]. The growing prevalence of divorce had mostly been neglected by the research community, within social sciences and social psychology too. In our paper we revealed that adolescents with divorce experience (DE) reported more somatic and emotional health complaints and unhealthy behaviors compared with peers from intact families.

According to a widely held view, the detrimental effects of divorce were mitigated by social welfare benefits protecting single mothers from poverty. Experiences from the Nordic welfare states could not be compared with research results from, for example, the United States, because single mothers had material standards that were acceptable, according to this view. Later, it was revealed that these opinions were mostly formed on the basis of wishful thinking[2]. The associations between parental divorce and several outcomes were generally very similar in Norway and the US, in spite of the great differences in family policy and welfare benefits. The mediational effects of family financial resources were similar in both countries and were most marked in the area of academic achievement. The predictive power of such variables was also quite similar.

Fathers matter

Another widely held opinion was that a hypothesized stigmatizing effect for children of divorce was mitigated by the fact that divorce became more prevalent and thus "normal". We were able to examine this hypothesis with data from four consecutive cross-sectional studies in the former county of Sogn og Fjordane during the years 1997–2009. The surveys were performed in the same context, with the same age group (late teens) and gained an equally high response rate.

Sogn og Fjordane was mostly a rural and a "traditional" spot on the Norwegian map, where the rise in the prevalence of divorce occurred later than in more urban areas of the country. During those years we observed a 34% relative increase in adolescents' DE. We identified no signs of attenuated effects on emotional health across the years of observation[3]. On the contrary, an increase in anxiety and psychosomatic complaints was detected. However, as a concomitant increase was also observed in the group with no DE, the changes probably expressed general secular trends or unspecific effects for the surveyed adolescents.

Furthermore, mental complaints were not attenuated as time since divorce increased. On the contrary, we revealed a borderline significant increase in depressive complaints with reported time since DE. If DE was a single traumatic event for adolescents, we should expect that health improved as time went by since the DE. Could a continuous factor impacting adolescents' mental health be the explanation for what we revealed?

When we separated the surveyed youth in one group with intact families, one group with DE but with preserved contact with both parents, and the last group with DE and loss of parental contact, interesting results emerged. The group with DE but preserved contact with both parents experienced significantly more mental distress, but the standardized beta-values were modest. However, adolescents with concomitant loss of parental contact experienced emotional distress to a far greater degree than their peers. The unadjusted b-values for this group were almost approaching the standard deviations (SDs) for the constructs used as measures of emotional distress, indicating large effect sizes[3].

During the survey period, the proportion of adolescents who experienced parental loss of contact slightly increased. As DE increased in relative and absolute terms, increased numbers of adolescents lost contact with one or both parents. Almost all adolescents who reported parental loss, lost contact with their fathers. The Norwegian authorities intend to promote preserved parental contact and mutual support from both parents after divorce. An increased number of parents voluntarily agree upon shared parenting after divorce[4], but it still seems that a sizable proportion of mothers divorcing exclude fathers from parenting or fathers abstain from parenting.

Statistics Norway has estimated that between 26,000 and 46,000 children (depending on which of the parents was asked) do not see their fathers during an average month, and a definite socioeconomic trend is observed. Most of the fathers want to regain contact with their children[5]. The present status of family and child policies in Norway is that a growing number of divorced parents choose shared parenting but that a sizable number of them experience conflict to such a degree that their children, especially those from disadvantaged socioeconomic backgrounds, lose contact with their fathers.

Supporting evidence

The findings from our cross-sectional studies are supported by a longitudinal cohort study conducted with a younger age group, in their early teens, including almost all students from grades 6 and 8 in Sogn og Fjordane, who were followed for two years. We investigated how divorce impacted their confidence when engaging in conversation and contact with their parents and how DE, confidence and contact with mothers and fathers impacted health complaints and self-esteem during the two-year period of observation and at the end of the study[6].

We investigated somatic health complaints, emotional complaints and self-esteem. The study revealed that former and recent DEs impacted the adolescents' confidence with fathers only. The impact was most evident for the more severe forms of conversational difficulties and with loss of paternal contact. Divorce had no impact on contact with or conversational difficulties with mothers. DE, in itself, predicted only self-esteem issues, which were mediated by confidence when engaging in conversation with parents. Confidence when talking about difficult issues with both mothers and fathers had strong temporal causal associations with the outcomes two years later. Only confidence experienced in conversation with fathers impacted changes in health complaints and self-esteem in full-model residual change analyses.

Interaction analyses revealed that interactions between DE and confidence with mothers were modest and statistically insignificant for all interaction terms. The level of confidence with fathers moderated, however, the impact of DE on all three outcomes[6].

In yet another study on the same population, we evaluated how self-rated health (SRH) was impacted by a more comprehensive set of predictors related to family life[7]. The most decisive factors impacting future SRH were linked to confidence in communication about difficult issues with both parents and the experience of parental support with schoolwork. In addition, adolescents' experience of having their opinions taken seriously within the family and the absence of excessive parental expectations impacted SRH after two years. Divorce impacted SRH modestly and was mediated by the other factors. Only the absence of contact with fathers moderated the effect of DE on SRH. We ascertained the causal relationships using residual change analyses.

Our longitudinal cohort studies had the following strengths. We evaluated comprehensively the important health consequences and self-conceptual problems that may affect adolescents' future health and well-being in adult life. We also examined a great variety of family factors, some of which have established associations with subjective health and others that do not. Both mediation and moderation were examined, and we performed both temporal causal and residual change analyses. The studies also adjusted for possible confounders, most importantly the self-rated socioeconomic status that is linked with both DE and subjective health.

Difficult or no contact: Does it matter?

The closeness between fathers and their children is important, according to the studies that we conducted. A question remains, however: If communication with their fathers is already difficult, may children benefit from losing contact with their fathers and thereby be protected from the effects of a difficult relationship? This question was addressed using a cross-sectional study, the results of which will be published shortly[8]. Subjective health complaints (both emotional and somatic) and life satisfaction were the outcomes surveyed in this study. A sizable proportion of this youth population reported difficult communication with their fathers and the percentage of those who had lost contact with their fathers increased from 5% among the 11 year olds to 12% among the 17 year olds.

The results of the study supported the hypothesis that adolescents reporting loss of paternal contact fared (slightly) better than those reporting very difficult communication with their fathers. The differences were small and only statistically significant for subjective health complaints. However, we revealed that any communication with fathers moderated the effect between DE and life satisfaction, whereas only the higher levels of communication quality moderated the effect on subjective health complaints[8].

Why does Norway lag behind?

There are several reasons why so many divorces in Norway end in battles during which children and parents suffer alike. First, we have a legal system that does not guarantee equal rights for both parents. Mothers have sole decision-making authority if the parents of a child are not living together before the child is born. Second, family law instructs judges to consider shared custody only in exceptional cases involving parental conflict regarding custody arrangements. Expert witnesses in the Norwegian legal system have an extraordinary influence on court decisions. The judges lean on these witnesses inappropriately[9].

The presumption that mothers are the primary attachment figures for children when they are young was mostly abandoned in the research literature during the 1970s[10]. The "mother presumption" was accordingly removed from Norwegian family law in the early 1980s. However, legal practice in Norwegian courts appears to have reintroduced this presumption in recent years[11].

We face another challenge linked to the way in which many psychologists and expert witnesses work within our legal system. Attachment is acknowledged as important; however, the downsides of exaggerated attachment, such as enmeshment, emotional control and parental alienation, are seldom acknowledged. Even though parental alienation has been documented in the research literature as detrimental to children's psychological and social health[12], it is noticeable that many Norwegian psychologists still deny its existence.

Norwegian family law is presently under revision and we hope that mutual care, shared custody and the best interests of children can be better promoted in our society as a result.

Notes

1 Breidablik HJ, Meland E. Familieoppløsning i barndom - helse og helseatferd i ungdommen [Family breakup in childhood: Health and health behavior in adolescence]. *Tidsskrift for den Norske lægeforening*, 1999; 119: 2331–5.
2 Breivik K, Olweus D. Children of divorce in a Scandinavian welfare state: Are they less affected than US children? *Scandinavian Journal of Psychology*, 2006; 47(1): 61–74.
3 Reiter SF, Hjorleifsson S, Breidablik HJ, Meland E. Impact of divorce and loss of parental contact on health complaints among adolescents. *Journal of Public Health*, 2013; 35(2): 278–85.

4 Andenæs A, Kjøs P, Tjersland OA. Delt bosted – hva sier forskningen [Shared parenting: What does science tell us?]. *Tidsskr for Norsk Psykologforening*, 2017; 55(3): 276–83.
5 Lyngstad J, Kitterød RH, Lidén H, Wiik KA. *Hvilke fedre har lite eller ingen kontakt med barna når foreldrene bor hver for seg? [Who are the fathers that have little or no contact with children after divorce?]*. Oslo: Statistics Norway; 2015.
6 Meland E, Breidablik HJ, Thuen F. Divorce and conversational difficulties with parents: Impact on adolescent health and self-esteem. *Scandinavian Journal of Public Health*, 2019; 1403494819888044.
7 Meland E, Breidablik HJ, Thuen F. Family factors predicting self-rated health during early adolescence. *Scandinavian Journal of Public Health*. 2020; 1403494820972282.
8 Thuen F, Meland E, Breidablik HJ. The effects of communication quality and lack of contact with fathers on subjective health complaints and life satisfaction among parental divorced youth. *Journal of Divorce & Remarriage*. 2021, doi.org/10.1080/10502556.2021.1871835.
9 Nordhelle G. Praktisering av sakkyndighetsarbeid i barnefordelingssaker – til barnas beste? *Tidsskrift for familierett, arverett og barnevernrettslige spørsmål*, 2011; 22(3): 176–97.
10 Davis PC. The good mother: A new look at psychological parent theory. *Review of Law & Social Change*, 1996; 22: 347–70.
11 Amundsen J. *"Barnets beste". Om "Foreldretvister" og hvordan begrepet "barnets beste" i barneloven §48 vurderes i avgjørelser om foreldreansvar, fast bosted og samvær. Analyse av lagmannsrettspraksis fra 2013 til 2015 i spørsmål om foreldreansvar [The best interests of the child]*. Oslo: Universitetet i Oslo; 2016.
12 Harman JJ, Kruk E, Hines DA. Parental alienating behaviors: An unacknowledged form of family violence. *Psychological Bulletin*, 2018; 144(12): 1275–99.

34

TRYING TO PUT SHARED PARENTING INTO SCOTTISH LAW

Ian Maxwell

Why enact legislation for shared parenting?

Shared parenting, in which separated parents take an equal part in the upbringing of their children, is already practised by many families. Like many other aspects of private family life, the state should hesitate to dictate what happens in the daily life of these families.

Many fundamental aspects of family life are already affected by legislation.

If parents are married or in civil partnerships, the law determines how these arrangements will end. It also determines how resources and property are divided when divorce occurs. In Scotland, there is also legal provision for the arrangements when cohabiting couples separate.

Ongoing child support maintenance arrangements are also based in law, and various aspects of the involvement of parents in the education of their children are also regulated. In Scotland, there is law concerning parental involvement in schools that interacts with legislation concerning parental rights and responsibilities and also the rights of children and young people to determine what involvement a father or a mother can have with their child's school.

Aspects of criminal law concerning domestic abuse and coercive control also have a part to play in regulating certain aspects of relationship breakdown.

None of these laws can force parents to conduct the break-up of a relationship in a particular manner or force them to share the care of their children in any particular pattern. But there is a strong case for changing the law in Scotland and many other countries to make it easier and more likely that shared parenting is the outcome of a court decision when both parents have a constructive and useful contribution to make to their children.

Shared parenting laws have already been passed in countries such as Belgium and in a range of states including Arizona. Portugal, Greece and a range of other countries across the world are currently considering whether to enact shared parenting legislation. Scotland is midway through reform of its own family law. By September 2020 we will know whether attempts to include a shared parenting provision have been successful–see the Success or Failure section below for the answer.

Changing the law *won't* force any family to share the parenting. But it will have a fundamental impact on the way that court disputes about the arrangements for children after separation are conducted. A law change, such as the one enacted in Belgium in 2006, *won't* even force the court to rule that care of the children should be shared on an equal basis. Either parent or the children can present reasons why equally shared care is not the best option for the children.

A shared parenting law *will* force the court to consider equally shared care if one of the parents requests it, and that is the fundamental change that such a law could bring about. When separated parents cannot agree on what living arrangements are best for the children, the case may be raised in court, either as a single issue or as part of legal action relating to other separation issues.

In many countries, including Scotland, the prevailing pattern of child residence decisions is to allocate the role of main carer to the mother, with the father getting anything from a few hours per week to the 'every second weekend and half the holidays' decision. In other countries, such as Sweden, social patterns have developed to the extent that shared care after separation is the norm, meaning that the courts are seldom required to settle such disputes.

This relic of the 'tender years' presumption is often taken as being a perfectly adequate approach – what more does a father need? (For it is usually the father who is excluded.) In a recent interlocuter (note of decision) in a court case, the sheriff (Scottish judge) said:

> The pursuer is looking for a shared parenting arrangement. It is difficult to make shared parenting work. Even with the greatest degree of cooperation between the parties it can rarely, if ever, be sustained in the case of a child of school age, certainly in my experience …

Even though this was maybe an extreme example, many sheriffs are likely to consider that, if the disagreement between the parents is serious enough to reach court, they couldn't possibly be expected to agree enough to make a shared parenting arrangement work.

Shared parenting law should turn this presumption on its head, making equal care the starting point and forcing anyone who doesn't agree to produce arguments why another pattern would be in the best interests of the children. It also overcomes another barrier to court decisions for shared parenting.

A court may order a more limited amount of time for one parent as the starting point, particularly if there has been a long period while that parent hasn't seen the children or if the child is very young. In theory, the court should be able to gradually increase that time once things settle down and the children become more familiar with that parent. But Scottish family law also has a 'no order' principle, stating that the court 'shall not make any such order unless it considers that it would be better for the child that the order be made than that none should be made at all'. This makes it difficult for a parent to return to court after a contact order has been made. Even if the matter can be raised in court, it will also be more difficult to obtain legal aid for court action once that parent is seeing the children for some of the time.

As discussed below, enacting a 'rebuttable presumption' for shared parenting is often misunderstood, sometimes wilfully, by the opponents of this law change. That is why it can be difficult to enact what could be considered as a very progressive, child-centred and gender-equality based measure.

Over the past few years, the Scottish government and parliament have been considering a range of changes to our main family law – the Children (Scotland) Act. The national charity, Shared Parenting Scotland, has been working to include a shared parenting provision within that law.

UK overview

The United Kingdom of Great Britain and Northern Ireland currently has a complex set of interlocking legislation. Many powers have already been devolved from the UK parliament to the parliaments or assemblies in Scotland, Wales and Northern Ireland. Aside from this relatively recent devolution process, Scotland has also maintained separate legal, court and educational systems, even though the 1707 Union of Parliaments brought Scotland under the Westminster parliament.

This means that Scotland has always been able to pass its own family laws, although some issues such as child support and parental leave are still determined for the whole of the UK. Scotland has its own court structure, although once a matter has been considered by the highest court (Inner House of the Court of Session) an appeal can be made to the UK Supreme Court and then to Europe. That ultimate appeal route may disappear in due course.

Scottish and English law are based on different principles. England is a common law country, whereas Scotland tends towards civil law, these differences having been maintained during nearly 300 years without a separate Scottish parliament because the courts have remained completely separate during that period. Quite often the two countries have made similar legal changes, but at different times.

In Scotland, we still have one ground of divorce, the irretrievable breakdown of the marriage, which is proven in four ways: adultery of the other spouse; 'unreasonable behaviour'; one year's separation if the other spouse consents; or two year's separation if the other spouse does not consent. In Scotland, separation grounds were shortened from two years and five years, respectively, in 2006. English law is currently undergoing similar changes, 15 years later than Scotland.

Not everything in Scotland happens first. The recognition of the rights of unmarried fathers whose name is on the children's birth certificate started on 1 December 2003 in England and Wales, whereas an equivalent unmarried father whose children were born in Scotland only obtained parental rights if his children were born on or after 4 May 2006 and his name was on their birth certificate. Another variation is in the length of time within which parents must register a birth: 42 days in England but only 21 days in Scotland.

Scotland also leads on some areas of law. The Scottish Schools (Parental Involvement) Act pioneered the way in 2006 by stressing the importance of involving both parents in their children's schooling. The terminology in the guidance to this legislation has recently been altered to ensure that both separated parents are shown as having equal status.

The Children (Scotland) Act enacted in 1995 made major changes to Scottish family law. It has some parallels with the equivalent law for England and Wales – the Children Act passed six years earlier, in 1989. Both laws were passed in the UK parliament at Westminster, but in 1999 the Scottish parliament at Holyrood resumed making laws for Scotland. Some changes were made by that parliament in 2006 in the Family Law (Scotland) Act, but overall revision has had to wait until the twenty-fifth anniversary of the Children (Scotland) Act.

The equivalent legislation for England was revised by the Conservative/Liberal coalition in the Children and Families Act 2014. The coalition government started out with a commitment to enact shared parenting legislation, but this resolve weakened under significant opposition, and the resulting law only includes the following statement:

> A court, in the circumstances mentioned in subsection (4)(a) or (7), is as respects each parent within subsection (6)(a) to presume, unless the contrary is shown, that involvement of that parent in the life of the child concerned will further the child's welfare.

This was further diluted by the following sub-section, which removed any presumption of equal time sharing: '"involvement" means involvement of some kind, either direct or indirect, but not any particular division of a child's time'.

Scottish family law background

For the 2016 Scottish Parliament election, the Scottish National Party (SNP) included the following commitment in their manifesto:

> And while we are rightly proud of the ground-breaking approach taken to parental rights and responsibilities in The Children (Scotland) Act 1995, we recognise that this legislation is now over 20 years old and the shape of families has changed considerably in that time. We will review the legislation to ensure the interests of children and their need to form and maintain relationships with key adults in their lives – parents, step-parents, grandparents and other family members – are at the heart of any new statutory measures.

Although the SNP didn't win an outright majority in 2016, it won more seats than any other party and remained in government as a minority, seeking support when needed from the Green Party.

The SNP government issued a consultation on 'Review of Part 1 of the Children (Scotland) Act 1995 and creation of a Family Justice Modernisation Strategy' in 2018.

From the outset the government was in no way convinced that a shared parenting presumption was a desirable part of family law. It knew that the battle lines had already been drawn across the border in England during consideration of the Children and Families Act in 2014.

Domestic violence and women's rights campaigners had strongly opposed the original plans for including shared parenting in the new law, and the amendments introduced as the English Bill passed through the UK parliament had removed any possibility that the law could be used to support equally-shared care.

A similar skirmish had occurred in Scotland just prior to the 2016 election when the Justice Committee of the Scottish Parliament conducted post-legislative scrutiny of the 2006 Family Law (Scotland) Act.

Scottish Women's Aid submitted a paper to that committee giving its views on shared parenting. It stated:

> There is no evidence that fathers' 'rights' are intrinsically discriminated against in child contact proceedings. A blanket and risk-averse approach to shared parenting which does not consider domestic abuse is not in the best interests of the child.

It went on to mention that a shared parenting presumption was rejected a few years earlier in England and Wales and that the Australian law reform in 2006 was abandoned after review, concluding that, 'Other research also supports the position against a presumption of shared parenting on the same grounds' (as in Australia).

Families Need Fathers Scotland (the previous name of Shared Parenting Scotland) made a submission that concluded:

> We believe it is probably time for a review of both the Children (Scotland) Acts of 1995 and 2006. We believe in the current climate they support contrived adversarial behaviour and airing of unfounded accusations aimed at controlling contact with a non-resident parent that damages children and both parents. This behaviour would be pre-empted by a presumption of 'shared parenting'. Shared parenting is not about a forced, arithmetical division of time that children should spend with each parent, shuttling between their respective homes. It is about a presumption that both parents should be accorded equal respect and recognition in discussions about contact and residence.

In response, Scottish Women's Aid made a supplementary submission on shared parenting:

> SWA is fully supportive of shared parenting where this means a 'flexible and child centred approach between parents', where the child's welfare is central and contact is safe for the children and parents. However, SWA is opposed to shared parenting where this is primarily concerned with a set amount of contact or residency time for parents, providing a guarantee that

both parents spend equal or substantial amounts of time with a child (i.e. 'shared care').

The weight of research evidence suggests that a legal presumption of shared care is at best a superfluous tool: unnecessary for parents who engage positively in negotiations for shared care and incapable of guaranteeing the quality of relationship (parent to parent and parent to child) on which successful shared parenting is predicated. At worse, such a presumption places children who have experienced domestic abuse at significant risk by generating an expectation of equal access of both parents to children even where such access is unsafe.

Both organisations also gave oral evidence to that committee, reiterating their respective views on shared parenting alongside all the other topics under consideration. While not taking sides on this question, the Justice Committee agreed that it was time for a wholesale review of Scottish family law.

Children (Scotland) Bill: Origins and early consultation

A consultation paper on the proposed legislation was launched in May 2018, seeking responses by August 2018. The introduction notes that it covers a wide range of issues that affect children, including how the court considers the views of the child, support for the child, who a child should have contact with and how contact should happen, how children and victims of domestic abuse can be protected and how to improve the process for children and young people.

In the section on shared parenting, it asks whether courts should presume that a child benefits from both parents being involved in their life. This presumption would be in line with arguments that children benefit from a shared parenting arrangement. It also asks whether courts should not make this presumption.

A total of 54 questions were asked in the consultation. In addition to the written consultation, the Scottish government held a series of 28 separate events across the country to seek views and feedback on the main consultation themes. These included meetings with fathers' groups and domestic violence organisations. The results of this massive consultation were published in May 2019.

For the main consultation, 254 responses were received; a separate young person's survey received 295 responses. As published, the responses to the shared parenting questions were not conclusive. In the main survey, the official version of the analysis states that only 50 per cent of respondents agreed that there be a presumption in law that a child benefits from both parents being involved in their life. But this percentage was calculated including the 58 people who didn't respond to that question. Looking only at those who answered yes or no, support for that question rose to 64 per cent (126 out of 196 responses).

In the young person's survey, the question 'Should a child have contact with both parents?' produced the following responses: 23 per cent said 'Yes, always' and 71 per cent said 'Yes, but only if it is good for the child'. Only 11 respondents felt that children should not have contact with both parents.

The comments that accompanied these answers were illuminating. While some did acknowledge the difficulties associated with those who may present a risk, it was felt unfair to penalise all (non-resident) parents.

Further, respondents felt that a rebuttable presumption would continue to provide flexibility for sheriffs to make orders that reflected the circumstances of individual cases, and for safeguards to be implemented when either parent presented a risk. Responses included:

> You cannot discriminate against the majority of good fathers because of the issues with a minority.
>
> *(Individual)*

> The current model adopted in family cases seems rooted in the 1970s and pays little attention to the changes that have taken place in family life in the last 40 years with more female participation in the workforce, more day-to-day hands on parenting by fathers and vastly different expectation among both parents and children of what involved parenting is in reality.
>
> *(Family Support Organisation)*

Given the range of vested interests amongst those responding to this consultation, it is not surprising that the responses were strongly divided. Very few people or organisations objected to the idea that children can benefit from the involvement of both parents, but many of the opponents of a legislative presumption considered that this would lead to unsuitable or abusive parents gaining court-ordered contact.

Around the time that these consultation responses were being obtained, Families Need Fathers Scotland conducted a Google poll on those issues to try to obtain views from a wider population sample. In a survey of 500 people that was balanced by age and sex, 81.5 per cent of responses supported a change in law to create a presumption of shared parenting, meaning children spend half their time with each parent unless there is good reason not to. Surveys conducted recently in other countries produce broadly similar results, indicating that there seems to be broad popular support for shared parenting. As usual, the views of politicians seem to lag behind those of the general public.

Progress of the Bill

The Children (Scotland) Bill was published in September 2019. The only move towards shared parenting at this stage was an addition to the list of factors to be considered before making an order: 'the effect that the order the court is deciding whether or not to make on the involvement of the child's parents in bringing the child up'.

The Bill also included new measures to encourage the hearing of views of younger children. This followed on from growing pressure for legislation about the rights of children. Scotland already had a Children's Commissioner and the Children and Young People (Scotland) Act had encouraged Scottish Ministers and public bodies to consider children's rights and required them to prepare reports on what they are doing to progress children's rights.

Now the Scottish government has decided to fully incorporate the UN Convention on Children's Rights (UNCRC) into Scottish law. This means that other planned legislation would need to comply with UNCRC. Consulting children and informing them about court decisions was therefore a major theme in the Bill. While this change is very welcome, there is some concern that the law also needs to have some provision to cover circumstances in which children have been unduly influenced by one of their parents.

Consideration by the Justice Committee

In the Scottish parliament each Bill is considered by one main committee, which takes written and oral evidence from interested parties and academics and then considers amendments. The Bill attracted 87 written submissions from a wide range of organisations and individuals. Oral evidence was taken over seven sessions between December 2019 and February 2020.

Also at this stage, an independent academic considered whether the Bill was compatible with UNCRC and also the European Convention on Human Rights, including whether the proposed amendments to the welfare checklist of factors in the Bill would comply with UNCRC. This assessment mentions that, amongst the elements that the UNCRC feels should be included, is the preservation of the family environment and maintaining relations. The UN Convention also states that, 'it is of the view that shared parental responsibilities are generally in the child's best interests' (Para 67 of General Comment no. 14)

In giving evidence to the Committee, Shared Parenting Scotland referred to the need for a comprehensive checklist in order to comply with UNCRC, and stated that one thing that is missing from the Bill is a statement on shared parenting.

At the end of this evidence-gathering stage, the Justice Committee published a stage 1 report that mentions various changes it felt to be necessary. On checklists, it recommended that an amendment should be placed at stage 2 to expand the list of factors to include those suggested by the UN Committee on the Rights of the Child.

But the Justice Committee was not persuaded that the Bill should include a presumption in favour of shared parenting, stating that the welfare of the child must remain the paramount consideration. Any shared parenting presumption could cut across that key principle and it considered that the statement on the involvement of the child's parents was sufficient.

Consideration of amendments

Following this stage 1 report and a response from the Scottish government, the committee moved on to stage 2 consideration and voting on amendments. This long and complex Bill might normally have had several stage 2 meetings, but because of the constraints caused by Covid-19, this was undertaken in one long meeting in June 2020.

An amendment based on the Belgian shared parenting law was tabled at this stage. It sought to insert the wording:

> In the absence of an agreement on the pattern of residence of a child and at the request of at least one of the parents, [consider] the possibility of ordering that the child should reside on an approximately equal basis with each of the child's parents.

Liam McArthur MSP (Member of the Scottish Parliament) stated, in proposing that amendment, that it seeks to make equally shared care the starting basis for contact orders, from which courts can move towards the most appropriate split. He stressed that the intention is not to make shared parenting mandatory or to be prescriptive with regard to any arithmetical split of time. It is simply to tell the court to start with that option when one of the parents requests it and then to consider any reasons why a different pattern is better for the child or children who are involved.

Despite this reassurance that the presumption would clearly be rebuttable, various comments seemed to misunderstand or simply ignore that point. Domestic abuse was raised several times in this discussion, with comments such as 'in my casework I constantly see cases in which contact and shared parenting are used to continue to perpetrate abuse'. Another MSP stated (incorrectly) that:

> the majority of contact cases that end up in court concern reports of domestic abuse, even those that are not are still likely to involve high conflict. All research on the matter suggests that a presumption of shared parenting in any high-conflict cases is likely to be harmful to the child. Being caught between warring parents is without doubt an adverse childhood experience which we would risk causing if the provision were to be included in the bill.

Other committee members were more supportive in their comments, mentioning the breaking down of gender stereotypes that could be accomplished. The amendment was not voted on at stage 2 but was reintroduced in the final debate in front of the whole Scottish parliament (stage 3). This debate took place on 25 August 2020.

The different factions

As noted above, the main opposition to a rebuttable presumption of shared parenting comes from the charity Scottish Women's Aid, which has concerns relating to court cases in which domestic violence is a factor. This concern was also expressed by a range of children's organisations. Given that many of them are mainly working with children and families who are seriously affected by domestic abuse or other problems, this is maybe not surprising.

During consideration of the Bill, the judiciary opposed the creation of a rebuttable presumption, largely on the grounds that sheriffs and judges don't need to be given these additional steers – they are perfectly capable of making decisions as to what is in the best interests of the child.

Some lawyers and legal academics were also against the shared parenting presumption, although others took a positive view, such as the head of family law in one of Scotland's major law firms. She published a paper in 2019 stating that:

> there is a growing body of consistent evidence pointing to the conclusion that shared care works for children, delivering more favourable outcomes over a range of key indicators than those found for children who do not benefit from living in shared care arrangements.

There are only a handful of organisations working with fathers in Scotland. One of them, the umbrella organisation Fathers Network Scotland, was successful in obtaining Scottish government support in proclaiming a 'Year of the Dad' in 2016. It sought to win support for fathers because society hasn't yet caught up with the huge cultural changes that have taken place in the home and workplace over the past 50 years, proclaiming that: 'It's time to ditch the gender stereotypes and celebrate the key contribution fathers make to child development, family and community life.'

But despite these gender equality statements, organisations representing or supporting fathers find it hard to dispel assumptions that they are advocating fathers' rights in opposition to the rights of women or children.

In order to clarify that our support for shared parenting isn't simply a 'fathers' rights campaign' the charity Families Need Fathers Scotland changed its name at the start of 2020 to Shared Parenting Scotland. Similar moves have been made by organisations in the USA, Portugal and Australia in recent years.

When it comes to the current politicians in the Scottish parliament, there is a wide spread of views but only comparatively few who are willing to openly support the shared parenting amendment. Many prefer to be identified with the strongly gendered domestic violence organisations given the prevalence of 'Me Too' and the moves towards equal involvement of women at all levels of society.

Support or opposition to shared parenting didn't follow party lines, although all politicians tend to show support in relation to issues in which domestic violence is cited as a key factor. Although some members of the SNP have been very supportive of shared parenting, particularly if they have personal or professional experience of contact problems following relationship breakdown, party allegiances caused them to resist any amendment that wasn't proposed by their own party. The timing of this stage 2 debate was unfortunately close to the time when SNP MSPs were being considered for reselection for the 2021 election – not a good time to rebel.

There has been strong support for the Cross Party Group on Shared Parenting, which was established in 2018. The group will identify, examine and promote policy and practice that supports parents in sharing parenting responsibilities. It will consider how gender stereotypes can be tackled in the pursuit of a better understanding of what we need to do to ensure the best possible childhood and most promising adult life for Scotland's children.

How to win the arguments

This five-year lobbying effort does produce some useful learning.

As with any campaigning effort, raising public awareness of an issue is crucial. A tiny charity with three staff and limited budget starts at a significant disadvantage when working against far larger and richer opposing organisations in both the statutory and charitable sector.

Shared Parenting Scotland simply doesn't have either the budget or the expertise to mount large publicity campaigns or mobilise opinion through social media. We are also swimming against the tide of public opinion in terms of both domestic violence and gender equality. Our protestations that shared parenting is neither a father's issue nor an attempt to subvert the protection of victims of domestic violence have had only limited success.

We know that the successful campaign in Arizona that produced the 2013 order that 'consistent with the child's best interests, the court shall adopt a parenting plan that maximises (parents') respective parenting time' was based on a major effort to bring domestic violence organisations and other potential opposing interested parties on side. We have attempted this dialogue in Scotland, but with limited success so far. Most often we find ourselves sitting in opposite lobbies.

We have managed to mobilise a limited number of the parents we work with, and some of these fathers, mothers and other family members have helped us to add their personal experience to our lobbying. Shared Parenting Scotland is contacted by around a thousand people every year in connection with problems experienced in trying to maintain contact with their children and move towards shared parenting.

A surprisingly small proportion of these people have been willing to make contact with their own MSPs, despite the strong emotions and expressions of unfairness that are raised at our local meetings across Scotland and on our online forums. This unwillingness to contact politicians is not limited to this issue – almost all campaigning organisations have difficulty in mobilising their supporters to lobby politicians in a constructive manner. We are incredibly grateful to the individuals who have sent emails and letters to their representatives and attended local surgeries as we know that even a handful of genuine personal messages on an issue can have a very powerful impact.

Success or failure: The resulting legislation

The Bill that was passed on 25 August 2020 did not include the shared parenting amendment. Because the debate had centred on children's views and domestic violence, the shared parenting amendment was only supported by one party, the Liberal Democrats. The other parties were influenced by the strong feminist and children's rights lobbies. The argument that children are being deprived of the involvement of worthwhile parents because of outdated judicial attitudes was not sufficient to counter these views.

The future: What still needs to change

Adding a rebuttable presumption of shared parenting to Scottish law would have sent a strong message to the judiciary and to parents intending to go to court. But, in itself, it won't lead to a significant increase in the proportion of Scottish parents who share the care of their children equally after separation. The new law will include a statement that the court should consider the involvement of the child's parents in bringing the child up. The accompanying Family Justice Modernisation Strategy has the potential to move family court actions away from the current adversarial process. A new generation of sheriffs should demonstrate less gender-biased attitudes towards the role of fathers and mothers in the upbringing of children. The wider changes in Scottish society should also support a more balanced approach to male and female parental roles.

And as these changes gradually take hold, children growing up in Scotland will learn that shared parenting is the way forward both within family relationships and following relationship breakdown.

References

Online sources for all the statements and discussion during the passage of the Bill can be found at www.sharedparenting.scot/campaigns-policy/family-law-reform/

The progress of the Bill is also detailed at https://beta.parliament.scot/bills/children-scotland-bill

35
FEATURES OF JOINT CUSTODY AND SHARED PARENTING IN SLOVAKIA

Dagmar Kopčanová

Introduction

Families in Slovakia face many socio-pathological phenomena (loss of jobs, rising prices, leading to rising crime, lack of time for children, rising divorce rates and many others). A married couple's failing relationship is often evidenced by failing communication between them. Partners in disharmonious family scenarios typically are unable to maintain constructive communication, strong ties or the functionality of an ideal family system. At this point, two essential functions of the family seem particularly lacking: *social support* (satisfying social–psychological needs) and *social control* (education, socialisation of children, etc.). Lacking these, a couple often opts for separation or even divorce (Folberg, 1991; Kopčanová, 2006; Mátel, 2010; Mydlíková, 2004; Plaňava, 2000; Sobotková, 2007; Verešová, 2011).

One potential hypothesis is that due to fear of divorce there has been a growing demographic of young couples who choose to cohabit instead of marrying and having children as in the traditional family unit, with the hope of more independence and less threat of divorce. This approach is something of a departure from the classic Slovakia – a country that traditionally had strong religious Catholic teachings and roots – with children in these unions born outside of the bonds of marriage. This form of family unit has been steadily increasing in recent years (see Figure 35.1).

However, the process of separation, whether through divorce or a cohabitating couple deciding to part ways, can be very difficult, particularly when children are involved. In both cases, partners must consider the issues of joint parenting so that the child will not be deprived of basic psychological needs, such as stability, safety and love from both parents. In these cases, more than ever, special counselling services are needed.

On 1 July 2011, new regulations in Slovak family law were adopted and the Judicial Institute of Shared Parenting and Joint Care was established. In line with other legislation in other countries, Slovakia now has, in addition to sole custody,

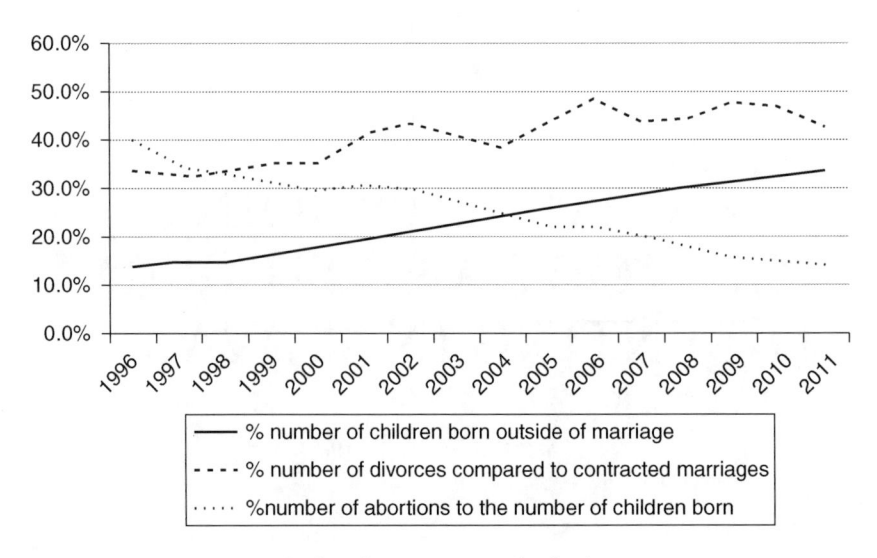

```
         % number of children born outside of marriage
    - - - % number of divorces compared to contracted marriages
    ····· %number of abortions to the number of children born
```

Figure 35.1 Divorce rate and other characteristic trends of today
Source: Slovstat, Statistical Office of Slovakia (www.statistics.sk)

the possibility of joint custody. In this arrangement, the parents reach an agreement (or the court decides) that for a part of each month, week, etc., the child or children will live with one parent, and for the other part, they will live with the other parent. This is not a new concept; shared parenting was established in the Czech Republic nearly 20 years ago, using the Cochem model. This model originated in Germany in 1992 as a grassroots initiative. The judge, Jürgen Rudolph, who hails from the small town of Cochem, was the main instigator of changes to the legislation. His aim was to establish joint parenting, provided equally by both parents, in order to de-escalate the divorce situation, speed up the divorce process as much as possible, and create a detailed plan for child rearing under the assumption that neither parent would receive sole custody (Rudolph, 2010). A very important principle of joint parenting is attachment to the family court, social welfare system, social workers, advocates and officially appointed experts in the region. Those involved hold joint meetings, usually once a month, and record approved decisions in the form of protocols, which are then monitored. Parents receive reports on the proceedings and proposals. The public plays a very important role in specific programmes related to joint care. The Cochem model has subsequently been introduced in other cities in Germany.

The terminology applied to joint parenting is often ambiguous. In the US and Canada, the terms joint custody, split custody or divided custody are employed and these terms are used interchangeably in different publications. Joint custody may also be referred to as *shared parenting*, joint parenting, co-custody, concurrent custody, shared custody or co-parenting (Folberg, 1991). The term joint custody will be used interchangeably with shared parenting and other similar co-custody terms throughout this chapter.

Research goals, sample and methods

The main goal of our explorative research was to verify whether the work of the Judicial Institute of Shared Parenting and Joint Care has proven to be, according to the views of mental health professionals, beneficial for children or whether it creates problems and the system thus needs to be re-evaluated.

The study sample ($N = 121$) was drawn from psychologists working at pedagogical–psychological counselling and prevention centres (CPPCPs), who were approached in the summer of 2016. An anonymous questionnaire was administered (using Google Forms) to gain data on the topics of joint custody and parental shared care. The research tool consisted of both closed (18) and open (5) questions, providing the opportunity to write more about selected issues. In this chapter we offer some of the more significant results, which illustrate the perception of the performance of the JC in practice, from the point of view of mental health specialists.

According to the Slovak Centre of Scientific and Technical Information, there were 434 psychologists working in these centres at that time, making for a response rate of approximately 25%. This is a low percentage, particularly taking into account that not every psychologist works with this sensitive issue of joint custody and shared parenting. However, it is still possible to consider the sample size as representative, as we received replies from all districts in Slovakia.

Research results

One of the key research questions relates to detection of how joint custody functions in practice. Being aware of other research results published in different countries (Anderson, 2014; Bauserman, 2002; Cashmore & Parkinson, 2011; Fabricius, 2003; Fidler-Bala, 2010; Früwirth, 2006; Haugen, 2010; Irving & Benjamin, 1991 ; Nielsen, 2018; Warshak, 1996), it is clear that the research results received in Slovakia are less in favour of joint custody. The majority of meta-analytical studies abroad find that children from divorced families are better adjusted when they live with both parents at different homes or spend significant time with both parents compared with children who interact with only one parent. For example, Bauserman (2002) reviewed 33 studies involving 1,846 sole-custody and 814 joint-custody children. Both groups of children were compared with a sample of 251 children in intact families. Bauserman found that children in joint-custody arrangements had fewer behavioural and emotional problems, higher self-esteem and better family relationships and school performance compared with those in sole-custody situations. He found no significant difference in adjustment among children in shared custody and those living in intact family situations. Joint-custody children probably fare better, according to Bauserman, because they have ongoing contact with both parents. Conversely, it is remarkable to observe that, in Slovakia, only 3% of respondents state that joint custody is an asset and nearly 30% do not agree with this arrangement at all. The majority of respondents (68%) state that joint custody is an asset but *only partially* (See Figure 35.2). Among restrictions, they usually raise issues such as gender, age of the child, distance from the house of the other parent, quality of communication between parents and other issues.

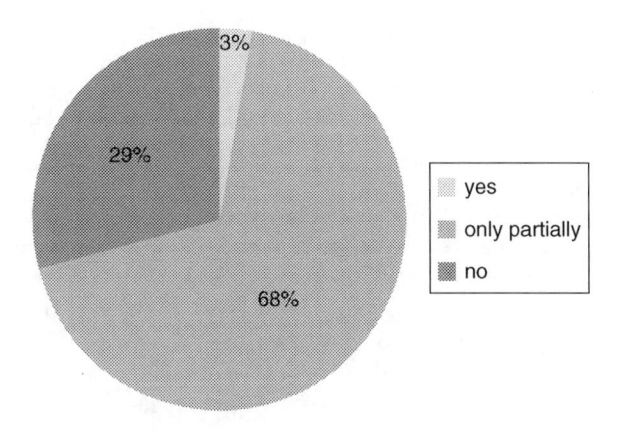

Figure 35.2 Views of CPPCP psychologists on joint custody functioning in practice
Source: Slovstat, Statistical Office of SR (online) (2015-09-30). Available at: http://www.statistics.sk

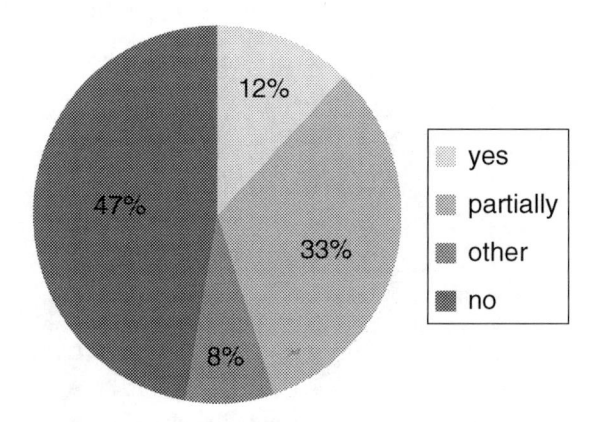

Figure 35.3 For joint custody implementation, it is enough when both parents agree...
Source: Slovstat, Statistical Office of SR (online) (2015-09-30). Available at: http://www.statistics.sk

The next question raised a rather provocative point: how is joint custody awarded automatically by Slovakian courts viewed – a situation that, unfortunately, occurs often? (See Figure 35.3).

Here, 47% of respondents did not agree with joint custody being awarded automatically and 12% supported this approach, which means that simple acceptance of the suitability of both parents to look after their children should not be sufficient and other preconditions should be met in order for the work of the Judicial Institute of Shared Parenting and Joint Care to be *truly effective*. One of the most important suggestions of respondents was that parents should take part in a special psychological training programme where they would be trained in efficient communication skills, conflict management, etc. Remarkably, 81% of the respondents identified this as an important issue (see Figure 35.4).

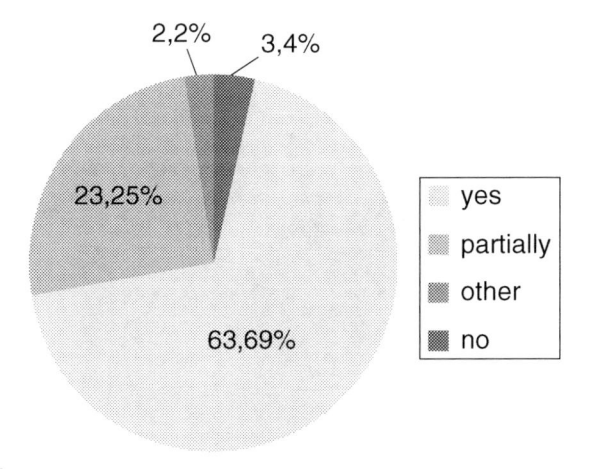

Figure 35.4 Parents should complete some special psychological training programme

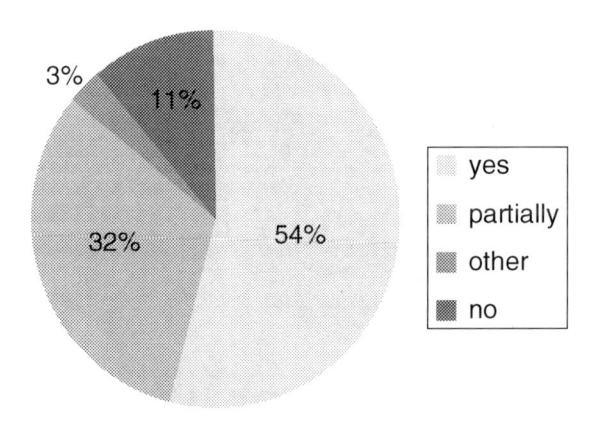

Figure 35.5 Importance of conditions under which joint custody arises and expires (for example, distance between parents' houses, methods of communication, moving abroad, etc.)

According to the respondents, joint custody should be tentatively approved by both parents who should also have completed a special psychological programme, focused on the communication competencies needed for effective cooperation. It is interesting that the psychologists are rather critical towards the contemporary wording of the law on joint custody. According to their views, it is important to have concrete, special rules set up in law, under which joint custody arises and expires. This might help to avoid some of the problems that arise due to each client interpreting the law in his or her own way (see Figure 35.5).

More than half of the respondents require some improvement in cooperation between courts and CPPCPs (54%). Other respondents (11%) do not because they rely on the fact that provision of psychological care is the remit of their colleagues working under the auspices of the Ministry of Labour, Social Affairs and Family (see Figure 35.6).

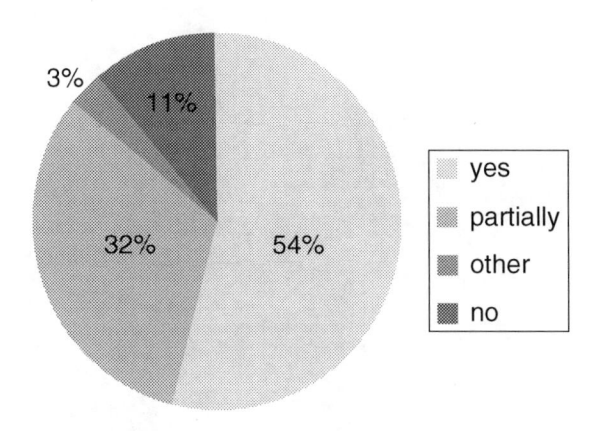

Figure 35.6 Importance of better cooperation between courts and CPPCPs

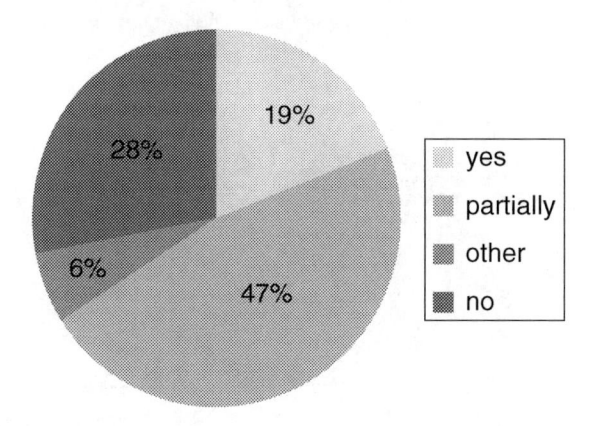

Figure 35.7 No benefits are available if parents are not able to communicate in a decent way

Another question addressed how much importance psychologists place on healthy communication between parents. Here, various views are expressed, although there is still a large percentage of respondents (47%) in agreement with the statement that decent communication is a core prerequisite for successful joint custody. Fewer than 20% of respondents were sceptical about this issue, believing nothing would help if partners were not able to communicate in a healthy way (see Figure 35.7).

In another question, the possibility of multiprofessional cooperation when dealing with the issue of joint custody was explored. Unfortunately, the results were not positive (see Figure 35.8). We are aware that there is still very little mutual cooperation between professionals on this issue, although in other countries multiprofessional teamwork has proved to be very productive and efficient, especially when dealing with multi-problem families (Kopčanová, 2016), which can describe many families separated by divorce.

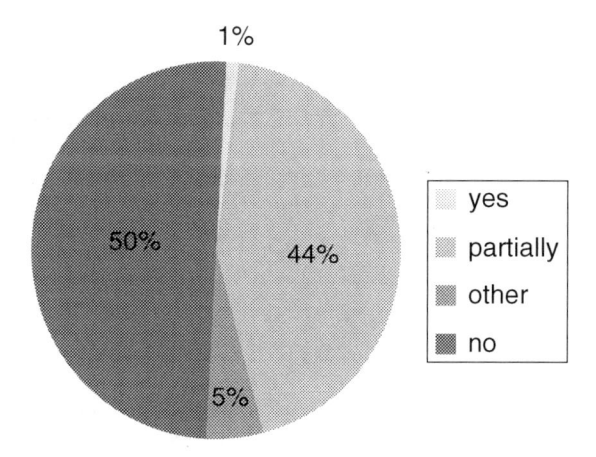

Figure 35.8 Is multiprofessional cooperation on behalf of joint custody successful in your team?

Discussion

The results presented above demonstrate that, according to the experience of mental health professionals, parents require further education in their communication skills. This means that more training and counselling care from mental health professionals for divorcing parents is necessary and highly recommended.

Regarding multiprofessional team work, it is clear that, in Slovakia, it has not yet proved to be very efficient (according to the views of psychologists), with specialists being very busy and unable to find time to meet and discuss their case studies together as a team. However, in other countries – for example, Israel – this experience is completely different. There, multiprofessional teamwork interventions, especially in the case of families in distress, can contribute substantially to the well-being of family members (Sharlin & Shamai, 2000). Other researchers also identify the need to understand and develop teamwork; for example, Littlechild and Smith (2013), Loewe and Herranen (1981) and Payne (2000). It is hoped that, in the near future, more Slovak experts will use multiprofessional teamwork in their special interventions.

In agreement with Warshak (1996), we suggest that joint custody could almost be described as 'a revolution' in post-divorce parenting, as it was not so long ago that children were automatically placed in the sole custody of their mothers . However, there are still some gaps in Slovak law that should be corrected and re-evaluated. For example, the description of joint custody is very brief and does not clearly state under what conditions it should start and finish.

The ideal rights of parents and their obligations to their children are very thoroughly addressed by the Cochem model, which can serve as a template for Slovakia in its future legal regulations on the matter.

Conclusion

In this chapter, selected results from ongoing research have been presented, which focus on the qualitative analysis of problems connected to joint custody and the shared care offered by parents after divorce.

There are some restrictions and biases that appear in the research, due to the fact that psychologists from CPPCPs work daily with clients in dramatic divorce and post-divorce situations, often dealing with very intense cases in which possibly even sole custody has failed, and only rarely do they deal with cases where joint custody has succeeded. Therefore, further qualitative research into this area is required. As a result, further work will be undertaken with a group of randomly selected parents who have asked for specialist help. Their experiences in shared parenting over a number of years will be analysed and the views and experiences of their children will also be studied.

Comparative quantitative research on the experiences, views and opinions of other experts cooperating with child psychologists in CPPCPs more closely on this issue will also be undertaken. These experts are psychologists, mediators and social workers working under the auspices of the Ministry of Labour, Social Affairs and Family. Through such research, the possibilities for joint professional cooperation in the process of special multidisciplinary intervention to families after divorce may be identified.

References

Anderson, J. 2014. The impact of family structure on the health of children: Effects of divorce. *The Linacre Quarterly*, 81(4), 378–387.

Bauserman, R. 2002. Child adjustment in joint-custody versus sole-custody arrangements: A meta-analytic review. *Journal of Family Psychology*, 16(1), 91–102.

Cashmore, J. & Parkinson, P. 2011. Parenting arrangements for young children: Messages for research. *Australian Journal of Family Law*, 25, 240–257.

Fabricius, W. 2003. Listening to children of divorce. *Family Relations*, 52, 405–396.

Fidler, B.J. & Bala, N. 2010. Children resisting postseparation contact with a parent: Concepts, controversies, and conundrums. *Family Court Review*, 48(1), 10–47.

Folberg, J. 1991. *Joint custody and shared parenting*. New York: Guilford Press.

Früwirth, J. 2006. Prehlad vedeckých výskumov o striedavke. Dostupné na internete. Retrieved from http://ligaotcov.sk/clanky/news_prehlad-vedeckych-vyskumov-o-striedavke.

Haugen, G. 2010. Children's perspectives on shared residence. *Children and Society*, 24, 112–122.

Irving, H. & Benjamin, M. 1991. Shared and sole custody parents. In J. Folberg (ed.), *Joint custody and shared parenting* (pp. 114–132). New York: Guilford Press.

Kopčanová, D. 2006. Násilie v rozvodovej rodine a jeho prevencia pomocou mediácie. In: *Dieťa v ohrození XV. Zborník z konferencie*. CD-rom. Bratislava: DF a VUDPaP.

Kopčanová, D. 2016. *Working with problem families: Use of a multiprofessional team*. SPAY International Conference, Bratislava.

Littlechild, B. & Smith, R. 2013. *A handbook for interprofessional practice in the human services: Learning to work together is an essential text for all students of inter-professional education, and for practitioners looking to understand and develop better inter-agency working*. Abingdon: Routledge.

Loewe, J.L. & Heranenn, M. 1989. Understanding team work: Another look at the concepts. *Social Work in Health Care*, 7(2), 1–11.

Mátel, A. 2010. Sociálna patológia rodiny. In Nečas, O.–Ondřej, J.–Hála, M. (eds.), *Sociální, ekonomické, právní a bezpečnostní otázky současnosti. Sborník příspěvků z 2. mezinárodní slovensko - české konference*. Praha: SVŠES.

Mydliková, E. 2004. *Dysfunkčná rodina ako klient sociálnej práce*. Martin: Šarkan.
Nielsen, L. 2018. Joint versus sole physical custody: Outcomes for children independent of family income or parental conflict, *Journal of Child Custody*, 15, 35–54.
Payne, G. 2000. *Social division*. Basingstoke: Palgrave Macmillan.
Pavelková, B. 2010. Inštitút striedavej starostlivosti v slovenskom rodinnom práve. In: *Personálny a mzdový poradca podnikateľa*. Ročník *2010*, č. *13–14*, str. *58*
Pavelková, B. 2012. *Právne postavenie rodiča vo výchove*. Habilitačná práca. Bratislava: Paneurópska Univerzita, Fakulta práva.
Plaňava, 0. 2000. *Manželství a rodiny. Struktura, dynamika, komunikace*. Brno: Doplněk.
Rudolph, J. 2010. *Du bist mein Kind: Die "Cochemer Praxis" – Wege zu einem menschlicheren Familienrecht*. Kindle edition.
Sharlin, S.A. & Shamai, M. 2000. *Therapeutic intervention with poor unorganized families: From distress to hope*. New York: Haworth Clinical Practice Press.
Sobotková I. 2007. *Psychologie rodiny. Druhé, prepracované vydanie*. Praha: Portál.
Správa o zdravotnom stave obyvateľstva SR za roky 2012–2014. 2015. Retrieved from www.rokovanie.sk.
Šprocha, B. & Vaňo, B. (eds). 2015. Populačný vývoj v Slovenskej republike 2014, Infostat–Inštitút informatiky a štatistiky. ISBN 978–80–89398–27–0, s. 25.
Verešová A. 2011. Kríza rodiny- deti ako prekážka pri sebarealizácii rodičov. In M. Hardy, T. Dudášová, E. Vranková, and A. Hrašková (eds), *Sociálna patológia rodiny*. Zborník z medzinárodnej vedeckej konferencie. Bratislava: VŠZaSP sv. Alžbety, 365.
Warshak, R.A. 1996. *Revoluce v porozvodové péči o děti*. Praha: Portál.

36

THE MERITS OF THE "ZAUNEGGER APPROACH" OF THE EUROPEAN COURT OF HUMAN RIGHTS

Martin Widrig

Introduction

We saw in Chapter 6 that the automatic exclusion of shared parenting by law or because one parent opposes it may lead to the unsatisfactory situation whereby, in a particular case, the better care or custody solution for the child cannot be imposed by the authorities involved. This situation is in contradiction with most fundamental human rights standards.[1] Notably, the child's best interests (Article 3 of the Convention on the Rights of the Child, CRC) cannot be taken into consideration and it cannot be verified whether the intervention with the child's right to be cared for by both parents was justified.[2] In this chapter, we shall discuss an approach developed by the European Court of Human Rights in its *Zaunegger judgment* from December 3, 2009.[3] By merely requesting the possibility of a judicial review, at the request of the child or a parent, a court largely solves these previously mentioned problems. Hence, with its "Zaunegger approach" the court has created a powerful tool to save the interests and human rights of children as well as parents by merely imposing a minimal obligation upon states.

The Court and the European Convention on Human Rights

The European Convention on Human Rights (ECHR, the Convention) is an international treaty under which the member states of the Council of Europe[4] promise to secure fundamental civil and political (human) rights for everyone within their jurisdiction. The treaty was signed on November 4, 1950 and entered into force in 1953.[5]

The European Court of Human Rights (ECtHR, the Court) is an international court, based in Strasbourg, France. It was set up in 1959 and rules on individual or state applications alleging violations of the rights set out in the Convention. The ECtHR has delivered more than 10,000 judgments, which are binding for the countries concerned and have led to important changes in their legislation and administrative practice. The Court has consolidated the rule of law and democracy in Europe and makes the Convention a "living (evolving) instrument".[6]

The Court's Zaunegger approach
The Zaunegger judgment
Circumstances of the case

Mr. Horst Zaunegger (the applicant) had lived with the child's mother for five years. Their child was born in 1995. In August 1998, they separated, and the child lived with the applicant until January 2001, when the mother decided that the child would live with her. When, in 2008, the mother wanted to move and their son clearly expressed the wish to live with his father, the latter started custody proceedings.[7]

According to German law, children born out of wedlock could, under normal conditions, only have a custodial father, when the mother agreed.[8] Unlike fathers who once held custody (because of marriage or a priori the mother of the child agreed), fathers of children born out of wedlock had no possibility of reviewing whether this measure was necessary to protect the child or not.[9]

Applicability and content of Article 14 ECHR

The Court considered that decisions with regard to custody (including decisions on education, care and the determination of where the child lives) fall into the ambit of the *right to respect for family life*, protected by Article 8 ECHR.[10] For this reason, Article 14 ECHR (prohibition of discrimination) was applicable.[11]

The judges concluded that, in Germany, with respect to the attribution of custody, different standards applied for fathers of children born out of wedlock compared with mothers and with fathers of children born during marriage.[12] Such differences in treatment are discriminatory, if they have no reasonable and objective justification. This means that a difference in treatment requires a legitimate aim and reasonable proportionality between the means employed and the aim sought to be realised.[13] Very weighty reasons must be put forward to justify a difference in treatment on the grounds of sex, birth out of or within wedlock and the marital status of fathers who share or shared the household of their children.[14]

Conviction and reasoning of the Court

The Court "accepted" the view that different life situations of children born out of wedlock exist and that it was justified to attribute sole parental authority over the child *initially* only to the mother.[15] It further "accepted" that, in a particular case, valid reasons might exist to deny an unmarried father participation in parental authority.[16] However, with regard to the specific circumstances of the present situation, the judges also made clear that, "the Court cannot share the assumption that joint custody against the will of the mother is *prima facie* not to be in the child's best interests".[17] In its reasoning, the Court pointed out that:

- The mother's objections to joint parental authority are not necessarily based on considerations related to the child's best interests,[18]
- "The applicant was excluded from the outset by force of law from seeking a judicial examination as to whether the attribution of joint parental authority would serve the child's best interests and from having a possible arbitrary objection of the mother to agree to joint custody replaced by a court order,"[19]
- "The common point of departure in the majority of Member States appears to be that decisions regarding the attribution of custody are to be based on the child's best interests and that in the event of a conflict between parents such attribution should be subject to scrutiny by the national courts,"[20] and finally
- The argument that, under the circumstances of the present case, "it could not be ruled out that the ordering of joint custody by a court would cause conflict between the parents and would therefore be contrary to the child's best interests" is not persuasive and insufficient to justify a difference in treatment of the applicant compared with fathers who originally held parental authority, being given that "the domestic law provides for a full judicial review of the attribution of parental authority and resolution of conflicts between separated parents in cases in which the father once held parental authority."[21]

For all these reasons, the Court concluded that there was no reasonable relationship of proportionality between the general exclusion of judicial review of the initial custody regulation and the aim pursued. Accordingly, there has been a violation of Article 8 taken together with Article 14 and it was not necessary to determine whether there has been a breach of Article 8 taken alone.[22]

Interpretations of the judgment

The view has been expressed that Germany's conviction was based (merely) on the difference in treatment between fathers.[23] However, the judgment appears to go beyond this discrimination,[24] which seemed to be only of "very subsidiary" importance in the reasoning of the Court.[25] The German Federal Constitutional Court, well-known Swiss scholars, the Swiss government and others shared the view that the essence of the Zaunegger judgment lies in the consideration that, "*the general exclusion of a judicial review* of the initial attribution of custody to the mother *was disproportionate* with regard to the aim" pursued to protect children born out of wedlock *and* that such a *judicial review has to be possible* in order to comply with the Convention.[26] This view has also been confirmed by subsequent judgments of the Court. Notably in the *Schneider judgment* the ECtHR pointed out that,

> The Court cannot but confirm ... its *approach taken in the ... case of Zaunegger v. Germany* ... which concerned the general exclusion from judicial review of the attribution of sole custody to the mother of a child born out of

wedlock [... in which] the domestic courts, applying the relevant provisions of the civil code, also considered parental rights of a father *prima facie* not to be in the child's best interest.[27]

(Italics added)

Definition of the Zaunegger approach

When referring to the Zaunegger approach, the author refers to an "obligation of a state to provide, on request by a child or a (potential) parent, at least a possibility for judicial review, in order to verify whether or not a restriction of children's or parental rights was necessary with respect to the child's best interests", which was established in the Court's Zaunegger judgment.[28] Although the judgments in question only concerned claims by (potential) fathers, it seems necessary to include children and mothers in the definition of the approach, since they could be in a similar situation as the fathers and claim on their own.

Confirmations, impact and views of other human rights bodies

Order of the German Federal Constitutional Court

In its Order – 1 BvR 420/09 – of July 21, 2010,[29] after Germany's conviction by the Zaunegger judgment, the German Federal Constitutional Court shared the view of the ECtHR. It considered, in particular, that:

- Parental custody is an essential component of parental human rights,[30]
- The general exclusion of the attribution of sole custody to the mother because of the mother's decision from a judicial review violates paternal human rights, since it excludes that the child's best interests can be taken into consideration in each particular case,[31]
- This general exclusion is a far-reaching intervention with parental human rights,[32]
- This dependence of paternal custody on the mother's "dominant will" discriminates fathers compared with mothers,[33]
- Only the child's best interests may justify the exclusion from paternal custody,[34]
- This regulation discriminates fathers that never have had custody as opposed to fathers that once held custody,[35]
- The dependence of the attribution of sole custody to the father on solely the mother's will violates paternal human rights.[36]

Subsequent judgments of the European Court of Human Rights

The Zaunegger judgment and the Zaunegger approach were confirmed by the *Sporer judgment* and several other decisions. As in Germany, the Austrian jurisdiction provided full judicial review of attribution of parental authority in cases in which fathers once held parental authority but did not do so for fathers of a child born out of wedlock who had assumed the role of father since the child was born.[37]

The Zaunegger approach has also been applied in other cases:

- In the *Anayo judgment*, the Court found a violation of private life. The authorities refused to allow the natural father to have contact with his twins who lived with their mother and their legal father. An examination of the question of whether contact would have been in the children's best interest was excluded by a mere legal assumption. Referring to the Zaunegger judgment, the Court concluded that the domestic courts failed to provide the applicant appropriate protection of his private life.[38]
- The *Schneider judgment* was found to be a violation of private life because the authorities refused a putative biological father's right to *contact* with and *information* on the development of his child (living with the mother and legal father) with no consideration of whether or not this right would have been in the child's best interest or whether such a judgment was overriding the interests of the child in favour of those of his or her mother and legal father. Again, the Court referred to and confirmed the approach of the Zaunegger judgment.[39]
- In the *Ahrens* and *Kautzor judgments* there was found to be no violation of private life, even though in proceedings started by the (putative) biological fathers concerning (1) the establishment of legal paternity, (2) a challenge to the legal paternity of legal and social (but not necessarily biological) fathers, and (3) clarification of a child's paternity via genetic testing without changing the child's legal status, it had not been determined whether the impugned measures served the child's best interests.[40] However, the Court confirmed, by referring to its Anayo and Schneider judgments (and for this reason, implicitly, the Zaunegger judgment), that Article 8 ECHR imposes "on the Member States an obligation to examine whether it is in the child's best interest to allow the biological father to establish a relationship with his child", for example by granting contact rights, and that this may even imply the establishment of biological paternity. Furthermore, the complete exclusion of the biological father from his child's life requires that there be relevant reasons relating to the child's best interests.[41]

View of the UN Committee on the Rights of the Child

The Zaunegger approach is in line with the recommendations of the UN Committee on the Rights of the Child to Liechtenstein in 2006 whereby the Committee expressed its concern that the fathers of children born out of wedlock had no legal standing from which to claim custody while custody was automatically given to the mother. It recommended that Liechtenstein amend its legislation and provide fathers with the opportunity to request, if possible, joint custody of their children.[42]

Impact on Swiss jurisdiction

The judgments mentioned above took place during a revision of the Swiss custody legislation, which entered into force on July 1, 2014.[43] Before this day, after divorce, granting shared legal and physical custody was only possible when both parents agreed and granting shared legal and physical custody to parents of a child born out of wedlock was only possible when the mother agreed and the father signed a contract in which they were frequently forced by the authorities to agree to a minimal contact right and to pay maintenance for the child to the mother in the case of parental separation – even if the father took care of the child alone.[44]

Well-known scholars and the Swiss government shared the view that a general exclusion of shared custody because of the lack of consent of both parents does not comply with Article 8 ECHR and thus Swiss custody legislation was contrary to the ECHR.[45] Notably, it has been argued, convincingly, that the general exclusion of shared legal custody because of the "veto" of one parent after a divorce does not comply with the reasoning of the Court's Zaunegger judgment.[46] Probably, the Court's case law has substantially influenced the revision of Swiss custody legislation and doctrine: on December 16, 2009 (which was only 13 days after the Zaunegger judgment), the government published its decision that custody of the father of children born out of wedlock should depend upon the agreement of the mother.[47] However, subsequently this view has changed and the new custody legislation, which entered into force on July 1, 2014, gives fathers of children born out of wedlock the possibility of a judicial review if mothers deny shared custody.[48] Since July 2014, shared legal custody remains the rule after divorce and sole custody is the exception that has to be justified.[49] Furthermore, two norms have been introduced into the Swiss Civil Code, which embody the Zaunegger approach, and assure that shared physical custody is now possible if only one parent or the child requests it.[50] Finally, yet importantly, with respect to relocation, the right to determine where the child lives belongs now to both parents. If they cannot agree, a court or child protection authority will decide and can now consider the child's best interests, other competing interests and the special circumstances of the case.[51]

Significance from a human rights perspective

In the cases mentioned above, the impugned measures interfered with rights of children and their parents. Because of general exclusions by irrefutable legal assumptions, the decision-making authorities were not allowed to consider the child's best interests or able to verify whether or not the interferences were necessary or able to create a fair balance between the competing interests involved. Such general exclusions by legal assumptions are highly problematic from a human rights perspective.[52]

By merely requesting the *possibility of a judicial review*, the Court and the UN Committee on the Rights of the Child have found an efficient way to assure that, *on request*, the child's best interests can be taken into consideration and respected in legal practice as requested by Article 3 CRC in every decision concerning children.[53] Furthermore, it can be verified whether a measure is necessary and the competing interests involved can be fairly balanced.[54] Finally, presuming that many parents are responsible and act in their children's best interests when they initiate a claim, the request of a judicial review might be the only way to assure that the child's best interests are being taken into consideration by a decision-making authority and for this reason contributes to the protection of the child.[55] These are the merits of the

Zaunegger approach,[56] which for the reasons mentioned above seems to be an appropriate (and necessary) minimal human rights standard for decisions concerning children and their relationship with a (potential) parent.

An important advantage of the Zaunegger approach is its simplicity and efficiency. Higher courts, in particular, frequently face the problem that lower courts are much closer to the families concerned and may be in a much better position to take appropriate decisions. For this reason, the ability of higher courts to order appropriate interventions is limited. However, what higher courts can do is assure the respect of most important rights and principles by lower courts. The Zaunegger approach provides an excellent tool with which to do so.

The Zaunegger approach and shared physical custody

There are many reasons to believe that the Zaunegger approach ought to apply as a minimal standard in decisions concerning physical custody. Although the approach proves to be a useful tool to protect the fundamental rights of children and parents, this does not necessarily mean that the Court will refer to it in care decisions.

Relevance as a minimal standard in care decisions

Empirical research clearly suggests that many cases exist in which shared physical custody against the will of one parent is in the child's best interests.[57] According to highly respected scholars, empirical research "clearly indicates" that limited contact schedules with one parent are not in the children's best interests, and an every-other-weekend parenting arrangement is associated with "a weakening of [parent]–child relationships and diminished closeness over time".[58] Hence, sufficient time with each parent seems to be essential for a meaningful child–parent relationship.[59] For these reasons, the view that joint physical custody is *always* contrary to the best interests of the child (unless both parents agree) finds no support. A general exclusion of joint physical custody (unless both parents agree) is untenable if the best interests of the child is supposed to be a relevant criterion in care decisions.

Furthermore, the German Federal Constitutional Court has pointed out, based on reliable research, that the dominant position as a result of the power of veto has been used by the privileged parent for personal reasons not related to the best interests of the child.[60] Even UNICEF recognizes that, too often, children lose the chance to maintain contact with a non-residential parent because of the needs of the residential parent.[61] The view that a parent who wants sole physical custody for him or herself *always* acts in the best interest of the child seems to be wrong. For this reason, a general dependence of joint physical custody on the consent of both parents is unacceptable, if Article 3 CRC is to be respected.

Finally, for children as well as parents, physical care and the corresponding child–parent bonds are substantially more important than legal bonds. It can be seen that the Court has attributed substantially more importance to contact and care than to legal bonds, as shown in the outcomes of the Ahrens and Anayo judgments, for example.[62] Enjoying each other's company is a fundamental aspect of *family life*, and

Article 8 of the Convention protects not only decisions on custody but also decisions on care and where a child lives.[63] While the Court has given Member States a wider margin of appreciation with respect to custody decisions, it has steadily pointed out that stricter scrutiny is necessary with respect to access. There is even a positive obligation imposed by Article 8 to unite children and their parents. To unite children and their parents has to be, if possible, the ultimate aim of all actions by the state, and a state must act in a manner calculated to enable family ties to be developed.[64] For these reasons, and also because the difference between contact and care is evident,[65] an application of the Zaunegger approach in care decisions would make even more sense than in custody decisions.

Caution concerning high expectations

One relevant aspect of the Zaunegger approach is that a well-known international Court has developed it. For this reason, the question of whether or not the Court would also apply this approach in a case in which extended contact rights or shared physical custody[66] depends only upon the will of one parent is of considerable interest.

As we have seen above, many points speak in favour of an application of the Zaunegger approach in care decisions. Nevertheless, this does not necessarily mean that the Court would apply its approach in such situations, since other factors may be considered. One relevant factor in the Court's jurisprudence is whether or to what extent a consensus exists among Member States with respect to a certain question. While all Member States have ratified the UN Convention on the Rights of the Child and are bound by its Article 3 CRC, some states remain in which contact or care decisions depend exclusively upon the will of one parent. Furthermore, in the Ahrens judgment, in which a biological father challenged the paternity of the social father in order to establish legal paternity, the Court did not impose its Zaunegger approach, even though a considerable majority (18 out of 26 – 69%) of Member States allow for a judicial review in equivalent circumstances.[67] Interestingly, in the X and others judgment, in which a second-parent challenged paternity of a legal and social (but non-residential) father in order to require a second-parent adoption, the Court decided that discrimination was evident, even though only 11 out of 39 (28%) Member States allow second-parent adoptions for unmarried parents, and, of these 11, only six (55%; and six (15%) of all 39 Member States) allow it for same-sex couples.[68] It could be that the Court still attributes more importance to non-discrimination than to respect of Article 3 CRC.

Conclusion

Convincing arguments were put forth by Swiss doctrine and acknowledged by the Swiss government supporting the notion that, according to the Court's reasoning in the Zaunegger judgment, the general exclusion of shared legal custody or its dependence on the will of one parent violates Article 8 of the Convention on the Rights of the Child. Bearing in mind the importance the Court ascribes to the protection and establishment of family bonds; contact and a relationship between children and parents; the greater relevance of shared physical custody than shared legal custody to protect and establish such relationships and bonds; and the positive results found for children living in shared care arrangements according to social science research, the expectation that shared physical custody has to be possible if only the child or one parent requests it seems reasonable and logical. Nevertheless, this does not necessarily mean that the Court would impose its Zaunegger approach if, in a national jurisdiction, care decisions depended exclusively on a parent's will.

However, independent of whatever the Court decides in future, the usefulness and brilliance of the Zaunegger approach will remain. With this approach, the Court has developed a powerful and convincing tool to assure that, in all decisions concerning children, the child's best interests can be taken into consideration, as requested by Article 3 CRC. In addition, the approach assures that it is possible to judicially review whether interventions on the basis of the human rights of children or parents are necessary. This is not the case, if, for example, shared physical custody is excluded by law or impossible if vetoed by one parent. For these reasons, the Court's Zaunegger approach is an appropriate minimal human rights standard for every jurisdiction in decisions concerning children and their relationship with their parents.

Notes

1 Chapter 6, this volume.
2 Ibid.
3 *Zaunegger v. Germany*, App. No. 22028/04 (ECtHR, judgment of December 3, 2009).
4 The Council of Europe is the leading Human Rights organization in Europe. It includes 47 member states (www.coe.int/en/web/about-us/our-member-states.
5 On the Court in brief, see www.echr.coe.int/Documents/Court_in_brief_ENG.pdf.
6 Ibid.
7 *Zaunegger v. Germany*, n. 3, para. 7 ff; 1 BvR 420/09 (German Constitutional Court, Order of the First Senate of July 21, 2010), paras. 26 ff.
8 § 1626a (1) aBGB (German Civil Code at the time of the Zaunegger judgment); 1 BvR 420/09, n. 7, paras. 2 ff.
9 *Zaunegger v. Germany*, n. 3, para. 44.
10 Ibid., para. 40.
11 Ibid., para. 40.
12 Ibid., para. 48.
13 Ibid., para. 49.
14 Ibid., para. 51.
15 Ibid., para. 55; 1 BvR 420/09, n. 7, para. 20.
16 *Zaunegger v. Germany*, n. 3, para. 56; 1 BvR 420/09, n. 7, para. 21.
17 *Zaunegger v. Germany*, n. 3, para. 59; Meier, P. 2010. L'autorité parentale conjointe—L'arrêt de la CourEDH Zaunegger c. Allemagne—quels effets sur le droit suisse? *Revue de la protection des mineurs et des adultes* 65/3: 246–256, p. 249 f.
18 *Zaunegger v. Germany*, n. 3, para. 58 and 57; 1 BvR 420/09, n. 7, para. 25; Deutscher Bundestag (German Parliament) 2008. *Drucksache 16/10047*. http://dip21.bundestag.de/dip21/btd/16/100/1610047.pdf, p. 12 ff.; Walper, S., and Jurczky, K. 2010. *Vorgezogener Endbericht für das Projekt "Gemeinsames Sorgerecht nicht miteinander verheirateter Eltern"*, www2.hs-fulda.de/fb/sw/BiB/Modul_O16/Studienbrief_3_1/Endbericht_Sorgerecht_final.pdf, p. 145 ff.
19 *Zaunegger v. Germany*, n. 3, para. 57.

20 *Zaunegger* v. *Germany*, n. 3, para. 26 f. and 60; among the 27 countries of the European Union two-thirds (18) treat unmarried parents completely or largely equally. Of the remaining nine countries, with the exception of Germany and Austria, seven provide a possibility for judicial review with respect to custody of the father (1 BvR 420/09, n. 7, para. 23).
21 *Zaunegger* v. *Germany*, n. 3, para. 61 f.; Meier 2010, n. 17, p. 249 f.
22 *Zaunegger* v. *Germany*, n. 3, para. 63 ff.; with respect to the entire judgment: Meier 2010, n. 17, p. 249 f.
23 Walper and Jurczky 2010, n. 18, p. 17.
24 Rumo-Jungo, A. 2010. *Gemeinsame elterliche Sorge geschiedener und unverheirateter Eltern, Der Vorentwurf und der geplante Entwurf des Bundesrates*. Jusletter of February 15, 2010, n. 15, suggesting that there is also discrimination between fathers and mothers.
25 Meier 2010, n. 17, p. 254.
26 1 BvR 420/09, n. 7, Headnote; Meier 2010, n. 17, p. 254; Government report concerning the revision of Swiss custody legislation of November 16, 2011, BBl 2011 9077, p. 9100; Wyttenbach, J., and Grohsmann, I. 2014. Welche Väter für das Kind? Der Europäische Gerichtshof für Menschenrechte und die Vielfalt von Elternschaft. *Aktuelle Juristische Praxis* 23/2: 149-166, p. 152; Sünderhauf, H., and Widrig, M. 2014. Gemeinsame elterliche Sorge und alternierende Obhut, eine entwicklungspsychologische und grundrechtliche Würdigung. *Aktuelle Juristische Praxis* 23/7: 885–904, p. 896 ff.; Widrig, M. 2013. Alternierende Obhut, Leitprinzip des Unterhaltsrechts aus grundrechtlicher Sicht. *Aktuelle Juristische Praxis* 22/6: 903–911, p. 906.
27 *Schneider* v. *Germany*, App. No. 17080/07 (ECtHR, judgment of September 15, 2011), para. 100.
28 Compare, for example, *Schneider* v. *Germany*, n. 27, para. 100.
29 An official English version of the Order 1 BvR 420/09 of the German Constitutional Court is available at www.bundesverfassungsgericht.de/SharedDocs/Entscheidungen/EN/2010/07/rs20100721_1bvr042009en.html;jsessionid=1A4329871C4E978C4BD82A421A2DA6AA.2_cid383.
30 1 BvR 420/09, n. 7, para. 47.
31 Ibid., n. 54.
32 Ibid., n. 55.
33 Ibid., n. 56 and 62; Rumo-Jungo 2010, n. 24, para. 15.
34 1 BvR 420/09, n. 7, para. 56.
35 Ibid., n. 57.
36 Ibid., n. 63.
37 *Sporer* v. *Austria*, App. No. 35637/03 (ECtHR, judgment of February 3, 2011), para. 88 ff.; *Sude* v. *Germany*, App. No. 38102/04 (ECtHR, decision of October 7, 2010); *Döring* v. *Germany*, App. No. 50216/09 (ECtHR, decision of February 21, 2009).
38 *Anayo* v. *Germany*, App. No. 20578/07 (ECtHR, judgment of December 21, 2010), para. 67 ff.
39 *Schneider* v. *Germany*, n. 27, para. 104.
40 *Ahrens* v. *Germany*, App. No. 45071/09 (ECtHR, judgment of March 22, 2012), para. 75; *Kautzor* v. *Germany*, App. No. 23338/09 (ECtHR, judgment of March 22, 2012), para. 68 and 78 f.
41 *Ahrens* v. *Germany*, n. 40, para. 74; *Kautzor* v. *Germany*, n. 40, para. 76.
42 Committee on the Rights of the Child 2009. *41ST session, Consideration of reports submitted by states parties under article 44 of the Convention, concluding observations: Liechtenstien*. March 16, 2006, CRC/C/LIE/CO/2, n. 18 f.
43 Revised norms of the Swiss Civil Code as decided on June 21, 2013 (AS 2014 357).
44 Former Article 298a of the Swiss Civil Code (see Revised norms of the Swiss Civil Code as decided on June 26, 1998 [AS 1999 1118]).

45 Meier 2010, n. 17, p. 254 ff.; Rumo-Jungo 2010, n. 24, para. 15; Widrig, M. 2012. *Elterliche Sorge–Ein Grundrecht?*. Jusletter July 23, 2012, n. 16; Widrig 2013, n. 26, p. 906; Sünderhauf and Widrig 2014, n. 26, p. 899; Government report concerning the revision of Swiss custody legislation of November 16, 2011, BBl 2011 9077, p. 9100; Protocol of the parliamentary debates AB 2012 N 1627 and 1632; Protocol of the parliamentary debates AB 2013 S 6.
46 Meier 2010, n. 17, p. 254. See, however, *Buchs v. Switzerland*, App. No. 9929/12 (ECtHR, judgment of May 27, 2014), in which a father had been awarded joint physical custody (42% of care time) but no legal custody. The Court accepted in an *obiter dicta* that, taking into account that the children and the father had extended contact rights, the experts considering the case recommended sole legal custody of the mother and, because there is no consensus with respect to the question of whether legal custody should depend on both parents' consent, joint legal custody may depend on both parents' consent (para. 55). With respect to the last reason, it is important to mention that, in its "relevant comparative law" analysis, the Court did not question in how many states joint legal custody after divorce depends on both parents' consent (paras. 22–24). Hence, we do not know whether there is consensus among Member States with respect to that question or not.
47 EJPD, *Gemeinsame elterliche Sorge mehrheitlich begrüsst, Bundesrat nimmt Vernehmlassungsergebnisse zur Kenntnis*, Medienmitteilung vom 16.12.2009 (www.bj.admin.ch/ejpd/de/home/aktuell/news/2009/2009-12-160.html). The EJPD is the government body that was responsible for the revision of Swiss custody legislation.
48 Article 298b Swiss Civil Code.
49 Article 133 Swiss Civil Code.
50 Articles 298 and 298b Swiss Civil Code; Swiss government message concerning the revision of Swiss care and alimony legislation of November 29, 2013, BBl. 2013 529, p. 565; Sünderhauf and Widrig 2014, n. 26, p. 893; Bernard S., and Meyer Löhrer, B. 2014. *Kontakte des Kindes zu getrennt lebenden Eltern–Skizze eines familienrechtlichen Paradigmenwechsels*. Jusletter May 12, 2014, n. 17 ff.; Gloor, U., and Schweighauser, J. 2014. Die Reform des Rechts der elterlichen Sorge–eine Würdigung aus praktischer Sicht. *Praxis des Familienrechts* 15/1: 1–25, p. 10; Widrig 2013, n. 26, p. 906.
51 Article 301a Swiss Civil Code.
52 Widrig 2020, n. 2; Widrig 2013, n. 26.
53 Article 3 CRC; Committee on the Rights of the Child, General Comment no. 14 (2013) On the right of the child to have his or her best interests taken as a primary consideration (Article 3, para. 1), May 29, 2013, CRC/C/GC/14, n. 6 and 17 ff.; Committee on the Rights of the Child, General Comment no. 5 (2003) General measures of implementation of the Convention on the Rights of the Child, November 27, 2003, CRC/GC/2003/5, n. 12; UNICEF 2007. *Implementation Handbook for the Convention on the Rights of the Child*. Geneva : UNICEF, Article 3 p. 36 f.; Zermatten, J. 2014. La Convention relative aux droits de l'enfant. In M. Hertig Randall, and M. Hottelier (eds), *Introduction aux droits de l'homme*. Zurich: Schulthess, 315–328, p. 324 f.; compare further: 1 BvR 420/09, n. 7, para. 54.
54 "Art. 8 requires that the domestic authorities should strike a fair balance between the interests of the child and those of the parents and that in the balancing process, particular importance should be attached to the best interest of the child which, depending on their nature and seriousness, may override those of the parents" (*Görgülü v. Germany*, App. No. 74969/01 [ECtHR, judgment of May 26, 2004], para. § 43).
55 This could particularly be the case in those situations where a parent has no custody.
56 The approach may not be the finest way in which to ensure the respect of human rights. Nevertheless, the approach assures that fundamental human rights principles can be respected on request, while only a minimal obligation is imposed upon Member States.
57 See, e.g., Nielsen, L. 2017. Re-examining the research on parental conflict, coparenting, and custody arrangements. *Psychology, Public Policy, and Law* 23/2: 211–231; Nielsen, L. 2018. Joint versus sole physical custody: Children's outcomes independent of parent–child relationships, income, and conflict in 60 studies. *Journal of Divorce & Remarriage* 59/4: 247–281, p. 271 f.

58 Kelly, J. B. 2014. Paternal involvement and child and adolescent adjustment after separation and divorce: Current research and implications for policy and practice. *International Family Law, Policy and Practice* 2/1: 5–23, 16; the problem is extensively discussed in Lamb, M., and Kelly, J. B. 2009. Improving the quality of parent–child contact in separating families with infants and young children: Empirical research foundations. In R. M. Galatzer-Levy, J. Kraus, and J. Galatzer-Levy (eds), *The scientific basis of child custody decisions*, 2nd ed. Hoboken, NJ: Wiley, p. 187–214.
59 Fabricius, W. V., Braver, S. L., Díaz, P. V., and Vélez, C. E. 2010. Custody and parenting time: Links to family relationships and well-being after divorce. In M. E. Lamb (ed.), *The role of the father in child development*, 5th ed. Hoboken, NJ: Wiley, p. 201–240; Sünderhauf and Widrig 2014, n. 26, p. 886 f.; Sünderhauf, H. 2013. *Wechselmodell, Psychologie–Recht–Praxis*. Wiesbaden: Springer, p. 237.
60 1 BvR 420/09, n. 7, para. 25.
61 UNICEF 2007, n. 53, art. 9 p. 130.
62 See III.C.2 above.
63 *Kutzner* v. *Germany*, App. No. 46544/99 (ECtHR, judgment of February 26, 2002), para. 58; *Zaunegger* v. *Germany*, n. 3, para. 40; *Sporer* v. *Austria*, n. 37, paras. 72 und 90; *Sude* v. *Germany*, n. 37; *Döring* v. *Germany*, n. 37, 2009), "THE LAW", para. 2; Widrig 2013, n. 26, p. 904 f.; BGE 136 I 178 (Swiss Supreme Court, judgment 5A_798/2009 of March 4, 2010), Cons. 5.2.
64 *Görgülü* v. *Germany*, n. 54, paras. 42, 45 and 49 ff.
65 Compare also: Nikolina, N. 2012. The influence of international law on the issue of co-parenting: Emerging trends in international and European instruments. *Utrecht Law Review* 8/1: 122–144, p. 123.
66 Understood as a care arrangement in which the child lives at least 30–35% with each parent.
67 The Court made a mistake in its comparative law research: contrary to the Court's allegations, in Switzerland, according to Article 260a (1) Swiss Civil Code, any interested party can challenge a fatherhood established by recognition; *Ahrens* v. *Germany*, n. 40, paras. 26 f.
68 *X and others* v. *Austria*, App. No. 19010/07 (ECtHR, Grand Chamber, judgment of February 19, 2013), para. 56 f.

References

Meier, P. 2010. L'autorité parentale conjointe–L'arrêt de la CourEDH Zaunegger c. Allemagne–quels effets sur le droit suisse? *Revue de la protection des mineurs et des adultes* 65/3: 246–256.
Rumo-Jungo, A. 2010. *Gemeinsame elterliche Sorge geschiedener und unverheirateter Eltern, Der Vorentwurf und der geplante Entwurf des Bundesrates*. Jusletter of February 15, 2010.
Sünderhauf, H., and Widrig, M. 2014. Gemeinsame elterliche Sorge und alternierende Obhut, eine entwicklungspsychologische und grundrechtliche Würdigung. Aktuelle Juristische Praxis 23/7: 885–904.
UNICEF 2007. *Implementation Handbook for the Convention on the Rights of the Child*. Geneva: UNICEF.
Widrig, M. 2013. Alternierende Obhut, Leitprinzip des Unterhaltsrechts aus grundrechtlicher Sicht. Aktuelle Juristische Praxis 22/6: 903–911, p. 906.

CONCLUSION

José Manuel de Torres Perea, Edward Kruk and Martin Widrig

Introduction

The University of Malaga and the International Council on Shared Parenting (ICSP) co-sponsored the International Conference on Shared Parenting and the Best Interests of Children, which took place at the University of Malaga, Spain, 1–2 December 2019. Preceding the Malaga conference, ICSP conducted four other international conventions held in Strasbourg in 2018, Boston in 2017 and Bonn in 2014 and 2015. This book includes a selection of contributions presented at the 2019 conference and conclusions from previous ICSP conferences. We then summarise the most important results from the contributions to the book and conclude with our thanks to all the contributors.

Conclusions of the first four ICSP international conferences

Our starting point is the conclusions of the first four international conferences of the International Council on Shared Parenting (ICSP), a multidisciplinary organisation established to develop evidence-based approaches to the needs and rights of children whose parents are living apart. The purpose of the Council is first, the dissemination and advancement of scientific knowledge on the needs and rights ("best interests") of children whose parents are living apart and, second, to formulate evidence-based recommendations about the legal, judicial, and practical implementation of shared parenting. Its aim is to find solutions for reducing the problems of children known to arise from family breakdown, such as diminished self-esteem, depression, and possible parental alienation, as well as educational failure, substance abuse, and trouble with the law.

The *first* International Conference on Shared Parenting reached a consensus that neither the discretionary best interests of the child standard nor sole custody or primary residence orders are serving the needs of children and families of divorce, as well as a consensus that shared parenting is a viable post-divorce parenting arrangement that is optimal to child development and well-being, including for children of high conflict parents. The amount of shared parenting time necessary to achieve child well-being and positive outcomes, it was concluded, is a minimum of one-third time with each parent, with additional benefits accruing up to and including equal (50–50) parenting time, including both weekday (routine) and weekend (leisure) time. There was also consensus that "shared parenting" be defined as encompassing both shared parental authority (decision-making) and shared parental responsibility for the day-to-day upbringing and welfare of children, between fathers and mothers, in keeping with children's age and stage of development. Thus "shared parenting" is defined as "the assumption of shared responsibilities and presumption of shared rights in regard to the parenting of children by fathers and mothers who are living together and apart". There was consensus that national family law should at least include the possibility to issue shared parenting orders, even if one parent opposes it, with a recognition that shared parenting is in line with constitutional rights in many countries and with international human rights, namely, the right of children to be raised by both of their parents. There was consensus that three principles should guide the legal determination of parenting after divorce: (1) shared parenting as an optimal arrangement for the majority of children of divorce, and in their best interests; (2) parental autonomy and self-determination; and (3) limitation of judicial discretion in regard to the best interests of children. There was consensus that the above apply to the majority of children and families, including high conflict families, but not to situations of substantiated family violence and child abuse. It was agreed that the priority for further research on shared parenting should focus on the intersection of child custody and family violence, including child maltreatment in all its forms, including parental alienation. Finally, there was consensus that an accessible network of family relationship centres that offer family mediation and other relevant support services are critical in the establishment of a legal presumption of shared parenting, and vital to the success of shared parenting arrangements.

The *second* conference, focusing on the legal and practical implementation of shared parenting, affirmed these conclusions and added to them with an agreement that, given recognition of the viability of shared parenting by the research community, as well as by legal and mental health practitioners, as a post-divorce arrangement that is optimal to child development and well-being, both the legal and psycho-social implementation of shared parenting as a presumption should proceed without delay, with the full sanction and support of professional bodies and associations. As shared parenting encompasses both shared parental authority (decision-making) and shared parental responsibility for the day-to-day upbringing and welfare of children, between fathers and mothers, in keeping with children's age and stage of development, there was agreement that the legal implementation of shared parenting, including both the assumption of shared responsibilities and presumption of shared rights in regard to the parenting of children by fathers and mothers who are living together or apart, be enshrined in law. As shared parenting is recognised as the most effective means for both reducing high parental conflict and preventing first-time family violence, there was consensus that legal and psychosocial implementation of shared parenting as a presumption should proceed with the goal of reducing parental conflict after divorce.

There was further consensus that legal and psychosocial implementation of shared parenting as a presumption be encouraged for high conflict families in particular, with the full sanction and support of professional bodies and associations. There was consensus that the above apply to most children and families, but not to situations of substantiated family violence and child abuse. In such cases, a rebuttable presumption against shared parenting should apply. There was further consensus that a priority for both the scientific and legal communities and mental health practitioners should be the development of legal statutes and practice guidelines with respect to safety measures in cases of established family violence. As there is mounting evidence that shared parenting can prevent parental alienation and is a potential remedy for existing situations of parental alienation in separated families, there was consensus that further exploration of the viability of a legal presumption of shared parenting in situations of parental alienation be undertaken. Finally, as therapeutic and mediation services are vital to the success of shared parenting arrangements, there was consensus that an accessible network of family relationship centres that offer family mediation and other relevant support services are critical components of any effort toward legislative and psychosocial implementation of shared parenting, with governments urged to establish such networks as a necessary adjunct to the establishment of a legal presumption of shared parenting.

The *third* conference related to the concept of the "best interests of the child" in family separation and divorce, the source of protracted debate within both the academic and professional practice communities. Many years ago, Hillary Rodham (now Clinton), then a family lawyer, declared that "children's best interests" are nothing more than an empty vessel into which adult prejudices are poured.[1] Since that time, however, family scholars have taken a much more child-focused approach to the study of children's needs and interests, a "best interests of the child from the perspective of the child". Thus, the question, "have we reached a watershed in understanding the best interests of children in situations of family separation and divorce?" was placed front and centre during conference deliberations. Specifically, it was asked, have we reached the point where we can conclude with some confidence that the best interests of children are commensurate with a legal presumption of shared parenting responsibility for children and families, rebuttable in cases of family violence and child abuse? Are we at a point where the scientific evidence points in the direction of mandating that shared parenting becomes the foundation of family law? The answer to these questions was distilled by Dr Sanford Braver, a leading figure on the best interests of children of separation and divorce, at the conclusion of the conference: "To my mind, we're over the hump … we've reached the watershed. On the basis of this evidence … social scientists can now cautiously recommend presumptive shared parenting to policy makers." He further added, "I think shared parenting now has enough evidence … [that] the burden of proof should now fall to those who oppose it rather than those who promote it."

The *fourth* conference, immediately preceding the Malaga conference, held under the patronage of the Council of Europe, focused on shared parenting, social justice and children's rights. The conference examined the degree to which shared parenting is in keeping with the principles and articles of the UN Convention on the Rights of the Child. Thus, the focus of the conference was to examine how shared parenting, viewed as in the best interests of children of separated parents, is a crucial issue for practitioners and policy makers around the globe, in regard to the realignment of national law and international practices in keeping with the articles of the Convention. The conference concluded that the time has come for both family law legislators and family practitioners to take action to establish co-parenting as the foundation of family law, as a fundamental social justice issue and right of the child. The conference called upon the UN Committee on the Rights of the Child, governments and professional associations to identify shared parenting as a fundamental right of the child.

This conference had as its central focus of study what was considered to be the specific need of children of separated and divorced parents to know and be raised by both parents, and the need to support shared parenting as the best way to ensure the protection of this need. It was considered that this should be done with respect for the views of children of separated and divorced parents on their stated preferences for living arrangements after separation. Article 9.1 of the Convention on the Rights of the Child clearly defines and implements the concept of the "best interests of the child" in the context of parental separation. The conference underlined that this article allows for an evidence-based and child-centred understanding of "best interests". From there, shared parenting could be identified as the best interest of the child, as it facilitates children's relationship with both parents and can reduce conflict between them, ensuring to the greatest extent possible the survival and development of children of separated and divorced parents.

This conference also called for the adoption of all appropriate legislative, administrative, social and educational measures to protect such children from all forms of physical or mental violence, injury or abuse, neglect or negligent treatment, maltreatment or exploitation, including parental alienation as a form of emotional abuse of the child and family violence. Finally, the conference called upon the UN Committee on the Rights of the Child to take measures to ensure that member states do not discriminate against children of separated and divorced parents on the basis of parental status, specifically in regard to removing a parent from the daily life of a child, and to encourage states that are signatories to the Convention to adopt shared parenting as the foundation of family law.

The Malaga conference and issues raised in this book: Answers to questions posed in the Introduction

We now return to the questions posed at the beginning of this book. We shall follow the structure of the Introduction, attempting to answer the questions left open. To this end, we present some of the conclusions and approaches offered within the chapters of this volume.

We share the view of Parkinson and Cashmore (Chapter 1) that three main logistical factors may be considered decisive in determining whether shared parenting is feasible in any given family situation. First, it is necessary that there exist two viable homes that are sufficient to allow the child to live and thrive in each home. Second, both parents should live reasonably close to each other to facilitate the child's life routines, for example to go to school and be connected to the local community. Third, there needs to be sufficient flexibility within each parent's work routine to make a co-parenting arrangement possible. However, we recommend caution in regard to automatically negating shared parenting due to any one of these factors. Even with respect to the distance between the parents' homes, there may be exceptions to the rule in which shared parenting may in fact be feasible; for example, in the case of a parent being willing and able to rent a second residence near the other parent's home where the children may comfortably reside.

There are other factors that affect the well-being of children, such as the strength of the child's attachment to each of his or her parents, parental capacity, the degree of conflict between parents, a history of family violence, safety issues, and the adjustment to new partners or stepfamilies.

Contra-indications to shared parenting

In the Introduction, we focused our attention on three factors that have been considered to be antithetical to shared parenting arrangements: the need of children to be protected from exposure to violence and protracted high conflict, family income that is at least sufficient to maintain two separate households, and the quality of a child's relationship with each parent and nature of the parent–child attachment being sufficiently close to warrant a shared parenting arrangement.

Importance of protection from violence, abuse and protracted high conflict

There is no question that children need to be protected from exposure to family violence and abuse, and protracted high conflict between parents. Many courts and custody evaluators, however, disavow shared parenting in the mere presence of parental conflict. There is an emerging consensus that the mere presence of (non-violent) parental conflict is not sufficient to deny children and parents the benefits of shared parenting. Nielsen (Chapter 3) analysed the results of 19 studies comparing outcomes for children in sole physical (SPC) and joint physical custody (JPC) homes that controlled for conflict. Only in three of these studies was there a negative outcome for JPC children, among equal or better outcomes. In all other studies, the outcomes were equal or better for JPC children. Children benefitted from JPC, even in studies in which conflicted parents did not mutually agree to a parenting plan. These findings undermine the traditional view that JPC requires the presence of little or no conflict for children to benefit from shared parenting. Based on her findings, Nielsen suggests that it seems to be more important to focus on strengthening and improving the child's relationship with both parents than on the presence of parental conflict, absent family violence situations.

Lamb and Braver (Chapter 2) consider that a distinction must be made between toxic and non-toxic conflict, as not all forms of conflict affect children in the same way. In fact, they claim that exposure to some degree of parental disagreement may promote child adaptation. A further explanation of this view is provided by Fabricius et al.'s research (Chapter 29): children should know that the other parent cares about them when they are not present, as many young children think that the other parent no longer loves them, when he or she "disappears" from their lives. If children see that a parent is fully present in their lives within a shared parenting arrangement, they know that they matter and that the parent cares. Lamb and Braver (Chapter 2) further point out that there are several strategies (such as dropping off and picking up children at school rather than at the other parent's home) that limit children's exposure to conflict, which may have benefits for parental cooperation over the long term.

Level of income

Nielsen (Chapter 3) found in her review that higher family incomes are not the reason why children fare better in JPC than in SPC. The exception is when a child lives in poverty. Based on a large body of research conducted over the last three decades, she concludes that family income is not closely linked to children's outcomes. For this reason, she was not surprised that the outcomes of the 25 studies comparing the well-being of children in JPC and SPC controlling for family income were better for children in JPC. Only in two studies was there a negative finding.

Quality instead of quantity

Some scholars oppose joint physical custody, arguing that only the quality of a parent–child relationship matters and that more time brings no additional benefit; that is, only quality matters, not quantity. Some even posit that better outcomes of JPC children are due to self-selection effects, implying that only those children who thrive in JPC arrangements have qualitatively better relationships with each parent prior to separation. Nielsen (Chapter 3) points out that this view ignores the reality that building a relationship with children requires sufficient time and that even the two most extensive reviews on this topic conclude that it is beneficial for a child to spend time in person with a loving and involved parent, bearing in mind that they only measured the frequency of face-to-face parenting time. For this reason, it is no surprise that more time for interaction through JPC leads to better outcomes for children.

This view is shared by Lamb and Braver (Chapter 2) and Fabricius et al. (Chapter 29). They consider that frequency can have very little meaning if it involves minimal contact time and share the view that what empiric studies seem to suggest is that quality requires sufficient time for interaction and that the child gets better results if she or he spends more time with both parents. From this perspective, it could be said that "quality" requires sufficient quantity of time between parents and children.

Finally, yet importantly in this context, Parkinson and Cashmore (Chapter 1) point out that spending more (overnight) time with fathers has no negative impact on children's closeness to their mothers.

Advantages and disadvantages of shared parenting

To provide a balanced examination of the benefits and drawbacks of joint physical custody, we must first determine the advantages and disadvantages of sole versus shared care arrangements. The main benefit of shared parenting seems to be that the child maintains optimal relationships with both parents. Other benefits of shared parenting pointed out in the literature are having some respite from one parent in the move to the other and contributing to a feeling of well-being in the child (Parkinson and Cashmore, Chapter 1).

As far as the disadvantages are concerned, the main one appears to be the transfer to and from parents' homes and the fact that a place to call "home" may be missing. In fact, in certain cases, when the child perceives the constant moving as a misfortune, he or she finds no reward in being able to spend more time with the non-resident parent (Parkinson and Cashmore, Chapter 1).

Joint physical custody may involve a significant effort in encouraging inter-parental cooperation and the overcoming of significant challenges, but is compensated by the benefit children gain from seeing a continuation in their family life after separation or divorce (Parkinson and Cashmore, Chapter 1).

Essential needs of children after parental separation

The essential needs of children of separated parents are little different from those of children in general, and children's needs are little different from those of human beings in general. Human needs, however, must be responded to in a way that is commensurate with their age and stage of development. Children are a special category, as human growth and integrity in the early years shape the rest of one's life. Parental involvement, especially during the early years, is critical to children's physical and emotional security and well-being.

The research on children and divorce has identified a wide range of factors affecting children's adjustment to the consequences of divorce. Principal among these are children's needs for the maintenance of meaningful relationships with and love of both parents; being shielded from ongoing parental conflict and family violence; stability in their daily routines; and financial security. These are all severely compromised in the context of adversarial divorce.

We live in an era in which justice for children is equated with children's rights. However, although children's rights are important, and the United Nations Convention on the Rights of the Child (UNCRC) provides us with a framework for understanding the essential needs of children, including children of separated parents, a strictly rights-based approach to addressing children's irreducible needs is not enough and does not address the needs of the most vulnerable children; thus, rights by themselves are inadequate. The notion of responsibilities comes before that of rights. The reason for this is that *a right is not effectual by itself, but only in relation to the responsibility to which it corresponds. The effective exercise of a right springs not from the child who possesses it, but from others who recognise that they have a responsibility toward that child.*[2]

It seems that the more concerned we are about rights, the less concerned we are about our responsibilities to others and to ensuring that essential needs are met. For every human need there is a corresponding responsibility and for every responsibility, a corresponding need. A responsibility-to-needs approach demands that we take action, in a way that a rights-based approach does not. And when it comes to the essential needs of children of divorce, more action and less rhetoric are urgently needed.

Today, an alternative approach is being advanced that suggests that our starting point in ensuring justice for children of separated parents is a covenant or charter of parental and social institutional responsibilities to children's essential needs. Primary among these responsibilities is to recognise our responsibility to ensure that the following needs are addressed: maintenance of meaningful parental relationships with acceptance and support from both parents, being protected from ongoing parental conflict that can lead to family violence, and providing daily stability and financial security.

The starting point of such a covenant or charter is the enumeration of the essential needs of children after parental separation. Physical needs are perhaps the easiest to identify: food, warmth, sleep, health, rest, exercise and fresh air. Psychological, social and spiritual needs, on the other hand, are a little more ambiguous, yet no less essential for the well-being of children of divorce.

What, then, are the essential "metaphysical" needs of children of separated parents? We refer to the work of child development theorists such as Greenspan and Brazelton (*The Irreducible Needs of Children: What Every Child Must Have to Grow, Learn, and Flourish*),[3] Robert Coles (*The Moral Intelligence of Children*),[4] Erik Erikson (*Identity: Youth and Crisis*)[5] and Abraham Maslow (*The Farther Reaches of Human Nature*)[6] in advancing some ideas about what may be considered the essential psychological, social, moral and spiritual needs of children of divorce. We also draw on the work of philosopher Simone Weil on essential human needs and corresponding obligations.

We begin with children's need for stability, predictability and routine in their daily lives. *Order* is the first essential metaphysical need; a stable environment provides a sense of constancy, predictability, routine and continuity essential to child well-being. An essential aspect of order in children's lives is that they are not caught in conflicts of loyalty between their parents and are assured that the care and nurture of each parent will continue and not be interrupted. Children need both parents (as parents, not visitors) in their lives. Shared parenting, inasmuch as it maintains the involvement of both parents in children's lives and reflects as closely as possible their existing relationships and routines, addresses children's need for order and stability in their lives during and after parental separation.

Protection and guidance are further core needs of children: maintaining safety and protection from physical and emotional harm. *Autonomy*, the freedom and ability to choose, within limits, is another essential need of children. This does not mean that we allow young children to choose their living arrangements after separation, as having to choose between their parents forces them into a conflict of loyalty. Rather, living arrangements should be based on empirical data on children's needs together with what children themselves identify as in their best interests. *Equality* is also an essential need of children, and part of this is respecting the needs of children whose parents are separated on an equal basis to children whose parents are living together.

Freedom of opinion and expression is also vital. The voice of the child must be taken into consideration and respected. As with children's need for autonomy, this does not mean that we allow young children to choose their living arrangements after separation. Rather, housing arrangements should be based on other foundations such as empirical data on children's needs. Consideration should also be given to what the children themselves identify as their best interest. The need for *truth* is, in many ways, a more important human need than any other. This requires that what we know about the effects of different custodial arrangements be universally accessible to family members, and not remote or distorted. In the domain of thought, the need for truth calls for protection from error and lies.

Responsibility is another vital human need. Initiative and responsibility, to feel useful and even indispensable, are vital to children's well-being. For this need to be satisfied self-efficacy is central: the ability to make decisions in matters affecting oneself and contribute to decisions in one's social environment. *Security, the feeling of safety*, is another need. Fear and terror are extremely harmful to children's well-being; security and a sense of safety are thus vitally important. Safe environments foster a child's feeling of security and belonging. At the same time, experiencing *risk* is a core need of children. Overprotection, shielding from boredom and absence of risk are detrimental to children's well-being.

Privacy, solitude and *confidentiality* are important needs. At the same time, *social life* and social connection are vital to children's well-being. Community involvement and participation in the collective allow children to flourish, to have a sense of belonging in a larger social milieu, and to develop a personal investment in their surrounding community. Caring community refers to the "village" it takes to raise a child. The community can positively affect the lives of its children. Child-friendly shopkeepers, family resource centres, green schoolyards, bicycle lanes and pesticide-free parks are some of the ways in which a community can support its young.

Finally, the need for roots, attachment bonds and nurturant relationships, love, belonging, connectedness to family, language, religion, culture, neighborhood, community, region and country are vital to a child's growth and integrity. A sense of belonging within various "natural environments" such as family and community is perhaps the most neglected human need, a tragic circumstance of modern consumer society in which individuals are disconnected from the milieux in which humans have naturally participated, and through which we live as moral, intellectual and spiritual beings. Attachment bonds and nurturant relationships, a sense of belonging and connectedness, are necessary to the well-being of the child. Everything that has the effect of uprooting a human being or of preventing one from becoming rooted is highly damaging. Needless to say, the loss of one of their parents subsequent to a court determination of sole custody cuts to the heart of children's well-being. Disconnection from a parent and one's extended family is a serious form of uprooting that has profound effects on child well-being, and parental disengagement from children's lives is the source of great malaise in the lives of children and youth today.

These are the essential needs of children of separated parents, essentially the same as the needs of all children, which are essentially the needs of all human beings. Certain needs stand out for children of separated parents, given the special vulnerability of children of divorce. The maintenance of meaningful relationships with both parents and the need to be shielded from ongoing parental conflict and family violence are primary.

Is there convincing evidence that shared parenting provides real benefits to children?

As emphasised in the Introduction, perhaps the central focus of this book lies in a simple question: Is there evidence that shared parenting benefits the child after separation or divorce? The answer to this question cannot be found in the legal sphere. It is up to experts in psychology to provide the answer.

The results of the 60 quantitative empirical studies summarised by Nielsen (Chapter 3) suggest that children who live with each parent at least 35% of the time usually have better outcomes than children who live mainly or exclusively with one parent on a broad range of measures, which include academic or cognitive skills, emotional or psychological well-being, behavioural problems (which include teenage drug, nicotine or alcohol use), physical health or stress-related physical problems and the quality of the parent–child relationship. In 34 of these 60 studies, the children in shared parenting had better results on all measures. In 14 studies the results were equal or better; in 6 they were always equal; and in another 6 they were worse on one measure but equal or better on all other measures. Nielsen concludes that these studies indicate (with the exception of conflict with physical abuse) that even when conflict is high and the family income is considered, most children still benefit more from shared parenting than from sole custody. Finally, she stresses that the conclusion reached by at least three different groups of researchers is clear: shared parenting is in the best interests of children of all ages, with the exception of children whose parents are abusive or neglectful.

Lamb and Braver (Chapter 2) refer to this matter when they present the views of 12 experts. They conclude that there is a remarkable degree of consensus that the empirical evidence currently available strongly suggests that children of divorce benefit, on average, substantially from shared parenting. They refer to the results of more than 50 individual studies that indicate that children whose parents share parenting fare better than those living in sole physical custody. According to the results of these studies, children living in joint physical custody benefit from lower levels of depression, anxiety and dissatisfaction; less aggression and reduced alcohol and substance abuse; better school performance and cognitive development; better physical health; lower rates of smoking; and better parent–child relationships.

Lamb and Braver stress that, in the language of attachment theory, children are at a disadvantage if they lack secure attachments to adult caregivers. Since children may form an attachment to several caregivers, JPC may provide an important advantage compared to children in SPC: if one attachment figure is (temporarily) deficient or unavailable, the attachment figure may compensate. The authors draw attention to the fact that, contrary to joint physical custody, sole physical custody deprives children of divorce of one of the key sources of social capital – the second parent. They add that many recent studies show that attachment relationships grow and change in quality over time. Thus, parenting time allocations must be flexible and subject to change as children mature.

Although Braver and Votruba (Chapter 5) consider existing research as sufficiently robust to carefully recommend a presumption in favour of shared parenting, they suggest ways in which to improve further research and receive even better answers.

Similarly, López Narbona, Moreno Mínguez and Ortega Gaspar (Chapter 13) share the view that, based on the literature available, there is consensus that joint physical custody is the best possible option for children as well as parents and that we have reached a stage at which science has to transmit the messages of research to the authorities responsible for policy and practice. In order to do so efficiently, they consider that there is a need for more databases, better studies and studies that take into account the impact of parental well-being upon the best interests of the child. We would like to supplement their last suggestion with the consideration of the impact that the child's well-being may have on the well-being of his or her parents.

Does a presumption in favour of shared parenting promote shared parenting?

Most of our contributors share the view that there is consensus that shared parenting promotes the well-being of the child and would most likely agree that, in overall terms, the promotion of joint physical custody is a matter of public health.

One of the questions frequently asked is whether a presumption in favour of shared parenting increases the number of children living in such an arrangement. Becerril Ruíz and Jiménez-Cabello (Chapter 12) studied the impact of law on both marital breakdown and the granting of child physical custody in Spain. They observed that the implementation of legislation that promotes shared parenting in several autonomous communities leads to a greater increase in joint physical custody arrangements in these communities than in others. While shared physical custody levels rose from 15% in 2011 to 35% in 2017 in autonomous communities with more favourable legislation, they also rose in the other autonomous communities from 9% in 2011 to 25% in 2017. Becerril Ruíz and Jiménez-Cabello established in their factor analysis that a presumption in favour of shared parenting promotes shared parenting.

However, a presumption in favour of shared parenting is not the only factor that led to an increase in this parenting arrangement. There were other factors that had a greater impact on the parenting arrangement than the presumption, as described below. Since 2009 the Spanish Supreme Court has developed case law in favour of shared parenting. The clearest example is the judgment of 29 April 2013, which created a precedent by stating that, despite the provisions of the Spanish Civil Code, in the absence of an agreement, shared parenting should not be considered as the exception but the best possible measure to be considered. Since then, the total percentage of shared parenting has increased throughout Spain, although as indicated above, more in regions with their own legislation than in those subject to the Civil Code. This suggests that not only legislative change, but also the attitudes of judges play a crucial role in the prevalence of shared parenting.

For these reasons, we consider a presumption in favour of shared parenting as a means by which policy makers could promote joint physical custody. It is important to mention this because some opponents of a presumption claim that policy and practice have no impact on social reality.

Finally, it may be worthwhile to mention other ways in which to promote shared parenting rather than a presumption. For instance, a German study shows that there are many divorced families that would like to share parenting but do not know how to do so. Assisting them in the implementation of a joint physical custody arrangement may be a very appropriate means of promoting shared parenting.[7] Another easy way may be to oblige family law professionals to inform parents about the benefits for children of having a meaningful relationship with both parents, as is occurring in Australia. Furthermore, there are many legal obstacles impeding the implementation of shared parenting, such as tax disadvantages and so on. Such futile problems would be better abolished today than tomorrow.

Is there evidence that a presumption of shared parenting promotes children's well-being?

Braver and Votruba (Chapter 5) study the impact of shared parenting presumptions on children's outcomes. They also examine outcomes in jurisdictions where a presumption is already the norm. They conclude that, according to evidence from recent research, shared parenting probably does benefit children on average, which undermines the major rival thesis that better outcomes for children observed in shared parenting arrangements are merely the result of self-selection. For these reasons, they consider that, in light of the research available to date, researchers can now cautiously recommend a presumption in favour of shared parenting.

Of the twelve experts whose views were reviewed by Lamb and Braver (Chapter 2), the majority share this view, although they caution against a one-size-fits-all solution. The presumption should notably be rebuttable on the basis of factors such as credible risk of abuse or neglect, too great a distance between parents' homes, threat of abduction by a parent, unreasonable or excessive gate-keeping or coercive controlling violence (the stereotypical male battering pattern, which is one of four subtypes of intimate partner violence). However, high parental conflict or opposition should not automatically preclude JPC. In fact, Linda Nielsen (Chapter 3) refers to one of the conclusions of her studies, which is that, even when conflict between parents is high and co-parenting is poor, children do not have worse outcomes in JPC than in SPC families.

In the words of Parkinson and Cashmore (Chapter 1), it is clear from the various studies of children's views and experiences that shared care has benefits for many children. They add that there is no one parenting arrangement that is best for all children and, in many cases, a shared care arrangement may not be logistically feasible. However, many children and young people express a preference for shared care.

Reasons include being able to maintain a close relationship with both parents and seeing this arrangement as fairer for the parents.

The results of an evaluation of Arizona's equal parent presumption by Fabricius et al. (Chapter 29) support the view that a presumption is practicable. They surveyed professionals involved in the family law decision-making process and assessed their perceptions of the legislation. The different professionals evaluated the presumption positively overall, regarding it as being in the children's best interests, having a neutral impact on parental conflict and leading to a small increase in allegations of domestic violence and abuse.

It therefore appears that evidence available to date supports shared parenting and even a rebuttable presumption. However, many open questions remain and, as our knowledge advances, the aforementioned conclusions may have to be adapted.

The presumption from a legal perspective

The frequently expressed objection that a presumption in favour of shared parenting would clash head-on with the principle of the best interests of the child is studied in Chapter 4 by de Torres Perea. He concludes that this principle can be interpreted and applied in two different ways. If it is considered as *a* primary consideration (among several others) to be taken into account by the courts, it is compatible with a presumption (understood as the starting point in care decisions). If it is considered *the* (and only) primary consideration, it is not. He concludes that only the first approach is compatible with the most fundamental legal standards, which allows for a presumption. Hence, from a legal perspective, a presumption is technically possible.

Widrig (Chapter 6) addresses the question from the perspective of the child. He concludes that the UN Convention on the Rights of the Child assumes children's care by their parents to be in the child's best interests. This coincides with a rebuttable presumption in favour of shared parenting from the perspective of adults but looks at the question from the perspective of the child. Starting from here, the best interests of the child must be determined in each particular case.

Further considerations

We share Parkinson and Cashmore's (Chapter 1) view that, in determining which parenting arrangement is best for the child, it is important to try to see the problems through the child's eyes. For this reason, choosing shared parenting is appropriate when decisions are made with the child in mind, his or her feelings are taken into consideration and when the time the child spends with his or her parents and siblings after the breakdown of the marriage is suitable for his or her well-being.

In addition, it should be noted that a parenting arrangement that works well early in a child's life may no longer be appropriate when the child grows older and eventually reaches adolescence. At this stage, the child tends to socialise and to be less frequently at home; he or she also tends to seek his or her identity by arguing with his or her parents. For this reason, the child must be heard, not only initially when the parental arrangement is agreed, but also and especially when she or he grows up and reaches a certain maturity. Children seem to desire "flexibility", especially as they grow older and become more independent (Parkinson and Cashmore, Chapter 1). If we want to respect a child's desire for flexibility, we may have to abolish the idea of *res iudicata* in care decisions.

Parental alienation dynamics

Lamb and Braver mention in Chapter 2 that researchers and courts often make confusing links between conflict, violence and parental alienation. They shared the view that this confusion should be avoided and claim that shared physical custody may successfully undermine attempts to alienate a child. A reason could be that children can directly assess the behaviour of both parents, recognising for themselves the discrepancies between the actual characteristics of the parent and those described by the alienating parent. Similarly, Kruk (Chapter 18) believes that, with the exception of situations with risk factors such as abuse or violence, shared parenting could reduce the risk and incidence of parental alienation dynamics, because children continue to have meaningful routines and relationships with both parents and are therefore less susceptible to alienating behaviours.

These views may be confusing to those who listen to critics of the so-called "parental alienation syndrome (PAS)" coined by Richard Gardner in 1985. In Spain and elsewhere, the existence of this syndrome is strongly rejected by many members of the doctrine, for example Iglesias Martín (Chapter 21). It should also be noted that the PAS has been used as a strategy to discredit allegations of child sexual abuse. For this reason, Ortiz-Tallo and Ferragut (Chapter 20) suggest investigating the possibility of child sexual abuse thoroughly and independently of PAS claims to ensure the well-being of the child.

In our view, it is necessary to distinguish clearly between the non-recognised PAS and the more general but widely accepted concept of parental alienation. In line with this, the judgment of the European Court of Human Rights (ECtHR) 23641/17, of 29 October 2019, studied by Sünderhauf-Kravets and Widrig (Chapter 22), recognises that there are "alienated children" and parents who negatively influence their children against the other parent (alienating behaviour). The ECtHR implicitly recognises parental alienation, although it does not recognise the existence of a syndrome. The Court condemns alienating behaviour as a form of emotional child abuse that may require rapid and carefully chosen interventions to protect the child and his or her relationship with a parent. The fact that a rejected parent uses the term "parental alienation syndrome" is no reason for the authorities to neglect their duty to investigate the matter and, if necessary in a particular case, to intervene appropriately.

Relocation

Lamb and Braver address relocation in Chapter 2. They observe that some jurisdictions place the burden of proof to justify relocation on the party wishing to relocate and others require the party not relocating to demonstrate why relocation should not be permitted. They state that, according to the group of experts, it is more appropriate to take individual decisions and to avoid presumptions in either direction. A court should take into consideration the history of involvement of the non-relocating parent when deciding in such cases and, importantly, ensure that children are able to maintain meaningful relationships with both parents, especially when such relationships existed prior to the change of residence.

Mazeh (Chapter 14) proposes a set of criteria to be considered in cases of relocation. He recommends that these include the quality of parenting of both parents, the level of parental involvement, past interference by the applicant parent in the relationship between the children and the other parent, as well as other factors such as the will of the child (where applicable), whether the parents had an existing agreement on this issue, the cause of the relocation and the potential harm to the children resulting from relocation.

Mazeh's approach focuses on the Israeli context, noting that in Israel judges frequently weigh up only one criterion – the needs of the parent requesting relocation with the children (usually the mother) – and assume that what is good for that parent is good for the children. He further disagrees with the premise that parents must differentiate between their own aspirations and the needs of their children, sacrificing the former. This view is close to the view of de Torres Perea in his philosophical note in Chapter 4, concerning the "Kantian objection". He considers that, from a philosophical perspective, the concept of dignity implies that each human being is an end in itself and cannot be relegated to a simple tool subjugated to the interests of another human being. Therefore, a strict interpretation of the best interest of the child that would absolutely subordinate the interests of a parent to that of his or her child could clash head-on with this Kantian formulation.

Cano Hurtado (Chapter 15) points out that, in any case, the decision on relocation cannot be taken unilaterally. Hence, if the relocation is not consensual, judicial intervention will be necessary. She describes the two main criteria considered by the Spanish Supreme Court when reaching a decision on the matter: first, it investigates whether shared parenting should be discarded when there is a great distance between parents' homes; second, it chooses the parent to be granted sole custody in such a case. The decision should be based mainly on the psychosocial report of an expert. This report should take into account the age of the child, the place of residence, the relationship with the parents and the other members of the family, while respecting the principle of the best interests of the child.

Judicial application of the best interests of the child principle

Chapter 9 is interesting from a legal perspective. Goñi Huarte points out that, under Spanish law, when the court delivers a judgment directly affecting minors, the judgment must be based on the best interests of the child. However, it is not sufficient to merely mention that the judgment is based on that principle; the judgment must also contain a statement of the reasoning behind how the best interests of the child have been applied in the particular case. If a judgment lacks this reasoning, deviates from the Supreme Court's case law concerning the application of the best interests of the child or ignores the existence of an expert's report on such application, it may be subject to appeal to the Supreme Court.

Sociological perspectives

Becerril Ruíz and Jiménez-Cabello (Chapter 12) study, from a sociological perspective, the impact of law on both marital breakdown and the granting of child custody in Spain. They conclude that, with respect to custody legislation, the implementation of laws passed by several autonomous communities that promote shared parenting has led to an interesting phenomenon. While shared parenting, at the expense of exclusive custody granted to the mother, has increased at a national level, this increase has been greater in regions with their own legislation, rising from 15% in 2011 to 35% in 2017. In communities without their own regulations, the increase was from 9% in 2011 to 25% in 2017. We can therefore conclude that the existence of a legal system that somehow favours the granting of joint custody increases its presence. One of the figures provided by Jiménez-Cabello at the conference in Malaga is interesting. He highlighted a relevant fact from his studies of statistical data, namely, that the percentage of shared parenting in the case of break-up of gay couples with children is much higher than in the case of heterosexual couples and subsequent litigation is also minimal.

In addition, López Narbona, Moreno Mínguez and Ortega Gaspar (Chapter 13) provide a critical literature review of empirical sociological studies on shared-parenting. They detected a serious lack of empirical evidence, lack of definition of the concept and a lack of databases and indicators or indexes based on solid theoretical foundations. As the studies provided by sociology are basic to the foundation of psychological and legal research, these shortcomings should be taken into consideration as one of the main challenges we face in this area.

New approaches from different scientific fields

Beyerlein (Chapter 10) provides a new approach from the fields of epigenetics and developmental biology. He claims that genome sequencing research allows us to reconstruct and understand the physiological mechanisms leading to cell differentiation, organ differentiation and the development of a person's character, that is, development into the physiological individuum. Memory and adaptation are the key concepts to understanding this process. The practical proof of the existence of a memory carrying all specialisation information is simple and understandable: within about seven years, almost all cells of the human body are substituted by their descendent cells. In addition, our development and differentiation never cease. And, of course, in this process cells continue to write the logbook and pass on its content to the next generation. Nature also performs a powerful "trick" that allows an efficient adaptation to the environment in which the organism is growing: adaptation by self-programming in the target environment. This is relevant for the development of the embryo and later the child at a biomolecular level. Beyerlein claims that 95% of the genetic code is highly variable and that children benefit most from the genetic potential of this 95% if they live with role models with a genetic code as similar as possible to their own. This may be relevant if we consider, for instance, an inherited genetic disease. Such natural preconditions and consequences of the genetic and epigenetic mechanisms are important to understand the biological impact of parentship, the biological difference of biological and foster parentship, the impact of divorce and after-divorce scenarios and of childhood traumatisation by parental separation or the follow-up settings. Beyerlein concludes that the principle of continuity serves the epigenetic needs of children. Continuity in terms of epigenetic health means: forming a legal and social system that promotes the establishment of an inseparable relationship between the child and both biological parents.

In the words of Vezzetti (Chapter 11), until now, the divorce of a couple with underage children has been considered by the authorities as a purely legal problem. He adds that biochemical and psychobiological studies allow for a completely different approach. Scientific research, also using animal models, demonstrates the biological basis of the problems associated with parental separation and the undisputed consequences for children's welfare and health. He concludes that judgments given by family courts can have a huge influence on human and public health, as they have an enormous impact on the probabilities of parental loss and other childhood adversities.

Conclusion and special thanks

We commenced the International Conference on Shared Parenting and the Best Interests of Child and this book with many open questions. Of course, we did not answer all of them (and even raised new ones). However, we can say that each contributor did his or her best to do so. We would like to particularly acknowledge and thank each of them for the tremendous effort made in making this *Routledge International Handbook of Shared Parenting and Best Interest of the Child* what it is today. Our gratitude also to all those whose efforts we could not include in the book.

Furthermore, we thank the University of Málaga, which is a leading research institution and an important pillar of innovation, human, socioeconomic and cultural development in the autonomous community of Andalucía and the Spanish nation, for co-organising and co-funding the conference, offering us the beautiful Aula Magna of the University of Málaga Law School to host the conference, amongst many other things.

We thank the University of Málaga's Law School (Faculty of Law), its dean, Juan José Hinojosa Torralvo, and the Department of Civil Law and its head, José Manuel Ruiz-Rico Ruiz, who ensured that both the academic and organisational aspects of the conference were dealt with efficiently. We also thank all members of the Law School who actively participated by mediating debates, presenting speakers, taking charge of the administration or presenting the results of their research.

We thank the International Council on Shared Parenting, a non-profit organisation devoted, first, to the disseminating and furthering of scientific knowledge on the needs and rights ("best interests") of children whose parents are living apart and, second, to formulating evidence-based recommendations on the legal, judicial and practical implementation of shared parenting. The ICSP co-organised this conference and provided valuable information and recommendations.

We thank the Obra Social la Caixa for its collaboration, support and funding of the simultaneous translation system used during the conference, with special thanks to Ángel Salar and Yolanda Solero.

We also thank the Málaga Bar Association for its participation in the Convention of Málaga, especially the Family Law section and its coordinator, Roberto García Alfonso.

We would like to thank Málaga City Council for supporting the event and offering us Loring Palace for the closing ceremony of the convention.

Finally, but no less importantly, we would like to express our special gratitude to Helen Pritt and our publisher Routledge and emphasise their enormous effort and support in bringing this fabulous Routledge International Handbook Series to the general public.

Notes

1 Hillary Rodham (1973). Children under the law. *Harvard Educational Review* 43/4: 487–514.
2 Paraphrased from the words of Simone Weil, French philosopher and political activist.
3 Stanley Greenspan and T. Berry Brazelton (2000). *The irreducible needs of children: What every child must have to grow, learn, and flourish.* Boston, MA: Da Capo Press.
4 Robert Coles (1998). *The moral intelligence of children.* London: Bloomsbury.
5 Erik Erikson (1968). *Identity: Youth and crisis.* London: W.W. Norton.
6 Abraham Maslow (1973). *The farther reaches of human nature.* London: Penguin.
7 This approach is taken by Sünderhauf, who, in a recent book, provides helpful insights on how to make shared parenting work (H. Sünderhauf. 2020. *Praxisratgeber Wechselmodell.* Wiesbaden: Springer).

INDEX

Note: Page numbers in *italics* indicate figures, **bold** numbers indicate tables, on the corresponding pages.

Aaron, M. 72
abuse in family relationships 244; *see also* child abuse; child sexual abuse (CSA)
Adamsons, K. 27, 31
additional children: child support credits 226; of child support payers 224–225; custodial parent, families of 223–224; incentive to have more 225–226; insufficient, child support as 224–225; non-custodial parent, families of 224; nondisclaimable duty 226–227; normative question 224–227; right to in intact families 223; second wife's income 225
Adolescent Views study 18, 19, 20–21, 22
age of child 464; joint physical custody and 40, 45; tender age presumption 186, 188–189, 192; Tender Age Rule (Philippine family law) 389–391; young children, joint physical custody and 40
aggression 139–140
Agid, O. 144
Ajenjo, A. 158, 175
Akins, F.R. 72
Albiston, C.R. 32
Alcázar, R. 175, 176
Alexander, M. 17
alienation *see* parental alienation; parental alienation syndrome (PAS)
Allen, D. 159, 161
Alsina, A.G. 175, 176

Amato, P.R. 31
Anayo judgement of the ECtHR 444
animals, effects of parental separation on 143
Arizona child custody reforms, evaluation of: background to reforms 370–371; child support payments 381; conflict between parents and 381; development of reforms 370–371; goal of reforms 370; limitations of evaluation 383; method of evaluation 372–374; mothers' attitudes 381; participants 372–374; positive evaluation 380–381; procedures 372; professional groups involved 371–372, 381–382; rebuttable presumption of equal parenting time 380, 382; results of 374–380, **375**, **376**, *377*, *378*, *379*
Assini, J.J. 72
attachment theory 30, 31
Atteneder, C. 161–162
Austin, W. 27
Australia: evolution of shared parenting in 356–358; mandatory mediation 311–313, *312*
autonomous communities in Spain: regulations of 160–161, 164–165, *166*; shared custody in 3–4, *4*
A. V. v. Slovenia 55

Bainham, A. 54, 361
Baker, A.J.L. 234, 292

Index

Bala, N. 362, 363
Balearic Islands, shared custody and 3, 4
Bambico, F.R. 143
Baude, A. 43, 63
Bauserman, R. 43, 63, 65, 67, 433
Becker, G. 159
Belgium, evolution of shared parenting in 364
benefits of shared parenting *see* children's experiences of shared parenting; panel discussions on shared parenting
Bercovitz Rodriguez-Cano, R. 110
Bergström, M. 27, 72, 86
Bernhardt, E. 171
best alternatives to a negotiated agreement (BATNA) 311
best interests of the child: as "a" or "the" primary consideration 8–9; conceptual map 51–52; critique of 79–80; deficits of incomplete Spanish system 98–99; direct/indirect measures 52; ECtHR case law 55–56; as a "general clause" 57; guidelines 83; indeterminacy of 79; International Council on Shared Parenting (ICSP) Conferences 454; interpretation of, UNCRC and 84; joint physical custody and 48–49; judicial application of principle 466–467; Kantian ethic objection 58–59; legal practice and research, UNCRC and 84–85; legal presumption of shared parenting 464; legal presumptions, BIC compatibility with 53–55; mistakes due to following 83; other considerations 52–53, 54; Philippine family law 384, 385–386, 389, 392–393; puzzling persistence of 80; reasoning of judgements in Spanish law 118–120; relocation of one parent 184, 205–206; Spanish case law 52–53, 57–58; Swiss custody legislation and 80–82; threefold perspective in 96; tool to assess 100; unaccompanied foreign minors 96–99; UNCRC and 83–85; United Kingdom 362; unreviewable discretion of 79–80; welfare of the child as paramount 56–58
Birnbaum, R. 23
Blasio, G. 162
Böheim, R. 162
Bordeianu v. Moldova 275
Bowlby, J. 30
Boyd, S.B. 357
Braver, S. 27–28, 29, 34, 67, 71, 73

Brazil, parental alienation syndrome (PAS) in 264
Brinig, M. 161
Briones, P. 162
Brullet, C. 175
Buchanan, C.M. 34, 74n2

Campbell, D.T. 69
Campo, M. 17
Canada, evolution of shared parenting in 362–363
Cancian, M. 359–360
capacity approach 58
Carbonell, X. 174
Carlberg, M. 16
case law in favour of shared parenting in Spain 4–5, *5*
Cham, H. 67, 68
Charter of Fundamental Rights of the European Union 200
charter of responsibilities to children's needs 459–461
child abduction, reasoning of judgements in Spanish law and 125
child abuse: International Council on Shared Parenting (ICSP) Conferences 453; parental alienation as **237**, 240, 290–291; *see also* child sexual abuse (CSA)
child-centred approach, change to 6
children *see* additional children; age of child; child abuse; children's experiences of shared parenting; child sexual abuse (CSA); unaccompanied foreign minors
Children Act (ChA) 1989 (UK) 51, 54, 360–361
Children Act (LOPJM) (Spain) 51, 59n2, 118–119, 121
Children (Scotland) Act (ChSA) 1995 51
Children (Scotland) Bill: amendments, consideration of 426–427; campaigning efforts 429; exclusion of shared parenting amendment 429–430; factions concerning 427–429; future changes needed 430; Justice Committee, consideration by 426; origins and early consultation 424–425; presumption of shared parenting 420, 421, 422, 423, 424, 425, 426, 427; progress of bill 425–426; United Nations Convention on the Rights of the Child (UNCRC) 426
children's experiences of shared parenting: *Adolescent Views* study 18, 19, 20–21, 22; benefits and costs 23–24; changes

471

over time 24; *Children's Voices* project 18, 21; closeness to parents 21–22; conflict between parents 22–23; equal time as preferred 19–20; factors making a difference 17; fair to both parents, desire to be 20; heterogeneity of 18–19; importance of children's views 23; logistics 22, 23; managing belongings 22; participation in decisions about 20–21; *Relocation* study 18, 19; research studies on 16–17; *Shared Care* study 18, 20, 21–22; stability 22
Children's Voices project 18, 21
child sexual abuse (CSA): custody and 265–266; defined 263; parental alienation syndrome (PAS) 265–266; prevalence 263; recommendations 268; testimonies 266–268
civil procedural law (LEC) (Spain) 117–118, 121–122
Cochem model of shared parenting in 423, 437
Cohen, B. 71
community, children's need for 460
compensation for parental alienation: ECtHR judgement 23641/17 283–284; *see also Pisică v. Republic of Moldova*
confidentiality, children's need for 460
conflict between parents: as argument against SP 40; Arizona child custody reforms, evaluation of 381; benefits of JPC and 64; children's experiences of shared parenting 22–23; decisions on shared parenting and 6–7; high-conflict post-separation cases 317–318; joint physical custody 42, 44; judicial management of high-conflict cases 318–320; mediation 319–320; panel discussions on shared parenting 34–35; parenting coordination as tool 320–324; parenting plans 320–322; protection from 456–457; protective factor for health, shared parenting as 146–147; religious and moral education of children 110–114; shared parenting as reducing 241, 244; Spanish Civil Procedure Act (LEC) 318–319, 320; statistical controls in research 66
conserved regions 137–138
constructive aggression 139–140
Convention for the Protection of Human Rights and Fundamental Freedoms 200
Cook, S.T. 359–360
Cookston, J. 71
cooperative parenting: appropriate behaviour 299; appropriate cooperation 299; attitude 298; benefits of 297; close cooperation method 299; communication 297, 298; conscious decision for 299–300; Cooperative Parenting Triangle 298, *300*, 300–301; everyday life 298; factors in 297–298; Finland 302–303; needs of the child after divorce 297; seamless cooperative parenting method 299; styles of 299; values 298; welfare of the child as priority 302
correlational research 48
Coster, M. 57
Council of Europe: Resolution 1714 (2010) 271–272; Resolution 2079 (2015) 313–314
covariance, analysis of 66
cross-sectional studies 64
C v. Finland 56

Dacasin v. Dacasin (Philippines) 390
Dallam, S. 265
Darnell, D. 234
definitions, diversity of 2–3
de Torres Perea, J.M. 404
Diaz, P. 71
dignity 58, 59
direct/indirect measures affecting the child 52
domestic violence: 'friendly parent' concept 276; International Council on Shared Parenting (ICSP) Conferences 453; intimate partner violence (IPV) as rebuttal factor 34; judicial investigation of 272–273; parental alienation syndrome (PAS) 273–276; protection of the child 272–273; strategies used in defence of 276; UNCRC and protection against 271
Douglas, E.M. 69
Dujo, V. 173–174, 176

education about shared parenting 244
effect sizes of research 48
Elster, J. 79
Emery, R. 34, 46, 65, 74n2, 80
enmeshment, principle of 188, 190
epigenetics 467–468; aggression 139–140; conserved regions 137–138; constructive aggression 139–140; deletion of adverse toggle patterns 137; epigenetic code 130–133; foster parents 137–138; health 134–135; individuum and 134; infanticide in mammals 135–136; joint imprint from both gender 138–139; learning 134–135;

missing parents 138–139; one-parent families 138–139; physiological "me" 134; toggles 130–133; traumas 136
equality, children's need for 460
equal time as preferred by children 19–20
Escobedo, A. 175, 176
Espiritu v. Court of Appeals (Philippines) 388–389
estrangement/alienation, distinction between 283
European Charter on Children's Rights 115n1, 200
European Commission on Family Law (CEFL) 199
European Convention for the Protection of Human Rights and Fundamental Freedoms 342
European Convention on Human Rights (ECHR) 53, 55; Zaunegger approach of the ECtHR 440–441
European Court of Human Rights (ECtHR) 51–52, 53, 54, 55–56, 314; *Anayo judgement* 444; *Bordeianu v. Moldova* 275; judgement 23641/17 465; parental alienation 465; religious and moral education of children 113; *Schneider judgement* 442–443, 444; *Sporer judgement* 443; Zaunegger approach 440–448; *see also* compensation for parental alienation
European Union Regulation 1347/2000 342
extraordinary scope, acts of 107–108

Fabricius, W. 19, 31, 71, 72, 147
fair to both parents, childrens's desire to be 20
families, dramatic changes in 1–2
Families Need Fathers Scotland 423, 425, 428
family income 42, 44; decisions on shared parenting and 6; shared parenting and 457; statistical controls in research 66–67
family relations: relocation of one parent 202–203; right to 198–201; shared parenting as best option 201–202; *see also* violence in family relationships
Fariña, F. 172
fathering time, quality/quantity of 41–42
Fathers Network Scotland 428
Fehlberg, B. 65, 358
financial interests, shared parenting and: case law 210–219; changes to arrangements, maintenance and 213–216; maintenance payments 210–213; reproachable, financial interests as 216–220; *see also* additional children
Finland, cooperative parenting in 302–303
Fisher, R. 311
Flaquer, L. 175, 176
flexibility of SP 31
foreign minors *see* unaccompanied foreign minors
France, parental alienation syndrome (PAS) in 264
Francesconi, M. 162
Fransson, E. 30, 72, 86
freedom, child's religious 108–109
freedom of opinion and expression, children's need for 460
'friendly parent' concept 276

Gardner, R.A. 263, 264, 273, 293
general clauses 57
genetic code 129, 130, 467–468; conserved regions 137–138; *see also* epigenetics
German Civil Code (BGB) 57
Germany *see* politics in Germany, shared parenting and; Zaunegger approach of the ECtHR
Gilbreth, J.G. 31
Gilmore, S. 54
Girard, R. 3
Glaser v. United Kingdom 55
Glenn, N. 159
Goldscheider, F. 171
Gómez-Casilla, A. 175
González, L. 175
grandparents: relationships with 46–47, 177; visiting rights 125
Grebin v. Grebin 223–224
guidance, children's need for 459–460
Gunnoe, M.L. 67

Hall, J. 19, 31
Halla, M. 161–162
Harman, J. 28
Haugen, G.M.D. 16
health, shared parenting as protective factor of 468; adversity, childhood, impact of 142; animals, effects of parental separation on 143; biological effects of parental loss 144–145; conflict between parents 146–147; emotional health 46; general well-being 147–151; infant health, psychobiological effects of adversity 143–144; parental loss 142–143, 146; public health point of view 150–151

473

Herring, J. 54, 56
high-conflict post-separation cases: judicial management of 318–320; mediation 319–320; parenting coordination as tool 320–324; parenting plans 320–322; realities and costs 317–318; Spanish Civil Procedure Act (LEC) 318–319, 320; Spanish judicial management of 318–320
Hjern, A. 72
Horcajo, P.J. 173–174, 176

illegitimate children: Philippine family law 387, 388; *see also* Zaunegger approach of the ECtHR
immigration *see* unaccompanied foreign minors
income, family 42, 44; decisions on shared parenting and 6; shared parenting and 457; statistical controls in research 66–67
indirect/direct measures affecting the child 52
individuality 130–131
infant health, psychobiological effects of adversity on 143–144
infanticide in mammals 135–136
informational physiology of individual development: aggression 139–140; constructive aggression 139–140; environment, importance of 129–130; epigenetic health 134–135; epigenetic learning 134–135; foster parents 137–138; genetic code 129, 130; individuality 130–131; infanticide in mammals 135–136; joint imprint from both gender 138–139; missing parents 138–139; one-parent families 138–139; one/two homes 140; physiological "me" 134; toggles, epigenetic 130–133
initial preferences of parents 71–72
International Convention on Children's Rights 342
International Council on Shared Parenting (ICSP) Conferences: best interests of the child 454; Bonn 2014 452–453; Bonn 2015 453–454; Boston 2017 452, 454; child abuse 453, 455; conclusions of first four 452–454; definition of shared parenting 453; further research 453; implementation of shared parenting 453–454; legal determination of parenting 453; national family law 453; purpose of ICSP 452; rights of the child 454–455; social justice 454–455; Strasbourg 2018 454–455; time, shared parenting 453; violence 453, 455; *see also* panel discussions on shared parenting
interrupted time-series 69–70, *70*
intimate partner violence (IPV) as rebuttal factor 34
Israeli case law in relocation of one parent 186–192

Jarne, A. 174
Johnson, M. 34
Johnson, S.K. 31
Johnston, J.R. 283
joint legal custody 31–32
joint physical custody: age of child 40, 45; arguments against 40–42, 74n2; as in best interest of the child 48–49; causality, probing 65–73, *70*; conflict between parents 40, 41, 42, 44, 47; correlational research 48; grandparents, relationships with 46–47; health, physical and mental 46; income, family 42, 44; limitations of research, acceptance of 48; meta-analyses of research 42–43, 63–64; methodology of research into, limitations of 64–65; opposition to as legal presumption 64; outcomes of 63–73, *70*; psychological research into outcomes 85–88; quality of parent-child relationships 44–45; quality/quantity of fathering time 41–42; research studies 43–49; worse outcomes for children 47; *see also* methodology of research into JPC; shared parenting
Jull, J. 139

Kaganas, F. 360, 362
Kantian ethic objection to BIC 58–59
Kelly, J.B. 82, 87, 183, 283
Keogh, E. 355
Kitterød, R.H. 356
Klaff, R.L. 188–189
Kornhauser, L. 71
Kosmopoulou v. Greece 55
Kreidl, M. 177
Kruk, E. 234
Kuppinger v. Germany 55

Lamb, M. 28, 30–31, 183
Lappegård, T. 171
LEC *see* civil procedural law (LEC) (Spain)
legal presumption of shared parenting 7–8, 33–34; Arizona child custody reforms, evaluation of 380; best interests of the

child 464; BIC compatibility with 53–55; Children (Scotland) Bill 420, 421, 422, 423, 424, 425, 426, 427; jurisdictions where JPC a presumption/norm 72–73; mandatory mediation 311; opposition to JPC as legal presumption 64; panel discussions on shared parenting 33–34; parental alienation 241–244; as promoting shared parenting 462–463; rebuttable presumption, shared parenting as 7–8; well-being of children as promoted by 463–464

Lesthaeghe, R.J. 171

literature review on shared care: children, effects of divorce on 173–174, 175; consensus on concepts, need for 178; data limitations 178; deficiencies in literature 170, 176, 467; empirical studies, need for 176–177; families, effects of divorce on 174–175; family compliance with agreements 178; first demographic transition 171; follow-up, lack of 178; gaps in research 177–178; methodology 172–173; parents, effects of divorce on 174–175; parents, effects of JPC on 177; purpose of 172–173; second demographic transition 171–172

Lodge, J. 17

logistics of shared parenting: children's experiences 22; parents' arrangements 23

longitudinal studies, power of 72

López Orozco, R.E. 266

Lowestein, L.F. 265

Ludolph, P. 28

Luecken, L.J. 147

Luepnitz, D. 71

Maccoby, E.E. 71, 358

maintenance payments 210–213; changes to arrangements and 213–215

mandatory mediation: arguments for 310; Australia 311–313, *312*; best alternatives to a negotiated agreement (BATNA) 311; definition of mediation 308; Europe, legal situation in 313–314; high-conflict post-separation cases 319–320; history of mediation 307–308; inappropriate, cases when 309; legal presumption of shared parenting 311; preconditions for success 308–309; refusal of 310; *versus* voluntary 309

Marín, M. 173–174, 176

Masardo, A. 355

Maslow, A.H. 171

McArthur, L. 427

McElroy, T. 72

McIntosh, J. 17, 45–46, 177

McLanahan, S. 238

mediation, mandatory: arguments for 310; Australia 311–313, *312*; best alternatives to a negotiated agreement (BATNA) 311; definition of mediation 308; Europe, legal situation in 313–314; high-conflict post-separation cases 319–320; history of mediation 307–308; inappropriate, cases when 309; legal presumption of shared parenting 311; preconditions for success 308–309; refusal of 310; *versus* voluntary 309

methodology of research into JPC: causality, probing 65–73, *70*; initial preferences of parents 71–72; jurisdictions where JPC a presumption/norm 72–73; limitations of 64–65; longitudinal studies, power of 72; natural experiments 68–69; propensity score analysis 67–68; quasi-experimental design *70*; statistical controls 66–67

Mexico, parental alienation syndrome (PAS) in 264

Meyer, D.R. 359–360

Minow, M. 226

Mnookin, R.H. 71, 358

moral education of children *see* religious and moral education of children

Moreno, C. 175, 176

multiprofessional teamwork 436, 437, *437*

Munby, J. 54, 361

Nakonezny, P. 159

natural experiments 68–69

Navarro Michel, M. 107

Netherlands, evolution of shared parenting in 363–364

Nielsen, L. 28, 31, 32, 34, 63, 64, 66–67, 71, 72, 148

non-governmental organizations (NGOs), unaccompanied foreign minors and 101

Nordic countries, evolution of shared parenting in 355–356

norms, importance of 32–33

Norway: evolution of shared parenting in 356; paternal contact, loss of 414–417

Nussbaum, M. 58

O'Connell, D. 71

O'Donohue, W. 65

Index

order, children's need for 459
ordinary scope, acts of 107
Otto, R. 65
outcomes of JPC: causality, probing 65–73, 70; initial preferences of parents 71–72; jurisdictions where JPC a presumption/norm 72–73; limitations of research design 64–65; longitudinal studies, power of 72; meta-analyses of research 63–64; natural experiments 68–69; propensity score analysis 67–68; quasi-experimental research design 70; statistical controls in research 66–67
Ovtscharoff, W. 143

Pablo-Gualberto v. Gualberto V (Philippines) 390–391
panel discussions on shared parenting: attachment theory 30, 31; benefits of SP, elements of 29–32; compensatory dynamics of shared parenting 29–31; conflict between parents 34–35; deficient skills of one parent, making up for 29–30; evidence on benefit of SP 29; flexibility of SP 31; legal presumption, SP as 33–34; norms, importance of 32–33; parental alienation 35–36; participants 27–29; public education 33; relocation of one parent 36; symbolic weight of SP 32–33
parental alienation: adversarial family law system 234, 241, 245–246; alienated parent, effect on 234, 293; child, effect on 234, 236–238, 292–293; as child abuse **237**, 240, 290–291; as child maltreatment 233; core elements of 233; defined 233; ECtHR judgement 23641/17 465; estrangement/alienation, distinction between 283; interventions 238–241; legal enforcement of shared parenting orders 240–241; legal presumption of shared parenting 241–244; mental health interventions 238–240; misunderstanding and denial of 234, 245; muilti-faceted approach to 245; panel discussions on shared parenting 35–36; passive approach by courts and authorities 293–294; as pathological condition 233–234; prevalence of 234; research into 245; shared parenting as prevention 241–244, 465; therapeutic interventions 238–240, 241; typologies of alienating strategies 234, **235–236**; *see also* compensation for parental alienation

parental alienation syndrome (PAS) 293, 465; child sexual abuse (CSA), custody and 265–266; child's opinion as not heard due to 264; concerns overs 273–276; controversy over 264; countries, differences between 264–265; defined 263; recommendations 268; testimonies 266–268; as unrecognised 264; violence in family relationships 273–276
parental authority 106–107; Philippine family law 384, 386–392, 393–394
parental conflict *see* conflict between parents
parental co-responsibility: case law of shared parenting, analysis of 342–344; introduction of 341–342; legislation 342; plans 345–348; shared parenting and 347
parental responsibility/ies 199–200
parenting arrangements: approach to decisions on 5–6; factors to consider when deciding 6–7
parenting coordination for high-conflict post-separation cases 320–324
parenting plans 320–322, 359
parenting skills of parents, decisions on shared parenting and 6
Parkinson, P. 28, 357, 358
participation in decisions about shared parenting, children's 20–21
Pérez Martín, A.J. 210
Peters, E. 159
Philippine family law: best interest of the child 384, 385–386, 389, 392–393; Constitution 384; *Dacasin v. Dacasin* 390; *Espiritu v. Court of Appeals* 388–389; Family Code 384, 386, 387, 389, 392, 393; illegitimate children 387, 388; legitimate children 387–388; mothers, deprivation of custody 390–391; *Pablo-Gualberto v. Gualberto V* 390–391; parental authority 384, 386–392, 393–394; separated parents 388–389; substitute parental authority 389; suspension of parental authority 392; Tender Age Rule 389–391; termination of parental authority 392; *Unson III v. Navarro* 391
PIFE (Processus D'Intervention Familiale Encadrée): both parents, meeting with 334; child, meeting with 333–334; child's needs, consideration of 329; closer parent, meeting with 332; conditions for optimal effectiveness 337; confidentiality 329; consent 329–331; distanced parent, meeting with 332–333; early intervention

328; evaluation stage 331; example of protocol consent 337–340; intervention phase 331–336; key principles 328–329; language used by 327; mandate 329–331; optimal parental collaboration 329; parent-child reconnection process 332–335; preliminary phase 329–331; proven worth of 327; rebalancing parental roles 336; re-establishment of parent-child bond 336; shared parenting as result of 327–328; systemic-strategic perspective 328; working alliance with parents 329

Pisică v. Republic of Moldova: absence of protection 288–289; analysis of ECtHR judgement 290–292; authorities' awareness of risks 288; best interest of the child 287, 292; child abuse, parental alienation as, ECtHR on 290–291; conclusions of ECtHR 290; diligence as needed 288; ECtHR commitment to parental alienation 290–291; ECtHR judgement 23641/17 283–284; ECtHR's assessment of case 286–290; enforcement of custody as insufficient 289; exceptional diligence, duty to perform 291–292; failure to review actions of domestic authorities 289; history of case 284–286; lack of evidence for sufficient implication by authorities 289; neutral placement as intervention 291; parties' submissions 287; scope of the right to respect for family life 287; serious treatment of claims of parental alienation 292; views of the child 287, 292; violation of exceptional diligence principle 289

politics in Germany, shared parenting and: assumptions regarding people's actions 252; comparison of 10 years ago 251; conservative actions of progressive parties 257–258; Die Grünen 249, 250, 253, 254, 255, 256; Die Linke 249, 250, 253, 254, 255, 256; inertia hypothesis 254–256; information on SP, progressive parties as needing 254; law changes as unnecessary to support SP 251; left-sided parties 252–258; political parties and SP 249–250; political situation 248–249; progressive parties 250, 252–258

Poortman, A.-R. 363–364
practical issues of shared parenting 22
Preamble to Organic Law (Spain) 119, 121
Principles on Parental Responsibilities 199
privacy, children's need for 460
Probert, R. 54

Processus D'Intervention Familiale Encadrée (PIFE) *see* PIFE (Processus D'Intervention Familiale Encadrée)
propensity score analysis 67–68
protection, children's need for 459–460
protective factor for health, shared parenting as: adversity, childhood, impact of 142; animals, effects of parental separation on 143; conflict between parents 146–147; emotional health 46; general well-being 147–151; infant health, psychobiological effects of adversity 143–144; parental loss 142–143, 146; public health point of view 150–151
proximity of parents' homes 203–204
psychological research into JPC outcomes 85–88

quality of parent-child relationships 44–45
quality of parenting skills decisions on shared parenting and 6
quality/quantity of fathering time 41–42
quantity of time spent with parents 457

randomized experiments 65
reasoning of judgements in Spanish law: child abduction 125; grandparents' visiting rights 125; minors 118–120; requirement for 117–118; shared parenting 120–125
rebuttable legal presumption: intimate partner violence (IPV) as rebuttal factor 34; shared parenting as 7–8; Western countries, evolution of shared parenting in 365; *see also* legal presumption of shared parenting
Reding, V. 150–151
Regnier-Loilier, A. 146
regression discontinuity 69–70, 70
religious and moral education of children: acts of extraordinary scope of parental authority 108; case law 110–113; conflict between parents and 108, 110–114; European Court of Human Rights (ECtHR) 113; freedom, child's religious 108–109; parental responsibility generally 106–108; rights of parents to ensure 108–109
relocation of one parent 465–466; best interest of the child 184, 205–206; cause of 185; child's will 185; custody 185–186; enmeshment, principle of 188, 190; family relations, right to 198–201; harm to the children 185; history of applying parent

477

184; impact on family relations 202–203; Israeli case law 186–192; in joint custody system 203–206; legal practice/normative criteria, gap between 192–194; level of parenting involvement 184; normative criteria to determine cases 184–186, 205–206; panel discussions on shared parenting 36; parental agreement 185; proximity of parents' homes 203–204; quality of parenting 184; severity of problems with 183; tender age presumption 192

Relocation study 18, 19

research design: causality, probing 65–73, *70*; initial preferences of parents 71–72; jurisdictions where JPC a presumption/norm 72–73; limitations of 64–65; longitudinal studies, power of 72; natural experiments 68–69; propensity score analysis 67–68; quasi-experimental design 69–70, *70*; statistical controls 66–67

responsibility, children's need for 460

responsibility-to-needs approach 459

right of first refusal provisions 30

rights of the child: as inadequate as approach 458–459; Swiss custody legislation and 80–82; UNCRC and BIC 83–85

Rivero Hernández, F. 115

Rodgers, J. 159

Rodríguez-Domínguez, C. 174

Ruiz, R.A. 174, 176

Ruiz-Callado, R. 174, 175, 176

Rupprecht v. Spain 113

Sadowski, C. 17

Saini, M. 23

Sandler, I. 28

Schneider, D. 238

Schneider judgement of the ECtHR 442–443, 444

Schöbi, F. 82

Scott, E.S. 80

Scottish law, shared parenting in: background to family law 422–424; Children (Scotland) Bill, development of 424–430; reasons for legislation 419–421; UK law comparison 421–422

Scottish National Party (SNP) 422

Scottish Women's Aid 423–424, 427

security, children's need for 460

self-selection, JPC research and 64–65

Sen, A. 58

Shared Care study 18, 20, 21–22

shared parenting: advantages and disadvantages 458; case law analysis 342–344; contra-indications 456–457; Council of Europe Resolution 2079 (2015) 313–314; defined 15; Europe, legal situation in 313–314; evidence of benefits to children 7, 461–462; exceptional nature of 341; factors to consider when deciding 6–7, 455; introduction of 341; legal systems favouring 467; main questions regarding 2; needs of children after parental separation 458–461; presumption in favor of 462–464; quantity of time spent with parents 457; tools and approaches to facilitate 9; *see also* Arizona child custody reforms, evaluation of; joint physical custody; literature review on shared care; methodology of research into JPC

Shared Parenting Scotland 428, 429

Shull, R. 159

Sillberg, J. 265

Simone, T. de 357

Slovakia, shared parenting in: automatic award of joint custody 434–435; Cochem model 423, 437; cohabitation, rise in 431; communication between parents 436, *436*; conditions for shared parenting 435, *435*; cooperation between courts and CPPCPs 435, *436*; future research 438; goals of research 433; method for research 433; multiprofessional cooperation 436, 437, *437*; restrictions and biases in research 438; results of research 433–436, *434*, *435*, *436*, *437*; sample for research 433; terminology 432; training for parents *434*, 434–435, *435*, 437; trends today 431, *432*; views on shared parenting 433, *434*

Smart, C. 16, 20

Smyth, B. 2–3, 355, 356, 362

social capital, access to 30

social life, children's need for 460

solitude, children's need for 460

Solsona, M. 158, 174, 175

Spain: autonomous communities 3–4, *4*, 467; case law, best interest of the child and 52–53, 57–58; case law in favour of shared parenting 4–5, *5*; evolution of shared parenting in 364–365; family law in 3; focus on 3–5, *4*, *5*; judicial management of high-conflict post-separation cases 318–320; parental alienation syndrome (PAS) 264–265; *see also* parental

co-responsibility; unaccompanied foreign minors
Spanish Civil Code 106, 120, 198–199, 342, 344, 404, 405, 408
Spanish civil procedural law (LEC) 121–122
Spanish Civil Procedure Act (LEC) 318–319, 320
Spanish Constitution 106, 108, 117–118, 119, 125, 198, 202, 212
Spanish law: 30/1981 158; 15/2005 158, 211; autonomous communities, regulations of 160–161, 164–165, *166*; breakdown of marriages and 157–160, *163*, 163–164, **164**, 166; child abduction 125; divorce and 157–160; grandparents' visiting rights 125; joint custody, granting of 160–162, 164–165, *165*, *166*, 167; methodology for research 162–163; minors 118–120; reasoning of judgements 117–125; shared parenting 120–125
Spanish Organic Law 3/2007 342
Spanish Supreme Court (TS), best interest of the child and: maintenance payments 411; modification of measures 408–411; shared custody 404–408; transformation of family law 403–404
Spjker, J. 158, 174
Sporer judgement of the ECtHR 443
Sta. Maria, M.S. 387, 388
Stahl, P.M. 34, 74n2
Stanford Child Custody Study 147
Stanley, J.C. 69
static group comparison 64
Steinbach, A. 43
Sternberg, K. J. 30–31
Stetson, D. 159
subjects of law, children as 78, 84
Suh, G.W. 71
Sünderhauf, H. 28, 32–33, 148
Swiss custody legislation, rights of the child and 80–82
symbolic weight of SP 32–33

Tach, L. 238
tender age presumption 186, 188–189, 192
Tender Age Rule (Philippine family law) 389–391
terminology, diversity of 2–3
therapeutic justice 177–178
therapeutic mediation 177
Thoemmes, F. 67, 68
Thompson, R.A. 30–31
timeshare arrangements as starting point 2

toggles, epigenetic 130–133
Tornello, S. 46
Trinder, L. 360
TS *see* Spanish Supreme Court (TS), best interest of the child and
Turunen, 150
Turunen, J. 150

unaccompanied foreign minors: best interest principle 96–99; deficits of incomplete Spanish system 98–99; dual-objective policies 100–101; lack of coordination between regions 100; NGOs, role of 101; numbers in Europe 96; regulatory framework in Spain 96–99; Spain, numbers in 96; Spanish Framework Protocol 97–98; tool to assess best interest 100
United Kingdom: best interest of the child 362; evolution of shared parenting in 360–362; parental alienation syndrome (PAS) 265; Scottish law and 421–422
United Nations Committee on the Rights of the Child (CRC Committee) 385; Zaunegger approach of the ECtHR 444
United Nations Convention on the Rights of the Child (UNCRC) 51, 52, 115n1, 118, 200, 385, 426, 454–455; best interest of the child and 83–85; protection against violence 271; psychological research into JPC outcomes 87; subjects of law, children as 78, 84
United States: evolution of shared parenting in 358–360; parental alienation syndrome (PAS) 264; *see also* Arizona child custody reforms, evaluation of
Unson III v. Navarro (Philippines) 391

van Gaalen, R. 363–364
variance, analysis of 66
Velez, C.S. 32, 71
Viitanen, T. 175
Villanueva, B. 162
violence in family relationships 244, 271–272; 'friendly parent' concept 276; International Council on Shared Parenting (ICSP) Conferences 453; intimate partner violence (IPV) as rebuttal factor 34; judicial investigation of 272–273; parental alienation syndrome (PAS) 273–276; protection of the child 272–273,

456; strategies used in defence of 276; UNCRC and protection against 271
Votruba, A.M. 29, 34
Vuri, D. 162

Warshak, R. 28–29, 148
Watson, J. 131
welfare of the child as paramount 56–58
West, S.G. 67, 68
Western countries, evolution of shared parenting in: Australia 356–358; Belgium 364; Canada 362–363; Netherlands 363–364; Nordic countries 355–356; rebuttable legal presumption 365; Spain 364–365; United Kingdom 360–362; United States 358–360; *see also* individual countries
Wiik, K.A. 356
Women's Aid 423
Wright, G. 159

young children, joint physical custody and 40, 45

Zaunegger approach of the ECtHR: Art. 14 ECHR, applicability and content of 441; caution concerning high expectations 447; circumstances of the case 441; conviction and reasoning of the court 441–442; definition of 443; European Convention on Human Rights (ECHR) 440–441; German Federal Constitutional Court, Order of the 443, 446; human rights perspective 445–446; interpretations of the judgement 442–443; as minimal standard 446–447; out of wedlock, children born 441; subsequent ECtHR judgements 443–444; Swiss jurisdiction, impact on 444–445; UNCRC views on 444
Žilinčíkova, Z. 177

Printed in the United States
by Baker & Taylor Publisher Services